THE NEW CENTURY

THE HISTORY OF CONTINENTAL PHILOSOPHY

General Editor: Alan D. Schrift

1. Kant, Kantianism, and Idealism: The Origins of Continental Philosophy
Edited by Thomas Nenon

2. Nineteenth-Century Philosophy: Revolutionary Responses to the Existing Order
Edited by Alan D. Schrift and Daniel Conway

3. The New Century: Bergsonism, Phenomenology, and Responses to Modern Science
Edited by Keith Ansell-Pearson and Alan D. Schrift

4. Phenomenology: Responses and Developments
Edited by Leonard Lawlor

5. Critical Theory to Structuralism: Philosophy, Politics, and the Human Sciences
Edited by David Ingram

6. Poststructuralism and Critical Theory's Second Generation
Edited by Alan D. Schrift

7. After Poststructuralism: Transitions and Transformations
Edited by Rosi Braidotti

8. Emerging Trends in Continental Philosophy
Edited by Todd May

THE NEW CENTURY

BERGSONISM, PHENOMENOLOGY, AND RESPONSES TO MODERN SCIENCE

Edited by Keith Ansell-Pearson and Alan D. Schrift

VOLUME 3

THE HISTORY OF CONTINENTAL PHILOSOPHY

General Editor: Alan D. Schrift

ACUMEN

SERIES PREFACE

"Continental philosophy" is itself a contested concept. For some, it is understood to be any philosophy after 1780 originating on the European continent (Germany, France, Italy, etc.). Such an understanding would make Georg von Wright or Rudolf Carnap – respectively, a Finnish-born philosopher of language and a German-born logician who taught for many years in the US – a "continental philosopher," an interpretation neither they nor their followers would easily accept. For others, "continental philosophy" refers to a style of philosophizing, one more attentive to the world of experience and less focused on a rigorous analysis of concepts or linguistic usage. In this and the accompanying seven volumes in this series, "continental philosophy" will be understood *historically* as a tradition that has its roots in several different ways of approaching and responding to Immanuel Kant's critical philosophy, a tradition that takes its definitive form at the beginning of the twentieth century as the phenomenological tradition, with its modern roots in the work of Edmund Husserl. As such, continental philosophy emerges as a tradition distinct from the tradition that has identified itself as "analytic" or "Anglo-American," and that locates its own origins in the logical analyses and philosophy of language of Gottlob Frege. Whether or not there is in fact a sharp divergence between the work of Husserl and Frege is itself a contested question, but what cannot be contested is that two distinct historical traditions emerged early in the twentieth century from these traditions' respective interpretations of Husserl (and Heidegger) and Frege (and Russell). The aim of this history of continental philosophy is to trace the developments in one of these traditions from its roots in Kant and his contemporaries through to its most recent manifestations. Together, these volumes present a coherent and comprehensive account of the continental philosophical tradition that offers readers a unique resource for understanding this tradition's complex and interconnected history.

Because history does not unfold in a perfectly linear fashion, telling the history of continental philosophy cannot simply take the form of a chronologically organized series of "great thinker" essays. And because continental philosophy has not developed in a vacuum, telling its history must attend to the impact of figures and developments outside philosophy (in the sciences, social sciences, mathematics, art, politics, and culture more generally) as well as to the work of some philosophers not usually associated with continental philosophy. Such a series also must attend to significant philosophical movements and schools of thought and to the extended influence of certain philosophers within this history, either because their careers spanned a period during which they engaged with a range of different theorists and theoretical positions or because their work has been appropriated and reinterpreted by subsequent thinkers. For these reasons, the volumes have been organized with an eye toward chronological development but, in so far as the years covered in each volume overlap those covered in the subsequent volume, they have been organized as well with the aim of coordinating certain philosophical developments that intersect in a fashion that is not always strictly chronological.

Volume 1 begins with the origins of continental philosophy in Kant and the earliest responses to his critical philosophy, and presents an overview of German idealism, the major movement in philosophy from the late eighteenth to the middle of the nineteenth century. In addition to Kant, the period covered in the first volume was dominated by Fichte, Schelling, and Hegel, and together their work influenced not just philosophy, but also art, theology, and politics. This volume thus covers Kant's younger contemporary Herder, and his readers Schiller and Schlegel – who shaped much of the subsequent reception of Kant in art, literature, and aesthetics; the "Young Hegelians" – including Bruno Bauer, Ludwig Feuerbach, and David Friedrich Strauss – whose writings would influence Engels and Marx; and the tradition of French utopian thinking in such figures as Saint-Simon, Fourier, and Proudhon. In addition to Kant's early critics – Jacobi, Reinhold, and Maimon – significant attention is also paid to the later critic of German idealism Arthur Schopenhauer, whose appropriation and criticism of theories of cognition later had a decisive influence on Friedrich Nietzsche.

Volume 2 addresses the second half of the nineteenth century, in part as a response to the dominance of Hegelian philosophy. These years saw revolutionary developments in both European politics and philosophy, and five great critics dominated the European intellectual scene: Feuerbach, Marx, Søren Kierkegaard, Fyodor Dostoevsky, and Nietzsche. Responding in various ways to Hegelian philosophy and to the shifting political landscape of Europe and the United States, these thinkers brought to philosophy two guiding orientations – materialism and existentialism – that introduced themes that would continue to play out throughout the twentieth century. The second half of the nineteenth century also saw the emergence of new schools of thought and new disciplinary thinking, including the birth of sociology and the social sciences, the development of French spiritualism, the beginning of American pragmatism, radical developments in science and mathematics, and the development of hermeneutics beyond the domains of theology and philology into an approach to understanding all varieties of human endeavor.

Volume 3 covers the period between the 1890s and 1930s, a period that witnessed revolutions in the arts, science, and society that set the agenda for the twentieth century. In philosophy, these years saw the beginnings of what would grow into two distinct approaches to doing philosophy: analytic and continental. It also saw the emergence of phenomenology as a new rigorous science, the birth of Freudian psychoanalysis, and the maturing of the discipline of sociology. Volume 3 thus examines the most influential work of a remarkable series of thinkers who reviewed, evaluated, and transformed nineteenth-century thought, among them Henri Bergson, Émile Durkheim, Sigmund Freud, Martin Heidegger, Edmund Husserl, Karl Jaspers, Max Scheler, and Ludwig Wittgenstein. It also initiated an approach to philosophizing that saw philosophy move from the lecture hall or the private study into an active engagement with the world, an approach that would continue to mark continental philosophy's subsequent history.

The developments and responses to phenomenology after Husserl are the focus of the essays in Volume 4. An ambiguity inherent in phenomenology – between conscious experience and structural conditions – lent itself to a range of interpretations. While some existentialists focused on applying phenomenology to the concrete data of human experience, others developed phenomenology as conscious experience in order to analyze ethics and religion. Still other phenomenologists developed notions of structural conditions to explore questions of science, mathematics, and conceptualization. Volume 4 covers all the major innovators in phenomenology – notably Sartre, Merleau-Ponty, and the later Heidegger – as well as its extension into religion, ethics, aesthetics, hermeneutics, and science.

Volume 5 concentrates on philosophical developments in political theory and the social sciences between 1920 and 1968, as European thinkers responded to the difficult and world-transforming events of the time. While some of the significant figures and movements of this period drew on phenomenology, many went back further into the continental tradition, looking to Kant or Hegel, Marx or Nietzsche, for philosophical inspiration. Key figures and movements discussed in this volume include Adorno, Horkheimer, and the Frankfurt School,

Schmitt, Marcuse, Benjamin, Arendt, Bataille, black existentialism, French Marxism, Saussure, and structuralism. These individuals and schools of thought responded to the "crisis of modernity" in different ways, but largely focused on what they perceived to be liberal democracy's betrayal of its own rationalist ideals of freedom, equality, and fraternity. One other point about the period covered in this volume is worthy of note: it is during these years that we see the initial spread of continental philosophy beyond the European continent. This happens largely because of the emigration of European Jewish intellectuals to the US and UK in the 1930s and 1940s, be it the temporary emigration of figures such as Adorno, Horkheimer, Lévi-Strauss, and Jakobson or the permanent emigration of Marcuse, Arendt, and Gurwitsch. As the succeeding volumes will attest, this becomes a central feature of continental philosophy's subsequent history.

Volume 6 examines the major figures associated with poststructuralism and the second generation of critical theory, the two dominant movements that emerged in the 1960s, which together brought continental philosophy to the forefront of scholarship in a variety of humanities and social science disciplines and set the agenda for philosophical thought on the continent and elsewhere from the 1960s to the present. In addition to essays that discuss the work of such influential thinkers as Althusser, Foucault, Deleuze, Derrida, Lyotard, Irigaray, Habermas, Serres, Bourdieu, and Rorty, Volume 6 also includes thematic essays on issues including the Nietzschean legacy, the linguistic turn in continental thinking, the phenomenological inheritance of Gadamer and Ricoeur, the influence of psychoanalysis, the emergence of feminist thought and a philosophy of sexual difference, and the importation of continental philosophy into literary theory.

Before turning to Volume 7, a few words on the *institutional* history of continental philosophy in the United States are in order, in part because the developments addressed in Volumes 6–8 cannot be fully appreciated without recognizing some of the events that conditioned their North American and anglophone reception. As has been mentioned, phenomenologists such as Alfred Schutz and Aron Gurwitsch, and other European continental philosophers such as Herbert Marcuse and Hannah Arendt, began relocating to the United States in the 1930s and 1940s. Many of these philosophers began their work in the United States at the University in Exile, established in 1933 as a graduate division of the New School for Social Research for displaced European intellectuals. While some continental philosophy was taught elsewhere around the United States (at Harvard University, Yale University, the University at Buffalo, and elsewhere), and while the journal *Philosophy and Phenomenological Research* began publishing in 1939, continental philosophy first truly began to become an institutional presence in the United States in the 1960s. In 1961, John Wild (1902–72) left Harvard to become Chair of the Department of Philosophy at Northwestern University. With a commitment from the provost of the university and the Northwestern University Press to enable him to launch the Northwestern Series in Phenomenology and Existential Philosophy, Wild joined William Earle and James Edie, thus making Northwestern a center for the study of continental philosophy. Wild set up an organizational committee including himself, Earle, Edie, George Schrader of Yale, and Calvin Schrag (a former student of Wild's at Harvard, who was teaching at Northwestern and had recently accepted an appointment at Purdue University), to establish a professional society devoted to the examination of recent continental philosophy. That organization, the Society for Phenomenology and Existential Philosophy (SPEP), held its first meeting at Northwestern in 1962, with Wild and Gurwitsch as the dominant figures arguing for an existential phenomenology or a more strictly Husserlian phenomenology, respectively. Others attending the small meeting included Erwin Straus, as well as Northwestern graduate students Edward Casey and Robert Scharff, and today SPEP has grown into the second largest society of philosophers in the United States. Since those early days, many smaller societies (Heidegger Circle, Husserl Circle, Nietzsche Society, etc.) have formed and many journals and graduate programs devoted to continental philosophy have appeared. In addition, many of the important continental philosophers who first became known in the 1960s – including Gadamer, Ricoeur, Foucault, Derrida, Lyotard, and Habermas – came to hold continuing appointments at major American universities (although, it must be mentioned, not always housed in departments of philosophy) and, since the 1960s, much of the transmission of continental philosophy has come directly through teaching as well as through publications.

The transatlantic migration of continental philosophy plays a central role in Volume 7, which looks at developments in continental philosophy between 1980 and 1995, a time of great upheaval and profound social change that saw the fruits of the continental works of the 1960s beginning to shift the center of gravity of continental philosophizing from the European continent to the anglophone philosophical world and, in particular, to North America. During these years, the pace of translation into English of French and German philosophical works from the early twentieth century as well as the very recent past increased tremendously, and it was not uncommon to find essays or lectures from significant European philosophers appearing first in English and then subsequently being published in French or German. In addition, the period covered in this volume also saw the spread of continental philosophy beyond the confines of philosophy departments, as students and faculty in centers of humanities and departments of comparative literature, communication studies, rhetoric, and other interdisciplinary fields increasingly drew on the work of recent continental philosophers. Volume 7 ranges across several developments during these years – the birth of postmodernism, the differing philosophical traditions of France, Germany, and Italy, the third generation of critical theory, and the so-called "ethical turn" – while also examining the extension of philosophy into questions of radical democracy, postcolonial theory, feminism, religion, and the rise of performativity and post-analytic philosophy. Fueled by an intense ethical and political desire to reflect changing social and political conditions, the philosophical work of this period reveals how continental thinkers responded to the changing world and to the key issues of the time, notably globalization, technology, and ethnicity.

The eighth and final volume in this series attempts to chart the most recent trends in continental philosophy, which has now developed into an approach to thinking that is present throughout the world and engaged with classical philosophical problems as well as current concerns. The essays in this volume focus more on thematic developments than individual figures as they explore how contemporary philosophers are drawing on the resources of the traditions surveyed in the preceding seven volumes to address issues relating to gender, race, politics, art, the environment, science, citizenship, and globalization. While by no means claiming to have the last word, this volume makes clear the dynamic and engaged quality of continental philosophy as it confronts some of the most pressing issues of the contemporary world.

As a designation, "continental philosophy" can be traced back at least as far as John Stuart Mill's *On Bentham and Coleridge* (1840), where he uses it to distinguish the British empiricism of Bentham from a tradition on the continent in which he sees the influence of Kant. Since that time, and especially since the early twentieth century, the term has been used to designate philosophies from a particular geographical region, or with a particular style (poetic or dialectical, rather than logical or scientistic). For some, it has been appropriated as an honorific, while for others it has been used more pejoratively or dismissively. Rather than enter into these polemics, what the volumes in this series have sought to do is make clear that one way to understand "continental philosophy" is as an approach to philosophy that is deeply engaged in reflecting on its own history, and that, as a consequence, it is important to understand the *history* of continental philosophy.

While each of the volumes in this series was organized by its respective editor as a volume that could stand alone, the eight volumes have been coordinated in order to highlight various points of contact, influence, or debate across the historical period that they collectively survey. To facilitate these connections across the eight volumes, cross-referencing footnotes have been added to many of the essays by the General Editor. To distinguish these footnotes from those of the authors, they are indicated by an asterisk (*).

Alan D. Schrift, General Editor

CONTRIBUTORS

Keith Ansell-Pearson holds a Personal Chair in Philosophy at the University of Warwick. His publications include *Nietzsche Contra Rousseau* (1991), *An Introduction to Nietzsche as Political Thinker: The Perfect Nihilist* (1994), *Germinal Life: The Difference and Repetition of Deleuze* (1999), and *Philosophy and the Adventure of the Virtual: Bergson and the Time of Life* (2002). He has also recently edited *The Nietzsche Reader* (2006) and *A Companion to Nietzsche* (2006).

Babette Babich is Professor of Philosophy at Fordham University with interests in aesthetics, the politics of philosophy (and science), and epistemology. She is the author of *Nietzsche's Philosophy of Science: Reflecting Science on the Ground of Art and Life* (1994; Italian 1996; German 2011), *Words in Blood, Like Flowers: Philosophy and Poetry, Music and Eros in Hölderlin, Nietzsche, Heidegger* (2006), *La fin de la pensée? Philosophie analytique contre philosophie continentale* (2012), and *The Hallelujah Effect: Philosophical Reflections on Music, Performance Practice and Technology* (2013). She founded and edits *New Nietzsche Studies*, and her edited books include *From Phenomenology to Thought, Errancy, and Desire* (1996), *Theories of Knowledge, Critical Theory, and the Sciences* (1999), *Nietzsche, Epistemology, and the Philosophy of Science* (1999), *Hermeneutic Philosophy of Science, Van Gogh's Eyes, and God* (2002), *Habermas, Nietzsche, and Critical Theory* (2003), and (co-edited) *Heidegger and Nietzsche* (2012).

Miguel de Beistegui is Professor of Philosophy at the University of Warwick. His areas of research include: the ontology of difference, the aesthetics of metaphor, and the ethics and politics of desire. His latest books include *Truth and Genesis: Philosophy as Differential Ontology* (2004), *The New Heidegger*

(2005), *Jouissance de Proust: Pour une esthétique de la métaphore* (2007), *Immanence and Philosophy: Deleuze* (2010), *Proust as Philosopher: The Art of Metaphor* (2012), and *Aesthetics After Metaphysics: From Mimesis to Metaphor* (2012).

Fabien Capeillères teaches philosophy at the University of Caen, France. A specialist of the neo-Kantian tradition, he is Directeur du Centre d'Études Critiques and general editor for Ernst Cassirer's complete works in French. He is currently writing a *History of Philosophical Scientificity*. The first volume, *Kant Philosophe Newtonien*, was published in 2004; *The First Crisis of French Philosophy: Science, Religion and Metaphysics 1850–1920* is forthcoming.

Leonard H. Ehrlich (1924–2011) was born in Vienna and immigrated to the US in 1939. He studied from 1948 to 1951 at the University of Basel with Karl Jaspers and Karl Barth, receiving his PhD from Yale University, began his career at the University of Massachusetts at Amherst in 1956, and retired from active teaching there as Professor Emeritus of Philosophy and Judaic Studies in 1990. Ehrlich is the founder and past president of The Karl Jaspers Society of North America, initiator and codirector of the first five International Jaspers Conferences, cofounder of the International Association of Jaspers Societies, and Founding and Honorary Member of the International Rosenzweig Society. He has published extensively on Jaspers, as author of *Karl Jaspers: Philosophy as Faith* (1975), coeditor and cotranslator of *Karl Jaspers: Basic Philosophical Writings, Selections* (1986, 1994), *Karl Jaspers: The Great Philosophers, Vol. III* (1993) and *Vol. IV* (1994), and coeditor of *Karl Jaspers Today: Philosophy at the Threshold of the Future* (1988), *Karl Jaspers: Philosophy on the Way to "World Philosophy"* (1998), and *Karl Jaspers's Philosophy: Rooted in the Present, Paradigm for the Future* (2003).

John Fennell is Associate Professor of Philosophy at Grinnell College. His work, which focuses principally on naturalist and antinaturalist approaches to meaning and mind, has appeared in *European Journal of Philosophy* and *International Journal of Philosophical Studies.*

Michael Friedman is Frederick P. Rehmus Family Professor of Humanities at Stanford University. His books include *Foundations of Space-Time Theories: Relativistic Physics and Philosophy of Science* (1983), *Kant and the Exact Sciences* (1992), *Reconsidering Logical Positivism* (1999), *A Parting of the Ways: Carnap, Cassirer, and Heidegger* (2000), *Dynamics of Reason* (2001), *The Kantian Legacy in Nineteenth Century Science* (2006), and *The Cambridge Companion to Carnap* (2007).

Mike Gane was a founder member of the Department of Social Sciences at Loughborough University in 1972, where he is now Emeritus Professor of Sociology. His main interest has been in the relation between science, philosophy, and the social sciences, particularly in the French tradition. He has published *On Durkheim's Rules of Sociological Method* (1988), *French Social Theory* (2003), and *Auguste Comte* (2006). He has also published edited collections: *Towards a Critique of Foucault* (1986), *Foucault's New Domains* (with T. Johnson; 1993), and *The Radical Sociology of Durkheim and Mauss* (1992). He has also published widely on the work of Jean Baudrillard and is a member of the editorial board of *Durkheimian Studies* (Berghahn).

Adrian Johnston is an Professor in the Department of Philosophy at the University of New Mexico at Albuquerque and an assistant teaching analyst at the Emory Psychoanalytic Institute in Atlanta. He is the author of *Time Driven: Metapsychology and the Splitting of the Drive* (2005), *Žižek's Ontology: A Transcendental Materialist Theory of Subjectivity* (2008), and *Badiou, Žižek, and Political Transformations: The Cadence of Change* (2009). With Catherine Malabou, he is presently coauthoring a book on affects reconsidered at the intersection of psychoanalysis, neuroscience, and philosophy (tentatively entitled *Auto-affection and Emotional Life: Psychoanalysis and Neurobiology*). And he is currently working on a project addressing forms of materialism ranging from historical and dialectical materialisms to such recent developments as speculative realism (tentatively entitled *A Weak Nature Alone: Prolegomena to Any Future Materialism*).

Sebastian Luft is Associate Professor of Philosophy at Marquette University. He has studied philosophy, classics, and German studies at the Universities of Freiburg, Heidelberg, SUNY Stony Brook, and Wuppertal, and was editorial assistant at the Husserl Archives in Leuven, Belgium from 1998 to 2002. He is the author of *"Phänomenologie der Phänomenologie": Systematik und Methodologie der Phänomenologie in der Auseinandersetzung zwischen Husserl und Fink*, *Subjectivity and Lifeworld in Transcendental Phsnomenology* (2011), and editor of *Husserliana* vol. 34, *Zur phänomenologischen Reduktion: Texte aus dem Nachlass (1926–1935)*, coeditor of *Neo-Kantianism in Contemporary Philosophy* (with Rudolf A. Makkreel; 2010), editor of *The Neo-Kantian Reader* (2013), and is working with Thane M. Naberhaus on a translation of Edmund Husserl's lecture course *Erste Philosophie*.

Paul-Antoine Miquel is Maître de Conférences in the Department of Philosophy at the University of Nice, and a member of the Centre d'Epistémologie et de Recherches Comparatives at the University of Provence. His publications include *Comment penser le désordre?* (2000), *Bio-logiques du vieillissement* (with Ladislas

Robert, 2004), *Qu'est-ce que la vie?* (2007), *Bergson ou l'imagination métaphysique* (2007), and *Biologie du XXIème siècle, évolution des concepts fondateurs* (2008).

John Mullarkey is Professor of Film and Television Studies at Kingston University, London. He is the author of *Bergson and Philosophy* (1999), *Post-Continental Philosophy: An Outline* (2006), *Philosophy and the Moving Image: Refractions of Reality* (2010), and editor, with Anthony Paul Smith, of *Laruelle and Non-Philosophy* (2012).

Thomas Nenon is Professor of Philosophy at the University of Memphis. He is the author of *Objectivitaet und endlich Erkenntnis* (1986), coeditor of vol. 25 (*Aufsätze und Vorträge 1911–21*) and vol. 27 (*Aufsätze und Vorträge 1922–37*) of the *Husserliana*, and author of a number of articles on Husserl, Heidegger, Kant and German idealism, hermeneutics, and the philosophy of the social sciences. He has served as review editor for *Husserl Studies*, President of the Center for Advanced Research in Phenomenology, and as Director of the Center for the Humanities at the University of Memphis. His current research interests include Husserl's theories of personhood and subjectivity, Husserl's ethical theory, and Kant and Hegel's practical philosophy.

Diane Perpich is Associate Professor of Philosophy at Clemson University. She is the author of *The Ethics of Emmanuel Levinas* (2008) and is currently working on a project considering the contributions of the phenomenological tradition to social ontologies.

Bob Plant has been Lecturer in Philosophy at the University of Aberdeen since 2005. He has published articles on Wittgenstein, Levinas, Derrida, Foucault, and Thomas Reid, and is the author of *Wittgenstein and Levinas: Ethical and Religious Thought* (2005).

Thomas Ryckman teaches philosophy of science and philosophy of physics at Stanford University. He is author of *The Reign of Relativity: Philosophy in Physics 1915–1925* (2005) and coauthor (with Zellig Harris and Michael Gottfried) of *The Form of Information in Science* (1987).

Alan D. Schrift is the F. Wendell Miller Professor of Philosophy at Grinnell College. In addition to his many published articles or book chapters on Nietzsche and French and German twentieth-century philosophy, he is the author of *Nietzsche and the Question of Interpretation: Between Hermeneutics and Deconstruction* (1990), *Nietzsche's French Legacy: A Genealogy of Poststructuralism* (1995), and *Twentieth-Century French Philosophy: Key Themes and*

Thinkers (2005). He has edited five collections on a variety of topics, including *The Logic of the Gift: Toward an Ethic of Generosity* (1997) and *Modernity and the Problem of Evil* (2005). In addition to serving as general editor of the eight-volume *The History of Continental Philosophy*, he serves as general editor of *The Complete Works of Friedrich Nietzsche*, the Stanford University Press translation of Nietzsche's *Kritische Studienausgabe*.

Michael Vaughan is currently at the University of Warwick, completing a PhD thesis entitled *Creative Revolution: Bergson's Social Thought*. He is coeditor of the centennial edition of Bergson's *Creative Evolution* (with Keith Ansell-Pearson and Michael Kolkman) and of a special issue of *SubStance* entitled "*Creative Evolution* one hundred years later" (with Michael Kolkman).

Dan Zahavi is Professor of Philosophy and Director of the Danish National Research Foundation's Center for Subjectivity Research at the University of Copenhagen. He has served as president of the Nordic Society for Phenomenology in the years 2001–7, and is currently coeditor in chief of the journal *Phenomenology and the Cognitive Sciences*. In his systematic work, Zahavi has mainly been investigating the nature of selfhood, self-consciousness, and intersubjectivity. His most important publications include *Husserl und die transzendentale Intersubjektivität* (1996), *Self-awareness and Alterity* (1999), *Husserl's Phenomenology* (2003), *Subjectivity and Selfhood* (2005), and *The Phenomenological Mind* (with Shaun Gallagher; 2008).

INTRODUCTION

Keith Ansell-Pearson

"The twentieth century began by insisting on its secession from the past." So writes Peter Conrad in his magisterial treatment of life and art in the twentieth century.[1] Between the 1890s and 1930s, a period that witnessed an acceleration of time and the dispersal of places, revolutions in the arts and society set the agenda for the rest of the century. In philosophy, too, it is a period in which we witness the birth and development of new programs and new modes of inquiry, including the phenomenon of "Bergsonism," the emergence of phenomenology as a new rigorous science, the birth of Freudian psychoanalysis, and the coming into maturity of sociology. As Michael Friedman and Thomas Ryckman note in their essay in this volume, all four of the major protagonists in both the analytic and continental traditions – Gottlob Frege and Rudolf Carnap, Edmund Husserl and Martin Heidegger – saw themselves as making revolutionary breaks with the philosophy of the past through the invention of new types of philosophical tools (Bertrand Russell is another relevant figure). In the period 1890–1930 we witness a remarkable series of thinkers, many of whom are covered in this volume, who review, evaluate, and transform into new directions the mixed results of nineteenth-century thought, and include Henri Bergson, Émile Durkheim, Sigmund Freud, Heidegger, Husserl, Karl Jaspers, Max Scheler, Georg Simmel, Max Weber, and Ludwig Wittgenstein. The results, according to one commentator, included wrestling with an ambivalent legacy, on the one hand, a dominant optimism based on the expansion of industrialization and democratization, and on the other hand, a subordinate pessimism centered on the

1. Peter Conrad, *Modern Times, Modern Places: Life and Art in the Twentieth Century* (London: Thames & Hudson, 1998), 8.

corrosive effects of the rationalism that presided over the tremendous processes of social change: "the turn-of-the century generation puts the brakes on intellectual progressivism, but fought not to give up on life, though the myth of rationalism, in both its materialist and spiritualist forms, had been shattered."[2] In short, a generation of thinkers completed the disenchantment of the world and sought a new re-enchantment, so continuing in key respects the task Nietzsche, whose philosophical work had ceased in 1889 with his mental collapse, had set philosophy in the 1880s: "there are so many dawns that have not yet broken."[3]

The period that this volume covers can fairly be identified as the period that witnesses the second scientific revolution, with our own era, with the rise of electronics, digitalization, genetic engineering, nanotechnology, and so on, being the third. In this period, a number of important discoveries take place, including the X-ray, radioactivity, and the electron, and out of this experimental research emerge atomic physics, the laws of relativity, and quantum theory. Writing in the 1890s, the French poet and critic Paul Valéry described the period as one "completely formed by the sciences, in perpetual technological transformation, where nothing escapes the will to innovation."[4] In its initial phases it is a period of technological progress and even utopianism, with the emergence of the motor car, the extension of travel by trains, bicycles, and tramcars, with countries now linked up by an international mail system and new modes of communication such as the telephone, and, finally, the rise of cinematography and the presentation of moving images. Valéry wrote of the "dizzying transformations of modern life," noting that the world had never before undergone such a rapid and profound transformation: "our ideas and our powers over matter, time, and space, conceived of and utilized completely differently than they were up to our time."[5] It has become impossible, he noted, to make a comparison between the way things were fifty years ago and how they are now in the time he is reflecting on. Values have been negated and ideas have been dissociated.

By the 1930s the tone of "energetic fascination" with which Valéry described the world has gone, being replaced by a mood of ambivalence and anxiety. Europe is undergoing a crisis both economically and intellectually. Between the 1890s and 1930s, several important political events have taken place and left an impact – the Dreyfus Affair in the mid-1890s, the Great War, and the rise of fascism among them – and the decade of the 1930s witnesses the coming into

2. Helmut Loiskandl, Deena Weinstein, and Michael Weinstein, "Introduction," in G. Simmel, *Schopenhauer and Nietzsche*, Helmut Loiskandl *et al.* (trans.) (Amherst, MA: University of Massachusetts Press, 1986), xi.
3. Nietzsche, *Ecce Homo* III iv.
4. Cited in Suzanne Guerlac, *Thinking in Time: An Introduction to Henri Bergson* (Ithaca, NY: Cornell University Press, 2006), 14.
5. *Ibid.*, 115.

power of Hitler's National Socialist Party.[6] As Guerlac also notes, for the poet, the intellectual crisis centered on a crisis of the sciences with our idea of the universe decomposing, "losing all hope of a single image" and giving rise to a culture of disorder and chaos.[7]

Valéry's mood finds sustained philosophical expression in Husserl's reflections on "the Crisis of the European Sciences" in the mid-1930s. For Husserl, the problem is centered on the positivistic concept of science that "decapitates philosophy."[8] He takes positivism to entail the reduction of the idea of science to mere factual science, giving rise to a crisis of science as the loss of its meaning for life: "Can we live in this world, where all historical occurrence is nothing but an unending concatenation of illusory progress and bitter disappointment?"[9] In the midst of the unreason sweeping over Europe in the 1930s he sought – vainly, some would say – to restore belief in the ideal of a universal philosophy in which humanity radically renews itself through the new philosophy. He speaks of "the new man," echoing Nietzsche's exhortation that the *Übermensch* is to be the meaning of the future of the new earth that comes into being in the wake of the death of God.[10] What guides this new human is the faith he has in securing a rational meaning for his individual and common existence; if this faith is being lost – which is Husserl's chief concern in the book – then this will entail a loss of faith in man's "own true being." Husserl insists that this "true being" is not a possession the human has, like the self-evidence of the "I am," but, and again echoing Nietzsche, a *task*: "True being is everywhere an ideal goal, a task of *epistēmē* or 'reason.'"[11] The task centers on the possibility of "universal knowledge." For Husserl, the true struggles of the time are spiritual ones between philosophies (skeptical and vital ones) and between a humanity that has collapsed and one struggling to find new roots. Husserl's perspective is Eurocentric – which is part of the reason why his analysis has been taken to task in our own time[12] – in which it needs to be decided, he argues, whether or not European humanity bears within itself an absolute idea, as opposed to "being merely an empirical anthropological type like 'China' or 'India,'" and, following from this, whether or not "the spectacle

6. *Ibid.*, 16.
7. *Ibid.*
8. Edmund Husserl, *The Crisis of European Sciences and Transcendental Phenomenology*, David Carr (trans.) (Evanston, IL: Northwestern University Press, 1970), 9.
9. *Ibid.*, 7.
10. For a recent, and typically thought-provoking, set of reflections on "the new man," see Alain Badiou, *The Century*, Alberto Toscano (trans.) (Cambridge: Polity, 2007), esp. 1–10.
11. Husserl, *The Crisis of European Sciences*, 13.
12. See Gilles Deleuze and Félix Guattari, *What is Philosophy?*, Graham Burchell (trans.) (London: Verso, 1994), "Geophilosophy."

of the Europeanization of all other civilizations bears witness to the rule of an absolute meaning," that is, a meaning that is not simply historically arbitrary or contingent.[13] In contrast to other sciences, such as psychology, what is at stake for philosophy, Husserl insists, are the ideas and ideals of "mankind," "humanity," and the future of our faith in the human as the being in search of truth and rational modes of being.

Historians in the early decades of the twentieth century were writing snapshots of philosophy as it was unfolding and what they privilege and focus attention on is quite different from how the history of this period is now conceived. Bergsonian thought was typically taken to be central to the era, but it is only in recent years, in our own time in fact, that Bergson's thought is being taken seriously once again. Until very recently Bergson has enjoyed a minimal presence in the rise and spread of academically practiced continental philosophy. Taking stock of the situation in philosophy at the beginning of the century, the Danish historian of philosophy Harald Höffding divided modern philosophers into three groupings corresponding to what he identified as three dominant tendencies: the "objective-systematic tendency" represented by the likes of Wilhelm Wundt in Germany, F. H. Bradley in the UK, and Alfred Fouillée in France; the "epistemological biological tendency" represented by various philosopher-scientists such as James Clerk Maxwell and Ernst Mach, and, finally, the "philosophy of value" represented by Nietzsche, Rudolf Eucken, and William James. For the 1913 edition, translated into English in 1915, Bergson was given a separate section on his own based on a series of lectures given by the author. Of course, this is one particular if revealing perspective on the changing philosophical scene. If one looks at Isaac Benrubi's *Contemporary Thought of France*, one finds a much wider range of authors and developments covered, but yet again prominence is given to Bergson with sections not only on him but also on "Bergsonians" (Edouard Le Roy, Georges Sorel) and "anti-Bergsonians" (Julien Benda, Jacques Maritain). Observing a great variety of currents and tendencies in the philosophical activity of his day, Benrubi identified three main tendencies of modern thought: empiric positivism, critico-epistemological idealism, and metaphysico-spiritual positivism. He also notes the closely interwoven character of contemporary French and German thought. We can also note certain developments in science that have an enormous impact on the philosophy being done in this period. Bergson, for example, was inspired by electromagnetism in his *Matter and Memory* of 1896, and he cites the likes of Michael Faraday and Maxwell in the text. For Bergson, it is the new science that is showing that "*modifications*, *perturbations*, changes of *tension* or of *energy* and nothing else"

13. Husserl, *The Crisis of European Sciences*, 16.

pervade extensity.[14] As one commentator has noted, electromagnetic physics confirms the intuition that a material point is a simple view of the mind by showing that solid bodies are not primary because "matter is first waves and light, indivisible energy and continuous flow."[15]

In the 1920s, a serious waning of Bergson's influence on the philosophical scene was in evidence and various reasons have been offered to account for this: he did not create a school, after the end of the Second World War no Bergson archive was established, and the philosophy of life was eclipsed by existentialism and phenomenology. But a dissident philosophical voice was evolving in the 1950s in the work of Gilles Deleuze and in which Bergson's texts and ideas play a vitally important role in the articulation of an innovative philosophy of difference.

The different trajectories and schools of thought that characterize this period are closely allied in that they offer a rich set of responses to a mid-nineteenth-century inheritance of positivism and scientism that sought to challenge and overturn philosophy's independence. Some, such as Bergson, sought liberation from a mechanistic paradigm represented by, but not restricted to, the work of Herbert Spencer, who was a major player on the world stage of philosophy in the second half of the nineteenth century. According to one commentator, "A whole generation had grown up under the Spencerian dispensation but had been made restive by a liberal and scientific progressive faith that had gone sour."[16] At the turn of the century, however, the world changed and the sense of a new consciousness and new reality was in the air. The feeling was that reality was permanently new, forever making itself afresh: "The new reality meant that reality was by its very nature continually new, that one now lived in a world of immanence, a world of incessant and unforeseeable change and possibility, a world always about to be."[17]

William James, for example, was convinced that a kind of new dawn was breaking in philosophy in the early years of the new century. Reflecting on "The Present Dilemma in Philosophy" (1907), James describes philosophy as at once the most sublime and the most trivial of pursuits: "It works in the minutest crannies and it opens out the widest vistas."[18] Although it "bakes no bread," it

14. Henri Bergson, *Matter and Memory*, Nancy Margaret Paul and W. Scott Palmer (trans.) (New York: Zone Books, 1991), 201.
15. Pierre Montebello, "Matter and Light in Bergson's *Creative Evolution*," Roxanne Lapidus (trans.), *SubStance* 114, 36(3) (2007), 93.
16. Tom Quirk, *Bergson and American Culture: The Worlds of Willa Cather and Wallace Stevens* (Chapel Hill, NC: University of North Carolina Press, 1990), 2.
17. *Ibid.*
18. William James, *Pragmatism and Four Essays from "The Meaning of Truth"* (New York: Meridian, 1974), 19.

emits "far-flashing beams of light … over the world's perspectives."[19] Bergsonism enjoyed an intellectual and social significance in what has been called the "Progressive Era." As Tom Quirk notes, "the Bergsonian universe is a universe of immanence, not transcendence."[20] At the Fourth International Congress in Philosophy held in Bologna in April 1911, Bergson gave one of the key lectures along with Hans Driesch, Paul Langevin, and Henri Poincaré. By the time of the Congress he had become the most celebrated thinker of the day and in his lecture he seeks to identify how philosophy relates to both science and art, something that also preoccupied the likes of Nietzsche and Wittgenstein, and that has been made central in our own time in Deleuze's consideration of the question "What is philosophy?"[21] For Bergson the future of philosophy resides in it finding its own sources of knowledge, not merely imitating developments in the method of science, and in this respect the activity of the philosopher is akin to that of the artist.

Bergson is also keen on occasion to tackle science head on in its claim to deal with facts and gain its superiority from this attachment to them. He pursues what we can call a "superior" positivism by conceiving metaphysics – the field of informed vision and speculation – as a mode of knowledge that can advance by the gradual accumulation of obtained results. In other words, metaphysics does not have to be "a take-it-or-leave-it system" that is forever in dispute and doomed to start afresh, thinking abstractly and vainly without the support of empirical science. Not only is it the case for Bergson that metaphysics can be a true empiricism, but it can also work with science in an intellectual effort to advance our knowledge of the various sources, tendencies, and directions of life. Bergson outlines his "superior positivism" in his Huxley lecture of 1911 on "Life and Consciousness": "it seems to me that in different regions of experience there are different groups of facts … we possess now a certain number of *lines of facts*, which do not go as far as we want, but which we can prolong hypothetically."[22] This is taken up again in the *Two Sources of Morality and Religion* of 1932, where he states that the different lines of fact indicate for us the direction of truth but none go far enough; the attainment of truth can take place only when the lines are prolonged to the point where they intersect.[23]

19. *Ibid.*
20. Quirk, *Bergson and American Culture*, 11.
21. Deleuze and Guattari, *What is Philosophy?*
22. Henri Bergson, "Life and Consciousness," in *Mind-Energy*, Keith Ansell-Pearson and Michael Kolkman (eds), H. Wildon Carr (trans.) (Basingstoke: Palgrave Macmillan, 2007), 4.
23. Henri Bergson, *The Two Sources of Morality and Religion*, R. Ashley Audra and Cloudesley Brereton (trans.), with the assistance of W. Horsfall Carter (Notre Dame, IN: University of Notre Dame Press, 1977), 248.

However, it is misleading, as is now customary, to simply label Bergson's project as standing for the renewal of spiritualism. This only reinstates the antinomies of modern thought, notably freedom and determinism, he was so keen to reconfigure and in a way that would significantly alter our appreciation of the problem. As one commentator has noted, his work reflects a lifelong interest in both the physical and mental realms and he was not an enemy of the inquiries of rational, physical science.[24] Moreover, like most intellectuals in the post-Darwinian era he felt compelled to confront the radical discoveries of natural science. In *Creative Evolution*, he holds that "transformism," as he calls the new science, "forces itself now upon all philosophy, as the dogmatic affirmation of transformism forces itself upon science."[25] Thus, to suggest that Bergson is the successor to French spiritualism who framed spiritualist ideas in terms that were appealing to a twentieth-century audience disillusioned with the rationalist and determinist society of the Third Republic is to present an oversimplified and distorting account of his work (it also ignores the fact that his academic training was in mathematics and physics; the same is also true of the founding figures of the analytic and continental traditions, Frege and Husserl). In insisting on a difference between the positive sciences and philosophy, Bergson is concerned with the purification of science from scientism, that is, a metaphysics that masquerades as positive scientific knowledge. Bergson's stance is one, of course, that would be met with widespread favor among philosophers of different persuasions today.

The reputation Bergson enjoyed at the time of the Fourth International Congress, and more generally in the intellectual life of the time, derived from him being able to offer fresh solutions to philosophical problems that were perceived at the time to resonate with social and global changes. In essence, he offered a philosophy of life to replace the philosophy of the closed system and predictable certainty, and the phenomenon of Bergsonism served as the main catalyst for the transformation of sensibility and appropriation of the new reality.[26] However, it was not alone in providing new methods and concepts to alter our understanding of, and participation in, the world.

Although today neo-Kantianism is unduly neglected, in this period it was one of the major philosophical forces in both France and Germany. As one commentator has noted, the view that it had reduced philosophy to the theory of

24. Mary Ann Gillies, *Henri Bergson and British Modernism* (Montreal: McGill-Queen's University Press, 1996), 9.
25. Henri Bergson, *Creative Evolution*, Arthur Mitchell (trans.) (Basingstoke: Palgrave Macmillan, 2007), 17.
26. Quirk, *Bergson and American Culture*, 14.

knowledge is unfair and was rejected by a number of neo-Kantians themselves.[27] Their achievements included: developing philological research that helped establish Kant's monumental role in the history of modern European philosophy, a role taken as a matter of course today; establishing important trajectories in epistemology and the philosophy of science; and developing Kantian thought in diverse areas such as the theory of value, ethics, and social and political philosophy. Taken together, these developments represent an attempt to restore the integrity of Kant's transcendental project against the nineteenth-century reduction of philosophy to a handmaiden of science as a result of the immature claims of positivism and scientism.

As Suzanne Guerlac notes, in the mid-nineteenth-century context, positivism was a progressive force that held out the promise of a radical secularization of knowledge, countering the fog of metaphysical dogmatism on the one hand and religion on the other.[28] The term "positivism" was first used by Auguste Comte (1798–1857) to denote a philosophy based on the positive facts of experience and that avoided metaphysical hypotheses. As Gary Gutting notes, it was applied to any view that privileged the empirical sciences over metaphysical thought.[29] In its classical expression in the work of Comte, positivism seemed to offer a grand narrative of human development from a theological phase (the age of gods or of God) through a metaphysical phase (the age of metaphysical abstractions) to that of positive scientific knowledge in which human maturity is reached with the abandonment of ultimate explanatory causes. With the arrival of positivism, the human mind contents itself with focusing on observed facts that it subsumes under general descriptive laws such as the law of gravitation. Our knowledge is relative, not absolute, and we relinquish the concern with ultimate causes insofar as we do not know the whole universe but only the universe as it appears to us. Recent studies have encouraged us to appreciate Comte as a much more subtle and delicate – even "continental" – thinker than is widely supposed. In his *Comte after Positivism*, for example, Robert Scharff seeks to show that Comte, while holding scientific philosophy to be the final stage of intellectual development, did not simply reject theology and metaphysics; rather, he has a historico-critical appreciation of the situation in which philosophy's past is relevant to its future practice, and this involves a *critical appropriation* of the theologico-metaphysical legacy.[30] Comte emerges, then, as a historically minded reflective thinker about

27. Herbert Schnädelbach, *Philosophy in Germany 1831–1933*, Eric Matthews (trans.) (Cambridge: Cambridge University Press, 1984), 106.
28. Guerlac, *Thinking in Time*, 21.
29. Gary Gutting, *French Philosophy in the Twentieth Century* (Cambridge: Cambridge University Press, 2001), 8.
30. Robert C. Scharff, *Comte after Positivism* (Cambridge: Cambridge University Press, 1995), 5.

scientific practice in which "positive philosophy" is to be practiced not in a "post-"metaphysical world but under transitional circumstances.[31]

In the period this volume covers, one important development in French philosophy advances in the direction of what has been called a "spiritual positivism," notably in the work of Bergson's immediate precursor, Émile Boutroux (1845–1921), who exerted a major influence as a teacher of the history of philosophy at the École Normale Supérieure and at the Sorbonne. Indeed, Boutroux dominated the academic philosophy of the Third Republic through the First World War.[32] Like other neo-Kantian philosophers of the period, Boutroux is wrestling with Kantian problems, especially freedom and determinism, and is dissatisfied with the Kantian solution, which places freedom and hence ethics in a sphere that is inaccessible to human consciousness. If we are to justify the claim that we are free, then it is necessary to establish that the phenomenal world as described by science is indeterministic.[33] In two of his most important books, his 1874 doctoral dissertation, *De la contingence des lois de la nature* (*The Contingency of the Laws of Nature*), and *Idée de loi naturelle dans la science et la philosophie contemporaines* (*Natural Law in Science and Philosophy*; 1895), Boutroux seeks to show that freedom is the fundamental element of reality and that science does not necessitate rigid determinism. Whatever happens, according to Boutroux, does so neither necessarily nor accidentally but contingently, and is the expression of a world consciousness conceived as an eternally creative activity. For science the law of causation is a practical principle; it is unable to explain the general interaction and interpenetration of things. Thus, in respect to quality, cause and effect are disproportionate to one another: the effect is different in nature from the cause and if nothing new were contained in the effect, then cause and effect would not vary from each other. This means for Boutroux that the laws of nature have no absolute existence and iron necessity but are to be regarded as the artificial picture of a model that is essentially a living and moving reality.[34]

Léon Brunschvicg (1869–1944) was the leading figure in the development of French idealism in this period who, as a professor at the Sorbonne from 1900 to 1939, exercised a tremendous influence, with all aspiring French philosophers of the time, including Jean-Paul Sartre and Maurice Merleau-Ponty, having to come to terms with his thought.[35] He was the author of important studies of

31. For Scharff's deft handling of Comte's "three-stage law" – theology, metaphysics, science – see *ibid.*, 73–91.
32. Gutting, *French Philosophy in the Twentieth Century*, 20.
33. *Ibid.*, 21.
34. Isaac Benrubi, *Contemporary Thought of France*, Ernest B. Dicker (trans.) (London: Williams & Norgate, 1926), 157.
35. Gutting, *French Philosophy in the Twentieth Century*, 40.

Pascal and Spinoza, and one of his major texts was on the modality of judgment. He formulates a critical idealism in the spirit of Kant as an alternative to positivism on the one hand and Hegelian rationalism on the other. Genuine knowledge consists for Brunschvicg not in the judgment of crude experience but in an independent interpretation by the mind of the data provided by observation and through the means of the analytical and synthetical forms of knowledge that are peculiar to it: reality is part of the mind's own development and self-realization. This is a view he called "mathematical intellectualism."[36] He rejects completely Kant's notion of the thing-in-itself since we can have no knowledge of something that exists independently of a relation to knowledge: a thing outside of knowledge would be equivalent to nothing. However, this does not lead him, *qua* his idealism, to reject external, material reality in favor of an inner spiritual reality since this would be to replace one thing-in-itself with another: "A consistent idealism must see *all* beings as the objects of a thought that is itself a function or act of thinking, not an independently existing thing."[37] The difference between science and philosophy is that whereas the former is concerned with objects of thought, the latter is concerned with thought itself in which thinking is identical with judging. As in the case of Boutroux, there is not an outright rejection of positivism. His project has been interpreted as a union of positivism and idealism: we know the truth through the experience of the historical progress of science and this history is the record of the mind's constitution of ever more successful frameworks for our interpretation of experience.[38] Like Boutroux he accords privilege to freedom and creativity over determinism and inertia: "consciousness is the creator of moral values, as it is of scientific values and of aesthetic values."[39] Speaking like Nietzsche, who appeals to philosophical legislators, and echoing Bergson in the *Two Sources of Morality and Religion*, Brunschvicg champions those heroes of spiritual life who "cast ahead of themselves lines of intelligence and truth" that are destined to create a new universe.[40]

Key figures in the history of sociology, such as Durkheim and Marcel Mauss, sought to assess the legacy of positivism (Comte and Émile Littré) and neo-Kantianism in France by reconfiguring the relation between philosophy and the social sciences, especially sociology and anthropology. Both preferred to be called rationalists rather than positivists. In political theory, they rejected Comte's "positive polity" and Marxian communism, as well as the political forms of the Third Republic. Against these developments, they sought to outline a theory of socialism in which political liberty and individualism could flourish.

36. Benrubi, *Contemporary Thought of France*, 133–4.
37. Gutting, *French Philosophy in the Twentieth Century*, 40.
38. *Ibid.*, 43.
39. Cited in *ibid.*, 47.
40. *Ibid.*

Their position was generally consistent with the development in the Third Republic of the laic state, the basis of which they argued would be civic secular ritual, institutional reforms underpinned by a new kind of moral and social scientific education. Their work influenced the theory of symbolic exchange developed by Georges Bataille and Jean Baudrillard, as well as the structural anthropology of Claude Lévi-Strauss. Mention should be made here of Mauss's "Essay on the Gift," which revolutionized the field of ethnology and, together with the aforementioned figures, has exerted a powerful influence on the reflections of Jacques Derrida on the economy of time and giving.[41] Mauss's text is not about religion but about economics and politics: "the theory of the gift is a theory of human solidarity."[42] Before the First World War, the open enemy of French political philosophy was Anglo-Saxon utilitarianism and liberalism, which was typically subjected to three criticisms: (i) that it was based on an impoverished concept of the person construed as an independent atom instead of a social being implicated in communities of exchange; (ii) that it neglected how social relations change with changes in the mode of production; (iii) that its concept of liberty was a negative one in which little role was given to the ethical importance of political participation. In the conclusion to his essay, Mauss stresses two aspects of his analysis: first, that the kind of analysis into gift exchange he has embarked on, in which the gift is conceived as a public drama, can lead to a "science of customs" in which the facts studied and observed are held to be "*total* social facts" involving the totality of society and its institutions, and, second, that it leads to a set of "moral conclusions" or, as he says, to adopt an old world "civility" or "civics." What is at stake in such a sociological inquiry is ultimately reflection on the nature and ends of "common life," "the conscious direction of which is the supreme art, *Politics*, in the Socratic sense of the word."[43]

In Germany, neo-Kantianism developed out of an academic context but also, as Sebastian Luft and Fabien Capeillères point out in their essay in this volume, out of sociopolitical discourses that responded to industrialization and the workers' question. The other relevant background, of course, as in France, is the progress of the natural sciences in an era of positivism. Hermann Cohen, one of the leading neo-Kantian figures in Germany, who promoted an ethical socialism, was dismissive of the rise of "Nietzschean" philosophy, seeing it as a withdrawal from scientific and scholastic rigor since it promoted a form of

41. See Jacques Derrida, *Given Time. I: Counterfeit Money*, Peggy Kamuf (trans.) (Chicago, IL: University of Chicago Press, 1994), and the essays in Alan D. Schrift (ed.), *The Logic of the Gift: Toward an Ethic of Generosity* (New York: Routledge, 1998).

42. Mary Douglas, "Foreword," in Marcel Mauss, *The Gift: The Form and Reason for Exchange in Archaic Societies* (London: Routledge, 2002), xiii.

43. Mauss, *The Gift*, 107.

cultural emancipation that could not be reconciled with the discipline of philosophy.[44] This did not stop, however, more intellectually independent figures, on the margins of academic philosophy and the neo-Kantian movement, from attempting a synthesis of Kant and Nietzsche, with the work of Simmel being the best-known example. It is usual to focus on two main schools of German neo-Kantianism: the southwest school based in the universities of Heidelberg and Freiburg, which includes figures such as Wilhelm Windelband and Heinrich Rickert, and the Marburg School located further north at the university there, which includes leading academic figures such as Cohen and Paul Natorp. At the risk of overgeneralization, it can be said that the southwest school tended to focus on questions of culture and value, with members of the Marburg School focusing more on issues of logic and epistemology.[45] Associated with the work of the southwest school, centered around its journal *Logos*, were major intellectual figures such as Weber, Simmel, and, interestingly, Husserl. What united the schools, in spite of their differences and quarrels, was their subscription to the battle cry of "Back to Kant" which came from Otto Liebmann's *Kant und die Epigonen* of 1865. This involved determining what Kant actually taught and said, or Kant philology. Cohen produced commentaries on each of Kant's three Critiques, while the edition of the Royal Prussian Academy, begun in 1900 under the general editorship of Wilhelm Dilthey, aimed to provide scholars with a definitive edition of Kant's writings. On the other hand, it also involved setting out what Kant *should* have said. While aiming to adhere to the spirit and letter of Kant's writings, "the neo-Kantians wished to return to Kant in order to use his principles and methodologies to answer both old and new philosophical problems."[46] A key concern and development was to extend the Kantian appreciation of what constituted universal and necessary knowledge. For Kant, such knowledge is exemplified by mathematics and the natural sciences; for the neo-Kantians, this could be extended to new sciences of man such as sociology and history. In refining and developing Kant in this way, Windelband argued that the aim was, in fact, to understand Kant by going beyond him.

In contrast to the case of Bergson, the legacies of Frege and Husserl were quite different, being both immediate and long-lasting. Frege, who taught mathematics at Jena University for the whole of his philosophical career, and who is today held to be, in the words of Michael Friedman and Thomas Ryckman, the "patriarch" of the analytic tradition, establishes modern mathematical logic

44. See Ralph M. Leck, *Georg Simmel and Avant-Garde Sociology: The Birth of Modernity 1880–1920* (New York: Humanity Books, 2000), 85.

45. Christopher Adair-Toteff, "Neo-Kantianism: The German Idealism Movement," in *The Cambridge History of Philosophy 1870–1945*, Thomas Baldwin (ed.) (Cambridge: Cambridge University Press, 2003), 28–9.

46. *Ibid.*, 30.

as both a technical subject and a foundational subject for philosophy. Frege took stock of the developments that had taken place in mathematics since Kant, including the construction of non-Euclidean geometries by figures such as János Bolyai and Bernhard Riemann, and advances made by analysis and algebra in axiomatization.[47] Under the influence of Rudolf Hermann Lotze, also read by Husserl, he arrived at the view that the propositions of arithmetic could not be synthetic *a priori* judgments but were instead analytic ones whose demonstration required no recourse to intuition. To show this, Frege aimed to free arithmetic from the bonds that tied it to natural languages and the way to do this was axiomatically, employing a system of conventional signs, namely, logic.[48] In his now famous article of 1892 entitled "Sense and Reference," Frege also formulated distinctions that were to prove invaluable not only for logical analysis but for linguistic analysis as well.

Husserl, the "patriarch" of the continental tradition, establishes the new method of transcendental phenomenology and seeks to constitute philosophy on new grounds as a rigorous "scientific" discipline. Although he did not invent the word "phenomenology" and was by no means the first to use it, the work he did under this title proved so influential that as a school of twentieth-century European philosophy, "phenomenology" became synonymous with his pioneering project. Husserl is one of the key philosophical figures of this period and his work undergoes a remarkable development, from *Philosophy of Arithmetic* of 1889 to *The Crisis of the European Sciences and Transcendental Phenomenology* of the mid-1930s. Against the imperial claims of a science that degenerates into scientism, Husserl is keen to show the necessity and validity of the human agent and person who belongs to a thematic world of intentional life. "Subjects cannot be dissolved into nature," Husserl maintains, "for in that case what gives nature its sense would be missing."[49] On the basis of this kind of claim, he seeks to show the necessity of moving from the "naturalistic attitude" to the "personalistic world," in which the researcher exists in a "surrounding world" of sense-bestowal. The other important aspect of Husserl's project of phenomenology is its attack, which it shares with the work of Frege, on the psychologism that reigned in philosophy from the middle of the nineteenth century until well into the twentieth century. This is the view that the structure and principles of logic are derived from the organization of the human psyche. There is a variant to this, which is the claim that psychology is the basis of the human

47. Christian Delacampagne, *A History of Philosophy in the Twentieth Century*, M. B. DeBevoise (trans.) (Baltimore, MD: Johns Hopkins University Press, 1999), 15.

48. *Ibid.*

49. Edmund Husserl, *Ideas Pertaining to a Pure Phenomenology and to a Phenomenological Philosophy, Second Book*, Richard Rojcewicz and André Schuwer (trans.) (Dordrecht: Kluwer, 1989), 311.

sciences including philosophy, a version of which Nietzsche promotes in *Beyond Good and Evil*,[50] and is a feature of the work of Wundt, Dilthey, and Simmel. The attempt to defeat psychologism and its influence, along with other philosophical reductions such as biologism, is what unites the work of Husserl, Scheler, and Heidegger. In short, phenomenology is an attempt to rehabilitate philosophy as a science with a special domain: as a rigorous science (*strenge Wissenschaft*), the attempt is made to describe phenomena as they are given and, through the famous *epochē*, refrain from "assumptions and affirmations of existence with regard to what it investigates in introspection … in this way, a vast field of enquiry, belonging only to 'phenomenological research,' is to be opened up."[51]

The phenomenological circles that flourished in the early part of the twentieth century – in Munich, Göttingen, Freiburg, and Vienna – served to extend the inquiries of phenomenology into the realms of aesthetics (Roman Ingarden), ethics (Max Scheler), social and political thought (Alfred Schutz and José Ortega y Gassett), and pushed it beyond its potentially narrow theoretical and geographical provincialism. The work of Scheler provides a good example of this. He was one of Husserl's most important associates but, in contrast to Husserl, his focus was not on founding a new scientific philosophy but rather on what he perceived to be the moral crisis of his time, "in which the values of a calculating and egotistic bourgeois capitalism replaced those of Christianity."[52] He set himself the task of reconstructing Christian ethics after Nietzsche's polemical attack on morality and showing that it was not the ethics of *ressentiment* Nietzsche claimed. To this end, he employed the resources of phenomenology, publishing in 1913 a phenomenological study of sympathy (and love and hate) and a work on ethics in which he sought to counter the tendency in philosophy of producing a formal ethics.

Heidegger published his epoch-making text *Being and Time* in 1927 and today it stands as perhaps the single most influential work of twentieth-century European philosophy, seeking to show why time is the phenomenon that can unlock the question of the meaning of being. As Herbert Schnädelbach astutely observes, it is a work that brings together a number of discussions that were at the time scattered and endeavors to resolve them all at once by posing the question at a more radical level.[53] This consists in offering a fundamental ontological theory of "understanding," showing that the phenomenology of Dasein is hermeneutics in the original sense of the word, referring to the "business of exposition." Heidegger's contention is that this hermeneutics is the elaboration

50. Nietzsche, *Beyond Good and Evil*, §23.
51. Schnädelbach, *Philosophy in Germany 1831–1933*, 107.
52. Herman Philipse, "The Phenomenological Movement," in Baldwin, *The Cambridge History of Philosophy*, 488.
53. Schnädelbach, *Philosophy in Germany 1831–1933*, 136.

of the conditions of the possibility of all ontological inquiry in which Dasein enjoys ontological priority over all beings: "Philosophy is universal phenomenological ontology, starting from the hermeneutics of Dasein, which, as an analytic of *existence*, has secured the end of the guiding thread of all philosophical questioning at the point from which it *originates* and to which it *returns*."[54] In effect, this means that "understanding" belongs to the fundamental structure of the human being (Dasein) and is a problem in the theory of science only at a secondary level. Heidegger insists that Dasein is a Being that cannot be understood as like all other beings since it is distinguished by the fact that in its very Being that Being is an issue for it: "*Understanding of Being is itself a definite characteristic of Dasein's Being*. Dasein is ontically distinctive in that it is ontological."[55] In this definition, Heidegger has carried out a major transformation of Husserl's project: while agreeing with Husserl that ontology is possible only as phenomenology, he uses phenomenology as a methodological concept and no longer as a definition of a field of objects.[56] As Heidegger says, the word "phenomenology" primarily informs us about "the '*how*' with which *what* is to be treated in this science gets exhibited and handled."[57] Phenomenology has become the science of the Being of beings, that is, of the manner in which things show themselves. Dasein is not to be approached in an objectivist fashion but as a special kind of "subject" of knowledge: it is distinguished by its "existential" mode of being and conditions of existence, and of course the claim that the essence of Dasein lies in its existence is what gives rise to existentialism, even though Heidegger was keen to disassociate his own position from it in his well-known *Letter on Humanism*.

On the one hand, this development in European thought of a philosophy of existence with Heidegger and Jaspers represents another attack on positivism and scientism; on the other hand, it also supersedes the philosophy of life in an equally deeper and more radicalized manner. It did this by seeking an integration in the concept of "existence" of the antithesis of life and understanding, or the irrational and rationality, especially in the work of Jaspers. Like Heidegger, Jaspers proposes that we need to think about the question of Being in a radically new way by asking what it means for us in our temporal existence. Truth for the human being under temporal conditions is a matter of historicity and active realization, being a matter of responsiveness to challenges and limit situations that confront us with the radical confines of our temporal existence. On

54. Martin Heidegger, *Being and Time*, John Macquarrie and Edward Robinson (trans.) (Oxford: Blackwell, 1962), 62.
55. *Ibid.*, 32.
56. Schnädelbach, *Philosophy in Germany 1831–1933*, 206.
57. Heidegger, *Being and Time*, 59.

the one hand, Jaspers follows life philosophies, such as we find in Dilthey, in holding that the cognitivist concept of the subject is seriously deficient and that it is through existential lived experience – and not simply through discursive understanding or science – that truth discloses itself to us. On the other hand, however, such an illumination of existence through existential means should not lead to a devaluation of understanding, reason, and science. Rather, Jaspers advises, the philosophy of existence needs to make use of all material knowledge.

Freud is highly relevant to the European philosophical tradition because he too places temporality and embodiment at the center of an understanding of human subjectivity. Although Freud himself was averse to relying on philosophers in the course of his psychoanalytic labors (finding it excessively speculative), from the vantage point of Jacques Lacan's return to Freud it is possible to discern important precursors of psychoanalysis in the modern era of the history of philosophy (Lacan takes great care to situate Freud in relation to the likes of Descartes, Kant, and Hegel), as well as appreciate the considerable impact Freud has had, and continues to have, on philosophy from his time through to the present. As Adrian Johnston notes in this volume, the topics Freud analyzes, such as temporality, subjectivity and intersubjectivity, embodiment, and affectivity are ones that are central to both the history of continental philosophy and its contemporary practice. A vulgar biological materialist would be of little interest to continental philosophers. But, as Johnston shows, for Freud the body with which psychical apparatus is in rapport is not construed along the lines of a piece of mechanistic matter moved by efficient causes. Thus, the picture of Freud as engaged in a reductive project shared by the likes of Heidegger and Sartre is fundamentally mistaken. As Johnston shows, Freud, like Husserl, has a debt to the work of Franz Brentano, which sought to show that the mental cannot be collapsed into the physical on account of the "intentional" quality and aspect of the mental. Where Freud's psychoanalysis does part company with Husserl's phenomenology, of course, is on the question of the unconscious. But with his all-important concept of the drive, Freud depicts the human subject as taking shape at the complex and tangled intersection of body and mind, nature, and nurture.

Wittgenstein's influence on linguistic philosophy is well known and has been well documented. Less well known perhaps is the relation of his philosophical therapeutics, which sets out to dissolve philosophical problems by showing them to be false problems, to both previous figures in modern thought who have played a seminal role in the development of continental philosophy (e.g. Nietzsche), and to major twentieth-century developments in continental philosophy (e.g. the work of Bergson, Derrida, and Lyotard). Although he is not doing either natural science or natural history, Wittgenstein's orientation is ultimately naturalistic: the conception of the "ordinary" is tightly woven with the general "facts of nature" in which propositions function in the context of concrete forms of human life and language games. Like Bergson, but for different reasons, Wittgenstein can be seen as suggesting that philosophy is more like an art than a science: "It has turned back from the quest for some more general and inclusive system, and the sense of wonder now finds its object and its satisfaction in the nuances of the particular case."[58]

Like several other thinkers whose work is treated in this volume, Wittgenstein occupies an important place in the development of a "superior" or "subtle" positivism. As one commentator has noted, "It is clear that Wittgenstein was not a destructive positivist. He did not reject all discourse but factual discourse. On the contrary, one of his reasons for plotting the limit of factual discourse was that he wanted to prevent it from encroaching on the others."[59] The "truths" of religion and morality cannot be defended in the way Kant sought, and although they lack factual sense this does not mean they are unintelligible or insignificant. When Wittgenstein famously says in the preface to the *Tractatus* that there is nothing outside the limit of language, he meant that there is nothing factual outside the limit of factual language, and in stating this he allows that there are things that cannot be said in factual language but that can still be "shown." Far from being an intolerant positivist, then, Wittgenstein shows in his approach to the phenomena of ethics, aesthetics, and religion that he is a "subtle" positivist.[60] On this model of knowledge, although the natural sciences disclose what can be said about the world and have no use for philosophy, the empirical sciences are to be regarded as providing not an explanation but only a simple *description* of the world.[61] Wittgenstein rejected the pseudo-scientific treatment of nonfactual modes of thought and defended their claim to independence. For example, a religious tenet is not a factual hypothesis but something that influences our thoughts and actions in a different way: "the meaning of a religious proposition is not a function of what would have to be the case if it were true but a function of the difference that it makes to the lives of those who maintain it."[62] Even when it appears that an "antiphilosophy" has been introduced into intellectual life, as in the cases of Nietzsche and Wittgenstein, it may be that such vexation is in fact, as one commentator has noted, a search for a new way of philosophizing.[63]

Indeed, it could be said that what emerges in philosophy in this decidedly modernist period of invention is, above all, a remarkable set of resources,

58. David Pears, *Wittgenstein* (London: Collins, 1971), 38.
59. *Ibid.*, 169.
60. See *ibid.*, 104, 172–4.
61. Delacampagne, *A History of Philosophy in the Twentieth Century*, 47.
62. Pears, *Wittgenstein*, 174.
63. Delacampagne, *A History of Philosophy in the Twentieth Century*, 60.

involving new methods, new concepts, and even new beings such as Dasein, that show the importance of philosophical subtlety, dexterity, and complexity, and these are vital instruments in combating the dogmatic self-assuredness of intellectual positivism and scientism. The thinkers of this period rediscover philosophy and invent it afresh, and they do so in many seminal ways that continue to exert a lively felt presence on its contemporary modes of practice.

1

HENRI BERGSON

John Mullarkey

For reasons too numerous to list here fully – many of them unrelated to what is normally called philosophy – Bergson's place in the history of continental philosophy is one that has always had to be contested.[1] By "continental philosophy" I understand the anglophone reception of the past hundred years of mainly French and German philosophy, a field in which one is as likely to come across Bergson's name as not at all. He appears as a central figure in one or two studies (in Eric Matthews's history, for example, all twentieth-century French philosophy is dubbed a "series of footnotes to Bergson"[2]) but he is mostly neglected in others. This is not always a product of laziness or ignorance; despite much recent work done by Bergson scholars in the US, Britain, and France on the centrality of Bergson to the French reception of phenomenology – or to the philosophy of time (or the body, or life, or difference) – Bergson still remains a blind spot, a repressed element that needs to be defended, resurrected, or rehabilitated time and time again. Of all the moderns named in Gilles Deleuze's famous counter-canon of philosophy – Spinoza, Leibniz, Hume, Nietzsche, and Bergson – it

1. Henri-Louis Bergson (October 18, 1859–January 3, 1941; born and died in Paris, France) was educated at the École Normale Supérieure (1878–81) and took his doctorate at the University of Paris (1888). His influences included Boutroux, Kant, Lachelier, Ravaisson, and Spencer. He held appointments at the lycée in Angers (1881–82), Lycée Blaise-Pascal, Clermont-Ferrand (1882–88), and Lycée Henri-IV, Paris (1888–97), and was appointed *maître de conférences* at the École Normale Supérieure (1897–1900), Chair of Ancient Philosophy at the Collège de France (1900–1904), and Chair of Modern Philosophy at the Collège de France (1904–12, 1914–20). He was elected to the Académie des Sciences Morales et Politiques in 1901 and the Académie Française in 1914, and was awarded the Nobel Prize for Literature in 1928.
2. Eric Matthews, *Twentieth-Century French Philosophy* (Oxford: Oxford University Press, 1996), 13.

is really only the last mentioned who has not been canonized *anywhere*.[3] The others have their long lists of disciples, societies, journals, schools, and recognized methods. Bergson has few or none, and remains an orphan within philosophical history, despite numerous efforts to reverse this; he appears as the perpetual outsider, uncategorizable, and anomalous in his place in the history of philosophy. It does not help, of course, that Bergson's complex theoretical positions make him resistant to assimilation within other movements: he has phenomenological aspects to his thought, and yet was not a phenomenologist; he was a naturalistic philosopher, but his was a far from standard naturalism; his work valorizes difference, but not through the structures of language. One is tempted to define Bergson in terms of his own concept of the "indefinite": as that which is always "on the move" and so incapable of being positioned.

It is not so surprising, therefore, that it has often fallen to the lot of the "Bergsonian" today to undo history's "damnation of Bergson," to make recompense for this unfair neglect, to show how he preempted Heidegger, influenced Merleau-Ponty, or shaped Deleuze's thinking (the strategy of tethering his name to more lustrous figures is a well-worn one). Yet anyone who has tried in vain to reverse this neglect over the past decade, and who has seen others attempt the same with little success over many decades, could be forgiven for growing weary of the cause.[4] The pressure of historical entropy seems to win out, its inertia irreversible: despite much evidence in favor of a Bergsonian dimension to their subject, most scholars (with a few of notable exceptions) of Merleau-Ponty or Deleuze (or Sartre, Henry, Levinas ...) rarely read Bergson. Not that this is surprising any longer, however, for it was rare for any of the major postwar French philosophers themselves to acknowledge an influence from Bergson, and without that clear expression of lineage it must be difficult to pursue lines of inquiry outside the *authorized* version of intellectual history. Apart from Deleuze (who did write extensively on Bergson), only Levinas takes time to credit Bergson with any sustained significance for him, but even then does so only in interviews rather than primary works.[5] The rest remain silent.

3. In *Negotiations*, Deleuze recalls being laughed at "simply for having written about Bergson at all" (*Negotiations 1972–1990*, Martin Joughin [trans.] [New York: Columbia University Press, 1995], 6).
4. Frederick Burwick and Paul Douglass (eds), *The Crisis in Modernism: Bergsonism and the Vitalist Controversy* (Cambridge: Cambridge University Press, 1992), 7.
5. See the interview with Levinas in Richard Kearney (ed.), *Dialogues with Contemporary Continental Thinkers* (Manchester: Manchester University Press, 1984), 49. Levinas does give something like a sustained philosophical treatment of Bergson in Richard A. Cohen's translated edition of Levinas's *Time and the Other* (Pittsburgh, PA: Duquesne University Press, 1987), but this still amounts to only one small part of a lesser work.

And yet for nearly twenty years Bergson was at the center of Western philosophy; for half of that time, from 1907 to 1917, he was *the* philosopher of Europe, with an influence spreading beyond philosophy and into the arts, sociology, psychology, history, and politics.[6] Although that influence had been severely diminished by the end of the First World War, all the same Bergson must have remained an important presence for the French philosophers born at the turn of the century. Whatever their reasons for not wishing to acknowledge that presence directly, there may be traces of it left in their work. One way to discover such traces is through the language used in their writing. And when one looks at Bergson's own vocabulary – the one he invented – one does have a sense of *déjà vu*. One discovers that the language that has been in use over the past hundred years of continental philosophy has an obvious Bergsonian provenance despite his own work's reversal of fortune. This is not direct enough to be a specific philosophical influence nor, alternatively, coherent enough to warrant it being called the *Weltanschauung* in which French thought conducted itself. But there is a range of words and terminological strategies that stands out because it is only after Bergson that this kind of language became *de rigueur* in French continental thought.

Alternatively, one all too visible trace of Bergson's presence that does not need any detection is what we should call "comic-book Bergsonism": in its pages we find the comical picture of a dualism that opposed all forms of space to time, a vitalism that argued for a special form of living energy determining the direction of evolution, and a monism that denied the existence and appearance of substance in favor of everything being in motion. All of these stereotypes of Bergson were and are straw men: implausible positions set up mostly in order to cast a favorable light on whatever supposedly stark alternative to Bergson was being forwarded at the time – a new phenomenology, logical positivism, structuralism, and so on. Yet Bergson would have found these views no less incredible, for he never opposed all space to time, did not think of the *élan vital* as a special kind of energy, did not think that evolution was heading in any direction, and did not deny the existence and appearance of substance (but only showed what substance was – a *complexity* of movement).

It is the task of what follows, then, to replace this comical image with a serious one: the image of a thinker whose influence on philosophy's language has been immense, yet rarely acknowledged by other philosophers. More often than not, of course, what philosophers say is at variance with what they do, and in the case at hand it will be the language of French philosophy that expresses a latent

6. See R. C. Grogin, *The Bergsonian Controversy in France, 1900–1914* (Calgary: University of Calgary Press, 1988); Mark Antliff, *Inventing Bergson: Cultural Politics and the Parisian Avant-Garde* (Princeton, NJ: Princeton University Press, 1993).

Bergsonism "acting itself out," so to speak. With this in mind, I shall set out a number of categories (not all of them explicitly used by Bergson – e.g. "holism") that tie together Bergson's terminology, while also linking them to his texts, to other philosophers, and to recent themes in continental philosophy. Although the terms will often overlap in usage, I shall try to separate them according to a number of linguistic practices:

- some of them *methodological* – the language of *holism* (vagueness, abstraction as immobilization, interpenetrating images, antibinarism, metaphoricity, thick descriptions that restore singular novelty, the concrete); the language of *intuition* (metaphysical perception, knowledge and sympathy, immanent thought as becoming the thing); the language of *immanence* (antitranscendence and the antitranscendental); the language of *pluralism* (multiplicity, levels, dissociation, qualitative difference and differentiation); and the language of *nonphilosophy* (philosophy in art, in mysticism);
- some of them *metaphysical* – the language of the *Real* (radical empiricism as metaphysics, the rejection of negativity, the critique of possibility); the language of *time* (novelty, becoming, change, process, movement, heterogeneity); and the language that goes *beyond subject and object* (refraction, endosmosis, mixture);
- some more *naturalistic* – the language of *Consciousness* (the unconscious, fractured ego, memory, the virtual); the language of the *body* (affectivity, motility, habit), and the language of *nature* (the animal, biology, evolution);
- and some more *normative* – the language of *Life*; the language of *ethics* (alterity, attention, sympathy, the Open and the Closed); the language of *antireductionism* (antimechanism, antiscientism); and the language of *freedom* (the given fact of liberty, the free act that dissolves *aporia*).

The philosophical origins of a term such as "multiplicity" are not exclusive to Bergson, of course (Husserl would also have to be brought into that account): no one can own a concept uniquely. But there is a critical mass attained by a large array of Bergson's favored terms that, only after him, became widespread and publicly owned, evolving by mutation in the hands of others. Nor is this Bergsonian inheritance operating in isolation; it coexists with the language of Greek philosophy, Cartesianism, and Kantianism that can be found in every Western philosophy. But it is the layers of Bergsonisms that especially characterize French thought this past hundred years, layers that might also reduce the gap between Matthews's comment on French philosophy as a "footnote" to Bergson, and the lack of actual footnotes to Bergson in its pages.

I. METHODOLOGIES

Holism

The mutation of Bergson's language also occurs in his own hands, for concepts such as "duration" or "space" do not hold the same meaning across his works. They evolve or, rather, they co-evolve in the presence of other concepts in other contexts (the duration of consciousness in *Time and Free Will* is somewhat different from the duration of life in *Creative Evolution*). This co-evolution is indicative of a Bergsonian principle that is now a commonplace: the holism of the Real. Bergson is a holist such that the analysis of ideas and of things never reveals their genuine inner reality, but only a set of immobile parts. Analysis does not reveal truth, but only our material intervention upon reality; it breaks things up, killing the Real while vivisecting it. And this very notion of holism is itself holistic, having different meanings when taken in the context of logical abstraction, psychological intuition, or the decomposition of movement. With regard to abstraction, the emphasis lies on the spatiality subtending it. According to *Creative Evolution*, our abstract logic is *physical* in its origins: "our logic," Bergson writes, "is, pre-eminently, the logic of solids." The binaries of this or that, here or there, are all variations of an all-or-nothing bivalent logic modeled on a kind of space, to be precise the space of solid, impenetrable bodies, where no two objects can simultaneously occupy the same location.[7] Other forms of logic – fuzzier, vaguer, more fluid – are no less possible; but, because we do not normally perceive how things do interpenetrate, how they do coexist in the same spaces, we separate everything into isolated, separable objects. Things are thrown apart – ob-jectified: "concepts, in fact, are outside each other, like objects in space; and they have the same stability as such objects."[8] It is for reasons of survival that our perception is keen enough only to see things in isolation. Were we to attempt to transcend our normal perception, we would see things much more fluidly, as movements that coexist, as indivisible continuities, shading into each other imperceptibly.[9] But then we would not be able to grasp them, hold them, and kill them.

---

7. Henri Bergson, *Creative Evolution*, Arthur Mitchell (trans.) (Basingstoke: Palgrave Macmillan, 2007), xxxv, in *Œuvres*, André Robinet (ed.) (Paris: Presses Universitaires de France, 1959), 489.
8. Bergson, *Creative Evolution*, 103, in *Œuvres*, 631.
9. Bruno Paradis has written about the vague or fuzzy nature of Bergson's concepts. He also points to an indetermination of conceptuality or "inexactitude" in Bergson's work ("Indétermination et mouvements de birfurcation chez Bergson," *Philosophie* 32 [1991], 19). A technical discussion here of the logic of vagueness would bring us far off the point, but the fact remains that Bergson clearly uses the notion of the indefinable and the indefinite, not in an attempt to perpetuate mystery, but to point to a genuine feature of the world.

These movements must be seen as individual, not as a movement in general or abstract, but in person. For Bergson, the individuality of movement *is* its metaphysical status. When seen normally, habitually, however, this movement has each of its various dynamic properties "extracted" as an abstract concept, leaving a putatively formless and static object behind. Abstraction is always extraction. Hence, the process of abstraction is a form of *inattention* to concrete specificity, whereby the individuating context (what makes a movement *this* movement) is extracted and immobilized to become a container for the content-object left behind by the very same process.[10]

Bergson's own language of vagueness and vague language, his use of metaphors across all his works (which was used by many critics against him), is, according to him, absolutely essential to expressing duration. Infamously, Bergson is said to condemn language as inadequate to "thinking in duration." But the truth is that he argues for new languages of thought, for the constant invention of metaphor, simile, and adjective, in order to provide the thick descriptions that will restore to the Real the novelty and concrete specificity extracted by the immobilizing general concept. In his seminal essay of 1903, *An Introduction to Metaphysics*, Bergson argues for a metaphysics that "frees itself from rigid and ready-made concepts in order to create a kind very different from those which we habitually use; I mean supple, mobile and almost fluid representations."[11] That is why Bergson demands that we "use metaphors seriously," because the transversal meanings of metaphor are the literal truth of a process reality.[12] This language of anti-abstraction, of the concrete, of antibinarism, the inseparability of dimensions and the ineliminability of context, is part of the atmosphere in which much poststructuralist thought breathes, and without it a good deal of what Jacques Derrida, or Luce Irigaray, or Deleuze write would make a good deal less sense. It gained its first prominence in French continental thought with Bergson, whether for good or (as Alan Sokal and Jean Bricmont argue[13]) for ill.

Intuition

Attached to the excessive interference of analysis is the excess of the intellect, which Bergson opposes to the noninterference of intuition. Clearly, intuition

10. For more on this, see my *Bergson and Philosophy* (Edinburgh: Edinburgh University Press, 1999), 175–7.
11. Henri Bergson, *An Introduction to Metaphysics*, T. E. Hulme (trans.) (Basingstoke: Palgrave Macmillan, 2007), 13, in *Œuvres*, 1401–2.
12. Henri Bergson, *Mélanges*, André Robinet (ed.) (Paris: Presses Universitaires de France, 1972), 980.
13. See Alan Sokal and Jean Bricmont, *Impostures intellectuelles* (Paris: Éditions Odile Jacob, 1997).

has a modern pedigree going back long before Bergson (be it to the rationalists on the one hand, or the Romantics on the other), so what is noteworthy about it in Bergsonism is a usage that is neither fully rationalist nor fully Romantic but accommodates aspects of both. With respect to the latter, intuition is taken as a sympathy with, or attention to, the object that approaches an immediate consciousness; with respect to the former, it is described as "supra-intellectual" or "ultra-intellectual," the immediacy with the object not being an easy achievement but something requiring "painful" effort.[14] Intuition is the painful exertion required to transcend our normal perception, to reverse the workings of the mind – for which analysis is not merely an intellectual habit but a vital necessity. By turning itself backwards in intuition, the mind attempts to reintegrate itself with the Real.

There is no "simple and geometrical definition of intuition," however. To be in sympathy with something requires "views of it that are multiple, complementary and not at all equivalent."[15] Intuition is this faculty of multiple perspectives. It is the power by which one subject is able to adjust itself to the alterity of the object (a changing process) by re-creating its movement within itself. But this re-creation is *not* a representation. Intuition is in fact antirepresentational: it is a thinking that is a part of the Real rather than a point of view that *represents* the Real. This is possible because intuition and the Real are both processes, and as such can participate with each other without representation. That is why Bergson made the claim that metaphysics is a form of knowledge without symbols. By symbol he meant representation. Hence, intuition dispenses with symbols in favor of a kind of presence (over re-presence), a material, processual, partial coincidence with the object (although it is never a perfect, complete coincidence).

The "metaphysical investigation" of the singularity of the concrete object is another name for Bergsonian intuition. In the effort to experience the object in itself, to sympathize with or attend to its movement, we differentiate between a generic image of it and a multitude of forms. And in doing so we have also, at one and the same time, integrated our movement into its own: we have participated in its becoming. This integration, though, is always dynamic, being the attempt to enter into the flux of another *durée* rather than to discover an eternal supersensory essence. Indeed, Bergson is adamant that his notion of intuition is non-Platonic and anti-Kantian, for he states clearly that "in order to reach

14. See Bergson, *Creative Evolution*, 113, 114, in *Œuvres*, 644, 645; *Introduction to Metaphysics*, 5, in *Œuvres*, 1395; *The Creative Mind: An Introduction to Metaphysics*, Mabelle L. Andison (trans.) (New York: Citadel Press, 2002), 32, 87–8, 30, in *Œuvres*, 1273, 1328, 1271. Bergson writes that he might have chosen to name this faculty "intelligence" instead of intuition. See *Mélanges*, 1322.
15. Bergson, *The Creative Mind*, 34, in *Œuvres*, 1274.

intuition it is not necessary to transport ourselves outside the domain of the senses." Intuition exists as the "*perception* of metaphysical reality." It is a form of attentive perception. Most philosophers since Plato have wished to "rise above" perception, Bergson claims, and some have seen intuition as their means to do it (Descartes and Spinoza being the two most obvious examples). Conversely, traditional skeptics of metaphysical intuition (such as Kant) have been no less unworldly in their positing of intuition: if it exists, then it will be "radically" different "from consciousness as well as from the senses" (which, for Kant, would be an impossibility). Bergson, by contrast, sees no need to escape perception, but instead argues for its promotion and primacy in a manner presaging Merleau-Ponty. Intuition is not the faculty for producing ever newer genera, but a superior empiricism that illuminates every "detail of the real" by "deepening," "widening," and "expanding" our perception.[16]

Immanence

This is not a valorization of human, anthropocentric, perception, however: it is the primacy of *inhuman* perception and the sensing body. Perception must be worked over, made attentive, given new forms. Despite the Romantic overtones of ecstatic empiricism in Bergsonian intuition (which raised the same levels of doubt and enthusiasm then as it does today), what really carries across from Bergson is the emphasis on transcending the *norms* of human perception, especially by means of *nonrepresentational* knowledge. It would be this kind of knowledge as sympathy, knowledge that attempts to go beyond power, that Levinas would later characterize as an ethical relation. Conversely, by locating this transcendent power in nature, by rendering metaphysics immanent, in other words, Bergson received Deleuze's approval. Indeed, reversing the effects of Platonism by annulling its unworldly view of metaphysics is perhaps Bergson's greatest contribution to twentieth-century philosophy. The idea that the "true empiricism" is the "true metaphysics" is central here. Yet it goes even further than many think, for Bergson was also the "adversary of Kant," as well as of Plato, inasmuch as he regarded the Critical Philosophy as simply another form of Platonism, only now applied to the human mind. There is no valid distinction between the "transcendent" and the "transcendental" (as Kantians claim), for the latter is simply the Platonization of deductive logic, making a certain kind of conceptual (and spatial) thought normative. But to make it normative, to make it the unconditioned condition of *all* experience is to render it transcendent to its immanent, mutable conditions. As we shall see, those conditions are multiple; *indeed they*

16. *Ibid.*, 127, 139, 140, 134, in *Œuvres*, 1364, 1374, 1375, 1370; *Creative Evolution*, 229–30, in *Œuvres*, 799.

are multiplicity or novelty itself, inasmuch as, for a process philosophy, there can be no condition of the new save for itself: the new comes out of no-thing – not substance, nor form, nor logic – nothing except itself, *de novo*. Its condition is to be unconditioned.

Pluralism

When speaking of method and multiplicity in Bergson, one must mention what has been called his "method of multiplicity," a method of proliferation in the face of philosophical paradox.[17] Indeed, intuition is another name for the method of multiplicity. This is quite the opposite of William of Ockham's principle – *entia non multiplicanda sunt praeter necessitatem* – which seeks the best explanation in parsimonious simplicity. The Bergsonian principle sees false problems and paradoxes arising *whenever we simplify too much*. Abstract intellect, of course, "loves simplicity," but that is because abstraction *is* simplicity itself, an extraction from and diminution of the Real. By contrast, intuition is the acknowledgment of or attention to the messy nuances of reality, because the Real is always *de trop*, whatever is in excess of our intelligence: it is the "*more than is necessary* – too much of this, too much of that, too much of everything."[18] Consequently, Bergson's axiom is one of disunity in the face of simplicity, be it a dis-uniting of space, of the ego, of memory, of order, of cause, of knowing, of religion, of morality. In each case, where we habitually see one kind of thing we can always be assured that a closer look will reveal many others, many kinds, or many levels. This is even true of multiplicity itself (it has two kinds, quantitative and qualitative) and Being as such (of which there are an indefinite number of levels). To break out of a false problematic or paradox, therefore, we must first multiply the number of variables at work within it: the problem of being ("why is there something rather than nothing?"), for example, emerges if one posits only one kind of ultimate being – "Being as such" – with an attendant non-being nipping at its heels. For Bergson, there is no one Being, but numerous, actual, levels or kinds of being, a proliferation of beings with no need for a ground in the One. As one commentator writes, Bergson's is a true "*metaphysics of degrees of reality*, on condition, however, that one specifies that it is not a question of the 'same' reality, but of *different* realities."[19] The multiple – another name for novelty, for process, for duration – is its own ground. Similarly, Zeno's paradoxes of movement only arise if one posits just one kind of space, homogeneous quantifiable

17. See Ann Game, *Undoing the Social: Towards a Deconstructive Sociology* (Toronto: University of Toronto Press, 1991), 91–6, 108–11.
18. Bergson, *The Creative Mind*, 209, 210, in *Œuvres*, 1440, 1441.
19. Frédéric Worms, *Introduction à "Matière et mémoire" de Bergson* (Paris: Presses Universitaires de France, 1997), 256.

space, instead of the other, numerous qualitative spaces wherein we walk, run, and commonly move with consummate ease.

It would be a mistake, however, to see Bergson's predilection for the multiple as gratuitous or unnecessary: it is immanent to or axiomatic of his method, given that intuition just is a *sensitivity* towards difference; it is not an intellectual decision, but an affective vision. There are many synonyms for multiplicity in Bergson's work: "dissociation," "dichotomy," "disharmony," "differentiation," "divergence." Picking just three from this list, the nineteenth-century psychopathological term of "dissociation," for instance, is transformed into a metaphysical principle: the *élan vital* itself is one example of dissociation, proceeding "*by dissociation and division*."[20] A living being is not a static composition or association of cells but an ongoing process that "has made the cells by means of [a] dissociation" of itself.[21] Because life proceeds by dissociation, the differences between species are more fundamental than the similarities. Likewise, knowledge and understanding are the "effect of a sudden dissociation," understanding being described as "a certain faculty of dissociating."[22] In *The Two Sources of Morality and Religion*, dissociation appears in the form of the "Law of Dichotomy," by which Bergson understands a natural tendency whereby every conceptual unity is actually only provisional, being destined to bifurcate indefinitely.[23] This constant dichotomization is not be confused with the Hegelian dialectic (or at least a stereotype of it), however, because this constant ramification proceeds without any subsequent synthesis. Indeed, Bergson's methodology is wholly different from Hegel's, being genealogical rather than teleological, dissociative rather than associative (or synthetic), and differential rather than negative. In fact, by contrast with the dialectical logic of Hegel, we might say that Bergson's pluralism posits itself in multiple logics: psycho-logic, bio-logic, epistemo-logic, socio-logic. Logic itself is multiple. Perhaps the nearest Bergson comes to an "orthodox" (abstract) logic of the multiple is in its mathematical implementation in the infinitesimal calculus, whose methods of differentiation and integration Bergson adopted as his own: "*the object of metaphysics is to perform qualitative differentiations and integrations*."[24]

Although Bergson is commonly regarded as a dualist (of life and matter, space and time), or even sometimes a monist (of Life), rather than a pluralist,

20. Bergson, *Creative Evolution*, 58, in *Œuvres*, 571.
21. *Ibid.*, 167, in *Œuvres*, 715.
22. Bergson, *The Creative Mind*, 137, in *Œuvres*, 1372; *Matter and Memory*, Nancy Margaret Paul and W. Scott Palmer (trans.) (New York: Zone Books, 1991), 181, in *Œuvres*, 318.
23. See Henri Bergson, *The Two Sources of Morality and Religion*, R. Ashley Audra and Cloudesley Brereton (trans.), with the assistance of W. Horsfall Carter (Notre Dame, IN: Notre Dame Press, 1977), 296ff., in *Œuvres*, 1227ff.
24. Bergson, *An Introduction to Metaphysics*, 42.

the closest examinations of his work agree that his thought embraces a "*dynamic* monism" allowing for "qualitative *diversity*"; he is neither a monist nor a dualist in the substantialist sense of these terms: the "infrastructure" of his philosophy is at once "dualist and unitary."[25] Unity is that which always splits or dissociates, being itself only a pragmatic, temporary unity, an impression of unity that must eventually bifurcate along with its object. At the origins of life, knowledge, the problems of philosophy, and even Being itself, there are always false unities, the fragmentation of which being the driving force that leads to other actual entities (with putative unified identities) that will in their turn disintegrate and differentiate. There are always divergent tendencies in Bergson's analyses, and a tendency is the movement between provisional, pragmatic states of the One or the Two or the Many. Movement is neither in a state of one, nor indeed in a state of many either, but is the transition between a kind of one and a new kind of many, the multiplicity of the multiple. His pluralism is a metapluralism, a plurality of pluralities. Although the provenance of the French philosophies of difference in the 1960s is clearly complex – Hegelian dialectic (or Alexandre Kojève's version of it in the 1930s), Heideggerian difference, Saussurean differentialism, even Husserl's own earlier use of "multiplicity" are all part of that story – the early and widespread use of pluralistic language throughout Bergson's work must still be regarded as a vital part of the confluence of ideas that made "difference" such a central term in their vocabulary.

Nonphilosophy

A final element of Bergson's methodological language concerns the sources of philosophy itself, for in taking metaphysics to be the indefinable intuition of the indefinite, the experience of a concrete multiplicity (which is *immanent* to or a part of the whole), philosophy itself can no longer be regarded as a predefined, autonomous inquiry. Philosophy becomes a self-fulfilling creative practice, and so that which one names "philosophy" only after the fact. It is a "bottom up," extensional characterization, one that is empirically based on the actuality of experiences that nominate themselves "philosophical" only *a posteriori*. Metaphysics is a thinking in duration, and although Bergson vacillated on whether science could or could not itself think (about) movement (in 1903 he thought that it could – with mathematical calculus being exemplary

25. Milič Čapek, *Bergson and Modern Physics* (The Hague: Martinus Nijhoff, 1971), 193, and "Bergson's Theory of the Mind–Brain Relation," in *Bergson and Modern Thought*: *Towards a Unified Science*, A. C. Papanicolaou and P. A. Y. Gunter (eds) (London: Harwood, 1987), 132; Georges Mourélos, *Bergson et les niveaux de réalité* (Paris: Presses Universitaires de France, 1964), 90.

in this regard – but in 1907 he restricted its role to the study of spatialized matter alone), Bergson is clear that both art and religion do have access to the metaphysical. Bergson's theory of art, best expressed in his study of humor in *Laughter* (1900), allows the artist the natural faculty to *perceive* difference, while *The Two Sources of Morality and Religion* sees the mystic as an individual endowed with "creation emotion" – a new name for intuition – that enables him or her to *feel* difference. In both cases, they have access to, or rather become a part of, the mobile Real, forming a triad, along with philosophy, of kinds of participation in the Absolute, which is change itself. Along with philosophy, they are forms of "attention to Life" or the Real. But what will count as Real – be it perceived, felt, or thought – always remains indefinite and indefinable. Bergson was adamant that even his own concepts of *durée* and qualitative multiplicity, for example, must not be seen as eternal names of the Real, but as conceptual placeholders that must eventually be surpassed: philosophy is not about discovering an eternal expression to represent reality perfectly; rather, it is the practice of continually creating new concepts that participate in the fluidity of the Real. The absolute is not comprehended "by giving it a name," but by *creating* a new expression.[26] And this creation can have its sources in nonphilosophy (art and religion) too. This tempering of the scope and sovereignty of philosophy, which nonetheless does not deny philosophy an ongoing role, makes Bergson appear particularly contemporary, for it avoids the postmodern clichés of philosophy being at its end (again), while also showing a maturity regarding philosophy's empirical basis and the extent to which it can maintain its autonomy from other disciplines. Philosophy is indeed conditioned (it is not exhaustive in its access to the Absolute but only partial), yet this conditioning is a mark of its Reality, of it being a part of the enduring, moving, whole.

II. METAPHYSICS

The Real

Moving from the language of method to the overlapping language of metaphysics itself, we are first reminded of Bergson's anti-Platonism as regards sensibility and anti-Kantianism as regards possibility. Bringing metaphysics down to earth from its Platonic heights renders it, in Bergson's views, a remedial procedure for our perception. In "An Introduction to Metaphysics," Bergson describes the percept as a "metaphysical object" and then continues: "a true empiricism is that which proposes to get as near to the original itself as possible, to search

26. Bergson, *The Creative Mind*, 49, in *Œuvres*, 1291.

deeply into its life, and so, by a kind of *intellectual auscultation*, to feel the throbbings of its soul; and this true empiricism is the true metaphysics."[27]

This is a radical empiricism, one practiced by Bergson even before William James had coined the term. Like James after him (and even more like Deleuze later again), Bergson argues that a true, metaphysical empiricism is not a contradictory mixture of supersensory abstraction and everyday experience, but the painful effort *to create* new realms of experiences, to expand perception such that we attend to the singularity of the concrete individual, the individual that can only be sensed rather than intellectualized. By this means, "metaphysics will then become experience itself," and concepts will be created to match each object rather than the other way around (in Procrustean fashion).[28] Metaphysics is not the contemplation of an alternative reality, therefore, but the heightened perception of reality, a perception Bergson also calls "intuition." There is also a link between Bergson and phenomenology in all of this: *Time and Free Will*'s resort to "immediate data," its proposal that we come "face to face with the sensations themselves," or *Matter and Memory*'s attempt to transcend "theory" in favor of "the presence of images," both appear to approximate a Husserlian *epochē* of sorts.[29] Nonetheless, although Bergson's proto-phenomenology must have helped to prepare the French soil for the implantation of German ideas, Bergsonism itself was never centered on a human representation (reworked or otherwise) of the *Ding an Sich* but something much more metaphysical, something transcending human representation: it is still experience, but experience before its human "turning," the *Ding* itself, the "very life of things" coming into thought.[30]

As already mentioned, the painful effort of intuition requires a reversal of the normal way in which we think, which goes from the particular to the general, extracting abstractions. Two particular abstractions are most culpable in this, according to Bergson: nothingness and possibility. Deleuze rightly states that in Bergsonism "there are differences in being and yet nothing negative."[31] To embrace the multitude of actual beings is far too fatiguing for the mind; indeed, it is contrary to what the mind is, to wit, the very extraction and simplification of this multitude. The positing of Being or Nothingness as the source from which the multitude supposedly come *simply is the immanent process of mentation*: it is not done *by* the mind, but just is one symptom of having a mind – it

27. *Ibid.*, 22, in *Œuvres*, 1408.
28. *Ibid.*, 18, in *Œuvres*, 1259.
29. H. Bergson, *Time and Free Will: An Essay on the Immediate Data of Consciousness*, F. L. Pogson (trans.) (New York: Dover, 2001), 47, in *Œuvres*, 34; *Matter and Memory*, 17, in *Œuvres*, 169.
30. *Ibid.*, 184–5, in *Œuvres*, 321; *An Introduction to Metaphysics*, 43, in *Œuvres*, 1424.
31. Gilles Deleuze, *Bergsonism*, Hugh Tomlinson and Barbara Habberjam (trans.) (New York: Zone Books, 1988), 46.

is the mind as performance, as process rather than substance, the process of extraction–abstraction. The symptoms of Being and Nothingness extend back as far as Parmenides and travel down through Plato and the Neoplatonists to Hegel, Heidegger, Sartre, Lacan, and Badiou today. In contrast to this, Bergson stands, alongside Nietzsche, at the head of a modern tradition of metaphysical positivism, or antinihilism, that has worked its way through to Deleuze in the contemporary era. The Real does not lack anything; it is its own full plenitude in all positivity. There is finitude and negation in Bergsonism, of course (Gaston Bachelard, for one, was wrong to think otherwise), but they are not primary, they are not the ground of our actuality; the nought is a derivative produced by either memory or expectation (*Creative Evolution*), that is, from a creative desire that produces its own supposed lack. But we can only realize this, we can only see it, if we reverse the way the mind works and interprets its own creativity.

The idea of possibility as a containment of the Real is another indication of this normal working of the mind. What we call the possibility of the Real is, in fact, *engendered* retrospectively by the Real, wherein "there is perpetual creation of possibility and not only of reality."[32] According to Bergson, it is extremely hard for the intellect to acknowledge that each present is really something radically new, that is, to attend to the actuality of the new. French nineteenth-century Romanticism, for example, was supposedly made possible because of the foregoing circumstances created by French Classicism. But Bergson argues instead that it was the Romanticism of Chateaubriand, Vigny, and Hugo that retroactively created the impression of a nascent Romanticism in the earlier classical writers. Romanticism, by its very coming into existence, created its own prefiguration in the past and, by that, a putative explanation of its emergence. This retroactive logic – what Foucault would later call (with self-critical awareness) the "history of the present" – also leads to a number of philosophical illusions. Our normal logic of retrospection perpetually recreates the actual present with elements of the past: meaning is reconstituted from words that are already meaningful (*Matter and Memory*), for example, or life is reconstructed from matter (a prebiotic soup) that is already vital (*Creative Evolution*), or consciousness is composed from brain cells that are already sentient ("Brain and Thought," in *Mind-Energy*), and so on. In each case, we reverse-engineer a generalized notion of the present phenomenon with a reductive mechanism as its supposed causal past. And we can do this only by extracting the novelty and singularity of the actual phenomenon in order to make it fit into (or reduce down to) our explanatory substratum. But duration is both the mark of reality *and* the agency behind our illusions concerning what makes any one reality possible. Because it is prior rather than subsequent to the possible, duration actually creates the

32. Bergson, *The Creative Mind*, 21, 23–4, in *Œuvres*, 1262, 1265.

latter retrospectively. And *this is also true of novelty itself*, which is its own real condition and has no "transcendental" conditions of possibility. Bergson's anti-Kantianism will not allow room for any form of abstract logic to act as the basis, the principle of sufficient reason, to understand time as duration. Duration does not need possibility, because it *makes* possibility.

Time

It must be admitted that what we described earlier as the comic-book Bergson, that of *durée* and the *élan vital* (time versus space and life versus matter), has nevertheless left to the French tradition an important set of terms for its vocabulary. Although there were important philosophers of time in France immediately preceding Bergson (Jean-Marie Guyau, Émile Boutroux), and he had a number of influential contemporaries outside France (Samuel Alexander and J. M. E. McTaggart especially), it was doubtless Bergson who made time and a whole family of associated terms – novelty, becoming, change, movement, process, and heterogeneity – an essential part of the intellectual milieu for the next century. Clearly, his was a dynamist theory of time, what McTaggart called an "A-Theory," emphasizing the perspectival determinants of flux, change, and unpredictability in the past, present, and future. The language of movement, of process, of change (along with that of freedom and creativity, as we shall see) is fundamental to Bergson's conception of time. *Durée* is "the uninterrupted up-surge of novelty," "radical novelty," "the radically new," or "complete novelty."[33] In contrast, clock-time is spatialized time, time understood in terms of eternal relations (of being before, simultaneous with, or after): this is the false time of Kant, of science, and of most contemporary thought. Indeed, this is another source of Bergson's anti-Kantianism. Far from being the first modern philosopher to liberate time from space (as some, like Deleuze, have argued), according to Bergson, Kant merely *inverted* the old binary opposition of time and space by making *measured* (spatially quantified) movement subordinate to the *measure of* (spatially quantified) time. Bergson's own thesis is not about the binary of space (movement) and time at all, but one concerning measure and immeasure, or quantity and quality. Kant simply internalized space and called it time. Bergson instead wants *time to be understood as qualitative movement, that is, to have its qualitative actuality restored.*

Bergson actually encompasses two approaches to temporality in his work, however, the one emphasizing the subjective experience of *durée* (in *Time and Free Will*), the other looking to the objective data of the contemporary sciences, physics and biology in particular (*Matter and Memory* and *Creative Evolution*),

33. *Ibid.*, 18, 99, 35, in *Œuvres*, 1259, 1339, 1276; *Creative Evolution*, 106, in *Œuvres*, 634.

and so extending the idea of continual, qualitative variation beyond human psychology and into the material universe. The idea that Bergson never goes beyond an implausible and old-fashioned dualism of psychological time (duration) versus static, homogeneous space, rests wholly on a (selective) reading of *Time and Free Will*.[34] By the time of *Matter and Memory*, it is homogeneity in equally spatial and temporal forms that is at issue. Homogeneous space and time are both the effects that we introduce into the "moving continuity of the real" in order to fix it, to control it, and to kill it (so that we can survive). They are the "diagrammatic design of our eventual action upon matter," not the other pole in an improbable Manichean system.[35] The *homogenizing* of space and time stems from our vital need to ignore their indigenous alterity, to reduce difference to sameness.[36] Real spatiality and real things, on the contrary, are not empty forms, but have depth and life all their own, in what Bergson calls "the extensive," which is "intermediate between divided extension and pure inextension."[37] It is only when we attend to their heterogeneity (in art, in mysticism, in metaphysical empiricism) that we see and feel and think the very life of things, that we see duration everywhere: in short, that we notice the constant upsurge of novelty or becoming, without any need for static space, or being, or nothingness, or even logic to support it. When we look elsewhere, when we abstract and extract – as we must to live – then it is we who immobilize, spatialize, or homogenize the Real.

Although it was a caricature of his thought that allowed Bergson's most obvious contribution – his theory of time – to be sidelined by the next generation of French philosophy, the fact remains that the philosophy of the new was a Bergsonian innovation, irrespective of its location (in the mind or in things), and it is one that remains a live issue today. For Badiou or Deleuze, for Lyotard or Derrida, for François Laruelle or Michel Henry, the problem of the new, of change, of the "Event," be it in politics, in philosophy, in "theory," in phenomenology, in art, or in literature, is obvious, and it is one that specifically marks out French continental thinking.[38]

34. Even *Time and Free Will* can be ambivalent about space, going so far as to say that "we shall not lay too much stress on the question of the absolute reality of space: perhaps we might as well ask whether space is or is not in space" (Bergson, *Time and Free Will*, 91, in *Œuvres*, 62).
35. Bergson, *Matter and Memory*, 211, in *Œuvres*, 345.
36. *Ibid.*, 247, in *Œuvres*, 376.
37. *Ibid.*, 245, in *Œuvres*, 374.
38. Indeed, even the term "Event" has a Bergsonian remit, *The Two Sources* arguing that the very notion of an event is already a spatialization of process, albeit in the special guise of what he calls "fabulation," which functions to collect (extract) numerous processes together under the singular name of "event" (sometimes even to give it a proto-personality – as an "earthquake," a "collision," a "hurricane," a bit of luck, my death, and so on). See *The Two Sources of Morality and Religion*, ch. 2 and my "Life, Movement, and the Fabulation of the Event," *Theory, Culture, and Society* 24(6) (2007), 53–70.

Beyond subject and object

The importance of understanding Bergson's purported dualism as actually processual, as a *dualization*, is critical. Alongside immanent intuition, Bergson also uses the language of mixture, "refraction," and "interpenetration" to move his philosophical thought even further beyond the dualism of subject and object. After the admittedly Cartesian propensity of *Time and Free Will*, *Matter and Memory*, for example, begins by thinking of perception without reference to self and world (in what could be taken as an *epochē* of sorts). But this is just one instance. Bergson's work is strewn with the language of contraction, "endosmosis," "interval," or "balance" understood as the condensation of opposed forces or movements, with seemingly subjective facets on one side and objective ones on the other. Impurity reigns everywhere, whereas purity is always only in theory, as a *hypothesis*, whether born from philosophy (like Nothingness) or the need to live (in homogeneous space). But what is real is the interval, the in between; what is unreal, or ideal, is the "extreme."

Admittedly, there are various subjectivist extremes put to work in Bergson's own thought – pure memory, *élan vital*, even pure duration – but they are ideal limits, entities with an "as if" ("*comme si*") existence, a "virtual" reality. In actuality, neither duration nor the *élan* are ever pure, but contain contradictions within themselves (duration is always spatialized, life is always found in embodied, material beings). And these are not contingent facts: life would not *be* life, that is, dissociative, unless it existed in biological form. These are not the poles of a dualism but the interpenetrating tendencies in a movement of dualization: the enduring mind *really can* become spatialized, and matter *really can* become vitalized (that is precisely what a living body is) because space and life are actually processes (spatialization and vitalization). These interpenetrating tendencies are seen most intensely in the optical metaphor of refraction found throughout Bergson's works, from the first to the last: space and time refract each other, free will and mechanism refract each other, open and closed morality refract each other, static and dynamic religion refract each other. Refraction as such is not tied to any privileged domain; it is seen in the psychological, social, and physical realms and so is relational rather than substantive. It is a form of movement. *The Two Sources of Morality and Religion* even ends with a prognosis for life on our "refractory planet" that must nonetheless be the means by which life evolves further.[39] To a lesser extent, Bergson also uses the language of interpenetration, or osmosis and endosmosis, always with the purpose of exemplifying the mixed nature of the Real. Without these ideas of mixture, Merleau-Ponty's chiasmic ontology of reversibility and subject–object

39. Bergson, *The Two Sources of Morality and Religion*, 317, in *Œuvres*, 1245.

intermingling would not have been written with the same facility or received with the same enthusiasm.[40]

And here is where metaphysics and methodology refract as well, for Bergsonism can also be seen as an attempt to move "beyond objectivism and relativism." According to *Matter and Memory*, when we try to transcend realism and idealism, all we are given are images, but these images are not representations; they are the universe set out in inhuman, nonrepresentational imagery. Objectivity can obviously be identified easily enough with a certain homogeneous physical reality. But Bergson sees this as merely the cancelling out of all perspectival differences, of all imagery whatsoever, "where everything balances and compensates and neutralizes everything else."[41] If everything is already a (nonrepresented) image, one could say that one purpose of Bergson's project is to relativize relativity. In *Duration and Simultaneity*, Bergson even forwards the idea of "full-relativity" as a relativism that actually reinstates a new kind of absolute, that of the Other's perspective, the perspective of otherness that continually frames or relativizes my own (relative) conceptual and perceptual frames of others.

Indeed, there is a connection between relativism and absolutism for Bergson or, rather, between relativism and absolutism of a certain kind. He regards the motive behind Kant's (relativizing) Copernican Revolution as itself a symptom of an absolutist intellect having failed in its attempt to totalize or subsume the world and that turns instead to a humble relativism that now dismisses the possibility of finding any absolutes whatsoever. If Kant banished metaphysics and with it the absolute, Bergson sees it as his task to reinstate them both, only now in a newly redeemed understanding rather than in the form to which Kant submitted them. Bergson's new absolute is not lost or found through the rigid concepts of Being, Nothingness, Space, the Transcendental, Logic, or Objectivity, but is grounded on the recognition of our selectivist, extractionist, tendency to centralize our own point of view by making everything else move relative to it, to be private absolutists. To say that everything exists (realism) is the same as to say that nothing exists save as an image *for me* (idealism). Relativism, or what Bergson says should more properly be called "half-relativism," always disguises

40. The "fundamental likeness" between Merleau-Ponty's project and Bergson's philosophy has struck a number of commentators, for example Ben-Ami Scharfstein, "Bergson and Merleau-Ponty: A Preliminary Comparison," *Journal of Philosophy* 52 (1955), 385. Edward Casey has noted that "Bergson is often the most effective escort into Merleau-Pontian reflection on many subjects" ("Habitual Body and Memory in Merleau-Ponty," *Man and World* 17 [1984], 283), and Eugene Kaelin went so far as to describe *La Phénoménologie de la perception* as a testament to the Bergsonian influence on Merleau-Ponty (*An Existentialist Aesthetic: The Theories of Sartre and Merleau-Ponty* [Madison, WI: University of Wisconsin Press, 1962], 339).

41. Bergson, *Matter and Memory*, 219, in *Œuvres*, 353.

a dogmatic absolutism. In contradistinction to both, Bergson's pluralism is also an absolute: an affirmation of the multiplicity of perspectives (images) that is nevertheless not an endorsement of the more customary representational form of relativism (because they are images *for themselves*). In place of relative knowledge Bergson puts partial knowledge, for while the relative implies a lost absolute, the part opens itself up immanently to the whole.[42]

III. NATURALISM

Consciousness

As regards the conscious subject (of supposed representation), Bergson's language also lent itself well to the project of decentering the self that became fundamental to French postmodernism. But it did so in a complex manner that involved Bergson's work in nonreductive naturalization. On the one hand, Bergson does everything he can to dismantle the integrity of the ego. From the very start, *Time and Free Will* split it into "superficial" and "profound" states: a state that is already a spatialized self – with sensations quantified on the model of social space – and another of continuous heterogeneous *durée* lying beneath the sameness of the public self. This "*moi profound*" was Bergson's own theory of the unconscious, quite separate from Freud's, although influenced by the psychologist Pierre Janet and as such closer to a theory of selective *inattention* than one of the unconscious *simpliciter*: Bergson does not divorce any one part of the personality from the other; the deeper self goes "not unperceived, but rather unnoticed."[43]

Matter and Memory and the subsequent works proliferated this dyadic model into numerous levels of stratified duration, dropping the language of "surface" and "depth" in favor of different rhythms of time.[44] In both versions, however, the idea of a self-identical ego was always an illusion for Bergson, there being neither "a series of distinct psychological states, each one invariable, which would produce the variations of the ego by their very succession … [nor] an ego, no less invariable, which would serve as support for them."[45]

Bergson once went so far as to liken the self to the pathology of multiple personality and even to a series of spiritual possessions in preference over any

42. See Bergson, *Mélanges*, 774.
43. See Bergson, *Time and Free Will*, 169, in *Œuvres*, 112; See also *Mélanges*, 810, for a rejection of an unconsciousness that is opaque to and inaccessibly cut off from consciousness.
44. See A. D. Lindsay, *The Philosophy of Bergson* (London: Dent, 1911), 5, 91–2, 156–7, 168–9, who makes a good deal of this development.
45. Bergson, *The Creative Mind*, 148–9, in *Œuvres*, 1383.

sovereign, autonomous agent.[46] As Simon Clarke observes regarding Bergson on this matter: "The 'death of the subject' … has roots that go back deep into French philosophy."[47]

On the other hand, though, Bergson extends the notion of consciousness or *psyche* to cosmic levels as well as devolving it to micro-selves. Here we see Bergson's nonreductive and even inflationary naturalism at work. In *Creative Evolution*, anything that is alive is regarded as conscious, although even matter at times is also treated as a kind of consciousness, albeit one that is turned in the opposite direction to life, physics being a "reversed psychology" or "psychics inverted."[48] Here is where Bergson approaches a Whiteheadian organicism. He never quite gets there, however, for the vital is not organic, but that which resists organization even as it must (provisionally) accommodate itself to it at any specific moment. Life, or consciousness, is not some subtle substance or vital energy, but a resistance movement. While Bergsonism is indeed a philosophy of consciousness, this consciousness or psyche is only a synonym for universal movement, cosmological rather than anthropological.

This other approach to decentering the (anthropomorphic) self, one that replaces it with the cosmos, has been adopted by Deleuze and his followers to huge acclaim. This is especially true with respect to *Matter and Memory* and its language of the "virtual" (or unrepresented memory). In Deleuze's reading, the virtual becomes ontological rather than psychological (although Bergson would not have opposed these terms as Deleuze does) and takes on the role of gathering all forms of difference together on to the same plane of immanence. All the same, the virtual remains alive, sentient, and moving – all Bergsonian characteristics – while also trying to rid itself of any *human* psychologism.

The body

Two other sites of Bergsonian naturalism are the body and nature itself. Following in the tradition of Maine de Biran (1766–1824) and Félix Ravaisson (1813–1900)[49] – while also modernizing them – the body is fundamental for philosophy in Bergson's view. It is the affective center of each individual; even further, it is the means by which our own sense of individuality is engendered. Through movement and affect, one image stands out among all other images: that of the body. Or rather, the image of the body is the image of mineness, of

46. Bergson, *Mélanges*, 858.
47. Simon Clarke, *The Foundations of Structuralism: A Critique of Lévi-Strauss and the Structuralist Movement* (Sussex: Harvester Press, 1981), 16.
48. Bergson, *Creative Evolution*, 134, 130, in *Œuvres*, 672, 666.
*49. This tradition is discussed in the essay by F. C. T. Moore in *The History of Continental Philosophy: Volume 2*.

my body. It is "a privileged image, perceived in its depths and no longer on the surface ... it is this particular image which I adopt as the center of my universe and as the physical basis of my personality."[50] "Mineness" is the product of an individuating movement-image, an act of nature rather than of an autonomous subject. The body has even more than this passive function, however, for it is also a center of action, of indeterminacy and choice. The "I" is given a "horizon" of possible interests that is constituted through the spatial relationship that other images have with my body: "*the objects which surround my body reflect its possible action upon them.*"[51] The body continues in importance in Bergson's work, from *Matter and Memory*, as the basis of recollection (through habit memory, a crucial discovery for 1896), all the way to *The Two Sources of Morality and Religion*, and its idea of a "logic of the body" as "extension of desire."[52] Time and again this lived body, based on movement, affect, and action, is contrasted with an objective, geometrical body, the body seen from the outside. The first, Bergsonian body is a true body-subject with its own consciousness, Bergson writing explicitly of an "intelligence of the body" and a "logic of the body" as well as "bodily memory," and both Merleau-Ponty and Irigaray are especially in his debt here.[53] In some quarters, Bergson has been acknowledged as the first thinker to see "the genuine significance and peculiarity of the body," as well as the earliest modern philosopher fully to realize "the body's pivotal position ... as a continual 'center of action.'"[54]

Nature

Ironically, it was precisely for such naturalism, however, that the early Merleau-Ponty actually criticized Bergson, sharing the opinion of Sartre and most of the next generation of French philosophers.[55] Naturalizing the human, emphasizing the continuity between culture and nature, attending to the animal and to biology as important sources of philosophy – these ideas were anathema to those like Sartre who thought that man was "the being whose appearance brings the world into existence," and so who "wanted man to be the measure of

50. Bergson, *Matter and Memory*, 61, in *Œuvres*, 209.
51. *Ibid.*, 21, in *Œuvres*, 172.
52. Bergson, *The Two Sources of Morality and Religion*, 167, in *Œuvres*, 1117.
53. Bergson, *Matter and Memory*, 111, 139, 152, in *Œuvres*, 256, 257, 293.
54. Richard M. Zaner, *The Problem of Embodiment: Some Contributions to a Phenomenology of the Body* (The Hague: Martinus Nijhoff, 1971), 243; Edward S. Casey, *Remembering: A Phenomenological Study* (Bloomington, IN: Indiana University Press, 1987), 179.
55. Merleau-Ponty would later return to Bergson at the same time that he discovered the attraction of creating his own philosophy of nature; see Maurice Merleau-Ponty, *Elogie de la philosophie et autres essais* (Paris: Gallimard, 1960).

everything."[56] Yet Bergson was also rebuked by philosophical naturalists at the time for what they saw as his residual subjectivism. What so dissatisfied both sides is the fact that Bergson's is a nonreductive naturalism: although he does want to "give to the word biology the very wide meaning it should have, and will perhaps have one day," this is not to reduce everything to one, worthless essence, because biology, as Bergson understands it, is what breaks all essences.[57] Bergson's is a process naturalism, and this is what gives it an irreducible value – the value of change. With regard to the sociobiology in *The Two Sources of Morality and Religion*, for example, there is no intent to deflate culture to the "merely" animal or biological; rather, in virtue of his antireductionist views in biology, his is an inflationary discourse – biology is a realm of value, not devaluation, and this value is the value of change. In process philosophy, norms and nature interpenetrate, refract each other and are only extracted as separate essences by the intellect (which is the faculty of separation, or spatialization).

IV. NORMATIVITY

Life

As already mentioned, the *élan vital* is a principle of change, and does not represent an alternative type of (living) substance (which would only beg the question of biological origins, anyway). It is a type of time, open and unpredictable. The values built into Bergson's philosophy of time are ones of openness, of open-ended creativity, of attention to otherness, to Life. These values are immanent within life, for the mark of the living is simply to continue evolving rather than to stay fixed in one form of species. "Attention to *life*," we recall, was always described in terms of an openness to the alterity, the singularity, of the other. Indeed, attention to life can appear in *Creative Evolution* as life's sole (immanent) imperative, for the only hierarchy found in life is not one based on complexity or rationality (although these may be attendant phenomena), but one that is created immanently within life when each species falls into self-absorption and a disregard for "almost all the rest of life."[58] There is a fundamental antifinalism in Bergson's thought that, for various reasons, has been obscured in the reception of his ideas. Against *both* Lamarck and the neo-Darwinians, Bergson argues

56. Quoted in Vincent Descombes, *Modern French Philosophy*, L. Scott-Fox and J. M. Harding (trans.) (Cambridge: Cambridge University Press, 1980), 30; quoted in Richard Kearney, *Modern Movements in European Philosophy*, 2nd edn (Manchester: Manchester University Press, 1986), 14.

57. Bergson, *The Two Sources of Morality and Religion*, 101, in *Œuvres*, 1061.

58. Bergson, *Creative Evolution*, 83–4, in *Œuvres*, 604.

for a nonteleological, dissociative life, and the *élan* is simply a principle of this endlessness, this constant dichotomization without synthesis, this continual creativity. The *élan* has no end, or, if you prefer, its only end is to creatively end all ends, to break all molds of speciation, to keep moving. To think of it as "stuff" is ridiculously unBergsonian, given that his is a meticulously processualist philosophy. Life is movement, a resistance movement, resisting whatever does not allow it to move, and that is its *immanent* value. No less than for Nietzsche before him or Deleuze (and Michel Henry) after him, creative Life is the supreme, self-positing or axiomatic value, once it is understood as that which remains open, moving, or, in Bergson's most renowned term, "creative" (which made Bergson a favored philosopher among artists).

Ethics

This normative dimension was always implicit in Bergson's work until *The Two Sources of Morality and Religion*, which at long last interprets the *élan vital* explicitly as an *élan d'amour*, a love or "open morality" forwarded as the end of life, that is, as the *open*-endedness of indefinite creativity (what Bergson calls "creative emotion"). This is embodied in the mystic or open soul, whose form of "dynamic" faith indicates a truly universal regard: it is not intentional – it has no particular end or object – for it is only disposed towards otherness *as such*:

> The other attitude is that of the open soul. What, in that case, is allowed in? Suppose we say that it embraces all humanity: we should not be going too far, we should hardly be going far enough, since its love may extend to animals, to plants, to all nature. And yet no one of these things which would thus fill it would suffice to define the attitude taken by the soul, for it could, strictly speaking, do without all of them. Its form is not dependent on its content. We have just filled it; we could as easily empty it again. "Charity" would persist in him who possesses "charity," though there be no other living creature on earth.[59]

The contrasting "closed morality" is not an affective regard toward alterity per se, but a set of rules, pressures, and obligations bearing down on the individual, homogenizing him or her as part of a group, a "closed society" of the same. Such a society tends to have an equally homogenizing form of faith, "static religion," a highly institutionalized religiosity that expresses the interests of the

---

59. Bergson, *The Two Sources of Morality and Religion*, 38, in *Œuvres*, 1006–7.

group through rules and obligations.[60] What is fundamental to such bounded groups is that, no matter how large and inclusive they may come to be, they *must remain closed to some form of outsider*: "their essential characteristic is nonetheless to include at any moment a certain number of individuals, and exclude others." Every in-group requires an out-group. Whatever feelings we have for the group, writes Bergson, "imply a choice, therefore an exclusion; they may act as incentives to strife, they do not exclude hatred."[61] Such closure, such hatred or disregard, indicates a differently oriented soul, centripetal rather than centrifugal. That is why closed morality cannot be transformed *gradually* (by steps of increasing enfranchisement) into open morality; there must be a leap from the one quality of closure to another of openness.[62]

The oppositions in *The Two Sources of Morality and Religion* between open and closed (morality and society), dynamic and static (faith), are simply new implementations of the mobile–immobile dyad pervading Bergson's work. The "creative emotion" linked to open morality is only another name for intuition, which was always both ethical and epistemological (as well as metaphysical), a *sympathy* with the object (that is also a partial coincidence with it).[63] This language of the "open" and openness – overtly adopted for political ends by Karl Popper, covertly appropriated by Heidegger for ontological ends – is simultaneously ethical and naturalistic, ethical in its regard for alterity (an idea taken up later by Levinas), naturalistic in its attention to singularity (subsequently given an ethico-metaphysical treatment by Deleuze using Spinoza). Indeed, it is arguable that the separated thought of Levinas and Deleuze is simply the dissociation of tendencies that remain fused in Bergson.

Antireductionism

If one could summarize the philosophical effects of the Bergsonian value system, both implicit and explicit, it would have to be in terms of antireductionism. Be it the critique of psychophysics in *Time and Free Will*, mind–brain localization in *Matter and Memory*, or neo-Darwinian gradualism in *Creative Evolution*, Bergson's intent was always to highlight the ineliminable remainder that refuses to be reduced (be it through a purported identity or a cause) to some nominated substratum, most often a mechanistic one. Such a reduction *is* a reduction, a diminution, because the substratum is always deemed to be less, to be *merely* mechanical, dumb, and inert. Bergsonism is a philosophy of levels of reality

60. *Ibid.*, 39, 205–7, in *Œuvres*, 1007, 1150–51.
61. *Ibid.*, 32, 18–19, 30, 31, in *Œuvres*, 1001, 989–90, 1000, 1001, 1002.
62. *Ibid.*, 36, in *Œuvres*, 1005.
63. *Ibid.*, 46, 64, in *Œuvres*, 1014, 1029.

that each have their own life and integrity. The "*esprit de système*" found in so much science (*and* philosophy), Bergson wrote, vainly tries to "embrace the totality of things in simple formulas."[64] *A contrario*, metaphysics for him must be the respect for, or sympathy with, the specificity of those levels of reality, for the complexity and excesses of nature. And with that respect comes a negative moment, namely the refusal to accommodate the intellect's systematic desire to simplify, to extract, to reduce the many to the one. Crucially, however, Bergson pursues this cause not against science, but against *scientism and mechanism*. As an empiricist, he strongly believes that science and philosophy must cooperate, and Bergson was undoubtedly a philosopher *of* science in every sense of the term, some commentators even going so far as to describe him as a positivist.[65]

Ironically, however, this desire to cooperate with science, to attend to its data for its own singularities and nuances, has been taken by others as a sign of Bergson's antirationalism. Significantly, where the English translation of Alan Sokal and Jean Bricmont's *Impostures Intellectuelles* focuses exclusively on contemporary figures such as Lacan and Baudrillard in an attempt to expose the alleged scientific charlatanry of French postmodernism, the original French text has an additional chapter on Bergson, as he represents for them *the* historical source for the turn to irrationalism and anti-science in French twentieth-century thought.[66] Contemporary French philosophy has indeed been a series of footnotes to Bergson, but according to Sokal and Bricmont they have been detrimental ones. But Sokal and Bricmont's reading of Bergson is hugely weakened by falling for the usual, shallow stereotypes of his philosophy. Bergson's extensive, long-term studies in psychology and biology are a testament to his respect for the methods and findings of the sciences. Of course, he never thought that philosophy itself could be reduced to science, but nor did he think that science could be reduced to philosophy (or language, or culture, or power). Philosophy is simply the space where we can, and have the duty to, interpret, or re-view, the *underdetermined* findings of science with new (metaphysical) ideas (rather than the lazy, mechanistic interpretations they usually acquire). The role of the philosopher is to engage with these scientific materials and provide them with the metaphysics – the vision of singularity – that they require.

64. Bergson, *The Creative Mind*, 207–8, in *Œuvres*, 1439. When Bergson proclaims "Je n'ai pas de système," there is no tone of apology in his voice (*Mélanges*, 362, 940).
65. See P. A. Y. Gunter, "The Dialectic of Intuition and Intellect: Fruitfulness as a Criterion," in Papanicolaou and Gunter, *Bergson and Modern Thought*. Vladimir Jankélévitch also commends what he calls Bergson's "superior positivism" (*Henri Bergson* [Paris: Presses Universitaires de France, 1959], 190).
66. See Sokal and Bricmont, *Impostures intellectuelles*, ch. 11.

Freedom

Philosophy has its freedoms, just as science has, but it is philosophy's peculiar function to take the *indeterminacy* of the object as its object. Moreover, that indeterminacy is not the object of philosophy's representation but, rather, philosophy simply *is* the indeterminacy immanent within the object. Freedom, indeterminacy, the underdetermined – these are only other names for the singularity and alterity that always attract Bergsonian thought, that are the indefinite end of its immanent regard (attention, sympathy, intuition). Freedom was the topic of Bergson's first work, *Time and Free Will*, which argued against free will being spatialized as a decision between possible choices, for real freedom creates the illusion of preexisting choices retrospectively; freedom was also the core idea of Bergson's most famous work, *Creative Evolution*, life being itself the freedom to create new forms of life; and freedom was also the final word of his most difficult work, *Matter and Memory*, which showed how freedom is always "intimately organized" with necessity and has its roots deep within it.[67] Freedom is a given fact for Bergson: the core immediate datum that is named and renamed in his works, but that remains the abiding value throughout. It is equally the value at the heart of his method and of his metaphysics. It is the free act that is able to "break the circle" of intellectual *aporia* by multiplying (by seeing) the number of variables creating the paradox.[68]

Perhaps this freedom, then, also provides a solution to the paradox of Bergson himself, whose influence seems all the more pronounced just as it is refused (or it refuses) a clear place in history. It is possible that there was never a need to reverse history's "damnation of Bergson," for history's neglect is perfectly adequate to the cause: Bergsonism = Freedom. Freedom does not exist in a vacuum: like its synonyms, Life, the Real, or duration, we must understand freedom to mean that which resists homogeneous space, that which resists static placement, that which resists historical identity. *Durée* itself is the freedom to resist. Consequently, Bergsonism is not the name of *a* philosophy, but the name of what resists (any one) naming. In this respect, Bergson's place is a non-place, invisible as an influence, although all the more influential nevertheless on account of that invisibility. If this means that Bergson cannot be given a place in history, cannot be spatialized with clear lines of influence streaming from his work down to his theoretical progeny, then perhaps this is something that we ourselves should not try to resist either. Rather than a history of Bergson, we might look for a Bergsonian history instead.

67. Bergson, *Matter and Memory*, 249, in *Œuvres*, 378.

68. See Bergson, *Creative Evolution*, 124, in *Œuvres*, 659–60.

MAJOR WORKS

Essai sur les données immédiates de la conscience. Paris: Félix Alcan, 1889. In *Œuvres*, 1–157. Published in English as *Time and Free Will: An Essay on the Immediate Data of Consciousness*, translated by F. L. Pogson. New York: Dover, 2001.

Matière et mémoire: Essai sur la relation du corps à l'esprit. Paris: Félix Alcan, 1896. In *Œuvres*, 159–379. Published in English as *Matter and Memory*, translated by Nancy Margaret Paul and W. Scott Palmer. New York: Zone Books, 1991.

Le Rire: Essai sur la signification du comique. Paris: Félix Alcan, 1900. In *Œuvres*, 381–485. Published in English as *Laughter: An Essay on the Meaning of the Comic*, translated by Cloudesley Brereton and Fred Rothwell. Los Angeles, CA: Green Integer Books, 1999.

Introduction à la métaphysique. Paris: Félix Alcan, 1903. Published in English as *An Introduction to Metaphysics*, translated by T. E. Hulme. Basingstoke: Palgrave Macmillan, 2007.

L'Évolution créatrice. Paris: Félix Alcan, 1907. In *Œuvres*, 487–809. Published in English as *Creative Evolution*, translated by Arthur Mitchell. Basingstoke: Palgrave Macmillan, 2007.

L'Énergie spirituelle: Essais et conférences. Paris: Félix Alcan, 1919. In *Œuvres*, 811–977. Published in English as *Mind-Energy*, edited by Keith Ansell-Pearson and Michael Kolkman, translated by H. Wildon Carr. Basingstoke: Palgrave Macmillan, 2007.

Durée et simultanéité à propos de la théorie d'Einstein. Paris: Firmin-Didot et Cie, 1922. In *Mélanges*, 57–244. Published in English as *Duration and Simultaneity: Bergson and the Einsteinian Universe*, translated by Leon Jacobsen. Manchester: Clinamen Press, 1999.

Les Deux sources de la morale et de la religion. Paris: Félix Alcan, 1932. In *Œuvres*, 979–1247. Published in English as *The Two Sources of Morality and Religion*, translated by R. Ashley Audra and Cloudesley Brereton, with the assistance of W. Horsfall Carter. Notre Dame, IN: Notre Dame Press, 1977.

La Pensée et le mouvant: Essais et conférences. Paris: Félix Alcan, 1934. In *Œuvres*, 1249–482. Published in English as *The Creative Mind: An Introduction to Metaphysics*, translated by Mabelle L. Andison. New York: Citadel Press, 2002.

Œuvres, edited by André Robinet. Paris: Presses Universitaires de France, 1959.

Mélanges, edited by André Robinet. Paris: Presses Universitaires de France, 1972.

2

NEO-KANTIANISM IN GERMANY AND FRANCE

Sebastian Luft and Fabien Capeillères

I. NEO-KANTIANISM IN GERMANY

"Neo-Kantianism" is the name for a broad philosophical movement that sought to revive Kant's philosophy in a radically changed philosophical and, more broadly, cultural landscape.[1] It flourished especially in Germany, but also in France and, to a lesser extent, in Italy and a few other European countries (including Eastern Europe). It reached its apex between 1880 and 1920. In Germany, it grew out of a decidedly academic context – as opposed to "renegade" writers such as Kierkegaard, Schopenhauer, and Nietzsche, who disdained academic philosophy – although its origins lie, in part, in sociopolitical discourses stemming from of the societal problems posed by the Industrial Revolution and the worker question (*Arbeiterfrage*). The other background is the challenge posed to philosophy by the impressively and quickly progressing natural sciences in the era of positivism. Both of these tendencies arose around the middle of the nineteenth century, in a time when, as was often noted, Hegel's system had "collapsed." In both cases, to be elucidated below, the call was issued, "*Back to Kant!*"[2]

1. Sebastian Luft is primarily responsible for the sections dealing with neo-Kantianism in Germany, while Fabien Capeillères is the primary author of the sections dealing with neo-Kantianism in France.
2. For a historical account of the origins of neo-Kantianism, see Klaus Christian Köhnke, *Entstehung und Aufstieg des Neukantianismus: Die Deutsche Universitätsphilosophie zwischen Idealismus und Positivismus* (Frankfurt: Suhrkamp, 1986), abridged English translation, *The Rise of Neo-Kantianism: German Academic Philosophy Between Idealism and Positivism*, R. J. Hollingdale (trans.) (Cambridge: Cambridge University Press, 1991), and Thomas Willey, *Back to Kant: The Revival of Kantianism in German Social and Historical Thought, 1860–1914*

The term "neo-Kantianism" was not used until the late 1880s, and then in a polemical fashion by its critics. The neo-Kantian movement, however, was (with the possible exception of the Marburg School), far from unitary and cohesive, as evidenced by the alternative names for this movement: (neo-)Criticism and neo-Fichteanism, among others. But around 1900, "neo-Kantianism" stuck. The demarcations concerning who belongs to this movement and who does not are to this day contested. Although it was a very broad movement, thinkers who might well be counted among its members – Nicolai Hartmann, Wilhelm Dilthey, or Edmund Husserl, for instance – are rarely included. In Germany, the neo-Kantian movement crystallized around the two "power centers": the "Marburg School" in Marburg, a small university town in the state of Hessia north of Frankfurt, and the "Southwest School" at the universities of Freiburg and Heidelberg.

Given its academic location – all the neo-Kantians were university professors or professional academics – the neo-Kantian movement is also a history of successful university politics: neo-Kantianism in Germany soon exerted its power over nearly all German-speaking universities (including Switzerland and Austria), and its representatives were heavily involved in shaping hiring policies and academic curricula. Around the turn of nineteenth century, neo-Kantianism had attained what Jürgen Habermas once called an "imperial stance" that lasted until its near collapse after the First World War and its total disintegration in Nazi Germany as of 1933. But its dissolution was in itself part of the legacy of neo-Kantianism: many of the leading neo-Kantians were Jews and, not surprisingly, prosecuted by Hitler's fascist regime. The removal of the main neo-Kantian philosophers from academia and from German culture – most of them were left-wing liberals anchoring the Weimar Republic in the values of the Enlightenment – was a consequence that reflected more than just official anti-Semitic policies. To many contemporaries, and Heidegger is here a good example of this attitude, the neo-Kantians represented not only a dated model of philosophy; in addition, their liberal politics, also diffusely associated with "Jewishness," reflected a politics whose time had passed. When Heidegger, in a letter from 1929, railed against the "jewification of the German spirit" (*Verjudung des deutschen Geistes*),

(Detroit, MI: Wayne State University Press, 1978). Brief overviews of the neo-Kantian movement can be found in Hans-Ludwig Ollig, *Der Neukantianismus* (Stuttgart: Metzler, 1979), and Manfred Pascher, *Einführung in den Neukantianismus* (Munich: UTB, 1997). A full-scale account of the neo-Kantian movement does not exist to this day, although certain thinkers or schools have been covered in greater detail. For work on the Marburg School, for example, cf. the important works by Holzhey (see bibliography), and for an historical account, cf. Ulrich Sieg, *Aufstieg und Niedergang des Marburger Neukantianismus: Die Geschichte einer philosophischen Schulgemeinschaft* (Würzburg: Königshausen & Neumann, 1994). The account here is indebted to and draws from all of these sources.

we see that "to be Jewish" was more than a creed; it was a philosophical as well as a political "lifestyle."[3]

Due to their dominant position between 1890 and 1914, the neo-Kantians were harshly attacked by nearly all the other philosophical movements that emerged after the First World War, including phenomenology, *Lebensphilosophie*, existentialism (Jaspers, the early Heidegger), and logical positivism. This critique of what was perceived as the dominant philosophical school in Germany became so much a part of the self-definition of these new tendencies that many, if not most, new philosophical movements and ideas cannot be understood without at least a basic knowledge of the neo-Kantian paradigms and theories that they argued against. Defining one's own project *vis-à-vis* the neo-Kantians became almost the *modus operandi* in many a philosopher's work, and we see this in Husserl's transcendental–eidetic phenomenology, Scheler's value ethics, Heidegger's hermeneutics of facticity, and Carnap's and the Vienna School's attempt at a "truly" scientific philosophy.

In short, the history of late-nineteenth- and early-twentieth-century philosophy cannot be adequately assessed without knowledge of neo-Kantianism. It is curious, then, to note that for over forty years (essentially after the Second World War), neo-Kantianism has been largely ignored by scholarship. As of the 1980s, however, increasing attention in Europe has been directed toward the work of the neo-Kantians and the importance of neo-Kantianism has also been brought to the fore by some scholars in North America. It is to be anticipated that neo-Kantianism will also become a widely discussed field of research in the next decade in North America for scholars working in the history of philosophy, history and philosophy of science, philosophy of culture, and "continental philosophy," broadly construed. This revival is evidenced by a good number of international conferences held in the past decade not only in Germany, France, and Italy, but also in the United States.

Despite the important role of neo-Kantianism in the philosophical landscape of the time, it is, ironically, hard to point to any seminal works by any of the major figures. Of these major figures, Hermann Cohen, Paul Natorp, Wilhelm Windelband, and Heinrich Rickert were the most famous, along with Ernst Cassirer, whose writings were widely received and translated. This is not to say that the literary output was not most impressive: all of these philosophers wrote books at the rate at which most academics today write articles. Nevertheless, some of the systematic approaches of the neo-Kantians have to be pieced together through a synopsis of several works. This dearth of "seminal works" also has philosophical reasons; it has to do with the nature of the neo-Kantian movement itself

3. Quoted in Peter E. Gordon, "Neo-Kantianism and the Politics of Enlightenment," *The Philosophical Forum* 39(2) (2008), 235.

and the type of work that it did and promoted – despite all differences of outlook and emphasis. Hence, to understand the distinct character of the neo-Kantian movement, let us return to its origins in the then-contemporary *political thought* and *natural science*.

Friedrich Albert Lange (1828–75) and Otto Liebmann (1840–1912) might both be considered "fathers" of neo-Kantianism. Lange published two works in 1865, which became defining works for the nascent movement, *Die Arbeiterfrage* (The worker question) and *Geschichte des Materialismus* (*History of Materialism*), while Liebmann's *Kant und die Epigonen* (1865) was very popular at the time. Both of Lange's books tackle the issue of the modern *conditio humana* and the problems arising from humankind's situation in the industrial age, which posed many new and hitherto unknown challenges (mass society, the problem of the working class, etc.). Lange also participated in the Vereinstag Deutscher Arbeitervereine, the German Workers' Association, an ancestor of the German Social Democratic Party (the SPD). However, as the title *Geschichte des Materialismus* indicates, Lange attempted to place these concrete problems into a larger philosophical context. The problem was, in his opinion, "materialism" and its disdain of human spirit and "idealistic" values in a broadly conceived sense of the term, along with materialism's tendency to reduce humans to functioning wheels in the machinery of modern industrial society. Hence, a decidedly political sense of "idealism" runs through neo-Kantianism. This tendency led to interesting and – judging from political debate among social democrats worldwide – still valid social-democratic ideas, which took hold especially in the Marburg School. Both Hermann Cohen and Natorp, for example, promoted what they called "social idealism" as an explicit rejection of a socialism stemming from the Marxist tradition. Thus, in reconstructing the origins of neo-Kantianism, one needs to keep in mind this political background and the societal context that the neo-Kantians attempted to address in a Kantian vein, while Marxist ideas were developing in elsewhere in Germany, England, and Russia.

The other origin, which connects more directly to Kant and hence constitutes the general alliance with the Sage of Königsberg and "Kantianism" in a broader sense, came, interestingly enough, from within the *natural sciences*. Here scientists confronted the problems that arose once natural science became "scientific" in the modern sense of the term, and the speculative *Naturphilosophie* of the German Idealists and the Romantics, especially Schelling,[4] became an object of ridicule. It was in fact a scientist – Hermann von Helmholtz (1821–94) – who, in his physical and optical experiments, discovered the influence of the observer on that which was being observed. In his famous speech *Über das*

*4. For a discussion of Schelling, see the essay by Joseph P. Lawrence in *The History of Continental Philosophy: Volume 1.*

Sehen des Menschen (On man's seeing, 1855), he attempted to formulate these ideas in Kantian terms, claiming that "all cognition of reality must be derived from experience." In this manner, he thought that his study of the physiology of the senses had confirmed in a scientific manner Kant's "organization of the mind," namely "that the manner of our perceptions is equally determined by the nature of our senses as through external objects."[5] Hence, experimental natural science seemed to confirm Kant's transcendental turn, without, however, the idealist baggage that burdened both Kant and his idealist aftermath. Early neo-Kantian philosophers such as Cohen soon took up this challenge and placed Helmholtz's ideas on a firmer philosophical foundation. While they welcomed the fact that an experimental scientist had made the way "back to Kant," they felt that this move took place in the (problematic) spirit of naturalism. As a result, the scientists' return to Kant received an enthusiastic reception on the part of philosophers of the Kantian stripe, but the neo-Kantians also felt that this scientific return to Kant needed to be monitored carefully. The close connections to the sciences became one of the trademarks of neo-Kantianism. In an unfavorable reading, which, however, became popular (and which one still finds quoted today), neo-Kantianism was criticized in this vein for reducing philosophy to the "handmaiden of the sciences." While this description is, as we shall see, unfair, it is true that the proximity to scientific endeavors and a reflection on the status and nature of the sciences – both the natural and the human sciences – became a dominant characteristic that defined and popularized neo-Kantian ideas.

Helmholtz's work exemplifies the rehabilitation of Kantian philosophy that emerged from discussions within the sciences and the philosophy of science. The call to return to Kant was soon taken up by philosophers or those – such as Cohen, who started out as an experimental psychologist – who turned to philosophy under this influence. Yet, once Kant had become re-established as an eminent philosophical figure with whom to approach epistemological questions in the sciences, another field of activity emerged that also helped to strengthen the overall stance of the neo-Kantian movement within Germany, namely *Kant philology* and *Kant scholarship*. With the development of rigorous philology in the nineteenth century and new editorial techniques arose the inauguration of critical Kant editions that adhered to these new standards. "Complete Works" editions had up to then either not existed or were, for example, in the notorious case of Hegel, not philologically sound in the light of contemporary editorial practices. Under the influence of Wilhelm Dilthey, the Kant edition initiated by the Berlin Academy of the Sciences, begun in 1900 and staffed by philosophers in the neo-Kantian vicinity – Erich Adickes, Benno Erdmann, and others – stands (for the

5. Quoted in Helmut Holzhey, "Der Neukantianismus," in *Geschichte der Philosophie*, vol. 12, H. Holzhey and W. Röd (eds) (Munich: Beck, 2004), 31.

most part) the test of modern editorial philology. The importance of this editorial work for the dissemination of Kant's philosophy cannot be overemphasized.

In addition to the Berlin edition, the late nineteenth century saw an impressive proliferation of *commentaries* on Kant's works. Some of the classical Kant scholarship produced then – commentaries by Cassirer, Cohen, Hans Vaihinger, and others – are to this day classics of Kant research. These basic readings defined the main avenues in which Kant would subsequently be read. In other words, what the neo-Kantians achieved, actively and conscientiously, was a *canonization* of Kant as he is perceived today: as the towering figure in modern philosophy. This is not to say that this status is not due to Kant's philosophy itself; however, a writer needs a functioning "transmission belt" that conveys one's thoughts to the readers. This is what the neo-Kantians achieved in an exemplary manner. While this might seem tangential to the actual *philosophical* importance of neo-Kantianism, it is indeed not to be dismissed, as it established both Kant in the position seen today and, in turn, the neo-Kantians as the "true" heirs of this seminal figure in the history of Western philosophy.

Since the neo-Kantian movement is anything but a unified school, we shall now turn to the Marburg School and the Southwestern School, respectively, to discuss their mutual contributions to modern philosophy. This short historical overview will have to confine itself to these two main groups.[6]

The Marburg School: Hermann Cohen, Paul Natorp, Ernst Cassirer

The Marburg School is the most "compact" group within neo-Kantianism, judging from its self-understanding and outward projection. This unity is due to the *method* that its founder, Hermann Cohen (1842–1918), developed out of his Kant interpretation. This method is called the *Transcendental Method*, in recognition of Kant's method, although the term is itself not to be found in Kant's *oeuvre*. This focus on method has led some to accuse the Marburg School of a "methodological fanaticism,"[7] although we shall see that the method itself plays a crucial role in the Marburg School's epistemological paradigm. Surrounded by a very

6. As mentioned, most philosophy departments in Germany and Austria were dominated by neo-Kantians and to do justice to this movement as a whole one would have to discuss figures whose names can merely be listed here: the largely independent Richard Hönigswald (1875–1947) in Breslau (Gadamer's first teacher there), later Munich; the critical realist Alois Riehl in Graz (1844–1924); the philosopher of law Leonard Nelson (1882–1927); Jonas Cohn (1869–1947) in Freiburg; Bruno Bauch (1877–1942), the editor of *Kant Studien*; and for the youngest generation of neo-Kantians after the Second World War, sometimes referred to as "neo-neo-Kantians" (a somewhat excessive title), Richard Zocher (1887–1976), Hans Wagner (1917–2000), and Wolfgang Cramer (1901–74), father of Konrad Cramer (1933–).
7. Cf. Hans-Georg Gadamer, "Paul Natorp," in Paul Natorp, *Philosophische Systematik* (Hamburg: Felix Meiner, 2000).

wide, national as well as international, circle of pupils and adherents, the main figures of this group are Hermann Cohen, Paul Natorp (1854–1924) and Ernst Cassirer (1874–1945). Cassirer is sometimes not counted as belonging to the Marburg School, although he is acknowledged to be one of the most significant philosophers who emerged from the neo-Kantian tradition as a whole. Unlike Cohen and Natorp, who were professorial colleagues at the University of Marburg and formed a unique coalition of great influence both within and outside the university, Cassirer was a generation younger and never actually taught in Marburg. The offspring of a rich Jewish family with relatives in Berlin, Munich, and Vienna, Cassirer rather disliked small-town life such as that of Marburg, a city with a population of some 30,000 at the time. Still, for reasons to be discussed, he deserves to be counted among the Marburg School and its method.

Cohen was by all accounts the dominant figure of this school; being also a charismatic and irritable character,[8] he was the main attraction for students who, after his arrival in Marburg in 1873, soon flocked around him. His ally Natorp was initially one of them, but soon secured his own position at the university, first as a librarian, then later, with Cohen's mentorship, as a professor. Cohen taught in Marburg until his retirement in 1912. He spent his last years living in Berlin teaching at the Lehranstalt für die Wissenschaft des Judentums (Academy for the Science of Judaism), where he taught mainly on Judaism and the philosophy of religion and was influential on a newer generation of thinkers such as Franz Rosenzweig and Martin Buber.[9]

Cohen first made a name for himself through his influential commentaries on Kant's three Critiques. The commentary on the First Critique, entitled *Kants Theorie der Erfahrung* (Kant's theory of experience), became especially influential for Kant scholarship as well as for the popularization of the "Marburg Method." Once these three voluminous commentaries were completed (1912), Cohen turned to composing his own "System of Philosophy" in three volumes analogous to Kant's Critiques – *Logik der Reinen Erkenntnis* (Logic of pure

8. As will become evident below in the treatment of Cohen's closest collaborator, Natorp, they seemed to have, as eyewitnesses report, polar opposite characters. Whereas Natorp was generally perceived as solid and reliable, Cohen seemed to have a choleric temper, which he did not even attempt to keep under wraps and which was directed at different people and peoples. To give just one example, Cohen, who discovered his Jewish roots after the Dreyfus affair, despised assimilated Jews and did not hold back judgment. One person whom he vilified in this way was, for instance, Husserl; see quotations from Cohen's correspondence with Natorp in Sebastian Luft, "Reconstruction and Reduction: Natorp and Husserl on Method and the Question of Subjectivity," in *Neo-Kantianism in Contemporary Philosophy*, Rudolf Makkreel and Sebastian Luft (eds) (Bloomington, IN: Indiana University Press, 2010), 84–5 n.3.
9. For a historical account of Cohen's interesting life, see Helmut Holzhey, "Cohen and the Marburg School in Context," in *Hermann Cohen's Critical Idealism*, Reinier Munk (ed.) (Dordrecht: Springer, 2004).

cognition), *Ethik des Reinen Willens* (Ethics of pure willing), and *Ästhetik des Reinen Gefühls* (Aesthetic of pure sentiment) – which appeared between 1902 and 1912. A transitional work, but from a developmental standpoint crucial, since it allowed Cohen to explicitly formulate his "transcendental method" (the centerpiece of the Marburg School), was the small study *Das Prinzip der Infinitesimal-Methode und seine Geschichte* (The principle of the infinitesimal method and its history). Cohen's system was supposed to be rounded off by a fourth part, a psychology explicating the "unity of cultural consciousness," but Cohen passed away before beginning it. Shortly before his death, Cohen completed his late manuscript on religion, *Religion der Vernunft aus den Quellen des Judentums* (Religion of reason out of the sources of Judaism), which was published posthumously and recently has attracted considerable attention in the philosophy of religion and Jewish studies.

To understand Cohen's original approach culminating in the "transcendental method," one must first assess his Kant interpretation. The thesis that Cohen boldly puts forth claims that with his Copernican turn Kant founded nothing less than a new concept of *experience*. Experience is not mere perception or intuition, but establishes *laws* about that which is experienced. In other words, according to Cohen, the experience Kant is talking about is that of the *scientist*. Cohen famously declares that Kant conceived his revolutionary Copernican turn as he meditated on Newton's *Principia Mathematica*. "Not the stars in the heavens," he writes, "are the phenomena, but the astronomical data that the scientist establishes, these are the contents of experience."[10] The experience of the scientist, in establishing laws of nature, thereby *constructs* nature as a mathematical universe. For Kant, Newtonian physics *exists* and, because of its mathematical method, is able to give rise to synthetic judgments *a priori*. In Cohen's interpretation, Kant's question concerning the transcendental condition of the possibility of *a priori* cognition is really concerned with the question of how those *a priori* truths established in natural (physical) science become possible and how they can be justified. The accepted cornerstone – which Kant called the *factum* – that philosophy has to clarify is the "factum of the sciences" (*das Faktum der Wissenschaften*) in which reality is constructed. Taking cues from the analytic method Kant pursues in the *Prolegomena*, this entails that philosophy's job is to *reconstruct* the conditions of possibility through which this *factum* comes about.

The manner in which Cohen recasts Kant's transcendental turn is, essentially, by rejecting the two stems doctrine (concepts and intuitions). His solution is Hegelian, as he grounds all knowledge and experience of reality in *a priori* concepts. Reality as experienced is *constructed* through and through, and

10. Hermann Cohen, *Kants Theorie der Erfahrung* (New York: Olms, [1871] 1987), 20–21. All translations from the German are my own.

this construction occurs through the use of *concepts* that are applied to what is experienced. Cohen grounds this premise on the discovery of the infinitesimal in mathematics, according to which all entities are constructed in thought on the basis of the category of the infinitesimally small.[11] Since these concepts are *a priori* (Cohen prefers the word "pure"), reality as we encounter it is *constructed in pure thought.* The task of philosophy is to lay the foundations of objective knowledge in pure thought, but the laying of these foundations is modified by scientific progress. That is, scientific progress makes new concepts necessary, and since all scientific cognition is in principle falsifiable, the foundations themselves are subject to constant re-evaluation and scrutiny. Philosophy is no longer a science of ultimate foundations (*Grundlagenwissenschaft*) – the traditional task of metaphysics prior to Kant's transcendental turn – but is a science of *laying foundations* (*Grundlegungswissenschaft*) in "pure thought."

Cohen's transcendental method grounds all knowledge of the world in pure thought. But Cohen's restatement of Kant's transcendental idealism operates on the basis of an unacknowledged Hegelian influence. This influence consists in the notion that the system of categories is not a "static" table of concepts, established once and for all, but something that evolves over time. This evolution, now departing from Hegelian idealism, is not that of absolute spirit but of scientific progress "on the ground." Theoretical philosophy becomes a logic of categories that have their origin in pure thought, and epistemology is recast as a "logic of origin" (*Ursprungslogik*), in which self-generated categories in thought (as their origin) become constituted as functional (not substantial) categories, forming a web of relations as a matrix for orientation in thought. This is to say that what Cassirer later formulated in his reconstruction of the shift from ancient to modern science – the move from a substance to a functional ontology – in effect already takes place in Cohen's logic. Cohen's late philosophy in his logic of origin differs from Hegel's, accordingly, in that thought categories lay the foundations for *scientific* thought. This logic is not, in other words, a "self-constructing path," as Hegel calls his method, but an *a priori* foundation of scientific thinking in an *a priori* category system that is itself dynamic and ever-evolving. For Cohen, philosophy is the justification of the *factum* that is already established (the mathematical sciences) and *reconstructs* their constructive activity, thereby *justifying* the knowledge claims of the scientist.

This abbreviated discussion of Cohen's philosophical system – his ethics, aesthetics, and political philosophy have been passed over[12] – has focused on

11. See Hermann Cohen, *Das Prinzip der Infinitesimal-Methode und seine Geschichte* (Berlin: Bruno Cassirer, 1883).

12. For more elaboration of his system, see Andrea Poma, *The Critical Philosophy of Hermann Cohen* (Albany, NY: SUNY Press, 1997); Geert Edel, *Von der Vernunftkritik zur Erkenntnislogik*

the transcendental method that forms the nodal point around which the other two significant thinkers of the Marburg School constructed their systems. The principle of human beings' *construction of reality* provides the crucial element for understanding this school. Reality, insofar as it is entirely constructed by the activities of the human spirit, of which scientific thought is merely one, albeit its most dignified, application, is the reality of humanity's *cultural* activities. The Marburg School is in this sense unified as outlining an encompassing transcendental philosophy of *culture*.[13] In the Marburg reading, to quote Cassirer, Kant's critique of reason is recast as a "critique of culture."

Natorp, after wavering between pursuing a career as a classical philologist, musician, or philosopher, finally came to focus on philosophy and moved to Marburg to study under Cohen. Cohen soon incorporated him into his growing group of collaborators. An avid student of the natural sciences and mathematics, Natorp was probably the most erudite member of this school. He wrote on ancient philosophy, ancient and modern science, social and political philosophy, and, last but not least – since his Chair was also dedicated to pedagogy – pedagogical philosophy, especially that of Heinrich Pestalozzi. A more agreeable character[14] and also a lucid writer – Cohen's writings were considered dense and difficult – Natorp helped the Marburg School gain a broader acceptance and popularity than Cohen himself would have been able to achieve. Given the openly anti-Semitic sentiment in large parts of German society and especially German academia, it is likely that, without Natorp on his side, Cohen, clearly the most innovative neo-Kantian, would have remained isolated and far less influential in the academic landscape of his time. The Marburg School must be seen as constituted by both individuals: Cohen, sometimes referred to as "minister of the exterior," and Natorp, dubbed "minister of the interior." Together they formed a powerful alliance and a functioning collaboration that lasted more than a quarter century.[15]

In addition to his writings on figures in the history of philosophy – most notably Plato – and on special problems in the philosophy of science, Natorp

---

(Freiburg and Munich: Alber, 1988); and the contributions in *Hermann Cohen's Critical Idealism*, Reinier Munk (ed.) (Dordrecht: Springer, 2004).

13. See Ursula Renz, *Die Rationalität der Kultur: Zur Kulturphilosophie und ihrer transzendentalen Begründung bei Cohen, Natorp und Cassirer* (Hamburg: Felix Meiner, 2002).
14. Cf. footnote 8 above for an illustration of Cohen's character. For an example of Natorp's greater effect on the scientific community of his day, one can point out that nearly all statements of the Marburg School that were received in the philosophical and wider public stemmed from Natorp's pen; for the logical method of the Marburg School, for example his *Die logischen Grundlagen der exakten Wissenschaften* (actually Cohen's domain), and for a general, and popular, expression of the Marburg School as a whole, one should note that Natorp's *Philosophie: Ihr Problem und ihre Probleme* (discussed in the main text above), was first published in 1911 and was re-edited four times during Natorp's lifetime.
15. Cf. Sieg, *Aufstieg und Niedergang des Marburger Neukantianismus.*

was also the only notable neo-Kantian who was able to write an unusually brief (150 pages) and bestselling treatise: *Philosophie: Ihr Problem und Ihre Probleme* (Philosophy: its problem and its problems). This text, which is a lucid "mission statement" of Marburg neo-Kantianism, has perhaps rightfully been considered the *Programmschrift* of the entire neo-Kantian movement. Yet Natorp's initial fame was based on his influential 1903 work on Plato: *Platos Ideenlehre: Eine Einführung in den Idealismus* (Plato's theory of ideas: an introduction to idealism). As the title indicates, Natorp's peculiar interpretation concerning Plato's theory of the Forms is that it is really an epistemological position – idealism – rather than a metaphysical one. More specifically, Natorp claims, Plato's ideas are nothing but natural laws that govern physical entities. Laws are that which make things what they are, what is "valid" about them. Soon after its publication, this bold thesis was harshly criticized, since it seems to read Newtonian physics and Kant's transcendental turn back into Plato's premodern thought; but given the close alliance with modern science, this reading is perhaps less surprising stemming from a Marburger than it first appears. In this sense, Natorp's *Plato* is less a work of Plato exegesis than a restatement of the type of idealism professed in the Marburg School.[16]

Natorp's most substantial philosophical contribution to the Marburg School was his psychology and concomitant theory of subjectivity. Dismissed by Cohen – although not openly – Natorp's idea of a philosophical psychology started out as a side project when he published in 1888 his short *Einleitung in die Psychologie nach Kritischer Methode* (Introduction to psychology according to critical method). This later turned into a full-fledged, yet ultimately abandoned, project when he published the "second edition" *Allgemeine Psychologie nach Kritischer Methode* (General psychology according to critical method), which had grown to 350 pages, more than three times its original size. In 1887, he published the influential article "Ueber Objective und Subjective Begründung der Erkenntniss" (On objective and subjective grounding of cognition), where he systematically laid out his idea of a *philosophical* – not experimental, as in the Brentano and Wundt Schools – psychology.

Natorp's psychology grew directly out of problems that he saw with the transcendental method. If the latter is about constructing reality, all that this method accounts for philosophically are the finished "products" such as scientific theories; these are the "outcome" of humanity's creative activity. In other words, all

16. It is interesting to note that Natorp somewhat recanted his earlier reading in a "Metacritical Appendix" of the second edition in 1921; cf. *Plato's Theory of Ideas: an Introduction to Idealism*, Vasilis Politis and John Connolly (trans.) (Sankt Augustin: Academia, 2004). For Natorp's Plato interpretation and its importance for the Marburg School, cf. Karl-Heinz Lembeck, *Platon in Marburg: Platon-Rezeption und Philosophiegeschichtsphilosophie bei Cohen und Natorp* (Würzburg: Königshausen & Neumann, 1994).

that philosophy was to do was justify *after the fact* what the sciences were "always already" doing. What was missing was an account of the creative, subjective *life* that creates these cultural products. This should be, Natorp asserted, the task of a critical psychology. Its purpose was, more precisely, to recover this creative, subjective life by going in the *opposite* direction of the transcendental, constructive method. That is to say, it should proceed *reconstructively* from the finished products back to the creative life that was involved in their constructive processes. Metaphorically, Natorp described the psychological, reconstructive method as a "minus" *vis-à-vis* a "plus" direction on one and the same line. What was to be regained would be this active, dynamic life that had come to a standstill once cultural products had been formed. This method should remain faithful to the essentially dynamic life of consciousness. All other psychological approaches treated consciousness with objectifying methods; when reading accounts of consciousness, Natorp complains, he feels as though he is walking through a morgue instead of studying bodies filled with life.[17] The reconstructive method was the method to finally overcome this problem. At the same time, given the metaphor of the plus and minus directions, it is clear that the reconstructive method is entirely dependent on the transcendental method; Natorp calls it its "inverse" application. That is, the reconstructive method of psychology serves a transcendental–philosophical function within the overall Marburg Method that was to account for subjectivity in all of its dimensions – in its cultural products and in its dynamic *status nascendi* – hence, psychology "according to critical method." Natorp's intention was not that this should replace or be in competition with experimental psychologies, but that it was intended to add a piece within the overall transcendental epistemology that the Marburg School had taken over from Kant, but which would remain incomplete unless this "subjective" part was supplied.

The subjective life, once it had been discovered through reconstruction, Natorp frames in terms of what he calls "*conscious-ity*" (*Bewusstheit*). Through this neologism he attempted to capture the very fact of "being conscious" of conscious life, with its conscious contents. Moreover, his reconstructive method would proceed *genetically*, that is, it would provide not static laws (of objectifying science), but genetic accounts of the dynamic life of consciousness, going down to the origins of consciousness where one cannot even speak of "consciousness" any longer. In his late work, Natorp simply calls it "life." Other than these principal philosophical insights, however, the actual results of Natorp's psychology were meager and Natorp himself abandoned the opposition between objective

17. Paul Natorp, *Allgemeine Psychologie nach Kritischer Methode* (Tübingen: Mohr/Siebeck, 1912), 16, 31. As Natorp explains there, an example of such "objectivist" treatment is the application of the mechanistic model of natural causality to the sphere of the psyche.

and subjective methods in favor of a more deeply grounded "all-method" that synthesized both subjectivist and objectivist methods. In his somewhat idiosyncratic late philosophical system, Natorp was seen to have departed from his Marburg roots (as some critics, clearly under the influence of Heidegger, have remarked),[18] and given this verdict, Natorp's late system has been vastly underappreciated. Challenging the fundamental assumptions of Kant's philosophy as well as that of the Marburg School as a whole, the question as to how one should ultimately interpret this school turns on the issue of whether it represents the final fulfillment of Kant's intentions if one spells out the implications of transcendental philosophy, or whether it is a radical departure from the Kantian paradigms. At any rate, his psychological method and his account of subjectivity have had significant impact on other theories, including Husserl's phenomenology and Heidegger's fundamental ontology of Dasein.

Cohen and Natorp formed such a close alliance that differences between them tended to remain subdued and unarticulated (either in public or even between them).[19] When Cohen left Marburg for Berlin in 1912, Natorp, who remained in Marburg until his death in 1924, experienced something of a renaissance. In his lectures he developed his original philosophical system, which he worked on until his last days. In his late thought he wanted to form an all-encompassing method, incorporating mystical elements into a totalizing philosophical system. The manuscript, which was prepared for publication by Natorp himself, remained unpublished until 1954. There has been some speculation that the publication was discouraged at the time by Heidegger, who was professor in Marburg as of 1921 and who was familiar with Natorp's latest developments.[20] In fact, Natorp's last intuitions, which focused on the simple and original fact of being simply being – the basic factum of the "*es gibt*" – bear some resemblance to Heidegger's *Seinsfrage*.

The most important and also most influential individual for twentieth-century philosophy stemming from the Marburg School was undoubtedly Ernst Cassirer. He ingeniously picked up the main lines from his teachers Cohen and Natorp, weaving them into his own philosophical system, while incorporating

18. Cf., for example, Christoph Von Wolzogen, *Die Autonome Relation: Zum Problem der Beziehung im Spätwerk Paul Natorps; Ein Beitrag zur Geschichte der Theorien der Relation* (Würzburg and Amsterdam: Rodopi, 1984), who also lists examples of such readings (von Wolzogen himself reads Natorp in this Heideggerian manner as well).
19. Helmut Holzhey's *Cohen und Natorp* (Basel and Stuttgart: Schwabe, 1986) does an excellent job at showing where the differences between Cohen and Natorp lay.
20. Cf. von Wolzogen, *Die Autonome Relation*, who lists some quotations from Heidegger's correspondence in support of this hypothesis. It would be, ironically, Gadamer, pupil of both Natorp and Heidegger, who later favored the publication of this text, as witnessed by his laudatory introduction "Paul Natorp," in Natorp, *Philosophische Systematik*, xi–xviii.

influences from such diverse fields as linguistics, anthropology, and other ("hard") sciences, such as contemporary physics. He was the most original and also most prolific offspring of the Marburg School. Coming from a wealthy family, he neither aspired to be a university professor, nor were his chances as a Jew ever very good in German academia at the time. Nevertheless, he was considered one of the strongest of his generation, earning his first recognition as a historian of philosophy through his studies on Leibniz and Renaissance and early modern thought. He was also involved in new editions of the works of Leibniz and Kant. His monograph, *Kant's Leben und Lehre* (*Kant's Life and Thought*), originally intended as the introductory essay to the Kant edition but not published until after the First World War, has become a classic in Kant scholarship, while his four-volume *Das Erkenntnisproblem in der Philosophie und Wissenschaft der Neueren Zeit* (The problem of knowledge in modern philosophy and science) is an excellent example of neo-Kantian *Problemgeschichte.*[21] One would, however, not do justice to his philosophical originality – which unfortunately has sometimes been the case – were he to be restricted to his early work on the history of philosophy.

After the First World War, Cassirer did receive a call as professor (*Ordinarius*) to the newly founded university of Hamburg, where he became Rektor (president) in 1929–30, the highest academic position that any Jew ever occupied in Germany. Quickly reading the signs of the times, he and his extended family left Nazi Germany in 1933. Cassirer emigrated first to England, then to Sweden, where he fled from the Nazis anew as they invaded that country in 1941. He was then invited to a visiting professorship at Yale, where he stayed for three years. In 1944, he assumed another visiting appointment at Columbia. Already in failing health and highly distressed by the war reports, he died of a heart attack on the streets of New York in 1945, shortly before the end of the Second World War. It has been speculated that his influence, especially in the US, would have been considerably stronger had he lived to see his original work, published in German and only slowly becoming translated, come to fruition in the New World.[22]

Sometimes referred to as a watershed event in twentieth-century philosophy, the famous encounter between Cassirer and Heidegger in the Swiss town of Davos in 1929 must be mentioned.[23] During the annually held *Hochschultage*

21. See the section on *Problemgeschichte* below.
22. Cf. Michael Friedman, "Ernst Cassirer," *Stanford Encyclopedia of Philosophy*, 2004 (http://plato.stanford.edu/entries/cassirer).
23. There is a smattering of literature on this event, beginning – at least in recent scholarship – with Michael Friedman, *A Parting of the Ways: Carnap, Cassirer, and Heidegger* (Chicago, IL: Open Court, 2000) Cf. also the recent article by Gordon, "Neo-Kantianism and the Politics of Enlightenment."

devoted to intellectual topics – in 1929, Kant's philosophy and its interpretation – Heidegger and Cassirer conducted a well-attended dispute regarding their different interpretations of Kant's philosophy. In truth, it amounted to a showdown between the two most prominent philosophers of the time: Heidegger, who had just published his groundbreaking *Being and Time* (1927); and Cassirer, who had just published the third volume of his philosophical system, the voluminous *Philosophy of Symbolic Forms*. While formally centering on the interpretation of Kant, the dispute was really about what, according to each, ought be considered the main purpose and intention of philosophy at large: for Cassirer, liberating the human being from his confinement in primitive and un-enlightened existence; for Heidegger, bringing human Dasein back into the "harshness and hardness of fate." Given the events that would ensue in Germany in 1933, Heidegger's role in them, and the fascist ideology the German people came to embrace – the country of the *Dichter und Denker* – it is not hard to see the wider and more profound implications of this encounter.[24] This is not to say that these implications were clear at the time to those in the audience. However, in hindsight, this encounter bears an almost eerie premonition of what was to come. The reasons why contemporaries believed that Cassirer had been so thoroughly bested by Heidegger cannot be spelled out straightforwardly either, but can perhaps best be described as "atmospherical." While the participants of the conference spent all day indoors debating, and dressed formally for the evening reception, Heidegger spent the days (presumably when he was not part of the program) skiing and showed up at the reception in his ski overalls, in total disregard of social etiquette. The "hardness of being" of the young and energetic Heidegger clashed against the bourgeois Cassirer, who seemed to be "in agreement with everything,"[25] implying weak compromises reminiscent of the politics of the Weimar Republic, which compromised itself out of existence.

Regarding Cassirer's character, it has been described as conciliatory and "Olympian," which extends to his writings. These display a remarkable lucidity and, at the same time, philosophical modesty. At times the philosophical core of his argument can be lost in the wealth of historical erudition that accompanies

24. This dispute is published as "Davos Disputation Between Ernst Cassirer and Martin Heidegger," in Martin Heidegger, *Kant and the Problem of Metaphysics*, Richard Taft (trans.) (Bloomington, IN: Indiana University Press, 1997). For important essays on this encounter, see Dominic Kaegi and Enno Rudolph (eds), *Cassirer–Heidegger: 70 Jahre Davoser Disputation* (Hamburg: Felix Meiner, 2000). Among those who travelled to Davos to witness this encounter were Rudolf Carnap, Eugen Fink, Herbert Marcuse, Joachim Ritter, Leo Strauss, Leon Brunschvicg, Emmanuel Levinas, Jean Cavaillès, and Maurice de Gandillac.

25. In a telling anecdote, reported in Gordon, "Neo-Kantianism and the Politics of Enlightenment," 223ff., students put on a mock debate between Heidegger and Cassirer one evening. Cassirer was played by the young Levinas, who supposedly let flour (= dust) trickle out of his sleeves, repeating the phrase "Ich bin mit allem einverstanden" (I agree with everything).

his accounts. Most of his writings focus on other thinkers and their theories, and he is content to raise philosophical issues in those contexts. Cassirer's first original contribution to critical philosophy, which came fairly late in this young shooting star's career, was his *Substanz- und Funktionsbegriff* (*Substance and Function*),[26] which appears to discuss a seemingly remote problem in scientific concept formation, but in fact raises an issue that will be the cornerstone of his philosophical systematic: the distinction between a substantial and functional ontology and its epistemological implications. This basic insight, stemming from the groundwork laid by Cohen, was cashed out in his three-volume *Philosophy of Symbolic Forms*. In addition to these substantial tomes, Cassirer wrote the four-volume study *The Problem of Knowledge in Modern Philosophy* and a wide array of articles and smaller studies on mythology, linguistics, modern physics, and intellectual history. Once in the United States, he summarized his system in the popular book *An Essay on Man* (written in English). His last work, *The Myth of the State*, offers a penetrating critique of modern fascism based on his interpretation of the role of myth in the hierarchy of cultural achievements and its relation to modern totalitarianism.

Returning to his first systematic work, *Substance and Function*, Cassirer, taking his cue from Cohen's paradigm of *construction*, traced the constructive activity of the human mind in the distinction between substantive and functional concepts in scientific nomenclature. Opposed to a substantial paradigm in which, following Aristotle's substance ontology, concepts mirror things as substances, a new type of concept formation has taken hold in modernity: that of functional concepts. Functional concepts place the objects that they mirror into a *function*, as in mathematical functions ($f(x)$). What functional concepts mirror, then, are not substantial things, but functions, that is relations. Being a function means that the functional concept formation actually *constructs* the object of a particular scientific endeavor. Hence, Cassirer discovered Cohen's constructive principle at the heart of scientific concept formation itself.

Whereas *Substance and Function* is largely a historical and programmatic work, drawing on critical reflections on late-nineteenth-century physics and mathematics by Richard Dedekind (1831–1916), Pierre Duhem (1861–1916), Hermann von Helmholtz (1821–94), and Heinrich Hertz (1857–94) as evidence for the core theme of functional concept formation, Cassirer subsequently wrote two monographs analyzing the revolutionary physical theories of the first half of the twentieth century – general relativity and quantum mechanics – as manifestations of this new mode of concept formation. *Zur Einstein'schen*

26. Published in English with a translation of his *Zur Einstein'schen Relativitätstheorie*, in *Substance and Function and Einstein's Theory of Relativity*, William Curtis Swabey & Marie Collins Swabey (eds) (New York: Dover, 1953).

Relativitätstheorie (1920; published in English as "On Einstein's Theory of Relativity: Considered from the Epistemological Standpoint" as a supplement to *Substance and Function*) identified the postulate of general covariance – that the laws of physics are the same in all reference frames, hence that the objects of fundamental physics must be represented as tensor expressions, valid in all coordinate systems – as a novel principle of objectifying unity, a significant further step away from anthropomorphic thing concepts toward an abstract and purely geometrical concept of object. Cassirer's epistemological examination of quantum mechanics, *Determinism and Indeterminism in Modern Physics*, written while in exile in Sweden in 1936, points to Heisenberg's uncertainty relations and quantum statistics as even more striking transformations of the concept of object, where the old classical notions of physical state and individual identity are transformed, acquiring functional form. The thrust of each of these two works is an insistence that the concept of object in physics is subordinate to that of physical law, and accordingly that "objectivity or objective reality, is attained only because and insofar as there is conformity to law – not vice versa."[27]

But this was only Cassirer's first step. For, Cassirer asserted, such a constructive activity is not present just in scientific concept formation – an activity of the human spirit, to be sure – but in *all* cultural activities. Construction is, in other words, a form of *interpretation* of something that could be completely different depending on the manner in which it is constructed. The sine curve (Cassirer's example) in the mathematical context is, in an artistic manner of seeing, an ornament, and may represent any number of other contexts. Prior to such an interpretation – *any* interpretation – the thing is simply nothing for us. What a thing is depends on its context, and the context is something *constructed* through the human mind. Cassirer calls the agent of this activity *spirit.* That which is constructed, or the medium of construction, he calls, nodding to Kant's "Transcendental Aesthetic," a *form.* There is no simple object given (as a substance or substratum) that *then* receives a supervening interpretation, but there are only objects-in-contexts. There is no "raw" datum. The term for such an object within a form Cassirer takes over from his favorite author, Goethe, in calling it a *symbol.* Cassirer therefore calls his system that of *symbolic forms.* They are the forms of manifestation into which human spirit's activity becomes

27. Ernst Cassirer, *Determinism and Indeterminism in Modern Physics: Historical and Systematic Studies of the Problem of Causality*, O. Theodor Benfey (trans.) (New Haven, CT: Yale University Press, [1936] 1956), 132. By showing that there is continuous progress toward pure signification in the process of objectification in physics, this book also rebuked the Nazis' characterization of relativity and quantum physics as "Jewish" and "degenerate" science. The authors would like to thank Thomas Ryckman for his suggestions on how to treat this issue. Interested readers should consult Ryckman's *The Reign of Relativity: Philosophy in Physics 1915–1925* (Oxford: Oxford University Press, 2005).

filled. Indeed, we live in a plurality of meaningful "contexts." The three symbolic forms that Cassirer discusses in his *magnum opus* are language, myth, and scientific cognition. They are products of human spirit's productive–constructive activity. His adaptation of the transcendental method traces the manner of construction in each form, respectively, while breaking with Cohen's exclusively scientific–logistic paradigm. The modes of construction in each form are more freely described as different "logics" inhering in them. Cassirer's system can also be described as a methodology of symbolic formation; thus, he is decidedly a methodological pluralist. But his methodological pluralism is incomprehensible without the fundamental constructive paradigm that is the signature of the "Marburg Method."

Owing to his systematizing work in describing symbolic formation in different cultural contexts, his writings have become influential for several sciences, both human (anthropology, linguistics, aesthetics) and natural (such as physics). Before leaving Cassirer, a brief comment on his interpretation of fascism is in order. *The Myth of the State* rivals other classical texts dealing with fascism in the twentieth century. In his interpretation of the rise of fascism in the twentieth century, he argues that the phenomenon of fascism is the result of political propaganda that has allowed myth to re-enter the political arena, making porous the borders between responsible, rational action and mythical power. Myth, once overcome by Greek enlightenment, raises its ugly head once political discourse has become corrupted in a manner that allows mythical elements – Hitler, the "divine *Führer*," the myth of the superior "Aryan Race," and so on – to dominate political, democratic discourse.

The Southwest School: Wilhelm Windelband, Heinrich Rickert, Emil Lask

The Southwest School is much less cohesive than the Marburg School; even the name "Southwest" indicates that this "movement" (to speak of a school is perhaps exaggerated) was localized in different university towns – Heidelberg and Freiburg im Breisgau, respectively.[28] The main representatives were Wilhelm Windelband (1848–1915) and his pupil Heinrich Rickert (1863–1936). An important member of this movement was Emil Lask (1875–1915), arguably the most interesting but also most difficult philosopher of this group and of significant influence for, among others, the young Heidegger. He died prematurely, however, in the trenches during the First World War. His "logic of philosophy" is a metaphilosophical category system for philosophy itself that, while highly

28. The Southwest School is sometimes also referred to as the "Baden School" after the state of Baden, part of the German Empire; the state was incorporated after the Second World War and is now called "Baden-Württemberg."

original, is arguably a departure from neo-Kantianism in its Southwest mode and will not receive further discussion here.[29]

The Southwesterners were quite successful at their respective universities and shaped several generations of students. Windelband, for instance, was professor in Zurich, Freiburg, and Strasbourg (then German territory), before settling into Heidelberg, where he lived from 1903 until his death. Rickert became professor in Freiburg in 1896 before receiving a call to Heidelberg in 1916 to succeed Windelband, who had died the year before. Despite a mental illness that prohibited Rickert from making public appearances (he suffered from agoraphobia), he nevertheless exerted a substantial influence through his – often polemical and piercing – writings.[30] While more loosely affiliated than the Marburg School, Rickert and Windelband nevertheless worked with certain core ideas that they shared, while not at all times agreeing in all details. Since their philosophical efforts displayed less of a systematic progression than the work of the members of the Marburg School, we shall be presenting the Southwest School in terms of their shared core ideas.[31]

(i) Writing the history of philosophy as a history of problems (Problemgeschichte)
Windelband, while best known as a historian of philosophy, is unfairly reduced to a historian insofar as he devised a new way of doing the history of philosophy, namely as the history of *problems*. While this might seem inconsequential today, to understand the history of philosophy as a development of philosophical problems was at the time quite innovative. Windelband's historiological method took the emphasis away from individual philosophers and a quasi-biographical reconstruction of their work and placed that emphasis instead on the rich historical "horizon" that provided a historical–scientific–philosophical setting in which these philosophers worked. This setting is the process in which "European humanity" exposes its view of world and life (*Welt- und Lebensauffassung*). It is not a Hegelian scenario, in which history is the process of increasing knowledge of freedom, but rather a process in which thinkers and scientists communicate and interact. In this historical process, there are relevant factors that need to

29. For an excellent treatment of Lask, see Steven Galt Crowell, *Husserl, Heidegger, and the Space of Meaning: Paths Towards Transcendental Phenomenology* (Evanston, IL: Northwestern University Press, 2001).
30. Rickert's reputation at the time indicates the significance of the acknowledgment given to the phenomenological movement when Husserl received the call to Freiburg in 1916 to succeed Rickert.
31. While the members of the Southwest School were no less respected in German academia than the Marburgers, their philosophical legacy has dwindled to nearly zero insofar as their achievements have become so much a part of the received idea of philosophical work that they can well be considered trivial.

be taken into account: pragmatic, cultural, and individual ones. A *pragmatic* consideration of the history of problems emphasizes that the same philosophical problems re-emerge throughout Western history in changed circumstances. The *cultural* aspect means that culture is the binding continuum that holds together seemingly incoherent scientific or philosophical discussions. And finally, the focus on *individuality* highlights the importance of individual characters in the history of philosophy. While this was the primary focus in earlier philosophical historiography, for the neo-Kantians this consideration now comes at the *end* of this historical reconstruction.[32] This type of philosophical historiography – in conjunction with the meticulous work that neo-Kantian philosophers carried out in their editing of the original sources – has become the standard for any historical writings in philosophy. It has also been the target of attempts to provide alternative ways of doing the history of philosophy, and Heidegger's "History of Being" and Gadamer's "History of Effects"[33] – both Heidegger and Gadamer knew this neo-Kantian method intimately – should be seen as direct critiques of the neo-Kantian method of doing history of philosophy.

(ii) Distinctions in theory of science: idiographic and nomothetic sciences

Perhaps the most famous legacy of the Southwest School is Windelband's distinction between idiographic and nomothetic sciences, that is, between a science of the individual and singular and a science of the general and lawlike.[34] Windelband lays out this influential distinction, at the height of his career, in his famous Presidential Address (*Rektoratsrede*) in Strasbourg in 1894.[35] His starting-point is a critique of the traditional distinction between rational and empirical sciences. This distinction is no longer satisfactory; indeed, the development of certain sciences – most notoriously psychology and physics – has shown that the true results of these disciplines are neither purely rational nor purely empirical. An overview of the scientific activities of his day reveals a different distinction that seems to better fit the actual status quo, namely that between sciences of nature (*Naturwissenschaften*) and sciences of the human world (*Geisteswissenschaften,* sometimes also translated as "human" or "spiritual sciences," or nowadays simply "humanities"). They are both sciences

32. Cf. Holzhey, "Der Neukantianismus," 59–60.

*33. This aspect of Gadamer's work is discussed in the essay by Wayne J. Froman in *The History of Continental Philosophy: Volume 6*.

34. Rickert expanded on this distinction and added some further details, but he was in general agreement with Windelband's line of thought. Although one reads time and again that this idiographic–nomothetic distinction was introduced by Rickert, it is Windelband, however, who conceived it.

35. Windelband, "Geschichte und Naturwissenschaft," in *Präludien: Aufsätze und Reden zur Philosophie und ihrer Geschichte* (Tübingen: Mohr/Siebeck, [1884] 1924).

– *Wissenschaften* – peculiar to the English ear, meaning, literally translated, "knowledge-doms." Such a distinction undercuts that of rational and empirical sciences and is indeed an advance over it. But such a distinction, although widely acknowledged in Windelband's day, rests on ontological assumptions concerning the ontic regions of nature and spirit that present a problem. The science that reveals the problem with this distinction is psychology: what kind of science is one to group it under? As it has the human psyche as its object, one would be inclined to call it a human science. Yet insofar as its goal is experimentally verifiable general results, it has the character of a natural science.

Here Windelband intervenes with an attempt to undercut this distinction. Arguing that all sciences, insofar as they treat objects of experience, are *empirical*, the only questions are *how* and *as what* to *interpret* these empirically ascertained results. This new distinction between *how* and *as what* is not an ontological one, but – in good Kantian fashion – a methodological one. The focal points of cognition are, generally, the individual or the general. Both are, however, not absolute but merely *relative* terms. Scientific cognition oscillates between these extreme focal points when interpreting its findings. The scientific cognition of something individual Windelband calls *idiographic* (i.e. describing the individual, singular), that of something general, *nomothetic* (i.e. positing the general, lawlike). "The latter are sciences of laws [*Gesetzeswissenschaften*], the former are sciences of events [*Ereigniswissenschaften*]; the latter teach what is always the case, the former what occurred only once."[36] For instance, if one wants to, as a historian, work on the French Revolution, one has to describe the individual characters and individual events that took place, and so on. On the other hand, if one wants to understand, as a chemist, the manner in which certain chemicals react together, one has to find out the general laws by which they function and react – always and in a reliable, repeatable pattern. But neither rests on an ontological premise. Indeed, the nomothetic and idiographic standards can be applied to one and the same ontic field. The classic example for this, according to Windelband, is the science of organic nature:

> As systematics, it is of nomothetic character, insofar as it describes the always fixed types of living creatures, which have been experienced within the millennia of human observation as their lawlike form. As developmental history, where it presents the order of earthly organisms as a process of descent and transformation of species [i.e. in evolutionary theory] ... there it is an idiographic discipline.[37]

36. *Ibid.*, 145.
37. *Ibid.*, 146.

This distinction stakes out a new *type* of science in the wake of the positivistic predicament that was rampant at the end of the nineteenth century, according to which naturalism was *the* method for all sciences. Contrary to the notion that human "disciplines" cannot be *sciences* precisely because they yield no general results, Windelband emphasized that the human sciences can indeed have the character of science with no less dignity than natural science *if* one has a different scientific ideal. The idiographic sciences have no less importance for the understanding of our world; indeed, if by "world" we mean not nature but *culture*, the idiographic sciences are *more* important. Windelband's distinction was, in effect, an assertion of the importance of a genuine "science of culture" over the reduced notion of science as *Wissenschaft* in the sense of "natural science."

As plausible as Windelband's distinction might seem, it was the focus of criticisms from, among others, Dilthey and Husserl, both of whom, albeit for different reasons, rejected this distinction when it came to describing the proper object of the human sciences. For Dilthey, a description of human historical development need not be only idiographic, but instead could posit types of worldviews and typical character forms (i.e. types, not laws), and hence need not have to choose between individual and universal accounts.[38] And Husserl's attempt at an *eidetic science* of subjectivity goes even further, asserting the possibility of a "rigorous" (i.e. *a priori*) science of subjectivity after the transcendental–phenomenological reduction. Finally, Heidegger's sketch of a hermeneutic of factical Dasein is predicated on a wholesale rejection of the (Platonic) distinction between the individual and the universal that underlies Windelband's account. Here again we see that the influence of neo-Kantianism on twentieth-century philosophy is *ex negativo*, as the seminal philosophers mentioned here derive their methodological paradigms from a rejection of this Windelbandian distinction.

(iii) Philosophy as value theory

The idea of an idiographic science as the proper method of accessing the life of spirit or human culture was cashed out especially in Rickert's work. Radicalizing Windelband, instead of seeing idiographic and nomothetic sciences as equally viable methods for cognition, Rickert privileges the idiographic over the nomothetic sciences. Informed by Rudolf Hermann Lotze's philosophy of value[39] – Lotze alleges that Plato's ideas ought properly to be conceived as valid values – Rickert asserts in his influential work *Der Gegenstand der Erkenntnis* (The object

*38. See the discussion of Dilthey in the essay by Eric Sean Nelson in *The History of Continental Philosophy: Volume 2.*

39. Rudolf Hermann Lotze (1817–81) was one of the leading German philosophers of the second half of the nineteenth century. A specialist in logic and philosophy of biology (he completed a medical degree along with his philosophy degree at Leipzig in 1838), he taught at Göttingen for almost forty years, beginning in 1844.

of cognition; first published in 1891 and re-edited six times, each time vastly reworked) that all cognition is in essence a form of *valuing*. Accepting Kant's thesis of the primacy of practical reason, this primacy asserts itself, according to Rickert, already in the field of cognition insofar as cognizing is not a passive apprehending but a *forming* of the object of cognition as something to be integrated into culture, that is, the world of values. At stake, for Rickert, is nothing less than a redefinition of the traditional task of epistemology. The object that is represented in cognition is not something *independent* of its being cognized, but is something that is being *formed* by the subject. Transcendent reality, which to Kant was always mind-independent, is therefore dependent on the culturally creative subject. This, concomitantly, changes the traditional notion of the cognizing subject as "we must form a different notion of the cognizing subject as only *representing* consciousness and, consequently, also a different notion of the object and the measure of cognition as that of a *transcendent reality*."[40] Given these two poles of cognition, one can approach the problem from both the subjective and objective sides. The subjective path leads to a transcendental psychology, the objective one to a transcendental logic; both are disciplines within transcendental philosophy. However, the empirical approach to the object of cognition remains valid in the empirical sciences; Rickert thus maps Kant's idealism–realism distinction onto that of philosophy and the empirical sciences. This dual approach is Rickert's restatement of Kant's transcendental idealism.

In his second famous work, *Die Grenzen der Naturwissenschaftlichen Begriffsbildung* (The limits of concept formation in natural science; first published in 1896), Rickert expands on the epistemological foundations while also drawing from Windelband's idiographic–nomothetic distinction. As the title indicates, concept formation in the natural sciences *has* limitations. It leads, if pursued to its extreme, into a purely naturalistic worldview. Contrary to Windelband, who considered both idiographic and nomothetic forms of scientific research to be on a relative scale (i.e. their difference was only a matter of degree), Rickert emphasizes the fundamental difference between them and goes on to favor the idiographic method. Nomothetic research winds up in a dangerous abstraction that threatens to cover up or make obsolete the historical life of culture (here anticipating Husserl's famous critique of the mathematization of science in *The Crisis of the European Sciences and Transcendental Phenomenology*). This is the negative part of this work. The positive is Rickert's description of the inner functioning of the human or cultural sciences. What makes them distinctly scientific in their own right is that they establish a relation to supra-individual *values*. Values, to Rickert, are neither physical nor mental, but are

40. Heinrich Rickert, *Der Gegenstand der Erkenntnis: Einführung in die Transzendentalphilosophie* (Tübingen: Mohr/Siebeck, [1892] 1928), 2.

"located" in an altogether different "third realm,"[41] where entities do not *exist* but *hold valid* (*gelten*). This realm is ontologically distinct from either the physical or the mental insofar as they both are forms of *being*, while the ontological status of values is their *validity*. Cultural scientific judgments, then, are characterized by making reference to this "world" of values. Hence the peculiarity of cultural scientific work is not primarily that it focuses on the individual – this is, as it were, taken for granted – but instead that *in* this individual attention it makes a connection to an independently existing realm of values.[42] This realm, moreover, is in itself systematically organized. Correct cultural as well as moral judgments can be discerned in their adequacy to the systematic hierarchy and order of values. Cultural or spiritual sciences are expressions of the ideal order of values. Therefore, the task of philosophy is to draft and describe this ideal system of values. In his later years, Rickert drafted a "system of values" based on the distinction of six different fields of values: logic, aesthetics, mysticism, ethics, the erotic, and philosophy of religion.[43] The true meaning of transcendental philosophy is thus redeemed in this draft of a system of values. Rickert began composing this sketch in his *System der Philosophie* (System of philosophy), of which only volume one appeared, and which has remained – despite Rickert's reputation in Germany at the time – largely ignored.[44]

II. NEO-KANTIANISM IN FRANCE

French neo-Kantianism emerged as the result of a conjunction of events including the demise of Victor Cousin's eclecticism under the "authoritarian" first period of the Second Empire (1851–60) and the development of spiritualism[45] under the "liberal" second period of the Empire. As a result of a very dense network of friendships, the extreme centralization of political power, and

41. Rickert also calls this realm – much earlier than 1933! – *das Dritte Reich*, the "Third Reich." I just mention this in order to clear up any confusion on the part of a stumped reader. The term was not exclusively used by the neo-Kantians; for instance, it was also used – in the same sense – by Frege.
42. In connecting the individual human being to the universal realm of values, Rickert is close to Cassirer's cultural anthropology, which defines the human being as a cultural being precisely in its capacity to lift itself out of the realm of nature and to become part of the world of spirit, which is intersubjective and universal.
43. Cf. Ollig, *Der Neukantianismus*, 63.
44. For a late recognition of Rickert's systematic philosophy, see Christian Krijnen, *Nachmetaphysischer Sinn: Eine Problemgeschichtliche und Systematische Studie zu den Prinzipien der Wertphilosophie Heinrich Rickerts* (Würzburg: Königshausen & Neumann, 2001).
*45. "French Spiritualist Philosophy" is discussed in the essay by F. C. T. Moore in *The History of Continental Philosophy: Volume 2.*

influential universities such as the École Normale Supérieure (ÉNS) and the Sorbonne, neo-Kantianism became the predominant philosophical trend in French academia under Victor Duruy's tenure as minister of education (1863–69). Charles Renouvier (1815–1903) and Jules Lachelier (1832–1918) initiated this trend, establishing two general and distinct forms that were never unified.[46]

Renouvier's works offer a system divided into the classical divisions of general and formal logic, rational psychology, and principles of nature.[47] In his *Essais de critique générale* (Essays in general critique), he writes: "I frankly confess that I follow in Kant's footsteps."[48] This Kantian program is described in general terms: "the analysis and the coordination of the principles of knowledge in general, and

---

46. The best studies of French philosophy between 1850 and 1930 are Isaac Benrubi, *Contemporary Thought of France*, Ernest B. Dicker (trans.) (London: Williams & Norgate, 1926), and Michel Espagne, *En deçà du Rhin: L'Allemagne des philosophes français au XIXe siècle* (Paris: Éditions du Cerf, 2004). In English, John Alexander Gunn, *Modern French Philosophy: A Study of the Development since Comte* (London: T. F. Unwin, 1922), has some interesting insights but, as Bergson noted, lacks a clear and firm guiding thread. The translation of Benrubi, *Les Sources et les courants de la philosophie contemporaine en France* (Paris: Félix Alcan, 1933), seems to be based on a shorter and schematic German version. Gary Gutting, *French Philosophy in the Twentieth Century* (Cambridge: Cambridge University Press, 2001), although interesting, is very partial, uses arguable classifications, and contains many inaccuracies: although different forms of Kantianism are mentioned, there is no analysis of the exchanges with Germany, a conceptually, institutionally, and politically essential point. Renouvier is not a spiritualist, he did not study at the ÉNS with Ravaisson, but was a student at the École Polytechnique, an important element for his scientific background and his relation to positivism, since this is how he met Comte. Hegel was indeed translated before the middle of the twentieth century: Charles Bénard translated the *Lectures on Aesthetics* in 1855, Augusto Vera's translation of the *Encyclopaedia* was published from 1859 to 1869, a fact that should be added to the file regarding Cousin's essential relation to Hegel, as well as Hippolyte Taine's. In *Twentieth-Century French Philosophy: Key Themes and Thinkers* (Malden, MA: Blackwell, 2006), Schrift's description of how the French system of education functions is fundamental and unique in English. Vincent Descombes, *Modern French Philosophy*, L. Scott-Fox and J. M. Harding (trans.) (Cambridge: Cambridge University Press, 1980) offers a witty picture of the latter trends in French philosophy (structuralisms, essentially), although the subtlety of the analysis as well as its irony may make it a difficult read for the unadvised reader.
47. On Renouvier, see Laurent Fédi, *Le Problème de la connaissance dans la philosophie de Ch. Renouvier* (Paris: L'Harmattan, 1999); Octave Hamelin, *Le Système de Renouvier* (Paris: J. Vrin, 1927); William Logue, *Charles Renouvier, Philosopher of Liberty* (Baton Rouge, LA: Louisiana State University Press, 1993). For Renouvier's conception of science and use of the hypothesis, cf. Warren Schmaus, "Kant's Reception in France: Theories of the Categories in Academic Philosophy, Psychology and Social Sciences," *Perspective on Science* 11(1) (2003). Schmaus's "Renouvier and the Method of Hypothesis," *Studies in History and Philosophy of Science* 38 (2007), is also interesting concerning the kind of neo-Kantianism that developed in France, and the typically neo-Kantian and phenomenological problem of the *Kategorienlehre* (doctrine of categories).
48. Charles Renouvier, *Essais de critique générale* (Paris: Lagrange, 1854–64), xv. Hereafter quotations from this foreword will be cited parenthetically by page number. Unless otherwise mentioned, all translations from the French are my own.

of those that the established sciences put at their foundations without making them explicit" (xx). The principles to which Renouvier refers are construed as fundamental *a priori* relations that constitute knowledge. Starting with the concept of representation in a very broad sense, Renouvier untangles its elements and the laws ruling knowledge. He is thereby led to rewrite the Kantian system of categories.

The Kantian inspiration is clear, and the influence of the forewords to the *Critique of Pure Reason*, in particular that of the second edition, is obvious. The question of the scientificity of philosophy is the guiding thread: "It is impossible to reasonably reject the *Critique*. For it is inspired by the spirit of science; it is that very spirit" (xii). For Renouvier, as for Kant, the *Critique* is opposed to traditional metaphysics, which was informed by theology and cosmology. As will soon be the case for the German neo-Kantians, Renouvier sees the *Critique*'s scientific character in its methodological dimension: "If the result of the *Critique* is to formulate a method, to provide a lasting logic, this is indeed very much; it is almost enough for its scientificity" (xiii). But a notable difference between Renouvier and the German neo-Kantians, especially the Marburg School, is that for Renouvier it is not so much that the *Critique as such* is the method (as Kant wrote in the B Foreword); rather, the method is the *result* of the *Critique* (namely, the ensuing Kantian methodologies themselves).

Nevertheless, Renouvier is quite critical of Kant. His last book, *Critique de la doctrine de Kant* (Critique of the Kantian doctrine), offers a systematic deconstruction of the *Critique of Pure Reason*. In Renouvier's idealism, as, arguably, in the Marburg School's idealism, the return to Leibniz[49] is nearly as important as the return to Kant.[50] But the very essence of Renouvier's concept of the transcendental remains deficient and psychological when compared to that found in more elaborate Kant interpretations, as well as in the main German neo-Kantian schools and Husserl's phenomenology.

Renouvier never taught and was extremely prolific. His influence was felt, however, only after 1867, the year he founded, with his friend François Pillon, the journal *L'Année philosophique* (The philosophical yearbook). At that time

---

49. In 1899, Renouvier published his *La Nouvelle monadologie*. A Leibnizian reconstruction of Kant relies on a long history, going back to Salomon Maimon's interpretation of Kant's Anticipations of Perception as an unconscious sum of "*petites perceptions*." Cohen's rejection of sensitive intuition relies on a similar conception. It is here important because in French neo-Kantianism, and particularly in the philosophy of mathematics, it will give birth to a strong opposition between the Kantian philosophy of intuition (Boutroux, Poincaré) and the Leibnizian philosophy of the concept (Couturat, Cavaillès).

50. This is a reason, among others, that it caught the attention of Cassirer; cf. Ernst Cassirer, "Das Problem des Unendlichen und Renouviers 'Gesetz der Zahl,'" in *Philosophische Abhandlungen: Hermann Cohen zum 70. Geburtstag Dargebracht* (Berlin: Bruno Cassirer, 1912), and "Review of Ch. Renouvier, *Essais de critique générale*," *Die Geisteswissenschaften* 1 (1914).

he started to have followers: François Evellin, the young Victor Brochard, Jean-Jacques Gourd, and his main disciple, Octave Hamelin.[51] It is also during this period that William James carefully read his work.

If Renouvier's neo-Kantianism can be described as a neocriticism insofar as it submits Kant himself to critique, Lachelier's can be described as a late evolution of spiritualism. His teacher, Félix Ravaisson (1813–1900), established an intellectual and institutional strain that would develop into Bergson's spiritualism as well as Émile Boutroux's neo-Kantianism. Ravaisson favored Schelling over Hegel, a preference that meant, in the French context, leaping over Cousin to return to Maine de Biran. True idealism is a spiritualism grounded in the will. Lachelier depicted, quite accurately, the intellectual situation framed by Ravaisson's *Report* (1868). As he writes in a letter to Paul Janet, on December 8, 1891:

> It is Ravaisson, I believe, who taught us all to conceive being not as objective forms of substances or phenomena, but as the subjective form of spiritual action, this action being – in its last resort – thought or will. I think you could find this idea in Bergson, in Ribot even, as well as in Boutroux and myself. It is perhaps the only trait that is common to all of us and that makes for the unity of the philosophical movement of the last twenty years.[52]

With such a common ground, how can one account for the fragmentation of spiritualism into Christian philosophy, Bergsonism, and neo-Kantianism?

---

51. Victor Brochard's (1848–1907) doctoral dissertation, *De l'erreur* (Paris, 1879), claims the influence of Kant and Renouvier. This is also the case for François Evellin's (1835–1910) dissertation: *Infini et quantité* (Paris: Germer Baillière, 1880). Jean-Jacques Gourd (1850–1909) was one of Renouvier's followers in Switzerland (see his *Le Phénomène* [Paris: Félix Alcan, 1888]). Octave Hamelin (1856–1907), the most prominent of Renouvier's followers, first exerted his influence by teaching at the University of Bordeaux (1884–1903), at the ÉNS (1903–7), and at the Sorbonne (1905–7). His acclaimed book, *Essai sur les éléments principaux de la représentation* (Paris: Félix Alcan, 1907; doctoral thesis), as well as his translation and commentary of Aristotle *Physics* II (complementary dissertation) were published the year of his death. Léon Robin, his student and another of the Sorbonne's major figures, published two thick volumes of Hamelin's lectures: *Le Système de Descartes* (Paris: Félix Alcan, 1911; with a foreword by Hamelin's friend Émile Durkheim), and *Le Système d'Aristote* (Paris: Félix Alcan, 1920; lectures given at the ÉNS in 1904–5). Indicative of his importance, other courses were later published, including *Le Système de Renouvier* (Sorbonne, 1906–7), *Les Philosophes présocratiques* (Strasbourg: Association des publications de l'université de Strasbourg, 1978; lectures 1905–6), and *Fichte* (Strasbourg: Presses Universitaires de Strasbourg, 1988; lectures 1887).
52. Jules Lachelier, *Lettres*, 1856–1918 (Paris: G. Girard, 1933), 139.

In 1861, Lachelier dissociated himself from Biran and hence from Ravaisson as well.[53] His courses on logic and on psychology demonstrate that he had already taken a Kantian position when he began teaching at the ÉNS. He exerted his remarkable influence through his lectures rather than through his – relatively few – publications.

The lectures on logic present a general elucidation of the theoretical principles of knowledge. From the very first lesson, the method is imbued with Kantian elements. "Let me explain: in any science one can differentiate what man knows and the way he knows, in other words, matter and form."[54] Both in his *Lectures on Logic* and in the *Critique of Pure Reason*, Kant had already made use of this conceptual distinction between logic in general (which is purely formal) and transcendental logic, which is both formal and material. Lachelier's lecture course then pursues a Kantian path. To circumscribe science, Lachelier takes a detour: "instead of saying in a few words what science is, it might be better to review the necessary conditions of science, the degrees spirit covers to reach science."[55] This path is very significant, for he borrows the conditions for science from the *Critique of Pure Reason*. The first condition for science is that an object is given. Lachelier takes an indirect path to introduce both forms of pure intuition, space and time: "the internal world of the successive states in time, the outside world of the simultaneous objects in space and also the successive states of these same objects in time."[56] Lachelier notes that space is integrated in time and, when dissociating the internal world from the external, he also intends to make room for that internal world that differs from the internalization of the external. A place is therefore reserved for feeling, desire, faith, and so on, opening the possibility for the fields of morality and religion, while avoiding a reductionist reading of Kant.

Sensation alone does not explain the possibility of science, since it is reduced to an indefinite number of atomistic elements: "impression, in itself, is reduced to an infinity of elementary impressions that is tied together by nothing and in which it vanishes."[57] Knowledge is constituted by a synthetic act of spirit, an intellectual synthesis that consists in the positing of pure relations. In addition to space and time, pure functions of synthesis are acknowledged as transcendental conditions of science. And when, in the middle of the chapter on induction, Lachelier intends to ground the determinism expressed by scientific law

53. Cf. Gaston Mauchaussat, *L'Idéalisme de Lachelier* (Paris: Presses Universitaires de France, 1961), 16–40.
54. Jules Lachelier, *Cours de logique*, École Normale Supérieure 1866–67 (Paris: Éditions Universitaires de France, 1990), 15.
55. *Ibid.*
56. *Ibid.*
57. *Ibid.*, 16.

and experimental method such as Claude Bernard[58] conceives it, he again refers to Kant, correcting the subjectivistic interpretation of the idealism:

> And, although it is attributed to Kant to have reduced the principles of understanding to a purely subjective value, it is to him that we owe the justification of the principle of determinism. We cannot know a priori things in themselves, but we can assert a priori that the phenomena of nature, which compose the weft of our thoughts, are possible to be thought. And the consciousness of our personal identity is the condition of any thought.[59]

Moving from the syntheses to individual unity, Lachelier again combines the original synthetic unity of apperception, the empirical unity of consciousness, and the paralogism of substantiality into one single thought.

The general method of his reflection, as well as the logical progression within these lectures, produce what one can call a transcendental idealism. They sketch an outline concerning induction that Lachelier's 1871 dissertation, *Du fondement de l'induction* (On the foundation of induction), will further develop; regarding determinism, they draw a frame Boutroux will fill, with a few gaps, in his dissertation, *De la contingence des lois de la nature* (On the contingency of the laws of nature).

Neo-Kantianism reached a preeminent position in French philosophy through Lachelier's teaching for the following reasons: he was a very charismatic professor; he taught at the ÉNS from 1864 to 1875; his lectures were copied and studied by at least twenty promotions of students,[60] some of whom in turn became the most influential professors of their time – Boutroux, Liard, Paul and Jules Tannery, Janet, Séailles, Brunschvicg.[61] And in addition to his teaching, Lachelier held important official positions such as the presidency of the *Agrégation,* a nationwide competitive examination one needed to take in order to teach in higher education, and the general inspector of public education.

In 1876, not even ten years after Ravaisson's *Rapport,* Désiré Nolen (1838–1904), in his Inaugural Lecture at the University of Montpellier succeeding

58. Claude Bernard (1813–78) was a French physiologist. His *Introduction à l'étude de la médecine expérimentale* (1865) was universally considered as a classic discourse on the scientific method, comparable only to the works of Newton. A professor at the Collège de France from 1847 to 1878, when he died he was given a public funeral, the first man of science to be awarded that honor in France.
59. *Ibid.*, 51; see also 122.
60. Entering classes in the École Normale are referred to as "promotions."
61. Cf. Celestin Bouglé, "Spiritualisme et Kantisme en France, Jules Lachelier," *La Revue de Paris* (May 1, 1934), as well as Léon Brunschvicg, *Préface* to *Œuvres de J. Lachelier* (Paris: Félix Alcan, 1933), xix.

Boutroux (another important figure of French neo-Kantianism), remarked that "over the last ten years, it seems that Kant's *Critique* has become the constant and common study of philosophical minds."[62] This, he continued, sets the stage for a truly European philosophy.[63] Boutroux, in his lectures on Kant delivered from 1894 to 1897 and 1900 to 1901 at the Sorbonne, writes:

> moreover, we, the French, have today a closer relationship with Kant's philosophy than we had fifty years ago. ...These studies contributed to the awakening of the metaphysical sense in our country .... Hence, to go back to Kant is not only to act as a scholar, as a historian, as a dilettante; it is to draw useful knowledge and forces us to face the problems imposed on us [today].[64]

Meanwhile Louis Liard (1846–1917),[65] a noteworthy neo-Kantian, student of Lachelier and friend of Boutroux, had become the director of the Enseignement Supérieur, France's university educational system between 1884 and 1902. Finally, almost half a century after Lachelier started teaching, Brunschvicg, the last great neo-Kantian of that period, concluded: "From 1870 on, a philosophical University has been built in France that should bear the name of Lachelier, just like the Old University bears the name of Victor Cousin."[66] The main neo-Kantian figures of this new "philosophical university" are Émile Boutroux, Émile Meyerson,[67] Léon Brunschvicg, and Octave Hamelin.

After Lachelier, Boutroux is the key figure in the development of French neo-Kantianism.[68] He is at the center of the intellectual and the institutional network

62. Désiré Nolen, *Kant et la philosophie du XIX siècle* (Montpellier: Martel Aîné, 1877), 12.
63. He neglected to mention the important contributions from Italian neo-Kantianism.
64. Émile Boutroux, *La Philosophie de Kant: Cours de M. Émile Boutroux (Sorbonne 1896–1897)* (Paris: Vrin, 1926), 12.
65. Cf. Charles Lyon-Caen, "Notice sur la vie et les travaux de M. Louis Liard," *Séances et travaux de l'Académie des Sciences Morales et Politiques* 81 (1921), and Alain Renaut, *Les Révolutions de l'université* (Paris: Calmann-Lévy, 1995), 156ff.
66. Léon Brunschvicg, *Écrits Philosophiques*, 3 vols (Paris: Presses Universitaires de France, 1951–58), vol. 2, 206.
67. Émile Meyerson (1859–1933), a Polish chemist who emigrated to Germany, then to France, exerted a strong influence on French philosophy, although, like Renouvier, he was never completely part of the system. His antipositivism, his Kantian and neocritical background as well as his discussion of contemporary science and his participation in discussions with Poincaré, Brunschvicg, and Langevin make him a noteworthy figure worthy of the renewed interest he is attracting.
68. Cf. Fabien Capeillères, "Généalogie d'un Néokantisme Français: à Propos d'Émile Boutroux," *Revue de métaphysique et de morale, Néokantismes* 3 (1997), and "To Reach for Metaphysics: Émile Boutroux's Philosophy of Science," in Luft and Makkreel, *Neo-Kantianism in Contemporary Philosophy*.

constitutive of the French higher education system. His work can be understood as an attempt to carry on the spiritualism of his masters, Ravaisson and Lachelier, in a Kantian guise. The problem around which his thought revolves is the reconciliation of the universal validity of scientific laws (which seems to involve an ontological necessity and therefore determinism), human freedom (the condition for morality), and religion.

This problem is precisely what he calls "Kant's problem": "How is science possible? How is morality possible? How is the reconciliation of science and morality possible?"[69] And later he states: "Kant's problem is ours. His writings talk about us: *nostra res agitur.*"[70] Despite several themes that can be considered Kantian, Boutroux's solution to the problem is not Kantian, and one cannot but assert that his understanding of the *a priori* and of the transcendental that he rejects is rather weak. One of the main interests is his treatment of science, which is both metaphysical and epistemological, and he is closely related to major scientists of the period such as his own son, Pierre Boutroux, and his brother-in-law, Henri Poincaré.[71] Boutroux's Kantianism has also been considered an influence on Poincaré's contributions to the problem of hypotheses, as well as on his conventionalism.[72] Within this constellation, the Tannery brothers were also of major importance.

Brunschvicg constitutes the apex of French neo-Kantianism, a status also claimed by Renouvier's heir, Hamelin.[73] Brunschvicg's achievement was a strictly methodological understanding of what he calls "the idea of critique." His achievement is deployed via a "wider and richer" use of "the truth of the transcendental method."[74] The general movement is similar to the "historization" and the "dynamization" of the transcendental operating in German neo-Kantianism, in particular, the Marburg School.

What will be left of the theory of transcendental consciousness, once one recognizes that algebra and geometry, mechanics and physics do not resign themselves to this docile immobility that Kant expected? And what will one

69. Boutroux, *La Philosophie de Kant*, 9; see also 266.
70. *Ibid.*, 11–12. This is a reference to Horace's "Nam tua res agitur, paries cum proximus ardet" (it becomes your concern when your neighbor's wall is on fire).
71. Cf. Mary Jo Nye, "The Boutroux Circle and Poincaré's Conventionalism," *Journal of the History of Ideas* 1 (1979).
72. Cf. *Les Sources et les courants de la philosophie contemporaine en France* (Paris: Félix Alcan, 1933), 351.
73. This is a perspective held for instance by Dominique Parodi; see *La Philosophie contemporaine en France* (Paris: Félix Alcan, 1919). Brunschvicg answers in "L'Orientation du rationalism" (*Écrits Philosophiques*, vol. 2, 25): "we do not find any trace of critical thought in neo-criticism."
74. Léon Brunschvicg, "L'Idée critique et le système Kantien," *Revue de métaphysique et de morale* 31(2) (1924), 153.

make of the fact that, during the nineteenth century, they broke the limits that the "Transcendental Aesthetic," the "Transcendental Analytic," and the *First Metaphysical Principles of the Science of Nature* had commanded them to respect as the final layout?[75]

The answer is somewhat brutal: "we should leave to some neo-Kantians and to Kant himself the postulate of this solidarity between the idea of critique and the table of the forms or the categories, since we know today that this solidarity expresses the most superficial and fragile aspect of the doctrine."[76] Brunschvicg then proceeds to point to a cleavage in the transcendental method: "The method put to work by the transcendental deduction is a *reflexive analysis*; it starts from science considered as a fact, and goes back to the a priori forms of intuitions and pure concepts of the understanding."[77] This first moment, reminiscent of Cohen, is legitimate in Brunschvicg's eyes, especially since it reverts to the unity of transcendental apperception, an important element for someone who also wants to claim the spiritualist inheritance. However, when a philosopher considers the system of categories as fixed once and for all, and limits deduction to that of the principles of a determined moment of physics (Newton, for instance), then the progressive synthesis that leads to all the dimensions of spirit will be lacking.

Brunschvicg's understanding of the "idea of critique" will be exercised as "reflexive analysis" on all fields of human knowledge: science, morality, religion, art, and history, in order to produce the system of critical idealism that presents the life of the spirit in all its directions as well as in its unity.

Brunschvicg's enormous influence was at its peak in the 1920s. Setting aside his impressive intellectual stature, we see that he exerted his influence through all dimensions of the French system: he held a key teaching position at the Sorbonne (for thirty years, beginning in 1909), was president of the *Agrégation* (1936–38), for many years was part of the academic–political network that oversaw the philosophy curriculum and the awarding of positions and grants, and was founder of the journal *Revue de Métaphysique et de Morale* (with Xavier Léon in 1893) and of the Société Française de Philosophie (1901, with Léon and André Lalande).

At the end of the nineteenth century, neo-Kantianism was not only the preeminent philosophy in France, but had also become the *philosophie officielle*. But soon Boutroux left center stage in favor of his most famous student and the true heir of spiritualism, Henri Bergson; Bachelard overshadowed Meyerson; Brunschvicg became the embodiment of the mandarin, confronted by young

75. *Ibid.*, 152.
76. *Ibid.*, 153.
77. *Ibid.*

materialists such as Georges Politzer[78] and Marxists such as Paul Nizan[79] or by philosophers such as Sartre and Merleau-Ponty. These thinkers found their inspirations in new figures in German philosophy – the early Husserl, Heidegger – and subscribed to their criticisms of Kant.

To take a look at the influence of neo-Kantianism on post-Second World War French intellectual life, one of the most interesting developments of French neo-Kantianism is the role it played in the rise of structuralism. Martial Guéroult's (1891–1976) reflections on the Kantian concept of architectonics, his familiarity with the neo-Kantian "quarrel of the system,"[80] and his reading of Karl Mannheim's *Die Strukturanalyse der Erkenntnistheorie* (The structural analysis of epistemology, 1922), resulted in his highly interesting structural methodology concerning the history of philosophy. Considering all genetic, chronological, and biographical studies merely preliminary steps, he argued that the analysis should proceed to an internal reconstruction of the philosophical work considered as a monument constructed by layers and successions of proofs. The more original rational conditions of the system consist in its transcendental conditions, just as, in Kant, the structure of the idea of pure reason forms a transcendental condition of a system. Victor Goldschmidt followed this path in his work in the history of philosophy.[81] But more important is the affiliation with Jules Vuillemin (1920–2001),[82] in which the meaning of the concept of structure shifted. It originally

78. See his 1926 attack in *Écrits*, Jacques Debouzy (ed.) (Paris: Éditions Sociales, 1969) I, 29.
79. Cf. Paul Nizan, *Les Chiens de garde* (Paris: Rieder, 1932).
80. The quarrel of the system was a fierce debate regarding two issues: (i) Could philosophy fulfill its claim to be a science only through the form of a system? And, given a positive answer to this first question: (ii) What kind of system should it be? Regarding the first claim, Hermann Cohen writes: "The philosophy reaches its concept only as system" (*Logik der reinen Erkenntniss*, 3rd ed. [Berlin: Bruno Cassirer, 1922], 601). Concerning the second claim, Natorp (like Cassirer) has a preference for the concept of a systematic: "Systematic, not system" (in *Philosophische Systematik* [Hamburg: Felix Meiner, 1958], 1). Rickert is also quite clear: "Unsystematic thought means unphilosophical thought" (in *Allgemeine Grundlegung der Philosophie* [Tübingen: J. C. B. Mohr, 1921], 11; see also *Grundprobleme der Philosophie* [Tübingen: J. C. B. Mohr, 1934], 1–25). He develops the concept of an "open system." What is here at stake is to be systematic without being dogmatic (or Hegelian!). See Christian Krijnen, *Philosophie als System: Prinzipientheoretische Untersuchungen zum Systemgedanken bei Hegel, im Neukantianismus und in der Gegenwartsphilosophie* (Würzburg: Königshausen & Neumann, 2008).
81. Victor Goldschmidt (1914–81) was well known for his application of a structuralist method of reading, inaugurated by Guéroult, to ancient philosophy (Plato, Aristotle, Epicurus, the Stoics, and so on) as well as to Rousseau. For some reservations, see Jacques Brunschwig, "Goldschmidt and Guéroult: Some Facts, Some Enigmas," *Archiv für Geschichte der Philosophie* 88 (2006).
82. Cf. Joseph Vidal-Rosset, "De Martial Guéroult à Jules Vuillemin, analyse d'une Filiation," in *Le Paradigme de la filiation*, Jean Gayon and Jean-Jacques Wunenberger (eds) (Paris: L'Harmattan, 1995).

referred to a scientificity gained through systematicity, but systematicity was now understood through logic and mathematical axiomatic. Gilles-Gaston Granger (1920–) played an important role in this transformation. These intellectual affinities (and friendships) resulted in academic appointments: Guéroult, who held the Chair of History and Technology of Philosophical Systems at the Collège de France (1951–62), nominated Vuillemin for a Chair of Philosophy of Knowledge (1962–90). And Vuillemin appointed Foucault to succeed him at the University of Clermont-Ferrand, then at the Collège de France (where he held a Chair of History of Systems of Thought, 1970–84); Granger succeeded Foucault in 1986, renaming the Chair "Comparative Epistemology."[83]

This logico-mathematical transformation of the concept of structure also impacted the writing of the history of philosophy (as well as history itself), leading, for instance, on the one hand, to the work of Michel Serres and Daniel Parrochia and, on the other, to Althusser's praxis in his reading of *Capital* and Foucault's "archeology."[84] The end of this story is better known, although often in a very confused fashion owing to the omission of the first episodes: to the mathematical paradigm a linguistic one would be added (Saussure, Benveniste) that in turn would lead, by a complete reversal, to neostructuralism or poststructuralism, while a Heideggerian intellectual background (blended with various proportions of Nietzsche, Marx, and Freud) would come to replace the Kantian paradigm.

Today, neo-Kantianism is still active in France: in epistemology, philosophy of mathematics, and philosophy of physics one might mention the work of Jean Petitot,[85] Michel Bitbol, Jean Seidengart, and Pierre Kerszberg; Alexis Philonenko in the history of philosophy; Alain Renaut in moral and political philosophy as well as education; and a neo-Kantian, Luc Ferry, became minister of education.

III. CONCLUSION

To summarize, the label "neo-Kantianism" was applied to a variety of tendencies within the philosophical scene in Europe, mainly Germany and France, to a

83. It is also worth noting that Jacques Bouveresse, who presented his 1995 Collège de France Chair of Philosophy of Language and of Knowledge as "in a way succeeding" those of Vuillemin and Granger, devoted his 2007 and 2008 lectures to a question formulated after a title of Vuillemin's book: "What are philosophical systems?" The lectures not only dealt explicitly with Vuillemin, but also with the tradition coming from Renouvier, Guéroult, and Hyppolite.

*84. Serres and Foucault are discussed in essays by Derek Robbins and Timothy O'Leary in *The History of Continental Philosophy: Volume 6*.

*85. The work of Jean Petitot is discussed in "The Structuralist Legacy" by Patrice Maniglier in *The History of Continental Philosophy: Volume 7*.

lesser extent Italy and the United Kingdom, at a certain period of time, roughly between 1870 and 1930.[86] While the peak of this movement can be said to have come to an end after the First World War, the Second World War seemingly sent it into oblivion. In the late 1970s, neo-Kantianism's importance and dominance in its own days began to be rediscovered in scholarship. This led to a philosophical revival, which is now palpable in nearly all fields of philosophical work. For instance, the question of *a priori* knowledge is discussed in contemporary philosophy of mind, epistemology, and philosophy of science. It is also remarkable that this European trend of "continental" philosophy is currently gaining leverage in the US, with the works and the influence of John Rawls in ethics and political philosophy and, for example, Michael Friedman in both philosophy of science and the genesis of analytical philosophy. Today, neo-Kantianism is slowly regaining its status as a major interlocutor with phenomenology and analytical philosophy, a status first exemplified, for instance, by the relations between Husserl and Natorp and its influence on Carnap.

In one sense, then, the term "neo-Kantianism" refers mainly to this period of time. In another sense, the term "neo-Kantian" can be understood in the manner in which philosophers today call themselves "neo-Fregean" or "neo-Pragmatist," by which they mean an alliance to these philosophers, not in the letter or in correct exegesis of the great thinker's true intentions, but in the *spirit* of the philosophers in question. It is in *this* sense that the neo-Kantians discussed here perceived themselves as furthering Kant's true intentions, be it in dismissing some elements in Kant's system for the sake of others or emphasizing those that they perceived to reveal a true kernel in the midst of other problematic intuitions in Kant's thought. In this effort, they not only brought forth highly original avenues of Kant interpretation that are still essentially pursued today, but also produced a range of interesting new systematic approaches and theories that are far from obsolete and deserve to be studied anew.[87]

If one were to summarize in the briefest terms its philosophical importance, one could call neo-Kantianism a philosophy of *culture*, whereby culture is itself the problematic philosophical term, the *terminus ad quem*. Philosophy, then, is placed in the service of human culture in modern society, which values and

86. Regarding Italian neo-Kantianism, see Massimo Ferrari, *Introduzione a il neocriticismo* (Rome: Laterza, 1997) and, more specifically, *I dati dell'esperienza: Il Neokantismo di Felice Tocco nella filosofia Italiana tra ottocento e novecento* (Florence: L. S. Olschki, 1990). UK neo-Kantianism is more difficult to characterize since it forms components of another complex philosophical movement: British idealism. Philosophers such as T. H. Green (1836–82), Edward Caird (1835–1908), and R. G. Collingwood (1889–1943) are often identified as neo-Kantians.

87. Two recent anthologies will help make neo-Kantianism more accessible for scholarship in the English language: Makkreel and Luft, *Neo-Kantianism in Contemporary Philosophy*, and Sebastian Luft (ed.), *The Neo-Kantian Reader* (London: Routledge, 2013).

upholds the fundamental beliefs of the Renaissance and the Enlightenment: reason, equality, freedom. Neo-Kantianism stands, to borrow a phrase from Ursula Renz, for a culture of rationality and the rationality of culture. Whether such an ideal and the consequences following from it will be allowed to survive in the so-called age of postmodernity is another question. Be that as it may, both as a starting-point for understanding the philosophical tendencies that would emerge and define the twentieth century, and as a vast quarry of inspiring ideas and timeless systematic approaches, one will need to reassess the neo-Kantian movement.[88]

MAJOR WORKS: THE MARBURG SCHOOL

Hermann Cohen

Kants Theorie der Erfahrung. New York: Olms, [1871] 1987.[89]
Kants Begründung der Ethik. Berlin: Dümmler, 1877.
Das Prinzip der Infinitesimal-Methode und seine Geschichte. Berlin: Bruno Cassirer, 1883.
Logik der Reinen Erkenntis. Berlin: Bruno Cassirer, 1902.
Ethik des Reinen Willens. Berlin: Bruno Cassirer, 1904.
Aesthetik des Reinen Gefühls. Berlin: Bruno Cassirer, 1912.
Religion der Vernunft aus den Quellen des Judentums. Leipzig: Fock, 1919 [Cohen's last work was published posthumously by his students in Berlin, Hans Rosenzweig and Martin Buber]. Published in English as *Religion of Reason out of the Sources of Judaism*, translated by Simon Kaplan. Atlanta, GA: Scholars Press, 1995.
Werke. Edited by the Hermann Cohen Archives at the Philosophical Seminar at the University of Zurich, under the leadership of Helmut Holzhey. Hildesheim/Zurich/New York: Olms, 1987ff.

Paul Natorp

Allgemeine Psychologie nach kritischer Methode. Tübingen: Mohr/Siebeck, 1912. First published as *Einleitung in die Psychologie nach kritischer Methode* (1888). New ed. Darmstadt: Wissenschaftliche Buchgesellschaft, 2013.
Philosophie: Ihr Problem und ihre Probleme. Einführung in den kritischen Idealismus [1911]. 3rd ed. Göttingen: Vandenhoeck & Ruprecht, 1921. New ed. Göttingen: Edition Ruprecht, 2008.

---

88. Special thanks go to Celeste Harvey for her help with assembling the bibliographical data and for correcting the grammar and style of this piece.

89. A note on the editions of the major works: As was customary in the days of the neo-Kantians, new editions did not get published without extensive authors' revisions, which not only eliminated typographical errors, but were also intended to capture the new developments the author had made since the first publication of the book in question. For this reason, in cases where there are different editions, we list the last – and presumably the latest and ultimately approved – version, or the critical edition, in the regular bibliography, preceded by the date of the first edition in brackets.

Platos Ideenlehre: Eine Einführung in den Idealismus. Hamburg: Felix Meiner, [1903] 1922. 2nd ed. with the important "Metacritical Appendix" (1922). Published in English as *Plato's Theory of Ideas: an Introduction to Idealism*, translated by Vasilis Politis and John Connolly. Sankt Augustin: Academia, 2004.

Philosophische Systematik. Hamburg: Felix Meiner, 1958 [posthumous publication of 1923 lecture course].

Ernst Cassirer

Substanzbegriff und Funktionsbegriff: Untersuchungen über die Grundfragen der Erkenntniskritik. Berlin: Cassirer, 1910. Published in English as *Substance and Function and Einstein's Theory of Relativity*, edited by William Curtis Swabey & Marie Collins Swabey. New York: Dover, 1953.

Kants Leben und Lehre. Hamburg: Felix Meiner, 1918. Published in English as *Kant's Life and Thought*, translated by James Haden. New Haven, CT: Yale University Press, 1981.

Philosophie der Symbolischen Formen. Erster Teil: Die Sprache. Berlin: B. Cassirer, 1923. Published in English as *The Philosophy of Symbolic Forms. Volume 1: Language*, translated by Ralph Manheim. New Haven, CT: Yale University Press, 1996.

Philosophie der Symbolischen Formen. Zweiter Teil: Das Mythische Denken. Berlin: B. Cassirer, 1925. Published in English as *The Philosophy of Symbolic Forms. Volume 2: Mythical Thought*, translated by Ralph Manheim. New Haven, CT: Yale University Press, 1996.

Philosophie der Symbolischen Formen. Dritte Teil: Phänomenologie der Erkenntnis. Berlin: B. Cassirer, 1929. Published in English as *The Philosophy of Symbolic Forms. Volume 3: The Phenomenology of Knowledge*, translated by Ralph Manheim. New Haven, CT: Yale University Press, 1996.

Nachgelassene Manuskripte und Texte. Edited by Klaus Christian Köhnke, John Michael Krois, and Oswald Schwemmer. Hamburg: Felix Meiner, 1995ff.

Gesammelte Werke. Edited by Birgit Recki. Hamburg: Felix Meiner, 2009.

MAJOR WORKS: THE SOUTHWEST SCHOOL

Emil Lask

Die Logik der Philosophie und die Kategorienlehre. Tübingen: Mohr/Siebeck, 1911. New ed. in vol. 2 of *Sämtliche Werke in zwei Bänden.* Jena: Dietrich Scheglmann Reprintverlag, 2002.

Heinrich Rickert

System der Philosophie, vol. 1. Tübingen: Mohr/Siebeck, 1921.

Der Gegenstand der Erkenntnis: Einführung in die Transzendentalphilosophie. Tübingen: Mohr/Siebeck, [1892] 1928.

Die Grenzen der Naturwissenschaftlichen Begriffsbildung. Eine Logische Einleitung in die historischen Wissenschaften. Tübingen: Mohr/Siebeck, [1896] 1929. Published in English as *The Limits of Concept Formation in Natural Science: A Logical Introduction to the Historical Sciences*, edited and translated by Guy Oakes. Cambridge: Cambridge University Press, 1986.

Wilhelm Windelband

Präludien: Aufsätze und Reden zur Philosophie und ihrer Geschichte. Tübingen: Mohr/Siebeck, [1884] 1924.

MAJOR WORKS: NEO-KANTIANISM IN FRANCE

Émile Boutroux

De la contingence des lois de la nature. Paris: Félix Alcan, 1874. Published in English as *The Contingency of the Laws of Nature*, translated by Fred Rothwell. Chicago, IL: Open Court Publishing Company, 1916.

De l'idée de loi naturelle dans la science et la philosophie contemporaines: Cours de M. Emile Boutroux (Sorbonne 1892–1893). Paris: Lecène, Oudin et cie, 1895. Published in English as *Natural Law in Science and Philosophy*, translated by Fred Rothwell. New York: Macmillan Company, 1914.

Science et religion dans la philosophie contemporaine. Paris: E. Flammarion, 1908. Published in English as *Science & Religion in Contemporary Philosophy*, translated by Jonathan Nield. London: Duckworth, 1909.

La Philosophie de Kant: Cours de M. Emile Boutroux (Sorbonne 1896–1897). Paris: Vrin, 1926.

Léon Brunschvicg

La Modalité du jugement. Paris: Félix Alcan, 1897.

Introduction à la vie de l'esprit. Paris: Félix Alcan, 1900.

L'Idéalisme contemporain. Paris: Félix Alcan, 1905.

Les Étapes de la philosophie mathématique. Paris: Félix Alcan, 1912.

Le Progrès de la conscience dans la philosophie occidentale. Paris: Presses Universitaires de France, 1924.

De la connaissance de soi. Paris: Félix Alcan, 1931.

Les Ages de l'intelligence. Paris: Félix Alcan, 1934.

La Raison et la religion. Paris: Félix Alcan, 1939.

Écrits philosophiques, 3 vols. Paris: Presses Universitaires de France, 1951–58.

Jules Lachelier

Lettres, 1856–1918. Paris: G. Girard, 1933.

Œuvres, 2 vols. Paris: Félix Alcan, 1933. Published in English as *The Philosophie of Jules Lachelier, Du fondement de l'induction, Psychologie et métaphysique, Notes sur le pari de Pascal, together with Contributions to Vocabulaire technique et critique de la philosophie, and a Selection From His Letters*, translated by Edward G. Ballard. The Hague: Martinus Nijhoff, 1960.

Cours de logique, École Normale Supérieure 1866–67. Paris: Éditions Universitaires de France, 1990.

Émile Meyerson

Identité et réalité. Paris: Félix Alcan, 1908. Published in English as *Identity & Reality*, translated by Kate Loewenberg. New York: Macmillan, 1930.

De l'explication dans les sciences. Paris: Payot, 1921. Published in English as *Explanation in the Sciences*, translated by Mary-Alice Sipfle & David A. Sipfle. Dordrecht: Kluwer, 1991. Published in English as *The Relativistic Deduction: Epistemological Implications of the Theory of Relativity*, translated by David A. Sipfle & Mary-Alice Sipfle. Dordrecht: Reidel, 1985.
Du Cheminement de la pensée, 3 vols. Paris: Félix Alcan, 1931.
Essais. Paris: J. Vrin, 1936.

Charles Renouvier

Essais de critique générale. Paris: Lagrange, 1854–64.
Critique de la doctrine de Kant. Paris: Félix Alcan, 1906.

3

THE EMERGENCE OF FRENCH SOCIOLOGY: ÉMILE DURKHEIM AND MARCEL MAUSS

Mike Gane

Durkheim's formation was in philosophy.[1] After attaining his Agrégation de Philosophie in 1882, he taught philosophy in schools in Sens, Quentin, and Troyes. However, he became dissatisfied with philosophy in its apparent struggle against the sciences, particularly the social sciences, very early on in his career, and in 1887 he accepted a position at the University of Bordeaux to organize courses in social sciences and in pedagogy (he became Professor in 1896). It was from this base that he published the results of his initial researches into sociology and the methodology that he had constructed to carry them out. He established a team of researchers that he, with his nephew Marcel Mauss,[2] organized around the journal *L'Année sociologique* from 1898. Mauss accepted a Chair at the École Pratique des Hautes Études in Paris in 1901 and, in 1902, Durkheim accepted a post in Paris at the Sorbonne, holding the Chair in the "Science of Education" (renamed as a Chair in Science of Education and Sociology in 1913). Durkheim did not promote himself as founder of sociology in France; this accolade came posthumously. He regarded his work as attempting a reorganization

1. Émile Durkheim (April 15, 1858–November 15, 1917; born in Épinal, France; died in Paris) was educated at the École Normale Supérieure (1879–82). His influences included Boutroux, Comte, Kant, Montesquieu, and Renouvier, and he held appointments at the University of Bordeaux (1887–1902) and the Sorbonne, Paris (1902–17).
2. Marcel Mauss (May 10, 1872–February 10, 1950; born in Épinal, France; died in Paris) was educated at the University of Bordeaux, and the École Pratique des Hautes Études, Paris (1895–1901). His influences included Comte, Durkheim, Renouvier, and Spinoza. He held appointments at the École Pratique des Hautes Etudes (1901–31), and the Collège de France (1931–40).

and correction of the sociology of Auguste Comte.[3] He regarded positivism as the greatest contribution of French thought in the nineteenth century both to philosophy and the social sciences. His appropriation and modification of the positivist tradition took place within the framework of French Kantianism, and particularly the writings of Charles Renouvier, against the background of academic eclectic philosophy dominated by the legacy of Victor Cousin. It was Durkheim rather than Mauss who engaged in a dialogue with philosophy, but, ironically, it has been the work of Mauss that has seemed more to interest philosophers.

I. LOCATING DURKHEIM AND MAUSS

Recent interpretations that suggest Durkheim can be read as a late-modern or even postmodern thinker (Stjepan Meštrović[4]) or as a thinker who imaginatively combined social science with a political and ethical vision derived from the Jewish tradition (Ivan Strenski[5]) are not representative. On the other hand, the view that Durkheim was essentially a conservative who worked with a precritical functionalist method has given way over the past twenty-five years to a view that he was a sophisticated democratic socialist who developed with various degrees of success a sociology based on structural theory and an inventive experimental method. Susan Stedman Jones's recent writings,[6] for example, develop the view that key subtleties of Durkheim's philosophy and epistemology are missed if the influence of Renouvier's neo-Kantianism is not taken into account. Her reconsideration is organized as an attack and refutation of the view that Durkheim was working with a crudely positivistic methodology. Her central thesis is that Durkheim adopts Renouvier's modification of Kant, which holds that reality is not a simple "thing" outside thought, but can exist only as a representation.[7]

---

*3. For a discussion of Comte, see the essay by Alan Sica in *The History of Continental Philosophy: Volume 2*.

4. Stjepan G. Meštrović, *Durkheim and Postmodern Culture* (New York: Aldine de Gruyter, 1992).

5. Ivan Strenski, *Durkheim and the Jews of France* (Chicago, IL: University of Chicago Press, 1997).

6. Susan Stedman Jones, *Durkheim Reconsidered* (Cambridge: Polity, 2001).

7. Any interpretation that wants Durkheim to depart from Kant risks reading him as positing knowledge as entirely relative to social structure. Thus, Stedman Jones's *Durkheim Reconsidered* holds on to the possibility of *a priori* knowledge through Renouvier's notion of the "skeleton" of representation. This *a priori* is "one which accommodates the historical and the relative" (*ibid.*, 70). This interpretation suggests: "Each culture is aware of reality as temporal and spatial, and as changing; of events as brought about or caused to be; of action as a pursuit of some end" (*ibid.*, 71). Relativism is not avoided by this sleight of hand, since

Durkheim's study of suicide is a crucial test for any interpretation that stresses the methodological impact of Renouvier. For Stedman Jones, the key to interpreting this work involves setting optimism, pessimism, solidarity, and hope in a dialectic of action, for the theory of suicide concerns the representation of psychic life. She holds that Durkheim adopts a kind of vitalist philosophy from Renouvier involving notions of passion, desires, disturbance, and frustration. Adopting Renouvier's notion of representation, the individual and the social become aspects of a unified field of causation; since they are one system of forces – relational and representational – the micro and the macro come together. The impact of Renouvier in this account becomes clear: it provides a nonpositivist explanation for those comments in Durkheim that relate to a universal condition of human action.

Watts Miller, on the other hand, has argued that Durkheim should be read as making a key contribution to liberal socialist ethics, to a communitarian defense of individualism within a significant continuation of the Enlightenment project. Miller also separates Durkheim from Comte and the Comtean tradition.[8] His central concern is to show how the problem of the relation between the individual as autonomous and as law governed – how individual freedom can be in harmony with a system of objective values – is not an insoluble problem for sociology. Miller tries to show that a purely rational construction of a scientific system cannot provide the structures for individual development and autonomy that are required by Durkheim's own conception of the "organic self." This requires not a mechanical enlightenment – based on the project of realizing a transparent society – but an organic enlightenment that works through the progressive dilemmas of modernity. Durkheim's real problem is how to secularize the kingdom of ends, or how to insert the reality of individual liberty and autonomy into the democratic frame that is at the same time legitimated through

---

any value, or any knowledge, can always be said to accommodate *to* the historical. What Durkheim set out to do – to analyze the ways in which representations are intimately bound up with the social – is occluded in this perspective.

8. Watts Willie Miller argues that Durkheim is concerned with the "rational deliberation of ends" and "not only to identify, clarify and rework ideals, but also to adjudicate on them" (*Durkheim, Morals and Modernity* [London: UCL Press, 1996], 1). The question that emerges concerns precisely the nature of the "ethical judge" (*ibid.*, 172), if this is not the individual, society, or social science. Miller suggests that the judge is the individual as man (*ibid.*, 177–8), but also "man," for "man is the enlightened republic's hidden god" (*ibid.*, 249). This view is expressed as a "vision that, in seeing the moral ideal's development through constant stirrings of new, obscure aspirations, builds in limits to a society with autonomous self-understanding. This in any case depends on the constitution, through collective processes, of a collective body of knowledge and experience ... So the human ideal must remain, in various if not very mysterious ways, elusive" (*ibid.*).

an ethics based on reason. In other words, Durkheim worked via an encounter with Kant toward a viable version of Comte's "religion of humanity."

Since the discovery in 1995 of the lectures Durkheim presented at the Lycée at Sens in 1882–84, many of the issues surrounding his relation to Kant and Renouvier have been resolved.[9] These lectures reveal that, far from marking a direct relation between Kant and Renouvier, Durkheim was working very systematically in the framework of Cousin's eclectic spiritualism. Cousin's influence dominated the curriculum of philosophy teaching from the 1830s and Durkheim had developed a position under this influence. The peculiarity of the French approach to philosophy, as opposed to the approach in Germany, was that it gave a founding role to psychology that, in Durkheim's time, was being radically reworked by Pierre Janet (1859–1947) within the eclectic framework of Cousin.[10] Durkheim, like Janet, held that philosophy was a science that had adopted experimental methods (guided by imaginative hypotheses controlled by empirical constraints). Thus in France, unlike in Germany, the philosophical tradition developed an analysis of the Kantian categories based on psychology rather than on logic. Emerging from this tradition, Durkheim sought to replace psychology with sociology as the foundation for philosophy, informed by a philosophical formation and terminology – particularly notions such as mental representation – that came from Cousin and Janet as well as Renouvier.[11]

Durkheim's sociology was therefore self-consciously embedded in the Kantian rationalism of the French philosophical tradition, a tradition that sidelined the positivism of Comte almost entirely during the nineteenth century. In order for rationalism to produce its potentially positive effects, Durkheim now argued that the Kantianism – through Cousin's spiritualist eclecticism – that had dominated the French rationalist tradition produced disastrous consequences – division, individualism, philosophy as art form, and in the end, an "anarchic dilettantism"[12] – that had to be faced.

Durkheim claimed that the political and social problems confronted by France – the particular effects of the Revolution – seen against the advantages

9. Neil Gross, "A Note on the Sociological Eye and the Discovery of a New Durkheim Text," *Journal of the History of the Behavioral Sciences* 32(2) (1996).

10. It is worth noting that in French universities, professors of psychology were located in departments of philosophy.

11. Émile Durkheim, *Durkheim's Philosophy Lectures: Notes from the Lycée de Sens Course, 1883–1884*, Neil Gross and Robert Alun Jones (trans.) (Cambridge: Cambridge University Press, 2004); see also Warren Schmaus, *Rethinking Durkheim and his Tradition* (Cambridge: Cambridge University Press, 2004); and for background John I. Brooks, *The Eclectic Legacy: Academic Philosophy and the Human Sciences in Nineteenth-Century France* (Newark, DE: University of Delaware Press, 1998).

12. Émile Durkheim, "L'Enseignement philosophique et l'agrégation de philosophie," in *Textes*, Victor Karady (ed.) (Paris: Éditions de Minuit, [1895] 1975), vol. 3, 418.

of its intellectual and rationalist heritage, meant that France was in a position to lead the development of the social sciences. This sociology would be theoretical, holistic, fundamentally evolutionist (it did not accept a radical break between anthropology and sociology), and linked in a complex way with the development of socialist ideas (while it rejected communism). It would be based in the relative independence from politics provided by the universities, yet it would certainly not be divorced from the central issues facing modern societies. Sociology would be a sophisticated therapeutic discipline that could work out objective analyses of social pathology. This, of course, had already been attempted by Comte, and indeed it was central to the positivists that the social sciences be aligned with the life sciences and embrace categories of health and illness. Far from prohibiting the definition of values and norms, Durkheim, following Comte, specifically elaborated them. Durkheim's particular version of Kantian rationalism was, from early on in his career, used critically to reconstruct and reinvigorate positive sociology through an encounter with the major sociologists influenced by Comte, in particular, John Stuart Mill (who was influenced early by Comte and then reacted strongly against him) and Herbert Spencer. Durkheim suggested it was precisely the moment of Saint-Simonian and early Comtean theory in the 1820s that reveals the decisive emergence of the modern notion of the "social" as such, and he provided one of the most notable accounts of this emergence in his lectures on *Socialism and Saint-Simon* (lectures given in 1895–96). His analysis of the French Revolution and the political instability in postrevolutionary France is not well known. Fundamentally it held that the dissolution of the guild-system in the prerevolutionary period initiated a deep-seated power imbalance within French society. He noted that for Henri de Saint-Simon, industry cannot advance without science and that therefore this too would have to be regulated in a new way.[13]

13. Durkheim notes that "practice presupposes science but is not to be confused with it. Human conduct is intelligent and enlightened only to the degree it is directed by theory – though theory cannot be productive except on condition of its not being limited to the pursuit of practical ends. In this light, science ceased to be a simple private occupation, a simple matter of individual curiosity. It became a social function…" (*Socialism and Saint-Simon*, Charlotte Sattler [trans.] [New York: Collier, (1928) 1962], 185). From the beginning of the nineteenth century two different issues are very clearly identified: "on the one hand are the 'political' and on the other, 'social' problems … [and] the more one advances in time, the more public attention turns from the former to the latter … Social questions … are those to which the economic state of modern societies give rise … [and] as Saint-Simon demonstrated, economic relations have become either the unique, or in any case, the principal substance of social life" (*ibid.*, 187–8).

Recent research has shown that a considerable amount of what was published under Saint-Simon's name when he was sketching out his vision for the new society was jointly written with Comte, who was his "secretary" for about five decisive years (Mary Pickering, *Auguste Comte: An Intellectual Biography* [Cambridge: Cambridge University Press, 1993]). The development

After having examined the Saint-Simonian socialist program and explained why it appeared when it did, Durkheim nonetheless thought its diagnoses were mistaken; indeed, "it seems to us that he was mistaken about what, in the present situation, is the cause of the uneasiness, and in having proposed, as a remedy, an aggravation of the evil."[14] This is also Durkheim's view of Marxism and any socialism in which the proletariat or class struggle is given the central role in and for such a program. For Durkheim the question was how to define whether the social state of revolutionary and postrevolutionary France was normal or abnormal. He concluded that it indeed had abnormal features. This abnormality did not lie within the sphere of political structures (as in liberal theory), or as a structurally inherent antagonism of the economic structure (as in Marxist theory), but in the insufficiency and imbalance of institutions in society as a whole.

Although some observers have found the term useful for defining the orientation of the Durkheim School, Durkheim himself clearly rejected the conception of the "positive polity" in Comte's sense. For Comte, popular sovereignty and democratic institutions were forms of the "metaphysical polity" linked structurally to egoistic individualism and, as such, were essentially unstable. Durkheim thought that Comte had not grasped the importance of the role of the democratic state in liberating the individual from bondage either to the family, or to secondary intermediary institutions. Nor had Comte grasped the way in which the social sciences could form the basis of a new curriculum in the schools and universities; for Comte education was to be controlled in detail by the sociocratic clergy. The key relationship was to be that between the state and secondary institutions remodeled as professions. Durkheim's ideal seems to have been a kind of liberal corporate socialism, or a "socialism of institutions," which would liberate a new individualism.

Thus Durkheim saw himself "following the path opened up" by Comte,[15] but in the context of a particular philosophical conjuncture dominated by the opposed influences of Renouvier and Spencer (who offered a more complex notion of social structure). Comte's fundamental three-state law of social evolution (theological, metaphysical, and positive) was rejected. This law did not

---

of the Saint-Simonian "Doctrine" after Saint-Simon's death in 1825 by Saint-Amand Bazard (1791–1832) and Barthélemy Enfantin (1796–1864) produced the first coherent theory of socialism, and it was in this form that Marx and Engels received the idea of socialism. Durkheim said of Saint-Simon, "in him we encounter the seeds already developed of all the ideas which have fed the thinking of our time ... we have found in it positive philosophy, positive sociology ... we ... also find socialism in it" (*Socialism and Saint-Simon*, 143).

14. *Ibid.*, 245.
15. See my "Durkheim contre Comte," in *La Methode Durkheimienne d'un siècle à l'autre*, Charles-Henri Cuin (ed.) (Paris: Presses Universitaires de France, 1997).

produce a valid conception of social types, or as he preferred to call them "social species." He held that "Comte's law correctly describes the way modern societies have developed from the tenth to the nineteenth century – but it does not apply to the entire course of human evolution."[16] He rejected Comte's historical method: "the genealogical tree of organized beings, instead of having the form of a geometric line, resembles more nearly a very bushy tree whose branches, issuing haphazardly all along the trunk, shoot out capriciously in all directions."[17] He distinguished between a genealogical analysis within a single real continuous society, a comparative analysis within a single society and between societies of the same type, and a more abstract comparative cross-cultural analysis that could form the basis of theoretical evolutionary typologies.

While Durkheim worked toward a critical reconstruction of Comte's sociology, he claimed that neither Hegel nor Marx had a direct influence on his thought. Certainly he debated with socialists, acknowledging that socialism and sociology were both profoundly indebted to Saint-Simon and Saint-Simonianism. In the mid-1890s, he began a lecture course on Saint-Simonianism that was conceived as the first in a series on socialist and communist ideas. After the initial lectures, however, Durkheim changed direction and began to work on religion; he was never to complete the series. It is clear that the very context of Durkheim's youth and early political awareness makes it unlikely that events such as the fall of the Second Empire, the Paris Commune, and the defeat of France in the Franco-Prussian war of 1870–71 did not leave their mark. The Third French Republic began under conditions of harsh political censorship. Durkheim passed his *baccalauréats* in 1875 and 1876, when the new political regime was beginning to settle into its republican and parliamentary routines. He came to maturity during the formation of the new regime, as a student at the École Normale Supérieure between 1879 and 1882. Durkheim's recently discovered (2004) early lectures of 1882–84 can be read as a critique of the limits of pure philosophy as a means for assessing and resolving the problem of social integration in France.[18] His early sociological publications suggest a change of perspective and that he worked to a position that would avoid the errors of the Commune on the one hand, and individualist liberalism (and anarchism – which took a turn to terrorism in the Third Republic in the years 1892–94) on the other, a position that formed the basis of his famous intervention in

16. Durkheim, *Socialism and Saint-Simon*, 268.
17. Émile Durkheim, *Durkheim on Institutional Analysis*, Mark Traugott (ed. and trans.) (Chicago, IL: University of Chicago Press, 1978), 53.
18. Neil Gross, "Introduction," in *Durkheim's Philosophy Lectures: Notes from the Lycée de Sens Course, 1883–1884* (Cambridge: Cambridge University Press, 2004).

the Dreyfus Affair (1894–1906).[19] Many commentators have seen Durkheim's position here as a valuable move beyond the confines of liberal political theory (Talcott Parsons[20]), while others have found that an absence of a theory of political parties constitutes the blind spot of Durkheimian sociology (Steven Lukes[21]). Clearly it is both since although Durkheim does not focus on political parties directly, he introduces a new analysis of state power.

From the mid-1890s Durkheim was working in close association with his nephew, Marcel Mauss. In the division of labor between them, Mauss seems to have been more closely involved in political practice. The phase of Western European socialism that developed after the Commune, particularly from 1876 to 1890, revealed, as Mauss later remarked in his *On Bolshevism*, a variety of practical developments of a new kind that left the heroic and utopian age of theory (Marx and Proudhon) behind; only from an existing nation, said Mauss, can the transition to socialism be conceived as an internal progression of an organic type. Thus the task for socialists within a nation is not primarily a political and revolutionary one, but a social engagement in building new organizations within and against the existing frame. This frame was not in itself an insuperable obstacle to this engagement, as Marxists claimed; quite the contrary, it alone makes it possible. Mauss was sent by *L'Humanité* as special envoy to conferences of the cooperative movement in Hamburg, Budapest, Paisley, and on a research mission to Russia in 1906, thus revealing the difference between the political involvement of Mauss and Durkheim reflected in their theorizing.

The primary aim of Durkheim and Mauss's project was not to establish or guide a political movement or party; it was clearly to insure the implantation of sociology within the universities as a reputable discipline with a pivotal role to play in the identification of the normal forms of the emerging institutional

19. Early on, Durkheim sided publicly with the Dreyfusards, taking an active role in support of the Ligue pour la défense des droits de l'homme (League for the defense of human rights) and becoming the secretary of its Bordeaux branch. He also was instrumental in getting his friend and former classmate at the École Normale, Jean Jaurès, to align the socialist movement with Dreyfus's defense. See Émile Durkheim, "Individualism and the Intellectuals," *Political Studies* 17(1) (1969), and another translation in *On Morality and Society: Selected Writings*, Robert N. Bellah (ed.) (Chicago, IL: University of Chicago Press, 1973). On the significance of this article, see Richard Bellamy, *Liberalism and Modern Society: A Historical Argument* (University Park, PA: Pennsylvania State University Press, 1992), 74–104. On the background crisis of the Third Republic see Robert Kaplan, *Forgotten Crisis: The Fin-de-Siècle Crisis of Democracy in France* (Oxford: Berg, 1995); see also Marcel Fournier, "Durkheim's Life and Context: Something New about Durkheim?" in *The Cambridge Companion to Durkheim*, Jeffrey C. Alexander and Phillip Smith (eds) (Cambridge: Cambridge University Press, 2005), 52–3.
20. Talcott Parsons, *The Structure of Social Action* (New York: McGraw Hill, 1937).
21. Steven Lukes, *Emile Durkheim* (London: Allen Lane, 1973).

structures of modern societies.[22] Durkheim stood at a distance from politics. Mauss said that even:

> the social and moral crisis of the Dreyfus Affair in which he played a large part, did not change his attitude. Even during the war, he was among those who put no hope in the so-called internationally organized working class. He therefore remained uncommitted – he "sympathized" … with the socialists, with Jaurès, with socialism. But he never gave himself to it.[23]

Durkheim's theoretical sociology, however, did not in fact shy away from the issues of the nature of the modern state and political power. Durkheim's argument suggests social theory is often mistaken in thinking the state is either a purely repressive machine, or that the purely political division of powers can deliver political and social liberty in the fullest sense. For Durkheim, the Spencerian thesis that freedom is freedom from the state ignores the fact that it is the state "that has rescued the child from family tyranny [and] the citizen from feudal groups and later from communal groups." Indeed Durkheim argued the state must not limit itself to the administration of "prohibitive justice … [but] must deploy energies equal to those for which it has to provide a counter-balance." Against the political illusion of power, for example as found in Montesquieu, Durkheim in effect tried to show that liberty is based on a particular form of the total social division of power: the state "must even permeate all those secondary groups of family, trade and professional association, Church, regional areas, and so on."[24]

Mary Ann Lamanna suggests that Durkheim's analysis of the family reveals how "[t]he tension between spouse and kin as heirs reflects the historic struggle of the conjugal family to emancipate itself from kin dominance."[25] This historic struggle, central to Durkheim's "grand narrative" of the movement from societies based on mechanical to those based on organic solidarity, is also the narrative of the modern state.

The legacy of Comte was not easily shaken off, however, for both Durkheim and Mauss, influenced by the Comtean view that war was incompatible with the advancement of industrial society, believed it impossible that there could really be deep-seated causes of war between advanced nations – by which they meant

22. Terry N. Clarke, *Prophets and Patrons: The French University and the Emergence of the Social Sciences* (Cambridge, MA: Harvard University Press, 1973), 162–95.
23. Mauss, Introduction to Durkheim, *Socialism and Saint-Simon*, 34–5.
24. Émile Durkheim, *Professional Ethics and Civic Morals*, Cornelia Brookfield (trans.) (London: Routledge, [1950] 1992), 64–5.
25. Mary Ann Lammana, *Emile Durkheim on the Family* (London: Sage, 2002), 91.

France, Britain, and Germany. The diplomatic activities of these nations were democratic, not divorced from popular control. In the run-up to the First World War, Mauss in particular contrasted the political maturity of these nations with the autocratic and feudal regimes of Eastern Europe, particularly Russia. His view was that German ambitions were eastward and the Western nations would not be drawn in. Close to Jean Jaurès, his position was pacifist.

When the war broke out, Mauss enlisted, immediately abandoning his pacifist stance. Durkheim again turned to his theory of social abnormalities. The state can become too strong and develop its own pathological dimensions and capacities: in his pamphlet "'Germany Above All': German Mentality and War" (1915), he critiqued the ideas of the German political philosopher Heinrich von Treitschke (1834–96), ideas that he took to be representative of the mentality that brought war to Europe in 1914. He was careful in fact to say that he was not analyzing the causes of war, but only examining one of the manifestations of a condition of social pathology.[26] Durkheim contrasted the democratic idea in which there is a continuity between government and people with Treitschke's thesis that there is a radical antagonism between state and civil society. Treitschke called for a state whose leaders are possessed of enormous ambition, unwavering determination, with personalities characterized by "something harsh, caustic, and more or less detestable" about them, a state with power capable of enforcing a mechanical obedience from its citizens, whose first duty was to obey its dictates.[27] These states flouted international law and conventions, and their idea of war pushed the development of military technology, which permitted the growth of states that were almost "exempt from the laws of gravity … [t]hey seem to transport us into an unreal world, where nothing can any longer resist the will of man."[28] Where there is a shift toward the concentration of power in the state, as occurs in wartime, the structures protecting individual values are weakened. In wartime there is to be expected not only an increase in altruistic suicide, most commonly associated with military discipline,[29] but also an increase in civil homicides since the individual as such is less protected by moral forces.[30]

After the war, Mauss took up a detailed analysis of the Bolshevik strategy in the Russian Revolution and its aftermath. The essay on Bolshevism, written he says as an "assessment" in Comtean style, would "criticize" in the style of

26. Émile Durkheim, *"Germany Above All": German Mentality and War* (Paris: Armand Colin, 1915), 46.
27. *Ibid.*, 30–34.
28. *Ibid.*, 46.
29. Émile Durkheim, *Suicide: A Study in Sociology*, John A. Spaulding and George Simpson (trans.) (New York: Free Press, [1951] 1970), 228ff.
30. Durkheim, *Professional Ethics and Civic Morals*, 110–20.

Renouvier.[31] He also suggested: "It would not be difficult here to pastiche Marx, to rewrite vis-à-vis this gigantic Commune his two famous pamphlets on the class struggles in France and on the Paris Commune. If I steer clear of such a parody, I hope I shall be allowed to follow fundamentally his example."[32] But he emphasized certain links with the Durkheimians. First, the idea of the soviet corresponds to Durkheim's conception of professional corporations as the basis of property statute; and second, "the establishment of a moral and political law of the group formed out of the economic association of those united in the same production" that is the professional occupation becomes the basis for political representation and social status on the model of the guild or the university.[33] Thus his interest in the Bolsheviks combined both scientific and personal concerns: "it was a socialism which among the options open to it had chosen my own, the professional organization"; indeed "Moscow seemed to many amongst us what it remains for many enlightened people … a kind of sanctuary incubating the very destiny of our ideas."[34]

All of these discussions are framed against a new evolutionary six-stage model – the elementary horde, simple clan-based tribe, tribal confederation, ancient city-state, medieval society, modern industrial nation[35] – that is underpinned by a simple theory of two fundamental forms of social solidarity: mechanical and organic. Societies that are mechanical add together elements (kinship groups) as "compound" or "doubly compound" compositions in Spencer's terms; societies that are organized on the basis of an "organic" division of labor and interdependent specialization of function (including medieval society, and the modern nation) have a form of social solidarity that is more and more complex. Whereas Durkheim outlined a theory of social structures, developing notably the distinction between segmental and organic forms of solidarity, Mauss retained the distinction as the basis of a theory of social evolution but introduced the concept of the nation as the key mediating term. Socialism is a modern idea and practice (after 1830), and is possible only as part of the development of the modern national form of organic solidarity; the project for a socialism where this form is absent, for example in Russia, can lead only to quite different results (for the

31. Marcel Mauss, "A Sociological Assessment of Bolshevism," in *The Radical Sociology of Durkheim and Mauss*, Mike Gane (ed.) (London: Routledge, 1992), 170. See the essay "Neo-Kantianism in Germany and France" in this volume for a discussion of Renouvier's *Criticisme*.
32. *Ibid.*, 171.
33. *Ibid.*, 172.
34. *Ibid.*, 173.
35. Ernest Wallwork, "Religion and Social Structure in The Division of Labor," *American Anthropologist* 86(1) (1984).

social elements are more like heterogeneous segments in an "Imperial sack").[36] But the way this framework was used by Durkheim and Mauss suggests there was a continuous and productive division of labor between them.[37] Each developed a style of work. Mauss's very large corpus of writings does not include a single book. Works like the famous essay on the gift were published as journal articles, as was the very long text Mauss wrote with Durkheim on social classification.[38] In fact, a large proportion of Mauss's output was coauthored, and appears as interventions in ongoing debates. He also favored work on social facts,[39] and was against what he called "the pretentious search for originality."[40] Mauss, however, claimed that the most important characteristic of his approach was not simply that he was a positivist and thus not interested in "the lofty realms of … metaphysical ideas," but that he was essentially a member of a school, a team, a workshop – in fact he had been Durkheim's "recruiting agent."[41] Theory, not philosophy, remained important and open. For example, although Mauss's studies were synthesized in Durkheim's 1912 study *The Elementary Forms of the Religious Life*, Mauss admitted in 1930 that Durkheim's argument about the nature of the sacred remained contested: "we were never sure that he was correct and I still continue to speak of the magico-religious."[42]

In 1893, Durkheim had referred to a specific group of acts as "gratuitous" and outside morals:

> the refinements of worldly urbanity, the ingenuities of politeness … the gifts, affectionate words or caresses between friends or relatives, up to the heroic sacrifices that no duty demands … The father of a family risks his life for a stranger; who would dare to say that was useful?[43]

36. Marcel Mauss, *Écrits politiques* (Paris: Fayard, 1997), 258ff.
37. See Émile Durkheim, *Lettres à Marcel Mauss* (Paris: Presses Universitaires de France, 1998).
38. See Émile Durkheim and Marcel Mauss, *Primitive Classification*, Rodney Needham (trans.) (Chicago, IL: University of Chicago Press, [1903] 1963).
39. A key concept in Mauss's "Essai sur le don", published in English as *The Gift*, by "total social fact" he named those social phenomena that involve "the totality of society and its institutions," that "are at the same time juridical, economic, religious, and even aesthetic and morphological, etc.," and that must be analyzed in terms of the totality of their connections (*The Gift: The Form and Reason for Exchange in Archaic Societies*, W. D. Halls [trans.] [London: Routledge, 1990], 78–9).
40. Phillippe Besnard (ed.), *The Sociological Domain: The Durkheimians and the Founding of French Sociology* (Cambridge: Cambridge University Press, 1983), 139.
41. *Ibid.*, 140.
42. *Ibid.*, 149.
43. Émile Durkheim, *The Division of Labor in Society*, George Simpson (trans.) (New York: Macmillan, [1933] 1964), 430–31.

In a marked departure from this view, Mauss's "Essai sur le don" clearly shifts from the notion that the gift is of no interest because it is merely a gratuitous act to the decisive discovery that it forms an obligatory form of exchange in all societies, whether or not it is the principle around which a particular society is organized.[44] This is to say, although the gift might appear free and disinterested, it is in fact neither, as Mauss argues that the gift is given in a context in which both its reception and its reciprocal return are obligated, and obligated in terms of well-articulated social rules. Thus, much of *The Gift* involves analyzing gift-giving practices in an effort to disclose the underlying rules that govern the ongoing circulation of gifts. The essay on *The Gift* was the basis of a quite new problematic, one that was to be made famous in Mauss's lectures at the Collège de France (1931–40). Mauss wrote an "intellectual self portrait" at the time of his election to the Collège that provides a restatement of his inductivist position: from the facts, he says, he

> drew out that at once religious, mythical and contractual idea of the gift. I also brought out the idea of total prestation between clans, between generations (usually staggered), between sexes and between descent groups ...: I established the collective nature of archaic forms ... and, above all, this notion of "total facts" which set the entire economic, moral, religious, aesthetic and mythical ... social whole in motion. Superimposed on reciprocity and conflict, a system of purely sumptuary, military, athletic, etc., rivalries developed within these societies ... the previous ways of posing questions have been surpassed and displaced.[45]

In his academic work, Mauss kept strictly to the sphere of those societies that the Durkheimians called polysegmental.[46] If academic sociology may, for Mauss,

44. "Essai sur le don" was published in the first issue of the second series of the *Année sociologique* in 1925, and all commentators have agreed that it marks a considerable move away from the problematic of the prewar *Année* (see Claude Lévi-Strauss, *Introduction to the Work of Marcel Mauss*, Felicity Baker [trans.] [London: Routledge, 1987]). Talcott Parsons likened the analysis to Mendel's discoveries in genetics (in Wilton Dillon, *Gifts and Nations* [The Hague: Mouton, 1968], 6); others argued that it marks the beginning of the analysis of power (Jean Baudrillard, *Symbolic Exchange and Death*, Iain Hamilton Grant [trans.] [London: Sage, 1993]), the "foundation of ethnology" (Marcel Fournier, *Marcel Mauss* [Paris Fayard, 1994], 501ff.), or even the "invention of the symbolic" (Camille Tarot, *De Durkheim à Mauss: L'invention du symbolique* [Paris: La Découverte, 1999]). For a review see Alain Caillé, *Don, intérêt et désintéressement: Bourdieu, Mauss, Platon et quelques autres* (Paris: La Découverte, 1994).
45. Besnard, *The Sociological Domain*, 147.
46. See N. J. Allen, *Categories and Classification: Maussian Reflections on the Social* (Oxford: Berghahn, 2000), 61–74.

even have been a "lost cause,"[47] this was not because Mauss ignored the political and social problems of the advanced nations.[48]

II. FUNDAMENTAL PROBLEMS OF METHODOLOGY

Following in Comte's footsteps, Durkheim attempted to specify the unique domain of sociological phenomena within the division of labor of the sciences. He insisted that rules of method are strictly parallel with other ethical and moral rules: "methodological rules are for science what rules of law and custom are for conduct," and whereas the natural sciences appear to have formed common ground, the "moral and social sciences" are in a state of anomie: "the jurist, the psychologist, the anthropologist, the economist, the statistician, the linguist, the historian, proceed with their investigations as if the different orders of fact they study constituted so many different worlds."[49] Rules of method organize and regulate the field, identify the ground for scientific strategies, and legitimate the way these strategies should be assessed. Methodology in the Durkheimian tradition was much more than a set of research techniques. It did not progress, however, without serious difficulties.

The methodological orientation was from the start one that strives for maximal objectivity of investigation: the primary definition of the terrain of sociology itself, the very object of social analysis, Durkheim formulated as "any way of acting, whether fixed or not, capable of exerting over the individual an external constraint."[50] On this *The Rules of Sociological Method* is insistent: all preconceptions must be discarded; never assume the voluntary character of a social institution; and always privilege the study of social phenomena that are detached from individual forms. The fundamental rule for observing social phenomena is "to consider social facts as things."[51] Durkheim considered the common ideological formation of the sociologist as modern citizen as in a sense, and paradoxically, both a support and a fundamental obstacle to positive research. His critical judgment is that in the absence of rules, "instead of observing, describing and comparing things, we … reflect on our ideas … Instead of a science which deals with realities, we carry out no more than an ideological analysis."[52] This partic-

47. Fournier, *Marcel Mauss*, 527ff.
48. Johan Heilbron, "Les Métamorphoses du durkheimisme, 1920–1940," *Revue française de sociologie* 26 (1985).
49. Durkheim, *The Division of Labor in Society*, 368.
50. Émile Durkheim, *The Rules of Sociological Method*, W. D. Halls (trans.) (London: Macmillan, 1982), 59.
51. *Ibid.*, 60.
52. *Ibid.*

ular text has been read as a revolutionary manifesto in sociology, for it essentially demands that each sociologist reverses habitual and everyday forms of thought.

When Mauss came to discuss the notion of the social fact, he gave it a different interpretation, more empirical and concrete in its emphasis. For example, when he presented socialism as a social fact, he departed from the classic definition of the social fact. Social facts are essentially psychological, and not to be found outside individuals in their social context, he says.[53] Durkheim's famous methodological definition of social facts as external to individuals appears abstract and formal against Mauss's formulation, which appears more in line with Durkheim's post-1898 position. It is clear, however, that these definitions and rules are also closely bound up with changing and developing political and research priorities; what seems at first to be Durkheim's attempt to produce a definitive text on methodology, *The Rules of Sociological Method*, is more complex than it appears. Durkheim and Mauss seemed able to produce definitive methodological rules that were only to be altered, or even abandoned, as soon as their researches progressed. The first definition of the field of study, for example, was not developed in terms of social facts at all, but rather of moral facts: "moral facts consist in a rule of sanctioned conduct."[54] Durkheim adopts this definition since the study of moral evolution no longer depends on the study of norms, but norms and sanctions. The terrain thus changes: the development of the "positive science of morality is a branch of sociology, for every sanction is principally a social thing."[55] When the focus is a moral social fact, Durkheim conceived the field in terms of the *conscience collective*; when the focus changed, from 1898 on, to social knowledge, it is conceived in terms of collective representations.[56] There is also a new conception toward 1912–14 that develops the conception of the articulation between the individual and society in terms of *homo duplex*.[57] With this concept Durkheim thought he had resolved the longstanding problem of the body (the basis of the sensation of individuality) and the soul (the reflection of the experience of social transcendence beyond the individual).

The (1893) discussion of method in *The Division of Labor in Society* was clearly the basis for much of what appears in *The Rules of Sociological Method* (published separately as articles in 1894 before appearing in modified book form in 1895). The characteristics of the moral fact are displaced and incorporated into the wider category of the social fact. In the 1894 formulations (that

53. Mauss, *Écrits politiques*, 76.
54. Durkheim, *The Division of Labor in Society*, 425.
55. *Ibid.*, 428.
56. Émile Durkheim, "Individual and Collective Representations," in *Sociology and Philosophy*, D. F. Pocock (trans.) (Glencoe, IL: Free Press, 1953).
57. Émile Durkheim, "The Dualism of Human Nature," in *Essays on Sociology and Philosophy*, Kurt Wolff (ed.) (New York: Harper, 1960).

is to say, in the first journal appearance of *The Rules of Sociological Method*), it is made clear nonetheless that the sociologist must choose to give primacy to the study of facts from "a viewpoint where they present a sufficient degree of consolidation."[58] By the time the book version of *The Rules of Sociological Method* was published in 1895, with a large number of revisions, this particular injunction was changed to the rule that the sociologist "must strive to consider [social facts] from a viewpoint where they present themselves in isolation from their individual manifestations."[59] *The Rules of Sociological Method* specifies a whole new range of ways in which external constraint occurs, from informal sanctions of ridicule and social ostracism to technical and organizational necessities. Moral obligation and sanction form the first domain of objects, but constraint and circumstantial necessity broaden this into the essential characteristics of (externally acting) social facts in general.

Durkheim maintains a continuing interest in moral statistics from the early essay on variations in birth rates through a range of studies of family, divorce, and political statistics.[60] This aspect of his sociology has attracted attention for installing an experimental rationalism as a founding moment in the modern discipline.[61] It seems clear that in 1895 he altered his research and decided to undertake a full-scale study of suicide statistics. He wrote in *The Rules of Sociological Method*: "if suicide depends on more than one cause it is because in reality there are several kinds of suicide."[62] The very existence of suicide statistics makes it possible for sociologists to study social currents as phenomena that are "independent of their individual manifestations." Far from fixing a unique definition of the object of sociology, such as social statistics, Durkheim gave himself a number of options. He does not seem to be worried if he does not follow to the letter his own hastily conceived prescriptive rules, as long as he remains consistent with basic principles.[63]

But there were important problems with this position in practice. Throughout the methodological writings to this point (1895), Durkheim insisted that the sociologist must start from things not ideas; indeed, the sociologist must start from "a group of phenomena defined beforehand by certain common external

58. Durkheim, *The Rules of Sociological Method*, 138.
59. *Ibid.*, 82–3.
60. Stephen Turner, "Durkheim among the Statisticians," *Journal of the History of the Behavioral Sciences* 32(4) (1996).
61. See Jean-Michel Berthelot, *1895: Durkheim: L'Avènement de la sociologie scientifique* (Toulouse: Presses Universitaires du Mirail, 1995), 75–105.
62. Durkheim, *The Rules of Sociological Method*, 150.
63. Émile Durkheim, *Contributions to L'Année Sociologique*, Yash Nandan (ed.) (New York: Free Press, 1980), 77.

characteristics."[64] Work must begin from these external features and move toward an understanding of their internal causal relationships. When investigating suicide, the procedure required that he group together those suicides with the same external features (e.g. how suicides were committed), and "would admit as many suicide currents as there were distinct types, then seek to determine their causes."[65] In the course of the analysis in *Suicide*, Durkheim says, however, that this procedure could not be used; instead, he proposed "to determine the social types of suicide by classifying them not directly by their preliminarily described characteristics, but by the causes which produce them."[66] Instead of proceeding from the characteristics in the facts themselves, he says "once the nature of the causes is known we shall try to deduce that nature of the effects ... Thus we shall descend from causes to effects and our aetiological classification will be completed by a morphological one."[67] He admitted that this was a complete reversal of the order of analysis prescribed in *The Rules of Sociological Method*, which was designed to discover social causes. It comes as something of a surprise to learn that the social causes of suicides (anomic, egoistic, altruistic) are already known.[68]

But there were other problems, particularly in defining abnormality in a society that was still in the process of formation. His primary rule here was: if the social fact is general in the average form of the social species under consideration, the fact is to be judged normal. Because there were problems with the very identification of the species French society belonged to, he introduced another much more theoretical consideration, requiring that it be demonstrated how a normal fact shows "that the general character of the phenomenon is related

64. Durkheim, *The Rules of Sociological Method*, 75.
65. Durkheim, *Suicide*, 146.
66. *Ibid.*, 147.
67. *Ibid.*
68. See my "The Deconstruction of Social Action: The 'Reversal' of Durkheimian Methodology," in *Durkheim's Suicide: A Century of Research and Debate*, W. S. F. Pickering and Geoffrey Walford (eds) (London: Routledge, 2000). If the results of Durkheim's analyses have often been challenged from outside the school, they were not immune from challenge from within either. Indeed, many observers have argued that Mauss sought to wrestle with the problems of Durkheim's initial conceptions and analyses to the end of his career (see Allen, *Categories and Classifications*). Others, such as Adam Kuper, have reviewed the criticisms of *The Elementary Forms of Religious Life* and concluded that Durkheim's "model of a segmentary structure based on unilineal descent groups is a sociological fantasy" ("Durkheim's Theory of Kinship," *British Journal of Sociology* 36[2] [1985]). The paradox therefore is: Why does Durkheim's work remain significant? Kuper suggests the "apparently paradoxical fruitfulness of Durkheim's work, despite its substantive failure, is ... due to the power of certain elements of his methodology; to the importance of some of the questions which he set on the agenda of the next generation; and, above all, to the sense which he communicated of the richness, complexity and sociological interest of ethnographic materials" (*ibid.*, 235).

to the general conditions of collective life in the social type under consideration," and this "verification is necessary when this fact relates to a social species which has not yet gone through its complete evolution."[69] The results of the analyses using these two rules tend to contradict each other in the case under discussion (one suggesting normality, the other abnormality). If the anomic forms of the division of labor are a continuation of segmental society, and "now increasingly dying out, we shall be forced to conclude that this now constitutes a morbid state, however universal it may be."[70] In other words, the theoretical analysis of the forms and functions of regulation suggest that economic anomie is pathological even if it is general; yet the principal rule suggests generality indicates normality. Because there is a problematic relation between rules and facts, Durkheim, reluctantly, is forced into a theoretical detour,[71] a detour that ultimately saved his sociology from a reductionist empiricism (unable to read social causation directly from facts, he had to take his detour through theory).

After Durkheim's death in 1917, the second series of *L'Année sociologique* also followed Durkheim's example by attempting to reflect on method. In Mauss's 1927 transitional text on method – "Sociology: Its Divisions and Their Relative Weightings" – it is clear that the old framework is bursting at the seams as Mauss attempted to reconstruct the sociological project in a new situation.[72] Mauss seems to have moved very strongly in the direction of anthropology, whether it be called ethnology or ethnography, and away from what was recognized as

69. Durkheim, *The Rules of Sociological Method*, 97.
70. *Ibid.*, 95.
71. Of course one of the reasons Durkheim choose suicide was to demonstrate that suicide rates could form a distinct object of study. Gabriel Tarde disputed this but nonetheless helped Durkheim to get access to statistics in Paris. Tarde held the view that there are only individuals and that society and social cause does not exist: "there can only be individual actions and interactions. The rest is only a metaphysical entity, mysticism" (*On Communication and Social Influence*, Terry N. Clark [ed.] [Chicago, IL: University of Chicago Press, 1969], 140). The help that Tarde gave Durkheim ironically became "the empirical basis for the sharpest attack that he ever received" (M. Borlandi, "Informations sur la rédaction du Suicide et sur l'état du conflit entre Durkheim et Tarde de 1895 à 1897," *Durkheim Studies* 6 [Fall 1994], 6). Durkheim developed in *Suicide* the classic case for the existence of unique structural social causes over and above individual interactions and *inter alia* presents one of his tactical critiques of Tarde (*Suicide*, 123–42, 306–25; my *On Durkheim's Rules of Sociological Method* [London: Routledge, 1988], 76–83).
72. A third set of publications – no longer called the *Année sociologique*, but the more accurate *Annales sociologique* – was started in 1934, and in its first volume Mauss published his essay "Fragment d'un sociologie générale descriptive," with a subtitle, "Classification et méthode d'observation des phénomènes généraux de la vie sociale dans les sociétés de type archaïques (phénomènes généraux spécifique de la vie intérieure de la société)" (in Mauss, *Œuvres* [Paris: Éditions de Minuit, 1968–9], vol. 3, 303–54), which continues this project in more detail; see the discussion in my "Introduction," in Marcel Mauss, *The Nature of Sociology*, W. Jeffrey [trans.] [Oxford: Berghahn, 2005], ix–xxii).

"sociology" in the years of the first *Année*.[73] Incontestably the essays published in that journal were dominated by themes of religion, ritual, classification, and sanctions in "primitive" societies. If Mauss even said, at one point, "I have never been a militant of sociology,"[74] what is striking is that, after Durkheim's death, Mauss began to work out a detailed conception of "general sociology" that is almost completely lacking in Durkheim's formulations. It has even been claimed, by Bruno Karsenti among others, that Mauss now began to restructure the anthropological field. Karsenti argues that:

> Relations are formed, connections established, and passages introduced which lead to a redistribution of knowledge. The latter, insofar as it no longer suffers from a foundational split, can now be seen from a unitary viewpoint and can take back the name of anthropology – although the old term has now acquired a new meaning.[75]

Indeed, for Karsenti, sociology in the Maussian scheme "has the imperative duty to fulfill itself on this basis and rediscover its place within anthropology."[76] Mauss also seemed to want to develop Durkheim's notion of *homo duplex*, but he did this in a way that did not confront the philosophers head on. The long-running dispute about reason and pure rationality, on the one hand, and social determinants, on the other, produced on Mauss's part some ingenious interventions. His early concern with bodily gestures, indicated in his 1909 thesis *On Prayer*, was continued throughout his career with essays on "techniques of the body" and technology.[77] He held that from *homo duplex* it was possible to think

73. Between 1898 and 1913 twelve volumes were published, although the volumes that contained significant analyses ended with volume 9 in 1906. A conspectus of the contributions of Durkheim and Mauss indicates that their work was already dominated by questions of the nature of the "elementary forms" of social and cultural structure. The first volume of 1898 contained Durkheim's essay on the origins of the incest taboo. The second published Durkheim's essay on the definition of religious phenomena and Mauss and Hubert's essay on sacrifice. The next major items by Durkheim appeared in volume 4 (1902), containing Durkheim's essay on penal evolution, and in volume 5 with Durkheim's essay on totemism. Volume 6 (1903) contained Durkheim and Mauss on "Primitive Classification." Volume 7 (1904) contained Mauss and Hubert's essay on magic. Volume 8 (1905) contained Durkheim's essay on "The Matrimonial Organization of Australian Societies'), and volume 9 (1906) contained Mauss and Beuchat's essay "Seasonal Variations of the Eskimo."
74. Besnard, *The Sociological Domain*, 142.
75. Bruno Karsenti, "The Maussian Shift: A Second Foundation for Sociology in France?" in *Marcel Mauss: A Centenary Tribute*, Wendy James and N. J. Allen (eds) (Oxford: Berghahn, 1998), 80.
76. *Ibid.*
77. See Marcel Mauss, *Techniques, Technology and Civilization*, Nathan Schlanger (ed.) (Oxford: Berghahn, 2006).

of "*homme total*," and of thinking not only with the brain but with the fingers.[78] It is not far fetched to think that Mauss was developing here a materialist conception of practice that anticipated the critique of Durkheim developed later by sociologists such as Peter Worsley.[79]

III. THEORETICAL REVISIONS

Durkheim developed his theory as his research grew more extensive. He began by suggesting that the earlier the society, the more likely it was to have repressive sanctions. He later revised this view completely. In his early lectures on *Moral Education*, for example, he argued that there was a plague of violent punishment in the schools of the Middle Ages, and the lash remained in constant use in schools up until the eighteenth century. After researching his lectures on educational thought in France,[80] he describes the thesis of the violent medieval colleges as simply "a legend." He had discovered that these educational communities remained essentially democratic and these forms "never have very harsh disciplinary regimes" because "he who is today judged may tomorrow become the judge."[81] The new analysis suggests that the turn towards a more oppressive disciplinary regime began at the end of the sixteenth century, just at the moment when the schools and colleges in France became centralized and isolated from the outside community.

But Durkheim faced up to the issue of punishment as a practical issue for teachers in his pedagogy classes. Between the offense and the punishment, he observed there is a hidden continuity, for they are not "two heterogeneous things coupled artificially."[82] This is the reason that erroneous theories of punishment arise. One such theory sees punishment as expiation or atonement; another sees punishment primarily as a way of intimidating or inhibiting further offenses. From a pedagogical point of view, the problem concerns the capacity to neutralize the demoralizing effects of an infringement of group norms. The effectiveness of punishment should be judged by how far it contributes to the solidarity of

78. Bruno Karsenti, *L'Homme total: Sociologie, anthropologie et philosophie chez Marcel Mauss* (Paris: Presses Universitaires de France, 1997); Nathan Schlanger, "Technological Commitments: Marcel Mauss and the Study of Techniques in the French Social Sciences," in *Techniques, Technology and Civilization* (Oxford: Berghahn, 2006).
79. Peter Worsley, "Emile Durkheim's Theory of Knowledge," *The Sociological Review* 4 (1956).
80. Émile Durkheim, *The Evolution of Educational Thought in France*, Peter Collins (trans.) (London: Routledge & Kegan Paul, [1938] 1977).
81. *Ibid.*, 155–7.
82. Émile Durkheim, *Moral Education*, Everett K. Wilson and Herman Schnurer (trans.) (London: Collier, [1925] 1973), 179.

the group as a whole, since certain kinds of punishment can contribute to the creation of further immoral acts.[83] Once applied, punishment seems to lose something of its power. A reign of terror is, in the end, a very weak system of sanctions often driven to extremes by its own ineffectiveness. Corporal punishment also involves an attack on the dignity of the individual, a dignity valued and fostered in modern societies.

The central theoretical issue here was addressed in his attempt to reconstruct the theses of *The Division of Labor in Society* in an article of 1900 called "Two Laws of Penal Evolution."[84] Durkheim criticized Spencer for thinking that the degree of absoluteness of governmental power is related to the number of functions it undertakes. But Durkheim worked toward the formulation: "the more or less absolute character of the government is not an inherent characteristic of any given social type"[85] – an idea to be found in Spencer's sociology. Durkheim presents an account of French society that is diametrically opposed to that of Marx, as he argues that "seventeenth-century France and nineteenth-century France belong to the same type."[86] To think there has been a change of type is to mistake a conjunctural event in the society (revolution) with its fundamental structure, since absolutism arises, not from the constituent features of a social form, but from "individual, transitory and contingent conditions"[87] in social evolution. In principle, the form of state is never a fundamental constituting feature of any social type.

Durkheim's work, then, involved considerable reworking of basic conceptions, and his theorizing was constructed with a view that made this possible. One such important example was the conceptualization of the notion of primitive society itself between *The Division* (1893) and *The Elementary Forms of the Religious Life* (1912). In the first of these studies, the fundamental fact of the early societies is that they are held together by bonds of similitude and characterized by intense and violent reactions to infringements of a highly uniform "collective consciousness." There is little social differentiation; even the gender division of labor is so slight there is no contractual regulation between the sexes, and relations between the sexes were characterized by sexual promiscuity.[88] Durkheim's more detailed investigations into Australian tribal society produced a more complex picture, as he began to see kinship organization as highly structured, and based on deeply embedded forms of sexual and age divisions. He came to view social structure as the outcome of symbolic practices, particularly those crystallized in rituals. He established the thesis that ritual beliefs were

83. *Ibid.*, 199.
84. Durkheim, *Durkheim on Institutional Analysis*, 157.
85. *Ibid.*
86. *Ibid.*
87. *Ibid.*
88. Durkheim, *The Division of Labor in Society*, 57–8.

structured on basic categories that were themselves socially produced and reproduced. Fundamental to such systems of religious categories were the concepts of the sacred and profane, good and evil, which were involved both in organizing such rituals and being at the same time reproduced by them. In this way, Durkheim thought he could arrive at a definitive sociological critique of Kantian apriorism on the one hand, and Spencerian individualism on the other. He also thought that this kind of investigation could shed light on the notion of the soul, developing further his notion of *homo duplex*, since evidence showed that representations of individual souls were intimately linked to the structure of social groups and their internal differentiation (in some Australian groups, for example, women did not have souls).[89]

Because Durkheim's attention had shifted to these symbolic processes and practices of intervention in and reproduction of such symbolic materials, it has been assumed in some interpretations that his whole sociology had itself become a subjective exercise in symbolic interactionism and a rapprochement with pragmatism.[90] Although there was no acknowledgment of this in Durkheim's writings on methodology, the focus of analysis was no longer on the external modes of sanctioned conduct (moral facts). It had moved to social epistemology, or what he called "the sociology of knowledge and religion," which examined the way immanent infrastructures imposed their exigencies on action. This shift of emphasis had already been signaled in his discussion paper on "The Determination of Moral Facts" (1906), where he had suggested that external constraint and obligation was one side only of moral discipline. Another dimension, neglected by Kant (but emphasized by Renouvier), was that aspect of morality beyond obligation that was "desirable and desired."[91] This he thought required a sociological analysis from the inside, to complement the analyses of the externality of obligation: "[t]his desirability peculiar to moral life participates of the … characteristic of obligation, and is not the same as the desirability of the objects that attract our ordinary desires."[92] Durkheim develops parallel ideas in his lectures on pragmatism with respect to truth.[93]

Mauss's political writings also reflect two important developments of Durkheimian theory after Durkheim's death in 1917. On the one hand, Mauss is much more influenced by the theory of capital and capitalism than Durkheim was, and this gives certain parts of his writing a critical and radical character. On

89. See my "Woman as Outsider," in Gane, *The Radical Sociology of Durkheim and Mauss*.
90. See Gregory Stone and Harvey Farberman, "On the Edge of Rapprochement: Was Durkheim Moving Towards the Perspective of Symbolic Interaction?" *Sociological Quarterly* 8 (1967).
91. Durkheim, *Sociology and Philosophy*, 45.
92. *Ibid.*
93. Émile Durkheim, *Pragmatism and Sociology*, J. C. Whitehouse (trans.) (Cambridge: Cambridge University Press, 1983), 73.

the other hand, Mauss attempted to think about politics directly. One aspect of this reflection can be found in his attempt to define the relation between sociology and politics;[94] another tended to look more to the practical development of socialism than to criticize socialist theory (although he also does this), and this leads him to assess progress on grounds that he claims are different from, and often in advance of, theory.[95]

Mauss did not give any great weight to the notion of social pathology, and so does not locate himself in Durkheim's scheme where the principal objective of theorists is to repair a social abnormality of structure through appeals to statesmen. In fact, the very category of "abnormal" and "pathological" social facts disappears with Mauss. But if Mauss kept his academic anthropology and his political writing separate, he drew practical political lessons for sociology whenever the opportunity arose. His judgment against the Bolsheviks draws some harsh ones: the Bolshevik Revolution was more a creature of the crisis in Russia than the outcome of the will of a people; it was not "methodically pursued … it was just a great adventure," in fact, "an accident, it has been grafted, overlaid onto the life of a people … it does not correspond to the movement of the mentality of the Russian people, any more than it is the pure realization of the ideas of its leaders."[96] Even the February Revolution of 1917, when Kerensky took power, was not the work of "a living society creating for itself by force a constitution," and even the socialist revolutionaries destroyed what political and civic organization there was. As for the Bolsheviks, "at least they had will power … savage will … not encumbered by any love for this immense people." The Bolsheviks "exploited" the revolution; they "seized Russia," but the opposition was even worse and even less popular.[97] It proves that all social revolution "must take a national character," "it must be the work of the 'general will' of the citizens." Indeed the communist and terrorist period of the Russian Revolution was not socialist. Socialism would organize the market and not attempt to produce a communism of consumption. Socialism would not "dispense with money" nor suppress the essential "industrial and commercial freedom" of the modern economy. Essentially socialism should maintain and "respect … intermediary collectivities." Indeed, "Durkheim's hypotheses about the moral and economic value of the professional group emerge further confirmed. The Soviets failed precisely because they undermined and destroyed this primordial organizational element."[98] Essential political conclusions follow: "violence is only legitimate via the law, via the legal order whose reign it supports: it is not itself order, still less faith"; second, "naïve sociologists,

94. Mauss, *The Nature of Sociology*, 80–84.

95. Mauss, *Écrits politiques*, 254ff.

96. Mauss, "A Sociological Assessment of Bolshevism," 175.

97. *Ibid.*, 178–9.

98. *Ibid.*, 187–91.

the Communists believed that the order of sovereignty, the law, can create … from nothing … the law does not create, it sanctions."[99]

The Durkheimians clearly aimed to decamp from philosophy, the discipline in which they were formed, into a positive science. They did not think that this involved an epistemological break, since their notion of philosophy was that it was already a science from the point of view of its methodology and logic. What they wanted was to put this science to use. The philosophers who did not take this route were, in their view, taking a path into a profoundly reactionary mysticism or scholasticism. But in their own practice, it seems clear to conclude that Durkheimian philosophy evolved into a radicalized Kantianism formed out of the French tradition of Cousin and Renouvier that they then applied to Comte in order to regenerate sociology and anthropology. What they produced was an experimental rationalism that had learning from errors as its objective.

MAJOR WORKS

Durkheim

De la division du travail social: Étude sur l'organisation des sociétés supérieures. Paris: Félix Alcan, 1893. Published in English as *The Division of Labor in Society*. (i) Translated by George Simpson. New York: Macmillan, 1933 [page references are to the 1964 edition]. (ii) Translated by W. D. Halls. New York: Free Press, 1984.

Les Règles de la méthode sociologique. Paris: Félix Alcan, 1895. Published in English as *The Rules of Sociological Method*. (i) Translated by Sarah A. Solovay and John H. Mueller. New York: Free Press, 1938. (ii) Translated by W. D. Halls. London: Macmillan, 1982.

Le Suicide: Étude de sociologie. Paris: Félix Alcan, 1897. Published in English as (i) *Suicide: A Study in Sociology*. Translated by John A. Spaulding and George Simpson. New York: Free Press, 1951 [page references are to the 1970 edition]. (ii) *On Suicide*. Translated by Robin Buss. London/New York: Penguin, 2006.

Les Formes elémentaires de la vie religieuse. Paris: Félix Alcan, 1912. Published in English as *The Elementary Forms of the Religious Life*. (i) Translated by Joseph W. Swain. New York: Free Press, 1915. (ii) Translated by Karen E. Fields. New York: Free Press, 1995. (iii) Translated by Carol Cosman. Oxford: Oxford University Press, 2001.

Mauss

"Essai sur le don: Forme et raison de l'échange dans les sociétés archaïques." *L'Année sociologique*, n.s. 1 (1925): 30–186. Published in English as: (i) *The Gift: Forms and Functions of Exchange in Archaic Societies*. Translated by Ian Cunnison. London: Cohen and West, 1954; (ii) *The Gift: The Form and Reason for Exchange in Archaic Societies*. Translated by W. D. Halls. London: Routledge, 1990.

Œuvres, 3 vols. Paris: Éditions de Minuit, 1968–9.

Sociologie et anthropologie. Paris: Presses Universitaires de France, 1968.

99. *Ibid.*, 198–9.

4

ANALYTIC AND CONTINENTAL TRADITIONS: FREGE, HUSSERL, CARNAP, AND HEIDEGGER

Michael Friedman and Thomas Ryckman

Gottlob Frege (1848–1925), Edmund Husserl (1859–1938), Rudolf Carnap (1891–1970), and Martin Heidegger (1889–1976) are universally acknowledged as key figures in the development of philosophy in the twentieth century and, in particular, as centrally important in the development of the well-known divide between what we now call the analytic and continental philosophical traditions. Frege, the patriarch of the analytic tradition, established modern mathematical logic as both a technical subject (now often pursued primarily in departments of mathematics and computer science) and a foundational discipline for philosophy. Carnap, one of Frege's very few students at the University of Jena in the years 1910–14, actively participated in the great transformation of mathematical logic that led to Kurt Gödel's fundamental contributions in the early 1930s;[1] and he also took Frege's (and Bertrand Russell's) conception of (mathematical) logic as the essence of philosophy several steps further – eventually leading (in 1934) to the radical idea that *Wissenschaftslogik* (the logic of science) should *replace* traditional philosophy entirely. Husserl, the patriarch of the twentieth-century continental tradition, established the new philosophical method of transcendental phenomenology, aiming (in a way quite different from Carnap) to "bracket" the ontological problems of traditional metaphysics and reconstitute philosophy as a scientific discipline. Heidegger, Husserl's most important assistant at the University of Freiburg in the late 1910s and early 1920s, then went on to disappoint his erstwhile mentor by establishing yet another radically new

1. See Erich Reck, "Carnap and Modern Logic," in *The Cambridge Companion to Carnap*, Michael Friedman and Richard Creath (eds) (Cambridge: Cambridge University Press, 2007), for discussion of Carnap's role in the further development of mathematical logic.

conception of philosophy – as phenomenological ontology or the existential hermeneutic of Dasein – in the late 1920s and early 1930s.

These two different traditions of philosophical thought appear, at first sight, to be completely at odds with one another. It is no wonder, then, that the increasing tension (and mutual incomprehension) between them crystallized in the early 1930s when Carnap published his well-known paper, "Überwindung der Metaphysik durch logische Analyse der Sprache" (Overcoming metaphysics through the logical analysis of language) (1932), featuring a blistering criticism of Heidegger's notorious sentence "*Das Nichts selbst nichtet*" (nothingness itself nothings) as a typical example of a metaphysical pseudo-sentence. After this, not surprisingly, the relationship between the two traditions went quickly downhill – hastened, in no small part, by the Nazi seizure of power in 1933 and the following migration of much of the German-speaking philosophical world (including Carnap) from central Europe to the United Kingdom or its dominions and the United States. The deep intellectual impasse characterizing most of the second half of the twentieth century between the analytic tradition, dominant in the English-speaking world, and the continental tradition, dominant in European lands, was the natural and inevitable result.[2]

Nevertheless, before the epoch-making events of the early 1930s, there was no such intellectual gulf within German academic philosophy. On the contrary, throughout the late 1910s and 1920s, logical empiricism (represented by Carnap and others), Husserlian transcendental phenomenology, neo-Kantianism (represented by the Southwest and Marburg Schools),[3] and Heidegger's new existential–hermeneutic variant of phenomenology were rather engaged in a fascinating series of philosophical exchanges and struggles, all addressed to the revolutionary changes that were then sweeping both the *Naturwissenschaften* and the *Geisteswissenschaften*. The differing philosophical movements of course disagreed with and opposed one another about the interpretation and significance of these revolutionary changes, but they still spoke the same philosophical language and actively engaged one another in a common set of philosophical problems. Moreover, many of these central points of both agreement and disagreement have their origin, as we shall see, in the earlier reactions of both Frege and Husserl to the profound developments in the foundations of mathematics of the late nineteenth century. For both were initially trained as mathema-

2. For a detailed consideration of the collision between Carnap and Heidegger over "metaphysical pseudo-sentences" in the early 1930s, together with extended discussion of its social and political context, see Michael Friedman, *A Parting of the Ways: Carnap, Cassirer, and Heidegger* (Chicago, IL: Open Court, 2000), on which we are drawing here. We shall return to this topic in §III below.

*3. For a detailed discussion of these schools, see the essay by Sebastian Luft and Fabien Capeillères in this volume.

ticians and were then led to philosophy by their deep (and somewhat different) interests in foundational problems.

Carnap's evolving engagement with these problems was also fundamentally shaped, unlike Frege's, by the influence of contemporary neo-Kantianism (especially as represented by the Marburg School), leading, in Carnap's case, to an even more serious divorce between formal logic and intuitive experience than in Frege. Whereas Heidegger's philosophy, after the fateful encounter with Carnap, was characterized by open hostility towards "logic and the scientific way of thinking," his earlier writings (including *Being and Time*) express a serious interest in early-twentieth-century developments in logic, the foundations of mathematics, and the foundations of natural science.[4] Moreover, although Heidegger's evolving perspective on these issues was importantly shaped by both Husserl and the historically oriented *Lebensphilosophie* of Wilhelm Dilthey,[5] he was also substantially influenced, like Carnap, by a thoroughgoing exposure to contemporary neo-Kantianism (here represented by the Southwest School). It turns out, therefore, that the original founders of the two traditions – even Carnap and Heidegger – had much more in common than may first appear. We shall argue, in particular, that one can go a long way toward understanding the divergent trajectories of the two traditions by concentrating on a single fundamental issue that divided them: the relative philosophical importance of the distinct but closely related disciplines Kant had called formal and transcendental logic.

I. FORMAL AND TRANSCENDENTAL LOGIC: THE KANTIAN LEGACY

Kant's *Critique of Pure Reason* is divided into two principal parts: a very long first part called the "Transcendental Doctrine of Elements," and a relatively brief second part called the "Transcendental Doctrine of Method." The "Transcendental Doctrine of Elements" is then divided, in turn, into a relatively brief first part called the "Transcendental Aesthetic" (concerning our two pure forms of sensible intuition, space and time) and a very long second part called the "Transcendental Logic" (comprising both the "Transcendental Analytic" and the "Transcendental Dialectic"). Kant begins the introduction to the second part (of the doctrine of elements) by enunciating his fundamental distinction between two distinct faculties of the mind, intuitive and conceptual:

4. We describe Heidegger's early writings on logic towards the end of §I (see, in particular, note 27 below). For Heidegger's interest in both the foundations of mathematics (formalism versus intuition) and the foundations of physics (relativity theory), see *Being and Time* §3.

*5. For a discussion of Dilthey, see the essay by Eric Sean Nelson in *The History of Continental Philosophy: Volume 2*.

> Our cognition arises from two fundamental sources in the mind, of which the first is [the faculty] to receive representations (receptivity of impressions), the second the faculty to cognize an object through these representations (spontaneity of concepts); through the first an object is *given* to us, through the second it is *thought* in relation to this representation (as mere determination of the mind). Intuition and concepts therefore constitute the elements of all our cognition, so that neither concepts without intuition in some way corresponding to them, nor intuition without concepts, can yield a cognition. Both are either pure or empirical.[6]

On this basis, Kant continues, "we distinguish the science of the rules of sensibility in general, i.e., aesthetic, from the science of the rules of the understanding in general, i.e., logic" (A52/B76). And what Kant first has in mind by "logic," in this context, is what he calls "general" or "formal" logic, characterized by the following two properties:

> 1) As general logic it abstracts from all contents of the cognition of the understanding and the diversity of its objects, and has to do with nothing but the mere form of thinking. 2) As pure logic it has no empirical principles, and thus it draws nothing from psychology (as one has sometimes allowed oneself to be persuaded), which therefore has no influence at all on the canon of the understanding. It is a demonstrated doctrine, and everything in it must be certain entirely a priori. (A54/B78)

Kant's own main concern, however, is a new type of logic, "transcendental" logic, which has the second property but not the first:

> General logic abstracts, as we have indicated, from all content of cognition, i.e., from all relation of it to the object, and considers only logical form in the relation of cognitions to one another, i.e., the form of thinking in general. But now since there are pure as well as empirical intuitions (as the transcendental aesthetic has shown), there could also be a distinction between pure and empirical thinking of objects. In this case there would be a logic [i.e., transcendental logic], in which one did not abstract from all content of

6. Kant, *Critique of Pure Reason*, A50/B74. All subsequent references to the *Critique of Pure Reason* are given parenthetically, as usual, via the A and B page numbers of the first (1781) and second (1787) editions respectively. All translations from the German are our own.

> cognitions; for that [logic] which contained merely the rules of the pure thinking of an object would exclude all those cognitions that were of empirical content. (A55/B79–80)

It is the task of transcendental logic, therefore, to relate the pure logical forms of thought comprising general logic to the pure forms of sensible intuition described in the "Transcendental Aesthetic"; and it is precisely this task that is then carried out in the "Transcendental Analytic."

But the rapid rise of scientific psychology in Germany in the second half of the nineteenth century prompted a renewed challenge to the sharp separation between logic and psychology originally ordained by Kant. With characteristic forthrightness, John Stuart Mill had already deemed logic to be a chapter of psychology:

> [Logic] is not a science distinct from, and coordinate with, Psychology. So far as it is a science at all, it is a part, or branch, of Psychology ... Its theoretical grounds are wholly borrowed from Psychology, and include as much of that science as is required to justify the rules of the art.[7]

A centerpiece of late-nineteenth-century materialism and naturalism, the reduction of logic to psychology was the research program of numerous psychologists and psychologistic logicians, who sought to show that the principles and laws of logic are rooted in empirical psychological (and ultimately, biological and chemical) laws governing actual mental processes. Accordingly, even the most basic principles of logic (including noncontradiction) were regarded as being about, and drawing their evidence from, a range of facts regarding the particular mental acts and processes of empirical cognizing subjects. The rejection of such views, first by Frege and then by Husserl, drew on the antipsychologism of German philosopher and logician Rudolph Hermann Lotze, and both Frege and Husserl accordingly attacked the psychological logicians' attempts to ground the objective and *a priori* validity of logical and mathematical principles or laws in the mental acts or psychic experiences (*Erlebnisse*) of the judging or reasoning subject.[8]

7. John Stuart Mill, *An Examination of Sir William Hamilton's Philosophy* (Boston, MA: William V. Spencer, 1865), 359.
8. For further discussion of this nineteenth-century background to both Frege and Husserl see Hans Sluga, *Gottlob Frege* (London: Routledge, 1980), and Michael Dummett, *The Origins of Analytic Philosophy* (Cambridge, MA: Harvard University Press, 1993). For the nineteenth-century logical background, more generally, to the analytic tradition compare J. Alberto Coffa, *The Semantic Tradition from Kant to Carnap: To the Vienna Station* (Cambridge: Cambridge

Frege's criticisms will be familiar to analytic philosophers. The laws of logic are not psychological laws, empirical generalizations describing how individuals actually reason, but are "laws prescribing the way one ought to think": universal laws of truth concerning what obtains with the utmost generality for all rational thinking. The domain of logic is neither more nor less than objective thought, considered solely with regard to truth and falsity. Descriptions of the mental are to be purged altogether from logic, where "psychological considerations have no more place … than they do in astronomy or geology." Indeed, logic is *sui generis*: a request for the justification of a law of logic is either answered by reduction to another law of logic or is not to be answered at all. Frege regarded any attempted justification of logic as inevitably circular, since logical laws and principles are presupposed by all rational inquiries. And this logocentrism is coupled with an objectivist and realist epistemology: knowledge is "an activity that does not create what is known but grasps what is already there," and, accordingly, "what is true" is "objective and independent of the judging subject." As the terminology of "grasping" suggests, Frege thus purchases his characterization of knowledge of logical and mathematical objects at the cost of a seeming Platonism about abstract objects, in particular, objective thoughts (*Gedanken*). Objective thoughts (e.g. the Pythagorean theorem) are not constituents of the stream of consciousness, but propositional bearers of truth-values: timeless objects of belief existing independently of being "grasped" by any subject.[9]

After Husserl had obtained a PhD in mathematics in Vienna in 1882, his interests turned to philosophy under the influence of Franz Brentano. Inspired by the latter's concept of intentionality as well as his injunction that philosophy can and must become scientific, Husserl began his philosophical career in earnest pursuit of Brentano's goal of showing that philosophy and logic are grounded in the laws of an empirical descriptive psychology. This is a principal thesis of his first book, *The Philosophy of Arithmetic* (1891), dedicated to Brentano. But Husserl's failure clearly to distinguish between numbers as ideal objects and as ideas or representations (*Vorstellungen*) in the cognitive acts of counting, collecting, and comparing was subjected to a withering review by Frege in 1894. It has been long and widely believed that Frege's caustic criti-

University Press, 1991). A more detailed discussion of this background in relation to both Husserl and Carnap is provided by Thomas Ryckman, "Carnap and Husserl," in Friedman and Creath, *The Cambridge Companion to Carnap*, on which we are drawing here.

9. See Gottlob Frege, *Grundgesetze der Arithmetik, begriffsschriftlich abgeleitet*, 2 vols (Jena: Pohle, 1893–1903), vol. 1, xv–xxvi; *The Basic Laws of Arithmetic: An Exposition of the System* (Berkeley, CA: University of California Press, 1967), 13–25, esp. 15, 23. In particular, Frege terms the laws of logic "the most general laws, which prescribe the way in which one ought to think if one is to think at all" (*Grundgesetze*, xv; *The Basic Laws*, 12). Compare Rudolf Hermann Lotze, *Logik* (Leipzig: Hirzel, 1874), §332.

cism converted Husserl from seeking a psychological foundation for logic and that subsequently Husserl joined Frege in a common critique of that program.[10] Nevertheless, recent studies argue in favor of Husserl's own later claim that he came independently to the rejection of psychologism in logic for motivations immanent within his own agenda.[11] One of these motivations, as evidenced by Husserl's generous references throughout the *Logical Investigations* (1900–1901), was his reading of Bernard Bolzano's (1781–1848) *Wissenschaftslehre* (1837). In the first two books of this neglected four-volume work (entitled *A Theory of Ideas in Themselves* and *A Theory of Propositions in Themselves*, respectively), Husserl found that "a complete plan of a 'pure' logic was already available."[12]

Furthermore, and in sharp contrast to Frege, Husserl regards the distinction between the descriptive and the normative as having little to do with the critique of psychologism. Instead, Husserl maintains that all normative sciences depend on theoretical sciences and, in particular, that applied logic, the technique of reasoning for a practical purpose, is itself grounded on a very general theoretical science termed, following Kant, Bolzano, and Lotze, "pure logic" (*reine Logik*). The basic error of psychologism is its conflation of pure and applied logic, resulting in a misinterpretation of the pure laws of logic as empirical laws of psychology. Like Frege, the first volume of the *Logical Investigations*, subtitled *Prolegomena to a Pure Logic* (1900), argues that psychologism in logic inexorably leads to skepticism and relativism. But already in the early 1890s, and perhaps even by 1891, Husserl had acquired the un-Fregean view that the fundamental contrast between logic and psychology lies in the circumstance that logical and mathematical objects are presented or given to the mind in a quite specific

10. See Marvin Farber, *The Foundation of Phenomenology: Edmund Husserl and the Quest for a Rigorous Science of Philosophy* (Albany, NY: SUNY Press, 1943), 54–8, and Dagfinn Føllesdal, *Husserl und Frege: Ein Beitrag zur Beleuchtung der Entstehung der phänomenologischen Philosophie* (Oslo: Aschehoug, 1958). Husserl indeed frankly criticized his earlier psychologism in the first volume (*Prolegomena to a Pure Logic*) of his *Logical Investigations* (1900–1901), but the alleged role of Frege in Husserl's conversion is puzzlingly not documented there, being limited to a footnote in which Husserl retracted his earlier criticism of Frege's antipsychologism while warmly commending the reader to the Preface to Frege's *Grundgesetze* (1893).
11. Edmund Husserl, "Entwurf einer 'Vorrede' zu den Logischen Untersuchungen," Eugen Fink (ed.), *Tijdschrift voor Philosophie* 1 (1939), §6. The case for Husserl's autonomous development is argued in Dallas Willard, *Logic and the Objectivity of Knowledge: A Study in Husserl's Early Philosophy* (Athens, OH: Ohio University Press, 1984), and J. N. Mohanty, "Husserl and Frege: A New Look at Their Relationship," in *Husserl, Intentionality and Cognitive Science*, Hubert Dreyfus (ed.); see, however, the reply to Mohanty by Føllesdal, "Response (to Mohanty)," in Dreyfus, *Husserl, Intentionality and Cognitive Science.*
12. See Edmund Husserl, *Introduction to the Logical Investigations: A Draft of a Preface to the Logical Investigations 1913*, P. J. Bossert and C. H. Peters (trans.) (The Hague: Martinus Nijhoff, 1975), 37.

fashion that lends them an identity distinct from the various individual psychic acts through which they are given. Thus, on the one hand, Husserl's alternative to Frege's antipsychologism took its first inspiration from Bolzano's conception of logic as the study of "propositions in themselves" (*Sätze an sich*), having no more relation to psychology than do the propositions of mathematics. And, on the other hand, Husserl regarded "propositions in themselves" as "metaphysical abstrusities (*sic*)"[13] – and so he rejected the Platonism common to both Bolzano and Frege. It was only on reading Lotze that Husserl came to see that reference to such entities was but reference to the "sense" of statements of a pure logic, and that they crucially possessed the property Lotze had termed "validity" (*Geltung*). In particular, Lotze interpreted the Platonism of earlier writers in the tradition of pure logic (such as Bolzano) in a deontologized fashion, so that the notion of "validity" pertains to the peculiar way in which the systematic forms of thought comprising pure logic are ideal and independent of particular thinkers but *not* independent of mind as such. In a sense to be further articulated by Husserl, pure logic is formal in that it is regarded as the science of these ideal forms of thought.[14]

Husserl's conception of pure logic thereby returns, in part, to Kant's conception of transcendental logic. For we are not concerned solely with abstract "propositions in themselves" (as in Bolzano or Frege) but also, and centrally, with the location or origin of these within the cognitive capacities of a pure or transcendental *subject*.[15] Unlike Kant, however, Husserl has no room for a sharp dichotomy

13. *Ibid.*, 37 n.12.
14. See Husserl in "A Reply to a Critic of My Refutation of Logical Psychologism": "I saw that under 'proposition in itself' is to be understood, then, what is designated in ordinary discourse – which objectifies the ideal – as the 'sense' of a statement. It is that which is explained as one and the same where, for example, different persons are said to have asserted the same thing. … And it further became clear to me that this identical sense could be nothing other than the universal, the species, which belongs to a certain *moment* or phase present in all actual assertions with the same sense, and which makes possible the identification [of sameness] just mentioned. … The proposition [*Satz*] thus relates to those acts of judgment to which it belongs as their identical intention [*Meinung*] in the same way as the species *redness* relates to individuals of 'the same' red color. Now with this view of things as a basis, Bolzano's theory, that propositions are objects which nonetheless have no 'existence' [*Existenz*], comes to have the following quite intelligible signification: They have the 'ideal' being [*Sein*] or validity [*Gelten*] of objects which are universals [*allgemeiner Gegenstände*]; and thus that being which is established, for example, in the 'existence proofs' of mathematics. But they do not have the real being of things, or of dependent, thing-like *moments* – of temporal particulars in general. Bolzano himself did not give the faintest intimation that these phenomenological relationships between signification, signification moment, and full act of signifying had been noticed by him" (in *Husserl: Shorter Works*, Peter McCormick and Frederick Elliston [eds] [Notre Dame, IN: University of Notre Dame Press, 1981], 154).
15. Compare Kant in the *Critique of Pure Reason*: "[Transcendental logic] would also concern the origin of our cognitions of objects, in so far as it cannot be ascribed to the objects; while general logic, by contrast, has nothing to do with this origin of cognition, but rather considers

between two distinct faculties of the mind, a purely conceptual faculty of understanding and a purely sensible faculty of intuition. On the contrary, all cognition, for Husserl, is necessarily both conceptual and intuitive, insofar as what Husserl calls "essential intuition" (*Wesenschau, Wesenserchauung*) immediately presents us (in the manner of direct intuition) with a (universal or conceptual) essence. Thus, whereas Bolzano, for example, explicitly opposed Kant on the need for intuition in mathematical analysis in favor of a purely logical, purely conceptual treatment of this subject,[16] Husserl rejected the very distinction between intuition and concepts with his doctrine that both logic and mathematical analysis rests on "formal" or "categorial" intuition having no relation (as does geometry) to any particular "material" subject matter given in sense perception.[17]

As programmatically outlined in the first volume of the *Logical Investigations*, pure logic is the domain of concepts such as truth, object, sense, proposition, syllogism, ground, and consequence. Inspired by the Leibnizean idea of a *mathesis universalis*, it considers "pure logico-grammatical forms" without regard to the actual knowing, judging, inferring, representing, and proving of any individual cognizing subject. The laws of pure logic possess "'eternal' validity" (*"ewige"*

representations, whether they are originally given a priori in ourselves or only empirically, merely according to those laws, in accordance with which the understanding brings them in relation to one another when it thinks, and therefore [general logic] deals only with the form of the understanding that can be provided for the representations, wherever they may have originated" (A55–6/B80).

16. As its title intimates, Bolzano's most significant mathematical work, his proof of the intermediate value theorem (1817), is explicitly a "purely conceptual" result, pointedly eschewing any reliance on spatiotemporal intuition (as in a spatial curve described by "continuous" motion). As such, it is an early precursor of the program of "arithmetization" of analysis subsequently carried out by Augustin-Louis Cauchy, Richard Dedekind, Leopold Kronecker, and Karl Weierstrass. Husserl studied under the latter two in Berlin in the late 1870s and early 1880s, serving as Weierstrass's assistant in 1883–84, and indeed Husserl would say that it was from Weierstrass that he had acquired "the ethos of my scientific endeavors"; see Karl Schuhmann, *Husserl-Kronik* (The Hague: Martinus Nijhoff, 1977), 7. While Husserl's conception of "Philosophy as a Rigorous Science" (1911) took as its model of rigor Weierstrass's grounding of higher analysis in elementary arithmetic, it is indicative of Husserl's more philosophically radical approach that he sought, in the *Philosophy of Arithmetic*, to extend Weierstrass's critical project by scrutinizing the concept of number itself. As described above, this led, once freed from the psychologism inherent in Brentano's conception of philosophy, to the development of phenomenology.
17. Husserl holds that, unlike logic and the sciences of number, pure geometry, as a formal conceptual structure, is an idealization of perceived space, which itself is an idealization from the space of actual experience. In the language of *Ideen zu einer reinen Phänomenologie und phänomenologischen Philosophie* (*Ideas Pertaining to a Pure Phenomenology and to a Phenomenological Philosophy*; hereafter *Ideas*) (1913), in *Husserliana* (hereafter *Hua*; Dordrecht: Kluwer, 1951–), vol. 3, §§8–9, geometry is thus a "material," not a "formal" eidetic science – "the *ontological discipline relating to an essential moment of material thinghood,* namely, *spatial form*." See also note 19 below.

Geltung), a validity guaranteed *a priori* through knowledge of their conceptual essence; and this knowledge, in turn, is obtained from intuition of categorial forms to which nothing perceptual corresponds. For Husserl, the ideality and *a priori* truth characteristic of the propositions of pure logic (and the more abstract parts of mathematics) involve a type of evidence presented only in directed intentional acts of categorial intuition. Unlike intuitions in Kant's sense, therefore, categorial intuitions present us with an "essence" (an abstract object) immediately and directly as an intentional unity of distinct acts of signification, a "givenness" that is inextricably conceptual as well as conceptually determined. In this way, intricate patterns of "validity-foundings" (*Geltungsfundierungen*) can be described, showing how particular ideal meanings are founded on or presuppose others.

By refashioning Lotze's inchoate doctrine of validity into the phenomenological method of essential intuition, Husserl's earlier analyses of the psychological origin of the basic concepts of arithmetic are transformed into descriptive phenomenological analyses of structures of intentionality underlying the ideal validity of the objects of logic and pure mathematics. Thus, whereas Frege (and, following him, Carnap) understood late-nineteenth-century mathematical developments (primarily the "rigorization" and eventual "arithmetization" of analysis) as pointing in the direction of a purely logical foundation for mathematics (arithmetic and analysis) making no reference to intuition whatsoever, Husserl drew from a different, more geometrical strand (involving the *n*-dimensional spaces or "manifolds" of Riemann and Helmholtz, Grassmann's *Ausdehnungslehre*, and Lie's continuous transformation groups[18]) in articulating a foundation in categorial intuition for the basic laws of logic themselves.[19]

18. Bernhard Riemann (1826–66) was a German mathematician whose 1854 *Habilitationsvortrag*, "On the Hypotheses which Lie at the Basis of Geometry," is among the most influential documents of modern mathematics. In it, Riemann extended differential geometry, hitherto applied only on two-dimensional surfaces, to what he termed *n-dimensional manifolds*, positing a differential expression for metrical relations between nearby points. Hermann von Helmholtz (1821–94) was a German physicist, physiologist, and philosopher of science. Helmholtz's (1868) paper "On the Facts Underlying Geometry" is an attempt to derive the Riemannian metrical expression from "facts" regarding the "free mobility" of rigid bodies. However, Helmholtz's condition of free mobility picks out only a restricted class of Riemannian manifolds: those with constant curvature. Sophus Lie (1842–99) was a Norwegian mathematician and founder of the theory of continuous transformation groups. These (so-called "Lie") groups were originally employed in the theory of differential equations, but Lie subsequently gave them a geometrical application, showing that they describe the set of rigid motions identified by Helmholtz's "free mobility." Hermann Grassmann (1809–77) was a German linguist and mathematician. Grassmann's major work, his 1844 *Die Lineare Ausdehnungslehre* (Theory of linear extension), formulated an algebraic theory of higher dimensional spaces, essentially *n-dimensional linear vector spaces*.
19. Although Frege sharply opposed Kant's doctrine of the role of pure intuition in arithmetic, looking for a foundation in pure logic for this science (and for the science of analysis), he

According to Husserl, phenomenology was transformed from a purely descriptive psychology to transcendental phenomenology by pursuit of the main themes of the *Logical Investigations*, resulting in the distinctive form of "transcendental phenomenological idealism" articulated in the *Ideen zu einer reinen Phänomenologie und phänomenologischen Philosophie* (*Ideas Pertaining to a Pure Phenomenology and to a Phenomenological Philosophy*, 1913).[20] Whereas the logician is concerned with *a priori* truths of ideal objectivities (just as the number theorist is concerned with numbers and the truths of arithmetic), the thesis of intentionality led to the view that meaning-constituting experiences (if only of an idealized subject) are necessarily correlated with any object of knowledge. Thus, the phenomenological discovery of the meaning-constituting acts of consciousness in the context of mathematical and logical idealities was extended to all objects. Through a step-wise progression of acts of reflection undertaken within inner intuition, each directed toward a normally unthematized particular conscious experience, the character and limitations of each are successively exhibited, together with their possible interconnections to strata more deeply embedded in preconscious experience. The goal is to uncover and bring to full consciousness the multiplicity and structure of the subjective acts through which the intended objects are invested with objective meaning.

For Husserl, therefore, transcendental phenomenology is constitutional analysis: that is, the intentional analysis of how an object is continuously constituted, with respect to its sense and validity, in the interconnections of all acts of consciousness directed towards it. But this is not to say that the object, whose

nonetheless followed the Kantian doctrine that the science of geometry, in particular, is based on our pure intuition of space (and is therefore *synthetic a priori*). Like Bolzano, then, Frege operated wholly within the Kantian conception of intuition, but he denied that any such intuition was needed in either arithmetic or analysis. Husserl, by contrast, is breaking with the Kantian conception completely: whereas arithmetic and analysis are based on formal or categorial intuition, the science of geometry is based on a *material* essential intuition having the essences of specifically spatial forms as its object (cf. note 17 above). In the terminology of *Ideas*, therefore, whereas logic, arithmetic, and analysis are completely universal or formal eidetic sciences, geometry is a regional or material eidetic science.

20. The characterization of phenomenology as "descriptive psychology" in the first edition of the *Logical Investigations* ("Introduction" to vol. 2, 1901) was later regarded as "misleading" and removed in the second (1913) edition: see "Translator's Note," in *Logical Investigations*, J. N. Findlay (trans.) (New York: Humanities Press, 1970), vol. 1, 262. Many phenomenologists resisted Husserl's "transcendental turn" away from "the things themselves [*die Sachen selbst*]" toward subjectivity as the ultimate stratum of phenomenological investigation, viewing it as a return to subjective idealism or even psychologism. For the controversy, see Herbert Spiegelberg, *The Phenomenological Movement: A Historical Introduction*, 3rd ed. (The Hague: Martinus Nijhoff, 1982). Husserl's own retrospective (1913) account of this transition – see his "Entwurf einer 'Vorrede' zu den Logischen Untersuchungen" – was not published during his lifetime.

sense may be that of a mind-transcendent object, is produced by consciousness, as subjective idealism absurdly maintains. Rather, constitution is a matter of "sense-bestowal through transcendental subjectivity," and the task of constitutive analysis is to investigate how objects, exclusively considered as accomplishments of intentional acts, are ongoing unities of "sense formation" arising against the background of previous sense formations. In this sense, transcendental constitution presupposes a purely methodological "bracketing" (*epochē*) or "phenomenological reduction," leaving the world of objects of science and everyday life "as is" but suspending or "putting out of action" the usual assumptions regarding the mind-independent existence of these objects. It is the attempt to understand the meaning of "mind-independent" being as arising within an object's "sedimented" sense-history, a history to be transcendentally reconstructed and clarified as an accumulating achievement within conscious experience in the broadest sense.[21]

Only in later works did Husserl consider extending the phenomenological reduction, the *epochē*, "to formal logic and *mathesis* in its entirety." By making these objects "essentially evident by observing consciousness itself in its pure immanence," transcendental phenomenology seeks to discover the "transcendental subjectivity" underlying the objects of logic and mathematics, "the a priori other side of genuine objectivity."[22] As in Kant, it then becomes the task of a transcendental logic to seek "in subjectivity, or more precisely, the correlation between subjectivity and the objective, the ultimate determination of the sense of objectivity, as apprehended in cognition."[23] These correlations of the

21. See Thomas Ryckman, *The Reign of Relativity: Philosophy in Physics 1915–1925* (Oxford: Oxford University Press, 2005), for a reconstruction of the mathematician Hermann Weyl's attempt to implement something like Husserl's program of transcendental phenomenological constitution in the context of classical field physics (Einstein's theory of general relativity and Maxwell's theory of electromagnetism). In 1918, Weyl formulated the first unified field theory of gravitation and electromagnetism; the theory's epistemological core, heavily indebted to Husserlian transcendental phenomenological idealism, rested on what Weyl termed "the principle of the relativity of magnitude" (*Raum–Zeit–Materie: Vorlesungen über allgemeinen Relativitätstheorie. Dritte Auflage* [Berlin: J. Springer, 1919], 243), which essentially states that the laws of nature should be invariant under "arbitrary" changes of scale at neighboring space-time points. Although originating in the context of classical fields, Weyl's principle, when reformulated for quantum mechanics (where it pertains not to a factor of length but to a factor of phase of the wave function, as Weyl himself later showed) is the progenitor of local gauge invariance, currently the unifying principle of the standard model of fundamental interactions, the cornerstone of the present understanding of elementary particles and the forces that act between them. See also Thomas Ryckman, "Hermann Weyl and 'First Philosophy': Constituting Gauge Invariance," in *Constituting Objectivity: Transcendental Perspectives on Modern Physics*, Michel Bitbol *et al.* (eds) (Dordrecht: Springer, 2009.
22. Edmund Husserl, *Formale und transzendentale Logik* (1929), in *Hua*, vol. 27, §100.
23. Edmund Husserl, *Erster Philosophie, I*, in *Hua*, vol. 7, 386.

formal objects of logic and mathematics with subjective processes of experiencing are treated schematically in the *Logical Investigations* but elaborated far more extensively in *Formal and Transcendental Logic* (1929) as well as other writings that remained unpublished in Husserl's lifetime. Transcendental logic is "foundational" only in a novel sense: its aim is the clarification of the fundamental concepts of logic and mathematics by showing how the sense of these ideal objectivities arises within "transcendental subjectivity," through "originary" sense-bestowing acts of pure consciousness. Increasingly prominent in these last writings, the account of the constitution of logical and mathematical objects within transcendental subjectivity ultimately rests on the phenomenological description of the "life-world" (*Lebenswelt*), the world of ordinary activities and beliefs whose prelogical validities act as grounds for the logical ones. Through the phenomenological reduction, these practices, as intentional acts, become the objects of phenomenological reflection, disclosing how their sense formations arise, structuring the experience characteristic of the life-world. In particular, Husserl famously argues that geometry originates within meaning-conferring acts, revealed through phenomenological investigation of the life-world.[24]

Carnap, as we noted, studied with Frege at the University of Jena in the years 1910–14. After the First World War he first returned to Jena in the years 1919–22, where he completed his doctoral dissertation, *Der Raum* (1921/2), and he then lived in the town of Buchenbach, near Freiburg, from 1922 to 1926. Carnap had already become seriously interested in phenomenology during the years 1919–22, for he makes very significant use of the Husserlian notion of essential intuition in his dissertation. Indeed, not only does he use this latter notion to defend a modified version of the Kantian conception of pure *spatial* intuition, but Carnap also embraces Husserl's notion of formal or categorial intuition for the most general laws of formal logic. After completing his dissertation, Carnap then turned in earnest to the project of *Der logische Aufbau der Welt* (hereafter *Aufbau*; 1928) in the years 1922–25, and it was this project, in particular, that then facilitated his introduction to the Philosophical Circle surrounding Moritz Schlick at the University of Vienna in 1925. While working on the *Aufbau*,

24. In his late work, *The Crisis of the European Sciences and Transcendental Phenomenology* (1936–37), the English translation of which includes his 1936 paper on "The Origin of Geometry," Husserl is concerned to exhibit the historical genesis through which the process of geometrical idealization has transpired, from practical activities of measuring and surveying to the triumph of the geometrical method in classical physics, as "a general method of knowing the real." This illustrates a highly significant shift in emphasis in Husserl's thought, from considering constitution principally as an achievement of the individual transcendental ego (termed, by later commentators, "static constitution") to viewing it more generally as an intersubjective achievement, in that the layers of meaning investing and informing a given constituted object may have origins extending back in cultural and historical time ("genetic constitution").

Carnap attended some of Husserl's seminars at Freiburg in 1924 and 1925, and the resulting philosophical conception very clearly shows this influence.[25]

In particular, the project of the *Aufbau* is also called a "constitutional theory" (*Konstitutionstheorie*), and, more specifically, a "constitutional theory of the objects of cognition."[26] Unlike in his doctoral dissertation, however, Carnap has now left all traces of Husserlian essential intuition (and of the Kantian synthetic *a priori*) entirely behind. In particular, the *Aufbau* presupposes only the theory of logical types of A. N. Whitehead and Russell's *Principia Mathematica* (1910–13) as the objectifying framework of a theory of constitution, lending the term "constitution" a precise meaning within the language of logic. It articulates the goal of a "rational reconstruction" of the (simply assumed) system of scientific knowledge via an extensional "constitutional system of concepts" wherein each scientific concept is definable in constructive step-by-step fashion from concepts of lower levels, ultimately from primitive concepts pertaining to the subjective sensory data or "elementary experiences" of a single subject. On account of the transitivity of reducibility, the principal thesis of Carnap's constitutional theory states that any scientific concept can be reduced, via logical chains of definition, to the primitive ones, thus reconstructing each concept in the epistemically privileged terms of first-person experiential content while simultaneously avoiding all (purely subjective) ostensive definitions (*Aufbau* §§1, 13–16). Logical construction thus provides "a rational justification of intuition," insofar as "intuitive understanding" is now everywhere replaced with "discursive reasoning" (§§54, 100, 143). This automatically excludes any extra-logical justification of logical laws and principles.

Carnap's *logocentrism* thus points to the vast abyss separating the constitutive approach of the *Aufbau* from transcendental phenomenology. Just as, for Carnap, all talk of "intuition" must be logically reconstructed, all talk of "acts of constitution" executed by a "transcendental subject" must similarly be replaced by purely logical constructions. Whereas all objects are indeed constituted from a "given" basis of first-personal (autopsychological) elementary experiences, it is a central thesis of Carnap's construction that "the given has no subject" (§65). More generally, whereas we can, if we like, describe Carnapian constitution in terms of the successive operations carried out by a cognitive subject, Carnap is very clear that this mode of speaking is merely a "fiction" whereby we vividly

25. See Herbert Spiegelberg, *The Context of the Phenomenological Movement* (The Hague: Martinus Nijhoff, 1981). Thomas Mormann, in *Rudolf Carnap* (Munich: C. H. Beck, 2000), speculates that Carnap moved to Buchenbach in 1922 to be in a position to interact and study with Husserl.

26. Carnap described the *Aufbau* project this way in his lectures to Schlick's Philosophical Circle in 1925; see Friedman, *A Parting of the Ways*, 70. It was on the basis of these lectures that Carnap then joined the Circle (soon to be named the Vienna Circle) as Schlick's assistant in 1926.

represent the true purely logical procedure of step-wise definition (§99). In particular, all it ultimately means to "constitute" an object from "the given" is that we have a chain of logical definitions within the type-theory of *Principia Mathematica* leading from a single basic relation between elementary experiences (remembrance of part-similarity) to the object in question. Formal logic, in this sense, wholly takes the place of transcendental logic.

Heidegger studied at the University of Freiburg in the years 1910–15, completing his habilitation in philosophy under Heinrich Rickert in 1915. Rickert was a neo-Kantian strongly influenced by the "pure logic" tradition; and Heidegger's earliest writings are largely concerned with this tradition and its ensuing problematic. Heidegger's first publication, "Neuere Forschungen über Logik" (1912), is a critical review of recent contributions to logic with particular emphasis on the need to overcome psychologism. His doctoral dissertation, *Die Lehre vom Urteil im Psychologismus* (1913), is a much more extended treatment of the same theme, which exposes some of the most popular current theories of judgment as psychologistic and therefore unacceptable. Finally, Heidegger's habilitation, *Die Kategorien- und Bedeutungslehre des Duns Scotus* (1915), is a reading of the *Grammaticae speculativae* (which was then attributed to Scotus) through the lenses of the contemporary logical investigations of Rickert, Husserl, and Emil Lask.[27]

Heidegger's early investigations revolve around the central distinctions between psychological act and logical content, between real thought process and ideal atemporal "sense," between being (*Sein*) and validity (*Geltung*). For, as Lotze in particular has shown, the realm of pure logic has a completely different mode of existence (validity) than that of the realm of actual spatiotemporal entities (being).[28] Moreover, as Rickert has shown, the realm of pure logic (the realm of validity) is also distinct from that of mathematics. For, although the latter is equally atemporal and hence ideal, it presupposes the existence of a particular object – the existence of "quantity" or a homogeneous serial order – and therefore lacks the complete generality characteristic of logic. It follows that we must sharply distinguish the realm of pure logic both from the given heterogeneous qualitative continuum of empirical reality and from the homogeneous quanti-

27. All three works are reprinted in Martin Heidegger, *Frühe Schriften*, *Gesamtausgabe* vol. 1 (Frankfurt: Klostermann, 1978), to which we refer in our citations. It is interesting to note that among the logical works Heidegger comments on are some of Frege's (on which Heidegger comments positively; cf. *Frühe Schriften*, 20) and Russell's (on which Heidegger comments negatively; cf. *Frühe Schriften*, 42–3, 174). Heidegger seems to see in Frege's ideas a concern for *meaning* appropriate to a "philosophical" logic, whereas Russell's work appears to him to tend in the direction of a mere "calculus," and is thereby divorced from the genuine problem of judgment. We shall return to the important influence of Lask in §II below.

28. The reference is to Lotze, *Logik*, §§316–20; see e.g. Heidegger, *Frühe Schriften*, 170.

tative continuum of mathematics.[29] In emphasizing these fundamental distinctions, and, above all, in maintaining "*the absolute primacy of valid sense* [*den absoluten Primat des geltenden Sinnes*],"[30] Heidegger shows himself indeed to be a faithful follower of Rickert.

It then becomes radically unclear, however, how the purely logical realm of valid sense is connected with the real world of temporal being (*Sein*): with either the realm of empirical nature where the objects of our (empirical) cognition reside or the realm of psychological happenings where our acts of judgment reside. Rickert himself responds to this problem by appealing to "transcendental psychology." As he explains in the Preface to the third edition of *Der Gegenstand der Erkenntnis* (1915), it is precisely the role of the transcendental subject (in Rickert's own terms, the "cognitive subject" or "theoretical subject") to bind the realms of being and validity together:

> We thus arrive at two worlds, a [world of] being [*einer seinden*] and a [world of] validity [*einer geltenden*]. But between them stands the theoretical subject, which binds the two together through its *judgments*, whose essence only becomes understandable in this way, and without which we could not meaningfully speak of existent [*seienden*] or real "objects" of cognition.[31]

Unfortunately, however, Rickert is never able to develop in any detail a transcendental psychology that could perform this "binding" role.

Heidegger, for his part, is very sensitive indeed to the difficult position in which Rickert has become entangled, and, accordingly, he also thinks that some version of transcendental psychology is necessary. For Heidegger, however, it is above all the phenomenology of Husserl that offers us a way out of Rickert's impasse:

> [T]he sharp separation of logic from psychology is perhaps not achievable. We must distinguish here. It is one question whether psychology founds logic in principle and secures its *validity* [*Geltungswert*], it is another whether it assumes the role of its primary theater of action and basis of operation. And the second is in fact the case; for we are

29. See Heidegger, *Frühe Schriften*, 214–89; as Heidegger notes, his discussion here is based on Rickert's "Das Eine, die Einheit und die Eins," *Logos* 2 (1911).
30. See Heidegger, *Frühe Schriften*, 273. The realm of valid sense enjoys this primacy because *all* realms of existence as such (the natural, the metaphysical–theological, the mathematical, and the logical itself) become objects of our cognition only through the mediation of the logical realm (*ibid.*, 287).
31. Heinrich Rickert, *Der Gegenstand der Erkenntnis*, 3rd ed. (Tübingen: J. C. B. Mohr, 1915), xi.

> here concerned precisely with the remarkable fact, which perhaps involves problems that can never be completely illuminated, that the logical is embedded in the psychological. But this just determined role of psychology requires to be made more precise. Experimental psychology remains irrelevant for logic. Moreover, even so-called introspective [*selbstbeobachtende*] psychology only becomes relevant from a particular point of view. The investigation concerns the *meanings*, the *sense* of the acts and thus becomes theory of meaning, *phenomenology* of consciousness. Husserl, simultaneously with the critical rejection of psychologism, also theoretically grounded phenomenology in a positive fashion and himself made fruitful contributions to this difficult subject.[32]

Whereas Rickert himself had serious doubts whether Husserl's phenomenology can fulfill the function of what he calls "transcendental psychology," Heidegger is now convinced that only Husserlian phenomenology can possibly play this role.

When, in 1916, Rickert left Freiburg to take Wilhelm Windelband's position at Heidelberg, and Husserl left Göttingen to take Rickert's position at Freiburg, Heidegger became an enthusiastic proponent of the new phenomenology and, in particular, distanced himself further and further from Rickert.[33] Nevertheless, in the very same year, in a concluding chapter added to the published version of his habilitation, there also appear rumblings in a new and quite un-Husserlian direction. For Heidegger this suggests that a genuine reconciliation of psychology and logic – here equated with a reconciliation of change and absolute validity, time and eternity – can be effected only through the concept of "living spirit" (*der lebendige Geist*) construed as a concrete and essentially historical subject. The "subjective logic" sought by Rickert and Husserl requires a radically new

32. Heidegger, *Frühe Schriften*, 29–30. Heidegger adds a note at "*phenomenology*" citing Husserl's "Philosophie als strenge Wissenschaft."

33. This distance from Rickert becomes quite extreme by 1925–26, when Heidegger was completing *Being and Time*, and can be graphically seen in lectures Heidegger presented at Marburg in the summer semester of 1925 on the concept of time – see Martin Heidegger, *Prolegomena zur Geschichte des Zeitbegriffs* (*Gesamtausgabe* vol. 20 [Frankfurt: Klostermann, 1979]) – and in the winter semester of 1925–26 on logic – see Heidegger, *Logik: Die Frage nach der Wahrheit* (*Gesamtausgabe* vol. 21 [Frankfurt: Klostermann, 1976]). Heidegger speaks of Rickert with almost entirely undisguised contempt, whereas Husserl appears as the leader of a new "breakthrough" in philosophy, which, in particular, has definitively overcome neo-Kantianism. Extensive discussion of these lectures, together with Heidegger's other lecture courses leading up to *Being and Time*, can be found in Theodore Kisiel, *The Genesis of Heidegger's "Being and Time"* (Berkeley, CA: University of California Press, 1993). See also the essay by Miguel de Beistegui in this volume.

point of view according to which the subject is no merely cognitive ("punctiform") subject, but rather an actual concrete subject comprehending the entire fullness of its temporal–historical involvements. And such an investigation of the concrete historical subject, according to Heidegger, must now be a "trans-logical" or "metaphysical" investigation. Thus, Heidegger is here already beginning to come to terms with the historically oriented *Lebensphilosophie* of Dilthey, an influence that will prove decisive in *Being and Time* (1927).[34]

II. THE CATEGORIES OF OBJECTIVE EXPERIENCE: CARNAP, HEIDEGGER, AND THE NEO-KANTIANS

Both Carnap and Heidegger were philosophically trained within a neo-Kantian tradition that dominated the German-speaking world at the end of the nineteenth and beginning of the twentieth centuries. The two most influential movements or "schools" in this tradition were the Marburg School, founded by Hermann Cohen and then continued by Paul Natorp and Ernst Cassirer, and the Southwest School, founded by Windelband and then systematically developed by Rickert. Heidegger, as we noted, studied with Rickert at Freiburg and, in fact, completed his habilitation under Rickert in 1915. Carnap, for his part, studied Kant at Jena with Bruno Bauch (1877–1942) – also a student of Rickert's from Freiburg – and, in fact, completed his doctoral dissertation (*Der Raum*) under Bauch in 1921.[35] It is clear, moreover, that Carnap carefully studied several

34. See Heidegger, *Frühe Schriften*, 341–411. For Heidegger's assessment of Dilthey's conception of the subject as "living person with an understanding of active history," in contrast to Husserl's more formal conception of the subject, see Heidegger, *Prolegomena zur Geschichte des Zeitbegriffs*, 161–71. As is well known, in *Being and Time* Heidegger is quite explicit that the crucial chapter on "Temporality and History" (Division Two, ch. 5, §§72–7) depends fundamentally on Dilthey: "The just completed analysis of the problem of history has arisen out of the appropriation of Dilthey's work" (§77). The influence of Dilthey is further exhibited in 1916 in Heidegger's preface to his habilitation, with its call for philosophy to become *weltanschaulich*, that is, engaged in the concrete historical events of the time; see Heidegger, *Frühe Schriften*, 191; and cf. 205 n.10. This call contrasts sharply with Husserl's own arguments (*contra* Dilthey) that philosophy *as a science* must be eternally valid and thus essentially ahistorical; see Edmund Husserl, "Philosophie als strenge Wissenschaft" (1911), in *Hua*, vol. 25, 323–41; "Philosophy as a Rigorous Science," Quentin Lauer (trans.), in *Phenomenology and the Crisis of Philosophy* (New York: Harper & Row, 1965), 122–47.
35. At Jena, Bauch was a close colleague and associate of Frege's. After the First World War, for example, Frege joined Bauch's conservative Deutsche Philosophische Gesellschaft and published his last three papers ("Logical Investigations") in the official journal of this society, *Beiträge des deutschen Idealismus*. For Bauch and his relationship to Frege, see Hans Sluga, *Gottlob Frege*, and *Heidegger's Crisis: Philosophy and Politics in Nazi Germany* (Cambridge, MA: Harvard University Press, 1993). For Carnap's relationship to Bauch and neo-Kantianism more generally – including discussions of *Der Raum* – see Alan Richardson, *Carnap's*

versions of neo-Kantianism, including, in particular, the writings of Natorp, Cassirer, and Rickert.

Common to both schools of neo-Kantianism is a conception of the object of knowledge or judgment inherited from Kant.[36] Our true judgments should not be construed as representing entities existing independently of them, whether as the "transcendent" objects of the metaphysical realist existing "behind" our sense experience or the raw unconceptualized sense experience itself beloved of the empiricist. In the first case, true judgment would be impossible for us, since, by hypothesis, we have no independent access to such objects by which we could verify the desired relation of representation between them and our judgments. In the second case, true judgment would be equally impossible, for the stream of unconceptualized sense experience is utterly chaotic and intrinsically undifferentiated. Comparing the articulated structure of our judgments to this chaos of sensations therefore makes no sense. How, then, is knowledge or true judgment possible? What does it mean for our judgments to relate to an object? The answer is given by Kant's "Copernican Revolution." The object of knowledge does not exist independently of our judgments at all. It is, rather, first "constituted" when the unconceptualized data of sense are organized within the *a priori* logical structures of judgment itself; the initially unconceptualized data are thereby brought under *a priori* "categories" and thus become capable of empirical objectivity.

Yet there is a crucially important difference between this neo-Kantian account of the object of knowledge and Kant's original account. For Kant, we cannot explain how the object of knowledge becomes possible on the basis of the *a priori* logical structures of judgment alone. We need additional *a priori* structures – the pure forms of sensible intuition – that mediate the pure forms of judgment comprising what Kant calls general (or formal) logic and the unconceptualized manifold of impressions supplied by the senses. The pure logical forms of judgment thus only become *categories* in virtue of the transcendental schematism of the understanding – that is, when pure forms of thought are given a determinate spatiotemporal content in relation to the pure forms of sensible intuition. The pure logical form of a categorical judgment, for example, becomes the category

Construction of the World: The "Aufbau" and the Emergence of Logical Empiricism (Cambridge: Cambridge University Press, 1998), and Friedman, *A Parting of the Ways*.

36. Some of the most important epistemological works of the two traditions are: Cassirer, *Substanzbegriff und Funktionsbegriff: Untersuchungen über die Grundfragen der Erkenntniskritik*; Cohen, *Logik der reinen Erkenntnis*; Natorp, *Die logischen Grundlagen der exakten Wissenschaften*; and Rickert, *Der Gegenstand der Erkenntnis*. Very useful summary presentations of the basic ideas of the two traditions can be found in Heinrich Rickert, "Zwei Wege der Erkenntnistheorie," *Kant-Studien* 14 (1909), and Paul Natorp, "Kant und die Marburger Schule," *Kant-Studien* 17 (1912).

of *substance* when it is schematized in terms of the temporal representation of permanence; the pure logical form of a hypothetical judgment becomes the category of *causality* when it is schematized in terms of the temporal representation of succession; and so on. For Kant, therefore, pure formal logic must, if it is to play an epistemological role, be supplemented by transcendental logic: an explanation of how logical forms become schematized in terms of pure spatio-temporal representations belonging to the independent faculty of pure intuition. And it is precisely this explanation, in particular, that forms the heart of the "Transcendental Analytic" of the *Critique of Pure Reason* – the so-called metaphysical and transcendental deductions of the categories.

Nevertheless, both versions of neo-Kantianism entirely reject the idea of an independent faculty of pure intuition. They here follow the tradition of post-Kantian idealism in vigorously opposing the dualistic conception of mind characteristic of Kant's own position: the radical distinction between a conceptual faculty of pure understanding and an intuitive faculty of pure sensibility. The *a priori* formal structures in virtue of which the object of knowledge becomes possible must therefore derive solely from the logical faculty of understanding. In particular, since space and time no longer function as independent forms of pure sensibility, the constitution of experience described by transcendental logic must now proceed on the basis of purely conceptual – *and thus essentially non-spatiotemporal* – *a priori* structures. And it is this last feature of their conception of epistemology that associates the neo-Kantians with the "pure logic" tradition derived from Bolzano, which had earlier arrived, as we have seen, at a conception of pure thought or pure logic whose subject matter is an essentially nontemporal, and therefore certainly not psychological, realm – an "ideal" (Platonic) realm of timeless formal logical structures.[37]

In any case, the "constitution" of experience described by transcendental logic must now proceed on the basis of purely conceptual *a priori* structures: formal logic must somehow take over the mediating role between *a priori* intellection and *a posteriori* sensible experience all by itself. The leading idea of the Marburg School – especially as developed in Cassirer's *Substance and Function*

37. As explained in Friedman, *A Parting of the Ways*, ch. 3, this point needs qualification in the case of the Marburg School, which attempted to avoid such Platonism by embedding formal logic within a transcendental logic depicting all cognitions of the understanding as belonging to a historical developmental process (in accordance with the "genetic" conception of knowledge). As we explained in §I above, Husserlian phenomenology is also predicated on a rejection of the original Kantian dichotomy between concepts and intuition. In contrast to both neo-Kantian traditions, however, Husserl does not give priority to concepts over intuition in his phenomenological method; on the contrary, he views all cognition, as we said, as a necessary *unity* of both elements (compare notes 17 and 19 above, together with the corresponding discussion in the main text).

– was to take as our most important "clue" to the fundamental structure of the intellect nineteenth-century developments in mathematics and mathematical physics, and not the traditional Aristotelian theory of the logical forms of judgment. For the modern concepts of function, relation, and series provide us with entirely new insights into our basic forms of concept formation, which we can then use to construct a new picture of the way in which the mind establishes a necessary relation to sense experience: namely, the so-called "genetic" conception of knowledge, wherein empirical knowledge, in particular, is now seen as a never-completed historical sequence of formal abstract structures somehow "converging" on the concrete object of experience as an ideal limit – as a forever unreachable ideal *X*.

The Southwest School, by contrast, decisively rejects this Marburg "mathematization" of formal logic. Formal logic remains Aristotelian syllogistic, so that mathematical thought, in particular, must be sharply distinguished from properly logical thought.[38] Hence, the concrete object of experience cannot be viewed as a formally constructed ideal limit (as conceived by the Marburg School), but must rather be viewed as a genuinely independent entity – given, as it was for Kant, in an independent "manifold of sensations" – standing over and against the original forms of thought expressing the purely logical structure of the intellect. Yet, since Kant's idea of an independent *a priori* faculty of pure intuition (to which the logical forms of thought are related by the transcendental schematism of the imagination) is also rejected, we are left with overwhelming problems in constructing any kind of mediating connection between formal logic on the one side and concrete sensory experience on the other. We are left with overwhelming problems, that is, in effecting a Kantian theory of the categories; and precisely these problems, as we shall see, then initiated the radically new (and explicitly anti-neo-Kantian) conception of the object of knowledge later articulated by Heidegger.

Although Carnap had defended a more orthodox Kantian position in his doctoral dissertation (where he retained an important role for the pure intuition of space), Carnap's own radical reconceptualization of epistemology in the *Aufbau* can be seen, at least in part, as a further development of the more mathematical "logicization" of experience effected by the Marburg School. In particular, by taking formal logic to be given by the new mathematical logic of Whitehead and Russell's *Principia Mathematica*, one can now show by logical construction how the initially entirely private and subjective "manifold of sensations" (Carnap's "elementary experiences") is successively "objectified" by application of the *a priori* formal structures of logic in a step-wise "constitution of reality."

38. See Rickert, "Das Eine, die Einheit und die Eins"; cf. note 29 above.

Carnap makes his debt to Cassirer and neo-Kantianism completely explicit here:

> Cassirer ([*Substanzbegriff und Funktionsbegriff*] 292ff.) has shown that a science having the goal of determining the individual through lawful interconnections [*Gesetzseszusammenhänge*] without its individuality being lost must apply, not class ("species") concepts, but rather relational concepts; for the latter can lead to the formation of series and thereby to the establishing of order-systems. It hereby also results that relations are necessary as first posits, since one can in fact easily make the transition from relations to classes, whereas the contrary procedure is only possible to a very limited extent.

The merit of having discovered the necessary basis of the constitutional system thereby belongs to two entirely different, and often mutually hostile, philosophical tendencies. *Positivism* has stressed that the sole *material* for cognition lies in the undigested [*unverarbeitet*] experiential *given*; here is to be sought the *basic elements* of the constitutional system. *Transcendental idealism*, however, especially the neo-Kantian tendency (Rickert, Cassirer, Bauch), has rightly emphasized that these elements do not suffice; *order-posits* [*Ordnungssetzungen*] must be added, our "basic relations" (*Aufbau* §75).

That Carnap has the genetic (*erzeugende*) conception of knowledge characteristic of the Marburg School specifically in mind here becomes especially clear later in the *Aufbau*, when Carnap describes his position this way:

> Constitutional theory and *transcendental idealism* agree in representing the following position: all objects of cognition are constituted (in idealistic language, are "generated in thought [*im Denken erzeugt*]"); and, moreover, the constituted objects are only objects of cognition *qua* logical forms constructed in a determinate way.
>
> (§177)

Nevertheless, constitutional theory does not conceive the real individual object of experience as an infinitely distant ideal limit; for, as Carnap emphasizes, all objects of knowledge are defined or "constituted" at definite finite ranks in the hierarchy of Russellian logical types:

> According to the conception of the Marburg School (cf. Natorp [*Die logischen Grundlagen der exakten Wissenschaften*] 18ff.), the object is the eternal X, its determination is an incompletable task. In opposition to this it is to be noted that finitely many determinations suffice

> for the constitution of the object – and thus for its univocal description among the objects in general. Once such a description is set up the object is no longer an X, but rather something univocally determined – whose complete description then certainly still remains an incompletable task. (§179)

As a result, as Carnap also emphasizes, there is no longer any need for the synthetic (as opposed to the purely logical or analytic) *a priori*. Since an object is always defined or "constituted" at a definite finite rank in the hierarchy of logical types, we can always separate those features of the object comprising its definition from those features that express further information about the object uncovered in the course of properly scientific investigation. Fully determining the latter is indeed an infinite task requiring the entire future progress of empirical science, but establishing the former is simply a matter of stipulation:

> After the first task, that of the constitution of the objects, follows as the second the task of investigating the remaining, non-constitutional properties and relations of the objects. The first task is solved through a stipulation, the second, on the other hand, through experience. (According to the conception of constitutional theory there are no other components in cognition than these two – the conventional and the empirical – and thus no synthetic a priori [components].) (§179)

Carnap thus overcomes even the attenuated version of the synthetic *a priori* characteristic of the Marburg genetic conception of knowledge, and, as we have already suggested, he thereby completely absorbs Kantian transcendental logic within pure formal logic.

We noted above that Heidegger's earliest writings revolved around the idea of pure logic and its resulting problematic. The most important of these writings, as we also suggested, was Heidegger's habilitation, *Die Kategorien- und Bedeutungslehre des Duns Scotus*, which examined logical doctrines then attributed to Scotus through the lens of the contemporary logical investigations of Rickert, Husserl, and Lask. What is now most important, from our present point of view, is that the work of Lask, in particular, was especially important for Heidegger's later development, for it was here that the deep tensions arising for the Southwest School in constructing a mediating connection between formal logic and concrete sensory experience emerged in their sharpest form.[39]

39. See note 33 above, together with the associated discussion in the main text, for Heidegger's evolving appreciation of these deep tensions arising within the Southwest School.

Lask was a brilliant student of Rickert's who held an associate professorship at Heidelberg before he was killed in the First World War in 1915. The basic argument of Lask's most important work, *Die Lehre vom Urteil* (1912), is that, whereas the Kantian philosophy has indeed closed the gap between knowledge and its object, we are nonetheless left with a new gap between what Lask calls "transcendental," "epistemological," or "material" logic on the one side and "formal" logic on the other. Formal logic is the subject matter of the theory of judgment: the realm of necessarily valid and timeless "senses," "objective thoughts," or "propositions in themselves" familiar under the rubric of pure logic. Transcendental or material logic, by contrast, is the theory of the categories: an explanation of how the concrete object of experience is made possible by the constitutive activity of thought. But, and here is the central point of Lask's argument, transcendental or material logic is *not* based on formal logic, and, accordingly, he explicitly rejects Kant's metaphysical deduction of the categories. For Lask, what is fundamental is the concrete, already categorized, real object of experience. The subject matter of formal logic (which includes all the structures of the traditional logical theory of judgment) only arises subsequently in an artificial process of abstraction, by which the originally unitary categorized object is broken down into form and matter, subject and predicate, and so on. Moreover, since this comes about owing to a fundamental weakness or peculiarity of our human understanding – our inability to grasp the unitary categorized object as a unity – the entire realm of "pure logic," despite its timeless and necessary character, is, in the end, nothing but an artificially constructed intermediary possessing no explanatory power whatsoever.

The importance of Lask's work for Heidegger's later development is clearly evident in a crucial section of *Being and Time* on "Dasein, Disclosedness, and Truth" (§44), where Heidegger explicitly rejects the Kantian "Copernican Revolution" in favor of an apparently "naive realist" conception of truth as direct "agreement with the object" (a view Heidegger associates with Aristotle). After explaining that "[t]he neo-Kantian theory of knowledge of the 19th century frequently characterized this definition of truth as an expression of a methodologically backward naive realism and described it as incompatible with a posing of the question having undergone Kant's 'Copernican Revolution,'" Heidegger articulates the "standard" epistemological position he wishes to oppose as follows: "Truth according to the general opinion is cognition. But cognition is judgment. And in the judgment we must distinguish between the judging as *real* psychical process and the judged as *ideal* content." Heidegger then protests vehemently against this latter distinction:

> And is not the separation of real execution and ideal content with reference to the "actual" judging of the judged as such unjustified? Is

> not the actuality of cognition and judging not broken apart into two types of being and "levels," whose piecing-together never touches the mode of being of knowing? Is not psychologism correct to resist this separation – even though it itself neither clarifies the mode of being of the thinking of the thought ontologically, nor even is acquainted with this as a problem?

Finally, Heidegger formulates his own "naive realist" account of truth:

> The meant being itself shows itself *so*, *as* it is in itself, i.e., that *it* in its self-sameness [*Selbigkeit*] is so, as how *it*, being pointed out in the assertion, is uncovered. Representations are not compared, either among themselves or in *relation* to the real thing. In identification there is not an agreement between knowing and object and certainly not between psychical and physical – but also not between "contents of consciousness" among themselves. In identification there is only the being-uncoveredness [*Entdeckt-sein*] of the being itself, *it* [itself] in the How of its uncoveredness. This [uncoveredness] proves true [*bewährt sich*] in that what is asserted – that is, the being itself – shows itself *as the same*. [Such] proof [*Bewährung*] means: *the showing itself of the being in its self-sameness.*

Heidegger finishes this passage with a footnote that refers us to the Sixth Investigation of volume two of Husserl's *Logical Investigations* (which introduces the idea of truth as "identification" – a direct relation of identity between the "intended" meaning and the real object) and to the work of Lask.[40]

40. The footnote warns us against relying exclusively on the first volume of the *Logical Investigations*, which may appear merely to represent the traditional theory of the proposition in itself derived from Bolzano. The relevant sections of volume two (1901, §§36–52), by contrast, present a conception of truth in which an intention or meaning is directly "identified" – in immediate intuition – with the very thing that is intended or meant. According to the theory of truth articulated in these sections of the *Logical Investigations*, truth in general is not even propositional. My representation of the table may be immediately compared with the table, just as my assertion that the table is brown may be immediately compared with the table's being brown. Thus, truth in general need involve none of the structures (subject and predicate, ground and consequent, and so on) studied in traditional formal logic. On the contrary, such peculiarly logical structures only emerge subsequently in the very special circumstances of "categorial intuition," where specifically propositional intentions or meanings are intuitively grasped in their most abstract – and, as it were, secondary and derivative – formal features. In this sense, Husserl's conception of the relationship between logical form and truth in general parallels Lask's view of the artificiality and subjectivity of logical form. In neither case can formal logic be in any way foundational or explanatory for truth as a "relation to an object." For Heidegger's assessment of the notion of "categorial intuition" in the

Heidegger is a "naive realist" here insofar as he begins with the idea of "being-in-the-world." We do not start with a cognitive subject together with its contents of consciousness, but rather with a living practical subject necessarily engaged with its environment. Assertion, as Heidegger explains earlier (§33), is a "derivative mode of interpretation" in which the "hermeneutical 'as'" of practical understanding of the "ready-to-hand" (where an item "ready-to-hand" is understood "as" suited for a given end or purpose) is transformed into the "apophantical 'as'" of theoretical understanding of the "present-at-hand" (where an item "present-at-hand" is understood "as" determined by a given predicate). Truth in the traditional (Aristotelian) sense – as a relation of agreement with an object – then emerges (§44) as itself a derivative phenomenon (where an assertion is compared with a "present-at-hand" object it points out in a relation that is itself "present-at-hand"). If we forget this derivative character, however, all the misunderstandings currently prevalent in the (neo-Kantian) "theory of judgment" then arise:

> If the phenomenon of the "as" remains hidden, and, above all, if its existential origin in the hermeneutical "as" remains covered over, then Aristotle's phenomenological approach to the analysis of the *logos* collapses into a superficial "theory of judgment" according to which judging is a connection and/or separation of representations and concepts. (§33)

In tracing the collapse of the "superficial 'theory of judgment'" prevalent in the contemporary neo-Kantian tradition to a neglect of the distinction between the "apophantical 'as'" of theoretical understanding and the "hermeneutical 'as'" of practical understanding, Heidegger has taken Husserl's theory of identification and Lask's emphasis on the primacy of the actual concrete object of experience an important – and absolutely decisive – step further. For Heidegger now conceives the concrete human subject neither as a cognitive or theoretical subject in the sense of Rickert nor as the subject of "pure consciousness" in the sense of Husserl. The concrete human subject (Dasein) is rather primarily and originally oriented towards pragmatic engagements and practical projects necessarily directed towards a temporal future; and it is in precisely this way, for Heidegger, that Dasein is an essentially finite, essentially temporal, being. And for such a being, in particular, the thought of temporal finitude is not simply the representation of an eventual limit or boundary to the sequence of passing phenomena and mental contents; it is rather the thought of the subject's own *death* – the

context of Husserl and Lask (which Heidegger sees as destroying once and for all the Kantian "mythology" of a synthesis of understanding and sensibility, form and matter) see Heidegger, *Prolegomena zur Geschichte des Zeitbegriffs*, 63–99.

radical possibility that, at any given moment, one's ongoing projects and pragmatic engagements may simply cease to be. Whereas, in its everyday understanding of itself, Dasein is completely unaware of its own peculiar character and is simply caught up in its projects and practical involvements, in "being-toward-death" Dasein is revealed to itself for what it is – as what Heidegger calls "*thrown* being-in-the-world."

Hence, temporality, for Heidegger, is neither the all-embracing public time within which events are dated and ordered nor the subjective time of "pure consciousness" in which experienced mental contents flow in review past the intentional "now." Temporality is rather first manifested in the being-towards-the-future of primarily practically oriented Dasein, a being-towards-the-future that necessarily includes being-towards-death and can therefore be either "authentic" or "inauthentic." Thus, in authentic existence, Dasein's concernful practical orientation (its "care" [*Sorge*]) is unified by a "resolute" and thoroughgoing decision. In inauthentic existence, by contrast, Dasein's "care" is dispersed and "fallen": Dasein has, so to speak, lost itself in its world.[41] Finally, in authentic existence, Dasein's practically oriented being-towards-the-future is at the same time a practically oriented (historical) being-towards-the-past. For, at precisely the moment of an authentic decision, Dasein must choose among possibilities that must themselves be already present and available in the historically given situation. Dasein, at the moment of its most authentic freedom, reveals itself as nonetheless dependent on *possibilities* that have been handed down or inherited. Dasein must thus appropriate its "fate" and is therefore necessarily historical.[42]

Heidegger's radical transformation of the neo-Kantianism of the Southwest School thus involves not only the deep influence of Husserlian phenomenology, but also a further appropriation of both the existential spirituality of Søren Kierkegaard and the historically oriented *Lebensphilosophie* of Dilthey.[43] The

41. See Heidegger, *Being and Time*: "Dasein *can* understand *itself* as understanding from the side of the 'world' and the other or from the side of its ownmost possibility-for-being [*aus seinem eigensten Seinkönnen*]. The last-mentioned possibility means: Dasein discloses itself to itself in and as its ownmost possibility-for-being. This *authentic* disclosedness shows the phenomenon of the most original truth in the mode of its authenticity. The most original and authentic disclosedness in which Dasein as possibility-for-being can be, is the *truth of existence*" (§44).
42. The temporality of "authentic" existence is articulated in Division Two, ch. 3 (§§ 61–6), the temporality of everyday "inauthentic" existence in ch. 4 (§§67–71), the temporality of "historicality" in ch. 5 (§§72–7). How the temporality of Dasein is actually the prior ground of the "ordinary conception of time" (viz. the all-embracing public time within which events are dated and ordered) is explained in ch. 6 (§§78–81). Note that the historicality of Dasein means only that the totality of its *possible* practical involvements is historically determined (and, indeed, by its own *interpretation* of this history). Dasein's *actual* practical involvements are up to its own free choice from among these historically determined possibilities. True authenticity, for Heidegger, rests on the correct understanding of precisely this situation.
43. For the importance of Dilthey, in particular, see note 34 above.

result is a breathtakingly original exploration of the spiritual and philosophical predicament of the early twentieth century; and Heidegger's decisive rejection of the authority and primacy of formal logic and the exact sciences in the dispute with Carnap over "metaphysical pseudo-sentences" can be properly understood, as we shall see, only against this particular background. Just as Carnap brings the mathematical "logicization" of experience begun by the Marburg School to completion using the new logic of *Principia Mathematica*, Heidegger, for his part, completes the "de-logicization" of experience implicit in the problematic of the Southwest School – which was made explicit, for the first time, in the work of Lask and then incorporated into Heidegger's own existential–hermeneutic version of phenomenology.

III. OVERCOMING METAPHYSICS

All four of our protagonists – Frege, Husserl, Carnap, and Heidegger – conceived themselves as making revolutionary breaks with the philosophy of the past through the invention (or discovery) of radically new types of philosophical tools. For Frege, this was the new form of logical language he created – the *Begriffsschrift* (1879) – where, in particular, a purely formal or conceptual treatment of the great mathematical discoveries of the nineteenth century (especially in the foundations of arithmetic and analysis) became completely clear and explicit for the first time.[44] This new logical language then constituted the indispensable basis for Frege's subsequent investigations into the philosophy of logic, language, and mathematics, which are still an essential part of the canon for an education within what we now call the analytic tradition.[45] The ambitions of this philosophical tradition to be "scientific" – and to leave behind the irresoluble obscurities of traditional metaphysics – rest squarely on the presumed scientific status of the new philosophical tool Frege created.

For Husserl, by contrast, although he, like Frege, drew very important inspiration from nineteenth-century mathematics, the formal language of modern logic

---

44. Cf. notes 17 and 19 above. Frege brings the process of showing that arithmetic and analysis are purely conceptual (and thus nonintuitive in Kant's sense) to a conclusion by finally articulating an explicit conception of purely formal logic adequate to the task.
45. See Gottlob Frege, *Die Grundlagen der Arithmetik: Eine logisch-mathematische Untersuchung über den Begriff der Zahl* (Breslau: Koebner, 1884); "Über Sinn und Bedeutung," *Zeitschrift für Philosophie und philosophische Kritik* 100 (1892); "Über Begriff und Gegenstand," *Vierteljahrsschrift für wissenschaftliche Philosophie* 18 (1892); and "Der Gedanke: Eine logische Untersuchung," *Beiträge zur Philosophie der deutschen Idealismus* 1 (1918). The last of these, "Thought" (*Der Gedanke*), is the first of Frege's final papers published under the title of "Logical Investigations."

(or any other formal language) was, by itself, quite insufficient to dissolve the obscurities of traditional metaphysics and now launch philosophy on a properly "scientific" path. Thus, as we have seen, Husserl found the modern logical tradition of Bolzano and Frege (and even Carnap) to be philosophically "naive," insofar as it appeared to give aid and comfort to a Platonistic ontology of timeless abstract objects and thereby render our supposed cognitive "grasp" of logic and mathematics completely obscure. Husserl addressed this difficulty, as we have also seen, by turning to a phenomenological investigation into the "mode of givenness" or "sense" of logical and mathematical objects as they first appear (immanently) to consciousness, while simultaneously "bracketing" all ontological questions as to their "real existence" (transcendently) independent of consciousness. And, more generally, Husserl applied the same method of "phenomenological reduction" to physical objects as well: what matters to phenomenology is again their distinctive "mode of givenness" to consciousness, not the question of their "real existence" independent of consciousness. The new discipline of transcendental phenomenology thereby achieved a distinctively philosophical standpoint that attempted to be entirely neutral with respect to all metaphysical disputes between conflicting "realist" and "idealist" tendencies in the philosophical tradition.

Carnap, in the *Aufbau*, attempted to do something very similar. We observed in §II above that, according to the *Aufbau*, constitutional theory and "transcendental idealism" agree that "all objects of cognition are constituted (in idealistic language, are 'generated in thought')" (§177); and, as we also observed, by "transcendental idealism" Carnap has primarily in mind the "logical idealism" of the Marburg School. Nevertheless, in the same section, Carnap also explicitly argues that "[*c*]*onstitution theory and realism do not contradict one another at any point*"; and, in an earlier section, he explains the precise sense of this metaphysical neutrality as follows:

> Are the constituted structures "generated in thought," as the Marburg School teaches, or "only recognized" by thought, as realism asserts? Constitutional theory employs a neutral language; according to it the structures are neither "generated" nor "recognized," but rather "constituted"; and even at this early stage it cannot be too strongly emphasized that this word "constitution" is always meant completely *neutrally*. From the point of view of constitutional theory the dispute involving "generation" versus "recognition" is therefore an idle linguistic dispute. (§5)

In particular, by "constitute," as we saw in §I, Carnap means only the construction of a sequence of logical definitions from his single autopsychological basic relation within the logic of *Principia Mathematica*, and he explicitly asserts, in addition, that all talk of "acts" of constitution by a cognitive subject is merely fictional (§99). Thus, although the *Aufbau* shows very clear signs of the influence of Husserl, it is ultimately modern mathematical logic, for Carnap, rather than transcendental phenomenology, that secures him a metaphysically neutral standpoint.[46]

Heidegger begins by following Husserl in taking the new phenomenological method decisively to transcend traditional philosophy and place philosophy on the path of a science. In part C of §7 of *Being and Time*, entitled "The Preliminary Concept of Phenomenology," Heidegger characterizes phenomenology as a "science 'of' phenomena," but he then turns in a quite un-Husserlian direction by asserting that, "with respect to its subject matter, phenomenology is the science of the being of beings – ontology." In particular, phenomenology, in its Husserlian form, now appears to Heidegger as excessively idealistic, because, as we have seen, he now takes being-in-the-world, rather than pure consciousness, as the subject of characteristically "phenomenological" investigation (within existential–hermeneutic phenomenology rather than Husserlian transcendental phenomenology). To be sure, the resulting "naive realism" still has an important transcendental dimension, insofar as we can pursue "fundamental ontology" only by means of an (existential–hermeneutic) "analytic of Dasein." It is quite clear, nonetheless, that Heidegger intends to rescue both fundamental ontology and traditional metaphysics, together with the real "being of the world," from precisely Husserl's phenomenological reduction.[47]

---

46. For more on Carnap's antimetaphysical standpoint in the *Aufbau*, see Michael Friedman, "Introduction: Carnap's Revolution in Philosophy," in Friedman and Creath, *The Cambridge Companion to Carnap*. Carnap famously uses the Husserlian terminology of the "*epochē*" when discussing his "autopsychological basis" of "elementary experiences": "At the beginning of the system the experiences are simply taken in as they are given; the postulations of reality and non-reality in them that are to follow are not yet made, but rather 'bracketed'; the phenomenological 'reduction' ('*epochē*') in the sense of Husserl is thus exerted" (*Aufbau* §64). Yet Carnap does not intend a reduction to the sphere of pure consciousness (of the transcendental subject), in the sense of Husserl. As he makes perfectly clear in the same section, Carnap simply has in mind the circumstance that all distinctions among "real" and "non-real" objects will be made at later stages (in the hierarchy of logical types of *Principia Mathematica*) of his purely logical sequence of constitutional definitions: "For the basis no distinction is made between those experiences which are distinguished from one another as perception, hallucination, dream, etc. on the basis of later constitution. This differentiation, and thereby that between actual and non-actual objects, only appears at a rather high constitutional level (cf. §170ff.)."
47. Thus, Husserlian transcendental phenomenology, from Heidegger's point of view, is still excessively "idealistic." See Heidegger's vehement rejection of the idea of a "pure" or "idealized" subject at the conclusion of *Being and Time* §44: "The ideas of a 'pure I' and of a 'consciousness in general' so little contain the a priori of the 'actual' subject that they either pass over the ontological character of the factuality and the constitution of being of Dasein or they do not see it at all. Rejection of a 'consciousness in general' does not mean the negation of the a priori, any more than the positing of an idealized subject guarantees the objectively

In the years following the publication of *Being and Time*, Heidegger embarked on something of a campaign on behalf of metaphysics. His first target was the neo-Kantian conception, especially as defended by the Marburg School, according to which the "return to Kant" they stood for implies that all traditional metaphysics (especially that of post-Kantian German idealism) should now be replaced by "theory of knowledge" (*Erkenntnistheorie*). To this end, Heidegger developed a "metaphysical" interpretation of the *Critique of Pure Reason* itself (still quite influential within German-language Kant scholarship[48]) explicitly opposed to the Marburg School. He first made this interpretation public in a celebrated disputation with Ernst Cassirer at Davos at the end of March and the beginning of April 1929,[49] which Heidegger then wrote up in a few short weeks and published as *Kant and the Problem of Metaphysics* (1929). In that same year, moreover, he took over Husserl's Chair at Freiburg and delivered "What is Metaphysics?" as his inaugural address. It appears, therefore, that Heidegger intended his new defense of metaphysics to represent not only the eclipse of Marburg neo-Kantianism, but also (at least symbolically) that of Husserl's transcendental phenomenology.

Now Carnap's collision with Heidegger over metaphysical pseudo-sentences was directed at precisely Heidegger's inaugural address (where the sentences in question appear). Indeed, Carnap attended the disputation with Cassirer at Davos in 1929, and he came away both impressed and alarmed by Heidegger. Carnap then returned to Vienna and undertook a rather serious study of *Being and Time*. He wrote up and delivered earlier drafts of "Overcoming Metaphysics" directly in the wake of this experience, as he struggled to find a professorship in Europe in the extraordinarily uneasy political climate of the early 1930s. Carnap finally secured a professorship at the German University in Prague (in the Division of Natural Sciences) in 1931, and he published "Overcoming Metaphysics" in *Erkenntnis* (the official journal of the Vienna Circle) in 1932. In December 1935, increasingly distressed by the "stifling political climate" and "danger of war" in Europe, he emigrated to the United States, taking up a position at the University of Chicago. Carnap's radical new attempt at overcoming metaphysics can only be properly understood against this background.[50]

---

grounded apriority of Dasein. The assertion of 'eternal truths,' together with the mixing up of the phenomenally grounded 'ideality' of Dasein with an idealized absolute subject, belong to the residues of Christian theology within the philosophical problematic that have still not yet been radically driven out."

*48. See, for example, the discussion of Dieter Henrich in the essay by Dieter Thomä in *The History of Continental Philosophy: Volume 7*.

49. See Friedman, *A Parting of the Ways*, ch. 1, for further discussion and references. See also the essay in this volume by Luft and Capeillères.

50. See Carnap's retrospective account in his "Intellectual Autobiography": "I was not only relieved to escape the stifling political and cultural atmosphere and the danger of war in Europe, but was also very gratified to see that in the United States there was a considerable interest,

In §5 of "Overcoming Metaphysics," entitled "Metaphysical Pseudo-Sentences," Carnap introduces his consideration of examples from Heidegger by remarking that, although "we could just as well have selected passages from any other of the numerous metaphysicians of the present or the past," Carnap has here chosen to "select a few sentences from that metaphysical doctrine which at present exerts the strongest influence in Germany."[51] There follows a discussion of several of Heidegger's sentences involving the concept of nothingness (*das Nichts*), including especially the notorious *Das Nichts selbst nichtet.*

Carnap's criticism is more sophisticated and penetrating then one might antecedently expect. For, in the first place, Carnap's complaint is not that the sentence in question is unverifiable in terms of sense data; nor is the most important problem that the sentence coins a bizarre new word (the verb *nichten*) and thus violates ordinary usage. The main problem is rather a violation of the logical form of the concept of nothing. Heidegger uses the concept both as a substantive and as a verb, whereas modern logic has shown that it is neither: the logical form of the concept of nothing is constituted solely by existential quantification and negation. In the second place, however, Carnap also clearly recognizes that this kind of criticism would not affect Heidegger himself in the slightest, for the real issue between the two lies in the circumstance that Heidegger denies while Carnap affirms the philosophical centrality of logic and the exact sciences. Carnap accordingly refers explicitly to such Heideggerian passages as the following:

> [N]othingness is the source of negation, not vice versa. If the power of the understanding in the field of questions concerning nothingness and being is thus broken, then the fate of the dominion of "logic" within philosophy is also decided therewith. The idea of "logic" itself dissolves in the turbulence of a more original questioning.

---

especially among the younger philosophers, in the scientific method of philosophy, based on modern logic, and that this interest was growing from year to year" (in *The Philosophy of Rudolf Carnap*, Paul A. Schilpp [ed.] [La Salle, IL: Open Court, 1963], 34). Compare also his remarks several pages later: "In 1936, when I came to this country, the traditional schools of philosophy did not have nearly the same influence as on the European continent. The movement of German idealism, in particular Hegelianism, which had earlier been quite influential in the United States, had by then almost completely disappeared. Neo-Kantian philosophical conceptions were represented here and there, not in an orthodox form but rather influenced by recent developments in scientific thinking, much like the conceptions of Cassirer in Germany. Phenomenology had a number of adherents mostly in a liberalized form, not in Husserl's orthodox form, and even less in Heidegger's version" (*ibid.*, 40).

51. Rudolf Carnap, "Überwindung der Metaphysik durch logische Analyse der Sprache," *Erkenntnis* 2 (1932), 229; "The Elimination of Metaphysics through Logical Analysis of Language," in *Logical Positivism*, A. J. Ayer (ed.) (New York: Free Press, 1959), 69.

> The supposed soberness and superiority of science becomes ridiculous if it does not take nothingness seriously. Only because nothingness is manifest can science make what is itself into an object of investigation. Only if science takes its existence from metaphysics can it always reclaim anew its essential task, which does not consist in the accumulation and ordering of objects of acquaintance but in the ever to be newly accomplished disclosure of the entire expanse of truth of nature and history.
>
> Therefore no rigor of a science can attain the seriousness of metaphysics. Philosophy can never be measured by the standard of the idea of science.[52]

Carnap concludes, in his own characteristically sober fashion: "We thus find a good confirmation for our thesis; a metaphysician here arrives himself at the statement that his questions and answers are not consistent with logic and the scientific mode of thinking."[53]

The "Postscript" to "What is Metaphysics?"[54] considers three types of criticism that have been made of the original lecture. Heidegger reserves his most extensive and militant response for the third criticism, namely, that "the lecture decides against 'logic.'" The heart of his response is as follows:

> The suspicion directed against "logic," whose conclusive degeneration may be seen in logistic [i.e. modern mathematical logic], arises from the knowledge of that thinking that finds its source in the truth of being, but not in the consideration of the objectivity [*Gegenständlichkeit*] of what is. Exact thinking is never the most rigorous thinking, if rigor [*Strenge*] receives its essence otherwise from the mode of strenuousness [*Anstrengung*] with which knowledge always maintains the relation to what is essential in what is. Exact thinking ties itself down solely in calculation with what is and serves this [end] exclusively.[55]

52. See Heidegger, *Was ist Metaphysik?* (Bonn: Friedrich Cohen, 1929), 14, 18; "What is Metaphysics?" in Martin Heidegger, *Basic Writings*, David F. Krell (ed.) (New York: Harper & Row, 1977), 107, 111–12. Carnap ("Überwindung der Metaphysik," 231–2; "The Elimination of Metaphysics," 71–2), quotes selections from these passages.
53. Carnap, "Überwindung der Metaphysik," 232; "The Elimination of Metaphysic," 72.
54. Martin Heidegger, "Nachwort," in *Was ist Metaphysik?*, 4th ed. (Frankfurt: Klostermann, 1943).
55. Heidegger, "Nachwort," 104; "Postscript" to "What is Metaphysics?," 356.

It is clear, then, that Heidegger and Carnap are actually in remarkable agreement. Metaphysical thought of the type Heidegger is trying to awaken is possible only on the basis of a prior overthrow of the philosophical authority and primacy of logic and the exact sciences. The difference is that Heidegger eagerly embraces such an overthrow, whereas Carnap is determined to resist it at all costs.

This sheds considerable light, we believe, on the context and force of Carnap's antimetaphysical attitude. For, by rejecting "metaphysics" as a field of cognitively meaningless pseudo-sentences, Carnap is by no means similarly rejecting all forms of traditional philosophy. He makes this perfectly clear, in fact, in his "Remarks by the Author" appended to the English translation "The Elimination of Metaphysics" in 1957:

> *To section 1, "metaphysics."* This term is used in this paper, as usually in Europe, for the field of alleged knowledge of the essence of things which transcends the realm of empirically founded, inductive science. Metaphysics in this sense includes systems like those of Fichte, Schelling, Hegel, Bergson, Heidegger. But it does not include endeavors towards a synthesis and generalization of the results of the various sciences.[56]

In Carnap's "Replies and Systematic Expositions," the point is made even more explicitly:

> Note that the characterization as pseudo-statements does not refer to all systems or theses in the field of metaphysics. At the time of the Vienna Circle, the characterization was applied mainly to those metaphysical systems which had exerted the greatest influence upon continental philosophy during the last century, viz., the post-Kantian systems of German idealism and, among contemporary ones, those of Bergson and Heidegger. On the basis of later, more cautious analyses, the judgment was not applied to the main theses of those philosophers whose thinking had been in close contact with the science of their times, as in the cases of Aristotle and Kant; the latter's epistemological theses about the synthetic a priori character of certain judgments were regarded by us as false, not as meaningless.[57]

56. Carnap, "The Elimination of Metaphysics," 80.
57. Rudolf Carnap, "Replies and Systematic Expositions," in *The Philosophy of Ernst Cassirer*, Paul A. Schilpp (ed.) (La Salle, IL: Open Court, 1963), 874–5. On the following page Carnap continues: "I think, however, that our [antimetaphysical] principle excludes not only a great number of assertions in systems like those of Hegel and Heidegger, especially since the latter

So Carnap is primarily concerned with "overcoming" a very particular kind of "metaphysics." The main target is the post-Kantian German idealism Carnap views as currently dominating European thought (in the early 1930s), and he views Heidegger, in particular, as the leading contemporary representative of this trend.

It is noteworthy, therefore, that Heidegger was aware of Carnap's attack and, indeed, explicitly responded to it – in a draft of his original 1935 lecture course, *Introduction to Metaphysics*, that does not appear in the published version (1953). Heidegger explains how, with the collapse of German idealism in the second half of the nineteenth century, the philosophical understanding of being degenerated into a consideration of the "is" – that is, a logical consideration of the propositional copula. He continues in a memorable paragraph that is worth quoting in full:

> Going further in this direction, which in a certain sense has been marked out since Aristotle, and which determines "being" from the "is" of the proposition and thus finally destroys it, is a tendency of thought that has been assembled in the journal *Erkenntnis*. Here the traditional logic is to be for the first time grounded with scientific rigor through mathematics and the mathematical calculus, in order to construct a "logically correct" language in which the sentences of metaphysics – which are all pseudo-sentences – are to become impossible in the future. Thus, an article in this Journal II (1931 f.), pp. 219 ff. bears the title "Überwindung der Metaphysik durch logische Analyse der Sprache." Here the most extreme flattening out and uprooting of the traditional theory of judgment is accomplished under the semblance of mathematical science. Here the last consequences of a mode of thinking which began with Descartes are brought to a conclusion: a mode of thinking according to which truth is no longer disclosedness of what is and thus accommodation and grounding of Dasein in the disclosing being, but truth is rather diverted into certainty – to the mere securing of thought, and in fact the securing of mathematical thought against all that is not thinkable by it. The conception of truth as the securing of thought led to the definitive profaning [*Entgötterung*] of the world.

---

says explicitly that logic is not applicable to statements in metaphysics, but also in contemporary discussions, e.g., those concerning the reality of space or of time." Cf.: "It is encouraging to remember that philosophical thinking has made great progress in the course of two thousand years through the work of men like Aristotle, Leibniz, Hume, Kant, Dewey, Russell, and many others, who were basically thinking in a scientific way" ("Intellectual Autobiography," 42–3).

> The supposed "philosophical" tendency of mathematico-physical positivism wishes to supply the grounding of this position. It is no accident that this kind of "philosophy" wishes to supply the foundations of modern physics, in which all relations to nature are in fact destroyed. It is also no accident that this kind of "philosophy" stands in internal and external connection with Russian communism. And it is no accident, moreover, that this kind of thinking celebrates its triumph in America. All of this is only the ultimate consequence of an apparently merely grammatical affair, according to which being is conceived through the "is," and the "is" is interpreted in accordance with one's conception of the proposition and of thought.[58]

Thus Heidegger once again expresses a rather remarkable agreement with Carnap concerning the underlying sources of their opposition – which, as is now clear, embrace both fundamental issues about the philosophical centrality of logic and the exact sciences, and the extremely fraught social and political climate of the late 1920s and early 1930s within which Heidegger's renewed defense of metaphysics first emerged.

It is even more remarkable, finally, that Carnap's and Heidegger's philosophical trajectories exhibited a surprising amount of convergence both before and after their collision over metaphysical pseudo-sentences. In particular, in the final section of "Overcoming Metaphysics," entitled "Metaphysics as expression of *Lebensgefühl*," Carnap refers very favorably to the *Lebensphilosophie* of Dilthey and his students (by which Carnap himself was considerably influenced during his own student years),[59] and he also refers very favorably to

58. See Heidegger, *Einführung in die Metaphysik* (*Gesamtausgabe* vol. 40 [Frankfurt: Klostermann, 1983], 227–8); the unpublished pages were apparently replaced by Heidegger, *Einführung in die Metaphysik* (Tübingen: Niemeyer, 1953), 78–90; *Introduction to Metaphysics* (New York: Doubleday, 1961), 86–99. Otto Pöggeler comments on this (1935) passage as follows: "Heidegger had sufficient taste not to deliver a previous version of his lecture in which Carnap's emigration to America was put forth as confirmation of the convergence between Russian communism and the 'type of thinking in America'" ("Heidegger's Political Self-Understanding," in *The Heidegger Controversy: A Critical Reader*, Richard Wolin [ed.] [New York: Columbia University Press, 1991], 218–19). Given that Carnap did not emigrate until December 1935, however, whereas Heidegger's lectures were held in the summer of that year, Heidegger cannot be referring to Carnap's emigration here. It is more likely, for example, that he is referring to Schlick's trip to Stanford University in 1929, which is prominently mentioned in the foreword to the Vienna Circle's manifesto *Wissenschaftliche Weltauffassung* (1929).
59. For Carnap's student years and *Lebensphilosophie*, see Gottfried Gabriel, "Introduction: Carnap brought Home," in *Carnap Brought Home: The View from Jena*, S. Awodey and C. Klein (eds) (Chicago, IL: Open Court, 2004), and André Carus, *Carnap and Twentieth-Century Thought: Explication as Enlightenment* (Cambridge: Cambridge University Press, 2007).

Nietzsche's *Also sprach Zarathustra*, in which, according to Carnap, the traditional confusion between metaphysics (as a supposed theoretical enterprise) and poetry (as the expression of *Lebensgefühl*) has been almost entirely avoided. Indeed, it is possible that Carnap took the wording of his title, "Überwindung der Metaphysik," directly from *Also sprach Zarathustra*, where the themes of the *Überwindung* and *Selbstüberwindung* of man (leading, of course, to the *Übermensch*) figure very prominently. Moreover, Heidegger, in the mid- to late 1930s (directly following his collision with Carnap), also began using the expression "overcoming metaphysics" to characterize his own philosophical ambitions, in connection with his work on Nietzsche and his increasing concern with technology.[60] This period, in particular, marks Heidegger's attempt to come to terms with the failure of his rectorate at Freiburg (1933–34), and his consequent disenchantment with the Nazi regime over its overwhelmingly technological character.[61] It also marks the boundary of Heidegger's famous *Kehre*, where he leaves behind the existential–hermeneutic analytic of Dasein once and for all in favor of a new appreciation for the inextricable connection between the type of philosophy he now wants to practice and poetry.[62]

It is during this same period, as we have seen, that Carnap, for his part, became increasingly distressed by the "stifling political and cultural atmosphere … in Europe,"[63] resulting in his emigration to the United States in December 1935. Carnap had just published his last major work written in German, *Logische Syntax der Sprache* (1934), where he announced a new type of philosophy – or rather what he calls a "replacement" for all traditional philosophy – devoted wholly to *Wissenschaftslogik*, the logic of science: this new discipline, he says, now "takes the place of the inextricable tangle of problems known as philosophy."[64] Moreover, just before leaving Europe, in September 1935, Carnap participated in the last great international congress devoted to the "scientific philosophy" of logical empiricism that took place before the advent of war. Among other things, Carnap delivered a programmatic paper, "Von der Erkenntistheorie zur Wissenschaftslogik" (From epistemology to the logic of science), where he asserts that all previous epistemology, including his own earlier epistemology developed in the *Aufbau*, must now be renounced as an "unclear mixture of

60. See e.g. Heidegger, "Überwindung der Metaphysik," written in the years 1936–41 (contemporaneous with his Nietzsche lectures).

61. See Rüdiger Safranski, *Ein Meister aus Deutschland: Heidegger und seine Zeit* (Munich: Hanser, 1994), ch. 17, for an illuminating description of this period.

*62. For a discussion of Heidegger's *Kehre*, see the essay by Dennis J. Schmidt in *The History of Continental Philosophy: Volume 4*.

63. Carnap, "Intellectual Autobiography," 34.

64. Rudolf Carnap, *Logische Syntax der Sprache* (Vienna: Springer, 1934), §72.

logical and psychological components."[65] The purely logical analysis of language – the purely logical analysis of *scientific* language – must now completely take its place.[66] Carnap here, and at virtually the same time as Heidegger's famous *Kehre*, has undergone a parallel *Kehre* of his own: he has not only rejected all of traditional metaphysics, but has also renounced the earlier post-metaphysical philosophies of Husserlian phenomenology, Marburg neo-Kantianism, and his own attempt logically to reconstruct both of these earlier revolutionary traditions in the *Aufbau*.[67]

We cannot pursue the further development of the (now entirely divergent) analytic and continental traditions beyond this point. Suffice it to say that the final philosophical history of the intricate and multifaceted web of interconnections between logic, intuitive experience, and the time-honored but always questionable enterprise of metaphysics has yet to be written. We believe, however, that it is only possible to make progress here by first adequately understanding how this web itself became "inextricably tangled" – to breaking point – between the two world wars of the twentieth century, and then proceeding (very patiently) to disentangle it.

65. Rudolf Carnap, "Von der Erkenntnistheorie zur Wissenschaftslogik," in *Actes du Congrès international de philosophie scientifique* (Paris: Hermann, 1936), vol. 1, 36.
66. For further discussion of Carnap's mature conception of philosophy as *Wissenschaftslogik*, see Michael Friedman, "The *Aufbau* and the Criticism of Metaphysics," in Friedman and Creath, *The Cambridge Companion to Carnap*.
67. Husserl's late work, *The Crisis of the European Sciences and Transcendental Phenomenology* (1936–37), represents his reaction to this most difficult time – and, in particular, to the now very alarming challenge he sees in Heidegger. Here, in particular, Husserl finally explicitly incorporates a fundamentally *historical* dimension into transcendental phenomenology (cf. note 24 above).

5
EDMUND HUSSERL

Thomas Nenon

It is possible to reconstruct a story about the development of twentieth-century continental philosophy that includes almost all of its major figures and movements either as extensions of the phenomenological tradition or as a critical response to it. Moreover, even though Edmund Husserl[1] was not, and never claimed to be, the inventor of the philosophical term "phenomenology," nor even the sole initiator of phenomenology as one the most important philosophical movements in twentieth-century philosophy, it is not an exaggeration to say that during the first few decades of the twentieth century, the term "phenomenology" as a philosophical method and direction of research became so closely associated with the thinking and the works of Husserl that the term "phenomenology" now usually means a kind of philosophizing associated with Husserl, his philosophical allies such as Max Scheler or Alexander Pfänder, and his successors such as Martin Heidegger or Maurice Merleau-Ponty. Hence, the philosophy of Edmund Husserl can legitimately be seen as the beginning of twentieth-century continental philosophy as an identifiable tradition and leading philosophical movement. Prior to Husserl's work, there may have been differences between some of the dominant tendencies in philosophy in various continental European countries as opposed to the British Isles and the United States, but these were hardly identifiable as a specific movement. But by the middle of the

1. Edmund Husserl (April 8, 1859–April 27, 1938; born Proßnitz [now Prostějov], formerly Austro-Hungarian Empire; died in Freiburg, Germany) was educated at the Universities of Leipzig (1876–78), Berlin (1878–81), and Vienna (1881–82) and took his doctoral degree at Vienna in 1882. His influences included Brentano, Cantor, Dilthey, Stumpf, and Windelband, and he held appointments at the Universities of Halle (1887–1901), Göttingen (1901–16), and Freiburg (1916–28).

twentieth century at the latest, those philosophical approaches that had developed as extensions of phenomenology in one way or another had come to be seen as something other than the predominant mode of philosophy in English-speaking countries at the time.

I. EARLY WORKS

Husserl was born in 1859 to a Jewish family that had long been settled in the town of Proßnitz (now Prostějov) in the district of Maehren, which is now part of the Czech Republic and was then part of the Austro-Hungarian Empire. Although many of his contemporaries still attended Jewish schools, Husserl was educated in a secular grade school and later attended and completed *Gymnasium* in the nearby provincial capital of Olmütz (now Olomouc). In 1876, he enrolled at the University of Leipzig, first studying astronomy and taking courses in mathematics, physics, and philosophy. This is also where he met and became lifelong friends with Thomas Masaryk (1850–1937), who was later to become the first President of Czechoslovakia. In 1878, he switched to the University of Berlin, where he studied mathematics under Karl Weierstraß (1815–97) and Leopold Kronecker (1823–91), and philosophy with Friedrich Paulsen (1846–1908). Husserl's special philosophical interests at this stage centered on investigations into the foundations of mathematics and logic. In 1881, he transferred to Vienna, where he completed his doctoral degree in mathematics under Leo Königsberger (1837–1921) with a dissertation on *Contributions to a Theory of Variable Calculus* in 1882. It was also in Vienna that Husserl began to work under Franz Brentano (1838–1917), who then recommended Husserl to his former student Carl Stumpf (1848–1936) in Halle. Under Stumpf's supervision, Husserl enjoyed his first regular academic appointment in philosophy and completed his first major work – *Concerning the Concept of Number. Psychological Analyses* – as a habilitation in 1887. This work was later revised and published as *The Philosophy of Arithmetic: Psychological and Logical Investigations* in 1891. During this period Husserl also came to know and be influenced by George Cantor (1845–1918) and his work in set theory. In these early studies, Husserl takes up the question of the foundation of mathematics as an inquiry into its origins. He attempts to show how the science of arithmetic and the concept of number on which it is founded are dependent on certain elementary operations. For example, to form the concept of "one," a person must abstract from the specific character of what that person experiences and form a notion of "something in general" as the basis for the idea of "unit." Forming the notion "multiplicity" involves the operation of collectively conjoining such abstract units. At this stage of his thinking, Husserl called this approach to explaining the origin of arithmetic as a discipline back to such elementary operations as abstraction and conjunction "psychological" analyses. He also argued that symbolic representation is a necessary element in arithmetic since the development of a system of integers for a finite discursive intellect necessarily involves the ability of consciousness to conceive of numbers that it cannot intuitively represent to itself. Hence symbolic representations such as numerals are required to conceive of larger numbers.

Husserl's general approach here is closely tied to Brentano's notion of "intentionality," which posits directedness to objects as an essential feature of all mental states, and thereby also sets the stage for an approach that analyzes objectivity as it presents itself to consciousness in certain mental acts. Thus the promising approach to questions concerning the foundation of mathematics and logic appears to be through an analysis of certain kinds of acts that must be presupposed if certain kinds of conceptions and entities are to be present for consciousness. However, both in substance and in the description of these investigations as "psychological analyses," there is a danger of confusing questions concerning the origin and status of mathematical entities with the question concerning the origin and status of the possible representation of those entities. The question of the implicit assumptions of certain kinds of simple concepts that are necessarily involved in more complex concepts such as that of a number is different from the question of the operations that are necessary to form those concepts. Moreover, there are important distinctions that would need to be made about what one means here by "operation" or "act," yet in Husserl's early work these distinctions are far from clear. One can easily gain the impression that Husserl is trying to suggest that the objects of mathematics and logic are psychological or subjective rather than genuinely objective, ideal entities.

Gottlob Frege was one critic who read Husserl's early work in this vein and voiced his objections in a well-known review of *The Philosophy of Arithmetic*. He accused Husserl of mixing logic and psychology so as to distort the status of the mathematical entities Husserl purports to analyze, such as "number," which is not a mental representation. When Husserl opened his next major published work, *The Logical Investigations* (1900), with a "Prolegomena" dedicated to the refutation of "psychologism" – the confusion of mathematical and logical principles with statements about psychological necessities or mental states – there was a common perception that Husserl had adopted as his own Frege's criticisms of his earlier work. While many assumed that it was in response to Frege's criticisms that Husserl had achieved a significant breakthrough towards a new approach that does not reduce ideal entities such as meanings or logical principles to mental acts, in fact it is now apparent from letters and minor publications such as book reviews written during the period between 1891 and 1900 that Husserl on his own had become aware of the ambiguities and possible confusions involved in his earlier work.[2] The *Logical Investigations* should, therefore, be understood more as an extension and clarification of the general approach taken in his earlier work than a repudiation of it.

II. *LOGICAL INVESTIGATIONS*

The *Logical Investigations* was Husserl's first introduction to a broader philosophical audience. It was published in two volumes – the *Prolegomena to a Pure Logic* as volume one in 1900, followed a year later by six specific investigations into topics pertaining to the foundation of such a pure logic in volume two. Husserl describes the pure logic it purports to found as a "*mathesis universalis*" for all individual sciences, that is, as a universal and formal theory of theories in general that could ground a universal system of all knowledge. The investigations thus center around such concepts as meaning, object, truth, and evidence, whose clarification is essential for any theory of science.

Given Frege's criticisms of Husserl's earlier position as "psychologism," it is ironic that it was the extended and devastating criticism of psychologism in volume one of the *Logical Investigations* that initially attracted the most attention. Here Husserl defines psychologism as the view that pure logic can ultimately be reduced to psychology, that is, that logical principles are at bottom nothing other than assertions about the predominant patterns of human cognition. Included in Husserl's list of those guilty of the sin of falling prey to this fallacious view is an array of thinkers from John Stuart Mill, Christoph Sigwart, Benno Erdmann, Richard Avenarius, and Hans Cornelius, who were all prominent in the fields of psychology and logical theory at the time. Husserl's refutation points to the differences in character between *a priori* logical principles and empirical generalizations about actual human thinking. Empirical laws are necessarily vague (i.e. always include *ceteris paribus* conditions), merely probable and, as supposed causal principles governing existing things, also have implicit existential import. Logical laws, by contrast, hold unconditionally. They are exact (i.e. are not restricted by *ceteris paribus* conditions), certain, and do not presuppose actually existing entities. The reality of logical principles is therefore of a fundamentally different kind than that of material or psychological objects. Husserl refers to them as "ideal objects," in a sense simply as the opposite of "real" objects, whereby their ideality does not make them any less genuine than

2. Edmund Husserl, "Rezension zu Schröder's *Vorlesungen über die Algebra der Logik* (1891)," in *Aufsätze und Rezensionen (1890–1910)*, in *Husserliana*, vol. 22, Bernard Rang (ed.) (Dordrecht: Kluwer, 1997), 3–43. See on this topic J. N. Mohanty, *Husserl and Frege* (Bloomington, IN: Indiana University Press, 1982), 1–17.

physical objects or mental states, although Husserl does not explicitly turn to ontological questions in the *Prolegomena* in order to begin to clarify how such nonphysical and nonmental objectivity might be possible.

In the course of the following investigations, however, Husserl does begin to address such questions. In the First Investigation, for instance, Husserl turns to the question of meaning: since the same expression may mean the same thing when uttered by the same speaker on different occasions, by different speakers, or even when the speaker may be unknown, Husserl again distinguishes the meaning of an expression from the mental state of the person uttering the expression. Thus the function of expressions as bearers of meaning is different from the function that they may play as indicators of the speaker's beliefs or emotions.[3] Husserl tries to show that the meaning of an expression must also be distinguished from the object that the expression refers to, since different expressions with different meanings may point to different aspects of the same object (e.g. the victor at Jena and the vanquished at Waterloo), and the same meaning (e.g. horse) can be used to refer to different objects. Meanings for Husserl are ways of relating to an object. For instance, one could intend the same object as a horse, a mammal, a quadruped, or – mistakenly perhaps – a mule. Each of these establishes a different intention and would have a different set of conditions that would confirm or refute it. Meanings are not identical to expressions, however, since there may be different expressions within a language or across languages for the same meaning, or different meanings for the same expression. Meanings are an abstract, ideal stratum of expressions, which have both a material and an ideal side, and can be viewed in terms of their function of expressing meaning or of indicating the mental state of the speaker.

Meanings and logical principles are not the only kinds of ideal entities for Husserl in the *Logical Investigations*. In the Second Investigation, he also defends the position that meanings may refer not only to individual physical objects, but also to ideal objects he call "species" or classes of things. "Red," for instance, is the object referred to by the general concept "red" and is neither itself a red object nor a mental operation. It emerges for a knower through the process of abstraction, but is not itself a mental process, as some empiricist theories might suggest. (This is one step along the way to the clarification of his own earlier positions in which he had not clearly enough distinguished the "meaning" or the concept from the operation through which the concept or meaning is grasped.) The Third Investigation makes clear, however, that Husserl does not view species and other

3. This view will be the subject of critical scrutiny in Jacques Derrida's *Speech and Phenomena, and Other Essays on Husserl's Theory of Signs*, David B. Allison (trans.) (Evanston, IL: Northwestern University Press, 1973), originally published as *La Voix et le phénomène: Introduction au problème du signe dans la phénoménologie de Husserl* (Paris: Presses Universitaires de France, 1967).

abstract objects as existing independently, but as nonindependent "moments" of concrete wholes in which they actually occur. Moreover, he argues that there are essential laws governing which kinds of meanings (and their corresponding objects) are independent and which kinds are dependent, and he asserts that there are essential laws that even stipulate which specific kinds of independent or concrete meanings and objects provide the foundation for specific kinds of dependent or abstract objects and meanings. The project of a pure phenomenological ontology, then, would be to investigate systematically and lay out these essential relationships. Closely related is the project of a pure grammar, described in the Fourth Investigation. A pure grammar would reflect on essential relationships that govern the kinds of meanings that are compatible with each other and those that are not, and which kinds of simpler meanings must be combined in which ways to result in more complex meanings such as those expressed in sentences.

The Fifth Investigation is particularly significant since it is here that Husserl introduces the notion of intentionality with explicit reference to Brentano and grants it a significant role in explicating the notion of meaning that has been functioning in the previous four investigations. Meanings become connected to intentionality since it is through meanings that a specific mode of directedness towards an object is established. Brentano had reintroduced the Scholastic notion of intentionality in his attempt to distinguish the realm of the mental from that of the nonmental. It is the unique property of mental acts to be about some object toward which they are directed, and Husserl adopts this view when he defines consciousness as intentional experiencing. In the Sixth Investigation Husserl complements this insight with the assertion that all objects for knowledge are at the same time intentional objects, that is, mediated through some meaning that governs the specific way in which they are intended.

Already in the Fifth Investigation, however, Husserl further distinguishes between the content or material and the quality of an intentional act, whereby the material names the particular object and the meaning through which consciousness is directed to it (e.g. an ice cream cone) and the quality of the act concerns the way that consciousness is directed to the object (imagining, desiring, or perceiving the ice cream cone). He also is careful to distinguish the material as the intentional object from the material of sense perception that may serve as the basis for the intention of that object, since from the phenomenological perspective those aspects of a sensibly perceptible object that are given through the senses (such as its specific color or taste) occur for consciousness only as aspects of the object as a whole (in this case, the ice cream cone) and not as independent objects. Thus, by "material" Husserl does not mean something like sense data, but rather intended objects that may include sensibly perceptible moments as part of their complete intention, but these sensibly perceptible moments are not separately intended objects.

Among the various kinds of intentions, Husserl identifies "representations" as the most basic units that are presupposed by others. He follows Brentano's analysis that it is indeed conceivable that one may represent, for instance, an ice cream cone to oneself without desiring it, but that one cannot desire it without implicitly representing it to oneself, so that there is a one-sided foundational relationship between them, in which representations found all other sorts of intentions.

In the Sixth Investigation, Husserl turns explicitly to the relationship between intentions and intended objects. He begins by focusing on the so-called "objectifying intentions," that is, those intentions that can be verified or falsified through appropriate intuitions. Thus, the traditional question about the relationship between subject and object, knowing and the object known, is approached in terms of the question of meaning-intentions and their fulfillment. An objectifying intention establishes a relationship to the object such that certain kinds of intuitions count as fulfilling the intention and thus presenting the intended object not merely as intended, but as actually known. The object of knowledge is just that which is given in a fulfilled intention. Hence, corresponding to every intention is an intended object, but in the case of an empty intending, that is, an intending not based on actual sense intuitions, there may or may not be an actual object that corresponds to the intention. In the case of a fulfilled intention, intuition confirms that there is an existent object that indeed corresponds to the intention and that the object is just as it has been intended, so that there is an identity between intended object and the actual object itself. The ideal of a completely fulfilled intention is captured in the notion *Evidenz*, the experience of an object being evidently given just as it has been intended, so that it is apparent that the actual object coincides precisely with the intention of it. In Husserl's view, the experience of the evidentness of the object for us as it is in itself lies at the basis of the notion of truth in all of its various manifestations, which all proceed from this notion of evidentness. Taken as a property of the intending or of a judgment expressing a specific intention, truth refers to the ability of an intention to be fulfilled by such an evidential experience. Truth can also be taken to be a property of the intended object or state of affairs, in the sense that something is indeed a true object or a true state of affairs if it can be evidentially experienced in the appropriate manner. Moreover, one can further distinguish between truth as the actual experience of the identity between the intention and the intended object by an observer and the claim that such an experience could be had by an ideal observer. But in any case, the claim that a proposition or a state of affairs is a true one ultimately must bear some possible or actual relationship to this experience of evidentness that is the fundamental phenomenon to which any truth claim must be referred.

The Sixth Investigation makes clear that the objects of legitimate intention are not limited to sensible individuals, but may also be states of affairs or other kinds of objectivities that may be founded in, but are not necessarily reducible to, that which may be directly perceived through the senses. Having articulated the general relationship between intention, fulfillment, and the objects of the intentions that are presented through the fulfillment of an intention in the first half of the Sixth Investigation, Husserl then turns to what he calls "categorial objects" such as states of affairs and the corresponding "categorial intuitions" that fulfill them. Not only does Husserl recognize as legitimate objects those states of affairs that are intended through complex meaningful expressions such as sentences, but he also maintains that there are other meaningful expressions, such as those referring to universals (or "species" as he called them in the Second Investigation), that each have their own appropriate and unique form of fulfillment. Thus, in addition to sense intuition, Husserl proposes that there are other forms of intuition, among them for instance categorial intuition (e.g. seeing that *a* is *b*) as the fulfillment of the intention of categorial objects (*a*'s being *b*), each with its own unique structure that is an appropriate topic for phenomenological investigation. Particularly important in this regard is his assertion that there may be kinds of intuitions parallel to categorial intuitions that could fulfill the intention of ideal objects, so that the fulfillment of intentions with regard to mathematical or logical truths would be possible, even though they are not reducible to sense intuitions. Husserl asserts that there is an essential sameness in character in the function that fulfillment plays in all of these forms of intuition in its ability to confirm or disappoint an intention. As a result, the parallel relations between intention, fulfillment, and objectivity make it necessary to recognize each fulfilling act of the confirming self-presentation of an object (even a complex object such as a state of affairs or an ideal object such as a logical principle) as a perception, each fulfilling act in general as an intuition, and its intentional object as an object (*Gegenstand*). Thus the realm of intuition extends beyond the realm of sense perception and the range of possible objects extends beyond that of mere individual physical objects to any sort of object whatsoever that can be intended and possibly fulfilled through an appropriate form of intuition in this extended sense of the term.

This opens the way for a whole range of investigations into the nature of these various realms or "regions" of objects, into the nature of the kinds of intentions and fulfillments appropriate to them, and into the relationship between the various kinds of objects, intentions, and fulfillments that belong to each of these realms to see how they are essentially related. The sensually perceivable or "real" objects are characterized as objects of the lowest stage of possible intuition; the categorial or ideal objects that are founded on them are by contrast higher-order objectivities. The project of spelling out just how they are related, what the essential structures of each of these regions are, and what essential relations obtain between the intention, fulfillments, and objects of the various regions is not carried out in the *Logical Investigations*, but the possibility of such a project is outlined and the necessity for it as part of an overall grounding for all of the particular sciences is asserted.

For all of Husserl's later work, this project will remain at the heart of phenomenology as a systematic field of study. However, a decisive question that remained at this stage of Husserl's thinking was the proper method for the execution of this project. What guarantees the necessary correlation between intention and object? How is reflection on such essential states of affairs possible and how is it different from the kind of internal observation of one's own mental states that would amount to nothing other than a new version of psychologism? What is the proper method for studying such essential correlations? Husserl's turn to transcendental phenomenology during the decade that followed the *Logical Investigations* was meant to answer such questions.

III. THE TURN TO TRANSCENDENTAL PHENOMENOLOGY

Shortly after the appearance of the *Logical Investigations*, Husserl received a professorship in Göttingen, where he would remain until 1916. During this period, he developed phenomenology as an explicit methodology and field of research, and he came to be regarded as the leading figure in phenomenology. It was also during this period that phenomenology became an intellectual movement centered on Husserl and his students in Göttingen (e.g. Winthrop Bell, Theodor Conrad, Hedwig Conrad-Martius, Adolf Grimme, Jean Hering, Dietrich von Hildebrand, Roman Ingarden, Fritz Kaufmann, Hans Lipp, Alfred Reinach, and Edith Stein) and a group of sympathetic scholars in Munich, some of whom were already well established on their own. The latter group had been introduced to Husserl's work by an independent scholar by the name of Johannes Daubert and included among others Theodor Lipps, Alexander Pfänder, Moritz Geiger, and Max Scheler. In his discussions with these circles as well as in critical yet friendly debates with leading representatives of neo-Kantianism such as Paul Natorp and of the philosophy of life such as Wilhelm Dilthey, Husserl comes to see phenomenology as the study of pure transcendental consciousness – both its intentional acts and the correlative forms of objectivity constituted through these acts. The process of "transcendental phenomenological reduction," through which all forms of objectivity are traced back to the processes in subjectivity through which they are constituted, was recognized as the key mode of access to the realm of pure phenomenology, which was now seen not as a reflection on the individual mental life of existing subjects within the world, but as an analysis of the realm of "pure transcendental subjectivity." What does this mean?

From the outset of his work, one of Husserl's problems had been distinguishing his own analysis of the essential processes through which various forms of objectivity become apparent to consciousness from a study of the mental processes that actually take place in individual subjects. In a polemical essay written for the journal *Logos* in 1911, Husserl described the need for a philosophical method that could make philosophy into a rigorous science, indeed the most rigorous of sciences, since it would presuppose no other. In order to fulfill this task, phenomenological philosophy must avoid the twin dangers of "naturalism," that is, approaching consciousness only from the standpoint of other natural, ultimately material phenomena, and "historicism," that is, reducing philosophical issues to matters of historical worldviews. As opposed to either of these ultimately empirical approaches, phenomenological philosophy, if it is to fulfill the task of philosophy as a rigorous science, must be a "pure," *a priori*, and hence certain discipline. If it is to study invariant, essential structures and not merely psychological patterns, then phenomenology must find a way to exclude all merely empirical elements from its analysis.

First in working manuscripts composed in 1905, then in lectures presented in 1907 and published posthumously under the title *The Idea of Phenomenology*, Husserl proposed the procedure of phenomenological reduction as the means for accomplishing this goal. The first step is to exclude, bracket out, or put out of play as fallible and thus not the source of genuine evidence those elements in any claim to knowledge that refer not to the processes through which the objects of knowledge are given to consciousness, but to the objects themselves. The technical term Husserl employs to name such suspension of belief on such matters of fact is the Greek term *epochē*, which arose in ancient Stoicism. Accordingly, it is not a phenomenological, but rather an empirical, question whether there actually is a tree outside my window, whether there are such things as magnetic force fields (or phlogiston, for that matter), or whether any particular physical object at all exists. The first step, then, toward moving from the natural or empirical attitude to the phenomenological attitude is to concentrate not on the tree that is seen or the magnetic force field that is proposed as an explanation for certain phenomena, but on the seeing of the tree or the explaining of the phenomena through the proposal of something like a force field, since – following a motif familiar to philosophers at least since Descartes – the seeing or explaining, at least at the moment they are going on, are indubitable occurrences for the subject that is performing the seeing or explaining. But even within this reflective attitude, it turns out that a further kind of reduction or bracketing is necessary to exclude all empirical and thus nonapodictic elements, since mental processes themselves are empirical facts about which one can be mistaken. It is not only possible to be mistaken about whether the tree is such as I perceive it, or even whether there is a tree there at all, but also, at least in principle, equally open to doubt whether it is I, the empirical person with this or that specific identity, physical or mental traits, and personal history, who is doing the perceiving. At least in principle, I could, for instance in a dream, be thinking of myself as a sixteen-year-old high-school student again talking to my father, who in reality has long since passed away. So in addition to bracketing out all commitments to the truth of the statement about whether the object is such as I perceive it, the phenomenologist must also bracket all empirical psychological claims about the perceiver. What is indubitable is the content and nature of the purported perceiving itself, including beliefs that the perceiver holds about his or her own identity and empirical character. The same holds not just for acts of perception, according to Husserl, but for any mental act whatsoever. The phenomenologist can reflect on those claims without any commitment to their empirical truth at all. Moreover, the phenomenologist can even reflect on what would count as good empirical evidence for those claims and the necessary limitations of such evidence. There can be doubt about whether there is anything that corresponds to these contents of consciousness, and even about the identity of the consciousness that is aware of them, but whenever these contents are present for consciousness there can be no doubt of their presence for the consciousness that is aware of them. Moreover, on reflection, one can also become aware of what would count as experiences that would validate the claims inherent in these beliefs about things like trees, our own identity, or anything else we might intend. Thus, if phenomenology limits itself to an analysis of these "pure" contents, that is the contents apart from all of the empirically dubitable claims attached to them, it has access to a sphere that is beyond doubt, a realm of apodictic certainty for its analyses.

Within this realm of pure self-givenness, Husserl's interest is and remains the analysis of essential structures and connections within cognition, of its various forms and correlative objectivities. Thus transcendental phenomenological reduction involves a third moment, which one might term eidetic reduction. Phenomenology's interest pertains to the eidetic, that is, the invariant and thus essential elements that present themselves to pure consciousness. In the Sixth Investigation, Husserl had maintained that such invariant structures or essences can be just as much an object for pure intuitions as an empirical physical object can be given to sense perception. With this reduction to the sphere of pure universal self-givenness, Husserl now believes he can distinguish phenomenology from descriptive psychology, since the investigation no longer concerns the immanent sphere of empirical consciousness, but rather the realm of the purely self-given contents that can be made apodictically evident to phenomenological reflection. Phenomenological reduction thus builds on and presupposes the procedure of imaginative variation through which those things that can conceivably be otherwise than they are may be separated from those that cannot conceivably change. This procedure, known as "eidetic variation," is a kind of thought experiment employed by the phenomenologist to distinguish empirical associations and contingent conjunctions from essential structures that cannot conceivably be different from the way they are. Phenomenology is thus a science of "pure possibilities" whose interest is directed to the necessities that underlie any such possibilities and consequently also hold for any conceivable actuality, so that they apply to all possible and actual relationships without implying any commitment to which actual relationships and objects genuinely exist.

Husserl introduced the phenomenological reduction for the first time to a wider audience outside his lecture halls in his major programmatic work, *Ideas Pertaining to a Pure Phenomenology and to a Phenomenological Philosophy, First Book*, which he described as a general introduction to pure phenomenology (commonly referred to simply as *Ideas I*). It was published in 1913 as the first volume of the *Yearbook for Philosophy and Phenomenological Research,* which he cofounded and edited together with Alexander Pfänder, Moritz Geiger, Max Scheler, and Adolf Reinach, and which was to remain the leading venue for phenomenological research until its final volume in 1930. In the general introduction, Husserl describes the sphere of phenomenological research as the "region of pure consciousness," as the "region of all regions," since it is within and for that sphere that all other regions are constituted. Transcendental phenomenology is said to be a kind of transcendental idealism, within which the pure or invariant structure of an act of consciousness (the "noesis"), its corresponding intentional object (the "noema"), and the necessary correlation between the two are investigated. It does not purport to replace the individual sciences that operate in the natural attitude and concern themselves with empirical facts. Instead, it seeks to ground all of them as well as formal disciplines such as logic and mathematics by showing how each of them presupposes certain essential structures or essences, whose description and explication can be properly executed only by transcendental phenomenology that brackets out or neutralizes the assumptions made within the natural attitude. The term Husserl now introduces to describe the process by which subjects come to intend objects is "constitution," through which he seeks to avoid causal terms that would imply a dependency relationship between two existing things such as consciousness and objects, but at the same time stresses the necessary role of specific cognitive operations (noeses) if various kinds of objects are to become present for consciousness (noemata).

In the final section of *Ideas I*, Husserl turns to the questions of reason and actuality. How does phenomenology fit in with the traditional philosophical project of rational foundation for knowledge and action, and what is the relationship between the eidetic analyses undertaken in phenomenology and actual existence? Husserl describes the two problems as interrelated, for to speak "reasonably" or rationally about objects involves a claim to justification or possible confirmation through evidence. Thus, under "reason" in this context Husserl understands the inherent directedness of intentions toward fulfillment. There is not only a corresponding noema for each noesis, but also the inherent directedness of objective consciousness toward the confirmation or fulfillment that would establish the relationship toward an actually existent object that would be identical to that noema. However, since there can be different kinds or "regions" of objectivities (such as physical objects, mathematical objects, cultural objects, etc.), there will also be correspondingly different kinds of confirming intuitions that fulfill them. Thus the philosophical project of reason is to lay out what these would be and systematically to delineate the various kinds of essential relationships that hold between them. Again, it is a nonphilosophical question which of these intentions is actually fulfilled, but that does not mean that phenomenology as the science of reason does not address questions of actual existence or actual objects, only that it addresses them exclusively in terms of their "meaning" and their structure. It analyzes the kinds of fulfillment that would be appropriate to these intentions and their corresponding objects, but does not claim to be able to take a stance as a pure science on which of them actually has been or will be fulfilled or not. This means that, for Husserl, the themes of reason, being, and truth are essentially interconnected in a way that presages how Heidegger's later analyses also attempt to establish an essential interconnection between *logos*, Being, and truth as *alētheia*.

It is during this period that, in addition to intentionality, temporality emerges for Husserl as the second significant essential structure of all consciousness. He demonstrates how consciousness occurs as a flow, so that each event in conscious life has a temporal location with regard to all others. The appearance of any object can necessarily be characterized in terms of a "now," a "before," or an "after." Moreover, Husserl's further analyses reveal that these distinct modes of past, present, and future are not only mutually related to each other, but also should not be conceived as discrete moments, each separated sharply from the other. Rather, the now appears always with a temporal fringe or horizon. The now taken as a moment around which past and future gather is never strictly an isolated point. Indeed, the very idea of the now as a point is merely a limit concept that is never experienced in itself, since in conscious life every now also involves the consciousness of a having-been that has immediately preceded it and a not-yet that is about to become now. Thus, the "now" for consciousness is always an extended "living presence" that, as the "originary temporal field," also includes the "no-longer" and the "not-yet."

One of Husserl's original contributions to the discussion of temporality, which he had taken up from Brentano, is his distinction between "retention" as that form of the no-longer that is part of the immediate horizon of the now, and "memory," which involves making present again to consciousness what was no longer immediately present for consciousness. Retention, along with "protention," its corresponding form of the not-yet, is a mode of what Husserl calls "impressional consciousness." Memory, by contrast, is a form of "representational consciousness." For example, when one hears a melody, a note runs off into the retentional past as it comes to be replaced by a new one, without disappearing from consciousness, since it would otherwise be impossible to hear a melody as such. Similarly, there arises at each moment a new anticipation of a coming note (its "protention") emanating from the present, which Husserl calls the "primal" impression in order to distinguish the way that it is present for retentive and protentive consciousness. All of these modes of temporal awareness of objects are ultimately grounded for Husserl in the temporality of consciousness itself, that is, in the self-constitution of its own identity throughout its different moments in the flow of consciousness. Another name for transcendental subjectivity is therefore "absolute primordially constituting consciousness" or "absolute primordial temporality," which has a specific structure that can be the object of phenomenological analysis and forms the horizon against which the constitution of the empirical consciousness of the individual and the objects of consciousness takes place. However, in *Ideas I* and other works from this period, Husserl does not trace back the constitution of specific kinds of objects to their ultimate temporal foundations, even though it is indeed during this period that the framework for such a project was laid.

IV. THE FREIBURG YEARS (1916–38)

A few years after the appearance of *Ideas I*, Husserl was named Chair of Philosophy at the University of Freiburg, succeeding Heinrich Rickert, who had accepted an appointment in Heidelberg and recommended Husserl to follow him. Here Husserl remained for the rest of his academic career until his retirement in 1928, and then until the end of his life in 1938. During these years, Husserl concentrated on the completion of phenomenology not just as a methodology, but as a concrete and comprehensive research project. This involved, on the one hand, pursuing a wide range of specific phenomenological constitutional analyses into the relationship between realms of nature and of spirit, or the correlative naturalistic and personalistic attitudes, as well as into the structure of the everyday life-world out of which science emerges; into intersubjectivity and into nature as the correlate of intersubjective intentionality; into the constitution of ideal objects such as numbers or geometrical shapes; into the foundations of sense experience and formal logic; and into the phenomenological foundation for normative sciences such as ethics and value theory. On the other hand, it also involved a deepened understanding of what phenomenological analysis must entail if it is indeed supposed to trace back the constitution of various kinds of objects to their ultimate origins. Instead of being a static description of various kinds of essential structures and the necessary relationships that obtain between them, if phenomenology is to be a genuine science of absolute origins, it will ultimately have to trace back all forms of objectivity to the structures of consciousness and its basic forms of intentionality and temporality. Constitutive phenomenology thus explicitly evolves into genetic phenomenology, which traces higher-order forms of objectivity back to lower-order forms, and these in turn to the most elementary structures of intentional consciousness that in turn have their ultimate basis in modes of temporality. Accordingly, phenomenology not only must provide a description of the essential relationships governing all of reality, but must also provide an account of the necessary origins of these relationships in and for consciousness in accordance with its most elementary structures. It must not only describe the constitution of the predicative realm and the operations most directly and easily accessible to reflection, but also trace these back to activities at the pre-predicative level that are generally thought of rather as passivities, the passive syntheses that take place at the most basic levels of consciousness as it organizes sense experience into the experience of individual material objects, on the basis of which higher-order objects are constituted.

One guiding theme throughout all of Husserl's work, and not only in this period, is his opposition to philosophy's recent attempt to model itself after the natural sciences and to reductionistic tendencies in many other sciences that have also falsely attempted to pattern themselves after that model. This is already a familiar theme developed in Husserl's earlier refutation of psychologism, where he argued against the attempt to reduce mathematics and logic to natural phenomena in the *Logical Investigations*, and then later again in his critique of naturalism, where he refutes the attempt to reduce all mental phenomena to externally observable physical entities in "Philosophy as a Rigorous Science." Already during his middle period, Husserl had discovered commonalities in this regard with the philosophy of life as represented by Dilthey, and with philosophers such as Wilhelm Windelband and Rickert, neo-Kantians of the Southwest School who stressed the independence of the cultural sciences from the natural sciences. Whereas the critique of naturalism in the *Logos* essay clearly demonstrated Husserl's common ground with them, the polemical tone of the critique of historicism offered in the second part of that essay (which exhibits Husserl's concern with the topic of history and the relationship between philosophy and the cultural sciences) stresses Husserl's differences from Dilthey and related thinkers instead of their commonalities. Indeed, not until the very last major published work by Husserl, *The Crisis of the European Sciences and Transcendental Phenomenology* (1936), does it become apparent that Husserl shares with the philosophers of life and of culture an appreciation of the cultural and historical dimensions that are constitutive of everyday human existence, dimensions that provide the background against which abstract disciplines such as the modern natural sciences arise. However, posthumously published writings such as Husserl's *Ideas II* reveal that Husserl had gained an appreciation for the non-naturalistic attitude that constitutes everyday life much earlier and that he had been decisively influenced in this regard by Dilthey, Windelband, and Rickert.

In *Ideas II*, Husserl contrasts the naturalistic and the personalistic attitudes. Each attitude may be described as a noetic stance, within which specific kinds of entities appear for consciousness. In the naturalistic attitude, everything appears as nature in the sense of modern natural science: what exists is spatially and temporally located, causally determined, and measurable. Husserl analyzes the fundamental concepts or categories that govern this region and shows how anything that does not fit into these categories is dismissed as nonexistent by these standards. However, Husserl makes clear that the naturalistic attitude is only one possible stance toward objects, and that other equally legitimate attitudes can reveal other kinds of equally genuine objects. For instance, in the personalistic attitude, governed by the category not of causality but of motivation, other human beings are encountered as subjects of intentional states who behave in the way they do not because of material causes, but on the basis of motivating mental states such as beliefs and desires. Moreover, even the everyday nonhuman objects that surround us are organized not in terms of the predicates of natural science, but rather in terms of their serviceability to our needs. In contrast to the world of "nature" and its seemingly objective properties, the everyday world in which we live as persons is filled with cultural objects such as tables and chairs and with other human beings who are also persons with beliefs, needs, and desires of their own.

In *Ideas II*, Husserl also examines the essential relationships that hold between the two different regions that emerge in the two different attitudes – that is, the naturalistic and the personalistic – and concludes not only that the personalistic realm is every bit as much a realm of genuine objects as the naturalistic realm, but also that the latter, that is, the scientific realm, is grounded in the former, the realm of everyday life, and not the other way round. Although it is true that the higher-order objects such as cultural objects or persons are founded on natural objects in the sense that each of these more complex, higher-order objects necessarily contains a stratum that can be described simply in naturalistic terms (its weight, spatial location, etc.), Husserl demonstrates that the realm of nature as such arises only through abstraction from the predicates that present themselves to us as genuine predicates of the objects in our everyday, concrete lived existence. The realm of nature or science is an abstraction derived from and therefore dependent on the realm of concrete everyday existence that we encounter in the personalistic attitude. Moreover, in the personalistic world, which Husserl calls the "*Umwelt*" ("environment" or literally "surrounding world") in contrast to nature, it is apparent that objectivities emerge for us in the way they do, show up as tables or chairs, in view of certain subjective acts. This realm makes the subjective role in the constitution of objects more easily apparent than an approach through the realm of nature, since the latter, in its search for universal and reliable structures of the objects, constitutes an idea of "objectivity" that is seemingly independent of any subjective acts or attitudes. Phenomenological investigation reveals, however, that this very notion of "objectivity" is itself a subjective construct that can be traced back to certain motivations and interests of persons. As such it is also subject to critical examination. If it is clear that the everyday surrounding world shows up the way it does in part as a result of the activity of a subject or a community of subjects, then critical reflection on its origins and justification is also possible. Whereas the world of science can tend to forget or hide its subjective origins and thus seem to remove itself from the necessity for critical scrutiny, the personalistic attitude is much closer to the truths that phenomenology reveals, namely that all supposed objectivities are correlates of subjective activities and attitudes that are amenable to reflective analysis and criticism.

One important insight developed for the first time in this work is the recognition that, in everyday perception, one is aware not only of the information provided to us about these objects through our senses, but also of information about the state and activity of ourselves as embodied agents as well. These ideas will be especially important for Merleau-Ponty in his *Phenomenology of Perception*. Using the notion of *kinaesthesis*, which in nineteenth-century psychology was used to describe our immediate sense of our bodies' own positions and movements that we can have without necessarily having to see or hear these movements, Husserl extends the term to refer not only to our awareness of our own bodily position and movements, but also to the way that we are actually engaged as embodied agents in the process of perception itself. We might walk around an object to get a better look at it or be in a better position to hear something. Moreover, whenever we are trying to make sense of what is going on in the world, we are constantly in the process of sorting out those changes in the perceptual field that come from changes in our bodily positioning and those that are independent of it. For instance, when I shake my head from right to left, what I see changes, but I attribute those changes not to changes in the objects seen, but to how my field of vision is changing because of the change in the direction I am looking. Moreover, in daily perception I am also aware that much of the way the world looks has to do with me and my own bodily states (where I am looking, whether I have good or poor eyesight, etc.), but also with the circumstances under which I perceive things (in a dark or well-illuminated room or in a room with a red light bulb that makes everything else appear with a reddish hue). In everyday life, then, the notion or "optimal" or "normal" perceptual conditions plays a constitutive role in our view about how objects "really" are.

Husserl also builds on these insight in the later sections of part one of *Ideas II*, where he shows how a modern notion of objectivity in the scientific sense emerged through an attempt to construct a conceptual framework that would not be contingent on accidental features of the human perceptual apparatus (e.g. the difference between primary and secondary qualities) or other "subjective" factors.

In fact, in Husserl's final works he returned to these themes and developed them further. In a 1935 essay entitled "Philosophy and the Crisis of European Humanity," he expanded his critique of naturalism into a sweeping indictment of the recent developments of Western culture in general under the heading of "objectivism." Objectivism, according to Husserl, is the belief that all genuine knowledge is objective knowledge and that objective knowledge is to be gained only by science after the model of modern natural science as it has developed since Galileo. Questions not accessible to the modern mathematical sciences are taken to be outside the realm of the rational; entities that cannot be captured in or reduced to these terms are taken to be nonexistent. Husserl, by contrast, claims that phenomenology realizes the true telos of Western science that was initiated by the Greeks and reawakened at the beginning of the modern age through its quest for absolute rational grounding of the subject and its activities by means of radical self-reflection. Rather than grounding all other sciences, modern mathematically oriented natural science must itself be grounded in a more radical and basic science, that of pure phenomenology.

In *The Crisis of the European Sciences and Transcendental Phenomenology*, Husserl presents an extended and detailed study of precisely how Galilean science emerged against the backdrop of a much broader attempt to capture nature in an all-encompassing rational framework. Husserl traces out how this ideal mathematization arose out of the everyday practice of measuring, then ultimately took on a dynamic of its own so that it came to appear as if nature as the construction of modern natural science bore no inherent relationship at all to human motivations and practices. Modern science involves a kind of subjective self-forgottenness in which human beings have come to take certain tenets about the nature of reality and knowledge for granted that now seem to be exempt from or even nullify the possibility of critical reflection on them. For instance, the assumption that all real knowledge can be or must be empirically verified is not itself an empirical tenet, nor is the modern assumption that all real entities are natural entities. These basic philosophical assumptions arise out of and express a specific worldview that cannot be justified or falsified through the procedures of modern natural science. The name for the ultimate sphere out of which science and all other human practices arise is now termed the "life-world."

Since it is the source for all other spheres of human activity and cognition, its investigation is the proper object of transcendental phenomenology.

The reference to Galileo and the mathematization of nature in modern science points to another central theme in Husserl's later work, namely the origin of ideal entities such as logical principles and mathematical entities out of the most basic tendencies in human cognitive life. This topic, the foundation and origin of mathematics and logic, had of course been one of Husserl's guiding concerns since his earliest work. In the other major published work from Husserl's later period, *The Formal and Transcendental Logic* (1929), Husserl once again returned to this problem, now not just in regard to arithmetic and its basic operations, nor to certain questions related to the general nature of formal logic, as in the first volume of the *Logical Investigations*; rather, he now tried to show in a very detailed way how the formalization of reason and its operations can result in the discipline of formal logic and its various divisions along with a pure science of manifolds or quantities. He also tried to show how even formal logic, since it necessarily aims at truth, still implicitly refers to and depends on its roots in the life-world out of which it arises. In this work, Husserl also introduces a distinction between apodicticity and adequacy that has far-reaching implications for his own phenomenological project. In his original formulations of the phenomenological method, Husserl had contrasted the apodicticity or certainty of phenomenological analysis under the presupposition of the transcendental reduction with the inherent inadequacy of empirical knowledge about external objects, suggesting that the difference between the two removed any source of uncertainty or error from phenomenological research. However, even nonempirical research such as phenomenological investigations always has absolute universality as part of its very intention, so that the attainment of such apodictic knowledge must at least in principle be reconfirmed over and again by the same researcher at different times and by other members of the community of researchers in order to test its adequacy. This, then, makes phenomenology not only an unending project that must be ever renewed, but also an inherently intersubjective enterprise to be carried out by individuals working in concert with one another, guided by the ideals of truth and self-responsibility.

This brings us to one final predominant theme in Husserl's later work that also deserves mention. If, on the one hand, phenomenology proceeds through pure reflection on the part of individual subjects, and yet on the other hand, as a genuine science, lays claim to intersubjective validity, then the problem of intersubjectivity and the idea of intersubjective validity will be especially pressing for phenomenology.[4] Husserl's most extended and best-known treatment of

*4. For a discussion of the question of the other in Husserl and Fichte, see the essay by Robert Williams in *The History of Continental Philosophy: Volume 1*.

the problem can be found in the fifth of his *Cartesian Meditations*, based on a series of lectures he gave at the Sorbonne in 1929 and published only in French translation during his lifetime. The intention of the Fifth Cartesian Meditation is to show that phenomenology is not a solipsistic enterprise. Consistent with his general project of showing how higher-level, more complicated intentions arise from simpler lower-order intentions, Husserl traces out the constitution of intersubjectivity for subjective consciousness. He begins by isolating that stratum of consciousness that is conceivable without any reference to other subjects. By abstracting from everything that involves a commitment to the existence of other subjects and any elements of consciousness that depend on others, Husserl identifies that stratum of conscious life he terms the "sphere of ownness." Within this primordial sphere, however, Husserl notes there is still a stratum of the world as the correlate of my isolated but ongoing experience, a stratum he calls "nature within ownness," that is different from the full notion of intersubjectively constituted nature that we intend in our everyday experience. Within this sphere there is also one unique object, namely one's own lived body (*Leib*) that is the organ of sense impressions and of movement and activity. Even as an isolated individual – if such a thing were empirically possible – one would thus be capable of recognizing objects within the world, of constituting oneself as a unity of body and soul, and of organizing the world in terms of use and value predicates. However, a subject that had constituted the notion of a lived body as a unity of mental and physical nature in his or her own case would also be capable of recognizing other perceivable entities that resemble his or her body in their appearance and behavior. Husserl calls the attribution of mental states to these other bodies on the basis of the observations of general similarities between my own lived body and theirs "pairing." The apprehension of these entities as lived bodies involves seeing them and their behavior as an expression (*Ausdruck*) of mental states. He refers to this apprehension as "empathy" (*Einfühlung*), although he admits that this term is easily misleading. He also describes it as an "appresentation," since the specifically subjective side of the other, the other's first-person awareness as such, is still never given to one directly. One can indeed have genuine and reliable awareness of at least some of another person's mental states, but only on the basis of some externally observable deed or statement. The experience of the other is therefore said to be founded on, but not reducible to, the physically observable states of his or her body as a material object in the world. In imputing to the other a subjectivity like mine, I also constitute the idea of a world that is the same for us all in spite of different perspectives, an intersubjective nature, and I can envisage myself as an object for others, as part of that intersubjective world. Moreover, it is also possible to constitute on this basis a world of shared values, a cultural world that could ultimately serve as the norm against which all individual beliefs and actions can be measured. Phenomenology as the realization of the inherent striving of all agents for rationality in the form of beliefs and norms that can be universally justified is thus necessarily an intersubjective enterprise, toward which Husserl viewed his own work as an important, but merely initial, contribution.

This analysis and most especially the reduction to the "primordial sphere" has been much discussed and criticized in subsequent phenomenological and post-phenomenological work, perhaps most notably by Emmanuel Levinas. Many question whether such a reduction is even possible. Others are concerned about the purported priority it seems to give to an isolated subject who is the source of the being of all other subjects. Can the concept of "pairing" do justice to the irreducible otherness of the other? Are community and language not so fundamentally presupposed for the constitution of any subject as such that the very notion of a primordial sphere as the foundation for intersubjectivity reverses the appropriate foundational order? Much of the answer to these questions will have to do with one's reading of the nature of Husserl's project in this brief Meditation.

From its beginnings as a theory in the foundations of logic and mathematics and as a method of reflection on the pure contents of the mental life of individual subjects, Husserl's phenomenology evolves into an all-encompassing research program that reveals the historical and intersubjective origins of the world in which we live and the objects within it. Husserl himself never rejects the centrality of the method of transcendental reduction, nor does he overlook the important foundational role of the simplest elements of conscious life, for example sense perception and an individual's direct first-person awareness of his or her own mental states. But Husserl's analyses demonstrate at the same time that the concrete world – the world in which we all live and which provides the basis from which any specialized scientific research, the world from which even phenomenology itself must proceed – is constituted historically and intersubjectively. Later successors to Husserl's phenomenological project, notably Heidegger, Eugen Fink,[5] Merleau-Ponty, Jacques Derrida, and Levinas, will attempt to go beyond Husserl by purging his approach and his results of what

5. Eugen Fink (1905–75) was Husserl's research assistant from 1928 until Husserl's death in 1938. In Husserl's final years, he collaborated closely with Fink and took steps to insure that Fink, and not Heidegger, would take his place at the center of the phenomenological research community. Fink also played a crucial role in assisting Father Herman Leo van Breda in the transfer of all of Husserl's manuscripts to Leuven, Belgium in 1938, and he emigrated to Belgium to continue working with the manuscripts in 1939. Following the German invasion of Belgium, Fink returned to Germany, and, after the war, he was instrumental in the establishment of the Husserl-Archiv in Freiburg in 1950, where he worked until 1971. His critical assessment of Husserl's phenomenology is described in great detail in Ronald Bruzina, *Edmund Husserl and Eugen Fink: Beginnings and Ends in Phenomenology, 1928–1938* (New Haven, CT: Yale University Press, 2004). Fink's interpretation of Husserl had an important influence on later French readers such as Merleau-Ponty and Derrida.

they perceive as undue Cartesian residues in the emphasis on logic, science, perception, theory, and subjective reflection. They consciously acknowledge their debt to the phenomenological method as developed by Husserl, but attempt to take his insights and develop them into a new way of doing philosophy that moves from the sphere of modern philosophy, in which he still located himself, into a new kind of philosophy that overcomes the modern scientifically oriented philosophy of subjective reflection. On this reading, Husserl represents an important transitional figure in the history of continental philosophy, since he stands as a leading and perhaps the last great representative of classical modern philosophy and a key figure in the transition to a philosophy that goes beyond it.

MAJOR WORKS

Husserliana, vols 1–30. Dordrecht: Kluwer, 1951ff. [The definitive and ongoing critical edition of Husserl's writings in German; abbreviated *Hua*.]

Logische Untersuchungen (1900, 1901), *Hua*, vol. 17 (1975) and *Hua*, vol. 19 (1984). Published in English as *Logical Investigations*, translated by J. N. Findlay. New York: Humanities Press, 1970.

"Philosophie als strenge Wissenschaft" (1911), *Hua*, vol. 25 (1987). Published in English as "Philosophy as a Rigorous Science," translated by Quentin Lauer. In *Phenomenology and the Crisis of Philosophy*, 69–147 (New York: Harper & Row, 1965).

Ideen zu einer reinen Phänomenologie und phänomenologischen Philosophie: Erstes Buch (1913), *Hua*, vol. 3 (1950). Published in English as *Ideas Pertaining to a Pure Phenomenology and to a Phenomenological Philosophy: First Book*, translated by F. Kersten. The Hague: Martinus Nijhoff, 1982.

Zur Phänomenologie des inneren Zeitbewußtseins (1928), *Hua*, vol. 10 (1966). Published in English as *Lectures on the Phenomenology of Inner Time Consciousness*, translated by John Brough. Dordrecht: Kluwer, 1991.

Formale und transzendentale Logik (1929), *Hua*, vol. 27 (1974). Published in English as *Formal and Transcendental Logic*, translated by Dorion Cairns. The Hague: Martinus Nijhoff, 1969.

Ideen zu einer reinen Phänomenologie und phänomenologischen Philosophie: Zweites Buch (1930), *Hua*, vol. 4 (1952). Published in English as *Ideas Pertaining to a Pure Phenomenology and to a Phenomenological Philosophy: Second Book*, translated by Richard Rojcewicz and André Schuwer. Dordrecht: Kluwer, 1989.

Cartesianische Meditationen (1931), *Hua*, vol. 1 (1951). Published in English as *Cartesian Meditations*, translated by Dorion Cairns. The Hague: Martinus Nijhoff, 1960.

Die Krisis der europäischen Wissenschaften und die transzendentale Phänomenologie (1936), *Hua*, vol. 6 (1954). Published in English as *The Crisis of European Sciences and Transcendental Phenomenology: An Introduction to Phenomenological Philosophy*, translated by David Carr. Evanston, IL: Northwestern University Press, 1970.

6

MAX SCHELER

Dan Zahavi

I. SCHELER'S LIFE AND WORK

Max Ferdinand Scheler was born in Munich on August 22, 1874, and brought up in an orthodox Jewish household. After completing high school in 1894, he started to study medicine, philosophy, and psychology. He studied with Theodor Lipps in Munich, with Georg Simmel and Wilhelm Dilthey in Berlin, and with Rudolf Eucken in Jena,[1] where he received his doctorate in 1897 with a thesis entitled *Beiträge zur Feststellung der Beziehungen zwischen den logischen und ethischen Prinzipien* (Contributions to an appraisal of the relations between the logical and ethical principles). Two years later this was followed by his habilitation thesis on *Die transzendentale und die psychologische Methode*.[2] In 1902, Scheler met Edmund Husserl for the first time at a reception in Halle given by Hans Vaihinger (1852–1933), the editor of *Kant-Studien*. Their discussion mainly turned on the relation between intuition and perception.[3] It was a meeting that would prove quite decisive for Scheler. As he was subsequently to write in the preface of *Der Formalismus in der Ethik und die materiale Wertethik*, "I owe the methodological consciousness of the unity and sense of the phenomenological

1. Theodor Lipps (1851–1914) was a prominent philosopher and psychologist known today mainly for his work on empathy. Georg Simmel (1858–1918) was an influential sociologist, and Rudolf Eucken (1846–1926) a philosopher, known mainly for his principle of ethical activism, who won the Nobel Prize for Literature in 1908.
2. Scheler's influences included Bergson, Dilthey, Eucken, Husserl, Kant, Nietzsche, and Pascal.
3. Max Scheler, *Die deutsche Philosophie der Gegenwart*, *Gesammelte Werke Band 7* (Bern/Munich: Francke, 1973), 308.

attitude to the work of Husserl," but as he then also continues, "I take full responsibility for the manner in which I understand and execute this attitude."[4]

Scheler is notorious for his rather tumultuous private life. In 1899, he converted to Catholicism and married Amélie von Dewitz-Krebs; it was an unhappy marriage that quickly fell apart, allegedly because of Scheler's many love affairs. In 1905–6, marital problems led to a public scandal that as a result had Scheler's wife confined in a psychiatric institution, whereas Scheler was forced to relinquish his teaching position in Jena and move to Munich. One consequence of this move was that Scheler was able to join the Munich Phenomenological Circle. This group consisted of students of Lipps (Theodor Conrad, Johannes Daubert, Moritz Geiger, Dietrich von Hildebrand, and Alexander Pfänder) who had all been devoted to phenomenology since the publication of Husserl's *Logical Investigations*. In the meantime, Scheler's unhappy marriage dragged on, and in 1910, as the result of yet another debacle, where his wife publicly accused Scheler of amoral behavior, Scheler lost his position, and had to begin earning his income as a free lecturer, essayist, and publicist. From 1910 to 1911, Scheler lectured in Göttingen, where he met the Göttingen phenomenologists (including Hedwig Conrad-Martius, Jean Hering, Roman Ingarden, Alexandre Koyré, and Adolf Reinach). Edith Stein was at this point one of his students. In 1912 Scheler finally managed to obtain a divorce, and shortly afterwards he married Märit Furtwängler – the sister of the noted conductor – and left for Berlin.[5]

Scheler had by then managed to establish himself as a phenomenological voice to count on, and in 1913 he was asked by Husserl to become coeditor of the *Jahrbuch für Philosophie und phänomenologische Forschung*, together with Pfänder, Geiger, and Reinach. It was in this venue that both parts of his *Formalismus* were published in 1913 and 1916, respectively. In 1913 he also published the work *Zur Phänomenologie und Theorie der Sympathiegefühle und von Liebe und Hass* (later republished in an extended version in 1923 under the better-known title *Wesen und Formen der Sympathie*).

Scheler's reputation continued to increase and by the end of the First World War he was considered one of the most influential Catholic thinkers in Germany. After a short interim, during which Scheler joined the German Foreign Office as a diplomat in Geneva and The Hague, he was in 1919 invited by Konrad Adenauer – then mayor in Cologne – to become one of the directors of the newly founded Forschungsinstitut für Sozialwissenschaft and at the same time professor of philosophy in Cologne. Shortly after taking up the position, however, Scheler

4. Max Scheler, *Formalism in Ethics and Non-Formal Ethics of Values: A New Attempt Toward a Foundation of an Ethical Personalism*, Manfred S. Frings and Roger L. Funk (trans.) (Evanston, IL: Northwestern University Press, 1973), xi.

*5. The work of many of the phenomenologists mentioned in this paragraph is touched on in the essay by Diane Perpich in this volume.

publicly distanced himself from the Catholic faith. This alienated him not only from his erstwhile supporters in Cologne, but also from many of his phenomenological colleagues who, owing to his influence, had converted to Catholicism. In the same period, Scheler fell in love with a young student, Maria Scheu. In 1923, he divorced his second wife and married Scheu the following year, a move that did little to improve his popularity in Catholic circles. During these years, Scheler's reputation as a phenomenologist continued to grow; he was the first of the leading phenomenologists to be invited to visit France, in 1924 and again in 1926, and his 1923 text *Wesen und Formen der Sympathie* was the first work of phenomenology to appear in French translation, published in 1928 as *Nature et formes de la sympathie: Contribution à l'étude des lois de la vie émotionnelle.* In 1928 Scheler was offered the Chair in Philosophy and Sociology at the University of Frankfurt. He accepted the position with pleasure, looking forward to future collaboration with thinkers such as Ernst Cassirer, Karl Mannheim, and Rudolf Otto, but on May 19, 1928, he died suddenly of heart failure. In his eulogy, Heidegger would praise him as "the strongest philosophical force in modern Germany, nay, in contemporary Europe and in contemporary philosophy as such."[6]

When reading Scheler, one is struck by the scope of his references. It is more wide-ranging than what one will find, for instance, in Husserl or Heidegger. The sources he drew on included not only classics from the history of Western philosophy as well as contemporary empirical research, but also works by figures such as Buddha, Freud, Muhammad, Goethe, Lao Tzu, Darwin, and Tagore.

When Scheler died in 1928, many of his writings remained unpublished. The publication of his posthumous writings commenced in 1933, but the enterprise came to a sudden halt with the rise of Nazism, which suppressed and banned Scheler's work owing to his Jewish background. Their publication resumed in 1954.

II. PHENOMENOLOGY AS EIDETIC ANALYSIS

Scheler worked on a wide variety of topics, and it is impossible to do justice to them all in a short overview such as this.[7] However, in his late text *Die Stellung des Menschen in Kosmos*, Scheler writes that the question concerning the ontological status of man had been central to him since the beginnings of his philosophical career, and that he had spent more time on this question than on any

6. Martin Heidegger, *The Metaphysical Foundations of Logic*, Michael Heim (trans.) (Bloomington, IN: Indiana University Press, 1984), 50.
7. For an excellent general introduction, see Angelika Sander, *Max Scheler zur Einführung* (Hamburg: Junius, 2001).

other.[8] Given Scheler's recognized status as a phenomenologist and as a pioneer of philosophical anthropology, these two domains will constitute the focal points in the following presentation. I shall start with a brief account of Scheler's phenomenological methodology, and then in turn discuss his concept of person, his description of the nature of sociality, and the in-depth analysis of expression and empathy found in *Wesen und Formen der Sympathie*. This selection, which pays scant attention to his value theory, is motivated by what I take to constitute Scheler's more enduring contribution, and also reflects the manner in which Scheler was received and discussed by contemporary and subsequent phenomenologists such as Stein, Husserl, Heidegger, Schutz, Sartre, and Merleau-Ponty.[9]

Scheler's understanding of phenomenology has many affinities with the early reception of Husserl's writings by the Munich and Göttingen phenomenologists. Scheler took the guiding idea of phenomenology to be the clear distinction between the essential and the existential, between the essence and the fact.[10] He consequently (mis)read Husserl's phenomenological reduction to be a question of ignoring the *hic et nunc* of objects in order to focus on their essential features. To put it differently, Scheler read Husserl's phenomenological reduction as an eidetic reduction, thereby disregarding the distinctly transcendental aspects of Husserl's enterprise. Indeed, rather than seeing phenomenology as a form of transcendental philosophy, Scheler primarily conceived of it as an intuitively based eidetic discipline.[11] For the same reason, Scheler distanced himself from Husserl's *Ideas I*, which Scheler characterized as a turn toward epistemological idealism and as a curbing of phenomenology to a mere eidetics of consciousness.[12]

Phenomenology is supposed to provide a rigorous intuitive method that will allow for the disclosure of *a priori* structures. This intuitive basis was stressed to such an extent by Scheler that his definition of phenomenology must count as decidedly antihermeneutical. On his account, the aim of phenomenology is to describe the given in as direct, unprejudiced, and pure a manner as possible, thereby allowing for a disclosure of its essence. As he writes in one of his posthumously published writings, phenomenology has achieved its goal when "there is no longer any transcendence and any symbol left."[13] Indeed, on his view, whereas nonphenomenological experience is experience through or by means of symbols

8. Max Scheler, *Die Stellung des Menschen im Kosmos* (Darmstadt: Otto Reichl, 1928), 9.
9. To illustrate (but see also the concluding section of this overview), of the six thinkers mentioned, the most extensive discussion of Scheler is found in a paper by Alfred Schutz entitled "Scheler's Theory of Intersubjectivity and the General Thesis of the Alter Ego."
10. Scheler, *Die deutsche Philosophie*, 307.
11. Scheler, *Formalism in Ethics*, 48; *Die deutsche Philosophie*, 308.
12. *Ibid.*, 311.
13. Max Scheler, *Schriften aus dem Nachlaß I: Zur Ethik und Erkenntnislehre, Gesammelte Werke Band 10* (Bern: Francke, 1957), 386.

and hence remains a mediated experience that never gives us the things themselves, phenomenological experience is in principle nonsymbolic. It alone yields facts themselves in an immediate and unmediated fashion. In phenomenological experience nothing is meant that is not given and nothing is given that is not meant: phenomenological experience contains no transcendence.[14]

Scheler's strength as a phenomenological thinker is undoubtedly to be found in his concrete analyses – in particular in his analyses of emotional life and sociality – rather than in his methodological considerations. It is for this very reason remarkable that he was quite explicit in his rejection and ridicule of what he termed "picture-book phenomenology," namely, the view that phenomenology should primarily be concerned with various eidetic analyses, and that any overarching systematization and systematic ambition should be avoided since it inevitably would involve distortions of the phenomena to be investigated.[15]

III. THE CONCEPT OF PERSON

According to Scheler, the task of philosophical anthropology is to show how all specifically human products, abilities, and activities are rooted in the fundamental ontological structures of man.[16] What then, on his account, uniquely characterizes human existence?

Scheler accepts the classical distinction between inorganic (or inanimate) being on the one hand and living creatures on the other. Whereas inorganic being lacks any kind of individual unity and interiority (*Innesein*) – it is in no way for-itself (*für-sich*) – all living creatures possess these features; they are more than merely objects for external observers. Scheler ultimately distinguishes three different levels of living creatures. At the bottom, we find plants, which although they possess unity and individuality (if you cut a plant in two, you destroy it), and even a certain interiority and expressivity (plants can appear as languishing, vigorous, etc.), lack both consciousness and self-consciousness. Next we find animals, which possess consciousness but which at the same time are bound to the environment. At the top level, we find human beings, who possess both consciousness and self-consciousness, and who in contrast to animals are not caught up in the world, but rather retain a certain distance from it: a distance that also enables them to objectify entities. To put it differently, in order to apperceive the given as objects, it is necessary to distance oneself somewhat from it. The ability to do so is a distinctive feature of human beings. Thus, on

14. Scheler, *Formalism in Ethics*, 50–51.

15. *Ibid.*, xix.

16. Scheler, *Die Stellung des Menschen im Kosmos*, 86.

Scheler's account, among all creatures human beings alone are able to distance themselves from the world and to objectify the world (and themselves). What provides human beings with this ability? The fact that human beings are spiritual creatures. Indeed, what characterizes human beings as human is precisely the presence of spirit (*Geist*). It is our spirituality that makes our human life highly independent of drives and independent of the attachment to a specific environment. It is our spirituality that allows us to transform and transcend the closed environment and makes us open to the world (*weltoffen*).[17] As he puts it at one point, man is "the one who can say 'no', the ascetic of life, the eternal protestant against all mere reality."[18]

Scheler next argues that the center from which human beings are able to perform these objectifying acts cannot be a part of the world, but must rather be appreciated as an aspatial and atemporal dimension.[19] Indeed, for Scheler the spiritual center or source of intentional acts – which he also calls the *person* – is not only not a substance or thing, but is in its core nonobjectifiable.[20] This holds true not only for our own personal being, but also for other persons. We cannot objectify them without losing them as other persons.[21]

Despite his occasional reference to the Kantian idea of a transcendental subject, however, Scheler's notion of person differs in certain crucial respects. For Scheler, the person is not some posited supra-individual principle behind or outside the immediately given. Rather, the person is the immediate coexperienced unity of experiencing. The person only exists and lives in the accomplishment or performance of intentional acts.[22] Furthermore, every person is individuated as a person, and not merely by virtue of their bodies, their spatiotemporal locations, and the content of experience. Indeed, for Scheler persons are absolute individuals in the sense that they and they alone are individuated in terms of themselves. So far, Scheler's concept of person might be different from Kant's but it seems to retain a high degree of formality. However, Scheler also claims that the possession of a fully sound mind is a prerequisite for being a person.[23] On this account, animals, as well as children, madmen, and slaves (!), are not persons. Your thoughts and actions must be bound by a unity of sense, must constitute parts of one meaningful life, if you are to qualify as a person.

17. *Ibid.*, 39.
18. *Ibid.*, 56.
19. *Ibid.*, 80.
20. *Ibid.*, 64, 79.
21. *Ibid.*, 49.
22. Scheler, *Formalism in Ethics*, 371, 386.
23. *Ibid.*, 476.

You must be the source of your own decisions, feelings, and thoughts; you must enjoy control and mastery over your own body.[24]

IV. SCHELER ON EMPATHY

Scheler's work *Wesen und Formen der Sympathie* (1923) is frequently listed as an example of a phenomenological investigation of emotional life. But in addition to presenting us with careful analyses of various emotional phenomena, the work must also be considered a significant contribution to the phenomenology of sociality and social cognition. It is no coincidence that Scheler at the outset states that the problem of how we understand other minds is a foundational problem for the human sciences. It is one that must be resolved if we are to determine the scientific status of history, psychology, sociology, and so on with any degree of adequacy.[25]

According to Scheler, sociality is not primarily a theoretical matter; rather, it is an essential aspect of our emotional life. Indeed, a fundamental Pascalian claim of Scheler's is that our emotions are characterized by an *a priori* content and are subject to *a priori* laws, and that one must recognize an *a priori* "order of the heart" or "logic of the heart."[26] It is in connection with his analysis of this emotional *a priori* that Scheler makes the claim that "all morally relevant acts, experiences, and states, in so far as they contain an intentional reference to other moral persons" (acts such as obligation, responsibility, loving, promising, etc.), "refer, by the very nature of the acts themselves, to other people," without implying that such others must already have been previously encountered in concrete experience (NS 229). Hence our relation to the other is not some empirical fact; on the contrary, the concrete experience of others presupposes an *a priori* relatedness to one another, and simply represents the unfolding of this possibility.[27]

Scheler elaborates on this by stating that every finite person is as originally a member of a community as he is an individual. A human being does not live a communal life with other persons "from pure accident"; rather, being a (finite) person as such "is just as originally a matter of being … 'together'" as it is a matter of being-for-oneself.[28] Thus, the experience of belonging to a community

24. *Ibid.*, 479.
25. Max Scheler, *The Nature of Sympathy*, P. Heath (trans.) (London: Routledge & Kegan Paul, 1954), xlviii–xlix. Hereafter cited as NS followed by the page number.
26. Scheler, *Formalism in Ethics*, 63.
27. *Ibid.*, 535.
28. Max Scheler, *On the Eternal in Man*, B. Noble (trans.) (New York: Harper & Brothers, 1960), 373.

is just as fundamental as self-experience and world-experience, and the intention "in the direction of community" exists completely independently of whether or not it finds fulfillment in a contingent experience of others. Scheler illustrates this idea by speaking of an epistemological Robinson Crusoe. Such a figure would be aware of his relatedness to an intersubjective community even if he had never had a concrete experience of others, and, indeed, would possess such an awareness by virtue of his experience of an emptiness or absence or lack in the fulfillment of intentions such as loving, promising, requesting, obeying, and so on, which can only form an objective unity of sense "*in conjunction with* the possibility of a social *response*" (NS 235).

Scheler obviously considers the relation between the individual and the community to be essential. But what kind of justification might we have for positing the real *de facto* existence of a specific other? How is the other given? To answer this question, we need to take a closer look at Scheler's analysis of empathy. Let us start by considering two groups of cases discussed by Scheler.

Consider first the situation where you see the face of a crying child, but rather than seeing it as expressing discomfort or distress, you see merely a certain distortion of the facial muscles; that is, you basically do not see it as emotionally expressive. Compare this (pathological case) with the situation where you see the same face as emotionally expressive, but without feeling any compassion, that is, while remaining indifferent. And finally consider the situation where you also feel compassion or concern for the child. For Scheler, the last situation counts as a case of sympathy, which he considers an ethically relevant act. But in order to feel sympathy – in order to feel compassion with, say, somebody's suffering – you need to realize or recognize that the other is indeed suffering. More basic than sympathy is what Scheler terms *Nachfühlen*, rendered in the following as *empathy*.[29] In short, whereas empathy has to do with a basic understanding of expressive others, sympathy adds care or concern for the other.

29. Unfortunately, Scheler does not stick to a single term when referring to this basic form of understanding. Rather, he uses terms such as *Nachfühlen* (reproduction of feeling), *Nachleben* (reproduction of experience), *Nacherleben* (visualizing of experience), *Verstehen* (understanding), and *Fremdwahrnehmung* (perception of other minds) (NS 9, 238). In some of the cases, the English translation might not be ideal, but Scheler himself must also be blamed for the inevitable confusion. How can *Nachfühlen* and *Fremdwahrnehmung* refer to one and the same phenomenon? As we shall see in a moment, Scheler rejects the view that our understanding of the emotional experience of others is based on an imitation or reproduction of the emotion in question, but why does he then himself use a term like *Nachfühlen*? The fact remains, however, that Scheler is quite unequivocal in his rejection of the view that our understanding of the emotional experiences of others requires us to have the same emotion ourselves (NS 9–10), and one must consequently simply note that his choice of terms left something to be desired. For want of a better term, I have decided to use "empathy" as the best way of capturing what Scheler was referring to when he spoke of a basic experience of others.

Now, apart from stressing the difference between empathy and sympathy, the point of Scheler's example is also to make it clear that it is possible to empathize with somebody without feeling any sympathy (NS 8–9). Just think of the skilled interrogator or the sadist. Sadistic cruelty does not consist merely in failing to notice the other's pain, but in empathically enjoying it (NS 14).

Consider now a second group of cases. You might enter a bar and be swept over by the jolly atmosphere. A distinctive feature of what is known as *emotional contagion* is that you literally catch the emotion in question (NS 15). It is transferred to you. It becomes your own emotion. Indeed you can be infected by the jolly or angry mood of others without even being aware of them as distinct individuals. But this is precisely what makes emotional contagion different from both empathy and sympathy. In empathy and sympathy, the experience you empathically understand or sympathetically care for remains that of the other. In both of the latter cases, the focus is on the other, the distance between self and other is preserved and upheld. Another distinctive feature of emotional contagion is that it concerns the emotional quality rather than the object of the emotion. You can be infected by cheerfulness or hilarity without knowing what it is about. This is what makes emotional contagion different from what Scheler calls *emotional sharing*. Consider the situation where a father and mother stand next to the corpse of a beloved child. For Scheler, this situation exemplifies the possibility of sharing both an emotion (sorrow or despair) and the object of the emotion. But emotional sharing must on its part still be distinguished from both empathy and sympathy. Consider the situation where a common friend approaches the despairing parents. He can empathize or more likely sympathize with their sorrow, without himself experiencing the despair in question, which is why his state of mind differs qualitatively from either of theirs. Indeed their sorrow and his empathy or sympathy are clearly two distinct states. Their sorrow is the intentional object of his empathy or sympathy (NS 12–13). On Scheler's account, empathy is not simply a question of an intellectual judgment that somebody else is undergoing a certain experience. It is not the mere thought that this is the case; rather, Scheler clearly defends the view that we are empathically able to *experience* other minds (NS 9). It is no coincidence that Scheler repeatedly speaks of the perception of others (*Fremdwahrnehmung*), and even entitles his own theory a *perceptual theory of other minds* (NS 220). Empathy

---

"Empathy" is usually considered the standard translation of *Einfühlung*, and it so happens that Scheler himself only used the latter term rather sparingly, and, when he did, frequently rather dismissively. However, Scheler's reservation was mainly due to his dissatisfaction with Lipps's projective theory of empathy, and it is telling that other contemporary phenomenologists, including Stein, also referred to Scheler's theory of empathy (*Einfühlung*); see Edith Stein, *On the Problem of Empathy*, Waltraut Stein (trans.) (Washington, DC: ICS Publications, 1989), 27.

is a basic, irreducible, form of intentionality that is directed toward the experiences of others. It is a question of understanding other experiencing subjects. But this does not entail that the other's experience is literally transmitted to us. It does not entail that we share his or her experience, and it does not entail that we ourselves undergo, say, the emotion we observe in the other. It might – as a consequence – but it is not a pre-requisite. We might encounter a furious neighbor and become furious ourselves, but our empathic understanding of our neighbor's emotion might also elicit a quite different response, namely, the feeling of fear.

To sum up, on Scheler's account empathy involves neither some kind of analogical inference, nor some kind of projection, simulation, or imitation (NS 12). In fact, Scheler insists that it is necessary to reject the projective theory of empathy in all its forms (NS xlviii), and he is also very dismissive of the attempt to account for the experience of others in terms of some imaginative transformation. In basic empathy, the focus is on the other, on his thoughts and feelings, and not on myself, not on how it would be like for me to be in the shoes of the other (NS 39).

V. ANALOGY AND EXPRESSION

Scheler's investigation of empathy and social understanding is restricted to the personal level. He is not concerned with the various sub-personal mechanisms that might be involved in interpersonal understanding. His main objection against competing theories seems to be that they are phenomenologically inadequate and that they fail to do justice to our actual experience. On this basis, it might be natural to conclude that his project is exclusively descriptive. It seeks to describe how we experience other minds, but it does not address the normative question concerning the justification or validity of that experience. But this is a mistake. Not only does Scheler provide more systematic arguments against the appeal to analogical inference, but ultimately he also seeks to provide an account of the nature of experience that makes comprehensible how we can experience other minds, and why such an experience can be justified.

According to Scheler, the argument from analogy presupposes that which it is meant to explain. In order for the argument to work, there has to be a similarity between the way in which my own body is given to me, and the way in which the body of the other is given to me. But if I am to see a similarity between, say, my laughing or crying and the laughing or crying of somebody else, I need to understand the bodily gestures and behavior as expressive phenomena, as manifestations of joy or pain, and not simply as physical movements. If such an understanding is required for the argument of analogy to proceed, however, the argument presupposes that which it is supposed to establish. To put it differently, in some cases we do employ analogical lines of reasoning, but we do so only when we are already convinced that we are facing minded creatures but are simply unsure about precisely how we are to interpret the expressive phenomena in question (NS 240).

In addition, Scheler questions two of the basic presuppositions behind the argument from analogy. First, it assumes that my point of departure is my own consciousness. This is what is at first given to me in a quite direct and unmediated fashion, and it is this purely mental self-experience that is then taken to precede and make possible the recognition of others. One is at home in oneself and one then has to project into the other, whom one does not know, what one already finds in oneself. Incidentally, this implies that one is able to understand only those psychological states in others that one has already experienced in oneself. Second, the argument also assumes that we never have direct access to another person's mind. We can never *experience* her thoughts or feelings. We can only infer that they must exist based on that which is actually given to us, namely, her bodily behavior. Although both of these assumptions might seem perfectly obvious, Scheler rejects both. As he points out, as philosophers it is our duty to question the obvious. We should pay attention to what is actually given, rather than letting some theory dictate what can be given (NS 244). On his view, the argument from analogy underestimates the difficulties involved in self-experience and overestimates the difficulties involved in the experience of others (NS 244–6). We should not ignore what can be directly perceived about others and we should not fail to acknowledge the embodied and embedded nature of self-experience. Scheler consequently denies that our initial self-acquaintance is of a purely mental nature, as if it anteceded our experience of our own expressive movements and actions, and as if it took place in isolation from others. He considers such an initial purely internal self-observation a mere fiction.

Scheler also denies that our basic acquaintance with others is inferential in nature. As he argues, there is something highly problematic about claiming that intersubjective understanding is a two-stage process, of which the first stage is the perception of meaningless behavior, and the second an intellectually based attribution of psychological meaning. Scheler argues that in the face-to-face encounter we are neither confronted with a mere body, nor with a pure soul, but with the unity of an embodied mind. He speaks of an "expressive unity" (*Ausdruckseinheit*), and claims that the notion of behavior is a psychophysically undifferentiated concept. It is only subsequently, through a process of abstraction, that this unity is divided and our interest then proceeds "inwards" toward the merely psychological or "outwards" toward the merely physical (NS 218, 261).

Foreshadowing something that both Sartre and Levinas would later discuss in more detail, Scheler writes that I experience, say, the hostility or love in the expression of another's gaze long before I can specify the color of his eyes (NS 244). Indeed, on Scheler's account, our primary knowledge of nature is knowledge of expressive phenomena. He finds this claim corroborated by newborns' preferential interest for expressive faces and human voices. This knowledge of a living world is taken to precede our knowledge of a dead and mechanical world. So, for Scheler, it is not the case that we first see inanimate objects and then animate them through a subsequent addition of mental components. Rather, at first we see everything as expressive, and then we go through a process of de-animation. Learning is a question of *Entseelung* (de-animation) rather than *Beseelung* (animation) (NS 239).

To sum up, Scheler opposed the view according to which our encounter with others is first and foremost an encounter with bodily and behavioral exteriorities devoid of any psychological properties. According to such a view, which has been defended by behaviorists and Cartesians alike, behavior, considered in itself, is neither expressive nor significant. All that is *given* is physical qualities and their changes. Seeing a radiant face means seeing certain characteristic distortions of the facial muscles. But, as Scheler pointed out, this account presents us with a distorted picture, not only of behavior but also of the mind. It is no coincidence that we use psychological terms to describe behavior and that we would be hard pressed to describe the latter in terms of bare movements. In most cases, it is quite hard (and artificial) to divide a phenomenon neatly into its psychological and behavioral aspect; think, for example, of a groan of pain, a handshake, an embrace, a leisurely stroll. In his view, affective and emotional states are not simply qualities of subjective experience; rather, they are given *in* expressive phenomena; that is, they are expressed in bodily gestures and actions, and they thereby become visible to others. Instead of attempting to secure an access to the minded life of others through technical detours, he argued that we need a new understanding of the given. If the realm of expressive phenomena is accepted as the primary datum or primitive stratum of perception, the access to the mind of others will no longer present the same kind of problem. What we see is the body of the other as a field expressive of his or her experiences (NS 10). Indeed, on Scheler's view, expressive phenomena – in particular facial expressions and gestures, but also verbal expressions – can present us with a direct and noninferential experience of the emotional life of others. As he eventually put it:

> For we certainly believe ourselves to be directly acquainted with another person's joy in his laughter, with his sorrow and pain in his tears, with his shame in his blushing, with his entreaty in his outstretched hands, with his love in his look of affection, with his

> rage in the gnashing of his teeth, with his threats in the clenching of his fist, and with the tenor of his thoughts in the sound of his words. If anyone tells me that this is not "perception," for it cannot be so, in view of the fact that a perception is simply a "complex of physical sensations," and that there is certainly no sensation of another person's mind nor any stimulus from such a source, I would beg him to turn aside from such questionable theories and address himself to the phenomenological facts. (NS 260)

It should by now be clear that Scheler took a solution to the problem of other minds to require a correct understanding of the relation between mind and body. And of course, the mind–body relation in question is not the mind–brain relation. Scheler was not concerned with the search for the neural correlates of consciousness. Rather, he was interested in the relation between experience and expressive behavior, and he obviously took the connection to be intimate and essential. He claimed that a repression of the emotional expression will necessarily lead to a reduction of the felt quality of the emotion (NS 251), and he even postulated the existence of what he called a universal grammar of expression, one that enables us to understand – to some extent at least – the expressions of other species, be it the gasping fish or the bird with the broken wing (NS 11, 82).

Despite his emphasis on the extent to which the life of the mind of others is visible in their expressions, Scheler insisted however that we should not commit the mistake of claiming that all aspects of the experiential life of an individual are equally accessible to others. Whereas we can in many cases intuit and even share the other's beliefs and emotions, there are, on Scheler's account, two limitations. On the one hand, we cannot literally share bodily sensations like a stomach ache (NS 255). I can have a similar stomach ache, but I cannot have the very same pain sensation as somebody else. On the other hand, although Scheler obviously concedes that we can learn something about the other from his *automatic* and *involuntary* expressions, he also insisted that there is a limit to how far this will get us. If we wish to grasp what Scheler called the intimate spiritual being of the other, that is the essence of his personhood, we need to rely on language and communication. More specifically, Scheler claimed that there will be aspects of the other that will remain concealed or hidden unless the other decides to reveal and communicate it freely (NS 225). Yet, even then, there will remain something ineffable in the other. There is an absolute intimate sphere of foreign personhood that even the act of free communicative intention cannot disclose (NS 66, 219). On some occasions, though, Scheler suggests that love is what can bring us closest to the essence of foreign individuality. As he would say, drives make blind, whereas love makes seeing (NS 71, 160).

VI. SCHELER'S RECEPTION BY AND INFLUENCE ON OTHER PHENOMENOLOGISTS

An early sustained engagement with Scheler's theory can be found in Stein's 1916 dissertation *On the Problem of Empathy*. Not surprisingly, her focus is on Scheler's account of how we come to understand others. Although she does raise critical points, her overall appraisal of his theory is positive, and she certainly takes it to constitute an improvement compared to Lipps's projective account of empathy.

After Scheler lost his position in 1910, Husserl wrote him a strong letter of reference, stating that Scheler was no second-rate thinker, but a very sharp, independent and scientifically rigorous scholar.[30] In his subsequent private correspondence, however, Husserl repeatedly expressed serious reservations about Scheler's work. Not surprisingly, his main objection concerned methodological issues. In letters to his friend Adolf Grimme (1889–1963) from 1917 and 1918, Husserl complained about Scheler's alleged attempt to hijack phenomenology for his own purposes, and even described Scheler as a genius of reproduction and secondary originality.[31] Indeed Husserl's main criticism was precisely that Scheler had misunderstood the sense of phenomenology by confusing the phenomenological reduction with the eidetic reduction, thereby missing its true transcendental character in favor of a philosophically naive anthropology.[32] In letters to Ingarden from 1927 and 1931, Husserl disputed that Scheler was a true phenomenologist, and made it clear that Scheler and Heidegger were the main targets of his 1931 lecture "Phenomenology and Anthropology" (although Scheler is mentioned only once by name, and Heidegger not at all).[33] In this lecture, Husserl referred very critically to the younger generation of German philosophers, who, inspired by Dilthey's philosophy of life, had turned toward philosophical anthropology and sought to renew philosophy through a focus on concrete existence.

At the beginning of his analysis of being-with (*Mitsein*) in *Being and Time,* Heidegger referred to Scheler's *The Nature of Sympathy* in support of his claim that a clarification of being-in-the-world leads us to the insight that a subject is never given in isolation from others.[34] But most of Heidegger's discussion of Scheler concerned the latter's analysis of personhood, in particular his attempt

30. Edmund Husserl, *Briefwechsel*, in collected works, *Husserliana*, Edmund Husserl Dokumente 3/1–10, Karl Schuhmann (ed.) (Dordrecht: Kluwer, 1994), *II*, 232.
31. Husserl, *Briefwechsel III*, 79–81.
32. Husserl, *Briefwechsel VI*, 429, 457, 459.
33. Husserl, *Briefwechsel III*, 232, 273–4.
34. Martin Heidegger, *Being and Time*, Joan Stambaugh (trans.) (Albany, NY: SUNY Press, 1996), 109.

to stress the nonobjectifiable character of the person.[35] According to Heidegger, Scheler failed to think the *being* of the person in a sufficiently radical manner. This criticism is more developed in Heidegger's 1925 lecture course *History of the Concept of Time*. As we have seen above, for Scheler the person exists in the performance of intentional acts. The person is neither a thing nor a substance. But Heidegger asked for a more positive determination of the being of the person, and argued that Scheler remained silent on this and failed to articulate or develop the concept of performance.[36]

Of the major phenomenologists, Merleau-Ponty was probably the one to appraise Scheler's work most positively. *Phenomenology of Perception* contains a number of references to Scheler, but Merleau-Ponty's most extensive reference to Scheler in that book touches on Scheler's conception of expression and on his criticism of the argument from analogy.[37] Scheler's contribution to both of these issues is also taken up in Merleau-Ponty's lectures on child psychology at the Sorbonne, where Merleau-Ponty, however, added a critical remark. He claimed that Scheler, in order to make the experience of others possible, ended up defending a kind of pan-psychism that led to a denial of the individuation of consciousness and thereby also to a destruction of the very distinction between self and other.[38] Although Scheler does at one point write that we can take the existence of emotional identification (*Einsfühlung*) – a limit case of emotional contagion – as an indication of the metaphysical unity of all organic life (NS 73–4), Merleau-Ponty's criticism is nevertheless unjustified, since Scheler is adamant in insisting that the existence of a unity on the level of organic life in no way rules out the *absolute difference* between individual persons (NS 65, 121). Indeed, one of the central findings of Scheler's analysis of empathy was precisely that it presupposes the difference between self and other.[39]

---

35. *Ibid.*, 44.
36. Martin Heidegger, *History of the Concept of Time: Prolegomena*, Theodore Kisiel (trans.) (Bloomington, IN: Indiana University Press, 1985), 126–8.
37. Maurice Merleau-Ponty, *Phenomenology of Perception*, Colin Smith (trans.) (New York: Routledge & Kegan Paul, 1962), 184, 352.
38. Maurice Merleau-Ponty, *Merleau-Ponty à la Sorbonne* (Grenoble: Cynara, 1988), 41–4.
39. Merleau-Ponty's criticism is nevertheless interesting since it throws an illuminating light on one of Merleau-Ponty's own famous claims, found in *Signs*, where he writes: "The solitude from which we emerge to intersubjective life is not that of the monad. It is only the haze of an anonymous life that separates us from being; and the barrier between us and others is impalpable. If there is a break, it is not between me and the other person; it is between a primordial generality we are intermingled in and the precise system, myself–the others. What 'precedes' intersubjective life cannot be numerically distinguished from it, precisely because at this level there is neither individuation nor numerical distinction" (*Signs*, Richard C. McCleary [trans.] [Evanston, IL: Northwestern University Press, 1964], 174).

Scheler's application of phenomenology to areas such as the emotional and affective domain, sociology, anthropology, and philosophy of religion was instrumental in making phenomenology known and appreciated outside academia. Indeed, in the period between Husserl's *Ideas I* (1913) and Heidegger's *Being and Time* (1927) – when neither of these thinkers published any major works – Scheler counted in the public eye as the most prominent phenomenologist.[40] Although Scheler was not a very systematic thinker, he proved a source of inspiration for many contemporaries, including neurologist Paul Schilder (1886–1940), physician and physiologist Viktor von Weizsäcker (1886–1957), psychiatrists Kurt Schneider (1887–1967), Viktor Frankl (1905–97), Ludwig Binswanger (1881–1966), psychologist F. J. J. Buytendijk (1887–1974), and sociologists Helmuth Plessner (1892–1985) and Arnold Gehlen (1904–76).[41]

MAJOR WORKS

Gesammelte Werke I–XV, edited by Maria Scheler (until 1969) and Manfred S. Frings. Bern/Munich: Francke, 1954–85; Bonn: Bouvier, 1985–97.

Der Formalismus in der Ethik und die materiale Wertethik: Neuer Versuch der Grundlegung eines ethischen Personalismus (1913, 1916), *Gesammelte Werke*, vol. 2. Bern/Munich: Francke, 1954. Published in English as *Formalism in Ethics and Non-Formal Ethics of Values: A New Attempt Toward a Foundation of an Ethical Personalism*, translated by Manfred S. Frings and Roger L. Funk. Evanston, IL: Northwestern University Press, 1973.

Vom Ewigen im Menschen (1921), *Gesammelte Werke*, vol. 5. Bern/Munich: Francke, 1954. Published in English as *On the Eternal in Man*, translated by Bernard Noble. New York: Harper & Brothers, 1960.

Wesen und Formen der Sympathie; Die deutsche Philosophie der Gegenwart (1923), *Gesammelte Werke*, vol. 7. Bern/Munich: Francke, 1973. Published in English as *The Nature of Sympathy*, translated by Peter Heath. London: Routledge & Kegan Paul, 1954.

Die Wissensformen und die Gesellschaft (1926), *Gesammelte Werke*, vol. 8. Bern/Munich: Francke, 1960. Published in English as *Problems of a Sociology of Knowledge*, translated by Manfred S. Frings. London: Routledge & Kegan Paul, 1980.

Die Stellung des Menschen im Kosmos (1928). Darmstadt: Otto Reichl, 1928. Published in English as *Man's Place in Nature*, translated by Hans Meyerhoff. New York: Noonday Press, 1961.

40. Wolfgang Henckmann, *Max Scheler* (Munich: C. H. Beck, 1988), 232.
41. Indeed, Gehlen argued that Scheler's *Die Stellung des Menschen im Kosmos* constituted the point of departure for modern philosophical anthropology; "Rückblick auf die Philosophie Max Schelers," in *Max Scheler im Gegenwartsgeschehen der Philosophie*, Paul Good (ed.) (Bern: Francke, 1975), 188.

7
THE EARLY HEIDEGGER

Miguel de Beistegui

Held by many to be the greatest philosopher of the twentieth century (and by others as an obscure philosopher whose involvement with National Socialism only highlighted the flaws of his philosophy), Martin Heidegger exercised, and continues to exercise, a deep fascination and considerable influence over generations of students and philosophers (Hannah Arendt, Hans-Georg Gadamer, Hans Jonas, Leo Strauss, Max Horkheimer, Herbert Marcuse, Jacques Derrida, and Emmanuel Levinas, to name only a few).[1] His personal and philosophical style was entirely new, and his understanding of the history, the aim, and the nature of philosophy nothing short of revolutionary. To this day, and despite the roughly eighty volumes of his *Complete Works* already published, it is his third book – *Being and Time* (1927) – that remains his most famous work. The reason for its success lies in the fact that it was the result of ten years of relentless and groundbreaking philosophical activity, carried out mostly in a series of lecture courses and seminars between 1916 (the year his previous work, in fact his habilitation dissertation, was published) and 1926. This is all the more remarkable in that the work in question was – and remains – incomplete. Its incompleteness was due partly to the sudden pressure under which Heidegger came to publish the results of his research and philosophical questioning in order to obtain a Chair at the University of Freiburg. More fundamentally, though, it was the

1. Martin Heidegger (September 26, 1889–May 26, 1976; born in Messkirch, Germany; died in Freiburg) was educated at the Gymnasium, Konstanz (1903–6), Gymnasium and archiepiscopal convent, Freiburg im Breisgau (1906–9), and Freiburg University (1909–15). His influences included Aristotle, Augustine, Dilthey, Hegel, Husserl, Kant, Kierkegaard, Lask, Luther, Nietzsche, and Rickert, and he held appointments at Freiburg University (1915–23, 1928–45), and Marburg University (1923–28).

sign that the project laid out in the book – and characterized as "fundamental ontology" – however groundbreaking, could not succeed on its own terms, and needed to be revised. This realization, in turn, forced Heidegger's thought into a new beginning, and triggered an extraordinary burst of philosophical creation in the 1930s and 1940s.[2] By following the itinerary of Heidegger's thought from his early years as a student to the publication of *Being and Time* and its immediate aftermath, we shall see how he arrived at the following conclusions, which are the central theses of his *magnum opus*: first, that the one and only question that philosophy always presupposes, but is never able to make explicit or answer adequately, is the question of being (*die Seinsfrage*), or the difference between beings (*das Seiende*) and being (*das Sein*) – a difference Heidegger also refers to as the ontico-ontological difference; second, that in order to be addressed properly, and solved, the question of being must be formulated in terms of *time* – time is the key to understanding what it means to be, not just for ourselves, but for all "beings." It was only by understanding being *in terms of* time, and by transforming classical ontology into onto-chronology, that Heidegger was able to revolutionize philosophy. But this is a revolution that occurred after many years of hard work and a series of breakthroughs.

I. THE STUDENT YEARS (1909–15)

(a) From theology to philosophy

Born in the quiet, rural, and conservative Swabian town of Messkirch, and into a modest, Catholic family, Heidegger gained access to secondary and higher education through the material and financial support of the Catholic Church. He was destined for the priesthood (his father was the sexton of the Church of St. Martin). His Catholicism, and his complex and tormented relation with it, should not be underestimated. He attributes his early interest in philosophy, and in the question that was to guide him through the writing of his *magnum opus*, *Being and Time*, to the reading in 1907 of Franz Brentano's doctoral thesis, *On the Manifold Senses of Being according to Aristotle* (1862).[3] If, as Aristotle claimed, we can rightly say of all the things that are (of "beings" or *das Seiende*) that they *are* in different ways, and that what it means for them *to be* varies in each instance (*to on legethai pollakos*), according to meanings or "categories" that we can list (being as "substance," "accident," "truth," "actuality," "potenti-

*2. For a discussion of Heidegger's work following the period covered by this essay, see the essay by Dennis J. Schmidt in *The History of Continental Philosophy: Volume 4*.

3. Martin Heidegger, "My Way to Phenomenology," in *On Time and Being*, Joan Stambaugh (trans.) (New York: Harper & Row, 1972).

ality," etc.), might it be possible to go further still and identify a single, unifying meaning of being (*Sein*) itself? And could this question be *the* question of philosophy? Also important for Heidegger at that time was the discovery of a book entitled *Vom Sein: Abriss der Ontologie* (1896) by Carl Braig, a Freiburg theologian who taught Heidegger a few years later. The reading of Brentano and Braig was key in introducing Heidegger to a puzzlement regarding what he later called the "question of being" (*die Seinsfrage*) and to the problematic of intentionality as a way of addressing it.

Between 1909 and 1911, Heidegger studied theology and philosophy at the Department of Philosophy at the University of Freiburg in preparation for the archdiocesan priesthood. In the winter semester of 1911–12, he withdrew from the Department of Theology and the Theological Seminary for health reasons and abandoned his career plans for the priesthood. He attended classes in mathematics (in analytic geometry of space, differential and integral calculus, algebraic analysis, and advanced algebra), experimental physics and chemistry, but also in logic and epistemology, epistemology, and metaphysics (with the neo-Kantian Heinrich Rickert), the history of philosophy, theology (dogmatic theology, Gospel of John), Hellenic mystery religions, and art history, before deciding to dedicate himself entirely to philosophy. In July 1913, he obtained his doctorate with *Die Lehre vom Urteil im Psychologismus* (The doctrine of judgment in psychologism). Immediately thereafter (August 1913), he applied to the Freiburg Archdiocesan Chancellery Office for a grant in order "to dedicate himself to the study of Christian philosophy and to pursue an academic career" through work on the habilitation and license to teach in German universities as a lecturer (*Privatdozent*). He was awarded a scholarship for two years with the expectation that he "would remain true to the spirit of Thomistic philosophy." In 1915, he submitted his habilitation thesis *Die Kategorien- und Bedeutungslehre des Duns Scotus* (The doctrine of categories and meaning according to Duns Scotus), directed by Rickert.[4]

(b) Phenomeno-logical investigations

After his early encounter with the works of Brentano and Braig, and his initial puzzlement concerning the manifold meaning of being, Heidegger seemed to be moving in a different direction. He devoted his initial investigations, written under the influence of Husserl's *Logical Investigations* and the neo-Kantian

4. Both of Heidegger's theses are now published in volume one of the collected works, *Gesamtausgabe*, hereafter cited as GA followed by the volume and page or section number (indicated by §). In cases where an English translation is available, the English page references will follow the German page references.

School of Baden (of Emil Lask, Rickert, and Wilhelm Windelband, in particular), to problems of judgment, categories, and meaning: in short, problems of logic.[5] A closer look at those early works, however, enables one to see how they in fact prepared the way for the type of questioning that eventually led to the publication of *Being and Time* by focusing on the status and origin of meaning as such. Where is the sphere or layer of meaning to be located? What should we attribute it to? What is it a matter for? Throughout his early period, Heidegger focuses on the question of judgment. Why judgment? Because it is through judgments or propositions that we know, and that the existing world makes sense: meaning is a prerequisite to knowledge. For Heidegger, logic is not the formal, symbolic logic of Frege and Russell – a conception that, in his mind, is too limited – but the study concerning "the conditions of knowing in general." In other words, logic is the "theory of theory," the "doctrine of science" (*Wissenschaftslehre*), or the science of the "primally theoretical" (*Urtheoretisches*) (GA 1, 23). Today, we would call it epistemology. Inasmuch as they deal with the conditions of knowledge, or truth, judgments constitute the "core" of logic, or its "archetype" (*Urgebilde*) (GA 1, 268). It is where meaning originates. Later on, as we shall see, Heidegger will reject that idea, and argue that life, not judgment, is the original source of meaning.

It is important to emphasize the fact that, following Husserl's critique of psychologism in the *Prolegomena* to *Logical Investigations*, Heidegger understands judgments not as psychic acts, or subjective representations, but as purely logical acts. Naturally, Heidegger writes, judgments involve a synthesis of representations. As such, they can be seen as psychic acts: the act of judging is a fleeting lived experience (*Erlebnis*) that comes and goes. Yet what distinguishes judgments from other representations is their reference to the true–untrue distinction (GA 1, 30). Now this distinction is one that we can attribute to neither our representations nor our volitions: if judgments, or propositions, were to be true only so long as the act of judging lasted, then there would be no truth in the first place. If, following Scotus, we can rightly claim that the *ens logicum* is an *ens rationis*, or an *ens in anima*, we cannot reduce it to a psychic reality (GA 1, 277). Translated into Husserlian, phenomenological language, Scotus's formulation means that the noematic sense or correlate of intentionality obviously cannot be distinguished from consciousness; equally, though, it means that it is not simply contained within consciousness, as a part is contained in a whole (GA 1, 277). What is expressed or intended in the judgment is something independent

5. In GA 1, we also find an early review essay entitled "Recent Research in Logic," originally published in 1912, and now partly translated and paraphrased in *Becoming Heidegger: On the Trail of his Early Occasional Writings, 1910–1927*, Theodore Kisiel and Thomas Sheehan (eds) (Evanston, IL: Northwestern University Press, 2007), 50.

of subjective experience. It is what §11 of Husserl's First Investigation refers to as the meaning (*Bedeutung*) of the judgment, and what Scotus called its *significatio* (GA 1, 328).

We must distinguish, therefore, between two aspects of the judgment, which are always intertwined: the judgment as *ideal* unity, or as *Bedeutung*; and the *real* judgment, the actual proposition that we can hear or read. Whereas psychology may have something to say about the latter, it has nothing to say regarding the former, which requires the construction of a "doctrine of meaning" (*Bedeutungslehre*), or, to use the Scholastic terminology, a *tractatus de modi significandi*. A "pure" logic only, and not, for example, a psychology, or a metaphysics, as Scotus made amply clear, can fulfill such an aim: insofar as the *ens logicum* is an *ens rationis*, it is not an *ens naturae*, that is, a natural or real thing, whether sensible or supra-sensible. It is autonomous with respect to the subjective (psychological) as well as the objective (real or actual) sphere. "Meaning," in that sense, refers neither to the psycho-physical act of judging – to the manner, that is, in which the act of knowledge is produced (for that is what psychology does) – nor to something real (*das Wirkliche*, *die Existenz*), but to what Husserl called the *Sachverhalt* (the content) of judgment, that is, its truth or cognitive character. This content, Heidegger goes on to explain, following this time Hermann Lotze,[6] is what "holds" or "values" (*gilt*) objectively, or with binding "validity" (*Geltung*): it is an atemporal mode of being that expresses a truth independent of our time-bound existence, our statements and thoughts, and the objects that we usually discuss (GA 1, 22).[7] We need to emphasize, at this point, the sharp distinction that Heidegger draws between "meaning," "truth," and "validity" as the object of logic, and "reality," "existence," and "actuality" as the object of the empirical sciences, and psychology in particular. The answer to the question regarding the meaning of being will require the convergence of those two opposed realms, and the reconciliation of *logos* and *being* in onto-logy.

Heidegger's habilitation dissertation reveals two traits that will remain decisive for his entire thought. The first, borrowed from Hegel, whom Heidegger quotes at the outset, is that philosophy and the history of philosophy are not two separate disciplines. In fact, the history of philosophy is the only way into

6. Rudolf Hermann Lotze (1817–81) made important contributions to the emerging project of neo-Kantian epistemology, especially in connection with the concept of validity. In his *Logik*, book III, §316, Lotze establishes a key distinction between being (or actuality), becoming (or events), and valuing (which applies to judgments). Propositions are neither actual, existing beings, nor events, but *validities*. Validities are themselves purely logical entities, as opposed to psycho-physiological acts. As a result, many subsequent philosophers, including Heidegger, credited Lotze with helping to forge one of the earliest criticisms of psychologism.

7. See also Richard Polt, *Heidegger: An Introduction* (Ithaca, NY: Cornell University Press, 1999), 12.

philosophy itself. While philosophy is something for the present, there is something forever present about great thinkers of the past. The second trait concerns the status of logic, language, and meaning. What Heidegger saw in Scotus, and especially in the "speculative grammar" (*grammatica speculativa*) that, at the time, scholars (wrongly) attributed to Scotus, is an investigation into the conditions of possibility of language and sense in general. In other words, Heidegger read Scotus as a proto-Husserlian who had developed a "theory of the forms of meaning," or a "logic of sense" very close to Husserl's "pure logical grammar." Scotus's logic is not purely syllogistic, that is, concerned with the art of formal demonstration, as in Aristotle. Rather, it is akin to what Husserl characterizes as a "formal apophantics." It is the part of logic that deals with the *a priori* laws of sense and that, as such, precedes the art of proof, or the logic of consequence (of reasoning). It is concerned with sense in its opposition to nonsense, and not to counter-sense. With the logic of sense, we arrive at the most primordial layer of logic, already developed by Husserl in his Fourth Investigation.

But before dealing with that logic in the second part of his habilitation, Heidegger deals with the doctrine of categories. In doing so, he comes closer to the question that will eventually shape his *magnum opus*. Toward the very beginning of the first chapter, he remarks that Scotus puts his finger on a decisive feature of our relation to the world in general, as a world made of objects, or things. Of an object in general, irrespective of the categories with which we can describe it, we can say that it is something, or that it *is*. No doubt influenced by Husserl's Sixth Investigation, and by his account of categorial intuition, Heidegger notes how we have all experienced having before us something, being aware of a presence, before actually knowing whether it is a substance or an accident, before being able to attribute a more precise categorial determination to the thing in question. In other words, before our intellectual gaze has been able to identify what is actually given in experience, something *has been* given. This means that we grasp something intuitively, prior to any determination of a categorial nature, or, better said perhaps, that we have a categorial *intuition* of things. Scotus calls this "primary object" "being" (*Ens*): *Ens*, or being-ness, is what is common to all things (*primum objectum est ens ut commune omnibus*). *Ens*, therefore, characterizes the feature that remains throughout the objective sphere: it is the category of all categories, or the primal category (*Urkategorie*). It precedes even the categories of unity (being-as-one) and veracity (being-as-true), that is, the idea that for something to be, it has to be *one*, and for it to be *truly* something, it needs to be an object of knowledge, or a "validity" in the sense spoken of above. Such is the reason, also, why scholasticism, and Scotus himself, refer to *Ens* as the *Transcendens* pure and simple. But can we say anything more of this *Ens*, more, that is, than the fact that it characterizes what is common to everything? Of *Ens*, can we say something other than the fact that it is the most general, and the most transcendent? Aristotle did not think so, and Scotus seems to agree with him: as soon as we ask something about this *Ens*, we ascribe to it something else; we understand it as being-ness in the sense of unity, veracity, goodness, and so on. In other words, we associate it with other *Transcendentia* (*Unum*, *Verum*, *Bonum*, etc.), which can be seen as quasi-properties of *Ens*, but which are not as originary as *Ens* itself. We clarify *Ens*, but we also lose it in its originarity. Even in the case of *esse* as *verum esse*, in the case of the copula as the vehicle of truth, the category does not coincide entirely with the object in its primitive or raw givenness. There has to be more to this *Ens* than meets the eye, and more than what the doctrine of categories has been able to express in its long history. There has to be a sense of *Ens*, or *esse*, that is not reducible to the senses of *esse* expressed in the categories. Yet what that excess might consist of, what that *Urkategorie* might be, is something that Heidegger is not in a position to discover in 1915.

It is only after engaging systematically and at length with Aristotle in the 1920s that Heidegger became fully aware of the nature of the problem, and came to terms with the metaphysical presuppositions underlying Scotus's own position. Aristotle was on the right track when he identified *ousia*, or beingness, as the unifying sense of being. *Ousia* is the name forged after the present participle of the verb *einai*, to be; the Latin *essentia* (from the infinitive *esse*) translates it literally. In and of itself, this category does not designate much. It is only when it is interpreted further as *parousia*, or *praes-ens*, that it becomes meaningful. Presence, Aristotle argues, is the primordial meaning of being: what *is* is first and foremost what is *present*. To the extent that this solution will influence an entire philosophical tradition, if not the whole of Western thought, Heidegger argues that the metaphysics inherited from Aristotle is a metaphysics of presence. But presence, he adds, is not the ultimate or most fundamental meaning of being. It actually presupposes a more hidden meaning, which it cannot access, namely, time. The meaning of being as presence presupposes the present as the origin of time. But this privileging of the present is precisely what metaphysics cannot think: it is the unthought of metaphysics, that is, its most fundamentally ingrained presupposition. Such is the reason why, in the end, Heidegger calls for the "deconstruction" (*Destruktion*, *Abbau*) of metaphysics, and for the reconstruction of philosophy as *fundamental* ontology. What metaphysics takes to be the origin of time, namely, the present, and the fundamental meaning of being, namely, presence, turns out to be only a secondary and derivative mode of what Heidegger calls the essence, or the temporalizing, of time. Time, in other words, is the key to solving the mystery of being or presence in general, the underlying and unifying phenomenon behind all the senses of being that Aristotle – and the entire philosophical tradition – sought (but failed) to discover in his *Metaphysics*. Time is the fundamental phenomenon, or the primordial event.

The first murmurs of Heidegger's own voice, and of what will become his question, can be heard in the conclusion to the book on Scotus. There, he claims that problems of logic must be envisaged within a broader context. In the long term, he writes, philosophy cannot do without what is after all its proper domain, namely, "*Metaphysics*" (GA 1, 348). Is judgment the ultimate site of meaning and truth, the key to understanding the Aristotelian question regarding the many senses of being, or does philosophy need to develop a metalogic that would reveal the ground of logic itself? In the conclusion to his book, Heidegger hints at what that ground could be when he writes that philosophy is "without force" when it is cut off from "life" and when he calls for a "teleological and metaphysical interpretation of consciousness" (GA 1, 352). It is all quite vague and very programmatic, but the spirit in which those final comments are made will carry Heidegger all the way to the publication of *Being and Time*.

Between 1915 and 1919, Heidegger did not make much progress with respect to his earlier work. Those were the difficult years of the war. In 1916, Heidegger met Elfride Petri, a Protestant, whom he married in 1917, thus bringing the plans for priesthood to an effective end. In 1916, Husserl had arrived in Freiburg, and began to collaborate with the young philosopher only a year later, despite Heidegger's eagerness to establish a working relationship with the founding father of phenomenology. That same year, Heidegger was called up for basic training as a reservist and received further training as airman in meteorology. He resumed his teaching in 1919.

II. FROM LOGIC TO ONTOLOGY (1919–23)

In 1919 Heidegger broke with what, in a letter to his friend from the early 1910s, Father Engelbert Krebs, he called "the system of Catholicism."[8] By that he meant the system of the Scholastics. Instead, he turned toward the more personal and passionate Christianity of Paul, Augustine, Luther, and Kierkegaard. In 1919, too, he became Husserl's assistant, and began to lecture extensively on phenomenology in connection with questions of value, of intuition and expression; with religion and the religious life; with historical figures such as Descartes, Augustine, and the Neoplatonists or, more importantly still, Husserl himself (*Logical Investigations*) and Aristotle. It is the teaching on Aristotle that struck the greatest chord with his audience, and gave him a national reputation,

8. The letter in question can be found in Martin Heidegger, *Supplements: From the Earliest Essays to "Being and Time" and Beyond*, John van Buren (ed.) (Albany, NY: SUNY Press, 2002), 69–70.

which resulted in an appointment as Associate Professor in Philosophy at the University of Marburg in 1923.

Theodore Kisiel, one of the most prominent interpreters of Heidegger, dates Heidegger's first breakthrough to his topic from 1919, and specifically from the "war-emergency semester" lecture course (GA 56/57).[9] In that lecture course, and very much as a response to claims made by others at the time, Heidegger begins by saying what philosophy is not. Contrary to what Jaspers argues, philosophy is not a worldview. And contrary to what the Marburg neo-Kantians, such as Ernst Cassirer, Herman Cohen, or Paul Natorp, argue, philosophy is not mere *Erkenntnistheorie*, or epistemology. In fact, the criticism aimed at the latter view is a criticism of Heidegger's own, earlier position. To the first, Heidegger responds that philosophy is a rigorous science, and the primordial science. To the second, he says that philosophy is the science not of the theoretical, and of the existing theoretical sciences, but of the *pretheoretical*. As we saw, in his very early work, Heidegger himself began by restricting questions of truth and meaning to the theoretical sphere. He now grants that it is easier and more practical to analyze them in that context, where they are universally valid. Mostly, though, "preference for the theoretical is grounded in the conviction that this is the basic level that grounds all other spheres in a specific way and that is manifested when one speaks, for example, of moral, artistic, or religious 'truth.'"[10] It is this assumption he now wants to challenge. The theoretical, it is assumed, colors all other domains of value, and does so all the more easily when it is itself conceived as a value, and the highest value. But, Heidegger claims, "this primacy of the theoretical must be broken, not in order to proclaim the primacy of the practical [in the sense of the ethical] … but because the theoretical itself and as such refers back to something pretheoretical."[11]

What, then, is this pretheoretical ground on which philosophy needs to focus? How can there be "meaning" at a pretheoretical, precategorial level? And how can that ground be accessed scientifically? Let me begin by addressing the latter question. What allows the discourse of the pretheoretical to be "scientific" is phenomenology. Since the scientificity of philosophy cannot be derived from the exact or natural sciences, or from the theoretical, which presuppose the very object philosophy sets out to analyze, it must be of its own making. Phenomenology, with its attentiveness to the things themselves, its methodological procedures and principle of "intuition," which are not borrowed from the empirical sciences, or mathematics, is the ideal tool to develop such a science.

9. Theodore Kisiel, *The Genesis of Heidegger's "Being and Time"* (Berkeley, CA: University of California Press, 1993), 38–59.

10. GA 56/57, 59/50.

11. *Ibid.*

It gives us eyes (or the conceptual tools) to "see" a lived experience in the very way in which it is lived, or experienced, that is, without adding to or subtracting anything from it, without transforming it in any way. Phenomenology, then, situates itself at the level at which the experience takes place.

As for the first set of questions, Heidegger sketches an answer in just one brief section (GA 56/57, §14) of his lecture course. It is remarkably programmatic, and can be seen as laying the ground for what will eventually become *Being and Time*. In that section, Heidegger no longer opposes "meaning" and "existence." He now understands being, and the being of beings around us, in terms of meaning, and meaning itself in terms of our own living. It is no coincidence if, in that same lecture course, Heidegger, for the first time, raises the question of the "various senses" in which "there is" something (§13): "being" now refers to the various ways in which "beings" are present or manifest before they are understood theoretically. Heidegger invites his audience to undergo a phenomenological exercise by focusing on what they actually see, or on what he, as a lecturer, actually sees when looking at the lectern in the lecture hall. Do I see, he asks, "brown surfaces, at right angles to one another?" Or do I see "a largish box with another smaller one set upon it?" In fact, he replies, I see neither. What I see is "the lectern at which I am to speak," and I see it right away, "in one fell swoop, so to speak." I see it in "a certain orientation, an illumination, a background." Naturally, he adds, "if a farmer from deep in the Black Forest" were to be led into the lecture room, he would have a different experience of the lectern. But he still would not see it "as a box, an arrangement of boards." He would see it as the place where the lecturer stands, from which he teaches. In other words – and this is the decisive conclusion – he would see the object as "fraught with meaning." Even someone culturally alien to the world of European universities, such as "a Negro from Senegal," would still see the lectern as something meaningful. "Even if he saw the lectern simply as a bare something that is there, it would have a meaning for him, a moment of signification." He would relate it immediately, and pretheoretically, to what he is familiar with. And even if he could not manage to make any sense of it, this would still testify to the fact that he, like everyone else, is caught up in a *meaningful world*. And that is the point: everything we see or experience, we see or experience *as*, or in terms of, something else – our own *world*, our own lived experience (*Erlebnis*), our own history, and so on. Meaning is first and foremost *worldly*, and not discursive. This "seeing *as*" is what, later on,[12] Heidegger will call the "hermeneutical as," in order to distinguish it from the "apophantical," or discursive "as," which is the "as" he had been analyzing up until then in the context of his logical investigations. What is so crucial about it is the fact that it signals a layer of meaning,

12. See Heidegger, *Being and Time*, §§32–3.

and a primordial one, that precedes any judgment or proposition regarding the world. It signals an originary layer of meaning that falls outside the operation of *Geltung* in which he had been considering it hitherto. Meaning turns out to be something much more, and quite literally, mundane: it is a decisive feature of the world as *my* world (*Welt*), or my environment (*Umwelt*). Everything, Heidegger concludes in that section, "signifies." And he adds, in what constitutes a remarkable revision of the position he held in his first two books: "It is everywhere the case that 'it worlds' [*es weltet*], which is something different from 'it values' [*es wertet*]" (§14). In other words, meaning is not so much a function of the judgments that we express about the world, and the "validities" they hold, as it is the result of our intimate and pretheoretical understanding of the world. There will be no turning back from that breakthrough.

What Heidegger calls the pretheoretical, therefore, is life (*Leben*) as it is lived and experienced (*Erlebnis*), or life as a meaningful nexus that is also a *world*. In that respect, every theoretical attitude, including that of the various natural and formal sciences, constitutes an abstraction from life and world thus understood. As such, it amounts to a process of de-vitalization, or de-vivication (*Ent-lebnis*) in which what is known is re-moved (*ent-fernt*), lifted out of the actual experience, and objectified (§15). The "reality" of the theoretical attitude is essentially different from that of philosophy: it is a reality of "mere things" with "thingly" qualities, such as color, hardness, extension, weight, and so on.[13] "Thingliness" is precisely what can be abstracted from, or distilled out of, the environment and the world of living "significations." This is how "significations" are turned into "things," and how the primordial sphere of the "it worlds" becomes a collection of fixed and de-vitalized qualities (§17). In the face of such a transformation, which has permeated philosophy itself, the task of philosophy becomes one of returning to life in its continuity and unity, and of using phenomenology as a way of being in "absolute *sympathy with life*,"[14] describing its basic features. If the operation of theory is described as a "process," the life that is to become the theme of philosophy is described as an "event" (*Ereignis*), both in the sense of something dynamic and something that, because I am closest to it, because I *am* it, can be ap-propriated (*er-eignet*), but precisely not as an object (§15). The categories of philosophy must not reflect personal views or opinions about the world, but fundamental structures of existence ("existentials") and actual, concrete possibilities of life. They are not abstract categories, empty generalities that we would somehow impose on life, or "logical forms" disconnected from the reality of factical life.

---

13. In the 1920s, and in *Being and Time* especially, Heidegger will designate that reality as *Vorhandenheit*, or objective presence.
14. GA 56/57, 110/92.

From then onward, it becomes a question of describing that life, as rigorously and methodically as possible. This is what Heidegger does throughout the 1920s, sometimes directly, but often indirectly, through a series of interpretations of Aristotle, and using the resources of phenomenology and hermeneutics. Heidegger's views from that period are perhaps most synthetically formulated in a short text from 1922, devoted to his "phenomenological interpretations of Aristotle," and written at Natorp's request for his appointment as an associate professor at the University of Marburg. "Phenomenology" and "hermeneutics" are now brought together to secure an access to the problem of life as the very problem of philosophy. To interpret, for Heidegger, is to engage in an activity of exegesis or explication (*Auslegung*) and comprehension (*Vernehmen*). The task of the interpreter is to *see*. And this seeing is directed toward a particular matter (*Sache*). Heidegger's concept of hermeneutics is essentially intuitionist, and very close to the ideal formulated by Husserl. "Seeing" or, more generally, "intuition" is the access to the *Sache*, and the guarantee of its givenness: from a phenomenological perspective, a matter or a phenomenon is "given," and so manifest as a phenomenon when it is grasped in an intuition. The ideal of intuition, and of hermeneutics, is transparency – not just, and not primarily, of philosophical texts, but of life itself. Following Wilhelm Dilthey, Heidegger claims that the ultimate goal of hermeneutics is to render the interpreter transparent to himself *as* life, and this means as a temporal, historical reality. Hermeneutics is directed toward the living present, or the "fundamental mobility" of life. The emphasis on seeing, intuition, and the living present means that hermeneutics is phenomenological through and through. Heidegger's own version and practice of hermeneutics is inseparable from his commitment to phenomenology.

In the very first sentence of the so-called "Natorp Report," Heidegger describes his investigations as a contribution "to the history of ontology and logic."[15] Ontology is now explicitly named as the object of philosophy, alongside logic. But the logic in question, Heidegger tells us, is no longer the logic of his early student years: it is now a "logic of the heart," a "logic of philosophy," or a "logic of thought" directed toward "pretheoretical and practical" existence.[16] It is, in other words, a logic of concrete, "factical" life (*das faktische Leben*), or "existence" (*Dasein*). If ontology designates the nature and object of philosophy (the *being* of factical life as the source and foundation of knowledge in general), logic designates the concepts or categories with which we can grasp that object in its very vitality and facticity. Philosophy is now understood as fundamental ontology, and more specifically as "the *phenomenological hermeneutics* of facticity."[17]

15. Heidegger, *Supplements*, 111.

16. *Ibid.*, 122.

17. *Ibid.*, 121.

In that respect, Heidegger's so-called "Natorp Report" can be seen as the first, embryonic version of *Being and Time*.

Factical life points, first of all, to the fact that we are always and from the start ex-posed to, or oriented toward, something (*das Aussein-auf-etwas*). This, according to Heidegger, is the fundamental meaning of intentionality. But because this primordial and irreducible relation is pretheoretical, and because there is no interiority into which it can withdraw, Heidegger no longer calls it "consciousness" (*Bewußtsein*), preferring instead to call it "existence" (*Dasein*). Dasein, Heidegger says in *Being and Time*, is essentially *ecstatic*: existence designates the essence of who we are (GA 2, 12). That toward which we are oriented or thrown is the "world" (*Welt*). It is only as *factical* life, or *as being-in-the world*, that human life can be distinguished from inert, lifeless presence, but also from the rest of biological life: on the one hand, my being is one that I must continue to be, it is an inescapable "having-to-be" (*Zu-sein*); on the other hand, it is a "being-able-to-be." Whereas the former points to something like the necessity of existence (so long as I am, I must continue to be), the latter points to its freedom (my being is a *Sein-können*, or a "being-able-to-be"). The ecstatic nature of existence, he will go on to say in the 1920s, and in *Being and Time* especially, is revealed in the following fundamental traits, known as "existentials": first, Dasein has the character of *being thrown* outside itself and into the world; second, Dasein is always ahead of itself, *projecting itself* into a world of possibilities, constantly anticipating itself; finally, Dasein is always *alongside* other beings, including other Dasein, and thus always in a world that is shared. "Thrownness" (*Geworfenheit*), "projection" (*Entwurf*), and "being-alongside" (*Sein bei*) are the three basic existentials.[18]

Heidegger describes the unity of factical life, or of the three existentials, as "concern," or "care." With this word, he wishes to characterize the "fundamental mobility" (*Grundbewegtheit*) of factical life.[19] We human beings *are* in such a way that we are "concerned" about our own being. This amounts to saying that our being is always at issue in the fact and the manner of our own being. We are concerned with ourselves. The concern of life is directed toward life itself. Yet to the extent that life is essentially factical, that is, always open to something, its concern is directed at the *world*. As a result, the movement of caring is characterized by the fact that factical life goes about its dealings (*Umgang*) with the world. And the world itself is always there, in this or that way, as having been taken up or addressed and claimed (*logos*) in care in one way or another. There are many ways in which factical life can be concerned about the world: it cares about needs, jobs, peace, tranquility, survival, pleasures, practical as

18. GA 2, §§12, 29, 31.

19. Heidegger, *Supplements*, 114; GA 2, §41.

well as theoretical knowledge, and so on. Every way of caring about the world amounts to a certain *understanding* of it: life moves itself in a horizon that is already understood, transmitted, reworked, or reshaped. What Heidegger calls "circumspection" (*Umsicht*) is the way in which life for the most part "sees" its world: its world is already *understood* on the basis of perspectives, priorities, aspirations, and specific circumstances. From the start, the world is organized as an *Umwelt*, an environmental milieu, and not as a theoretical (especially mathematical) "reality" that stands opposed; this is to say, not as "nature" in the modern, scientific sense that we have come to take for granted, and which continues to inform today's debates around realism and idealism, naturalism, and the philosophy of mind. No doubt the world can be envisaged from the point of view of its "look" (*eidos*), or "form" (*idea*), in which case it becomes an object of wonder and curiosity – an object of scientific investigation. At the most primordial level, though, the *meaning* of the world is pretheoretical: we do not understand and navigate the world as a result of its theoretical representation, but of our pragmatic comportment toward it. Our understanding (*Verstehen*) of the world is primarily practical.

Yet, precisely to the extent that the movement of caring is a living *inclination* toward the world, life tends to lose itself in the world, to be sucked into it. It takes the form of a *propensity* toward becoming absorbed in the world, and "forgetting" its own being (and freedom, as was suggested a moment ago) in this absorption. There is, in other words, a basic factical tendency in life toward *falling away* from itself (*Abfallen*), a fall through which life detaches itself from itself and falls into the world. Life is naturally decline (*Verfallen*) and *falling into ruin* or self-ruin (*Zerfall seiner selbst*). Terminologically, Heidegger writes, we can describe this basic characteristic of the movement of caring as "the *inclination* of factical life toward *falling*" or, in abbreviated form, simply as "*falling into* …" (*Verfallen an*).[20] *Verfallen* is not a mere occurrence, something that happens occasionally to life. Rather, it is a *how* of life itself, a basic "intentional" modality, or a fundamental manner in which life is open to the world. In fact, this propensity (*Hang*) is "the most intimate fate [*Verhängnis*] that life factically has to endure within itself."[21] What does this mean? That this characteristic of movement is not an "evil feature of life" appearing from time to time, or structurally there as a result of some primordial sin, which, one day, we could hope to atone. We must resist diabolizing this natural declivity, despite its obvious biblical resonances (which were, most probably, an initial source of inspiration for Heidegger). This state of life does not point to a higher, more perfect "paradisiacal naturality," whether in the old, biblical sense, or in the more recent, say

20. See also GA 2, §§35–8.
21. Heidegger, *Supplements*, 117.

Rousseauist, sense of a "natural state" of innocence and goodness among men before the introduction of culture and society. In short, it cannot be a question of eradicating life's propensity toward falling. What it does mean, though, is that life tends to understand and interpret itself on the basis of its own fallen state, that is, on the basis of its own practical, concernful absorption in the world. This is a natural tendency, and an alienating (*entfremdend*) one, insofar as it drives life to avoid itself, that is, to pass by its other, more genuine possibilities (which *Being and Time* describes at length). At the same time, however, this tendency is reassuring and *tranquilizing*: it allows Dasein to carry on with its life without further questioning or complication. For the most part, life is *habit* (and in that sense not far from the life of other living beings).[22] Heidegger will want to contrast these circumstances, or this state of affairs (*Lage*), in which life is somehow lost in its own fallen state, with the situation (*Situation*) in which life makes itself transparent to itself in its own fallen state, takes a stance with respect to itself, cares about itself in a concrete manner, and takes itself up as a possible *counter-movement* to its fallen state.

What lies in the inclination toward falling is the fact that factical life, which is in each case the factical life of the individual, is for the most part not lived *as such*. It is lived, of course, but only as something else, as something other than life in its ownmost and most extreme possibility. It is only an *average* life. It moves itself within the *averageness* (*Durschnittlichkeit*) that belongs to its caring, its going about its dealings, its circumspection, and its understanding of the world. This averageness is that of the *publicness* that reigns at any given time. It is the averageness of the *entourage*, the dominant trends and opinions, the "just like everyone else." But this "everyone" is at the same time no one in particular, an anonymous "I" that factically lives the life of the individual: everyone is concerned about such and such, everyone sees it, judges it to be so, enjoys it, does it, asks about it, etc. For the most part, factical life is the life that is lived by "*no one*," or by what Heidegger calls "the one" (*das Man*).[23] In this way of being (often considered a way of life), life *conceals* itself from itself in the world in which it is absorbed and in the averageness in which it goes about its dealings. In the tendency toward falling, Heidegger insists, it is as if life goes out of its way to avoid itself.[24]

But what is it that life turns away from, or turns it back to, when it conceals and avoids itself in that way? With that question, Heidegger is on the verge of his major discovery, insofar as answering it will allow him to identify the meaning of the being of factical life, or existence, as well as – later on – the meaning of

22. *Ibid.*, 116.

23. *Ibid.*, 118; GA 2, §27.

24. Heidegger, *Supplements*, 118.

the being of all beings. With that question, he will finally be able to answer the question that, he claims, was guiding his philosophical curiosity from the start, namely, the question regarding the meaning of being. Let me reformulate the question slightly differently. What is it that Dasein is afraid of, such that it would want, or feel naturally inclined, to flee? We know that it is itself, as factical life – and not some "innerworldly" thing – that Dasein flees, and that this fleeing takes the form of an absorption into worldly concerns. But what does this "itself" consist in? What is Dasein's ownmost self, the feature that separates it from other beings? Thus far, we have described life only negatively. as it were, as habitual, "fallen" life. We need to understand why Dasein avoids itself in that way, and what it is actually retreating from. Also, we need to find out if there is a distinct possibility for Dasein of grasping and appropriating itself *as* factical life, a possibility, that is, of becoming transparent to itself. Finally, we need to ask how time emerges as the answer to the question regarding the meaning of being. All those questions are intimately linked, and are given a preliminary, programmatic answer in the Natorp Report, which reveals *death* as a key phenomenon for accessing the meaning of the being of factical life. This may sound paradoxical, of course, as death is normally opposed to life. If anything, a concern with death is normally associated with a flight from life. Not so for Heidegger, who writes: "The forced absence of worry about death in the caring of life actualizes itself in a flight into worldly concerns and apprehensions."[25] Looking away from death does not mean grasping factical life, but evading what is most distinctive about it. Paradoxically, experiencing the phenomenon of death, and thinking about it, makes life itself "visible" and transparent to itself, and reveals its specific temporality. But what is death, and how does it manifest itself *positively* to Dasein, outside "fallenness"? This is a question that Heidegger leaves unanswered in 1922, but one to which he returns soon thereafter (GA 20, §§33–4), and thematizes most explicitly in *Being and Time*, Division Two, chapter one.

III. "BEING" AS "TIME" (1923–27)

It is what is usually referred to as the Marburg period that really marks Heidegger's philosophical breakthrough, of which the publication of *Being and Time* in 1927 is the crowning achievement. For it is in that period that Heidegger is able to bring together being and time explicitly, and concretely, by thinking the distinct nature of death for Dasein.

There is indeed something quite distinctive about the death of Dasein. Naturally, there is nothing distinctive about dying as such. All living things die,

25. *Ibid.*, 119.

or rather, perish. They all come to an end. Yet the death of Dasein is different, inasmuch as Dasein relates to its *own* death, not when it is actually taking place, not at the time of its death, but from the start. Dasein's death is distinctive in that it is not an event, or something that takes place in time, but a possibility, toward which Dasein is constantly projecting itself. Yet death is a possibility unlike other possibilities. First, it is Dasein's *ownmost* possibility, that is, the possibility that it cannot delegate, and of which it cannot be relieved. Second, it is the *ultimate* possibility, or the possibility of the impossibility of existence: we have the distinct sense, and even knowledge, that our being (*Sein*) *qua* potentiality (*Seinkönnen*) is not unlimited, and that our openness to the world is not absolute. Somehow, we know that there is a horizon that delimits our world, and therefore limits our possibilities. This limit or horizon is precisely *death*. Finally, it is a *pure* possibility, or a possibility that, unlike all other possibilities, can never be actualized (for as soon as it is actualized, Dasein is no longer): death is always "not yet" for Dasein. It testifies to the fact that, so long as Dasein continues to exist, there is something outstanding, something to come. In that respect, death keeps the world open, and allows possibilities to emerge. As such, it is the possibility of all possibilities, or *the* condition of possibility. By virtue of being "only" a possibility, however, it is not as if death were a *remote* possibility. On the contrary: Heidegger insists that it is always impending, always there in a way, threatening to bring to an end that which it opens up. Such is the paradox of death: it is both the condition of possibility *and* impossibility of the world. As the end *toward* which existence ex-ists, death is at once the possibility of closure of existence and the horizon from which the world opens up and unfolds for Dasein, the limit from which "it worlds." Such is the reason why Heidegger qualifies further the openness of existence, and the fundamental state of being-in-the-world, as "disclosedness" (*Erschlossenheit*): the openness and manifestness of the world presuppose a more originary closure.

Remarkably, the word *Erschlossenheit* is also Heidegger's translation of the Greek, and especially Aristotelian, *alētheia* ("truth"). By investigating the fundamental structure of life, and identifying death as its horizon, Heidegger is able to uncover the hidden and forgotten meaning of truth. It is no longer judgment (*logos apophantikos*), or even speech (*logos semantikos*), as he once thought, but existence, which is the place and origin of truth.[26] The sense of being as truth (*esse* as *verum esse*), which Heidegger had tried to understand in his habilitation

26. This discovery emerges in the context of Heidegger's sustained phenomenological–hermeneutical interpretations of Aristotle. The Natorp Report provides an early, still-tentative version of it: "*Hon os alethes* [being as being true] is not the authentic being of true judgments and their domain of being or validity but rather beings themselves in the how (*os*) of their unveiled being-meant [*seines unverhüllten Vermeintseins*]" (*ibid*., 132); see also GA 19, §26; GA 2, 32–4.

thesis, and to which he returns time and again in his phenomenological interpretations of Aristotle, is now finally established. It presupposes a move from logic to its ontological, and specifically existential, ground. But it is not just the question regarding the sense of being as truth that is solved; it is also the question regarding the sense of sense, or the meaning of meaning – it is meaning itself that Heidegger now wrests from logic, by understanding it as an ontological *a priori*. "Meaning" now designates the transcendental *x*, or the horizon, on the basis of which something (in this instance, "being") becomes intelligible.

Finally, and more importantly still, it is the meaning of being as time that Heidegger is now in a position to reveal. Traditionally, time was considered to originate in the present. The present was the primordial reality from which the rest of time flowed: the past was understood as what was no longer, and the future as what was not yet. As a result of this present-centrism, and as early as Plato and Aristotle, *presence* (*parousia*) defined the underlying meaning of being (*ousia*): to *be* always (implicitly) meant to be *present*. What Aristotle called *ousia* (*essentia*) was the fundamental, primordial meaning of being, from which all the other meanings (or "categories") of being were derived. But, Heidegger claims, this understanding of being as presence stems from an inability to understand our own being as existence, and to draw the temporal consequences of that discovery. With Heidegger, "being" no longer means "presence," but coming-into-presence (dis-closedness), and coming into presence itself presupposes an originary concealment (*lethe*), which, for Dasein, is death. As the extreme possibility toward which we find ourselves always oriented, death reveals existence as always ahead of itself, projecting itself in a world of projects and possibilities, anticipating itself. "Project" (*Entwurf*) and "anticipation" (*Vorlaufen*) are fundamental features of factical life. But what those existentials reveal is the fact that life unfolds from the future, and that the future is its source.[27] What we witness with Heidegger, then, is a decisive shift in the perception of where time originates: the center of gravity of temporality is no longer the present, as was the case in the philosophical tradition, but the future (*die Zukunft*). The future is the source or the origin from which time flows.

For the most part, though, Heidegger tells us, we do not see time (or ourselves) for what it is: we see the result of the event of time – presence, and not presenc*ing*. We see things at the end of the process, as things that we can use (or not), with a view to this or that, always in a certain light, without asking ourselves about the source of that light. As a result, we also tend to understand ourselves, our own being, on the basis of the being of those very things, on the basis, that is, of presence (whether practical or objective). We do that naturally, and the metaphysical conception of being is born of that natural tendency.

27. GA 2, 325.

From a phenomenological perspective, however, the question is one of knowing whether we ever encounter time itself, whether we ever experience ourselves on the basis of our own being. Now Heidegger claims that we do, for example in immediately tangible "moods" or "dispositions" (*Stimmungen*), such as anxiety, or boredom.[28] In both instances, we experience a total withdrawal of the world, or, better said perhaps, of familiar, ordinary, worldly things. We come face to face with ourselves, with our own worldliness and temporality. In boredom especially, we feel very strongly that all "there is" is time, and that makes us feel uneasy. As a result, we look for a way back into the familiar, practical world in which we feel safe. The question, though, is one of knowing whether there is some kind of experience that could reveal our temporal being and bear witness to the temporal meaning of being in general and that we would not want to flee, but to embrace and sustain. Furthermore, could this experience, this "attunement," reveal more precisely the way in which time unfolds or temporalizes itself? It is in the phenomenon that *Being and Time* describes as "anticipatory, resolute disclosedness" (*vorlaufende Entschlossenheit*) that Dasein is said to understand itself "authentically," that is, on the basis of its own being-towards-death.[29] This phenomenon reveals a distinct possibility of existence, one in which existence is disclosed to itself *as* disclosedness, or in its totality (as "care"). In resolute disclosedness, Dasein does not flee its own mortality and finitude, but anticipates it, that is, brings it to bear on its comportment toward the world. This means that Dasein does not look forward to its own death, or, worse still, that it anticipates its own death through suicide. Rather, it means that Dasein lives in the full awareness of its own finitude, and of the fact that time itself is finite. This, in turn, has an effect on the intensity with which it lives its life: possibilities are chosen, decisions are made, on the basis of such an awareness.

Even Dasein's own past, and not just its present, is modified as a result of its ability to relate positively to its own end. We need to emphasize the point that, although Heidegger locates the source of time in the future, and understands life as projection (*Entwurf*), he also recognizes that existence is not entirely its own ground, and that it is always thrown (*geworfen*) into situations that are not of its choosing. This, after all, is what moods and dispositions reveal, namely, the irreducible passivity of life, the fact that thrownness (*Geworfenheit*) can never be erased. To understand itself as being-towards-death, "authentic" Dasein must also take over its thrownness. Now to take over one's thrownness means nothing other than to be "authentically" or "properly" what one already was "inauthentically" or "improperly." What Dasein *can* be is nothing other than what it already is, nothing other than its *having-been* (*Gewesen*). It is only in the anticipation

28. On anxiety, see GA 2, §40; "What is Metaphysics?" On boredom, see GA 29/30, part one.
29. GA 2, §62.

of its end that Dasein can correspond to its original condition. Only insofar as Dasein ex-ists, that is, comes *toward* itself futurally, can it come *back* (*zurückkommen*) to itself and what it already is:

> Anticipation of one's ownmost and uttermost possibility is coming back understandingly to one's ownmost "been." Only so far as it is futural can Dasein *be* authentically as having-been. The "having been" [*die Gewesenheit*, and not *die Vergangenheit*, the past] arises, in a certain way, from the future.[30]

This is tantamount to saying that Dasein can *be* its past only insofar as it comes back to it on the basis of its own future. If the having-been arises from the future, it is because there can be facticity only within the horizon of a can-be (*Seinkönnen*). So, once again, the future, properly understood, is not a now that is not yet actual, but Dasein's coming toward its ownmost can-be, which occurs in the anticipation of death. Likewise, because Dasein is not a pregiven entity, an entity present-at-hand, it is not, strictly speaking, "past," but has always already been and *is* this very having-been: the "having been" (*gewesen sein*) is the original phenomenon of what we call the past. Traditionally, the past is what is no longer. But the temporal dimension associated with Dasein's thrownness is not past in that sense. On the contrary, it is a dimension that persists and insists, although not as something present. Thrownness indicates that Dasein exists in the mode of having-been, a mode that is irreducible to a mere "modification" or variation of the present. What we normally call the present is not the founding moment of time. In fact, it is a derivative mode of time. For presence always arises out of the futurity and pastness of existence. Anticipatory resoluteness, in which existentiality is disclosed as essentially futural, also discloses the present. Indeed, anticipatory resoluteness reveals what Heidegger calls a "situation" by making present an entity. The present as a mode of temporality is originally a making present, or a presencing (*ein Gegenwärtigen*). Coming back to itself futurally, resoluteness makes present the beings that it encounters environmentally. This is the phenomenon Heidegger designates as temporality (*Zeitlichkeit*). It has the unity of a future that makes present in having-been (*gewesend-gewärtigende Zukunft*).

Our present is the effect of the way in which our having-been-ness (*Gewesenheit*) and our futurity (*Zukünftigkeit*) come together. Now, the present that is opened up in resolute disclosedness is radically different from that of this or that particular situation. It differs from the kind of present that is linked to a punctual and practical situation; in other words, from the mostly "concerned"

30. GA 2, 326.

and "absorbed" present of our everyday life, the present of needs and ordinary dealings with the world. Furthermore, it is also to be distinguished from the abstract present (the "now") of the theoretical attitude, which we now unquestioningly consider to be the very form of the present, unaware of the spatial, and specifically linear, understanding of time such an attitude presupposes, the ontologico-existential ground of which we can trace back to the ordinary, fallen nature of our relation to the world in everyday life. Rather, the present that is at issue in the "moment" is the present in which existence is present to itself as the very operation of disclosure, or as the very *there* of being. In the "moment of vision," or the *Augen-blick*, Dasein "brings itself before itself": it *sees* itself for the first time for what it is, that is, the originary "clearing" (*Lichtung*) or the "truth" of being. Thus, the "moment" is not linked to the disclosure of a particular situation, but to the disclosure of situatedness as such: "The moment of vision is nothing other than the *look of resolute disclosedness* [*Blick der Entschlossenheit*] in which the full situation of an action opens itself and keeps itself open."[31] Thus, in the moment, Dasein has an eye for action in the most essential sense, insofar as the moment of vision is what makes Dasein possible as Da-sein, there-being. It is to this that the human *must* resolutely disclose itself. The human must first create "for himself *once again* a genuine knowing concerning that wherein whatever makes Dasein itself possible consists."[32] Thus, in the moment of vision, existence resolves itself to itself, to itself as Da-sein, thus allowing it to become free for the first time: free not to *do* this or that, at least not primarily, but free to be its own being, free to be in the most intense and generous sense, that is, free to be for its own freedom or its own ability to be.

Being and Time is the culmination of Heidegger's early thought, which sets out to construe a fundamental ontology by revealing the unifying meaning of being as time. It corresponds to Heidegger's first major effort to wrest being from inert substantiality and recover its forgotten origin as pure becoming. "Being and Time" really reads: "Being as Time." But time itself, pure becoming, must be distinguished from the time of the world and of actuality, the fallen time, as Heidegger puts it, in which things and events seem to succeed one another in what amounts to a merely sequential order. Real time, on the other hand, is not the time of succession, or the linear, actual time in which events replace one another. Nor is it the time of eternity, of the absolute present, which events occupy for a while before vanishing into the past. And the past itself is not what is no-longer-present and held in reserve, waiting to be reactivated or brought back into the present. The present is only an *effect* of time, not its point of departure. To think time from the present alone, then, is to think abstractly,

31. GA 29/30, 224/148.
32. GA 29/30, 247/165, emphasis added.

for it amounts to taking the effect for the cause, even if no actual cause can be associated with the unfolding, or the temporalizing of time. It also amounts to constructing time as a sequence of instants, which, in turn, can be represented as a line made of points and segments. In doing so, time is spatialized, and denied its own temporal essence. Heidegger's concept of time, on the other hand, is precisely aimed at despatializing and de-reifying time in order to uncover its eventful or ontological power. Time, he says, "is" not, but temporalizes itself; there is no such *thing* as time, only a temporalizing, and from out of this primordial and ongoing event, everything takes place and finds its place, possibilities emerge, and a world begins to take shape. So when Heidegger claims that temporality *is* the meaning of care, we need to understand that only in the self-temporalizing of temporality does Dasein exist according to its own possibilities of being. As Heidegger emphasizes at the beginning of *Being and Time* §65, by "meaning" we need to understand that wherein the understandability of something lies. The meaning of something, therefore, is that which is necessarily presupposed in that thing for it to become understandable. In other words, it is the condition of possibility of that thing. In that respect, when we say that time is the meaning of care, we say that it is only on the basis of the temporalization of temporality that Dasein's being as care can come to be understood. How are we to understand the temporalization of temporality? What does Heidegger mean by that? To say that time is essentially a temporalizing is tantamount to saying that time does not constitute the "internal sense" or the "interiority" of a "subject," but that it is "the *ekstatikon* pure and simple," "the original outside-of-itself in and for itself." Heidegger borrows the term *ekstatikon* from Aristotle's *Physics*, where it designates the nature of change (*metabole*). It is to be understood in its literal Greek sense as a coming out of oneself, and must hence be related to the notion of existence (or ek-sistence, as Heidegger will later begin to write). By defining the future, the having-been, and the present as the *ecstasies* of temporality, Heidegger emphasizes the temporalizing of temporality as a movement or an event, and not as the coming out of itself of a hitherto self-contained subject: "Temporality is not, prior to this, a being that first emerges from itself; its essence is a process of temporalizing in the unity of the ecstasies."[33] Thus temporality needs to be understood as an ekstatic unfolding, and not, as thought by the "ordinary understanding," as a pure sequence of "nows," without beginning and without end. Ek-sistence, then, as the event of being, is entirely outside: it is not an interiority that externalizes itself, but the outside as such, pure exteriority, pure throwing (pro- and retro-ject). It is only with the characterization of our being in terms of time that Heidegger is able to understand fully the meaning of factical life as being-outside-itself-and-toward-something.

33. GA 2, 329.

By way of summary, we can bring Heidegger's analysis of originary temporality under four theses: (i) Insofar as time makes possible the constitution of the structure of care, time is the originary *temporalizing* of temporality. (ii) This implies that temporality does not refer to the interiority of a subject, but that it is essentially *ekstatic*. (iii) Temporality temporalizes itself primordially on the basis of a priority given to the *future*. (iv) Such an ekstatic–existential temporality characterizes primordial time as *finite* time. Time, in short, is horizonal, finite, futural, and ekstatic.

IV. AFTER *BEING AND TIME* (1928–30)

Despite this considerable achievement, *Being and Time* goes only so far in establishing time as the meaning of all beings (and not just that of the human being), and wresting philosophy from anthropology once and for all. We must bear in mind that the book contains only one of two parts initially planned, and only two of three divisions. This means that the third division of the first part, which was to reveal time as the meaning of the being of all beings, was never written, or at least not until 1962 (in a conference entitled "Time and Being"). But by then the project had been transformed so radically that it was no longer possible to envisage the lecture as the missing third division of *Being and Time*. What *Being and Time* planned to do – this is clearly stated in the Introduction (§8) – was to reveal time as the transcendental horizon for the question of being. In a way, this program is accomplished in the lecture course from 1927 that immediately followed the publication of *Being and Time* (GA 24). Yet what Heidegger does not manage to achieve, whether in *Being and Time* or in the lecture course, is to think the time or the temporality of being itself. He finds himself always drawn back into what Division Two of *Being and Time* had established, namely, "the interpretation of Dasein in terms of temporality" (GA 2, 40). In order to carry out his initial intention, and fulfill the program he had initially defined in the Introduction to *Being and Time*, namely, to reveal the meaning of being itself (as opposed to that of the human Dasein), Heidegger will have to transform his project radically, and abandon the project of a fundamental ontology rooted in human existence. Soon after the publication of *Being and Time*, Heidegger's thought began to shift from a transcendental–horizonal conception of the *meaning* of being, in which being temporalizes itself in the ekstatic temporality of Dasein, to what we could call an aletheic–ekstatic conception of the *truth* of being, in which Dasein finds its stance and to which it co-responds. This turning marks the point where being is no longer temporal because it constitutes the horizonal unity of Dasein's ekstatic temporality, but rather because it is historical in itself. There is a shift from historical time as rooted in the historicity of Dasein to history understood as a sending and a destiny that belongs to the truth of being itself. The conference "Time and Being" concludes by saying that instead of "being" and "time" we should now speak of "clearing" (*Lichtung*) and the presencing of "presence" (*Anwesenheit*).

In addition, soon after the publication of *Being and Time*, in a few enigmatic and complex pages devoted to a "Characterization of the Idea and Function of a Fundamental Ontology" (GA 26, 196–202), Heidegger suggests that in redefining the task of philosophy as fundamental ontology, one cannot remain content simply with revealing the sense of being as time. For insofar as this task is carried out as a possibility of Dasein itself, it must itself be submitted to the rigor of the ontological analysis. Thus, in what amounts to the ultimate phase of the project of fundamental ontology, the analysis is to turn back on the way in which the transcendence of Dasein is involved in the very elaboration of that project, back on the way in which this task is made possible and limited at the same time by the very way in which the factical existence of Dasein is folded into it. For what characterizes Dasein in its factical existence is precisely the fact that it is always and from the very start confronted with "nature," or with the totality of beings. Heidegger introduces this problematic of *das Seiende-im-Ganzen*, or of "beings as a whole," under the name metontology (*Metontologie*), and the latter constitutes the very heart of his reflection in the years 1929–30.[34] It is only with the exposition of the way in which ontology runs back into the metaphysical ontic in which it is caught from the very start that philosophy radicalizes itself and is turned over into meta-ontology. Heidegger announces the programmatic nature of this fully developed concept of metaphysics toward the end of the *Kantbuch*, claiming that "fundamental ontology, however, is only the first level of the metaphysics of Dasein."[35] Whereas the 1928 lecture course still conceived of philosophy as a whole, including its last phase (metontology), under the name "fundamental ontology," the texts and lecture courses written and delivered immediately thereafter identify fundamental ontology with only the first phase of what came to be characterized as metaphysics. Yet this metaphysics of Dasein, or this metontology, which led to fascinating developments in themselves, was itself abandoned, and replaced by yet another way into the question of being. This shift – known as the "turning" (*die Kehre*) – is apparent in Heidegger's pivotal lecture course of 1929–30 (GA 29/30). In the first part of the lecture course, entitled "Awakening a Fundamental Attunement [*Grundstimmung*] in our Philosophizing," Heidegger sets out to unveil the ground or the soil from out of which philosophizing might be possible. In other words, this first part is supposed to bring us to the very threshold of metaphysics

34. See also "What is Metaphysics?" and "On the Essence of Ground," and GA 29/30.
35. GA 3, 232.

and of its fundamental concepts by turning to the buried source of a concrete disposition of our existence (this is what Heidegger calls the ontical–existentiell level, which he distinguishes from the structural, or ontological–existential level). Thus, the preliminary task to which Heidegger devotes himself in that lecture course is the awakening within us of a metaphysical disposition that, as existents, is proper to us, and on the basis of which the entry into metaphysics should take place. But things will turn out to be more complicated. Indeed, the analysis of the fundamental disposition that is supposed to take us to the very threshold of metaphysics or, to be more precise, the historical diagnosis to which Heidegger submits this disposition, is introduced at the cost of a tension that the 1929–30 lecture course is not in a position to resolve. The solution to this tension will be found only when Heidegger will reformulate the project of the question concerning the *meaning* of being and transform it into the question concerning the *history* of being. In other words – and this constitutes the truly paradoxical nature of Heidegger's enterprise – the progressively revealed access to the fundamental concepts of metaphysics is eventually inscribed in a context that itself is such as to call into question existence as the primal and originary source of metaphysics. Metaphysics itself will turn out to be grounded not in the transcendence of Dasein, but in history, understood as the history of being: metaphysics itself turns out to be an effect of history, and not just a possibility of Dasein.

MAJOR WORKS

Frühe Schriften (1912–1916). Gesamtausgabe, vol. 1. Frankfurt: Klostermann, 1978.

Zur Bestimmung der Philosophie. Gesamtausgabe, vol. 56/57. Frankfurt: Klostermann, 1987. Published in English as *Towards the Definition of Philosophy*, translated by Ted Sadler. London: Athlone, 2000. [Freiburg lecture courses 1919.]

Ontologie (Hermeneutik der Faktizität). Gesamtausgabe, vol. 63. Frankfurt: Klostermann, 1982. Published in English as *Ontology – The Hermeneutics of Facticity*, translated by John van Buren. Bloomington, IN: Indiana University Press, 1999. [Freiburg lecture courses of 1923.]

Platon: Sophistes. Gesamtausgabe, vol. 19. Frankfurt: Klostermann, 1992. Published in English as *Plato's Sophist*, translated by Richard Rojcewicz and André Schuwer. Bloomington, IN: Indiana University Press, 1997. [Marburg lecture course of WS 1924–25.]

Prolegomena zur Geschichte des Zeitbegriffs. Gesamtausgabe, vol. 20. Frankfurt: Klostermann, 1979. Published in English as *History of the Concept of Time: Prolegomena*, translated by Theodore Kisiel. Bloomington, IN: Indiana University Press, 1985. [Marburg lecture course of SS 1925.]

Logik. Die Frage nach der Wahrheit. Gesamtausgabe, vol. 21. Frankfurt: Klostermann, 1976. [Marburg lecture course of WS 1925–26.]

Sein und Zeit (1927). *Gesamtausgabe*, vol. 2. Frankfurt: Klostermann, 1977. Published in English as *Being and Time*. (i) Translated by John Macquarrie and Edward Robinson. New York: Harper & Row, 1962. (ii) Translated by Joan Stambaugh. Albany, NY: SUNY Press, 1996.

Die Grundprobleme der Phänomenologie. Gesamtausgabe, vol. 24. Frankfurt: Klostermann, 1975.

Published in English as *The Basic Problems of Phenomenology*, translated by Albert Hofstadter. Bloomington, IN: Indiana University Press, 1982. [Marburg lecture course of SS 1927.]

Kant und das Problem der Metaphysik (1929). *Gesamtausgabe*, vol. 3. Frankfurt: Klostermann, 1991. Published in English as *Kant and the Problem of Metaphysics*, translated by Richard Taft. Bloomington, IN: Indiana University Press, 1990.

Was ist Metaphysik? Bonn: Friedrich Cohen, 1929. Published in English as "What is Metaphysics?" translated by David Farrell Krell. In Martin Heidegger, *Pathmarks*, 82–96. Cambridge: Cambridge University Press, 1998. [Inaugural public lecture at the University of Freiburg, July 24, 1929.]

Vom Wesen des Grundes. Halle: Max Niemeyer, 1929. Published in English as "On the Essence of Ground," translated by William McNeill. In Martin Heidegger, *Pathmarks*, 97–135. Cambridge: Cambridge University Press, 1998. [Contribution to a *Festschrift* for Edmund Husserl on his seventieth birthday.]

Die Grundbegriffe der Metaphysik. Welt – Endlichkeit – Einsamkeit. Gesamtausgabe, vol. 29/30. Frankfurt: Klostermann, 1983. Published in English as *The Fundamental Concepts of Metaphysics: World, Finitude, Solitude*, translated by William McNeill and Nicholas Walker. Bloomington, IN: Indiana University Press, 1995. [Freiburg lecture course of WS 1929–30.]

8

KARL JASPERS

Leonard H. Ehrlich

I. RENEWAL OF THE QUESTION OF BEING

> The question "what Being is" is "the question which was raised of old and is raised now and always, and is always irresolvable."
> (Aristotle, *Metaphysics* 1028b)

Citing this passage from Aristotle's *Metaphysics*,[1] Jaspers[2] takes up the question of Being as the perennially most fundamental question of philosophy. Coming to terms with its *irresolvable* nature, Jaspers thinks that the question requires not a radically new departure, but a fresh approach that draws on humanity's experience of thought about it. Jaspers's thinking constitutes a *renewal* of the question of Being, based on a *reorientation* whereby its possibility is clarified and its significance reconfirmed. The reorientation of the question of Being is the achievement of the first of his two main works, *Philosophy*. On the basis of the reorientation, Jaspers's later main work, *Von der Wahrheit*, provided the

1. Karl Jaspers, *Von der Wahrheit: Philosophische Logik. Erster Band* (hereafter VdW; translations throughout are my own) (Munich: Piper, 1947), 35.
2. Karl Theodor Jaspers (February 23, 1883–February 26, 1969; born in Oldenburg, Germany; died in Basel, Switzerland) was educated at the Humanistic Gymnasium Oldenburg (1892–1901) and universities in Berlin and Göttingen, and took his medical doctorate at the University of Heidelberg (1908). His influences included Husserl, Kant, Kierkegaard, Nietzsche, and Max Weber, and held appointments at Heidelberg Psychiatric Clinic (1909–15) and the University of Heidelberg Department of Psychology (1913–20) and Department of Philosophy (1920–48). He was forced to retire by the Nazi regime in 1937 because his wife was Jewish, and in 1945 was reinstated under US Army auspices. He was honorary University Senator of the University of Basel (1948–), and emeritus (1961).

elaboration in the form of a radical treatment. The two works are not separate departures, but two stages of Jaspers's renewal of the question.

Jaspers speaks mainly of "truth" rather than of "Being." We do not confront Being per se, but only as it is "for us": "Truth" is "Being for us." Thus the question of truth coincides with Being for us. Most thought and action is valid by virtue of a specific truth or kind of truth, for example scientific inference, pragmatic expediency, justification by faith, representation of interest, formal deduction. The fundamental question of truth is distinct: it underlies any and all manner of "special truth," it is the question of truth in its fundamental unity. The tradition of metaphysics assumed that the underlying fundamental truth has an object, and can be determinately grasped. Yet a system of Being, no matter how inclusive, is, by virtue of its determinate foundation, limited. Since thought is, as such, determinative, truth in its unity, transcending determination, is not present to it as an object. Therein lies the "irresolvability" of truth in its unity.

Yet the question of truth has been "raised of old and always." In history it has been perennially significant because it concerns the source of meaningfulness of a thoughtful life and of a life of purposive action and endeavor. Hence the philosophical concern over truth that is *the* truth calls for "operating with this indeterminacy." Accordingly, Jaspers's philosophy culminates in the idea of the truth of Being as *encompassing* man's temporal perspective.

II. THE FIRST STAGE: REORIENTING THE QUESTION OF BEING

The idea of Being and truth as "encompassing" is adumbrated in Jaspers's earliest works.[3] The adumbrated motives are taken up in the three volumes of *Philosophy* (1932). The focus there is on the question of Being.[4] In light of those motives, the

3. See the methodological pluralism in *General Psychopathology*, J. Hoenig and Marian W. Hamilton (trans.) (Chicago, IL: University of Chicago Press, 1963) and the phenomenology of *Weltanschauungen* in *Psychologie der Weltanschauungen* (Berlin: Springer, 1919).
4. Jaspers and Heidegger met at the observance of Husserl's sixtieth birthday, and soon formed a close philosophical friendship. Jaspers was six years older than Heidegger, and, at that time, had more experience in thinking against the stream. In the 1920s, while writing their first major philosophical works, they met frequently for intense discussions. It is not known what they discussed. Although they went divergent ways, they found their contact challenging and fruitful. The fact that the first volume of Heidegger's *Being and Time* was published several years before Jaspers's complete three volumes of *Philosophy* does not mean that the latter was written in response to the former, as Heidegger hastily published his volume to qualify for a professorship. Neither knew what the other was writing, and when the respective works came out, neither of them understood nor appreciated that of the other. Both addressed the question of Being. After *Being and Time*, Heidegger would make attempts to envisage how it would be if "what calls for thinking" is "Being itself." Jaspers, realizing that "Being itself" transcends man's thought, would elaborate on the question of "Being for man in time." Jaspers

"search after Being" is posed from the limited perspective of man's historicity, that is, of man in his situation and within his temporality. From this perspective, Being ruptures into modes of Being. It is a kind of thinking that steps beyond the multiplicity of beings and kinds of Being, beyond the determinate objectivities of cognitive thought, and beyond the phenomena of which we are conscious. It is the basic operation of philosophical thought; Jaspers calls it "transcending."

These themes determine the division of *Philosophy* into the three "books." We first ask how Being presents itself as "world" within the confines of man's situation and temporality; second, what are the characteristic phenomena of man, the being that exists thinkingly, such that they determine man's search after Being; and finally, how man relates to the ground of Being that as such transcends man's grasp.

World-orientation

The Being of the world shows itself to transcending thought not as it is in itself but according to man's orientation within the world. Among the most prominent modes of world-orientation, Jaspers discusses "purposive action" in the world as well as knowledge about the world, in particular modern scientific thought.

The phenomenon of orientation divides into many modes. World-orientation is not a pursuit designed to lead to a closed and finished structure of the kind envisaged by, for example, idealism or positivism. Especially scientific world-orientation calls for a representation of knowledge achieved at any one time; it is at best an open, ever-changing systematic order, never a system. Systems such as positivism and idealism are the opposite of a systematic order, because they absolutize knowledge gained through a specific kind of world-orientation that, in its specificity, is relative.

The perspective of man's temporality

The second book is a transcendental reflection on the being of man as *Existenz*. Dealing with its subject matter in a manner different from Heidegger's fundamental–ontological analysis of Dasein, Jaspers characterizes the prominent phenomena of man's being-in-time. This can be regarded as the basic text of modern existential philosophy. Its wider significance is determined by the context of the whole

mentioned that in working on *Von der Wahrheit*, he had Heidegger in mind; he was referring to a theme of his later work, namely, that philosophy has political import. To him Heidegger's (brief) alignment with the Nazi movement was an appalling and telling misstep. See Jaspers's *Notizen zu Martin Heidegger*, Hans Saner (ed.) (Munich: Piper, 1978), as well as the posthumously published chapter "Heidegger," Hans R. Rudnick (trans.), in *The Philosophy of Karl Jaspers*, rev. 2nd ed., Paul. A. Schilpp (ed.) (La Salle, IL: Open Court, 1974).

work, according to which the search for Being is thrown back to the question concerning the one who is searching. In this way one can prevent confusing Being with Being-as-it-is-for-man in his historicity. This is the primary concern and main achievement of this part of *Philosophy*, entitled "Illumination of Existenz."

The modalities of the question of Being become actual and articulated to man, not in his being of and in the world but by existing self-consciously in his temporality. Existenz can be approached by transcendental phenomenology but not cognitively; it can be illumined, not in its actuality as a living person, but only as "possible Existenz." In order to emphasize this, Jaspers often speaks in polarities reminiscent of Kierkegaard's Anti-Climacus.[5] This procedure stands in marked contrast to Heidegger's phenomenology of the structures (*existentialia*) of the being of Dasein in *Being and Time*, written at the same time that Jaspers wrote *Philosophy*.

Accordingly, historicity and communication are the leading themes of Jaspers's phenomenology of "possible Existenz." In Jaspers's conception, historicity refers to whatever becomes historic out of the ground of Being through the agency of thinking man. It refers not only to time, but to man's temporality. It means not only history (what is realized in public time), but history as the realization of what a person is committed to, and for which he offers his temporality. Man finds himself tied to situations that challenge him to make choices and decisions. This involves the risk of offering up one's limited temporality, as well as proving oneself with respect to what one regards to be one's grounding in truth by virtue of fundamental convictions (faith). It entails the assumption of obligation for what is to be actualized, and responsibility for the success or failure of one's action.

The truth of Being is not realized through action wholly and with finality. Instead, what is true within the bounds of one's temporality is – not infallibly – decided in one's original realizations. Moreover, man exists and acts with respect to fellow man; one stands essentially in communication, for one's truth is not all the truth. Concern over one's truth means to be engaged in a struggle for the truth with or against fellow man. Jaspers indicates the relevance of communication to realms of human realization that are wider than that of interpersonal transaction, including the political.

Obligation and responsibility call for a discussion of freedom as distinguished from free choice. Freedom cannot be grasped like a knowable object or an observable trait, which would reduce it to conditionality. Freedom is unconditional; it is a capacity drawn from the ground of Being by which man finds

*5. For a discussion of Kierkegaard, see the essay by Alastair Hannay in *The History of Continental Philosophy: Volume 2*.

himself, and, finding himself, participates in the determination of truth for man in time.

The unconditionality of Existenz is at play in Jaspers's conception of other phenomena. Man's coming to be takes place in the context of cultural, biological, social, historical, and everyday situations; as mere Dasein, man's being is tenuous, is "never without struggle and suffering,"[6] is inevitably entangled in obligation and guilt, experiences failure and shipwreck, and is confronted with death and having to die. While such limits are conditions of man's being, Jaspers points to their import when they are encountered as *limit situations*. They are *limit* situations not by setting limits, but in being confronted. Confronting "limit situations" can direct us to choices on which depend whatever truth can become actual within those limits.

Man does not merely function as the instrument – for example, of the World-Spirit (Hegel) – of actualizing whatever comes about through him, since one's personal fate and destiny are involved no matter what cause, lord, or god one serves. Where man effects his actualization out of possibilities that are not cognitively derivable but require fundamental commitment and choice, he draws them from the ground in which he is rooted. Jaspers refers to this phenomenon of one's originality as *absolute consciousness,* in distinction from cognitive consciousness and from Hegel's mediating particularization of the Absolute Universal. Absolute consciousness is to be understood as daring to bring meanings and actualities to bear on the here-and-now that are not native to it. Jaspers recognizes absolute consciousness in the phenomena faith, love, and the creative imagination. By means of the illumination of those phenomena of "possible Existenz," Jaspers provided the groundwork for reorienting the question of the search for Being by way of the question concerning the one who is searching.

The transcendence of the ground of Being

The question of the truth of Being is the fundamental topic of philosophy; it is therefore with respect to the enterprise of philosophy that Jaspers applies the most radical reorientation effected through the "illumination of Existenz." While "Metaphysics" is the title of the third book of *Philosophy*, Jaspers's treatment of the subject is a departure from traditional metaphysics. He rejects metaphysical thought that lays claim to universal validity which, in his view, has been preempted by modern science. The question of the ground of Being must be thought as transcending determinacy – hence its unresolvability. In light of the reorientation, metaphysics is now regarded as the thinking being's relation to the ground of Being, rather than as the forms and traditions of objectification.

6. Karl Jaspers, *Philosophie. Vol. 2: Existenzerhellung* (Berlin: Springer, 1932), 246.

Consequently Jaspers's treatment focuses on the ways of thought about metaphysical topics.

Jaspers raises the question: "Is that which had been the foundation of personalities and of singular creations an aberration. ... would it be high time to extirpate it once and for all?" And he poses the opposite question, "is there within us a sense of forlornness and a longing for the retrieval of an experience of authentic Being?"[7] In light of the critical distinction between cognitive–scientific and metaphysical thought, Jaspers says that if the latter is meant to refer to knowable objects, then it is illusory; however, it is actual for Existenz in its relation to the transcendent ground of Being, especially in light of the unconditionality of freedom and the originality of choice. For Existenz, metaphysical thought is historic, that is, actual in the exercise of one's freedom.

To Jaspers, received testimonies of the relation to transcendence, such as scriptures, myths, theological treatises, texts of philosophy, and, in particular, of metaphysics, are the dry bones of the vital appearance of authentic Being for an Existenz in its freedom. Their significance for us consists in that, by studying them. These testimonies may, by assimilation or by rejection, awaken in us our own historic grounding in the truth of Being.

Jaspers elaborates on this significant aspect of traditional metaphysics under the heading "formal transcending." On the surface, his is a critical examination of a thinking that has traditionally prevailed in metaphysics and systematic theology. The criticism is aimed at the supposition that formal thought, operating with categories of cognition, can produce valid and cogent knowledge concerning transcendent matters; in this sense Jaspers sees a reason to depart from traditional metaphysics. But his criticism also shows that metaphysical speculation, pursued without the pretense of cognition but with the courage to proceed with clarity of thought and the risk of shipwreck, can be an indicator that the relation to transcendence is *actual* in the *historicity* of Existenz. Traditional metaphysics can then gain a new significance.

The centerpiece of Jaspers's metaphysics is his phenomenology of *existential relations to transcendence*, that is, what posture Existenz takes as it directs itself to transcendence. Jaspers explores four pairs of such postures. These are not alternatives, but in each case exhibit the tension of polar opposites. It is one of the most original parts of the work, spanning worldwide theological thought; I indicate them in brief.

Defiance and *devotion*[8] (or piety) are postures taken when merely living one's existence in the world and in everyday life becomes questionable, as in

7. Karl Jaspers, *Philosophie. Vol. 3: Metaphysik* (Berlin: Springer, 1932), 13.
8. What Jaspers means by *Hingabe* is difficult to render in English; "devotion" or "piety," which I favor, come closer to the intended meaning than Ashton's translation "surrender."

the confrontation with limit situations. It is the refusal to remain blind with respect to the questions of the meaningfulness, worth, justice, and justification of existence. Jaspers recalls Ivan Karamazov's defiant protest against a world in which even one innocent child has to suffer. Like Job, Ivan wants to know. The will to know is a primary note of defiance. Devotion is the polar opposite, but not in the sense of surrendering the insistence on understanding what transcends comprehension. Instead, as with Job, it is a knowing piety, born of the knowledge of one's fundamental ignorance, and knowing that, even though one stands by oneself in one's freedom, one, as it were, did not create oneself; one is "not the ultimate." In its knowing ignorance (as in Cusanus's *docta ignorantia*), devotion is the chance of accepting one's freedom and one's temporal existence in the world as a gift to be used for the actualization of what can be only through oneself.

The confines of time and temporality determine the second polarity, that of *descent* and *ascent*. Within temporality, the relation to transcendence is not a state but an ongoing process of uncertain outcome. It is a matter of invoking ideals of meaningfulness, aspirations, standards of responsible action, causes and purposes to be fulfilled. These are not determinants of our existence, for what we become is subject to our decisions. They function as measures with respect to which we prove ourselves or fail to do so. It is a way of descent to regard the truth to which one ascends as the only truth, without conceding the validity, for the other, of his other truth. Being in process within time, one is never whole; one is torn between the voice of the genius and the voice of the demon, the slide into abject nothingness and the realization of immortal Being.

The existential positions, which Jaspers characterizes with the metaphoric imagery *law of day* and *passion for night*, are a fundamental polarity reminiscent of the Greek *cosmos* and *chaos*. The position "law of day" obliges us to order, clarity, reason, hence to being loyal and dependable, to "actualization in the world, to building in time, to complete temporal existence on a never-ending path."[9] Thus to Jaspers the light of reason is not extraneous but fundamentally proper to Existenz. Yet "night," the wholly other, also demands its due, for it is, like Schopenhauer's cosmic will, a felt actuality that, blind to thought and reason, brings forth and destroys. It affects us in our coming forth out of the darkness of not-being, in this age, at this place on earth, and among these people; in the inevitability of our death and of the eventual ruin of all we have built. Truly a *passion* for night, it is active in us, most prominently in that "incomprehensible fetter" of eroticism beyond mere sexuality. Night is not evil; the distinction between good and evil prevails in day, and night is beyond good and evil.

9. Jaspers, *Philosophie. Vol. 3: Metaphysik*, 102.

The idea of transcendence as the One is the focus of the final pair of existential relations to transcendence, namely the "Wealth of the Many and the One." Jaspers wonders about the perennial fascination with the One, beginning especially during times that Jaspers later identifies as the "axial times." He recalls, for example, the idea of the one universal deity of Greek philosophy (Xenophanes, Plato), and of "the God of the Jewish prophets experienced in the soul's solitude."[10] What is at play is oneness as the existential relation to transcendence, which, in the testimony of untold generations, has been thought of as the divinity. Jaspers explains: if we decide by whim, or let ourselves be tossed about by the vicissitudes coming our way, then we fail to be an identity. It is different if we make choices and act out of what is fundamentally important to us, if we know where we stand and are true to ourselves. Yet the transcendent One on which one grounds oneself is in each case one's own truth. It is not a matter of partaking in what one can know to be an all-embracing ultimate truth. My truth is not everybody's truth. Even in mutual struggle one has to concede each other's relation to God. While one's God is subject to one's choice and risk, the truly One is beyond one's limit. "Authentic Existenz will not lose sight of the far God beyond one's near God."[11]

Ciphers of transcendence

If the relation to transcendence is fundamentally existential, what is the meaning of the articulation of that relation, whether in images, myths, symbols, metaphysical systems, or religious doctrines? Jaspers takes up this question in the last chapter of *Philosophy*, "The Reading of the Cipher-Script."[12] The basic thought is as follows: Transcendence to which one relates as one's ground in Being cannot be encountered as an actuality in the world, nor thought in the manner of a cognitive object. Yet actual objects and determinate thoughts are the unavoidable means of articulating that relation. Thus transcendence is present only as mediated through one's thoughts or in experienced actualities, and such thoughts or experiences are "ciphers" of transcendence. In ciphers one does not understand or hear but can be addressed by transcendence. Any thought, any experience, can be taken as expressive of that relation, but only to us in our "absolute consciousness," not in our cognitive understanding. With regard to the inevitable

10. *Ibid.*, 124.
11. Karl Jaspers, *Philosophie. Vol. 3: Metaphysik*, 122; *Philosophy. Vol. 3: Metaphysics*, E. B. Ashton (Chicago, IL: University of Chicago Press, 1969–71), 107.
12. Although an original approach to metaphysics, it is rooted in the experience and history of thought, especially modern thought. Jaspers refers to Paul Tillich and Friedrich T. Vischer; but see also Ernst Cassirer (symbolic forms) and Emmanuel Levinas (Trace).

objectification of ciphers, Jaspers distinguishes between the levels of immediate experience, of objective configuration, and of speculative elaboration.[13]

To illustrate: In Golding's *The Lord of the Flies*, schoolboys stranded on a deserted island kill a pig, sever its head, and triumphantly mount it on a pole. Fascinated by the ugly sight of flies swarming around the decaying head, one of the boys is overwhelmed by the display of what to him is the presence of an awesome and implacable happening beyond comprehension. This is the cipher at the level of existential immediacy. At the next level, immediacy is replaced by objectification, such as institutional religion, mythic imagery, art, doctrine. In such objectification, the cipher does not remain the vehicle of one's personally exclusive relation to transcendence. It can be regarded by anyone; one can appreciate it without being addressed by it; it can be debated, criticized; it can attract or repel. It is then no more than a symbol; but to the extent that one can be addressed by it, the symbol is a cipher.

In the public domain, a cipher is a determinate object; its meaning can vary with the observer's standpoint. But insofar as the cipher is expressive of one's grounding, in freedom, on transcendence, it represents the indeterminacy of transcendence. The meaning it conveys is not verified by interpretation or speculation – the third level – but through one's commitment and the difference it makes here and now. But personal verification is neither evidential inference nor conceptual finality. Transcendence is as such unfathomable to man thinking determinately and existing in time; the meanings of the cipher are multiple, and transcendence can manifest itself in other ways.

Jaspers's conception of metaphysical (including theological) thought as the existential reading of the cipher script is the basis of his view of the foundation of religion. This view was challenged by proponents of revealed religion, to whom the tenets of faith are neither myths nor symbols but revealed accounts of mysterious occurrences. Jaspers has met the challenge, whether in the demythologizing controversy with Rudolf Bultmann,[14] or in the confrontation of revealed faith with philosophical faith. In most of his works, we find his interpretations of

13. Jaspers speaks of "three languages" rather than levels.

14. The Protestant theologian Rudolf Bultmann, inspired by Heidegger, proposed to demythologize the Bible by translating the myths of the New Testament into a nonmythical idiom, leaning on modern science. The only exception is the event of salvation, that is, Jesus's death on the cross and his resurrection; this is to be accepted as literal fact by virtue of the kerygma. Jaspers countered that the truth of myths, symbols, and ciphers is translatable only into other myths, and verified not simply by confessing to it, but by its impact on the conduct of life. See Karl Jaspers and Rudolf Bultmann, *Die Frage der Entmythologisierung* (Munich: Piper, 1954), published in English as *Myth and Christianity: An Inquiry into the Possibility of Religion Without Myth*, Norbert Guterman (trans.) (New York: Noonday Press, 1958). [*] For a discussion of Bultmann, see the essay by Andreas Grossman in *The History of Continental Philosophy: Volume 4*.

testimonies of existential relations to transcendence as ciphers, such as religious doctrines, works of literature, myths, works of art, and traditional metaphysics. The last, while rejected as literal, cognitive thought, is seen by Jaspers, especially in his *The Great Philosophers*, in its significance as the cipher-like articulation of relations to transcendence.

Personal temporality as the pivotal factor in the reorientation of the question of Being and truth is especially at play where reading the cipher-script ends and culminates in the phenomenon of *shipwreck*. This is neither the deliberate pursuit of foundering, nor the nihilistic resignation from life seen as an exercise in futility. Instead, it is the actual *experience* of the inevitability of shipwreck by one engaged in realizing whatever Being and truth can humanly be realized.[15] The ultimate cipher is the one where man, attempting to fathom meaning, runs aground. We cannot find life-giving meaning, for example, in memories lost that are the last repository of what has been achieved, realized, attained by way of Being for man in time. Being as such is the abyss at which thought fails.

The phenomenology of "reading the cipher script" shows that "the question 'what Being is' … is unresolvable." Insofar as Being "calls for man's thinking," Being does not provide man with direction by his stepping back and "letting Being be," as Heidegger suggests. Instead, we are turned to Being as it is for man bringing himself forth in time.

The triple helix

By virtue of the reorientation elaborated in *Philosophy*, Jaspers proceeds with the renewal of the question of Being with respect to the *unity of Being and truth*, the basic theme of *Von der Wahrheit*. Several undercurrents motivate Jaspers's pursuit of the question in *Von der Wahrheit*.

One is the *unresolvability* of the question of Being: "We do not and we shall not possess the one truth, and yet the truth can only be one."[16] The question therefore turns on how the unity of the truth of Being can be regarded through thought determined by man's temporality.

Another motive is the reference to the *testimony* of humanity's concern over that question in the history of philosophy as well as in literature and religion. Jaspers's leaning on this testimony is so programmatic a feature that parallel to his systematic elaboration of the testimony that informed the reorientation, Jaspers devoted much of his later years to a major and original conception of a "world history of philosophy," which, by its conception, was integral to and

15. Jaspers, *Philosophie. Vol. 3: Metaphysik*, 226; *Philosophy. Vol. 3: Metaphysics*, 199.
16. VdW, 839.

intertwined with the philosophic elaboration of the second stage in *Von der Wahrheit*.

Finally, since truth for man in time is historic, there is no truth for man without testimony through choice, action, and responsibility. Authentic philosophy is the *practice of philosophy*. Inasmuch as action affects others, action as testimony of one's truth is potentially of political import. If we add to that the importance of communication for interpersonal transaction, we find that for Jaspers the question of the unity of truth carries with it a concern over the unity of the human community and of its challenges and tasks past and present, including the unity of the enterprise of research in the university, the meaning of history, and above all, the political motive. The concern over praxis is integral to and intertwined with the substance of the philosophic elaboration of *Von der Wahrheit*, and is the subject matter of major and minor works of Jaspers's later years dealing with fundamental political thought, critical studies of current political topics, the criticism of modernity, philosophy of history, the future of scientific research, of the practice of medicine, of education, and the university. Consequent on the earlier reorientation, Jaspers's thinking in each of the three strands is intertwined with the others, each informing the other. These are: the question of the unity of Being and Truth for man in time; regard for man's experience with that question; and concern over the active realization of Truth. This *triple helix* of his thought – fundamental thought, history of testimony, testimony through praxis[17] – more or less indicated in *Philosophy*, is deliberately at play in his later writings.

III. THE SECOND STAGE: BEING FOR MAN IN TIME

Being and its modes: the encompassing

In light of the reorientation we now have to ask how we can speak of Being from the perspective of the historicity of man. For man, Being in its oneness is absolutely transcendent, it surrounds man's temporality, it is the "Encompassing." For man, Being ruptures into modes, which are also encompassing as they appear to man. They are encompassing horizons in that they recede no matter how far we progress in realizing what is for man in time.

Pursuing a radical train of thought, Jaspers discloses such horizons, characterizes them, and shows the relations between them. Jaspers calls this a doctrine

17. The three strands are displayed in the list of Jaspers's major works: "Fundamental philosophy"; "Philosophy of faith and religion"; "History of philosophy"; praxis: "Political philosophy," "Philosophy of modernity and history," "Psychiatry and psychology".

of the modes of encompassing Being, or "periechontology,"[18] in distinction from traditional ontology, that is the doctrine of Being. Jaspers eschews both the constructive thinking (traditional metaphysics) and the antimetaphysical de-constructive phenomenology (Heidegger). Instead, he refers to the testimony of humanity's hitherto achieved realization of Being and truth, the testimony of philosophy as well as that of language, literature, art, science, praxis, religion, and myth.

Jaspers meant his periechontology to be suited to the contemporary tasks and challenges of peoples meeting in what has irreversibly become one world since it provides an "open horizon" for them to meet in communication. He insists that his periechontology is a personal philosophical perception, not a claim to universal validity. The idea of periechontology is historic, hence open and modifiable. Jaspers does not regard it to be original with him, but at play in all great philosophers, beginning with Plato. It is the open space where people who are divided in their respective fundamental faith can meet in mutual tolerance.

The primary rupture of Being for man is the subject–object dichotomy. Whatever is for us is within this dichotomy. Being-as-such, encompassing both subject and object, is not amenable to being an object for us. Within the primary rupture, Jaspers distinguishes being-object as "Being itself," and being-subject as "Being that we [human beings] are or can be."

"*Being that we are or can be*" divides into several modes: being-there (*Dasein*), consciousness-as-such, spirit, and Existenz.

Being-there.[19] We are as *Dasein*, that is, we are there (*da-sein* means "being-there") as beings in our environment, in and part of the spatiotemporal world, as life in the biological sense. Whatever else we are, we are actual in the concreteness of our being-there. Being-there is the arena of our actuality. The subject–object dichotomy with respect to being-there consists of the distinction of one's personal life from one's surrounding world, one's environment.

Consciousness-as-such.[20] The term (*Bewußtsein überhaupt*) stems from Kant. It refers to thought-as-such in the sense that whatever else we human beings may be said to be, we are it thinkingly. Thought, Jaspers says, is a primal phenomenon; it accompanies all other phenomena. Being-thinking includes not only

18. Jaspers reached back to a similar use of the word in Aristotle's *Metaphysics*; Aristotle reports that according to Anaximander the *apeiron* (the unbounded) cannot be a single thing but encompasses (*periechein)* single things, and cannot be something that is itself encompassed (*periechomenon*).
19. VdW, 53–64; in English in *Karl Jaspers: Basic Philosophical Writings*, Edith Ehrlich *et al.* (eds and trans.) (Athens, OH: Ohio University Press 1986), selection 17.
20. VdW, 64–70; in English in *Karl Jaspers: Basic Philosophical Writings*, selection 18.

cognition, but also self-consciousness and the inner act of experiencing; hence the designation "consciousness-as-such." It is by virtue of our being consciousness that Being for us is split into subject and object. Being thinking, we can transcend any being that is for us as object, and, thinking it, we think it in the form of objectivity. No mode of encompassing Being is for us except insofar as we think it. Even the fundamental ("pre-logical") distinction of the modes of the Encompassing is the work of thought. However, it is cognition that is the proper fulfillment of thought. Hence the nature of thought merits an extensive treatise in Jaspers's *Von der Wahrheit*.[21]

Spirit. Jaspers reintroduces spirit into philosophic discourse as an encompassing mode of the being that we are. In his conception of the spirit, Jaspers, inclining toward Kant's transcendental idea,[22] stresses the articulation of spirit in the form of ideas. Ideas express transcendental wholenesses and serve as practical or theoretical measures, as motivating aspirations, and as configurations, metaphors, symbols, or ciphers of transcending thought. For example, over the decades Jaspers published three versions of "the idea of the university," each containing the same core idea, but differing in its application to changing conditions; they are meant not as descriptions of extant universities, but as measures that existing universities might refer to in the realization of the idea. In the form of ideas Jaspers sees encompassing spirit as carrying the formidable weight of humanity's directing itself to its tasks, to creativity, to investing life and reality with respect to meaning.

Existenz: self-being. We do not need to reiterate here Jaspers's phenomenology of possible Existenz (freedom, historicity, communication, *et al.*). But Jaspers also speaks of "self-being." Being oneself means being engaged in an unending task of becoming by virtue of the risk and responsibility of decisions and choices made in confrontation with challenges, choices out of possibilities that are not always at hand but are invoked from the ground of one's being. It is for this reason that, with respect to man's temporality, he speaks of self-being as Existenz, that is, as deliberately coming to be in time out of infinite possibility. Existenz is thus more than (transcends) the immanent modes. Jaspers says, "I am not merely there [being-there], not merely the subject of consciousness-as-such, not merely the place of spiritual movement and spiritual creation, but in all of them I can [either] be myself or be lost in them."[23]

21. VdW, 225–449.
22. See Jaspers's early essay on "Kant's Doctrine of Ideas" appended to his *Psychologie der Weltanschauungen*.
23. VdW, 77. See also *Karl Jaspers: Basic Philosophical Writings*, 154.

Jaspers discusses the relations and distinctions between Existenz and the immanent modes extensively; we mention only one aspect concerning spirit, namely the question of time and historicity. To Hegel, human actualizations are the particular concretions of the spirit's universality. But Existenz is not a derivative and cannot be subsumed under a universal; Existenz is on its own responsibility, at its own risk. Existenz leans on spirit for its self-articulation; it is not an item of the world spirit's comprehensive historical universality. For universal spirit, time is the panorama of its timeless wholeness. For Existenz, time is one's own temporality on which one brings to bear timeless sources of possibility in a never-ending search for wholeness.

How can Existenz be discerned as a mode of man's being that transcends the immanent modes? One indicator is the motive of immortality among peoples of all kinds, of all times. Jaspers does not mean immortality as "the continuation of life in another form"; he means a sense of being borne by an eternity (transcending temporality) that manifests itself in persistently filling one's temporality with effective activity. In Jaspers's words:

> We have but one actuality: here and now. What we miss by our evasion will never return, but we lose Being also if we squander ourselves. Each day is precious: a moment can be everything. We are remiss in our task if we lose ourselves in past or future. The timeless is accessible only by way of present actuality; only by taking hold of time do we get to where all time is extinguished.[24]

The subject–object dichotomy with respect to Existenz is the polar relation of Existenz to its other, to transcendence, as the "dark ground" and source of our being "out of which I encounter myself in freedom … [and] bring myself forth, yet am given to myself as a gift."[25] In this sense, Jaspers regards faith – as in *Philosophy* – as an expression of the fundamental certainty of Being.[26]

"*The encompassing that is Being itself*" appears as *world* and is, as *transcendence*, the ground of Being of Existenz. Jaspers takes a critical stance against the view that there is no indication of Being independently of being for us and radically other than the Being that we are. He takes particular issue with the Nietzschean view that all that is is interpretation originating with us as inter-

24. Karl Jaspers, *Einführung in die Philosophie* (Zurich: Artemis, 1950), 136; see *Way to Wisdom: An Introduction to Philosophy*, R. Manheim (trans.) (New Haven, CT: Yale University Press, 1951), 144.
25. VdW, 77.
26. In *Philosophy* Jaspers mentions faith, love, and creative imagination (*Phantasie*) as the forms of fundamental certainty. In the writings of the second stage, imagination makes its appearance as the ideas of the spirit by means of which we articulate our faith.

preters. Leaning on Kant, he points out that while we – never adequately, never with finality – bring forth the world and transcendence in their appearance to our thoughtful apprehension, we thereby do not bring forth Being in itself. Against German idealism Jaspers counters Hegel's dictum: "Whatever might not be known by consciousness would have neither meaning for it nor power over it":

> What does not enter our consciousness is actual power even if unknown … The unknown is effective at the limit of even the most far-reaching consciousness. Without our knowledge it affects us, determines us, overwhelms us; it is discernible … at two limits: every encountered fact indicates Being that we are not and which, in its totality, we call "the world." [And:] The Encompassing that we are cannot be comprehended out of itself, but indicates an other through which it is …[27]

World. The world is neither an illusory backdrop to what is no more than subject to our interpretation, nor is it Being in itself, independent of man but adequately reflected in our knowledge. Instead, the world in its totality is an idea, cognitively inconceivable. What we do know is always *in* the world, always a perspective on the world, never *the* world. And even though we bring forth perspectives on the world in its appearance to our thinking being, we do not bring forth the being of the world. The being of the world, independently of its being known, intimates itself at the limit of our knowledge, in the unyielding givenness of encountered factualities.

What is the relation of world and the modes of being human? As being-there, we too are in and of the world; the expressions of meanings entertained in consciousness are events in the world, the effects of spirit are manifest in the concreteness of the world. Yet no mode of being that we are is reducible to the world; each in its own way is radically originary. There are, then, two aspects of the Encompassing of the world. It means the sheer endlessness of whatever can be an object of our cognition. And, the world is "the Encompassing that we are not, the simply other, that in its core is not present to us as our own essence."[28] The world contains the conditions for our being-there, for our being consciousness, for our being spirit. If this were to mean that the being that we are is derived from the world, then man would be a microcosm of the cosmos, and the world, indwelling in us, would not be the unfathomable other. But Jaspers recalls that even Aristotle, who sees man within the natural continuum of living beings,

27. VdW, 84. See also *Karl Jaspers: Basic Philosophical Writings*, 159.
28. VdW, 87. See also *Karl Jaspers: Basic Philosophical Writings*, 160.

regards *nous* as coming to man from outside. The world remains extraneous to what we are; encompassing whatever we can cognitively know, it remains a mysterious other. As the condition for our very being, it is that by which we are borne; and it is that which is utterly indifferent to our being.

The conception of the world is not unitary. It is always someone's world, and every human being has her own world. One's world is not only one's physical environment, but differs according to how one acts in it, or makes use of it. It also differs according to how one shapes it, and consists of the different kinds of interpersonal transaction (social, political, etc.). Different still is the world as object of our understanding and cognition, such as history and scientific research. The world ruptures into many worlds; in each, in its own way, we encounter only factualities *in* the world. Jaspers cautions against absolutizing any one conception.

The realization of the world as encompassing is of weighty political import. Any particular world taken as the true world as such enables one to regard the world as at one's disposal for ordering it in accordance with one's vision. Breaking through every limited perspective on the world sheds light on the fathomless ground in which the world is for us and in which we are as beings who, in our historic originality, gain perspective on it. Thus, to Jaspers, our realization of the world as encompassing also points to our freedom in the following three senses:

- "We become free for the world": that is, we are able to recover from any particular realization, and proceed in our never-ending quest for knowledge of and meaningfulness in the world.
- "We become free for ourselves in the world": that is, we can discover, beyond our being *of* the world, the source of our own becoming within ourselves.[29]
- "We become free for ourselves in relation to transcendence": that is, we proceed within the world free for our grounding on transcendence. This calls for our testimony in the form of finite cognition, specific actions, or of the difference we make in shaping the world and our lives.[30]

Transcendence. Existenz in its freedom is central in pointing to the actuality of transcendence. In Jaspers's words: "Where I am truly myself, I know that I am given to myself [in the manner of a gift]. The more decisively I am conscious of my freedom, the more undisputed also is the transcendence through which I am." And he adds, including a phrase from Kierkegaard: "I am Existenz only together with knowledge about transcendence as the power through which I

29. VdW, 104.
30. *Ibid.*, 104–5.

am myself."[31] The reason is that only relatedness to transcendence can affirm one's independence from the conditionality of world-being, and thus confirm one's freedom.

The different ways of experiencing the – as such hidden – transcendence remain as characterized by Jaspers in the first stage, namely: formal transcending, the existential relations, the reading of the cipher-script. Now, however, Jaspers refers to some of the many names by which, in the history of man's experience, transcendence has been referred to.

- *Being*. Within philosophy, Being has long been regarded as transcendence, especially in Scholastic thought.[32] And Jaspers, as well as Heidegger, have renewed the question of Being, each in his own way. To Jaspers, Being is transcendence only for abstract thought. Hence – in keeping with the renewal of the question of Being – Jaspers turns to historically more concrete cipher-imagery.
- *Authentic actuality*. The conception of transcendence in this sense of *Wirklichkeit* (actuality that brings forth) has a long tradition, rooted in the biblical God as creator, in Plato's *demiourgos*, and in Aristotle's prime mover being pure *energeia*;[33] it is reflected in the Scholastic idea of God as *actus purus*,[34] and in later conceptions derived therefrom (Descartes, Leibniz). To Jaspers, transcendence as actuality is perceived as that which touches and involves us, to which we are drawn, which offers guidance.[35]
- *Divinity* is the experience of transcendence as the actuality that governs us, that, surrounding us with its presence, addresses us and makes demands upon us.
- *God* is transcendence as person of concern to us as singular persons; God is experienced as the person-to-person relation to us as individuals. It is the idea of transcendence derived from the Hebrew Bible, determining the fundamental experience of transcendence in the West.

Jaspers traces the historical rise of man's relation to transcendence. The decisive step is the realization of transcendence as "simply other"; the world is no longer

31. *Ibid*., 110; in English in *Karl Jaspers: Basic Philosophical Writings*, 175. Kierkegaard's pseudonym Anti-Climacus, as orthodox Christian, says of the redeemed self: "in relating itself to itself and in willing to be itself, the self rests transparently in the power that establishes it" (*The Sickness unto Death*, Howard V. Hong and Edna H. Hong [trans.] [Princeton, NJ: Princeton University Press, 2001], 14).
32. See e.g. Thomas Aquinas, *Summa theologica*, q. 3, a. 4.
33. See Aristotle, *Met*. bk. XII, ch. 7, 1072b.
34. See Aquinas, *Summa theologica*, q. 3, a. 2.
35. Paraphrasing "das uns ... Angehende, das uns Anziehende, Haltgebende" (VdW, 111).

regarded as Being as such, sufficient in itself. Akhenaten's inspiration of the sun as the one fundamental divinity, although monotheistic, is merely a step in that direction.[36] In the traceable history of humanity, taking that step is a feature in what Jaspers calls the axial times, the period he sees as the axis of history. He says: "Posing radical questions and confronting the abyss, [man] seeks liberation and salvation. Fully conscious of his limits, he sets himself the highest goals. He experiences unconditionality in the depth of his self-being and in the clarity of transcendence."[37]

In the Hebrew Bible, Jaspers sees one of the most decisive realizations of transcendence in the axial age. Interpreting the first two of the Ten Commandments as ciphers, Jaspers says,

> *The one God*: Polytheism is in keeping with natural man and with all of us. … Man stands in contradiction with himself; by serving some gods he offends others. And then the power of Oneness appears with strange force.
>
> *No image and no symbol*: Transcendence lies beyond all ciphers. Therein lies the truth of all philosophizing.[38]

Reason: the bond within us of all modes of the Encompassing. In both stages of Jaspers's renewal of the question of Being, we noted his perception of the rupture of Being into modes, and of the ruptures within the immanent modes. Jaspers raises the question of unity in connection with the rupture of Being into encompassing modes: "[The] source of the unrelenting urge to unity lies in the Encompassing that we are – not only the internal unity of each Encompassing but that of all modes of the Encompassing, that which we are and that which we encounter: *Unity is through Existenz and reason*."[39] While the motive of unity may arise as an existential concern over personal integrity, the driving force toward unity is a matter of *reason*.

In Jaspers's phenomenology, reason is a deliberate bonding force: it is the will of reason to "reclaim whatever there is from … mutual indifference and to return it to a movement of belonging together."[40] Reason does not have any

36. Akhenaten (Amenhotep IV), was an eighteenth-dynasty Pharaoh, and sponsor of the short-lived Amarna culture centered on the sun as predominant deity.
37. Jaspers, *Einführung in die Philosophie*, 98; *Way to Wisdom*, 100.
38. Karl Jaspers, *Kleine Schule des philosophischen Denkens* (Munich: Piper, 1965), 125; in English in *Philosophy is for Everyman: A Short Course in Philosophical Thinking*, R. F. C. Hull and Grete Wels (trans.) (New York: Harcourt, Brace & World, 1967), 88.
39. VdW, 113, emphasis added; see also *Karl Jaspers: Basic Philosophical Writings*, 179.
40. VdW, 114; see also *Karl Jaspers: Basic Philosophical Writings*, 179–80.

content specific to it, but by virtue of reason we direct ourselves to the content of the other modes of Being. Through reason we bring what is disparate, other and strange, incompatible and indifferent into relation, not to subdue one to the other, but to recognize and to be concerned that there is otherness that claims to be and to be true.

Jaspers exemplifies the working of reason in the sciences, which, as such, seem to be purely a matter of the understanding. As the motivating force of unity, reason is the impetus of research, a never-ending process of testing and of interim solutions in the form of theoretical constructs. Never satisfied, reason impels us to further questioning and research. The task of reason is, then, not to bond segments of the ruptured wholeness of Being. Instead, it is a decisive force in the history of humanity concerned with the realization of truth, which is never at an end.

Reason is definitive of Jaspers's conception of the axial age. It is not a coincidence that, together with tragic poetry and scriptural testimonies of man's hearkening to a transcendent one and singular God who addresses man with demands and guidance, it was the time of the rise of philosophy. For transcending thought, concern over unity and restless questing of truth are the marks of both reason and philosophizing. In modernity, Jaspers sees humanity facing a fundamental challenge second only to that of the axial age. With science having preempted the realm of cogent knowledge, with the irreversible encounter of disparate fundamental truths, differing social norms, conflicting political ideologies, and incompatible cultural values, Jaspers regards reason as the taskmaster of humanity in meeting that challenge – albeit reason in a deliberately communicative mode. We find this at play in all the major aspects of Jaspers's philosophical work that are the outgrowths of the culmination of his renewal of the question of Being in the philosophy of the Encompassing: the philosophy of modernity and history; the philosophy of science coupled with his idea of the research university; his conception of the statesman as a man of reason, and of politics as grounded in the supra-political; his consideration of the mutual encounter of religious beliefs, and his own encounter with revealed religion; his vision of a world philosophy to come; his project of a world history of philosophy.

IV. TRUTH FOR MAN IN TIME

In light of the reorientation, culminating in the disclosure of Being and its modes as encompassing, Jaspers approaches the question of truth with respect to unity. But truth in its unity, encompassing any human realization, is transcendent. Hence an inquiry into truth with respect to its unity can be only an illumination, with shafts of light that are finite and defined, of the encompassing truth within which we find ourselves.

While traditional theories of truth are valid within respective bounds, they stop short of addressing the question as now defined. In his discussion of the theories of validity of propositions, correspondence, and *alētheia* (Heidegger), Jaspers finds that they are directed to the rupture of Being. And the Scholastic principle of *omne ens est verum, unum, bonum*, while addressing unity, eschews the perspective of human temporality.

Another theory of truth that Jaspers discusses is truth as origin and goal. A conception of truth with no recognizable historical precedent, it is proposed by Jaspers in opposition to the relativism of historicism current in the early twentieth century. Truth as origin and goal means that there is no fundamental determinant as to what is truth for man in time, for it encompasses time and temporality:

> Our will to truth is not satisfied with any [realized] truth. … [C]ertain that it is derived from a ground and on the way to a goal … no configuration of truth will satisfy as we are still on the way. … Even though this ultimate goal … is never reached in time, it can guide us … The idea of encompassing truth means … the rejection … of all false anticipation of redemption … We prefer open honesty, whatever its consequences, to a happy sense of security protected by means of blinders … [The] thought of "being-true" as endless promotes the strength of carrying on the restless search.[41]

Accordingly, Jaspers sets himself the task of illuminating encompassing truth, and, with reference to the historical experience of thought, he does so in three ways, in a phenomenology spread over 600 pages of *Von der Wahrheit*, to which we cannot do justice in brief. The ways of illumination are distinct and are not derived from a common principle; nor do they function as elements or stages of a coherent construct. They merely intersect.

The first of these ways concerns "*Truth and Falsehood*."[42] The meaning of "being true" is here illuminated from the perspective that, for man, truth functions as a criterion rather than as an actuality. Measured against the criterion, however conceived, what man realizes is not fully truth but is, in fact, untruth. Truth in its encompassing unity is manifest, as it appears to man, as being less

41. VdW, 461–2.
42. VdW, 453–600; see *Karl Jaspers: Basic Philosophical Writings*, selections 35–7.

than truth. "*Il n'y a point, pour nous, – êtres imparfaits, – de vérité parfaite*,"[43] Jean Paumen says. Not only are we deceived and deceptive; not only is realized untruth the path in our search for truth; not only is untruth, even lying, a deliberately chosen vehicle of human realization in thought, in action, and in interpersonal relations; but untruth is an indispensable mode of the very being of truth for man.

A familiar instance is the theological function of the symbol.[44] The symbol is a falsehood in a sense in which the sign is not, that is, by representing what is never as such present to our consciousness. If the symbol or the analogy is meant as the presentation of transcendent actuality, it is a deception. The deceptiveness is reduced – not eliminated – by exposing the untruth of the symbol as the vehicle of the irreducible transcendence, for example of the divinity. The phenomenon of shipwreck of thought is, to Jaspers, a prime mode of exposing thought as inadequate to the realization of transcendent truth, thus dependent on the vehicle of untruth.[45]

Configurations of Truth is the second way of illumination, as Jaspers turns to the forms in which truth in its unity can be discerned as a phenomenon of the concreteness of truth for man in time. Truth manifest to us is a matter of many truths and modes of truth. As we seek the unity of this multiplicity it becomes more elusive and obscure. The deity, however conceived, that might be posited as the fulfillment of unity, is present within received traditions functioning in the form of institutional structures, established orders, and cultural dispositions. Yet, since these do not only include but exclude, they dismantle the unity vouchsafed by our directedness toward the one God. Thus the very pursuit of the wholeness of truth brings into focus the fragmentation of truth.

We attain truth in time through inquiry or enactment, through the order we live in or try to establish, through the guidance we receive that may pit us against others in their truth. In any of these instances truth in time can be seen as

43. "There is nothing at all for us – imperfect beings – of perfect truth"; Jean Paumen, *Raison et existence chez Karl Jaspers* (Brussels: Éditions du Parthenon, 1958), 251.

44. VdW, 487–8.

45. Xavier Tilliette, Professor at the Gregoriana, shows how, in the broad sweep of Jaspers's theory of truth, what is true for man in time is defined in its limitation over against the transcendence of truth in its oneness. Yet Tilliette looks for some cognitive assurance of the groundedness of man's limitation in transcendence, which he fails to find in Jaspers. As a way to such assurance he suggests the theological doctrine of analogy. But what pertains to the symbol pertains to the theological use of analogy: the divine actuality that is inferred analogically differs from all other analogically inferred actualities in that it remains an inferred actuality. (With respect to proofs for the existence of God, Jaspers is wont to point out that an inferred God is not God; God in his transcendence is a matter of existential faith or not at all.) See Xavier Tilliette SJ, *Karl Jaspers: Théorie de la verité, métaphysique des chiffres, foi philosophique* (Paris: Aubier, 1960), esp. 149ff.

limited and encompassed by truth in its transcendent unity. Truth in time does not take the place of truth in its encompassing unity, but the one truth functions within truth in time by breaking into its confines. Neither derivable nor expectable from the knowledge or power of human realization, it will burst into our lives and into human history, signaling a truth that encompasses man's truth. This can take many forms, but for Jaspers the main concrete configurations by which truth in its unity functions in its breakthrough for man in time are those of *authority* and the *exception*. They are polar opposites, but both are indispensable intimations of the unity of truth in the face of the immanent fragmentation, disruption, and limitation of truth. The mark of authority[46] is the sort of universality that, in its intention and potentiality, comprises and concerns all men. But human universality is itself limited, hence truth for man in its encompassing unity requires the challenge of the exception.[47] Even as the truth of authority can become an atrophied caricature of truth unless breached by the exception, so man, in the exception of his truth, will intensify his own limitation unless nourished and challenged by authority.

To Jaspers, the ultimate configurations are not authority and exception but *reason* and *catholicity*, each functioning within authority as well as exception. Reason, perennially in search of unity, is not fulfilled in time. The position of the fulfillment of truth in time is the rival of the rule of communicative reason. Jaspers calls this rival – whether appearing in culture, politics, or religion – the position of catholicity. Although the impulse toward unity springs from reason in either case, there is a fundamental difference in executing this impulse, whether oneness of truth is a matter of communicative openness or a matter of realizing a vision of truth deemed to be valid for and binding on all.

The first two illuminations focus on more formal features of the question of truth; in the third illumination Jaspers means to approach the question from the perspective of man's intimacy with what is true for him. The title of this approach is "Vollendung des Wahrseins" ("The Being of Truth in its Completion").[48] Radically speaking, the form in which truth is effectively complete is a matter of the singular Existenz; in philosophical abstraction we can only generalize about such forms. The two types of existentially effective completion that Jaspers characterizes are "original intuitions" and "philosophizing."

---

46. Gadamer misreads Jaspers's conception of authority as a configuration of transcendent truth for man in time by claiming that Jaspers means the authoritarian demand of deference, and not cognitive information. See Hans-Georg Gadamer, *Wahrheit und Methode* (Tübingen: J. C. B. Mohr, 1960), 264.
47. Jaspers leans on both Kierkegaard's and Nietzsche's realization of being exceptions. See Jaspers's interpretation of Kierkegaard and Nietzsche in *Reason and Existenz*, William Earle (trans.) (New York: Noonday Press, 1955).
48. VdW, 869–1054.

He begins the discussion of original intuitions as follows: "It is characteristic of man as man to direct his gaze into the ground of truth. Truth is there for him at all times, and it is within him by means of some language, be it ever so rough or opaque."[49] Religion, art, and poetry are the ordinary designations of what, for Jaspers, are the intuitions that afford visions of the ground of truth. They are the life-founding completion of truth for man in time, and accomplish this in a manner that is original, that is, not primarily reflective, although their expressions and traditions can reach pinnacles of spiritual sophistication in the form of scriptural legacies, mythic traditions, literary creations, iconic art, and so on.

Jaspers exemplifies the manner in which original intuitions have been effective as the completion of truth in time – particularly in light of inevitable limit situations and the phenomenon of foundering – by means of an essay on the tragic and its relation to the idea of redemption. To Jaspers, tragic knowledge is not the perception of the indifferent observer but the cognition of one who is affected at the limit of possibility, in the face of limit situations, where the realization of truth in thought and in deed experiences shipwreck. Jaspers sees Shakespeare's Hamlet as "steadfast in his will to truth ..., fully committed to the here-and-now, who does not deny himself to the world but is excluded from it, who fully delivers himself to his destiny and, in his heroism, is devoid of pathos."[50] Tragic knowledge signals a man's transformation, leading either to rising beyond the tragic in the direction of redemptive grounding in the source of Being, or to a nihilism of aesthetic contemplation, detached, without grounding. Jaspers traces the conception of redemption to the axial times of the millennium before Christianity, when knowledge of the dire state of humanity no longer referred merely to the everyday facts of illness, old age, and death. It was now seen as the fundamental human condition.

Jaspers discusses redemption in Greek tragedy (Aeschylus, Sophocles; absent in Euripides), the dissolution of tragedy in Christian redemptive grace (Dante, Calderón), the philosophical tragedies of Goethe (*Faust*) and Lessing (*Nathan the Wise*), the perversion of tragic knowledge in tragic worldviews (Unamuno). Jaspers cautions that the tragic is not absolute, that there are limits to the interpretation of the tragic, that original intuition of the tragic must be maintained lest its significance be lost. In its true historic intuition, the tragic is "questioning and thinking ... as well as the overcoming of the tragic, but not through doctrines and revelation, but with respect to order, right, love of fellow man; in trust, in not making final decisions, in the question that has no answer."[51]

49. *Ibid.*, 915.
50. *Ibid.*, 942–3.
51. *Ibid.*, 959.

Within philosophic reflection on the encompassing unity of truth, religion, as with the tragic, is identified in its absolute personal significance as the original intuition of the completion of truth in time. This is an additional basis for Jaspers's stand in regard to the demythologizing controversy, his idea of a "philosophic faith," and the confrontation of revealed religion with faith philosophically conceived.

It is deliberate reflection that is the mark of distinction of the philosophic concern over the completion of truth in time for man. The stress is on philosophizing – whichever form it takes – as the preeminent existentially effective completion of truth in time. Philosophizing is activity, neither doctrine nor a distinctive way of crafting a doctrine. Hence the key and culmination of Jaspers's exploration of the completion of truth is an essay on reason. Here the completion of truth in its unity is seen as impossible for man in time, but completion of truth in time is turned into the task of self-realization through exercising a will to total communication. And, conversely, communication is seen as the ultimate vehicle of the concretion of truth in time. Truth in time is, then, not something we can realize in its completeness, but its completion is the task of our temporal career. It is by virtue of communicative reason that, for Jaspers, philosophizing is the "ground and completion" of truth.[52] It is that because communicative reason is present wherever there is testimony to one's own finitude in the face of encompassing truth, testimony that consists in communicative openness to the other, no matter how crude and how far removed from the sophistication of the philosophic craftsman. In Jaspers, the problem of truth for man in time, although informed by the testimony of man's experience, is turned to the enactments of human life, the everyday life as well as the bigger arenas such as politics, religion, the life of the spirit.

In each of the three illuminations of truth on the way between origin and goal, truth in its unity is seen as exceeding man's capacity, and thereby it is left in its encompassing transcendence. The transcendence of *the* truth does not reduce either man or man's truths to insignificance. Through the transcendence of truth, the finitude that is man, in which he finds himself, which he confronts, shapes, and realizes, is the field of truth for man in time. Man is invested with the task of actualizing truth through the capacities given to him, most fundamentally

52. *Ibid.*, 960. Readers should not be led by this reference to "communicative reason" into thinking that Jaspers's thought has had an influence on Jürgen Habermas. Habermas's use of "reason" differs from Jaspers's; what Habermas means by "reason" is what Jaspers means by the "understanding." Also, what Habermas means by "communication" differs from Jaspers, as Jaspers's "communication" falls within the area of what Buber means by "dialogue," although there are significant differences between them. See "Dialogue and Communication – Buber and Jaspers," in my *Karl Jaspers: Philosophy as Faith* (Amherst, MA: University of Massachusetts Press, 1975), 77–97.

communicative reason, and thereby of gaining the actualization of his freedom. But the measure of the truth of the various pursuits and ways is the unity of truth in its encompassing transcendence, a cipher functioning as a measure: in the first, in the sense of the perfection of truth; in the second, as truth in its wholeness; in the third, as truth in its completion.

Jaspers's treatment in *Von der Wahrheit* of truth for man in time is a completion of what he began in *Philosophie*. The earlier work reopens the question of Being and truth in its unity as an existential exigency, and the later work subjects the question to radical exploration.

MAJOR WORKS

Fundamental philosophy

Philosophie. Vol. 1: Philosophische Weltorientierung; Vol. 2: Existenzerhellung; Vol. 3: Metaphysik. Berlin: Springer, 1932. Published in English as *Philosophy. Vol. 1: Philosophical World Orientation*; *Vol. 2: Existential Elucidation*; *Vol. 3: Metaphysics*, translated by E. B. Ashton. Chicago, IL: University of Chicago Press, 1969–71.

Von der Wahrheit: Philosophische Logik. Erster Band. Munich: Piper, 1947. Excerpts published in English in *Karl Jaspers: Basic Philosophical Writings*, edited and translated by Edith Ehrlich, Leonard H. Ehrlich, and George B. Pepper. Athens, OH: Ohio University Press 1986.

Philosophy of faith and religion

Der philosophische Glaube. Zurich: Artemis, 1948. Published in English as *The Perennial Scope of Philosophy*, translated by Ralph Manheim. London: Routledge, 1949.

Die Frage der Entmythologisierung (with Rudolf Bultmann). Munich: Piper, 1954. Published in English as *Myth and Christianity: An Inquiry into the Possibility of Religion Without Myth*, translated by Norbert Guterman. New York: Noonday Press, 1958.

Der Philosophische Glaube angesichts der Offenbarung. Munich: Piper, 1962. Published in English as *Philosophical Faith and Revelation*, translated by E. B. Ashton. Chicago, IL: University of Chicago Press, 1967.

History of philosophy

Nietzsche: Einführung in das Verständnis seines Philosophierens. Berlin: de Gruyter, 1936. Published in English as *Nietzsche: An Introduction to the Understanding of His Philosophical Activity*, translated by Charles F. Wallraff and Frederick J. Schmitz. Tucson, AZ: University Arizona Press, 1965.

Die grossen Philosophen, Vol. 1. Munich: Piper, 1957. Published in English as *The Great Philosophers,* vols 1 and 2, translated by Ralph Manheim. New York: Harcourt, Brace, and World, 1962, 1966.

Die grossen Philosophen. Nachlass, vols 1 and 2. Edited by Hans Saner. Munich: Piper 1981. Published in English as *The Great Philosophers*, vols 3 and 4, translated by Edith Ehrlich and Leonard H. Ehrlich. New York: Harcourt, Brace, and World, 1993, 1994.

Political philosophy

Die Schuldfrage. Zurich: Artemis, 1946. Published in English as *The Question of German Guilt*, translated by E. B. Ashton. New York: Dial Press, 1947.

Die Atombombe und die Zukunft des Menschen: Politisches Bewusstsein unserer Zeit. Munich: Piper, 1958. Published in English as *The Future of Mankind*, translated by E. B. Ashton. Chicago, IL: University of Chicago Press, 1961.

Philosophy of modernity and history

Die geistige Situation der Zeit. Berlin: de Gruyter, 1931. Published in English as *Man in the Modern Age*, translated by Eden Paul and Cedar Paul. New York: Holt, 1933.

Vom Ursprung und Ziel der Geschichte. Zurich: Artemis, 1949. Published in English as *The Origin and Goal of History*, translated by Michael Bullock. New Haven, CT: Yale University Press, 1953.

Psychiatry and psychology

Allgemeine Psychopathologie: Ein Leitfaden für Studierende, Ärzte und Psychologen. Berlin: Springer, 1913. 4th rev. and aug. ed. Berlin: Springer, 1946. Published in English as *General Psychopathology*, translated by J. Hoenig and Marian W. Hamilton. Chicago, IL: University of Chicago Press, 1963.

9

PHENOMENOLOGY AT HOME AND ABROAD

Diane Perpich

A full century has passed since Edmund Husserl (1859–1938) published his two-volume *Logical Investigations* (1900/1901), which set in motion the phenomenological movement as we know it. Bertrand Russell proposed to review this "monumental" work for the journal *Mind* in 1917, although the review was never completed and a friend later described the task as being "very much like trying to swallow a whale."[1] The predicament of the reader one hundred years later has only worsened, since grasping the movement now requires digesting not only one whale but a whole pod – not only Husserl, but also Martin Heidegger (1889–1976), Hans-Georg Gadamer (1900–2002), Jean-Paul Sartre (1905–80), Emmanuel Levinas (1906–95), Maurice Merleau-Ponty (1908–61), Paul Ricoeur (1913–2005), and Jacques Derrida (1930–2004), to name but a few of the most important and prolific – and to follow the philosophical currents set in motion by these thinkers whose intellectual heritage can be traced back to Husserl and phenomenology.

Some fifty years after the publication of the *Logical Investigations*, Merleau-Ponty lamented that the question "What is phenomenology?" had yet to be answered in a definitive way.[2] Ricoeur, also writing mid-century, suggested that we view Husserl as the knot tying the movement together; but he was also quick to note that what we count as phenomenology must include not only the various formulations of it in Husserl's own writings, but also the "heresies" of those who

1. The remark comes from Constance Malleson, as reported by Ronald W. Clark in *The Life of Bertrand Russell* (London: Jonathan Cape, 1957), 348. Russell's review never appeared owing to a delay in the translation of the Sixth Investigation.
2. Maurice Merleau-Ponty, *Phenomenology of Perception*, Colin Smith (trans.) (New York: Routledge & Kegan Paul, 1962), vii.

came after him.[3] Herbert Spiegelberg, whose treatise on *The Phenomenological Movement* (1960) remains unsurpassed as an introduction to the thinkers and themes of this tradition, writes that it would be a "misconception" to think "that there is such a thing as a system or school called 'phenomenology' with a solid body of teachings."[4] This is so not because phenomenology has been unable to achieve an adequate level of clarity about its own task, but because it was substantially reinvented and reinvigorated by each successive generation of phenomenologists and, as a result, became one of the richest and most diverse movements in twentieth-century Western thought. This essay provides a historical introduction to the phenomenological movement and to the main developments within it. After considering the history of phenomenology in Germany, the essay traces its reception in France, and ends with a consideration of its status as an international movement and the question of its future.

I. HUSSERL AND THE PHENOMENOLOGICAL CIRCLES AT MUNICH AND GÖTTINGEN

Husserl's earliest writings cannot properly be considered phenomenological, although they were to lead him to problems that put him on the path to phenomenology as he ultimately came to understand it. His first book, *The Philosophy of Arithmetic* (1891), attempted to derive the fundamental concepts of mathematics by means of a descriptive psychology of acts of mathematical thinking. The attempt was roundly criticized by Gottlieb Frege, although the latter's target was not Husserl alone but the "widespread philosophical sickness" of employing psychology to answer questions in logic.[5] The planned second

---

3. Quoted in Herbert Spiegelberg, *The Phenomenological Movement: A Historical Introduction*, 3rd rev. and enlarged ed. (The Hague: Martinus Nijhoff, 1982), 586. Ricoeur was the French translator of Husserl's *Ideas I* and also published a line-by-line analysis of that work. Born in Provence, he was strongly influenced by the philosophy of Gabriel Marcel. Ricoeur had a synthetic turn of mind and a sure grasp of the grand sweep of contemporary philosophy, both European and Anglo-American. He published important works in the philosophy of language and hermeneutics, on metaphor and narrative, on Freud and psychoanalysis, on phenomenology, and in his last works on subjectivity and ethics. [*] His work is discussed in the essay by Wayne J. Froman in *The History of Continental Philosophy: Volume 6*.
4. Spiegelberg, *The Phenomenological Movement*, xxvii.
5. For an overview of Frege's relation to Husserl, see Clair Ortiz Hill, "Frege's Attack on Husserl and Cantor," *The Monist* 77(3) (July 1994). See also Michael Dummett, *Frege: Philosophy of Mathematics* (Cambridge, MA: Harvard University Press, 1991); Dagfinn Føllesdal, "Husserl and Frege: A Contribution to Elucidating the Origins of Phenomenological Philosophy," in *Mind, Meaning and Mathematics: Essays on the Philosophical Views of Husserl and Frege*, Leila Haaparanta (ed.) (Dordrecht: Kluwer, 1994); Clair Ortiz Hill, *Word and Object in Husserl, Frege, and Russell* (Athens, OH: Ohio University Press, 1991); J. N. Mohanty, *Husserl and*

volume of Husserl's work on arithmetic never appeared and Husserl himself remarked that although the descriptive analyses he had attempted brought a certain clarity to the origin of subjective acts of mathematical thinking, he could discover no way to pass from the subjective connections between ideas to the distinctive objectivity and theoretical unity of mathematics as such. In effect, there was no way to "reconcile the objectivity of mathematics, and of all science in general, with a psychological foundation for logic."[6] The first volume of the *Logical Investigations* was subsequently devoted to a thoroughgoing critique of psychologism in logic while the second volume, appearing a year later, contained six studies devoted respectively to expression and meaning, the problem of universals, the theory of parts and wholes, acts of meaning and the idea of a pure grammar, intentional experience, and the elements of a phenomenological account of knowledge.[7]

The elucidation of the intentional structure of consciousness remains a primary contribution of the *Logical Investigations* and of phenomenology generally. Franz Brentano (1838–1917), from whom Husserl takes the term "intentionality," argued that all conscious experience is intentional, by which he meant that it is directed *toward something*: there is no perceiving without something perceived, no imagining without something imagined, no judging without something judged.[8] Husserl uses intentionality in largely the same way to indicate that all consciousness is consciousness *of* something, although he also recognizes that some mental phenomena, such as sensations or sensation complexes, are not themselves intentional. Intentionality, as it is understood by Husserl and Brentano alike, is not to be understood in terms of the relation of a mental act to an extra-mental object or really existing thing. Imagining and hallucinating, for example, are both intentional acts but neither is directed toward objects that *exist* or are real in our usual sense of the term. In later works, Husserl will seek to clarify the status of the intentional object and to articulate more fully its relation to the intentional act, but what initially interested him was not the act–object relationship but the connections between different intentional acts or between different aspects of a single complex act. For example,

Frege (Bloomington, IN: Indiana University Press, 1982); David Woodruff Smith and Ronald McIntyre, *Husserl on Intentionality* (Dordrecht: Reidel, 1982).

6. Edmund Husserl, *Logical Investigations*, J. N. Findlay (trans.) (New York: Humanities Press, 1970), vol. 1, 42.

*7. For a detailed discussion of Husserl's *Logical Investigations*, see the essay by Thomas Nenon in this volume.

8. Brentano writes, "Every psychical phenomenon is characterized by what the Scholastics of the Middle Ages called the intentional, (or sometimes the mental) inexistence of an object, and what we should like to call … the directedness (*Richtung*) toward an object (which in this context is not to be understood as something real)" (*Psychologie vom empirischen Standpunkt I*, Buch II, Kapitel I §5, 125–6, quoted in Spiegelberg, *The Phenomenological Movement*, 36).

the complex intentional act judging that "the cup is white" points back to, or in Husserl's terms, is "founded," in a prior act in which the whiteness of the cup is given in a "fulfilling" perception. This act of perception, in turn, has both complete and incomplete aspects: the back of the cup is only emptily intended in my perception of the front of the cup, although this empty intention can only be filled in by certain kinds of contents and not others.[9] The idea that every act of consciousness – no matter how seemingly simple – is determined as a set of relations between "founded" and unfounded acts, and between "empty" or "merely signative" acts and "fulfilling" or "intuitive" acts becomes evident from a careful reflection on the nature of these acts considered ideally. A full, descriptive account of the structural relations governing the manner in which objects or states of affairs are given in consciousness was the central aim of Husserl's early phenomenology.

Over the next decade, phenomenological circles inspired by Husserl's work sprang up in both Munich and Göttingen. The *Akademischer Verein für Psychologie*, attended by the more advanced students of Theodore Lipps (1851–1914), was already in existence in Munich when the *Logical Investigations* appeared with Husserl's extended attack on Lipps's psychologism. Lipps defended his position before the group with the unexpected result that many of them became confirmed opponents of his position and converted, as it were, to phenomenology. This was the case for both Alexander Pfänder (1871–1941) and Johannes Daubert (1877–1947), who were the leading members of the group at the time. Several members of the Munich Circle went on to work as phenomenologists for the duration of their academic careers. Pfänder became one of Husserl's collaborators on the *Jahrbuch für Philosophie und phänomenologische Forschung*, as did Moritz Geiger (1880–1937), Max Scheler (1874–1928), and Adolf Reinach (1883–1917). The *Jahrbuch* would publish some of the most significant contributions to phenomenology, including the first volume of Husserl's *Ideas Pertaining to a Pure Phenomenology and Phenomenological Philosophy* (1913) and the first two divisions of Heidegger's *Being and Time* (1927). Pfänder and Geiger made modest but noteworthy contributions to phenomenology during academic careers spent chiefly in Munich (although Geiger fled Germany during the Second World War and spent his last years as a professor at Vassar College in New York). Pfänder's contribution was primarily in the domain of psychology, his work consisting mainly of descriptive analyses of various acts of willing, and of the structure of other-directed positive and

9. An exceptionally clear and succinct discussion of Husserl's thought, including its early phases, is to be found in Steven Galt Crowell, "Husserlian Phenomenology," in *A Companion to Phenomenology and Existentialism*, Hubert L. Dreyfus and Mark A. Wrathall (eds) (Malden, MA: Blackwell, 2006).

negative sentiments (e.g. benevolence, friendliness, ill-will, or hostility).[10] Geiger also made contributions to a phenomenologically based descriptive psychology, focusing like Pfänder on questions of the will, but he was better known for his contributions to a phenomenology of aesthetic acts and attitudes.[11]

Max Scheler was a major figure in phenomenology and in the intellectual life of Germany during his lifetime. Scheler completed both his doctoral dissertation and his habilitation thesis (by the age of twenty-five) under the direction of Jena philosopher Rudolf Eucken (1846–1926).[12] Eucken believed that the philosopher had a special role to play in measuring the practices and attitudes of contemporary society against the unchanging and transcendent moral values that could be discerned by philosophy. Scheler inherited Eucken's commitment to the idea of unchanging values as well as the latter's concern for contemporary life and society; what he sought from phenomenology was a method by which to discern transcendent values and to preserve their status independent of the workings of logic and cognition. By Scheler's own account, he met Husserl at a party in Halle in 1901 and found his ideas about nonsensuous or categorial intuition immediately useful to his own projects. Brilliant and charismatic, Scheler rose to prominence in both the Munich and Göttingen circles, writing major works on the notion of resentment and *The Nature of Sympathy* (1923). His most enduring phenomenological work was his *Formalism in Ethics and Non-Formal Ethics of Value* (1913), although he was better known to the general reading public for

10. Pfänder's most significant contributions to phenomenology were still in fragmentary form at the time of his death, but have since been edited and published by his students. Of the works published during his lifetime, *Die Seele des Menschen* (1933) was undoubtedly the most mature expression of his views. A translation of his seminal essay, "Motive and Motivation," and of some of his early work on the will and on logic may be found in *Phenomenology of Willing and Motivation and Other Phaenomenologica*, Herbert Spiegelberg (ed.) (Evanston, IL: Northwestern University Press, 1967).
11. Klaus Berger reports that Geiger's lectures in aesthetics, given in Munich between 1909 and 1922, "were among the more important events at the University" (in Moritz Geiger, *The Significance of Art: A Phenomenological Approach to Aesthetics*, Klaus Berger [ed. and trans.] [Washington, DC: University Press of America, 1986], xvii). Geiger's *Zugange zur Ästhetik* was published in 1928, at which time he also announced plans for a major work in aesthetics. At the time of his death in 1937, an initial section of this book, looking at the foundations of value aesthetics, was fairly well developed although not in final form. A second section on the differentiated structures of various art forms was left in a very fragmentary state. Berger collected the more developed parts of this manuscript together with selections from Geiger's earlier work on aesthetics and published the whole under the title *The Significance of Art*.
12. Eucken lectured widely in Europe and America after the First World War, speaking of the unity of humankind and the need to overcome the self-destructive impulses that had fueled the war. He was awarded the Nobel Prize in Literature in 1908. An overview of Eucken's influence on Scheler's philosophy can be found in H. Bershady, "Introduction," in M. Scheler, *On Feeling, Knowing, and Valuing: Selected Writings*, H. Bershady (ed.) (Chicago, IL: University of Chicago Press, 1992).

an essay that appeared on the eve of the First World War. There in "The Genius of War" he advocated going to war, arguing that a refined German spirit (*Geist*) could cure Europe of what ailed it, specifically the draining forces of autocracy in Russia, the dry and sterile rationalism of France, and the crude utilitarianism of England.[13]

Adolf Reinach, the fourth member of the *Jahrbuch* editorial team, may well be the least known of Husserl's early collaborators but he played a significant role in propagating a realist strain of phenomenology and did as much as anyone in the early years to promote the phenomenological movement. As a *Privatdozent* in Göttingen during Husserl's tenure there, Reinach[14] had a profound influence on members of the Göttingen Circle, including Alexandre Koyré, Roman Ingarden, and Edith Stein.[15] Koyré and Stein, for example, both

*13. Scheler's work is discussed in more detail elsewhere in this volume.

14. Reinach was part of the "Munich invasion" of 1905, when a number of Lipps's students began coming regularly to Göttingen to attend Husserl's seminars. Daubert was among the first to come, and with him came Reinach. They would be followed by Geiger and Scheler, among others.

15. Koyré (1892–1964) studied with Husserl and the mathematician David Hilbert at the University of Göttingen (1908–11) before coming to Paris, where he followed Bergson's lectures at the Collège de France and studied with Léon Brunschvicg and Étienne Gilson at the Sorbonne (1912–14). After the First World War, he emigrated to Paris, where he taught at the École Pratique des Hautes Études (1922–32, 1950s), Fuad University (later Cairo University) (1932–34, 1936–38, 1940–41), Johns Hopkins University (1950s), and the Princeton Institute for Advanced Study (starting in 1956). Koyré was the first to introduce Bergson's work in Germany in 1911 at the Göttingen Circle and was the first to bring Husserl's phenomenology to France. His emphasis on phenomenology in the interpretation of Hegel was influential for the Hegelianism of Alexandre Kojève and Jean-Paul Sartre. While best known for his work on Descartes and Hegel, Koyré also made important contributions to the history of science. His most important text, *Études galiléennes*, was published in three volumes in 1939 (*Vol. 1: A l'aube de la science classique; Vol. 2: La Loi de la chute des corps: Descartes et Galilée; Vol. 3: Galilée et la loi d'inertie*) and was dedicated to Émile Meyerson (1859–1933), whose own work on epistemology played a significant role in Koyré's thinking. Some aspects of Koyré's role in bringing phenomenology to France are noted below. [*] His contribution to French Hegelianism is also discussed in an essay by John Russon in *The History of Continental Philosophy: Volume 4*.

Ingarden (1893–1970) studied with Husserl from 1912 to 1918 in Göttingen and remained in touch with Husserl by letter until the latter died in 1938. Ingarden is best known for his phenomenological investigations of works of art, including literature, music, and the plastic arts. He pursued painstaking descriptions of the various "strata" that make up the work of art, arguing that even the lowest, most material strata were imbued with cultural constructions. In a move that resonates well with reader-response theory in literature as well as with other contemporary theories of art, Ingarden argued that the work of art was not complete in and of itself and that its meaning emerged as it was concretized by the reader, viewer, or listener. Ingarden was also interested in essential methodological questions concerning the foundation of phenomenology and did not fully embrace Husserl's transcendental turn. His major works in phenomenological aesthetics include *Das literarische Kunstwerk* (1965; *The*

report that they learned phenomenology from Reinach rather than Husserl. It is no doubt under Reinach's influence that the group came to see phenomenology not only as a study of the essential structures of consciousness, but even more so as a universal philosophy of essences. And it was during this period that some in Germany began to equate phenomenological intuition with an untenable rebirth of Platonism.[16] Husserl himself was inclined to dismiss some of the discussions of his students during this time as a "picture book phenomenology" overly concerned with the essences of everyday objects, perceptions, and states of affairs.[17] But even as Husserl disavowed his own earlier characterization of phenomenology as a descriptive psychology, Reinach and many in the Göttingen Circle insisted on the legitimacy and fruitfulness of this understanding and of the inquiry into essences arrived at through careful and precise investigation or intuiting with respect to ideal cases.[18] The Göttingen phase of phenomenology ended when Husserl moved to Freiburg in 1916, but there can be no doubt that Reinach's death in action in 1917 also spelled the end of an independent realist phenomenology.[19]

Literary Work of Art) and *Vom Erkennen des literarischen Kunstwerks* (1968; *The Cognition of the Literary Work of Art*). [*] For a discussion of Ingarden's work, see the essay by Galen A. Johnson in *The History of Continental Philosophy: Volume 4.*

Stein (1891–1942) was Husserl's first Freiburg PhD student. She is as well known for the details of her biography as for her philosophical works. Born to Jewish parents, Stein converted to Catholicism and joined the Carmelite order; she was deported to and died in Auschwitz during the Second World War. Stein's major philosophical contributions lie in Thomistic philosophy, especially in her posthumously published *Finite and Eternal Being* (1950), but her debt to phenomenology is readily apparent. See *Endliches und ewiges Sein: Versuch eines Aufsteigs zum Sinn des Seins* (1950; *Finite and Eternal Being: An Attempt at an Ascent to the Meaning of Being*).

16. Reinach was deeply influenced by Plato even before beginning his university studies, and in 1919 gave a lecture course on "Plato's Philosophy and Its Relation to Contemporary Problems in the Theory of Cognition" (Karl Schumann and Barry Smith, "Adolf Reinach: An Intellectual Biography," in *Speech Act and Sachverhalt: Reinach and the Foundations of Realist Phenomenology*, Kevin Mulligan [ed.] [The Hague: Martinus Nijhoff, 1987], 20).
17. Spiegelberg, *The Phenomenological Movement*, 168.
18. Schumann and Smith, "Adolf Reinach," 20. Reinach was the managing editor of the first volume of the *Jahrbuch*, which appeared in 1913, containing the first part of Husserl's *Ideas* as well as contributions by the other coeditors. It is around this time that he began to take his distance from Husserl's thought and its transcendental idealism.
19. Despite their growing intellectual differences, Husserl's memorial to Reinach, published in *Kantstudien* in 1919, spoke of the *Privatdozent* in the most glowing terms praising the "independence and power of his mind" as well as the "seriousness of his scientific striving" (Edmund Husserl, "Adolf Reinach," *Philosophy and Phenomenological Research* 35[4] [(June 1975], 571; originally published in *Kantstudien* 23 [1919], 147).

II. HUSSERL'S TRANSCENDENTAL PHENOMENOLOGY

Husserl's journals and personal correspondence from the Göttingen years paint a picture of the philosopher struggling to win clarity on the fundamental issue of the relation of the intentional act to its object.[20] In his earlier work, Husserl had already branded the traditional epistemological problem of how subjective thoughts reach a world of external objects a pseudo-problem bred by lack of clarity. However, he remained puzzled by the "enigma" of cognition and particularly by the problem of how the really immanent components of the stream of conscious experience (*this* perception of whiteness) are related to the nonimmanent or transcendent meanings that make our experience an experience *of something* (a white cup). The solution to this problem was broached first in a short text on *The Idea of Phenomenology* (1907) and then in detail in *Ideas I* (1913). It involved the insight that the relation between transcendence and immanence was itself something that could be immanently given and thus made the object of a pure, phenomenological description. In setting out to develop a pure, presuppositionless critique of cognition, Husserl had to describe the manner in which cognition and its object are bound together, but this description could not use anything that was not self-evidently or intuitively given to consciousness.[21] The famous transcendental–phenomenological reductions that make up the phenomenological method were developed precisely to secure the givenness of the phenomenological datum, in this case the relation of the intentional act and its object.

Like much else in Husserlian phenomenology, the reductions are reworked numerous times both in the published texts and in unpublished writings – of which there are forty thousand shorthand pages in Husserl's *Nachlass*. A first kind of reduction to essences – an *eidetic* reduction – was already in use in the *Logical Investigations*, where Husserl recognized that the experience of a

20. Crowell, "Husserlian Phenomenology," 16–17.

21. Edmund Husserl, *The Idea of Phenomenology*, William P. Alston and George Nakhnikian (trans.) (Dordrecht: Kluwer, 1964), 37. Eduard Marbach explains that for the *Logical Investigations*, "Only intentional *acts*, given in phenomenological reflection, count as presuppositionless epistemological data. The acts of cognition relevant for the basic epistemological question about truth are intentionally fulfilled acts in which the intended objects comes to intuitional self-givenness. Strictly speaking, nothing can be said about the object of cognition except that it is intended in an act that must be more closely determined. When, from the end of 1906 on, Husserl proceeded to designate as a phenomenologically evident datum not only the act but also the intentional correlate of this act, that is, the intentional object just as it is intended in this act, there followed very decisive consequences for carrying through the phenomenological theory of cognition" (Rudolf Bernet, Iso Kern, and Eduard Marbach, *An Introduction to Husserlian Phenomenology* [Evanston, IL: Northwestern University Press, 1993], 55–6).

particular object will always be limited by contingent features of the subject's physical situation *vis-à-vis* the object and by her personal history and any associations she may connect with the object. Phenomenological reflection, in performing an eidetic reduction, abstracts from these contingent features (e.g. the dim light in which the cup is right now seen or the fact that it bears the logo of this particular café) and attends to universal and essential features of the cognizing act. Nor is this reduction limited to phenomenology; it is a standard feature of all kinds of conceptual and mathematical analyses.

The reductions that belong more particularly to the transcendental period of Husserl's thought are the *epochē* and the full set of reductions that Husserl simply calls transcendental–phenomenological. The *epochē* concerns the possibility of suspending or bracketing presuppositions about the object that belong to our everyday or "natural" attitude. In the natural attitude, the subject takes for granted that the chair in which she sits or the paper on which she writes are really there in front of her with just these physical and perceptual properties. Likewise, the subject in the natural attitude takes for granted the results of various sciences and subscribes to various unquestioned beliefs handed down to her by her society or culture. The effect of the *epochē* and its accompanying transcendental–phenomenological reductions is not so much that the subject comes to *doubt* these beliefs, as that she *suspends* them or makes no use of them. The upshot for the critique of cognition is that one no longer worries whether or not the cup being perceived right now "really exists"; the question of existence is put into brackets or put out of play. Similarly bracketed is any account of perception that depends on an acquaintance with theories that come from biology, neuroscience, psychology, or any other science. The *epochē* is not like radical Cartesian doubt in which I lose the world temporarily in order later to regain my certainty about it. As long as I am engaged in phenomenological reflection, the *epochē* remains in play. Its function is only to make possible a pure presuppositionless description of the objective correlate of the intentional act as such. The "exclusion of Nature" is "the methodic means for initially making possible the turning of regard to transcendentally pure consciousness."[22]

The transcendental–phenomenological reductions go on to expose the remaining kinds of transcendencies (that is, those nonimmanent elements of conscious experience) that must be put out of play or bracketed in a phenomenological description. In *Ideas I*, Husserl writes that "it is immediately understandable" that the suspension of the natural world brings along with it a bracketing of "all sorts of cultural formations, all works of the technical and fine arts, of sciences" and "aesthetic and practical values of every form" including

22. Husserl, *Ideas Pertaining to a Pure Phenomenology and to a Phenomenological Philosophy: First Book*, F. Kersten (trans.) (The Hague: Martinus Nijhoff, 1982); *Ideas I*, 131.

our ideas of the reality of political states, moral customs, law, and religion.[23] Again, the idea is not to *doubt* the reality of such things but to make no use of beliefs imported from these realms in developing pure descriptions of the operations or essential structures of different types of cognition and conscious experience. While the suspension of the natural and social sciences and all social and cultural values was, for Husserl, an obvious extension of the original reduction, he was less certain about whether (and to what extent) the ego could be reduced, and about whether a suspension of pure logic and of phenomenology itself was possible. Husserl would return to these topics in later writings and his struggles to win a truly presuppositionless starting-point for a critique of cognition would prove to be a lifetime concern. For Husserl, phenomenology was to be a rigorous philosophical science clarifying the epistemological norms governing every region of human consciousness, but the success of this project was directly dependent on whether the phenomenological datum – consciousness and its essential structures – could be given in a pure presuppositionless form.

When Husserl's thought took its transcendental turn, it cost him many of his former students and thus he arrived in Freiburg in 1916 having to make a fresh start. It was there that he met Heidegger, a junior professor who would become his assistant and whose impact on phenomenology would be at least as important as Husserl's own, even as it spelled the end of Husserl's dream of phenomenology as a collectively pursued pure presuppositionless science of conscious experience.

III. HEIDEGGER AND FUNDAMENTAL ONTOLOGY

To what extent should Heidegger be considered a phenomenologist? Today few doubt his central place in the history of the movement, but it is noteworthy that scholars writing in the 1960s could earnestly debate this question. Early treatments of phenomenology in English, if they mention Heidegger at all, tend to emphasize the differences between Husserl and Heidegger and, depending on the camp, extol the rigor and scientific spirit of the former or the brilliance and originality of the latter. Husserlians, in particular, wanted to distance phenomenology from the seemingly impenetrable language of Heidegger's philosophy and from its existential overtones. By contrast, Heideggerians were anxious to preserve the independence of the question of the meaning of Being and touted Heidegger's work, as he did himself, not as phenomenology but as fundamental ontology. French accounts of phenomenology, then as now, were more inclined to see Husserl's and Heidegger's work as roughly continuous. Levinas, for

23. Emmanuel Levinas and Richard Kearney, "Dialogue with Emmanuel Levinas," in *Face to Face with Levinas*, Richard A. Cohen (ed.) (Albany, NY: SUNY Press, 1986), 15.

example, who studied with both Husserl and Heidegger in Freiburg, thought of Heidegger's work as "the fruition and flowering of Husserlian phenomenology,"[24] although he readily acknowledges that Heidegger in no way proposed a transcendental phenomenology along the lines of *Ideas I*.[25]

Although Heidegger seems to have had no early personal contact with Husserl or members of the phenomenological circles,[26] his interest in phenomenology dates to his student days at Freiburg University. In a famous essay – "My Way to Phenomenology" (1963) – Heidegger reports having had Husserl's *Logical Investigations* on his desk for two years in the student dormitories and having read it "again and again … without gaining sufficient insight into what fascinated me."[27] Of course, the other book that Heidegger speaks of as being "the chief help and guide of my first awkward attempt to penetrate into philosophy" was Brentano's dissertation "On the Manifold Meaning of Being since Aristotle" (1862).[28] The young Heidegger received this book from his high-school teacher and the story of this gift is often told as a reminder that, for Heidegger, prior to phenomenology there was the question of the meaning of Being. Theodore Kisiel convincingly proposes that Heidegger's two principal influences – Aristotle's account of the ways in which Being is said (the problem of the "categories") and phenomenology's account of the intentional structure of conscious experience – were knit together in an important way by the mediating influence of Emil Lask (1875–1915). Like Heidegger, Lask was a student of the neo-Kantian Heinrich Rickert (1863–1936) and was also deeply influenced by Husserl's thought. Lask was interested in what Fichte had described as *facticity*: our brute encounter with the world. But whereas for Fichte the factic is the "irrational par excellence … the 'matter' *given* to thought," Lask maintained (*pace* Husserl) that the world is given not only in sensuous intuition but in categorial intuition as well: for Lask, there is "a precognitive moment in which the initial categories or forms first present themselves as simply given in experience before

24. Emmanuel Levinas, *Ethics and Infinity: Conversations with Philippe Nemo*, Richard A. Cohen (trans.) (Pittsburgh, PA: Duquesne University Press, 1985), 38.
25. In a lecture course from 1925, Heidegger is especially dismissive of the Munich tradition of phenomenology, saying that although the *Logical Investigations* influenced Lipps's Munich students, the book "was regarded simply as an improved descriptive psychology." Heidegger makes it clear that this is a misinterpretation, although one that Husserl himself briefly labored under. See Martin Heidegger, *History of the Concept of Time: Prolegomena*, Theodore Kisiel (trans.) (Bloomington, IN: Indiana University Press, 1985), 25.
26. Martin Heidegger, "My Way to Phenomenology," in *On Time and Being*, Joan Stambaugh (trans.) (New York: Harper & Row, 1972), 74.
27. *Ibid.*
28. Theodore Kisiel, *The Genesis of Heidegger's "Being and Time"* (Berkeley, CA: University of California Press, 1993), 27.

they are known."[29] We "live" in this pretheoretical moment before we explicitly "know" anything of it and it is life in this sense that Lask claims is especially worthy of philosophical investigation: what is philosophically significant is "not brute factic life but rather the sphere of immediate experience replete with value, of life already made worthwhile."[30] This claim resonates with the fundamental task undertaken in Heidegger's best-known work, *Being and Time* (1927), where the aim is an analysis of the complex and irreducible relationships that structure our everyday understanding of the world and remain concealed within the apparent immediacy of that understanding.

After writing his thesis on Duns Scotus (which Rickert suggested was more in thrall to Lask's work than might be desirable), Heidegger joined the Freiburg faculty as a *Privatdozent* or junior professor. Husserl arrived the following year to fill Rickert's Chair. Heidegger reports that it was only when he had a chance to work directly with Husserl that he came fully to understand the method of phenomenological "seeing."[31] He also remarks, however, that the better he came to understand phenomenology, the more he saw it as "fruitful for the interpretation of Aristotle's writing" and the less able he was to separate his own thinking from that of Aristotle and the Greeks.[32] As for their personal relationship, Heidegger served as Husserl's assistant in Freiburg until 1923,[33] regularly teaching a "Phenomenological Practicum" for beginners (usually in conjunction with a reading of either Aristotle or Descartes) while Husserl offered a corresponding seminar for more advanced students. In 1923, Heidegger left Freiburg for a position at Marburg and there began the most fruitful period of his career. As before, he taught courses on phenomenology and continued the tradition of

29. Emil Lask, *Gesammelte Schriften* (Tübingen: Mohr, 1923), vol. 2, 196; quoted in Kisiel, *The Genesis of Heidegger's "Being and Time,"* 28.
30. Heidegger, "My Way to Phenomenology," 79.
31. *Ibid.*, 78. There were other decisive influences on Heidegger's work as well as phenomenology and the Greeks. Early encounters with the writings of Nietzsche, Kierkegaard, Schelling, Hegel, Rilke, Trakl, and Dilthey were formative for the questions developed in *Being and Time* and for Heidegger's later writings.
32. During the period from 1917 to 1919, Heidegger served for a time in the German military, completing basic training in May 1918 and then serving in the meteorological services until the end of the First World War. There has been some dispute about just when and where he served. Kisiel collects the relevant evidence in *The Genesis of Heidegger's "Being and Time,"* 553 n.6. The period from 1917 to 1919 is also noteworthy as the time when Heidegger appears to have set aside his religious convictions. In a letter to Englebert Krebs, he writes of a "transformation of my fundamental standpoint" during this time which "made the *system* of Catholicism problematic and unacceptable to me" (quoted in *ibid.*, 553 n.6).
33. *Being and Time* was rushed into publication when Heidegger was recommended by the faculty at Marburg for a full professorship. Husserl was instrumental in having the completed parts published in the *Jahrbuch* and also in a separate edition by Niemeyer. For Heidegger's account of the publication history, see Heidegger, "My Way to Phenomenology," 74–82.

offering a phenomenology "practicum" for beginning and advanced students. It was during the Marburg years that Husserl and Heidegger collaborated (with limited success) on an article on "Phenomenology" for the *Encyclopædia Britannica*. It was also during this period that Heidegger wrote the bulk of *Being and Time*. In 1928, when Husserl retired, he named Heidegger as the only adequate successor to his Chair. Husserl seems to have recommended his younger colleague for this post without having read *Being and Time*, although he was instrumental in the publication of this work.[34] Had he read Heidegger's *magnum opus*, he might have been reluctant to see in his former assistant the successor to his own phenomenological project. Indeed, it is clear from later correspondence that he came to feel that Heidegger's work neglected the fundamental importance of the phenomenological reductions, with the result that his thought ended up effecting a return to the anthropologism and psychologism Husserl had been at pains to eradicate from philosophy. While there was no formal break between the two men, it is striking that after his first semester back in Freiburg, Heidegger never again offered a course with phenomenology in the title (with the single exception of a seminar on Hegel's thought).

Heidegger's most intense engagement with phenomenology thus took place between 1916 and 1929, during which time it is fair to say that he both promoted the philosophical breakthrough achieved by Husserl and significantly reformulated the basic problems of phenomenology. Most importantly, while Heidegger applauded Husserl's phenomenology for having shown that intentionality is the fundamental structure of all lived, conscious experience, he repeatedly stressed the inadequacy of the phenomenological characterization of intentionality to date. The guiding theme of the 1927 lecture course published as *The Basic Problems of Phenomenology* is the need to "*conceive intentionality itself more radically*."[35] Intentionality is there said to be "founded" in Dasein's "transcendence" or "transposition" over to things.[36] Transcendence, in turn, is identified with Dasein's understanding itself "*from a world*"[37] – the elucidation of the "world-concept" being for Heidegger one of the central problems of philosophy,[38] inattention to which has involved the discipline in "remarkable insoluble aporia."[39] In *Being and*

34. Martin Heidegger, *The Basic Problems of Phenomenology*, Albert Hofstadter (trans.) (Bloomington, IN: Indiana University Press, 1982), 162.
35. *Ibid.*
36. *Ibid.*, 300.
37. *Ibid.*, 164.
38. *Ibid.*, 162.
39. Heidegger, *Being and Time*, §4. *Dasein* was translated into French as *réalité-humaine* ("human reality") and left in the original German in English translations of Heidegger's work. While neither choice is fully adequate, both are legitimate solutions to the translation problem posed by the unique manner in which Heidegger uses this term.

Time, Heidegger explicitly abandons the term "intentionality" and such corresponding concepts as "consciousness," "ego," and "subjectivity." All, he argues, are inextricably mired in the problematic ontology of modern philosophy where the subject is envisioned as an inner sphere set over against the extant objects of the world. In opposition to this picture, which fails to capture the phenomena of lived conscious existence, Heidegger develops a rich description of what he terms Dasein's being-in-the-world (*In-der-Welt-sein*). In German, *Dasein* is an ordinary word meaning "existence"; in Heidegger's work, by contrast, it functions as a technical term indicating human existing or that being which each of us is and that has an understanding of being as a definite characteristic of its being.[40] This way of designating human subjectivity may seem willfully obscure unless we remember that Heidegger's aim is to give a description of our factical existing, that is, of the manner in which the world is manifestly *there* for us and of the way in which we ourselves are *in* the world understandingly. For Heidegger, central to an adequate understanding of being-in-the-world is the recognition that it is lived and experienced in a unitary fashion. Although being-in-the-world is analyzed in *Being and Time* in terms of its constituent parts (Dasein, the *worldhood* of the world, and the mode of Dasein's *being-in*), the aim of the work is to elucidate the unitary character of this overarching structure.

Heidegger's analyses of things as present-to-hand and ready-to-hand, his elaboration of moods, of our average or everyday way of understanding and its dependence on undifferentiated public understandings, of anxiety, death, temporality, and other elements of being-in-the-world had an enormous influence on twentieth-century thought in fields as diverse as literature, sociology, psychology, art, history, and education. Heidegger also produced numerous students, including, most notably, Hannah Arendt and Gadamer, the latter of whom developed an important philosophical hermeneutics on the basis of Heidegger's work.[41] But the most immediate and possibly the most significant impact of Heidegger's thought came in the form of French existentialism, to which we turn next.

IV. PHENOMENOLOGY IN FRANCE

Phenomenology crossed into France at the Alsatian border. Jean Hering (1889–1966), a professor at the University of Strasbourg, published his *Phénoménologie et philosophie religieuse* (Phenomenology and religious philosophy) in 1925.

40. Gadamer (1900–2002) was born in Marburg and grew up in Breslau (now Poland). He studied with Heidegger in Marburg from 1923 until 1928. [*] For further information, see the essay by Daniel L. Tate in *The History of Continental Philosophy: Volume 4*, and the essay by Wayne J. Froman in *The History of Continental Philosophy: Volume 6*.

41. Levinas, *Ethics and Infinity*, 30.

He also encouraged a young Lithuanian student, Emmanuel Levinas, to travel from Strasbourg to Freiburg to study directly with Husserl. Levinas was initially greatly attracted to Henri Bergson's account of intuition and when a friend gave him a copy of the *Logical Investigations*, containing Husserl's account of nonsensuous intuition, he read it with great perseverance and interest but also, as he says himself, "without guide."[42] Levinas reports that the truth of Husserl's perspective dawned on him slowly but surely and he determined to study directly with the philosopher himself. When Levinas arrived in Freiburg, Husserl had just retired but was still teaching, and Levinas attended his lectures on phenomenological psychology and the constitution of intersubjectivity.[43] Later, Levinas would translate into French (and not altogether to Husserl's satisfaction) the crucial fifth chapter of the *Cartesian Meditations*:[44] – the chapter in which Husserl takes up the problem of how the other person can be constituted as other for consciousness. The real discovery of Levinas's study year abroad, however, was Heidegger, then even less well known in France than Husserl. In contrast to the "abstract" and "ponderous" approach of Husserl's phenomenology, Heidegger, in Levinas's view, "brought the phenomenological method to life and gave it a contemporary style and relevance."[45] Levinas subsequently wrote his dissertation in 1930 on *La Théorie de l'intuition dans la phénoménologie de Husserl* (*The Theory of Intuition in Husserl's Phenomenology*), and it would be the first work in French wholly devoted to Husserl's thought. Levinas's presentation in this early book is admittedly influenced by Heidegger and criticizes Husserl for a certain "intellectualism," by which Levinas means that Husserl uncritically maintains that a theoretical or "thetic" positing lies at the basis of all intentional acts. In Heidegger, by contrast, there is an emphasis on the practical and affective dimensions of our involvement in the world and an insistence that these modes of relating to things are not secondary to acts of representation, but primary and disclosive of the world itself.

Having published his book on Husserl, Levinas turned to writing a similarly expository work on Heidegger. He abandoned this project in 1934, however, when he learned that Heidegger had joined the Nazi Party. Those who would argue that it was not possible in the early 1930s to discern the direction National Socialism would take, or who excused Heidegger's involvement on such grounds, need look no further than Levinas's 1934 "Reflections on the Philosophy of Hitlerism" to see that sharp eyes and a keen moral compass were

42. *Ibid.*, 33.
43. Levinas translated only the fifth chapter; the remainder of *Méditations cartésiennes: Introduction à la phenomenologie* was translated by Gabrielle Pfeiffer.
44. Levinas and Kearney, "Dialogue with Emmanuel Levinas," 16.
45. Emmanuel Levinas, "Reflections on the Philosophy of Hitlerism," *Critical Inquiry* 17 (August 1990), 71.

able to expose the racism of National Socialism and to predict that it harbored a threat to "the very humanity" of humankind.[46] Levinas would lose his entire extended family in Lithuania to Nazi violence and was never able to exculpate or forgive Heidegger's involvement with National Socialism. Nonetheless, Levinas recognized *Being and Time* as among the four or five greatest works of Western philosophy and his own first attempts at developing an original philosophy were recognizably modeled on the existential analytic of *Being and Time*, although they were also meant as a corrective to that account. Specifically, Levinas revisits the ontological difference and inverts the Heideggerian schema that privileges Being over beings or existents. Levinas's *De l'existence à l'existent* (1947) – whose translated title, *Existence and Existents*, fails to capture this inversion from Being to beings – looks to phenomena such as fatigue, indolence, and insomnia to disclose the suffocating immanence of Being, a horror in existing itself and not only an anxiety about human finitude. Levinas suggests that this immanence cannot be pierced or evaded by the usual forms of transcendence that ultimately rely on a world behind the world, a "place" to which one can flee: after all, such places still *are* and thus remain within Being. Being, as Levinas presented it in this very early work (and in *Time and the Other*, also published in 1947), is an encumbrance that cannot be shaken off or transcended *except* in the relation to an Other, *l'Autrui*, who is absolutely other. Levinas would spend the rest of his career pursuing this line of thought, which is indebted to Heidegger but also determined to "leave the climate of Heidegger's thought."[47] Thirty years after his dissertation on Husserl, he published *Totality and Infinity* (1961), the first mature statement of his ethics, and then significantly revised his position in *Otherwise Than Being, or Beyond Essence* (1974). Today, these works are considered among the most significant challenges to Heidegger's fundamental ontology and are credited with effecting an ethical turn in French philosophy. But, if Levinas played an important (and long unacknowledged) role in the reception of phenomenology and its promotion within the French philosophical tradition, it is a role that unfolded in several distinct phases and over the space of decades rather than years.

Other forces and persons contributed equally to the rise of phenomenology in France during the 1930s. The role of Koyré deserves special mention. A Russian emigré who studied Bergson's intuitionism in Paris and then phenomenology as a member of the Göttingen Circle, Koyré moved back to Paris from Germany in 1912 and became an important conduit for the transmission of phenomenology

46. Emmanuel Levinas, *Existence and Existents*, Alfonso Lingis (trans.) (Pittsburgh, PA: Duquesne University Press, 2001), 4.

*47. For a discussion of the role Levinas played in this ethical turn, see the essay by Robert Eaglestone in *The History of Continental Philosophy: Volume 7*.

to France. In 1931, Koyré founded the journal *Recherches philosophiques*, which regularly devoted space to phenomenological essays and reviews, publishing translations of works by Husserl, Karl Jaspers (1883–1969), and Heidegger, as well as phenomenological studies by budding French phenomenologists. Koyré's seminar at the École Pratique des Hautes Études (EPHE) also played a role in bringing phenomenology to France, attracting Georges Bataille (1897–1962) and Alexandre Kojève (1902–68), among others. Indeed, Koyré served as a kind of mentor to his Russian countryman Kojève (who was briefly married to Koyré's former sister-in-law). It was at Koyré's instigation that Kojève pursued a French doctorate and with Koyré's recommendation that Kojève succeeded him at the EPHE in 1933. Kojève's seminar at the EPHE between 1933 and 1939 developed a reading of Hegel that still casts its shadow on French thought.[48] Reading Hegel line by line, translating it into French on the spot, Kojève fascinated his audience as he brought Bergson, Husserl, Heidegger, Einstein, and, most significantly, Marx to bear on Hegel's text (and reciprocally read those figures through a Hegelian lens). The list of those who attended the seminar now reads like a who's who of French philosophy, and Kojève's interpretation of Heidegger no doubt had its influence on these thinkers. Bataille and Jacques Lacan (1901–81) were regulars at the seminar, while Raymond Aron (1905–83), André Breton (1896–1966), Levinas, Merleau-Ponty, and Eric Weil (1904–77), among others, were known to have attended at one time or another.[49]

In France, the purest continuation of phenomenology may well have come in Merleau-Ponty's *Phenomenology of Perception* (1945). Like almost everyone else in his generation in France who came under the influence of phenomenology, Merleau-Ponty initially reacted against the rationalism of Léon Brunschvicg (1869–1944) by turning to Bergson's intuitionism. (He would later accede to Bergson's Chair at the prestigious Collège de France). Merleau-Ponty was introduced to phenomenology through Georges Gurvitch's (1894–1965) seminar at the Sorbonne (from 1928 to 1930) and attended Husserl's lectures at the Sorbonne in 1929 (although, by his own report, he spoke no German at the time). Interested in the relationship between consciousness and nature, Merleau-Ponty proposed to investigate the nature of perception as that which accomplishes our primary relation to the world. Initially he proposed to do this by returning to the insights of Gestalt psychology, although after his discovery of Husserl he saw phenomenology as the principal means by which perception could be described and analyzed, since phenomenology avoids both a

*48. Kojève's reading of Hegel is also discussed in the essay by John Russon in *The History of Continental Philosophy: Volume 4*.

49. See Ethan Kleinberg's account of the seminar and its impact for the reception of Heidegger's thought in *Generation Existential: Heidegger's Philosophy in France, 1927–1961* (Ithaca, NY: Cornell University Press, 2005), 49–108.

crude naturalism and an overly rationalist intellectualism. Husserl's influence is evident when Merleau-Ponty writes,

> Our task will be … to rediscover phenomena, the layer of living experience through which other people and things are first given to us …; to reawaken perception and foil its trick of allowing us to forget it as a fact and as perception in the interest of the object which it presents to us and of the rational tradition to which it gives rise.[50]

In reawakening an interest in perception as the original modality of consciousness, Merleau-Ponty also developed a rich and persuasive account of the role of the body and embodiment in the structure of experience. The body is neither a mere object in the world, nor the passive instrument of perception, but the unseen pathway or open-ended system by which we are *in*-the-world. Especially in Merleau-Ponty's later work, the body is described as an "ensemble" of "routes" that prepare the possibility of consciousness without necessarily being conscious as such.[51] Merleau-Ponty was only fifty-three years old when he died in 1961, but his thought has been exceptionally influential and is employed not only by those who continue the phenomenological tradition, but by philosophers of mind, philosophers of the body, and those interested generally in the philosophy of perception.[52]

Merleau-Ponty's schoolmate and sometimes friend Jean-Paul Sartre probably did more than anyone to popularize phenomenology in France. Simone de Beauvoir (1908–86) reports that Sartre became interested in phenomenology after a discussion with Aron in a cafe in 1932. Aron was just back from a year at the Institut français de Berlin where he had carried out research on the philosophy of history and had also read Husserl and Heidegger. Pointing to his drink, Aron announced that phenomenology made it possible to philosophize from the concrete things themselves and convinced Sartre that with phenomenology one could avoid Cartesian dualism while still crediting the irreducible difference between consciousness and the givenness of the world. In then looking for a book on phenomenology, Sartre came across Levinas's book on Husserl and, deciding to study this new philosophy seriously, Sartre made the necessary arrangements to succeed his friend Aron at the Institut français. It is a puzzling fact about Sartre's time in Germany that he never went to Freiburg to study directly with either Husserl or Heidegger and met the latter for the first time

50. Merleau-Ponty, *Phenomenology of Perception*, 57.
51. Maurice Merleau-Ponty, *The Visible and the Invisible*, Alfonso Lingis (trans.) (Evanston, IL: Northwestern University Press, 1968), 247–8.
*52. For a discussion of Merleau-Ponty, see the essay by Mauro Carbone in *The History of Continental Philosophy: Volume 4*.

only in 1952, by which time both men had moved significantly beyond their phenomenological beginnings and, as Ethan Kleinberg speculates, "had very little to talk about."[53]

Much like Heidegger, who transformed phenomenology rather than merely transmitting it, Sartre's engagement with phenomenology was revolutionary. His early work *The Transcendence of the Ego* (1936/7) largely accepts Husserl's project of a pure presuppositionless description of lived conscious experience and acknowledges the fundamentally intentional structure of consciousness, but rejects the idea of a transcendental ego remaining after the reductions have been carried out. In the consciousness of an object, the cogito is prereflective, Sartre argues, but the ego itself is constituted in reflection and thus is an object in the world like any other. This view not only dispenses with the threat of solipsism, but, more importantly for Sartre, it returns the ego to the world and subjects it to all the vicissitudes of existence. Phenomenology can be credited with having "plunged man back into the world," but only if it lets go of the transcendental ego that would once more pull "a part of man out of the world" and set it up as the creator of all that is.[54] For Sartre, intentionality heralds the idea that the world and the self or "me" are contemporaneous. This supposition is enough, says Sartre, to make the "subject–object duality, which is purely logical, definitively disappear from philosophical preoccupations."[55] Much like Heidegger, then, Sartre understands phenomenology as tasked with producing a description of our being-in-the-world that does not fall back into the trap of positing the subject over against a world of objects. In his masterwork, *Being and Nothingness* (1943), Sartre distinguishes being-for-itself (*l'être-pour-soi*) or consciousness and being-in-itself (*l'être-en-soi*) or the being of phenomena.[56] Being-in-itself simply is what it is: in itself it is solid and massive. Being-for-itself, by contrast, is "the locus of possibility, negativity, and lack."[57] Phenomena, in short, are identified with "thingness" while consciousness is fundamentally "nothingness."[58] Whereas Heidegger defines Dasein as that being for whom its own being is in question, Sartre defines Dasein or *réalité-humaine* as "a being such that in its Being, the Nothingness of its Being is in question."[59] To put this

53. Kleinberg, *Generation Existential*, 168.
54. Jean-Paul Sartre, *The Transcendence of the Ego: An Existentialist Theory of Consciousness*, Forrest Williams and Robert Kirkpatrick (trans.) (New York: Farrar, Straus & Giroux, 1972), 105.
55. *Ibid.*
56. Jean-Paul Sartre, *Being and Nothingness*, Hazel E. Barnes (trans.) (New York: Washington Square Press, 1956), 25.
57. Thomas Flynn, "Sartre," in *A Companion to Continental Philosophy*, Simon Critchley and William R. Schroeder (eds) (Oxford: Blackwell, 1998), 258.
58. *Ibid.*
59. Sartre, *Being and Nothingness*, 57.

idea in the famous slogan of existentialism, this is just to say that for human being or being-for-itself, existing precedes any essence. A human being is not a particular *kind* or *type* of existent object with a specific essence or excellence. Rather, as consciousness, human being or being-for-itself is a spontaneity and freedom through which nothingness comes into the world.[60]

Sartre's existentialism was developed on this ontological basis. For Sartre, we are factically existing beings – that is, we live in a situation that is in some respects given – but we have absolute freedom when it comes to how we regard our situation and the actions we undertake within that situation. To think otherwise and to blame one's choices on the circumstantial constraints is a matter of bad faith. But bad faith is not just a condemnation of cowardice in the face of absolute freedom (and a correspondingly absolute responsibility). It plays the ontologically disclosive role of showing once again that human reality begins with an act of negation. In order to say that I am courageous when I am not, I have to have the power of negation. Similarly, this power is manifested when I deny that my act was courageous and say that I only did what anyone in the circumstances would do. As many have pointed out, in France at the end of the Second World War, when French society was coming to terms both with occupation and collaboration, Sartre's existentialism showed how it was possible to move forward in hope without denying the moral failings and horror of the recent past.

Kleinberg explains that "Sartre's use of Heidegger led to the widespread supposition in France that Heidegger was an existential humanist, and Sartre's own political affiliations with various left-wing political groups led to the vague impression that Heidegger had similar concerns."[61] Neither supposition was borne out. As for the second, the intellectual Left in France was stunned when it learned of Heidegger's involvement with National Socialism, and the debate over whether and to what extent Heidegger's philosophy is compatible with or contains Nazi sentiments lead to the so-called Heidegger Affair of 1946–47, when the issue was debated in newspapers and through academic journals such as Sartre's *Les Temps modernes*. The Affair has been revived several times since, both inside and outside France, each time reigniting the furor of the original tempest. As for the first supposition, it is widely known that Heidegger himself eschewed the title "existentialist." Through a go-between, Heidegger was made aware of the influence of his thought in France and had the opportunity to read the major works of Sartre and Merleau-Ponty. While deeply interested in Sartre's work in particular, he felt that the young scholar had overemphasized the human agent and his freedom, thus falling prey, as did Husserl, to a repeti-

60. *Ibid.*, 60.
61. Kleinberg, *Generation Existential*, 153.

tion of Cartesianism. Heidegger's "Letter on Humanism," written in response to an invitation by Jean Beaufret (1907–82) to expand his thought in the direction of an ethics, was his most important effort in writing to correct what he felt was the misleading existentialist interpretation of his work in France. The force of this document on French letters and philosophy was exceptional and played an important role in the rise of French antihumanism as seen in the works of Lacan, Michel Foucault (1926–84), and Jacques Derrida.

The philosophical currents begun by these three philosophers enriched and enlivened French philosophy in the second half of the twentieth century. Foucault's archaeological and genealogical philosophy, Lacan's revivification of Freudian psychoanalysis, and Derrida's deconstruction all owe a debt to phenomenology that must be recognized, although it cannot be explored in detail here. Instead, we turn to a final summation of the international status and future of the phenomenological movement.

V. PHENOMENOLOGY AS AN INTERNATIONAL MOVEMENT

Phenomenology has always been an international movement. Many of those who visited Husserl or studied with him came from abroad and were central in the spread of phenomenology. Notably, there was Ingarden from Poland, Koyré from Russia, Aron Gurwitsch from Lithuania, Alfred Schutz from Vienna, Marvin Farber, among others, from the United States, and José Ortega y Gassett from Spain, although the last was never a thoroughgoing phenomenologist.[62] Jewish scholars fleeing Germany during the Second World War were also a

62. Gurwitsch (1901–73) spent a year studying with Husserl and Heidegger in the early 1920s and wrote his dissertation under Scheler and then, after Scheler's death, Moritz Geiger. He was strongly attracted to Gestalt psychology and integrates insights from this tradition with his understanding of transcendental phenomenology. Gurwitsch fled Germany during the Second World War and spent seven years in France before moving to the United States. There he taught at Johns Hopkins University, Brandeis University, and, most famously, from 1959 to 1973 at the New School for Social Research. His major original work was *The Field of Consciousness*, published originally in French in 1957, then in English in 1964. His *Studies in Phenomenology and Psychology* contains excellent critical studies of key concepts in phenomenology as well as original essays reflecting his wide interests in philosophy and psychology. Schutz (1899–1959) was a native of Vienna introduced to Husserl by Felix Kaufmann in 1932. Picking up Husserl's notion of the lifeworld, Schutz developed a phenomenology of the social world with particular attention to the identification of the various sub-worlds that make up the lifeworld and their structural interrelation. Representative works include *Der sinnhafte Aufbau der sozialen Welt* (*The Phenomenology of the Social World*).

Farber (1901–80) studied with Husserl in Freiburg in 1923–24 and wrote his dissertation on Husserl's philosophy. In 1939 he founded the International Phenomenological Society and in 1940 the journal *Philosophy and Phenomenological Research*. He taught at the University of

factor in establishing phenomenology in North America. Arendt as well as Felix Kaufmann, Fritz Kaufmann, Schutz, Gurwitsch, and Moritz Geiger all taught in the United States in the postwar years,[63] many of them at the New School for Social Research in New York. After moving into France in the 1930s, phenomenology was exported worldwide first in the form of existentialism and later in the deconstruction of Derrida. Everywhere it has traveled, geographically and outside the discipline of philosophy, phenomenology has been mixed with local concerns and questions. In Latin America, phenomenology became a resource for liberation theology; in the United States and Canada, it has intersected with and informed the work of feminist philosophers as well as philosophers

---

Buffalo and made it a leading center for phenomenological studies in the United States. He published his main work on Husserl, *The Foundation of Phenomenology*, in 1943.

José Ortega y Gassett (1883–1955) was a Spanish philosopher and public intellectual. He received his doctorate from Complutense University in Madrid in 1904 and spent the next few years studying in Germany at a number of different universities. He was appointed to a Chair in Metaphysics at his alma mater in 1909 and became a leading figure in Spanish philosophy and politics. He was not a phenomenologist *per se*, but visited Husserl in Freiburg in 1934 and impressed him greatly. Ortega played a leading role in the translation of contemporary German philosophy, including phenomenology, into Spanish and it was his students who effectively introduced phenomenology into Mexico and Latin America.

63. Arendt (1906–75) was born in Hanover and studied philosophy in Marburg with Heidegger and then with Jaspers in Heidelberg. She became one of the most influential and important political philosophers of the twentieth century, and both Heidegger, with whom she had a brief love affair, and Jaspers were crucial influences on her thought. Arendt fled Germany when the Nazis came to power in 1933, spending six years in Paris before she was again forced to flee, this time to the United States, where she spent the remainder of her life teaching at prestigious institutions such as the University of California, Berkeley, Princeton University, and finally the New School for Social Research. Major works include *The Human Condition* (1958), *Eichmann in Jerusalem* (1963), *The Origins of Totalitarianism* (1973), and *The Life of the Mind* (1978). [*] Arendt's work is discussed in detail in an essay by Peg Birmingham in *The History of Continental Philosophy: Volume 5*.

Felix Kaufmann (1895–1949) was interested in mathematics and physics as well as law and the social sciences. He visited Husserl repeatedly in Freiburg, after first contacting him by letter in 1922, and kept up a prodigious correspondence with him. In Vienna, Kaufmann was marginally connected with the Vienna Circle and tried to strengthen the relations between phenomenology and logical empiricism. In 1935, he organized a visit with Husserl in Vienna and was instrumental in trying to move the philosopher and his papers to Prague, although the attempt ultimately had to be abandoned. Fleeing to the United States, Kaufmann was the first of Husserl's students to teach at the New School for Social Research, offering courses beginning in 1939.

Fritz Kaufmann (1891–1958), no relation to Felix Kaufmann, began his studies with Husserl and Heidegger in Freiburg in 1919. He wrote his dissertation on "The Picture as Aesthetic Experience," and a book-length study of Thomas Mann. His main work was *Das Reich des Schönen: Bausteine zu einer Philosophie der Kunst* (1960). He fled Nazi Germany during the Second World War and spent twenty years teaching in the United States at Northwestern University and then the University of Buffalo, before returning to Europe at the end of his life.

of mind, and has had an important impact in psychology and sociology. It has spawned numerous academic organizations worldwide (of which the Society for Phenomenology and Existential Philosophy in the United States is among the largest) and has, of course, spawned a veritable industry of smaller conferences, research circles, translations, publications, and the like. What phenomenology has not had, however, at least not since the generation of Sartre and Levinas, is a major reinterpretation based on its dual origin in Husserl and Heidegger. This suggests perhaps that phenomenology is at risk of becoming a historical curiosity: retaining its ability to philosophize about the "things themselves" but failing to speak urgently to the central problems of human existing or of philosophy in our time. Indeed, already in 1963, Heidegger remarked that the "age of phenomenology seems to be over. It is already taken as something past which is only recorded historically along with other schools of philosophy."[64] But this judgment is as premature now as it was in 1963. Heidegger suggests that phenomenology is not a technique employed by a certain "school" of philosophers. "It is," he says, "the possibility of thinking" and even if the name disappears as such, wherever there is attention paid to what manifests itself and to how it is given, we are in the vicinity of phenomenology.[65] We may add to these sentiments that we are far from having digested all that is given to be thought in the works of Husserl, Heidegger, Sartre, Levinas, Merleau-Ponty, Derrida, and others, and this suggests that the future of the phenomenological *movement* no less than that of phenomenology in Heidegger's sense remains invitingly open, ready for renewal and reinvention.

64. Heidegger, "My Way to Phenomenology," 82.
65. *Ibid.*

10

EARLY CONTINENTAL PHILOSOPHY OF SCIENCE

Babette Babich

During the years leading up to and after 1890–1930, the continental conception of science had a far broader scope than the anglophone notion of science today. Even today, the German term *Wissenschaft* embraces not only the natural and the social sciences, including economics,[1] but also the full panoply of the so-called humanities, including the theoretical study of art and theology, both important in the nineteenth century for, among other things, the formation of the life sciences.[2] Philosophy itself was also counted as a science and was, in its phenomenological articulation, nothing less than the science of scientific origins or "original science" – the "*Urwissenschaft*" – as Martin Heidegger defined it in 1919,[3] following his own intensive engagement with Edmund Husserl's *Logical Investigations*.

It is also crucial for any discussion of continental philosophy of science between 1890 and 1930 to emphasize that these were, in Winston Churchill's words, "precarious times," times of technological and social change and of revolution, scientific and political. In a positive reflection on the transformations of

1. See Ernst Haeckel, *Systematische Phylogenie: Entwurf eines natürlichen Systems der Organismen auf Grund ihrer Stammesgeschichte* (Berlin: Georg Reimer, 1894–96).
2. See Bernhard Kleeberg, "God–Nature Progressing: Natural Theology in German Monism," *Science in Context* 20(3) (2007), as well as Mario Di Gregorio, *From Here to Eternity: Ernst Haeckel and Scientific Faith* (Göttingen: Vandenhoeck & Ruprecht, 2005), and Burkhardt Gladigow, "Pantheismus und Naturmystik," in *Die Trennung von Natur und Geist*, Rüdiger Bubner (ed.) (Munich: Fink, 1990).
3. Martin Heidegger, *Towards the Definition of Philosophy*, Ted Sadler (trans.) (London: Continuum, 2000), 3, 11ff. See for a broader discussion, Theodore Kisiel, *Heidegger's Way of Thought* (London: Continuum, 2002), 17ff.

this period, Heidegger refers, as will Husserl later, to the "crisis of philosophy as science," noting in 1925 that all "sciences and groups of sciences are undergoing a great revolution of a productive kind that has opened up new modes of questioning, new possibilities, and new horizons."[4]

These same critical years also saw astonishing industrial innovations, yielding many of the still-familiar achievements of modern technology, from cars (the four-wheeled automobile in 1892), airplanes (1903), and even moving sidewalks (1893); from moving pictures (1895) to public radio broadcasting (in 1922, although Marconi first transmitted a radio signal in 1895) and television broadcasting (1929). Wilhelm Röntgen took the first X-rays in 1895, while the development of modern artillery began in 1897, and Robert Goddard launched the first liquid-fueled rockets in 1926.

Continental philosophy of science has always featured reflection not only on the technologies of scientific investigation but also on human perception and technological circumspection. Louis Basso's 1925 essay, "Induction technique et science expérimentale" was central to Gaston Bachelard's 1928 dissertation, *Essai sur la connaissance approchée*, because Basso raised the question of the industrial arts as involving an inherently encompassing coordination of mechanization and technique.[5] Heidegger had already emphasized in 1927 the interaction between theoretical world-disclosure and scientific research equipment, points that continue in Patrick A. Heelan's (1926–) reflections on Werner Heisenberg's (1901–76) physical philosophy and Heelan's own subsequent elaboration of the phenomenology of perception as a phenomenology of laboratory discovery.[6] A similar focus on the researcher's art also characterizes Ernst

4. Martin Heidegger, "Wilhelm Dilthey's Research and the Struggle for a Historical Worldview," Charles Bambach (trans.), in *Supplements: From the Earliest Essays to "Being and Time" and Beyond*, John van Buren (ed.) (Albany, NY: SUNY Press, 2002), 148. Heidegger goes on to detail the theory of relativity in physics along with the crisis of foundations in mathematics, to which one must add quantum mechanics and the movement against mechanistic thinking in the biological sciences.
5. Basso's "Induction technique et science expérimentale," *Revue philosophique de la France et de l'etranger* 99 (1925), with its focus on the industrial arts and the relation between practical application and science along with its emphasis on technological style would be continued in Jacques Ellul and Jean Baudrillard and in still more comprehensive detail in Siegfried Giedion's *Mechanization Takes Command: A Contribution to Anonymous History* (New York: Norton, 1948). An account of the historical context of the development of French philosophy of science may be found in the introduction to Anastasios Brenner and Jean Gayon (eds), *French Studies in the Philosophy of Science* (Frankfurt: Springer, 2009).
6. Patrick A. Heelan, *Quantum Mechanics and Objectivity: The Physical Philosophy of Werner Heisenberg* (The Hague: Martinus Nijhoff, 1965). A new book by Kristian Camilleri, *Heisenberg and the Interpretation of Quantum Mechanics: The Physicist as Philosopher* (Cambridge: Cambridge University Press, 2009), also considers Heisenberg's philosophy of science and quantum mechanics.

Mach's (1838–1916) philosophical reflections on science and can be said to drive Ludwik Fleck's (1896–1961) philosophical sociology of medical science.[7]

For his part, Heidegger's critical reflections on science anticipate the turn to the history of science and indeed the social and historical studies of technology that increasingly inform science studies.[8] Heidegger's reflective critique of mathematics and science in his 1927 *Being and Time*, together with the questioning he undertakes with regard to thinking the essence of modern technology, provides the basis for his hermeneutic phenomenology of both scientific theory and practice. As he writes in the later 1930s, using what would turn out to be a timely example taken from the same experimental physics that would herald the development of the atom bomb in the mid-1940s, "Within the complex of machinery that is necessary to physics in order to carry out the smashing of the atom lies the whole of physics."[9]

Heidegger's point is echoed in the argument Heelan makes in *Quantum Mechanics and Objectivity* with respect to Heisenberg's perturbation theory of measurement in his 1925–27 contributions to quantum mechanics.[10] Measurement, as Heelan points out with special emphasis on the technological instruments that are used to obtain such measurements – that is, what Heidegger calls "the complex of machinery" – makes all the difference for the "new scientific spirit" – using Bachelard's terminology – of physics.[11] For Heidegger, what is at issue is the *constitution* of modern technological and mathematizable (measurable, calculable, model-oriented) science, conceived in both the Husserlian phenomenological sense and the mechanically explicit sense of standardized manufacture and institutional technology.[12] It is thus in this sense that

7. See Jerzy Giedymin, "Polish Philosophy in the Interwar Period and Ludwik Fleck's Theory of Thought Styles and Thought Collectives," in *Cognition and Fact: Materials on Ludwik Fleck*, Robert Cohen and Ludwig Schnelle (eds) (Boston, MA: Reidel, 1986), 184, for a comparison of Fleck and Mach; and Friedrich Steinle, "Experiment, Concept Formation and the Limits of Justification: 'Discovering' the Two Electricities," in *Revisiting Discovery and Justification*, Jutta Schickore and Friedrich Steinle (eds) (Frankfurt: Springer, 2006), 191.

*8. For a discussion of science studies, see the essay by Dorothea Olkowski in *The History of Continental Philosophy: Volume 8*.

9. Martin Heidegger, "The Age of World Picture," William Lovitt (trans.), in *The Question Concerning Technology* (New York: Harper & Row, 1977), 127. See too Paul Forman, "The Primacy of Science in Modernity, of Technology in Postmodernity, and of Ideology in the History of Technology," *History and Technology* 23(1) (2007).

10. Heelan, *Quantum Mechanics and Objectivity*, chs 4 and 5.

11. See Patrick A. Heelan, "Preface," in Gaston Bachelard, *The New Scientific Spirit* (Boston, MA: Beacon Press, 1984). With reference to the laboratory embodiments of research, Heelan's study of Heisenberg discusses Ernst Cassirer, Erwin Schrödinger, and Eugene Wigner along with Hanson.

12. See Dmitri Ginev, *The Context of Constitution: Beyond the Edge of Epistemological Justification* (Dordrecht: Springer, 2006) for an analysis of this concept in continental philosophy of science.

the Heidegger of the 1930s describes the trajectory of modern technology as a "humanism," much as Friedrich Nietzsche in *The Gay Science* and in his posthumous notes characterizes mathematics and the sciences in general as what he named, in a Kantian voice, so many modalities of "humanization."[13]

I. LIMIT-CONCEPTS, METHOD, AND THE TENSIONS OF FRENCH PRAGMATISM

In his address in Paris to the 1900 World Congress of Mathematicians, David Hilbert (1862–1943) adumbrated his famous programmatic plan for mathematics, articulating his positive conviction that "However unapproachable these problems may seem to us and however helpless we stand before them, we have, nevertheless, the firm conviction that their solution must follow by a finite number of purely logical processes."[14] In 1930, Kurt Gödel (1906–78) would announce the results of his own research disproving Hilbert's program at a congress on the epistemology of the exact sciences in Königsberg at which Hilbert himself gave the culminating public lecture of his life, publicly broadcast on the radio, and proclaiming in conclusion "*We must know – we will know*."[15] One did not, however, have to wait for Gödel. The crisis in the foundational program is coterminous with Hilbert's project. It is already present in the neo-Kantianism that dominated continental thinking on science and mathematics in all its modalities from the empiriocriticism or environmental positivism of Richard Avenarius (1843–96) and Mach, in the logical positivism of the Vienna Circle that emerged from this tradition, in Henri Poincaré and Henri Bergson, and in Husserl and Heidegger.

To the question of foundations must be added the question of method. Heinrich Rickert's *The Limits of Concept Formation in Natural Science* (1896–1902) distinguishes the different traditions of science as such, and Wilhelm Dilthey (1833–1911) extends this reflection to the human sciences. Inaugurating the then-influential turn to what was called *Lebensphilosophie*,[16] Dilthey

13. Cf. Friedrich Nietzsche, *Sämtliche Werke: Kritische Studienausgabe*, Giorgio Colli and Mazzino Montinari (eds) (Berlin: de Gruyter, 1980) (hereafter KSA), vol. 11, 191.

14. David Hilbert, "Mathematical Problems," *Bulletin of the American Mathematical Society* 8 (1902), 445. [*] For a discussion of developments in sicence and mathematics in the latter half of the nineteenth century, see the essay by Dale Jacquette in *The History of Continental Philosophy: Volume 2*.

15. Contending that there is in mathematics no "Ignorabimus," Hilbert refers to Emil du Bois-Reymond's (1818–96) claim that there are limits to human knowledge; see Victor Vinnikov, "We Shall Know: Hilbert's Apology," *Mathematical Intelligencer* 21 (1999).

16. Dilthey invokes the notion of limit-concepts in *The Formation of the Historical World in the Human Sciences*. For a 1939 account, see Carl Theodore Glock, *Wilhelm Diltheys Grundlegung einer wissenschaftlichen Lebensphilosophie* (Berlin: Junker und Dünnhaupt, 1939). On the

emphasized lived experience as central to the opposition between *explanation* and *understanding*. The same focus on method can be read in the reflections of social scientists such as Max Weber (1864–1920), as well as in the *Existenz-philosophie* of the physician turned philosopher, Karl Jaspers (1883–1969). Even Nietzsche emphasized that "the scientific spirit rests upon insight into method,"[17] a claim that included classical philology and history as well as the physical sciences.[18] Yet Nietzsche also argued that "the triumph of science distinguishes our 19th century less than does the triumph of scientific method over science."[19] Although there were clear differences between them, Nietzsche shared Mach's emphasis on the role of error in scientific rationality along with Mach's opposition to atomism.[20] Indeed, one commentator's introductory assessment of the general reaction to Mach in this context should be compared to common responses to the conjunction of Nietzsche and science: "Mach's viewpoint provides a basis only for destructive criticism, and tends to discourage the development of hypotheses that may turn out to be fruitful."[21]

It is Nietzsche's critical thinking on the sciences and on logic and mathematics, conjoined with his influence on certain scientists and mathematicians, that constitutes one of the earliest instantiations of continental philosophy of science. During the period under discussion here, Nietzsche's critical

social and natural sciences, see Joseph J. Kockelmans, "Science and Discipline: Some Historical and Critical Reflections," in *Interdisciplinarity and Higher Education*, Joseph J. Kockelmans (ed.) (University Park, PA: Pennsylvania State University Press, 1979) and Charles Bambach, *Heidegger, Dilthey, and the Crisis of Historicism* (Ithaca, NY: Cornell University Press, 1995).

17. Nietzsche, *Human, All Too Human*, §635, in KSA, vol. 2, 360–61; cf. *ibid.*, §278, 228–9. On Nietzsche and method, see my "'The Problem of Science' in Nietzsche and Heidegger," *Revista Portuguesa de Filosofia* 63 (2007).
18. Nietzsche, *On the Use and Disadvantage of History*, §7, in KSA, vol. 1, 295.
19. Nietzsche, KSA, vol. 13, 442. The same question of method later animates Paul Feyerabend, but although there are parallels – see Gordon Bearn, "Nietzsche, Feyerabend, and the Voices of Relativism," *Metaphilosophy* 17(2–3) (1986), as well as my *Nietzsche's Philosophy of Science: Reflecting Science on the Ground of Art and Life* (Albany, NY: SUNY Press, 1994), 48ff., and, more broadly, Angèle Kremer-Marietti, *Seven Epistemological Essays* (Paris: Buenos Books America, 2007) – Feyerabend himself disclaimed any influence. On the 1930s background to the deep complexities of such influence see Val Dusek, "Brecht and Lukács as Teachers of Feyerabend and Lakatos: The Feyerabend–Lakatos Debate as Scientific Recapitulation of the Brecht–Lukács Debate," *History of the Human Sciences* 11(2) (1998).
20. Hans Kleinpeter emphasizes the connection with Mach in *Der Phänomenalismus: Eine naturwissenschaftliche Weltanschauung* (Leipzig: Johann Ambrosius Barth, 1913), 226ff., citing his 1912 essay on Nietzsche's epistemology. Mach also shared Nietzsche's radical skepticism, as Carl Friedrich von Weizsäcker notes in "Nietzsche: Perceptions of Modernity," in *Nietzsche, Epistemology, and Philosophy of Science*, B. Babich and R. S. Cohen (eds) (Dordrecht: Springer, 1999), 227. See too Renate Reschke, *Denkumbrüche mit Nietzsche: Zur anspornenden Verachtung der Zeit* (Berlin: Akademie, 2000), 187ff., and my "Mach, Duhem, Bachelard," in *Twentieth-Century Continental Philosophy*, Richard Kearney (ed.) (London: Routledge, 1996).
21. Stephen Brush, "Mach and Atomism," *Synthese* 18 (1968), 192.

philosophical spirit, including his theory of eternal recurrence,[22] influences not only literary and artistic traditions but also philosophical discussions of Darwinism, the debate on entropy and thermodynamics,[23] and the tradition of Victorian relativity antedating Einstein, even if we set aside, for the moment, the impact of Nietzsche's thinking on Heidegger's early philosophy of science.

Highlighting Nietzsche's practical emphases together with his skepticism, the Belgian philosopher René Berthelot in 1911 coordinates American pragmatist and continental philosophy of science, comparing Nietzsche not only to the pragmatism of Charles Sanders Peirce and William James but also to Poincaré.[24] Linking the American pragmatists in this way with the work of scientists is no fluke. In fact, it is difficult to parse French philosophers of science during this period without referring to Peirce and, especially, to James, who was familiar with and shared a number of interests with Bergson.[25] Bergson began his intellectual life with a prize essay in mathematics, and in addition to his reflections on evolution he contributed also to the philosophy of mathematics inasmuch as he undertook the critically important step at the turn of the twentieth century of

---

*22. For a discussion of Nietzsche's eternal recurrence, see the essay on Nietzsche by Daniel Conway in *The History of Continental Philosophy: Volume 2*.

23. Drawing on Henri Poincaré's argument that a closed system of atoms must recur, in an infinitesimal approximation, to its initial state, infinitely many times, von Weizsäcker notes that Ernst "Zermelo in 1900 raised objection to the statistical interpretations of the second law of thermodynamics, the so-called Recurrence Objection" ("Nietzsche: Perceptions of Modernity," 227). This objection against entropy seemed to provide support for Nietzsche's and other theories of recurrence. For a discussion, including references to Nietzsche and Poincaré, see Stephen Brush, *The Temperature of History: Phases of Science and Culture in the Nineteenth Century* (New York: Bart Franklin, 1978); more recently, Péter Érdi cites the same tradition in *Complexity Explained* (Frankfurt: Springer, 2007). For an overview, including a reference to Nietzsche, see Christopher Herbert on the tradition of relativity before Einstein in *Victorian Relativity: Radical Thought and Scientific Discovery* (Chicago, IL: University of Chicago Press, 2001).

24. See René Berthelot, *Un Romantisme utilitaire: Etude sur le mouvement pragmatiste. 1, Le pragmatisme chez Nietzsche et chez Poincaré* (Paris: Félix Alcan, 1911). Peirce, it should be noted, was not pleased with this comparison.

25. See Henri Bergson, "On the Pragmatism of William James: Truth and Reality," Melissa McMahon (trans.), in *Key Writings*, Keith Ansell-Pearson and John Mullarkey (eds) (New York: Continuum, 2002) as well as Émile Boutroux's *William James*, Archibald Henderson and Barbara Henderson (trans.) (New York: Longman's, Green, 1912). Horace Kallen's *William James and Henri Bergson: A Study in Contrasting Theories of Life* (Chicago, IL: University of Chicago Press, 1914) begins by focusing on the perceptual contrast between, and hence affinity of, the artist and the philosopher. It should not be supposed, however, that French philosophers of the turn of the century read the American pragmatists in the way they are read today, a difference still evident, for example, in Paul Ricoeur's *Freedom and Nature: The Voluntary and the Involuntary*, Erazim Kohak (trans.) (Evanston, IL: Northwestern University Press, 1966), where, in addition to a discussion of James and eidetic phenomenology, Ricoeur also compares James with Bergson and Jaspers.

"rereading both Kant's philosophy and Riemann's mathematics of the manifold and gave the term *intuition* a central place in his reasoning."[26]

II. THE MEDIEVAL FOUNDATIONS OF MODERN SCIENCE: HISTORY OF SCIENCE AND IDEOLOGY

Contemporary analytic philosophy of science rests, implicitly or explicitly, on the crucial idea of the "scientific revolution". In this same tradition of philosophy of science, it is well known that Pierre Duhem's famous theoretical underdeterminism was influential for Einstein and Quine.[27] What is less well known is that Duhem also wrote a key account of the story of Catholic (and Islamic and Jewish[28]) science in the Middle Ages – the ten-volume *Le Système du monde* – undermining nothing less threatening to modern science's conception of itself (in contrast with the medieval and ancient worlds[29]) than the very idea of the scientific revolution. Most historians and philosophers of science are hard pressed to fit the conceptual traditions of medieval science into the developmental tradition of modern science,[30] and ancient science presents an even more difficult task.

26. Julian Rohrhuber, "Intuitions/Anschaungen," *Faits divers* 1 (2007), 2. As Jean Milet notes, in *Bergson et le calcul infinitésimal: Ou, la raison et le temps* (Paris: Presses Universitaires de France, 1974), while widely celebrated in many fields in the early part of the twentieth century, Bergson came to be denounced with rhetorically savage criticism, as some raised what Milet regards as baseless claims challenging Bergson's mathematical proficiency. In contrast, Gaston Bachelard's reflections on science were widely appreciated, perhaps because of his enthusiasm for subordinating "empirical diversity to the power of reason," as Bernadette Bensaud-Vincent insightfully puts it in her discussion of Bachelard and chemistry, "Chemistry in the French Tradition of Philosophy of Science: Duhem, Meyerson, Metzger and Bachelard," *Studies in History and Philosophy of Science Part A* 36(4) (December 2005), 633.
27. Don Howard, "Einstein and Duhem," *Synthese* 83(3) (June 1990).
28. See e.g. Gad Freudenthal, "Maimonides' Guide of the Perplexed and the Transmission of the Mathematical Tract 'On the Asymptotic Lines' in the Arabic, Latin, Hebrew Medieval Tradition," *Vivarium* 26 (1988); Max Lejbowicz, "Pierre Duhem et l'histoire des sciences arabes," *Revue des questions scientifiques* 175(1) (2004); F. Jamil Ragep, "Duhem, The Arabs, and the History of Cosmology," *Synthese* 83 (1990); and David B. Ruderman, *Jewish Thought and Scientific Discovery in Early Modern Europe* (New Haven, CT: Yale University Press, 1995).
29. Paul Feyerabend, *Science in a Free Society* (London: Verso, 1978), 33ff., is both wry and unparalleled on philosophy of science and history of science. On the reciprocal exclusions of the history of science and philosophy of science, see John R. Wetterstein, "The Philosophy of Science and the History of Science: Separate Domains vs. Separate Aspects," *The Philosophical Forum* 14(1) (Fall 1982), and Klaus Hentschel, "Der Vergleich als Brücke zwischen Wissenschaftsgeschichte und Wissenschaftstheorie," *Journal for General Philosophy of Science* 34 (2003).
30. But see, generally, Edward Grant, *The Foundations of Modern Science in the Middle Ages: Their Religious, Institutional and Intellectual Contexts* (Cambridge: Cambridge University Press, 1996).

On the subject matter of ancient science, and challenging the ongoing presumption that supposes Aristotle incapable of observation, Paul Feyerabend reminds us of the stubbornly acontextual tendencies of the Vienna Circle.[31] In accord with Duhem's continuationist point *vis-à-vis* the scientific revolution, Feyerabend argues that the "Vienna Circle shares with the enlightenment an exaggerated faith in the powers of reason and an almost total ignorance concerning past achievements."[32] Like Nietzsche before him, Feyerabend calls for greater historical sensitivity, a hermeneutic attention to context that would increase the rigor of scientific historiography.

Duhem's 1903 discovery of themes from Leonardo's notebooks in a medieval manuscript (of one Jordanus Nemorarius) exemplifies this point.[33] As one scholar notes, so far "from seeing Leonardo as the forerunner of modern science, Duhem fairly rooted him in the then-hitherto unexplored context of late medieval scholastic thought."[34] Using a metaphor borrowed from Nietzsche to speak of the Greeks' unique discoveries,[35] Ernst Cassirer has drawn our attention to the detail of Duhem's account of "how Leonardo received a great number of problems immediately from the hands of Cusanus and how he took them up precisely at the point Cusanus had left them."[36] As Duhem further details, Domingo de Soto (1494–1570) had described free fall eighty years before Galileo in his 1551 commentary on Aristotle's *Physics*.[37] Duhem's approach became the basis for an important change in the history of science. As Jeanne Peiffer explains, "Duhem exploited long-neglected sources and enlarged the body of knowledge concerned with scholastic mathematics and philosophy. He defended the thesis that, through an uninterrupted sequence of barely perceptible improvements, modern science arose from doctrines taught in the medieval schools."[38]

Together with a focus on interpretation and context, hermeneutic and phenomenological philosophy of science also attends to the kind of historical

31. Here Feyerabend repudiates "the historical illiteracy of most contemporary philosophers and of their low standards of hero worship" (*Science in a Free Society*, 59).
32. *Ibid.*
33. See Duhem's three-volume study *Études sur Leonard de Vinci: Ceux qu'il a lus et ceux qui l'ont lu* (Paris: A. Hermann, 1906).
34. A. Richard Turner, *Inventing Leonardo* (New York: Knopf, 1992), 141.
35. Nietzsche, KSA, vol. 1, 804.
36. Ernst Cassirer, *The Individual and the Cosmos in Renaissance Philosophy*, Mario Domandi (trans.) (New York: Dover, 2000), 50; see also Lynn Thorndike, *History of Magic and Experimental Science* (New York: Columbia University Press, 1941).
37. See on this, among many others, William Wallace, "Duhem and Koyré on Domingo de Soto," *Synthese* 83(2) (1990).
38. Jeanne Peiffer, "France," in *Writing the History of Mathematics*, Joseph W. Dauben and Christoph J. Scriba (eds) (Basel: Birkhäuser, 2002), 30. Feyerabend invokes Duhem to argue that "logic was on the side of … Bellarmine … not Galileo" (*Farewell to Reason* [London: Verso, 1989], 134).

specificity or perspective emphasized by Herbert Butterfield, as does Nietzsche, and later still Foucault and Georges Canguilhem.[39] Mainstream history of science by contrast continues to tend toward "leaving things out,"[40] perhaps in the interest of minimizing complexity, which may be why it prefers the more neutral "presentist" to Butterfield's "whig" terminology. But the language of "presentism" exemplifies the problem of presentism. Thus Butterfield argues that:

> behind the Whig interpretation – the theory that we study the past for the sake of the present – is one that is really introduced for the purpose of facilitating the abridgment of history; and its effect is to provide us with a handy rule of thumb by which we can easily discover what was important in the past, for the simple reason that, by definition, we mean what is important "from our point of view."[41]

III. BEYOND PHYSICS: EXEMPLARS OF SCIENCE

(i) Grounding physical science: geology and deep time

A relatively new science that developed in the nineteenth century, geology is a science typically neglected in mainstream discussions of the philosophy of science.[42] Like evolution and paleontology, geology counts as a "palaetiological" science in William Whewell's language that has had a correspondingly diverse range of influences, not least in the mid-nineteenth century via Charles Lyell's influence on Darwin.[43] The Scottish physicist William Thomson (1824–1907), who later became Lord Kelvin, challenged the Hytton–Lyell "uniformitarian" theory of geology[44] in the 1860s. Although his challenge to uniformitarian

*39. For a discussion of Foucault and Canguilhem in this regard, see the essay by Pierre Cassou-Noguès in *The History of Continental Philosophy: Volume 4*.

40. Palle Yourgrau uses this expression to characterize the exclusion of Gödel from the philosophy of physics in *A World Without Time: The Forgotten Legacy of Gödel and Einstein* (New York: Basic Books, 2005), 24. See also the discussion below.

41. Herbert Butterfield, *The Whig Interpretation of History* (New York: Norton, 1931).

42. The paleontologist and geologist Karl Alfred von Zittel (1839–1904) authored a comprehensive overview of both sciences in *Geschichte der Geologie und Paläontologie bis Ende des 19. Jahrhundert*. See too Peter J. Bowler, "The Whig Interpretation of Geology," *Biology and Philosophy* 3 (1988) and Rachel Laudan, *From Mineralogy to Geology: The Foundations of a Science, 1650–1830* (Chicago, IL: University of Chicago Press, 1987).

43. See Roy Porter, "Charles Lyell and the Principles of the History of Geology," *British Journal for the History of Science* 9(32) (1976).

44. The uniformitarian theory of geology, as the name suggests, assumes the constancy of the earth's relative position in the solar system and the stability of the geological features of the earth itself over long periods of time.

theories of the age of the earth was well founded, Lord Kelvin's own simple or "elegant" mathematical model failed to represent the complex dynamics of the earth's geological evolution (and indeed its present), and hence his estimate of the age of the earth, for all its mathematical "correctness," was nonetheless erroneous.[45] Incorporated in the second law of thermodynamics as expressed in 1865 by Rudolf Clausius (1822–88), Thomson's challenge, although not itself productive for geology *per se*, was enormously influential and culminated in the concept of entropy, one of the most profoundly philosophical scientific notions of the nineteenth century. This vision in turn inspired Poincaré's recurrence theorem, which stated that in a closed or bounded system all events return, infinitely many times, to their initial state, much as Nietzsche also argued with his own theory of the eternal recurrence of the same.[46] In the spirit of "deep time," both Poincaré's and Nietzsche's articulations highlight an already-consummate past.

Beyond its nineteenth-century preludes and in addition to thermodynamics and evolution, geology saw further important innovations in the polar explorer and geologist Alfred Lothar Wegener's (1880–1930) 1912 theory of continental drift.[47] Quintessentially revolutionary, Wegener's discovery dramatizes some of the difficulties of paradigm change, as it was ridiculed for nearly fifty years (indeed, it was still the object of ridicule by professors of earth science when this author was at university) before being finally accepted as today relevant for the sciences of ecology, evolution, and climate change. Wegener is thus a paradigmatic example for the obstacles faced by any revolutionary theory.[48] Both for theoretical as well as contextually hermeneutic reasons, including the develop-

45. See, for a discussion, in a context attuned to both geology and mathematical modeling in science, Orrin H. Pilkey and Linda Pilkey Jarvis, *Useless Arithmetic: Why Environmental Scientists Can't Predict the Future* (New York: Columbia University Press, 2007), 27ff.
46. For a discussion of the nineteenth-century context, relevant to Poincaré as well as Nietzsche, see Brush, *The Temperature of History*, as well as Milič Čapek, *The Philosophical Impact of Contemporary Physics* (New York: Van Nostrand-Reinhold, 1961). For a discussion of Poincaré, see the first part of Barry Gower, "Cassirer, Schlick, and 'Structural' Realism: The Philosophy of the Exact Sciences in the Background to Early Logical Empiricism," *British Journal for the History of Philosophy* 8(1) (2000), esp. 80–86, as well as Érdi, *Complexity Explained*. See also Eli Zahar, *Poincaré's Philosophy: From Conventionalism to Phenomenology* (La Salle, IL: Open Court, 2001), esp. ch. 4.
47. Alfred Wegener, "Die Entstehung der Kontinente," *Geologische Rundschau* 3 (1912).
48. In addition to Ronald Giere's central discussion of Wegener and revolution in geology in *Explaining Science* (Chicago, IL: University of Chicago Press, 1988), ch. 8, see Homer Eugene LeGrand, *Drifting Continents and Shifting Theories* (Cambridge: Cambridge University Press, 1989), 37–54, as well as, with specific reference to philosophy of science, Carol E. Cleland, "Methodological and Epistemic Differences between Historical Science and Experimental Science," *Philosophy of Science* 69 (September 2002).

ment of nuclear weapons,[49] but also given new interest in environmental philosophy, geology continues to be relevant for continental philosophy of science to this day.[50]

(ii) Chemistry contra *physics*

Like the reductionist tendency to translate continental philosophy into analytic philosophy, all other sciences are thought, at least in theory, to be amenable to a translation into the terms of physics. This presupposition is inherently problematic in chemistry, even though chemistry, unlike biology or psychology, can appear to be the most physics-like of the nonphysics natural sciences. This point is exemplified by the writings of a chemist whose work is increasingly relevant in the philosophy of chemistry today, Friedrich Adolf Paneth (1887–1958).[51]

49. The science of geology is essential to detecting covert nuclear tests. See John Cloud, "Imaging the World in a Barrel: CORONA and the Clandestine Convergence of the Earth Sciences," *Social Studies of Science* 31(2) (2001), and Paul Forman, "*Kausalität, Anschaulichkeit,* and *Individualität*, or How Cultural Values Prescribed the Character and the Lessons Ascribed to Quantum Mechanics," in *Society and Knowledge: Contemporary Perspectives in the Sociology of Knowledge*, Nico Stehr and Volker Meja (eds) (New Brunswick, NJ: Transaction Books, 1984). But also see Kai-Henrik Barth, "The Politics of Seismology," *Social Studies of Science* 33(5) (2003).
50. See Michael Aaron Dennis, "Earthly Matters: On the Cold War and the Earth Sciences," *Social Studies of Science* 33(5) (2003). For continental philosophies of geology, see Robert Frodeman, *Geo-Logic: Breaking Ground between Philosophy and the Earth Sciences* (Albany, NY: SUNY Press, 2003) and Thomas Raab and Robert Frodeman, "What is it Like to be a Geologist? A Phenomenology of Geology and its Epistemological Implications," *Philosophy and Geography* 5(1) (2002).
51. See Eric Scerri, *The Periodic Table: Its Story and its Significance* (Oxford: Oxford University Press, 2006) for a discussion of the conceptual and theoretical implications of Paneth's work for the philosophy of chemistry. Although the discussion to follow will highlight Paneth's work, we have already cited several chemists, notably Bachelard but also Duhem and Berthelot. To these names, Bensaud-Vincent adds Émile Meyerson (1859–1933), who began his career as a German trained chemist, and Hélène Metzger (1889–1944) ("Chemistry in the French Tradition," 634–5). For Bensaud-Vincent, the considerations of feminist philosophy and history of science are indispensable because philosophers and historians of science tend to overlook otherwise significant scientific work owing to a double prejudice against women that extends to those who lack the "prestigious diplomas" and not less (and this is the contrast as Bensaud-Vincent notes with Myerson) the crucial academic appointments that make all the difference for scholarly recognition (*ibid.*, 644). To Metzger's name in chemistry may be added in physics the name of Mileva Marič or Marity (1875–1948), Albert Einstein's first wife and his mathematical and scientific collaborator, controversially listed as the coauthor of his 1905 "Zur Elektrodynamik bewegter Körper," received by the Swiss journal *Annalen der Physik* on June 30, 1905, signed Einstein-Marity. Alberto Martínez argues the mainstream view *contra* the significance of Mileva Marity-Einstein, but cites the Russian physicist Abram Joffe's 1955 account in "Handling Evidence in History: The Case of Einstein's Wife," *School Science Review*

As a scientist, Paneth is known for his work on isotopes, collaborating in 1921 on the use of radium D as a tracer with the Hungarian chemist George de Hevesy (1885–1966).[52] Paneth is also well known for theorizing the natural scientific limit-concept of the chemical element as such. Paneth underlines the dangers of the reductionist tradition of representing chemistry on the model of physics, writing that "As a rule, chemistry is presented by the philosophers as a science which is well on the way to transforming itself into physics, and to which, therefore, the same considerations will apply in due course."[53] But where Paneth sought to make these points from the perspective of the philosophy of chemistry in the 1930s, response, as Jaap van Brackel details, has been either utterly absent or glacially slow in mainstream philosophy of science. Indeed, as Joachim Schummer argues, the "one-sided picture of science tailored to physics"[54] has often meant that analytic philosophers of science are unaware of the philosophy of chemistry in terms of the specific differences between chemistry and physics rather in the way they are generally unaware of the philosophy of biology or the philosophy of economics in spite of the important work of continental scientists and theorists such as Friedrich von Hayek and Michael Polanyi.[55]

Duhem, himself a physical chemist, would emphasize the exceptionality of chemistry in the same way, pointing to Kant's observation that "the theory of bodies can only become a science of nature when mathematics is applied to it."[56] The point of drawing a parallel with chemistry (like other sciences such as geology, as noted above) has been to underline the fact that analytic philosophers

---

86(316) (March 2005), 51–2. Inasmuch as the original manuscript has vanished, no resolution is in fact possible.

52. Hevesy, an independent researcher, won the Nobel Prize in Chemistry in 1943 for work that grew out of this earlier collaboration with Paneth. Michael Polanyi (1891–1976) was Hevesy's assistant in Budapest in 1919 before returning to Germany where he had studied physical chemistry.

53. See Friedrich A. Paneth, "The Epistemological Status of the Chemical Concept of Element," *Foundations of Chemistry* 5 (2003), 114. See Eric Scerri, "Realism, Reduction and the 'Intermediate Position," in *Of Minds and Molecules*, Nalini Bhushan and Stuart M. Rosenfeld (eds) (Oxford: Oxford University Press, 2000) as well as Scerri, "Normative and Descriptive Philosophy of Science and the Role of Chemistry," in *Philosophy of Chemistry: Synthesis of a New Discipline*, David Baird *et al.* (eds) (Dordrecht: Springer, 2006).

54. Joachim Schummer, "The Philosophy of Chemistry," *Endeavor* 27(1) (2003), 37. See further Christoph Liegener and Giuseppe Del Re, "Chemistry versus Physics, the Reduction Myth, and the Unity of Science," *Zeitschrift für allgemeine Wissenschaftstheorie* 18 (1987), as well as, for an instructively comprehensive account, Jaap Van Brakel, "On the Neglect of the Philosophy of Chemistry," *Foundations of Chemistry* 1 (1999).

55. For a discussion of Hayek's (1899–1992) and Polanyi's philosophies of science, see Peter Medawar, *The Art of the Soluble* (London: Methuen, 1967) and Philip Mirowski, *The Effortless Economy of Science* (Durham, NC: Duke University Press, 2004).

56. Pierre Duhem, *German Science: Some Reflections on German Science and German Virtues*, J. Lyon (trans.) (La Salle, IL: Open Court, 1991), 31. Duhem goes on to cite Adolphe Wurtz,

of science ignore both chemistry and the philosophy of chemistry rather in the way continental philosophy of science is similarly discounted.

But the parallel runs deeper. Paneth's own work is itself steeped in the early continental tradition of the philosophy of science. Thus Paneth's theoretical reflections on the nature of the chemical element cannot be read apart from his engagement with the epistemological reflections of Rickert's limit-concepts or the philosopher Eduard von Hartmann (1842–1906), or Meyerson's own chemical insights or Polanyi's, or of Wilhelm Wundt (1832–1920), the father of experimental psychology so important for cognitive science. Additional influences on Paneth's thinking include the theoretical insights of Hermann Weyl (1885–1955) and the physicalist and phenomenological reflections of the 1902 Nobel prize-winning chemist Emil Fischer (1852–1919).

In his "On the Epistemological Status of the Chemical Concept of Element," Paneth repudiates the reduction of chemistry to physics for the very phenomenological and critical reason that the aim of physics is ultimately to reduce "sensory qualities to quantitative determinations."[57] Like Duhem, Paneth cites Kant's mathematical conventionality as justifying the exclusion of chemistry as a science. By contrast, Paneth argues that inasmuch as "chemistry is essentially non-mathematical,"[58] it was the "chemist, unhampered by mathematics or indeed almost any theory, who discovered the majority of all chemical elements on the basis of the most primitive *concept* of substance!"[59] The effectively unchanged basis of chemistry, that is, the basic schema of the periodic table itself in the wake of relativity and quantum theory, offers a corroboration, as Paneth underscores: "already in the seventies of the last century, the elements had been arranged by the chemists into a scheme, the so-called 'natural system of the elements'"[60] – a system thus unchanged in its character by the innovations of twentieth-century atomic theory.

Dictionnaire de chimie: Pure et appliquée (Paris: Librairie Hachette, 1874): "Chemistry is a French science."

57. Paneth, "The Epistemological Status," 16.
58. *Ibid.*, 118. In a related but ultimately different point, some philosophers of science have argued that the difference between chemists and physicists can be found in the central role of the "thought experiment" in physics just where it is conspicuously absent in chemistry.
59. *Ibid.*, emphasis added. See Jaap Van Brakel, "Chemistry as the Science of the Transformation of Substances," *Synthese* 111 (1997).
60. Scerri notes that the French geologist Alexandre-Émile Béguyer de Chancourtois (1820–86) was the first to propose a periodic arrangement of the elements according to atomic weights. Others include the English chemist John Alexander Reina Newlands (1837–98) and the German chemist Julius Lothar Meyer (1830–95) in addition to Dmitri Mendeleev (1834–1907). Mendeleev is celebrated as the first to use the table to predict elements as yet undiscovered.

Speaking here of substance as either basic (nonobservable, theoretical, or, in some philosophic expressions, constructed) or simple (observable), Paneth seeks to explain the notion of an element as such: "the whole body of chemical theory lies in the assumption that the substances which produce the phenomenon of 'simple substances' serve in the quality-less, objectively real sphere of nature as 'basic substances.'"[61] Rather than progressing toward a more mathematized chemical science on the model of physics, one would do well to return to the philosophical origins of the concept of the "elemental" (and Paneth means such a return in earnest as he invokes the ancient atomists but also the Epicurean notion of "mixing"), in order to avoid the dangers of equivocation when speaking of either the permanence of substance as such or the signal chemical and even alchemical achievement that is the "creation of a new substance by mixing two known ones."[62]

In other words, chemical synthesis generates new compounds, and what we understand by "substance" (here regarded as much philosophically as scientifically) matters for a phenomenological understanding of such new compounds. If Paneth refers to Karl Joel's 1906 allusion to the "genesis of nature philosophy in the spirit of mysticism,"[63] Bensaud-Vincent reminds us that "the challenge posed by chemistry is that its irrationals are incorporated in matter: they are everywhere, in a glass of sugared water or in the kitchen salt that we use every day."[64]

61. Paneth, "The Epistemological Status," 130. For a discussion of the difference between Paneth's transcendental approach and František Wald's Machian phenomenalism, see Klaus Ruthenberg, "Chemistry Without Atoms," in *Stuff: The Nature of Chemical Substances*, Klaus Ruthenberg and Jaap van Brakel (eds) (Würzburg: Königshausen & Neuman, 2008).
62. Paneth, "The Epistemological Status," 123. Bensaud-Vincent cites Duhem's discussion of the very idea of a new chemical compound by way of his revival of the Aristotelian term "mixt" and other related concepts *contra* "the prevailing atomist and mechanistic views" ("Chemistry in the French Tradition," 637). Thus Duhem, in *Le Mixte et la combinaison chimique*, argues that in "this mixt, the elements no longer have any actual existence. They exist there only potentially because on destruction the mixt can regenerate them" (cited in Bensaud-Vincent, "Chemistry in the French Tradition," 637).
63. Paneth, "The Epistemological Status," 24.
64. Bensaud-Vicent, "Chemistry in the French Tradition," 646. The distinction between physics and chemistry, a political order of rank, seems to have made all the political, theoretical difference for the scientific estimation and investigation of the first reports of cold fusion inasmuch as these reports were made by scientists who happened to be not physicists but chemists. Mainstream philosophy of science continues to regard cold fusion as an example either of pseudo-science or straightforward fraud. See Jean-Paul Biberian, "Condensed Matter Nuclear Science (Cold Fusion): An Update," *International Journal of Nuclear Energy Science and Technology* 3(1) (2007).

IV. THE THINGS THEMSELVES: HUSSERL'S PHENOMENOLOGICAL PHILOSOPHY OF SCIENCE

We have noted that Husserl's philosophy of science must be set into the wider scope of Hilbert's foundational program. For Husserl, this is the concern of philosophy as a rigorous science but that is only inasmuch as philosophy is concerned with truth (and not only with what is upheld as what is as good as truth).[65] Indeed, Husserl was associated with nearly every key mathematician of the day, from Georg Cantor (1845–1918), Husserl's friend and colleague at the University of Halle between 1890 and 1910,[66] and Gottlob Frege to Hilbert, Weyl, L. E. J. Brouwer, and Gödel.[67] For this reason, Husserl's *Philosophy of Arithmetic,* which first appeared in 1891, is key to the period of continental philosophy of science under discussion.[68] Heelan uses both Husserl's and Heidegger's reflections to develop a philosophical reflection on objectivity, particularly in Niels Bohr's and Heisenberg's theoretical interpretations, thereby suggesting that phenomenology offers an indispensable route to a clarification of quantum mechanics. Others have highlighted Einstein's role in Husserl's philosophy of science, while yet others emphasize the coordination of Poincaré with Husserl's criticisms of

65. See, however, on Husserl and pragmatism, the work of Richard Cobb-Stevens and others.

66. It has been argued that Cantor was an important influence on Husserl; see Clair Ortiz Hill, "Did Georg Cantor Influence Edmund Husserl?" *Synthese* 113 (1997) and David Woodruff Smith, "What is 'Logical' in Husserl's Logical Investigations? The Copenhagen Interpretation," in *One Hundred Years of Phenomenology: Husserl's Logical Investigations Revisited*, Dan Zahavi and Frederik Stjernfelt (eds) (Dordrecht: Kluwer, 2002). But see also David Bell, "A Brentanian Philosophy of Arithmetic," *Brentano Studien: Internationales Jahrbuch der Franz Brentano Forschung* 2 (1989), who argues that Husserl was principally influenced by Brentano. Alain Badiou likewise alludes to this influence with his own claim that Husserl reads Galilean science on a par with (post-Cantor) set theory in *Being and Event*, Oliver Feltham (trans.) (London: Continuum, 2005), 3.

67. Even Einstein is said to have been tempted to name his theory of relativity "*Invariantentheorie*," in an explicit echo of Husserl's phenomenological method; see Richard Tieszen, *Phenomenology, Logic, and the Philosophy of Mathematics* (Cambridge: Cambridge University Press, 2005), 87.

68. In addition to Heelan's *Quantum Mechanics and Objectivity* (The Hague: Martinus Nijhoff, 1965) (which remains important for its emphasis on the crucial role of continental philosophers in their theoretical engagement with scientists, and thereby with Heelan's analysis of the hermeneutics of natural science within the experimental practice of the sciences themselves), and his *Space-Perception and the Philosophy of Science* (Berkeley, CA: University of California Press, 1983), a book on, among other things, Husserl and the metrics of vision from Luneberg to Marr, see Thomas Ryckman, *The Reign of Relativity: Philosophy in Physics 1915–1925* (Oxford: Oxford University Press, 2005) for an account attuned to the history of science (on Husserl and Weyl as well as Einstein, Schlick, Reichenbach, and Eddington); see also Tieszen, *Phenomenology, Logic, and the Philosophy of Mathematics* (on Husserl and Gödel as well as on Cantor and Brouwer, Heyting and Poincaré).

logicism and formalism.[69] Where Ryckman and Clair Ortiz Hill point to the decades Husserl spent in Halle (and the importance of Cantor), Heelan highlights, as do others, the significance of Husserl's tenure in Göttingen during the dynamic years of Hilbert's foundational program in mathematics.[70]

Echoing René Descartes's remark in his *Discourse on Method*, Einstein famously quipped that we should attend to what scientists do, not to what they say. Richard Tieszen thus commends the value of Husserl's "philosophy of mathematics" as it bears witness to the attempt "to do justice to mathematics as it is actually given and practiced."[71] Such a coordinated reference to the history and practice of science exemplifies both phenomenological and hermeneutic approaches to the philosophy of science, and we have seen its relevance for Nietzsche. In this spirit, Ryckman can refer to Husserl's claim to be the "true positivist,"[72] a claim that Steven Crowell likewise cites as being "only" slightly ironic.[73]

For Descartes, as for the entire Enlightenment order of philosophizing about cognition and perception, what the mind knows is mind. Thought must be submitted to logical analysis to gain any sure knowledge of it, which leaves the gap between mind and world, thought and object. What Eugene Wigner (1902 –95) would describe in a later recollection of this early period, and with patent reference to both Hilbert and Gödel, as the "unreasonable effectiveness" of mathematics in the natural sciences reflects a number of theoretically (if not to be sure "effectively" or "practically") unbridgeable chasms. While this is the traditional issue of objective versus subjective logic for both Husserl and Heidegger, Husserl's account of intentionality sidesteps just this separation insofar as "the

69. Ryckman, *The Reign of Relativity*, argues that Husserl, via Weyl, was an influence on Einstein. In addition to Tieszen, *Phenomenology, Logic, and the Philosophy of Mathematics*, for a discussion of Brouwer and Weyl in this particular context, see Günther Neumann, *Die phänomenologische Frage nach dem Ursprung der mathematisch-naturwissenschaftlichen Raumauffassung bei Husserl und Heidegger* (Berlin: Duncker & Humblot, 1999), 23–33. In this same connection, see Zahar, *Poincaré's Philosophy*, 216ff. Indeed, Zahar argues that Husserl's notion of intentionality clarifies Poincaré's "constructivist *yet* anti-psychologistic conception of the foundations of mathematics" (*ibid.*, 206).
70. See Patrick A. Heelan, "Husserl, Hilbert and the Critique of Galilean Science," in *Edmund Husserl and the Phenomenological Tradition*, R. Sokolowski (ed.) (Washington, DC: The Catholic University of America Press, 1988) and Philip Buckley, "Husserl's Göttingen Years and the Genesis of a Theory of Community," in *Reinterpreting the Political*, Lenore Langsdorf *et al.* (eds) (Albany, NY: SUNY Press, 1998). See also Martin Eger, "Hermeneutics as an Approach to Science, Parts I and II," *Science and Education* 2 (1993). The same viewpoint recurs in Norwood Russell Hanson, *Patterns of Discovery: An Inquiry into the Conceptual Foundations of Science* (Cambridge: Cambridge University Press, 1958), a parallel Heelan traces in *Quantum Mechanics and Objectivity*.
71. Tieszen, *Phenomenology, Logic*, 50.
72. Ryckman, *The Reign of Relativity*, 15.
73. See Steven Galt Crowell, *Husserl, Heidegger, and the Space of Meaning: Paths Towards Transcendental Phenomenology* (Evanston, IL: Northwestern University Press, 2001), 46.

intentional object of a presentation is the same as its actual object."[74] What is known by any intentional act is the intentional object or "noematic" correlate, hence the *directive* direction of Husserl's classic cry: "*zu den Sachen selbst*" (to the things themselves).[75]

Following the error of what Husserl calls "Galilean science" and Rickert had named "positivist" science, the worldview of modern science inaugurates the opposition between pragmaticism and realism that still stands for many as the central problem of the philosophy of science today. Modern science limits or reduces reality to its scientifically measurable, calculable, or quantifiable properties, taking reality here in the common-sense (but still counter-intuitive) meaning of *scientific realism*. As Husserl saw it, the technological, practical, and theoretical mathematical projects articulating the essence of modern science are fundamentally rather than incidentally opposed to one another. Galilean science (Heidegger's *calculative* rationality) *substitutes* "the mathematically substructed world of identities for the only real world,"[76] and in this way, so Husserl suggests, Galilean science itself comes to stand in the place of the world "that is actually given through perception … [that is,] our everyday life-world."[77]

The Galilean distinction between primary and secondary properties privileges the measurable as primary, so that what began as a convenience led with Descartes to the division of subjective experience (mind) and objective world (body). And in the end, only the objective or measurable world became the real world, with the subjective and leftover worlds of "meaning" and "value," "mind" or "spirit," correspondingly eliminated or "reduced" to the domain of the unreal as mere phenomena. As Husserl writes in *The Crisis of European Sciences and Transcendental Phenomenology*, the scientific worldview "excluded in principle precisely the questions which man, given over in our unhappy times to the

74. Edmund Husserl, *Logical Investigations*, J. N. Findlay (trans.) (New York: Humanities Press, 1970), vol. 2, 595.

75. In this way, Husserl extended the concept of the life-world beyond its Romantic origins to connect the worlds of science and mathematics to the world we inhabit, a project continued in Heidegger's philosophical reflections on the worldview of science and technology and further revitalized and ultimately radicalized in Maurice Merleau-Ponty; see Heelan's discussion of Merleau-Ponty and Husserl in *Space-Perception and the Philosophy of Science*, and for a discussion of Merleau-Ponty and Derrida with respect to Husserl, see Leonard Lawlor, "The Legacy of Husserl's '*Ursprung der Geometrie*': The Limits of Phenomenology in Merleau-Ponty and Derrida," in *Merleau-Ponty's Reading of Husserl*, Ted Toadvine and Lester Embree (eds) (Dordrecht: Kluwer, 2003). Florence Caeymaex also traces the connection between Merleau-Ponty and Husserl via Bergson in her *Sartre, Merleau-Ponty, Bergson: Les Phénoménologies existentialistes et leur héritage bergsonien* (Hildesheim: Olms, 2005).

76. Edmund Husserl, *The Crisis of European Sciences and Transcendental Phenomenology: An Introduction to Phenomenological Philosophy*, David Carr (trans.) (Evanston, IL: Northwestern University Press, 1970), 48–9.

77. *Ibid.*, 49.

most portentous upheavals, finds the most burning: questions of the meaning or meaninglessness of the whole of this hard existence."[78] The greatest threat for Husserl is thus the devaluation of consciousness, the loss of spirit or meaning.

V. HEIDEGGER: HERMENEUTIC PHENOMENOLOGY OF SCIENCE

If, as Theodore Kisiel argues, "the Husserlian approach to science is strikingly evident in the early pages of *Being and Time*,"[79] Joseph J. Kockelmans (1923–2008) emphasizes that "in most of his publications Heidegger deals explicitly with problems which pertain specifically to the realm of philosophy of science."[80] Like Nietzsche, Heidegger argues that beyond theoretical reflection or scientific analysis, philosophy is an explicitly active questioning, especially so in the case of the philosophy of science and modern technology. It is in terms of the importance of reflection in philosophy that Heidegger argues that "all science is perhaps only a servant with respect to philosophy."[81] The critical spirit of this early account of the specific difference of philosophical reflection and scientific theorizing finds its most famous expression in the later Heidegger's provocative dictum "science does not think,"[82] a claim that is already to be heard in his 1927 *Being and Time*: "ontological inquiry is more primordial or original than the ontic inquiry of the positive sciences."[83]

Opposing sense-oriented reflection [*Besinnung*] to the calculative project of Western technologically articulated and advancing science, Heidegger varies

78. *Ibid.*
79. Theodore Kisiel, "Science, Phenomenology and the Thinking of Being," in *Phenomenology and the Natural Sciences*, Joseph J. Kockelmans and Theodore J. Kisiel (eds) (Evanston, IL: Northwestern University Press, 1970), 168. Kisiel here goes on to parallel Heidegger's *Being and Time* with Husserl's *Logical Investigations*, where Heidegger characterizes science as "the coherent totality of proofs which ground propositions" (*ibid.*).
80. Joseph J. Kockelmans, "The Era of the World-as-Picture," in Kockelmans and Kisiel, *Phenomenology and the Natural Sciences*, 184.
81. Martin Heidegger, *The Fundamental Concepts of Metaphysics: World, Finitude, Solitude*, William McNeill and Nicholas Walker (trans.) (Bloomington, IN: Indiana University Press, 1995), 5; Tieszen, *Phenomenology, Logic, and the Philosophy of Mathematics*, emphasizes the importance for Gödel of this emphasis on the role of philosophy, which Gödel shared with both Husserl and Heidegger.
82. Martin Heidegger, *What is Called Thinking?* F. D. Wieck and J. G. Gray (trans.) (New York: Harper & Row, 1968), 8ff. For discussion, see Dmitri Ginev, *A Passage to the Idea for a Hermeneutic Philosophy of Science* (Amsterdam: Rodopi, 1997), as well as the contributions to B. Babich (ed.), *Hermeneutic Philosophy of Science, Van Gogh's Eyes, and God: Essays in Honor of Patrick A. Heelan, SJ* (Dordrecht: Kluwer, 2002), and Jean-Michel Salanskis, "Die Wissenschaft denkt nicht," *Tekhnema* 2 (1995).
83. Martin Heidegger, *Being and Time*, J. Macquarrie and E. Robinson (trans.) (New York: Harper & Row, 1962), 11.

but he does not alter his early discussion of the relation between science and philosophy in *Being and Time*, writing that "all scientific thought is merely a derived form of philosophical thinking."[84] With this claim, Heidegger maintains that with respect to science, philosophy "is prior in rank."[85] In *Being and Time*, this priority is characterized as a "*productive* logic"[86] that leaps ahead "into some area of Being, discloses it for the first time, in the constitution of its Being, and, after thus arriving at the structures within it, makes these available to the positive sciences as transparent assignments for their inquiry."[87] Heidegger thus opposes the creatively foundational activity of philosophic reflection to the then popular articulations of epistemological investigations into the sciences of his era as the kind of "logic" (Heidegger sets this off in quotes) following after science, "'limping along in its wake,' investigating the status of [any given] science as it chances to find it in order to discover its 'method.'"[88]

"What is decisive" for Heidegger – who here writes in Husserl's critical foundational spirit – in the development of mathematical physics is "the mathematical project of nature itself" inasmuch as the project "discovers in advance something constantly objectively present (matter) and opens the horizon for the scientific perspective on its quantitatively definable moments (motion, force, location, and time)."[89] The "founding" of "factual science" is "possible only because the researcher understood that there are in principle no 'bare facts,'"[90] that, in other words, the material project of nature must be given in advance, *a priori*. Only then is it possible for a science to be "*capable* of a crisis in its basic concepts."[91]

Heidegger, who remained committed to phenomenology throughout his life, emphasizes that beyond any superficially obvious call "to the things themselves,"[92] phenomenology "presupposed life."[93] To understand Heidegger here requires a specific and hermeneutic attention to the biological transformation that was then under way. Including and exceeding Claude Bernard's *milieu intérieur*, as the evolution beyond Cartesian mechanism, Heidegger's reference was critically ecological, radically environmental: "Life is that kind of reality which is in the

84. Heidegger, *The Fundamental Concepts of Metaphysics*, 26.
85. *Ibid.* For a reading of Heidegger's discussion of philosophy and science in the 1930s, see my "Heideggers 'Beiträge' zwischen politische Kritik und die Frage nach der Technik," Harald Seubert (trans.), in *Eugenik und die Zukunft*, Stefan Sorgner *et al.* (eds) (Freiburg: Karl Alber, 2006).
86. Heidegger, *Being and Time*, 30, emphasis added.
87. *Ibid.*, 31.
88. *Ibid.*, translation modified.
89. *Ibid.*, 362.
90. *Ibid.*
91. *Ibid.*, 29.
92. Heidegger, "Wilhelm Dilthey's Research," 160.
93. *Ibid.*, 162.

world and indeed in such a way that it has a world. Every living creature has its environing world not as something extant next to it but as something that is there [*da ist*] for it as disclosed, uncovered."[94] And in 1925, Heidegger emphasized that "for a primitive animal, the world can be very simple," explaining that we run the risk of missing "the essential thing here if we don't see that the animal has a world."[95] Heidegger's original continuum of complexity and/or simplicity must be added to contemporary readings of Heidegger's subsequent discussions of the world-poverty of the animal in terms of *indigence*.

In his 1929–30 lecture course, *The Fundamental Concepts of Metaphysics*, Heidegger alluded to the work of Hans Driesch (1867–1941), who theorized chemical gradients in embryological development.[96] In that same course, Heidegger also invokes the theoretical biologist Jakob von Uexküll's (1864–1944) 1909 expression of the "*Umwelt*," citing the Czech biologist Emanuel Rádl (1873–1942) on the significance of animal phototropism[97] in order to emphasize the gulf (*Abgrund*) between human and animal,[98] but also as a biologistic contrast to the Cartesian tendency of modern scientific biology to define both animals and human beings in mechanistic terms. This tendency remains in modern experimental biology, underlying its reliance on "models," specifically in animal experimentation.[99] Here Heidegger reprises his hermeneutico-phenomenological case for the interpretive ontology of the human being as an animal bound to world-invention, or what Heidegger called, in an ecological modality, world-making.[100] In this way, Heidegger had earlier cited Nietzsche's perspectival sense of the human as the "yet to be finished animal."[101] It is in this projective, that is, yet-unfinished but to-be-finished, sense that "The world that is closest to us is one of practical concern. The environing world [*Umwelt*] and its objects are in space, but the space of the world is not that of geometry."[102] Historically, the mechanistic conception of life would return to triumph over the notion of "vital movement" nascent in Driesch (although it is an error to reduce Driesch's concerns to sheer vitalism, as is evident in his emphasis on electro-

94. *Ibid.*, 163.
95. *Ibid.*
96. Heidegger, *The Fundamental Concepts of Metaphysics*, 261ff. Driesch published his theory of organic development using the example of sea urchin development in 1894.
97. *Ibid.*, 242ff., esp. 244.
98. *Ibid.*, 264.
99. For a discussion of the epistemological implications of experimentation, see Shiv Visvanathan, "On the Annals of the Laboratory State," in *Science, Hegemony, and Violence: A Requiem for Modernity*, Ashis Nandy (ed.) (Oxford: Oxford University Press, 1988). And for models and complexity in environmental science, see, again, Pilkey and Pilkey-Jarvis, *Useless Arithmetic.*
100. Heidegger, *The Fundamental Concepts of Metaphysics*, 274.
101. Nietzsche, *Beyond Good and Evil*, sec. 62 (KSA, vol. 5, 81).
102. Heidegger, "Wilhelm Dilthey's Research," 163.

chemical gradients), whereas Heidegger explored the living trajectory of life as opposed to its "calculable" course.[103]

Heidegger's focus on life also recurs in his reference to chemistry in 1929 in order to speak of the biological and organic sciences, to underline how little is said about "the living being" when we "define it in terms of the organic as opposed to the inorganic."[104] Echoing Nietzsche's contrastive differentiation of reductively identical kinds in chemistry,[105] Heidegger reminds us to consider the example of "organic and inorganic chemistry" precisely inasmuch as "organic chemistry is anything but a science of the organic in the sense of the living being as such. It is called organic chemistry precisely because the organic in the sense of the living being remains inaccessible to it in principle."[106]

Heidegger began *Being and Time* with a reference to the crisis in the sciences and arguing for the importance of philosophical reflection. Each particular science articulates its own regional ontology in terms of its basic constitution (*Grundverfassung*),[107] beginning with the example of the foundational controversy of mathematics in his (and still in our own) day, "between the formalists and the intuitionists."[108] Thus Heidegger adds, in good Husserlian fashion, that what is at stake in this debate turns on "obtaining and securing the primary way of access to what are supposedly the objects"[109] of mathematical science. Heidegger articulates the same foundational revolution in physics as he invokes the theory of relativity. This means that science begins with or alongside its own fundamental concepts, and inquiry into these foundations is not then a matter of scientific research, for such research is possible only on the basis of such concepts. Hence philosophical inquiry, or what Heidegger calls "ontological inquiry," can only be "more primordial, as over against the ontical inquiry of the positive sciences."[110]

For Heidegger, philosophy is, and can be, in Husserl's terminology, the science of science not because of a venerable tradition of so regarding philosophy but

103. See Keith Ansell-Pearson, *Viroid Life: Perspectives on Nietzsche and the Transhuman Condition* (London: Routledge, 1997) for an innovative exploration of this theme with reference to Bergson and others.

104. Heidegger, *The Fundamental Concepts of Metaphysics*, 212.

105. Nietzsche repudiates the notion that there is "nothing unchanging in chemistry" as "a scholastic prejudice. We have dragged in the unchanging, my physicist friends, deriving it from metaphysics as always. To assert that diamond, graphite, and coal are identical is to read off the facts naively from the surface. Why? Merely because no loss in substance can be shown on the scales?" (KSA, vol. 13, 374).

106. Heidegger, *The Fundamental Concepts of Metaphysics*, 212.

107. Heidegger, *Being and Time*, 29.

108. *Ibid.*, 30. Cf. 121–2.

109. *Ibid.*

110. *Ibid.*, 31. Cf. 91.

because specifically philosophical research must and "*can*," as Heidegger claims, "run ahead of the positive sciences."[111] Thus, as Heidegger clarifies this point, the contribution of Kant's *Critique of Pure Reason* "lies in what it has contributed towards the working out of what belongs to any Nature whatsoever."[112] Rather than epistemology, Kant's "transcendental logic is an *a priori* logic for the subject matter of that region of Being called 'Nature.'"[113]

In this productive, disclosing sense, which Heidegger also expresses as the constitutional eventuality of aletheic truth as discovery or "uncovering," the scientist effectively opens up the truth of nature. In the aletheic context of such a specifically scientific disclosure, it can be said that *before* "Newton's laws were discovered, they were not 'true.'"[114] By way of Dasein's "being in the truth,"[115] the laws of Newtonian physics only first "became true." "Newton's laws, the principle of contradiction, any truth whatever – these are true only as long as Dasein *is*."[116] But to say this is also to say that through "Newton the laws became true: and with them entities became accessible in themselves to Dasein. Once entities have been uncovered, they show themselves as the entities which beforehand they already were. Such uncovering is the kind of Being which belongs to 'truth.'"[117]

VI. GÖDEL: MATHEMATICS, TIME, AND THE COLLAPSE OF DIALOGUE

At the outset, we noted the importance of Hilbert's 1900 program to set mathematics on the "completed" path of a science, expressed as Hilbert's "conviction (which every mathematician shares, but which no one has as yet supported by a proof) that every definite mathematical problem must necessarily be susceptible of an exact settlement."[118] And we have already noted that thirty years later, Hilbert's conviction would be proven unfounded by a young mathematician who initially thought himself to be taking up Hilbert's program.[119] As is already evident in the title of Gödel's 1931 first incompleteness theorem, "On Formally Undecidable Propositions of Principia Mathematica and Related Systems, "all consistent formulations of such formal systems as number theory include unde-

111. *Ibid.*, 30.
112. *Ibid.*, 31.
113. *Ibid.* See P. Kerzberg, *Kant et la nature* (Paris: Les Belles-Lettres, 1999).
114. Heidegger, *Being and Time*, 269.
115. *Ibid.*
116. *Ibid.*
117. *Ibid.*, translation modified.
118. Hilbert, "Mathematical Problems," 444.
119. Although Gödel and Hilbert never met (this is not surprising given the difference in age and, indeed, prestige), they were not unconnected given Gödel's friendship with Hilbert's assistant, Paul Bernays (1888–1977).

cidable statements (*unentscheidbare Sätze*).[120] As such, Gödel's incompleteness theorem undermines Hilbert's ideal of axiomatic consummation. The second incompleteness theorem states that the consistency of arithmetic cannot be proved in arithmetic itself or on its own terms, using the methods of first-order predicate calculus. As Jean Cavaillès (1903–44) has articulated Gödel's second theorem, "noncontradiction of a theory can be demonstrated *only* within a more powerful theory."[121] But this means that consistency can be proven only if the formal system is inconsistent, and insofar as one needs a higher-order or more powerful system in order to prove consistency, this too falls short of the foundationalist ideal of a complete axiomatic system.

The significance of Gödel's work for mathematics and logic has been widely acknowledged. As Cavaillès[122] notes, the "result of Gödel's work is well-known: every theory containing the arithmetic of whole numbers is necessarily non-saturated. A proposition can be asserted within them which is neither the consequence of the axioms nor in contradiction with them."[123] Which is to say, no formal system can be both consistent and complete. And beyond his engagement with Hilbert and contributions to mathematics, there is also a case to be made for the relevance of Gödel's incompleteness theorem for Heisenberg's quantum mechanics and the most promising discussions look to John von Neumann (1903–57) and his quantum measurement theory.[124] Yet while Gödel's contributions are readily acknowledged by many, there is significant debate in the literature regarding Gödel's *philosophical* accomplishments in the field of logic, and many scholars like to claim that it is easy to overstate the consequences of Gödel's incompleteness theorems.[125]

This is noteworthy because beyond his work in mathematical logic, Gödel's ambitions were philosophical. As he wrote to the phenomenologically oriented mathematician and philosopher Gian-Carlo Rota (1932–99), "Transcendental

120. Kurt Gödel, "Über formal unentscheidbare Sätze der Principia Mathematica und verwandter Systeme I," *Monatshefte für Mathematik* 149(1) [1931] (September 2006): 1–29.

121. Jean Cavaillès, "On Logic and the Theory of Science," in Kockelmans and Kisiel, *Phenomenology and the Natural Sciences*, 406, emphasis added.

122. For general context including a specific discussion of Cavaillès, see Alan D. Schrift, *Twentieth-Century French Philosophy: Key Themes and Thinkers* (Malden, MA: Blackwell, 2006), 36ff.; for discussion including Husserl and axiomatization, see Michael Roubach, "Heidegger, Science, and the Mathematical Age," *Science in Context* 10(1) (1997). Lawlor also discusses Cavaillès in *Derrida and Husserl: The Basic Problem of Phenomenology* (Bloomington, IN: Indiana University Press, 2002), 62ff.

123. Cavaillès, "On Logic and the Theory of Science," 405.

124. J. W. Dawson, Jr., "What Hath Gödel Wrought," *Synthese* 114 (1998).

125. The one unifying characteristic of both popular and more recondite books on Gödel seems to be impatience with other treatments of Gödel in philosophical literature, cultural studies, and in other books on Gödel and mathematics.

philosophy … carried through, would be nothing more nor less than Kant's critique of pure reason transformed into an exact science."[126] In particular, Gödel's interest in time was expressed in the same Kantian spirit, as Gödel believed, in Palle Yourgrau's paraphrase, that "the attempt to discover what is fundamental about our thinking about time can receive no assistance from physics which, he argued, combines concepts without analyzing them."[127] We have instead to "reconstruct the original nature of our thinking."[128]

It is regrettable, but unremarkable, given the differences between Anglo-American and continental styles of philosophizing, that throughout his life Gödel himself would be excluded from mainstream debate on the philosophical reflections on the problems of physics and mathematical logic, and especially on the philosophy of time. Yourgrau outlines one such example in detail: Gödel's contribution to Paul Schilpp's 1949 *Albert Einstein: Philosopher-Scientist* was judged to be mistaken, a judgment Yourgrau argues as seemingly made "on principle" insofar as the presumption of error was not the *result of* but made in *advance of* debate.[129] Even in the long course of the more than half century of scholarship to follow, Yourgrau observes, "Gödel's contribution to the Schilpp volume had almost no impact on the community of philosophers."[130] In his view, Gödel was judged to lack the credentials needed to theorize as a philosopher and, as a consequence, Gödel's reflective efforts were denied a proper reception, a refusal that continues within analytic philosophy to this day.[131]

The phenomenon of such academic exclusion is the common, all-too-political, academic tendency to refuse what is not expressed in the style of the "profession": just as Gödel failed to employ the then-current writing style of analytic philosophy, and failed to refer to the "right" names in American analytic philosophy, his own contributions to philosophy were refused access to the conversation. In this sense, Gödel stands as an example, one among many, of the closed nature of certain domains within academic discourse and the unwillingness to allow dissenting voices and voices coming from other traditions to have a share in the conversation of philosophy. Sadly, this has been as true of philosophy of science as it has been in the more "obviously" politicized discourses of social, ethical, and political philosophy.

126. Citation in Yourgrau, *A World without Time*, 107.
127. *Ibid*., cf. Heidegger, *History of the Concept of Time*.
128. Yourgrau, *A World without Time*, 170.
129. *Ibid*., 119–20.
130. *Ibid*.
131. *Ibid*., 121.

11

LUDWIG WITTGENSTEIN

John Fennell and Bob Plant

> [T]he nature of men, however various and subject to change, must possess some generic character if it is to be called human at all. This holds … of differences between entire cultures. There is a limit beyond which we can no longer understand what a given creature is at; what kinds of rules it follows in its behavior; what its gestures mean. In such situations, when the possibility of communication breaks down, we speak of derangement, of incomplete humanity.
>
> (Isaiah Berlin, *The Crooked Timber of Humanity*)[1]

Brilliant, intense, socially inept, and preoccupied with his sins, Wittgenstein continues to nourish our appetite for tales of tortured genius.[2] Likewise, his fragmented, agonistic prose has generated considerable literary interest. Nevertheless, these biographical and stylistic peculiarities are not without philosophical import, for they reflect the awkward terrain of his "long and involved journeyings."[3] Wittgenstein's various journeyings have, of course, impacted

1. Isaiah Berlin, *The Crooked Timber of Humanity*, Henry Hardy (ed.) (London: John Murray, 1990), 80.
2. Ludwig Wittgenstein (April 26, 1889–April 28, 1951; born in Vienna; died in Cambridge) was educated at the Technische Hochschule, Berlin (1906–8), the University of Manchester (1908–11), and the University of Cambridge (1911–13, 1929–30). His influences included Boltzmann, Frege, Hertz, Kierkegaard, Kraus, Loos, Moore, Russell, Schopenhauer, Spengler, Straffa, Tolstoy, and Weininger, and he held appointments at the University of Cambridge (1930–36, 1939–41, 1944–47).
3. Ludwig Wittgenstein, *Philosophical Investigations*, G. E. M. Anscombe and Rush Rhees (eds), G. E. M. Anscombe (trans.) (Oxford: Basil Blackwell, 1953), ix. Hereafter cited as PI followed by the page or section number.

most conspicuously on the development of the analytic philosophical tradition. But even here his influence has not been unanimously welcomed. Indeed, Wittgenstein's later descriptive, therapeutic approach has often been seen as a lamentable diversion for academic (and now highly professionalized) philosophy. Although many analytic philosophers continue to appeal to "ordinary language," few, if any, think that philosophical questions are really grammatical confusions waiting to be "dissolved … like a lump of sugar in water."[4] Instead, Wittgenstein's writings have been excavated for serviceable arguments and theses. Given that his later work was never intended for publication, this interpretive methodology has obvious pedagogical advantages, but only by understating Wittgenstein's broader metaphilosophical aims: namely, the dissolution of philosophy itself.

What then about the relation between Wittgenstein and so-called continental philosophy? This is even less clear. For while he mentions Hegel, Schopenhauer, Kierkegaard, and Heidegger, these allusions remain tangential; Dostoevsky and Tolstoy were closer to Wittgenstein's heart. Moreover, he has received little sustained attention from continental thinkers. Despite all of this, we are going to outline a few possible correlations between Wittgenstein and the continental tradition; specifically, Nietzsche, Schutz, Lyotard, and Levinas. (Obviously, these correlations are not exhaustive.) Before doing so, however, we shall begin by laying out some of the basic theses of the *Tractatus Logico-Philosophicus* that provide the background for introducing the contrasting set of concepts central to Wittgenstein's later philosophy; namely, "language games," "grammatical investigation," "forms of life," and "family resemblance."

I. THE *TRACTATUS*

One way of understanding the profound shift in Wittgenstein's thought from the *Tractatus* to *Philosophical Investigations* and *On Certainty* is to see his account of linguistic meaning as transitioning from the former to the latter notions in the following series of oppositions: abstract–concrete, general–particular, one–many, monism–pluralism, theory–practice, necessary–contingent, essence–accident, individual–social, atomism–holism, logical-analysis–grammatical-description, and theoretical–therapeutic. That is, if the *Tractatus* conceives of linguistic meaning as atomistic, abstract, and general, as necessarily having a monistic essence expressible in the pure, crystalline (PI §108) formalism of first-order logic, *Philosophical Investigations* and *On Certainty*, by describing the

4. Ludwig Wittgenstein, *Philosophical Occasions 1912–1951*, James Klagge and Alfred Nordmann (eds) (Indianapolis, IN: Hackett, 1993), 183. Hereafter cited as PO followed by the page number.

multifarious ways in which language is concretely used in the context of purposive activity, present a pluralist, particular-case-oriented, context-specific, and practical action-embedded account.

The *Tractatus* was, at least on Wittgenstein's own reckoning, the culmination of the project of early analytic philosophy started by Frege and Russell. The basic assumption of the program is that natural language is a deceptive medium that conceals the true meaning of its sentences and sub-sentential expressions, and in so doing is responsible for a host of philosophical problems, such as the meaningfulness of nonreferring singular terms, the possibility of true negative existential claims, the informativeness of true contingent identity statements, and so on. What is needed is logical analysis (thus the name "*analytic* philosophy"), which involves parsing the sentences of ordinary language into the forms and expressive resources of first-order quantification theory, the logic that Frege, Russell, and early Wittgenstein were developing. Doing so reveals their true underlying logical form, that is, what their correct meaning consists in, and once this is revealed, the philosophical problems surrounding them evaporate.

A paradigm of such logical analysis was the logical atomism of the *Tractatus*, in which sentences of ordinary language are analyzable into elementary propositions that are in turn ultimately analyzable into combinations of simple names that mean by virtue of picking out simple objects. These simple names come with their possibilities for combining with other simple names built into them; such a possible combination of simple names constitutes an elementary proposition and the totality of such combinatorial possibilities of simple names with each other (the totality of elementary propositions) delimits the expanse of logical space, that is, of all that can be meaningful (meaningfully true or false). As possibilities, some may be realized (and become true propositions) while others may not (and express false propositions); thus false statements can be meaningful and statements denying the existence of something can be meaningful and true (they say that a certain possible arrangement of simple objects, which exist, is not actualized). The problem of nonreferring singular terms is dealt with in a similar way. Such terms are understood to be complex, that is, composed of simple names that do refer, which ensures their meaningfulness. It is just that the particular combination of simple names that is the complex name in question does not pick out anything actual, so the term, while meaningful, is nonreferring. In this way, simple objects referred to by simple names must exist for such sentences and terms to have any determinate meaning at all, and logical analysis into simple names corresponding to simple objects (the true logical form of ordinary names and sentences) solves outstanding philosophical problems. The job of philosophy is clearly demarcated: to furnish such logical analyses, that is, to map the workings of natural language onto the abstract, universally applicable formalism of first-order logic.

II. LANGUAGE GAMES, GRAMMATICAL INVESTIGATIONS, FORMS OF LIFE, FAMILY RESEMBLANCES

The notion of a language game and the examples of language games introduced in the early sections of *Philosophical Investigations* (e.g. the builders' and grocer's language games) are clearly meant to contrast fundamentally with this earlier model of language.[5] As the word "game" brings out, the concept of a language game highlights the fact that for the later Wittgenstein linguistic meaning is inextricably linked with the concrete, practical activities of speakers in their particular natural and social environments. Importantly, with the introduction of language games, the unit of semantic concern is not the declarative *sentence* but the *utterance* (e.g. of a desire, "I want five red apples," or a command, "Bring me a slab"), that is, a social – involving a speaker and hearer – use of language embedded in some practical activity. Thus, the object of investigation is not a symbolic structure excised from its practical context, something whose meaning is then amenable to expression in the abstract formalism of first-order logic; rather, it is a speech *act* that takes place at a particular time and place, in the context of purposive social activity (buying produce from a vendor, building a structure as part of a work crew), and thus something that involves others and that has a particular practical goal or purpose in view. By foregrounding language's embeddedness in the practical, social activities of our everyday lives, the focus on language games moves from an approach to meaning that sees it in terms of its ability to be modeled in some abstract logical formalism to one in which the meaning of a speech act is particularized to what is, in the context of the activity in question, the purpose of the speech act. The meaning of "slab" in the language game of the builders is just what someone who understands the term in this context understands by it, as manifested by responding appropriately (in the way established by the language game as correct) to the utterance – which in this example would be bringing a particular shape of stone (a slab rather than a block, beam, or pillar) to a designated place (PI §§2, 8–10, 19–20). It is "what happens before and after" the speech act (PI §35), the whole surrounding context, the pattern of activity within which it is embedded, that determines its meaning. Change this background in certain ways (imagine the workman is not laboring as part of a work crew but is ostensively instructing his child in the names for the various building materials, e.g. pointing to a particular shape of stone and saying "slab") and the meaning of the utterance will change: for example from a demand for certain building materials to an identifying

5. The discussion of this section has benefited from Robert Fogelin, *Wittgenstein*, 2nd ed. (London: Routledge, 1987), ch. IX, and Marie McGinn, *Routledge Philosophy Guidebook to Wittgenstein and the Philosophical Investigations* (London: Routledge, 1997), ch. 2.

reference to a particular object, for the language game now being played is one of identifying or ostensively defining masonry items and not constructing a building.

Interestingly, the emphasis on the actual use of ordinary language in practical contexts does not mean that Wittgenstein now believes that the "surface grammar" (PI §664) of natural language provides a transparent medium in which to read off the meaning of natural language expressions. Indeed, a deep commonality in early and late Wittgenstein is the belief in the capacity of ordinary language to disguise through misleading surface similarities the disparate uses of seemingly similar expressions of natural language. What is different in the later work is that the remedy for these confusions is not logical analysis, but in-depth investigation and description of ordinary-language locutions in the contexts of their use. For the later Wittgenstein, then, if ordinary language is the *source* of confusions, it – and not logical analysis – is also the *resource* for overcoming them. The confusions created by ordinary language are to be remedied by looking into the detailed workings of the concrete, context-specific, multifarious but indeterminate phenomenon of language-in-use, by attending carefully to how particular words function in particular contexts of use in the everyday lives of speakers engaged in particular practical activities (i.e. language games). One does this by painstakingly describing the range of particular, concrete uses of a word, not by trying to constrain such uses by imposing on them some decontextualized logical form. This kind of context-specific immersion in, and description of, our ordinary uses of language is what Wittgenstein means by a "grammatical investigation" (PI §90). *Philosophical Investigations* and *On Certainty* are thus collections of such grammatical investigations that examine a domain of language that has become the source of philosophical confusion or myth, for example how names, mathematical expressions, and sensation terms get their meaning, or when it does and does not make sense to claim to know something, doubt it, be certain of it, and so on.

In Wittgenstein's usage, "grammar" is not a syntactic notion that refers to some Chomsky-like innate, universal schema or set of transformational rules, and nor, of course, is it the notion of logical form; rather, it refers to the patterns of the actual uses of particular words in specific practical situations. Attending to these patterns of use involves, *inter alia*: considering how we teach children certain expressions (e.g. arithmetic terms, sensation words, epistemic terms like "know," "doubt," "justify"); thinking about how we would teach them to linguistic aliens who had no prior use for them; exploring whether certain of their uses would still occur if certain facts about ourselves and the world were different, and so on. The focus on language games and the technique of grammatical investigation, then, does not aim for a systemization of *the* determinate set of rules that govern *all* uses of *all* words in *all* circumstances – as the project of arriving at the logical form of language does – but at laying out the distinctive patterns of use that characterize the actual employment of them. Thus the account of meaning grammatical investigations ushers in is one that replaces the former monism of logical form with the pluralism of patterns of use.

A related notion is "form of life" (PI 226). Like the idea of language games, Wittgenstein's notion of forms of life contrasts with the Tractarian conception of language as an abstract, formal system of signs. And just as the former notion emphasizes that language is something that is used by speakers in the context of their nonlinguistic activities in the natural and social worlds, so forms of life, which are made up of language games and the nonlinguistic activities that they are embedded in, also view language as something that is enmeshed in the lives of human agents and their significant activities. "Life," then, is not understood merely as a naturalistic–biological category but also as a cultural one. It refers to the shared set of linguistic and nonlinguistic practices and traditions that determine what is correct and incorrect, what appropriate and inappropriate, in what a historical group of individuals says and does, and in so doing constitutes their culture.[6] To be sure, a form of life is *based* in biological facts and capacities (PI 230), but insofar as it is structured by normatively rich practices of instruction, evaluation, criticism, correction, and so on, it is not *reducible* to them but is deeply cultural or meaning laden. In his notion of a form of life, then, Wittgenstein naturalizes the normative without naturalistically reducing it, for a form of life is not independent of natural facts but neither is it thereby identified with such facts. "Form of life" is his term for that nonreductive complex involving natural facts about us and the world we live in as well as the normative practices of language, customs, and traditions that give a community its identity.[7]

The descriptive, particularist, and pluralist character of language games, forms of life, and grammatical investigations dovetails with another impor-

---

6. Thus there is a marked similarity between the Wittgensteinian concept of "form of life" and Husserl's notion of "life-world," which underwrites the similarity between Schutz and Wittgenstein that we will later discuss. The life-world for Husserl concerns the sociocultural structure of meanings or senses established and inculcated in the linguistic and nonlinguistic practices of a community, which delimits the bounds of comprehensibility for the community. As with a form of life, a life-world may well be based on general natural facts and be founded evolutionarily, but it is importantly a cultural entity: the meaning-laden structures that constitute a community's worldview, the norms of meaningfulness that condition the way it understands itself, the world and others. Hence it is a life-world that individuals from different communities must to some extent share if it is to be possible for them to understand each other.

*7. For more on Wittgenstein's nonreductive brand of naturalism, see the discussion in the next section as well as the essay by John Fennell in *The History of Continental Philosophy: Volume 8*.

tant notion of the later Wittgenstein: family resemblance. Wittgenstein initially introduces this notion by considering the language game of the term "game" itself. He argues that if we examine the actual uses of the term "game," we do not find any single property or set of properties, any common essence, to the activities we rightly call "games." Some games are amusing and do not necessarily involve any element of competition, of there being a winner or a loser; others are more about competition and less about fun; some others involve skill and not that much luck, while others luck and not that much skill, and in those that require skill there may be very different kinds of skill involved, and so on. The conclusion he draws is that the use of the term "game" does not come with a sharply circumscribed set of individually necessary and jointly sufficient conditions for its correct application, such that the term does not apply if the conditions are lacked, but does if they are satisfied; rather, attending to actual use shows "a complicated network of similarities overlapping and criss-crossing: sometimes overall similarities, sometimes similarities in detail" (PI §66). However, for all that, the term "game" has a perfectly good use, and thus a perfectly serviceable meaning. To be sure, it does not have determinate rules for its correct application, rules that would determine its application in all possible future contexts; but Wittgenstein's point is that it does not need such universalist, determinate rules to have a use and thus be meaningful. He therefore cautions, "Don't say: 'There *must* be something in common, or they would not be called "games"' – but *look and see* whether there is anything common at all" (PI §66). This is a warning not to be tempted, as Wittgenstein himself was in the *Tractatus*, by the thought that unless there is complete determinacy of meaning there is no meaning at all, which is at the heart of his argument for the necessity of simples. *A priori* arguments for the necessity of the determinacy of meaning in his early work give way to empirical, "look and see" descriptions of the actual use of terms in specific circumstances in his later work. And what these descriptions show is that in order to have a legitimate use and meaning, terms need not have a strictly determinate meaning-essence. The family resemblances obtaining between uses that emerge from grammatical investigations into the actual uses of words in specific contexts, then, do not issue in conclusions that generalize to the essence of all linguistic meaning; their particularist, context-specific character ensures that any conclusions reached about the meaning of a certain kind of term are highly contingent and provisional: contingent on certain environmental features and social practices of speakers remaining the same, such that if they were to change so might the patterns of use, and thus the grammar (meaning) of the expressions involved. Nevertheless, as long as the range of a term's applications displays some recognizable continuity, similarity, or family resemblance, however loose this may be, a use is determined for the term, and thus a meaning.

III. RELATIVISM, NATURALISM, AND GRAMMATICAL PROPOSITIONS

Although the notion of family resemblance introduces a certain looseness or anti-essentialism into the later Wittgenstein's picture of meaning, he does not think that this entails that words have no meaning (meaning indeterminacy) nor that they can mean anything at all, that however we use a word is consonant with its meaning (meaning relativism). Regarding the potential threat of meaning indeterminacy, as we have just seen, all the looseness shows is that absolutely determinate meaning is not necessary for meaning. With regard to the problem of meaning relativism, the later Wittgenstein has two resources at his disposal: his "naturalism," and the category of grammatical (as opposed to empirical) propositions. We shall explain these notions in turn.

By naturalism, we mean Wittgenstein's insistence that language games, and the family resemblances among uses of terms that emerge in them, are underpinned by a shared human nature possessed by all human beings and a common natural world that we all live in, no matter what the historical, cultural, and individual differences between us. (As we shall see later, this idea is developed in *Zettel* and "Remarks on Frazer's *Golden Bough*.") The kind of common nature that Wittgenstein has in mind here consists of very general facts of nature, such as our mortality and biological needs for food and to reproduce, as well as very general facts about our environment, such as that it does not rain gold filigree, that trees do not speak Latin, or that human beings cannot fly or breathe under water unaided. Such general facts of nature to do with us (where "us" here means "us human beings," not, say, "us early twenty-first-century postmoderns") and our world act as boundary conditions for what is comprehensible to us, what language games are possible for creatures like us, what uses our words can enter into, and so on. While allowing for some differences between conceptual schemes, such general natural facts do place boundary constraints on the scope of difference. In this way these natural facts permit a plurality of language games, novel extensions of extant language games and differences in the assessment of claims made within them, while at the same time providing a bulwark against an "anything goes" conceptual relativism by placing limits (albeit minimal and general) on what it is possible for us to think, say, and understand. Put another way, they insure that other ways of thinking and using language cannot be completely, radically, *other*. The radical other must be somewhat familiar, for our nature simply does not allow the truly radically other to be intelligible to us. (We shall return to this later in our discussion of Levinas.) Of course this is a very weak form of naturalism since it does not entail any commitment to reductionism: it is merely the claim that what forms of life and language games are comprehensible to us *arise out of* general facts of nature, not that they are *reducible to* them; that such normative practices are not *independent* of natural facts but nor are they *identifiable* with them. The present point is that although minimal, this form of naturalism still forestalls strong versions of relativism. What it leaves us with is a plurality of language games within certain kinds of boundary conditions; not an "anything goes" relativism but an "a lot of things go" pluralism, where the parameters for what goes and what does not go are not determined *a priori* by logic but empirically by contingent, general facts of nature. At least this is part of the story.

Not only are there external constraints on the plurality of language games imposed by general facts of nature, but there are internal constraints inside particular language games that limit the intelligibility of claims made within them. These internal constraints on intelligibility are expressed by "grammatical truths" (which are contrasted with empirical claims). This notion is introduced in the discussion of the meter stick (PI §50) and "bedrock" propositions (PI §217), and gets extensive treatment in *On Certainty*. The idea is that certain statements inside a language game have the special role of acting as conditions for the possibility of other statements in the language game being meaningful. For example, in the language game of measuring objects in meters, the statement that "The standard meter stick is a meter long" does not have the same status as the statement "My desk is a meter long." The latter is an empirical statement, the former a grammatical one: rather than representing some object as being a certain length in meters, in expressing the standard for what it is to be a meter long, it is what makes all such representations of objects' lengths in meters possible and so cannot itself be represented in the language game of representing the lengths of objects in meters. To say of the meter stick that it is a meter long in this language game is in effect to say that the meter stick has the same length as the meter stick. That is, it is analogous to an empty tautology, and as with other tautologies – for example "Either it is raining or it is not raining" – which do not describe, represent, or tell us something about the world (it does not say that it is raining, nor does it say that it is not raining), so this does not make an empirical claim about the length of some object but is a condition for other claims doing so. As the repeated reference to the "language game of representing the length of objects in meters" in the foregoing should make clear, its role as a grammatical statement is language-game specific. That it is rather like a tautology or necessary truth in that language game – in other words, that it is a presupposition for other statements to be meaningful in that language game – does not mean that it universally has this status. In another language game, for example the language game of assessing the accuracy of standards of measurement, the statement that the standard meter is a meter long *is* an empirical claim that attributes a length to a particular object and so stands in need of verification.[8]

8. Indeed, its being taken as such resulted in its being replaced; at present, the standard is the distance travelled by light through a vacuum in a certain, very small, fraction of a second.

In *On Certainty*, which is discussed in greater depth below, Wittgenstein makes the same point, but this time with regard to the language game of philosophical skepticism and anti-skepticism and the use of the terms "knowledge," "doubt," and "certainty." There Wittgenstein points out that Moorean propositions such as "Here is one hand, here is another," "My name is LW," "I have never been far from the surface of the earth," and so on are grammatical propositions in the language game of ordinary knowledge claims. As such they are statements that have no justification, indeed, they do not need such justification; to think that they do (as the skeptic does) is to misunderstand their grammatical role in the language game (or grammar) of justification – namely, that justification has to end somewhere (with them, as it turns out). Thus, they are epistemic primitives, the justificatory "bedrock" where our epistemic "spade is turned" (PI §217). The important point here is that one cannot be a pluralist about such grammatical propositions and continue to "play" the language game in question: reject them and one is opting out of the specific language game (e.g. moving from the language game of representing the lengths in meters of objects to the language game of assessing standards of measurement, or moving from the language game of ordinary knowledge claims into paranoia or madness[9]). Grammatical propositions "hold fast" (OC §173), at least for the language game in question. Disagreement about them is not possible inside the language game they govern; it bespeaks a misunderstanding, not a different understanding of the concepts involved, and in this way grammatical propositions also act to constrain the possibilities for difference or "otherness."

IV. METAPHILOSOPHY

With this family of concepts (language games, grammatical investigations, forms of life, family resemblance), Wittgenstein is not so much objecting to this or that semantic theory – for example the truth-conditional account of sentential meaning, the referentialist account of names, and so on – with the aim of replacing it with another theory of meaning, namely, the so-called "use theory" of meaning. The use *theory* of meaning often attributed to the later Wittgenstein is a misnomer. His move to looking at how words are actually used in particular social situations given certain natural facts about us and the world is not directed toward installing another, different *philosophical* theory of meaning (the use theory) in place of these other theories. It is better seen as the rejection of

9. Ludwig Wittgenstein, *On Certainty*, G. E. M. Anscombe and G. H. von Wright (eds), Denis Paul and G. E. M. Anscombe (trans.) (Oxford: Basil Blackwell, 1969), §155. Hereafter cited as OC followed by the section number.

the whole "will-to-theorizing" about linguistic meaning characteristic of philosophy; the rejection of the quintessentially philosophical drive to get "behind" or "beneath" actual linguistic usage and arrive at *a* theory that would explain once and for all what linguistic meaning consists in. In other words, his concentration on actual use is expressive of an antitheory, *meta*philosophical attitude. For Wittgenstein, philosophy should consist of piecemeal, particular descriptions of actual concrete uses of language in specific practical situations and under certain natural world conditions. When so practiced, traditional philosophical problems, like the problem of knowledge, the meaningfulness of nonreferring singular terms, the determinacy of the meaning of mathematical expressions, and so on, are not so much answered as do not even arise. Philosophical problems will not be solved but *dissolved*: they will not even be formable in the first place. Philosophy so practiced will therefore be therapeutic (PI §133); it will not supply the single, unified explanatory theory of how words mean, but will instead cure us of the disease of thinking that we need such a theory.

This conception of philosophy as therapy foregrounds an important aspect of Wittgenstein's later work, namely, his conception of what philosophy *should* be. This normative dimension is important because Wittgenstein's methodological commitment to leave "everything as it is" (PI §124) does not extend to traditional philosophical practice itself. Indeed, he repeatedly characterizes philosophers as idiotic, deranged, and infantile. For Wittgenstein, then, philosophy *ought* to be therapeutically oriented toward attaining "[t]houghts that are at peace."[10] He therefore describes philosophical puzzlement as an illness or disease, and his own practice as the requisite treatment (PI §255, §593). This therapeutic analogy is crucial, for just as there is no *intrinsic* value in medicine, there is no *intrinsic* value in philosophy; both are valuable relative to their curative capacities. (In this sense, Wittgenstein's later method might be described as broadly ethical in orientation.) Philosophers should therefore eschew theorizing, as this merely intensifies conceptual suffering. Rather, philosophy's task lies in "clearing up the ground of language" (PI §118), thereby leaving one "capable of stopping doing philosophy" (PI §133).

Although Wittgenstein is a deeply *anti*-philosophical thinker, his metaphilosophy is not wholly idiosyncratic. For while he cared little for the history of philosophy, Wittgenstein's approach has significant resonances with ancient Pyrrhonism, Franz Rosenzweig, and Nietzsche. Indeed, despite his concerns about psychoanalysis, Wittgenstein explicitly aligns himself with Freud to the extent that both are engaged in "persuasion" or "making propaganda for one

10. Ludwig Wittgenstein, *Culture and Value*, G. H. von Wright (ed.), Peter Winch (trans.) (Oxford: Blackwell, 1994), 43. Hereafter cited as CV followed by the page number.

style of thinking."[11] Why? Because what the patient requires is a wholesale perspectival shift: something akin to a *conversion*.

Beset by dogmatism, superstition, and an impulse to theorize (notably about language), philosophers routinely employ preconceived ideas of that "to which reality *must* correspond" (PI §131), as Wittgenstein himself had done in the *Tractatus*. All this he offsets in his later work with the "weighing of linguistic facts"[12] and "description alone" (PI §109). So, whenever philosophers talk of "knowledge," "being," "object," "I," "proposition," and "name," and thereby "try to grasp the *essence* of the thing," we should ask: "is the word ever actually used in this way in the language game that is its original home?" What Wittgenstein attempts to do then is "bring words back from their metaphysical to their everyday use" (PI §116), for our confusions are generated by surface similarities "between the forms of expression in different regions of language" (PI §90). Philosophy can neither interfere with how language is actually used, nor provide it with a foundation. Rather, philosophers' task is to "only describe" (PI §124).

Notwithstanding his criticisms of philosophy, Wittgenstein does not think that our conceptual illnesses are *created* by philosophers. Rather, *language itself* routinely misleads us (CV 18). For example, because the "verb 'to be' ... seems to function like 'to eat' and 'to drink'" (because we habitually talk of a "flow of time and an expanse of space," etc.), we continually "bump up against the same mysterious difficulties" (PO 185–7). Although philosophers certainly exacerbate such confusions, they do not generate them *ex nihilo*. Our battle is therefore against the seductions of language itself, and not least our "urge to misunderstand" (PI §109). Because it is often as hard to avoid using certain expressions – just as it is hard to "hold back tears, or an outburst of anger" (PO 161) – neither the force of "grammatical illusions" (PI §110) nor the demands of Wittgenstein's therapy should be underestimated or thought to trivialize philosophy.

At this juncture, we should note Nietzsche's own warning against the seduction of words.[13] Just as Wittgenstein counters our essentialist urges by introducing language games and family resemblances, Nietzsche similarly cautions that the "unity of the word is no guarantee of the unity of the thing."[14] Not only are we routinely misled by the "similarity of words and concepts,"[15] but the

11. Ludwig Wittgenstein, *Lectures and Conversations on Aesthetics, Psychology and Religious Belief*, Cyril Barrett (ed.) (Oxford: Blackwell, 1994), 27–8. Hereafter cited as L&C followed by the page number.
12. Ludwig Wittgenstein, *Zettel*, G. E. M. Anscombe and G. H. von Wright (eds), G. E. M. Anscombe (trans.) (Oxford: Blackwell, 1990), §447. Hereafter cited as Z.
13. See Nietzsche, *Beyond Good and Evil*, §20, and *On the Genealogy of Morality*, I §13.
14. Nietzsche, *Human, All Too Human*, §14.
15. Nietzsche, *Daybreak*, §195.

latter are inherited from more primitive times.[16] Although he would not share Nietzsche's haughtiness regarding "primitive mankind" (see our later discussion of "Remarks on Frazer's *Golden Bough*"), Wittgenstein concedes that "our language has remained the same and seduces us into asking the same questions over and over" (PO 185). Likewise, his caution that an "entire mythology is laid down in our language" (PO 199) is prefigured by Nietzsche's own warning: "A philosophical mythology lies concealed in *language*."[17] Illustrating how the deepest philosophical prejudices are already contained within language, Nietzsche thus directs our attention to the supposition that "the subject 'I' is the condition of the predicate 'think,'" for the "inference here is in accordance with the habit of grammar: 'thinking is an activity, to every activity pertains one who acts, consequently.'"[18] Both Wittgenstein and Nietzsche thus highlight the manifold dangers of getting "tangled up in the snares of grammar."[19] Indeed, on this point at least, it is hard to know where Nietzsche ends and Wittgenstein begins.[20]

For Wittgenstein, then, ordinary language is both the source of our confusions *and* where these confusions are remedied.[21] But his later therapeutic method might be arduous for other reasons. Recalling Wittgenstein's allusion to our "urge" to misunderstand, in *Culture and Value* he conjectures: "It is sometimes said that a man's philosophy is a matter of temperament, and there is something in this. A preference for certain similes could be called a matter of temperament and it underlies far more disagreements than you might think" (CV 20). Again, this has striking Nietzschean resonances, for Nietzsche similarly describes the tendency of philosophers to cast their rivals as "anarchists, unbelievers, opponents of authority"[22] in terms of those *instincts* that are "active behind all … *pure* theoreticians." In other words, philosophers have, "under the spell of the instincts, gone fatalistically for something that was 'truth' *for them* …" As such, the rancor between philosophical systems and "epistemological scruples" is really just a "conflict between quite definite instincts."[23]

That philosophers rarely ask what instincts motivate them is hardly surprising, for this would undermine their universalist, aprioristic pretensions. But here Nietzsche happily blurs the line between philosophy and autobiography:

16. Nietzsche, *The Will to Power*, §409.
17. Nietzsche, *The Wanderer and His Shadow*, §11.
18. Nietzsche, *Beyond Good and Evil*, §17.
19. Nietzsche, *The Gay Science*, §354.
20. See Erich Heller, *The Importance of Nietzsche: Ten Essays* (Chicago, IL: University of Chicago Press, 1988), 152.
21. Heller suspects that Wittgenstein's preoccupation with "everyday" or "natural" language was, in part, due to a "Tolstoyan belief in the virtue of the simple life" (*The Importance of Nietzsche*, 155).
22. Nietzsche, *The Will to Power*, §447.
23. *Ibid.*, §423. Cf. Nietzsche, *Beyond Good and Evil*, §8.

> [W]hat happens … is that a prejudice, a notion, an "inspiration," generally a desire of the heart sifted and made abstract, is defended … with reasons sought after the event … It has gradually become clearer to me what every great philosophy has hitherto been: a confession on the part of its author and a kind of involuntary and unconscious memoir … [a] decisive testimony to *who he is* …[24]

When considering even the philosopher's most abstract metaphysical claims, we should therefore ask: what "morality" does he or she aim at? Here there is nothing "impersonal";[25] indeed, for Nietzsche, even the laws of logic merely express an empirical human "inability," and thereby function as "*imperative*[*s*] concerning that which *should* count as true."[26] Although less radical than Nietzsche, Wittgenstein would probably agree that philosophy "creates the world in its own image,"[27] and rarely (if ever) for purely rational considerations.

V. THE ORDINARY, KNOWLEDGE, AND TRUST

As will have become clear from our discussion thus far, appeals to the "ordinary" play a crucial methodological role in Wittgenstein's later work. To dissolve our perplexities and cure philosophical disease, language must be returned "home" from its metaphysical to its everyday usage (PI §116). In short, problems arise "when language *goes on holiday*" (PI §38). Here Wittgenstein thus seems to polarize two realms: one of safe familiarity, the other of hazardous disorientation. But might one not object that Wittgenstein himself has here been seduced by "forms of expression"; namely, the picture of *being-at-home* in the "ordinary"? As we have seen, such a conclusion would be hasty insofar as ordinary language is both curse *and* cure (the "things that are most important" are "hidden because of their simplicity and familiarity" [PI §129]). Still, it is worth exploring other aspects of the ordinary.

In the *Investigations*, Wittgenstein remarks: "What has to be accepted, the given, is … *forms of life*" (PI 226). Precisely what this encompasses remains unclear – not least for Wittgenstein himself – but as we saw above, he uses "forms of life" to refer alternatively to a collection of interwoven language games, to the practical dimension of language games, and even to human life in both its natural–biological and normatively rich aspects. We have referred to "forms

24. *Ibid.*, §§5–6.
25. *Ibid.*, §6.
26. Nietzsche, *The Will to Power*, §516.
27. *Ibid.*, §9.

of life" here to highlight two things about the ordinary: (i) When Wittgenstein insists that forms of life are *given*, and thereby must be accepted, he is countering the urge to uncover some esoteric, hidden reality (PI §126). The philosopher's rightful task is instead to describe how language *actually* works *in situ*. Moreover, one has to accept *something* as "given." In philosophy, no less than history, geography, physics[28] and even our prephilosophical life, at *some* point one's "spade is turned" (PI §217). What are given are our mundane language games, embedded in more complex forms of life, and expressed by the propositions that are grammatical for them. Thus we are similarly instructed to accept language games "as the *primary* thing" (PI §656), for they require "no justification" (PI 200). In *On Certainty*, then, Wittgenstein claims that the language game is "something unpredictable"; that is to say, it is "not based on grounds. It is not reasonable (or unreasonable). It is there – like our life" (OC §559). (ii) Wittgenstein's various appeals to the ordinary function as a methodological constraint. He has no aspiration to intrude on other disciplines (e.g. evolutionary theory[29]), for he is doing neither natural science nor natural history. Nevertheless, as noted earlier, his "interest certainly includes the correspondence between concepts and very general facts of nature. (Such facts as mostly do not strike us)" (PI 230). This is important, for Wittgenstein's orientation (like Nietzsche's) is deeply naturalistic. As such, his conception of the ordinary cannot be divorced from those general facts of nature only within which human life is truly *human* life. Our language games are therefore to be understood as being "as much a part of our natural history as walking, eating, drinking, playing" (PI §25).

Wittgenstein once claimed that he could imagine philosophy written entirely as jokes.[30] Although "making a joke" is included in his inventory of language games (PI §23), it is not obvious why Wittgenstein thought joking to be *philosophically* important. An answer to this is suggested in the *Investigations*:

> The problems arising through a misinterpretation of our forms of language have the character of *depth*. They are deep disquietudes; their roots are as deep in us as the forms of our language and their significance is as great as the importance of our language. – Let us ask ourselves: why do we feel a grammatical joke to be *deep*? (And that is what the depth of philosophy is.) (PI §111)

28. See OC §§162, 206, 234, 600, 608.
29. Ludwig Wittgenstein, "Remarks on Frazer's *Golden Bough*," John Beversluis (trans.), in *Wittgenstein: Sources and Perspectives*, C. G. Luckhardt (ed.) (Bristol: Thoemmes Press, 1996), 69. Hereafter cited as RFGB followed by the page number.
30. See Norman Malcolm, *Ludwig Wittgenstein: A Memoir* (Oxford: Clarendon, 2001), 27–8.

The depth of grammatical jokes (e.g. "I have a pain in my pocket"[31]) thus corresponds to Wittgenstein's insistence that confusions arise when language goes "on holiday." That such jokes might provide therapeutic "reminders" (PI §127) of how language ordinarily works is clear. Nevertheless, we would like to pursue this topic further.

Wittgenstein's introduction of language games foregrounds that the "*speaking* of language is part of an activity" (PI §23), a more complex "form of life" that includes nonlinguistic activities. Because the ordinary encompasses typical human behaviors, only of what "resembles (behaves like) a living human being can one say: it has sensations; it sees; is blind; hears; is deaf; is conscious or unconscious" (PI §281). As we will see later, these behaviors are crucial for understanding Wittgenstein's relevance to ethics. For the moment, we simply need to note that Wittgenstein is not only concerned with everyday ways of *speaking*, but with how concepts such as "pain" function in the complex "weave of our life" (PI 174). For, as he insists, it is the "common behavior of mankind" that provides the "system of reference" for understanding others – even those of an "unknown country" (PI §206).

According to Wittgenstein, then, if we attend to our actual use of language, what is "hidden" is of "no interest" (PI §126). But in one sense he *is* interested in something hidden, albeit due to its mundane "familiarity" (PI §129). For what Wittgenstein finds "mysterious" and unable to express is the "background against which whatever I could express has its meaning" (CV 16). Although this may sound distinctly Tractarian, the "background" against which life ordinarily functions is a recurrent theme throughout Wittgenstein's work. As already noted, the horizon of normal human actions remains elusive because of its extreme proximity. To get a clearer sense of this, let us return to Wittgenstein's *On Certainty*.

As was pointed out earlier, in these last notebooks Wittgenstein focuses on Moore's common-sense examples of things he knows to be true[32] – most famously: "'Here is one hand, and here is another.'"[33] What troubles Wittgenstein here is not Moore's general antiskepticism, but rather his specific claims to *knowledge*. Why? Because if we attend to how "know" functions in ordinary life, free from philosophers' "metaphysical emphasis" (OC §482), we find that "I know" entails the possibility of providing further justification, proof, or supporting evidence. In short, "I know" is conditional or "restricted" (OC §554). More specifically, "know" and "doubt" are mutually parasitic, for "I know" implies that "I doubt" *makes sense*. Wittgenstein thus inquires: "How does someone judge

31. This example is taken from Raimond Gaita, *The Philosopher's Dog: Friendship with Animals* (New York: Routledge, 2003), 53, 56.
32. See G. E. Moore, "A Defense of Common Sense," in *Classics of Analytic Philosophy*, Robert R. Ammerman (ed.) (Indianapolis, IN: Hackett, 1994), 48.
33. G. E. Moore, "Proof of an External World," in Ammerman, *Classics of Analytic Philosophy*, 82.

which is his right and which his left hand? How do I know that my judgment will agree with someone else's?" and continues: "If I don't trust *myself* here, why should I trust anyone else's judgment? Is there a why? Must I not begin to trust somewhere? That is to say: somewhere I must begin with not-doubting; and that is not, so to speak, hasty but excusable: it is part of judging" (OC §150). To the question "Why don't you satisfy yourself that you have two feet?" one cannot provide evidence more certain than what is in doubt; hence Wittgenstein's own response: "There is no why. I simply don't. This is how I act" (OC §148). What therefore remains interesting about Moore's propositions is that they neither require nor permit epistemic bolstering – they are, one might say, more fundamental than epistemology. Subsuming these claims under the rubric of "knowledge" therefore trivializes them, and even perhaps generates comic incongruity (OC §§463–4).

It is crucial to note here that Wittgenstein does not simply rebuff Moore. For although Moore "does not *know* what he asserts he knows," it nevertheless "stands fast" (OC §151) for both him *and* Wittgenstein (not to mention the rest of us). Indeed, if Moore's propositions *were* knowable, and thereby open to critical interrogation, then "a doubt would … drag everything with it and plunge it into chaos" (OC §613). Wittgenstein thus undercuts the entire skeptic/anti-skeptic debate by suggesting that "know" and "doubt" are two sides of the same conceptual–linguistic coin. But this requires clarification, for he also insists that the "game of doubting itself presupposes certainty" (OC §115). In short, while "know" and "doubt" are inextricably connected, the entire knowledge/doubt language game is underpinned by *certainty*. So, Wittgenstein is not only concerned with describing the knowledge/doubt language game, but also interested in what underpins *all* our language games; hence his allusions to "something universal" (OC §440), "something animal" (OC §359), and even (rather oddly) "the human language-game" (OC §554). Wittgenstein patently struggles to articulate this background certainty without employing the vocabulary of "knowledge" and "doubt."[34] Because the latter generate "misfiring attempt[s] to express what can't be expressed like that" (OC §37), he alludes instead to *trust*: "I really want to say that a language-game is only possible if one trusts something. (I did not say 'can trust something')" (OC §509). The parenthetical qualification here is important, for such trust is not deliberative or hypothetical, but rather "trust … without any reservation" (OC §337). Such trust is "primitive" in that it is both unconditional and manifest (shown) in our ordinary linguistic and

34. This shifting vocabulary is most apparent where Wittgenstein discusses learning a whole "world-picture" (OC §§95, 162, 167) or "system of propositions" (OC §141). It should be noted that Moore himself struggles to articulate his certitude; see Moore, "A Defense of Common Sense," 56–7, and "Proof of an External World," 83–4.

nonlinguistic behavior.[35] Insofar as trust is "anchored in all my *questions and answers*, so anchored that I cannot touch it" (OC §103), it thus resists explicit articulation. Indeed, even in our most theoretical and/or skeptical moments we do not evade trust, and as such any metadiscourse *on* trust (Wittgenstein's included) itself *presupposes* such trust. This then is why Moore's "Here is one hand, and here is another" contributes only philosophical confusion to the course of daily life in which hands ordinarily have a role.

Mindful of this, just as Wittgenstein's conceptual vocabulary shifts throughout *On Certainty*, we find a similar array of descriptions in Alfred Schutz's discussions of what is taken for granted in the "everyday life-world."[36] Like Wittgenstein, Schutz similarly seems to struggle to articulate this "unquestioned background."[37] But, as we shall see shortly, what is especially interesting is how Schutz's phenomenology of the life-world highlights problems he appears to share with Wittgenstein.

Although Schutz maintains that the pretheoretical attitude of common sense is dominated by the pragmatic know-how involved in pursuing concrete objectives, most of our worldly knowledge is received from our sociocultural heritage. This inherited stock of knowledge is not static, however; "radical surprises"[38] sometimes occur, which are either subsumed into our existent body of knowledge or undermine our hitherto "unquestioned course of experience."[39] At what point such anomalies endanger one's stock of knowledge is not possible to determine in advance because the latter provides the criteria for what is *relevant* in one's "biographically determined situation"[40] and what *counts* as a genuine problem. Like Wittgenstein, Schutz thus thinks that the taken-for-granted world constitutes the realm in which doubting and questioning become possible, and as such lies at the "foundation of any possible doubt."[41] Moreover, intersubjectivity permeates the life-world. Not only is the taken-for-granted world essentially sociocultural; even one's pragmatic dealings with objects refer to past, present, and futural activities of human beings. Indeed, while face-to-face encounters

35. See Jerry H. Gill, "Saying and Showing: Radical Themes in Wittgenstein's *On Certainty*," *Religious Studies* 10(3) (September 1974), 283–5, 290.
36. Alfred Schutz, with Thomas Luckmann, *The Structures of the Life-World*, Richard M. Zaner and H. Tristam Engelhardt, Jr. (trans.) (London: Heinemann, 1974), 4.
37. Alfred Schutz, *Collected Papers II: Studies in Social Theory*, Arvid Brodersen (ed.) (The Hague: Martinus Nijhoff, 1964), 234.
38. Schutz, *The Structures of the Life-World*, 169.
39. Alfred Schutz, *Reflections on the Problem of Relevance*, Richard M. Zaner (ed.) (New Haven, CT: Yale University Press, 1970), 69.
40. Alfred Schutz, *Collected Papers I: The Problem of Social Reality*, Maurice Natanson (ed.) (The Hague: Martinus Nijhoff, 1971), 9.
41. *Ibid. I*, 74.

are immediate,[42] here one takes for granted not only the bodily reality of one's fellow human beings (including their conscious life and possibility of mutual understanding),[43] but also the interchangeability of our respective standpoints;[44] namely, that "I and my fellow-man would have typically the same experiences of the common world if we changed places."[45]

However reassuring all this may sound, Schutz's work is haunted by a persistent ambiguity. Like specific passages in *On Certainty* (especially OC §§162, 167, 608–12), Schutz's life-world often sounds relativistic. A tension thus emerges between "relative-natural world view[s]," on the one hand, and "the fundamental structures of … the life-world"[46] on the other, and likewise between "the life-world"[47] and "our life-world"[48] – where the "our" pertains to a historically and culturally specific community. In a similar vein, Schutz refers to others being so radically different that *we* do not have "any principles of interpretation"; *their* world lies "beyond the grasp" of *our* understanding.[49] (Indeed, he even suggests that not even the "so-called biological needs for food, shelter, and sex" are basic enough to support a "theory of the equality of men grounded on the equal needs of mankind."[50]) We have begun to see – and will discuss further later – how Wittgenstein's apparent relativism is tempered by his naturalism, but does Schutz have similar resources available? It seems to us that he does. For Wittgenstein, we will recall, the "common behavior of mankind" provides our hermeneutic "system of reference" (PI §206). Only with this background in place can we *possibly* understand others. As such, this common behavior binds us across history, culture, and our respective stocks of knowledge. Despite the fact that Schutz seems to think that sociocultural groups can be unintelligible to one another, partaking in mutually untranslatable (incommensurable) forms of life, he nevertheless maintains that "Certain features … are common to all social worlds because they are rooted in the human condition."[51] Every situation is therefore "'limited' through the prior givenness of my body"[52] and the given "ontological structure of the world."[53] Together these impose a limit on

42. Schutz, *Collected Papers II*, 22–3.
43. Schutz, *Collected Papers I*, 313.
44. *Ibid.*, 12.
45. *Ibid.*, 315–16.
46. Schutz, *The Structures of the Life-World*, 104.
47. Alfred Schutz, *Collected Papers III: Studies in Phenomenological Philosophy*, I. Schutz (ed.) (The Hague: Martinus Nijhoff, 1966), 117.
48. *Ibid.*, 119.
49. Schutz, *Collected Papers II*, 62.
50. *Ibid.*, 230.
51. *Ibid.*, 229.
52. Schutz, *The Structures of the Life-World*, 101.
53. *Ibid.*, 114.

historical, cultural, and individual difference.[54] Accordingly, these features are universal; they are "on hand for everyone; they are the same in whatever relative-natural world view [one is] … socialized."[55] As such, the other *is* "in principle 'understandable' to me."[56] Putting this in Wittgensteinian terms, then, difference is confined by "very general facts of nature" (PI 230) pertaining to "the natural history of human beings" (PI §415).

VI. ETHICS, THE BODY, AND "OTHERNESS"

Discussing Wittgenstein's relevance for ethics may seem odd. For when he laments "the harm philosophers do in ethics,"[57] he is not objecting to specific positions in moral philosophy, but to the philosophical treatment of ethics *as such*. Wittgenstein thus insists that we should "put an end to all the idle talk about Ethics – whether there be knowledge, whether there be values, whether the Good can be defined, etc."[58] In short, our tendency to talk about ethics is ultimately hopeless (PO 44).

Wittgenstein's broader treatment of ethics seems similarly discouraging. In the *Investigations* he simply (and unsurprisingly) notes that the word "good" has a "family of meanings" (PI §77) rather than any determinable essence. Elsewhere he suggests that between different moral principles there cannot be "argument and proof," and that context is all-important when trying to understand moral concepts.[59] In keeping with these latter suggestions, in *On Certainty* Wittgenstein imagines encountering another culture. For *us* the propositions of physics constitute good grounds (OC §608), but how are we to judge those who instead consult an oracle (and for which we "consider them primitive")? If we think it is wrong or mistaken for their actions to be guided in this way, would we not be merely "using our language-game as a base from which to *combat* theirs?" (OC §609). Wittgenstein thus proceeds to caution:

> Where two principles really do meet which cannot be reconciled with one another, then each man declares the other a fool and heretic

54. *Ibid.*, 111.
55. *Ibid.*, 109.
56. *Ibid.*, 18.
57. O. K. Bouwsma, *Wittgenstein: Conversations 1949–1951*, J. L. Craft and Ronald E. Hustwit (eds) (Indianapolis, IN Hackett, 1986), 39.
58. Ludwig Wittgenstein, "On Heidegger on Being and Dread," Michael Murray (trans.), in *Heidegger and Modern Philosophy: Critical Essays*, Michael Murray (ed.) (New Haven, CT: Yale University Press, 1978), 80–81.
59. Bouwsma, *Wittgenstein: Conversations 1949–1951*, 4–5.

> … I said I would "combat" the other man, – but wouldn't I give him *reasons*? Certainly; but how far do they go? At the end of reasons comes *persuasion*. (Think what happens when missionaries convert natives.) (OC §§611–12)

So, if such principles can be *radically* divergent (and reasons must terminate *somewhere* [OC §§34, 192, 204, 262]), then noncoercive interaction becomes problematic. Reading Wittgenstein as endorsing a radical incommensurability thesis is doubtless tempting, but as we have begun to see, it is far from unproblematic. Still, we would like to pursue this idea a little further, with reference first to Lyotard, and then to Levinas.

Mindful of the above passages from *On Certainty*, if there is no site of arbitration *outside* all language games (no God's-eye view), then any inter-game judgment will inevitably be framed in the conceptual vocabulary of a specific language game, thereby generating conflict. These broadly Wittgensteinian concerns preoccupy Lyotard insofar as he thinks that the multiplicity of language games (e.g. those governing "science, literature and the arts"[60]) are irreducible and heterogeneous. Simply put, "we have no common measure"[61] here, and the resultant incredulity toward metanarratives (i.e. "narrations with a legitimating function"[62]) constitutes our postmodern condition. If metanarrative legitimation is problematic, then the emancipatory quest for consensus itself becomes ethically and politically questionable. After all, why assume that it is "always *better* to play together"?[63]

Clearly, Lyotard's use of "language game" is rather different from Wittgenstein's.[64] For while the former extends its application to cover complex sociocultural phenomena, Wittgenstein's own examples in the *Investigations* (e.g. "Giving orders, and obeying them … Reporting an event … Forming and testing a hypothesis …Translating from one language into another … Asking, thanking, cursing, greeting, praying" [PI §§23–5]) are significantly more mundane, and thereby cut *across* science, religion, art, and so on. Lyotard's extension of "language game" thus enables him – rightly or otherwise – to draw explicit ethico-political conclusions; specifically that the imposition of one

60. Jean-François Lyotard, *The Postmodern Condition: A Report on Knowledge*, Geoff Bennington (trans.) (Minneapolis, MN: University of Minnesota Press, 1984), xxiii.
61. Jean-François Lyotard, *Just Gaming*, Wlad Godzich (trans.) (Minneapolis, MN: University of Minnesota Press, 1985), 50.
62. Jean-François Lyotard, *The Postmodern Explained to Children: Correspondence 1982–1985*, Julian Pefanis and Morgan Thomas (eds), Don Barry (trans.) (London: Turnaround, 1992), 31.
63. Jean-François Lyotard, *Postmodern Fables*, Georges Van Den Abbeele (trans.) (Minneapolis, MN: University of Minnesota Press, 1997), 144.
64. The striking exception to this is OC §§608–12.

set of rules across the social field "entails a certain level of terror"; a more-or-less tacit injunction: "be operational (… commensurable) or disappear."[65] To translate conflicting parties, even for the sake of consensual harmony, violates the given heterogeneity of (Lyotardian) language games. Because different language games have their own operational criteria for how to move,[66] and cannot be externally justified (i.e. their rules are local), the tension between language games cuts deep. However, such tension is not due to a problem of mere *litigation* or disagreement about the application of a shared rule. Rather, what interests Lyotard is what he calls the "*differend*," where even the criteria for *playing* differ between subjects or collections thereof. Such conflict constitutes a *differend* because "the success (or the validation) proper to one genre is not the one proper to others."[67]

Although bolstered by his philosophy of language and appeal to a quasi-Kantian sublime, the political implications of Lyotard's incommensurability thesis are pretty clear. He therefore advocates a "pagan" attitude of celebration and multiplication of differences – even a "war on totality."[68] Privileging one language game would be as absurd as claiming that chess or poker was the only true game. The pagan recognizes that there is no such privilege, for one can play numerous games each of which is "interesting in itself." Conversely, a sure indication that people are insufficiently pagan is that "they think that they are in the true."[69] The flourishing of difference, nourished by an experimental attitude,[70] is therefore what Lyotard thinks we postmoderns *should* desire, not least because questions of justice cannot be solved by models or rules.[71] The alternative to this "pagan" attitude is the sort of dogmatism that, ultimately, leads to imperialism and genocide. Lyotard's avowed openness to "difference" may sound cozy, but for him *dissensus* is the cost of recognizing the heterogeneous nature of language games.[72] Although agonistic,[73] Lyotard is

65. Lyotard, *The Postmodern Condition*, xxiv.
66. Although even *within* a language game there is no *necessity* to "move" one way rather than another; see Jean-François Lyotard, *The Differend: Phrases in Dispute*, Georges Van Den Abbeele (trans.) (Minneapolis, MN: University of Minnesota Press, 2002), 66, 80–81.
67. *Ibid.*, 136.
68. Lyotard, *The Postmodern Condition*, 82.
69. Lyotard, *Just Gaming*, 60–62.
70. Avant-garde art is the paradigm case here, for its only "rule" is to search for (and question) its own rules; see Lyotard, *The Differend*, 139, and *The Postmodern Explained to Children*, 24.
71. Lyotard, *Just Gaming*, 25, 65, 98.
72. See Lyotard, *The Postmodern Condition*, 66.
73. Lyotard's shifting vocabulary of language games, little narratives, phrases, and so on similarly bears witness to his agonistic desire to avoid totalizing discourse. The agonism of the phrase amounts to this: to phrase is inescapable; it is given, but *how* to phrase remains open (see Lyotard, *The Differend*, 66; *The Postmodern Explained to Children*, 54). Owing to the multiplicity of possible linkages, there is a corresponding multiplicity of possible disputes about

not therefore despairing, for politics is simply inseparable from the "threat of the differend."[74]

These concerns seem in keeping with Wittgenstein's insistence that all we can ultimately say is "*this language-game is played*" (PI §654), for at *some* point justification is exhausted (PI §217). Indeed, as noted earlier, the language game is "something unpredictable … it is not based on grounds. It is not reasonable (or unreasonable). It is there – like our life" (OC §559). Thus, when Lyotard writes "All we can do is gaze in wonderment at the diversity of discursive species,"[75] we might well hear an echo of Wittgenstein's own amazement at the given multiplicity of language games and forms of life (PI 226). On a Lyotardian reading, then, Wittgenstein's anti-essentialism bears witness to "what the postmodern world is all about"; namely, the delegitimation of homogenizing metanarratives.[76]

While there are some striking correlations between Lyotard and Wittgenstein – especially the latter's remarks in §§608–12 of *On Certainty* quoted earlier – we would now like to shift focus from Lyotard's *differend* (and associated themes[77]) to Levinas – one of the most prominent continental philosophers of "difference."[78] Like Lyotard's, Levinas's work resists easy summary. As such, we will concentrate on a couple of themes that relate most conspicuously to Wittgenstein's later thinking.

Levinas's central preoccupation throughout his work is with the singularity of the "other" – specifically, other human beings.[79] In this he draws on our prephilosophical experience of others, placing special emphasis on face-to-face encounters. According to Levinas, traditional philosophy has tended to characterize the other as essentially a member of a common species, an instance of humanity, or to use philosophical jargon, a token of a type. Typically, the other here figures as a source of epistemological concern – hence the problem of other minds and associated puzzles. But this way of construing our relation to others misses something much more fundamental; namely, that I am routinely faced by concrete, singular, vulnerable others – each with their own distinct

---

each linkage. Moreover, every specific linkage is made at the expense of other linkages (*The Differend*, 136).

74. *Ibid.*, 138.
75. Lyotard, *The Postmodern Condition*, 26.
76. *Ibid.*, 41.
77. For an interesting, though problematic, application of Lyotardian themes, see Bill Readings, "Pagans, Perverts or Primitives? Experimental Justice in the Empire of Capital," in *Judging Lyotard*, Andrew Benjamin (ed.) (London: Routledge, 1992).
78. For more on the relation between Wittgenstein and Levinas, see Bob Plant, *Wittgenstein and Levinas: Ethical and Religious Thought* (London: Routledge, 2005).
79. For Levinas's views on other animals, see especially "The Paradox of Morality: An Interview with Emmanuel Levinas," A. Benjamin and T. Wright (trans.), in *The Provocation of Levinas: Rethinking the Other*, Robert Bernasconi and David Wood (eds) (New York: Routledge, 1988).

life-narratives, needs, desires, etc.[80] (We might say, borrowing Wittgensteinian terms, that Levinas is here *reminding* us of something mundane we nevertheless tend to overlook due to its "familiarity" [PI §129].)

Much of Levinas's work thus focuses on what it means to be faced by a finite, vulnerable, embodied other. The general claim he makes here is that "access to the face is straightaway ethical."[81] In other words, my "access" to the other is not dependent on any analogical inference or chain of reasoning on my part; rather, it is *immediate*. As Levinas remarks, what the face expresses

> is not just a thought which animates the other; it is also the other present in that thought ... [for the] expression does not speak about someone, is not information about a coexistence, does not invoke an attitude in addition to knowledge ... Expression is ... the archetype of direct relationship.[82]

Levinas goes further, however, for the face is not merely a collection of discernible features to be recognized, deciphered, or comprehended.[83] Rather, the face has an active ethical dimension, for I am *faced* by the other's face, not merely presented with one more worldly object for cool contemplation. Here, then, Levinas maintains that the other's face embodies three things: first, the biblical command "Thou shalt not kill";[84] second, the appeal "Do not kill me" (and even "Do not abandon me"[85]); and third, the face accuses me of already having killed, of being an (albeit unwitting) accomplice in others' deaths.[86] So, the other's face simultaneously *commands*, *appeals*, and *accuses*. Combined, the moral claim made on me here is inescapable.[87] Thus, when Levinas says that the "face speaks,"[88] the point is not merely physiological. Rather, the face provides the

80. *Ibid.*, 169.
81. Emmanuel Levinas, *Ethics and Infinity: Conversations with Philippe Nemo*, Richard A. Cohen (trans.) (Pittsburgh, PA: Duquesne University Press, 1985), 85.
82. Emmanuel Levinas, *Collected Philosophical Papers*, Alphonso Lingis (trans.) (The Hague: Martinus Nijhoff, 1987), 21.
83. Emmanuel Levinas, *Difficult Freedom: Essays on Judaism*, Seán Hand (trans.) (Baltimore, MD: Johns Hopkins University Press, 1997), 8.
84. Levinas, *Ethics and Infinity*, 89.
85. Emmanuel Levinas, *Outside the Subject*, Michael B. Smith (trans.) (London: Athlone, 1993), 44.
86. Emmanuel Levinas, *Entre Nous: Thinking-of-the-Other*, Michael B. Smith and Barbara Harshav (trans.) (New York: Columbia University Press, 1998), 186.
87. See Emmanuel Levinas, *Basic Philosophical Writings*, Adriaan T. Peperzak *et al.* (eds) (Bloomington, IN: Indiana University Press, 1996), 54, and "Ethics of the Infinite," in *Dialogues with Contemporary Continental Thinkers: The Phenomenological Heritage*, Richard Kearney (ed.) (Manchester: Manchester University Press, 1984), 63.
88. Levinas, *Ethics and Infinity*, 87.

ethical conditions of possibility for discourse. For it is *from* the (vulnerable) authority of the other's face that the silent demand that I justify myself first comes, and *toward* the (authoritative) vulnerability of the face that my response is ultimately addressed. It is in this sense that responsibility is "not a simple attribute of subjectivity"; rather, I am "initially for another."[89]

That being faced by the other demands that I *justify* myself is one of Levinas's most persistent themes, for he repeatedly insists that the face "calls me into question."[90] The natural "egoism" of the self – what Levinas sees as its instinctive prioritization of its own welfare, needs, and desires over others' – is therefore undermined in the face-to-face encounter. For here I am (albeit silently) required to justify to the other my very "right to be."[91] Why? Because my simply *being-here* constitutes a "usurpation of someone's place." This then helps to explain why Levinas insists that "bad conscience … comes to me from the face of the other."[92] The command of the face "Thou shalt not kill" is therefore an impossible injunction, for I have *already* sacrificed others, and continue to do so. For no matter how sensitive and generous I might be toward *this* other, I thereby neglect all the *other* others who are just as singular and needy.[93] It is in this sense then that responsibility is, strictly speaking, "infinite." For what Levinas rules out is the *good conscience* involved in thinking that one's responsibilities have been accomplished. (This latter theme plays a central role in Derrida's ethical and political writings on hospitality, forgiveness, and the gift.)

These, in brief, are some of the central motifs of Levinas's work. Mindful of all this, it is striking that Wittgenstein also draws our attention to the human face. In a sense this is unsurprising, for face-to-face encounters clearly play a central role in our everyday dealings with others.[94] But Wittgenstein's remarks on the human face (and the body more generally) have more notable Levinasian resonances. For he too wants to undermine the general philosophical view that others are essentially another species of object to be *known*. Like Levinas, Wittgenstein insists that the meaningful presence of the other is *immediate*. For example, one *sees* consciousness, and even a "particular *shade* of consciousness," in the other's face. When encountering others one does not first look into *oneself* and then "make inferences … to joy, grief, boredom" (Z §225) concerning *them*. (This is why a facial expression cannot adequately be described in terms of "the

89. *Ibid.*, 96.
90. Emmanuel Levinas, *The Levinas Reader*, Seán Hand (ed.) (Oxford: Blackwell, 1996), 83.
91. Levinas, "Ethics of the Infinite," 63.
92. Levinas, *Entre Nous*, 148.
93. See *ibid.*, 21, 82–3, 104; "The Paradox of Morality," 173.
94. See PI §286; David Cockburn, *Other Human Beings* (London: Macmillan, 1990), 66–7, 70–71, 77.

distribution of matter in space" [CV 82].) Rather, we normally "describe a face immediately as sad, radiant, bored" (Z §225); its meaning "is there as clearly as in your own breast" (Z §220). The face, one might therefore say, *manifests* joy, grief, boredom, suffering, and so on. It is not incidental then that some recent Wittgensteinians describe embodiment, and specifically the human face, as a "moral space," for the face is "the locus of the possibility of all those expressions that are at the basis of moral life."[95]

Despite all of this, we should not overstate the similarities between Levinas and Wittgenstein. For while Levinas constantly stresses the radical "otherness" of the other (although he gives this a distinctly ethical twist), Wittgenstein repeatedly emphasizes the regularities and commonalities of human behavior (PI §206). For example, he remarks: "If a man's bodily expression of sorrow and of joy alternated, say with the ticking of a clock, here we should not have the characteristic formation of the pattern of sorrow or of the pattern of joy" (PI 174). In a similar vein, elsewhere Wittgenstein writes:

> Isn't it as if one were trying to imagine a facial expression not susceptible of alterations which were gradual and difficult to catch hold of, but which had, say, just five positions; when it changed it would snap straight from one to another. Now would this fixed smile, for example, really be a smile? And why not? (Z §527)

Such a face or body would signal, not radical "otherness," but rather abnormality, dysfunction, or someone acting or making a joke.[96] Wittgenstein thus asks us to imagine meeting people whose facial features were identical. Here, he suggests, this "would be enough for us not to know where we are with them" (CV 75) – just as we would falter if we were to encounter others whose linguistic and nonlinguistic behavior was *completely* predictable.

Given Wittgenstein's preoccupation with human embodiment, his occasional references to the "soul" may seem rather surprising. But what interests Wittgenstein here is, predictably enough, how this term actually functions in our ordinary intercourse. If we "look and see," rather than impose preconceived ideas of what "soul" means, we find that the term does not name some mysterious inner substance. Saying that someone "has a soul" is manifested, not in one's hypothetical beliefs about their metaphysical constitution, but rather through one's practical orientation toward them. In other words, to "believe that men have souls" lies in the application of this "picture" (PI §422), and this

95. Benjamin R. Tilghman, *Wittgenstein, Ethics and Aesthetics: The View from Eternity* (Albany, NY: SUNY Press, 1991), 115.
96. Bergson's *Laughter* is in large part an extended meditation on this point.

is why, regarding concrete others facing me, I have "an attitude towards a soul. I am not of the *opinion* that he has a soul" (PI 178). Given this very practical characterization of "attitude," it becomes clear why such a picture is central to our sense of ethical concern for finite, embodied, vulnerable others. There is something primordially significant about the human form, so much so that it determines the limits of to what or whom the concepts pain, consciousness, soul (etc.) can be meaningfully attributed. It is in this sense then that caution is needed when speaking of the intractable or radical "otherness" of the other. For while other human beings may not be transparent to us (hardly something we should bemoan), that does not mean that they are inherently mysterious or that an unfathomable gulf separates us. Certainly the lives of others are singular; each of us has our own physical, psychological, emotional, and cognitive peculiarities, not to mention our own distinct life-narratives. In this sense we are unique and irreplaceable. But it is misleading to suggest that our uniqueness betokens some *radical* difference between us. For this ignores the mundane fact that, simply in virtue of being human, we share a considerable amount. Indeed, as suggested earlier, if others were truly *radically* "other," how could we possibly be cognizant of this fact? Surely they would not even register on our cognitive, affective, and empathic radar.[97]

Both Wittgenstein and Levinas insist on the *immediacy* of our intersubjective encounters; our responsiveness to others is not essentially deliberative, nor does it result from our reasoning by analogy (Z §537). But here is where Wittgenstein and Levinas part company in the most significant way. As noted above, Levinas conceives of the face-to-face as undermining the natural "egoism of the I."[98] That is to say, for Levinas ethics is fundamentally "*against nature* because it forbids the murderousness of my natural will to put my own existence first."[99] This markedly bleak vision of the natural is crucially at odds with Wittgenstein's naturalism, and specifically his insistence that "it is a primitive reaction to tend, to treat, the part that hurts when someone else is in pain; and not merely when oneself is." By "primitive," Wittgenstein does not mean anything derogatory, but rather that such responses are "*pre-linguistic*: that a language-game is based *on it*, that it is the prototype of a way of thinking and not the result of thought" (Z §541). ("'Putting the cart before the horse' may be said of an explanation like the following: we tend someone else because by analogy with our own case we believe that he is experiencing pain too" [Z §§540–42].) Thus:

97. A similar point is made by Derrida, "Violence and Metaphysics," in *Writing and Difference* (New York: Routledge, 1997), 114–16, 121–3, 125, 127, 132, 143.

98. Levinas, *Basic Philosophical Writings*, 54.

99. Levinas, "Ethics of the Infinite," 60; cf. "The Paradox of Morality," 172.

> Being sure that someone is in pain, doubting whether he is, and so on, are so many natural, instinctive, kinds of behavior towards other human beings, and our language is merely an auxiliary to, and further extension of, this relation. Our language-game is an extension of primitive behavior. (Z §545)

Of course, there are times when the meaning and sincerity of others' behavior is far from obvious. But Wittgenstein's point is that, in the ordinary course of our lives, "'I can only *believe* that someone else is in pain, but I *know* it if I am'" is only to say that "one can make the decision to say 'I believe he is in pain' instead of 'He is in pain'. But that is all … Just try – in a real case – to doubt someone else's fear or pain" (PI §303). Put slightly differently, in such circumstances one needs "reasons for leaving a familiar track," for "[d]oubt is a moment of hesitation and is, *essentially*, an exception to the rule" (PO 379). In an especially striking passage, Wittgenstein proceeds:

> The game doesn't begin with doubting whether someone has a toothache, because that doesn't – as it were – fit the game's biological function in our life. In its most primitive form it is a reaction to somebody's cries and gestures, a reaction of sympathy or something of the sort. We comfort him, try to help him. (PO 381)

The important point here is that if, as Wittgenstein maintains, language is an extension, refinement, or replacement of primitive reactions (Z §545; CV 31; PI §244), then moral deliberation concerning *when*, *how* and *to whom* we should attend is ultimately rooted in prelinguistic natural or "primitive" reactions toward others. This is not to contest the obvious anthropological fact that the manner in which different cultures organize and implement their moral values may vary considerably. (Nor is it to contest the existence of sociopaths and moral blindness.) What it does suggest, however, is that the depth of such cultural diversity is *not* unfathomable, but rather circumscribed both by prelinguistic behaviors and given natural facts about human beings – not least their finitude and vulnerability. This then is why Wittgenstein insists:

> The concept of pain is characterized by its particular function in our life.
>
> Pain has *this* position in our life; has *these* connexions; (That is to say: we only call "pain" what has *this* position, *these* connexions).
>
> Only surrounded by certain normal manifestations of life, is there such a thing as an expression of pain. Only surrounded by an even more far-reaching particular manifestation of life, such a thing as the expression of sorrow or affection. And so on. (Z §§532–4)

Moral problems force themselves on us insofar as they arise from the "common life between men and do not presuppose any particular forms of activity in which men engage together."[100] Thus, for example, what constitutes suffering is not primarily an epistemic or hypothetical matter; it is central to the natural life of human beings. The other's suffering *commands* us to help (whether or not we actually do); his misery "calls for action: his wounds must be tended."[101] As such, the various trajectories taken in the course of historical and cultural practice and rational ethical and political deliberation are only possible on the grounds of a much more natural responsiveness toward others. Unlike Levinas's ethics of radical otherness, then, what Wittgenstein is reminding us of in all this is the *natural* backdrop our lives share; our "agreement … in form of life" (PI §241).

In the previous discussion we have been stressing Wittgenstein's (albeit minimal) naturalism, and how this figures in thinking about the relevance of his later work for ethics. Before concluding, however, it is worth saying something about "Remarks on Frazer's *Golden Bough*," for here Wittgenstein's naturalism plays an even more tangible role. In these notes, Frazer is taken to task for portraying the magical and religious views of humankind as pseudo-scientific "*errors*" or "pieces of stupidity" (RFGB 61). According to Wittgenstein, however, religious beliefs can be erroneous only to the extent that they offer a theory or opinion. But "[n]o *opinion* serves as the foundation for a religious symbol" (RFGB 64); indeed, the "characteristic feature of primitive man is that he does not act from *opinions*" (RFGB 71). Frazer's assessment is driven by his desire to *explain* religious practices. True to form, Wittgenstein opposes this by insisting that one must "only *describe* and say: this is what human life is like" (RFGB 63). Under these methodological constraints, then, "all one can say is: where that practice and these views occur together, the practice does not spring from the view, but they are both just there" (RFGB 62). These sentiments are therefore in keeping with Wittgenstein's remarks in *On Certainty* that he wants to "regard man here as an animal … a primitive being to which one grants instinct but not ratiocination." After all, "[a]ny logic good enough for a primitive means of communication needs no apology from us. Language did not emerge from some kind of ratiocination" (OC §475). For Wittgenstein, neither religious practices nor language itself are founded on reason; rather, the "origin and the primitive form of the language game is a reaction; only from this can more complicated forms develop" (CV 31). In short, Wittgenstein's focus in "Remarks on Frazer's *Golden Bough*" is not on (allegedly) "primitive" *human beings*, but rather on the "primitive" *within* human beings.

100. Peter Winch, "Nature and Convention," *Proceedings of the Aristotelian Society* 20 (1960), 239–40.

101. Tilghman, *Wittgenstein, Ethics and Aesthetics*, 113.

Wittgenstein thus provides a continuity thesis regarding primitive behaviors and language games. Indeed, this is why he suggests that "one could begin a book on anthropology by saying: When one examines the life and behavior of mankind throughout the world, one sees that … [human beings] perform actions which bear a characteristic peculiar to themselves, and these could be called ritualistic actions" (RFGB 67). Not only does Wittgenstein narrow the apparent rift between Frazer's "savages" and us postmoderns, but this underlying commonality is something Frazer himself presupposes. For if his explanations did not already appeal to a natural tendency in *us*, then they would have little explanatory force. What Wittgenstein is stressing is the kinship between the behavior of Frazer's "savages" and "any genuinely religious action of today" (RFGB 64). Because these various practices show a "common spirit" (RFGB 80), were one to invent a religious ritual, it would either perish or be "modified in such a manner that it corresponds to a general inclination of the people" (RFGB 78). (Indeed, we should remember *our own* ritualistic behaviors, such as kicking the ground in anger or kissing the photograph or name of a loved one.) Moreover, on closer inspection, Frazer's "savages" understand perfectly the natural boundaries of their rituals, for the "same savage, who stabs the picture of his enemy apparently in order to kill him, really builds his hut out of wood and carves his arrow skillfully and not in effigy" (RFGB 64). Hence, Wittgenstein concludes that if they were to document their knowledge of nature, it "would not differ *fundamentally* from ours" (RFGB 74). Judging the religious practices of Frazer's "savages" by our scientific criteria is misguided, perhaps also unjust, but not because of some radical *differend* or unfathomable "otherness." Rather, the injustice here lies in Frazer's underestimating our *natural commonality*. It is therefore unsurprising that "in relation to man, the phenomena of death, birth, and sexual life, in short, everything we observe around us year in and year out … will play a part in his thinking … and in his practices" (RFGB 66–7).[102]

102. In the same vein, Winch maintains: "[T]he very conception of human life involves certain fundamental notions – which I shall call 'limiting notions' – which have an obvious ethical dimension, and which indeed in a sense determine the 'ethical space', within which the possibilities of good and evil in human life can be exercised … [specifically] birth, death, sexual relationships. Their significance here is that they are inescapably involved in the life of all known human societies in a way which gives us a clue where to look, if we are puzzled about the point of an alien system of institutions … In trying to understand the life of an alien society, then, it will be of the utmost importance to be clear about the way in which these notions enter into it … [T]he very notion of human life is limited by these conceptions" ("Understanding a Primitive Society," *American Philosophical Quarterly* 1[4] [October 1964], 322). Passages such as these undermine the common view that Winch is some sort of cultural relativist.

VII. CONCLUSION

Wittgenstein introduces the concept "language game" (and associated terms) to shake us from our grammar-induced urge to think that language functions *in one way*. Rejecting such essentialism thus leads him to embrace a contextual, descriptive–therapeutic (rather than aprioristic, speculative–theoretical) approach. The early part of our discussion focused on this aspect of Wittgenstein's work. What is of broader significance, however, is that while he emphasizes sensitivity toward the "multiplicity of language-games" (PI §24), he does not think that the horizon of human life is radically open. While we must be attuned to diversity in the social, historical, and cultural realm, insofar as language games emerge from shared "primitive behavior" (Z §545), it is misleading to interpret Wittgenstein as having "developed the theory of the irreducible plurality of language games," and who thereby "sought to resolve the difficult question of values in terms of *plurality*."[103] It is even more misleading to think that Wittgenstein faced intractable problems "surmounting the heterogeneity of language games and the corresponding forms of life."[104] While specific passages in his later work (not only in *On Certainty*[105]) lend themselves to this sort of interpretation, Wittgenstein's naturalism situates him *at least* as close to "common-sense" philosophy as to Lyotard's postmodernism or Levinas's ethics of radical otherness.

Inevitably in an essay of this sort it, is impossible to provide a comprehensive analysis of a given philosopher. As such, we have doubtless presented Wittgenstein in a partial light, foregrounding what we considered to be the most interesting and salient facets of his work. Specifically, we have emphasized his naturalism and tried to explain how this bears on a number of issues – not least those of a broadly ethical sort. But, one might reasonably ask, where does this leave us? What *is* the relationship between Wittgenstein and so-called "continental philosophy"? The answer to this question, it seems to us, remains contentious. Or rather, if we expect a neat answer to this question, then we will likely be disappointed, for Wittgenstein's is not the sort of work to permit such an unequivocal answer. To borrow a good Wittgensteinian metaphor, Wittgenstein's own work is held together by a network of "family resemblances": a "complicated network of similarities overlapping and crisscrossing: sometimes overall similarities, sometimes similarities in detail" (PI §66). But this should not be cause for despair, among continental philosophers or anyone else. For Wittgenstein's

103. Jean Greisch, "Ethics and Lifeworlds," in *Questioning Ethics: Contemporary Debates in Philosophy*, Richard Kearney and Mark Dooley (eds) (New York: Routledge, 1999), 46.

104. *Ibid.*, 58.

105. See, for example, Wittgenstein's remarks on religious believers and nonbelievers being "on an entirely different plane" (L&C 53; cf. 56, 59–60) insofar as they "think entirely differently" (L&C 55). As such, he suggests, there is no "contradiction" between them (L&C 53, 55).

work requires reconstruction. What we have provided here is just part of that much larger – albeit disparate – ongoing project. Ours has been a cautionary tale, specifically against reading Wittgenstein as a champion of unbounded radical difference and otherness. Such a reading, we think, misses an important, although often neglected, aspect of his work: namely, his minimal naturalism. But other commentators – for example, Simon Glendinning, Stephen Mulhall, Chris Lawn, and Søren Overgaard[106] – have traced other points of contact between Wittgenstein and continental philosophy. During the twenty-first century, no doubt, there will be other similarly insightful and challenging reconstructions of Wittgenstein's work. In this sense at least, the future for thinking about Wittgenstein in relation to continental philosophy remains open.

MAJOR WORKS

Logisch-Philosophische Abhandlung. In *Annalen der Naturphilosophie*, 1921. Published in English as *Tractatus Logico-Philosophicus*, translated by David F. Pears and Brian F. McGuinness. London: Routledge & Kegan Paul, 1961. First English edition 1922, translated by C. K. Ogden.

Philosophische Untersuchungen. Published in English as *Philosophical Investigations*, translated by G. E. M. Anscombe, edited by G. E. M. Anscombe and Rush Rhees. Oxford: Basil Blackwell, 1953.

Über Gewissheit. Published in English as *On Certainty*, translated by Denis Paul and G. E. M. Anscombe, edited by G. E. M. Anscombe and G. H. von Wright. Oxford: Basil Blackwell, 1969.

106. See Simon Glendinning, *On Being With Others: Heidegger, Wittgenstein, Derrida* (London: Routledge, 1998); Chris Lawn, *Wittgenstein and Gadamer: Towards a Post-Analytic Philosophy of Language* (London: Continuum, 2005); Stephen Mulhall, *Inheritance and Originality: Wittgenstein, Heidegger, Kierkegaard* (Oxford: Oxford University Press, 2001); Søren Overgaard, *Wittgenstein and Other Minds: Subjectivity and Intersubjectivity in Wittgenstein, Levinas, and Husserl* (London: Routledge, 2007).

12

FREUD AND CONTINENTAL PHILOSOPHY

Adrian Johnston

I. INTRODUCTION: THE FREUDIAN DIFFERENCE IN CONTINENTAL PHILOSOPHY – THE DISCOVERY OF THE UNCONSCIOUS

Sigmund Freud[1] is a momentously important figure not only in relation to the history of the continental philosophical tradition; he casts a prominent long shadow over the entirety of the past century.[2] In addition to informing certain varieties of therapy linked to specific theoretical models of the mind, Freud's invention of psychoanalysis has exerted (and continues to exert) enormous influence on Western culture and the history of ideas, even transforming the very manners in which people think and speak about themselves at an everyday level. Who does not occasionally suspect that he or she and others are moved by obscure or hidden mental forces, that the reasons for observed behavior are not always what they superficially seem? And few thinkers from one hundred years ago continue to provoke controversy in the here-and-now. Freud's writings, rather than being highly specialized psychological texts focusing on sexuality and family life, are incredibly rich and wide-ranging reflections on numerous aspects of the human condition, such as the workings of memory, the relation-

1. Sigmund Freud (May 6, 1856–September 23, 1939; born in Freiberg, Moravia [present-day Czech Republic]; died in London, England) took his MD at the University of Vienna (1881). His influences included Brentano, Josef Breuer, Ernst Wilhelm von Brücke, Jean-Martin Charcot, Charles Darwin, Empedocles, Gustav Fechner, Wilhelm Fliess, Johann Wolfgang von Goethe, Hermann von Helmholtz, Nietzsche, Plato, Schopenhauer, William Shakespeare, and Sophocles.

*2. Freud's influence is discussed in the essay on "Psychoanalysis and Desire" by Rosi Braidotti and Alan D. Schrift in *The History of Continental Philosophy: Volume 6.*

ship between mind and body, the meaning of literature and art, the nature of the emotions, the function of religion, and the structure of social groups. In several senses, for one to understand oneself today requires understanding Freud.

Thanks to his formidable erudition and amazing breadth of interests, Freud's texts have something to say about nearly every issue and topic of concern to philosophers (as well as to anyone who pauses to ponder the mysteries of being human). However, whereas Anglo-American philosophical orientations generally have, with a few exceptions, skirted around serious engagement with the implications of Freudian psychoanalysis for accounts of mind and subjective agency, every significant philosophical movement forming part of the history of thought in twentieth-century Europe has, at a minimum, felt obligated to rise to the challenge of reconsidering the multifaceted enigmas of existence and subjectivity in response to Freud. It would be no exaggeration to assert that what is designated nowadays by the phrase "continental philosophy" involves, almost by definition at the current historical juncture, various relations with Freudian psychoanalysis and its diverse offshoots.

Along with Karl Marx and Friedrich Nietzsche, Freud is an essential, unavoidable point of reference for those continental philosophers working in his wake (with Marx, Nietzsche, and Freud functioning as a sort of foundational triumvirate for continental philosophy from the twentieth century through the present). Likewise, for all who seek to comprehend these philosophers, a certain comprehension of Freud's key concepts and claims is mandatory. At the most basic and fundamental of levels, what Marx, Nietzsche, and Freud have in common is an emphasis on the subtle and insidious ways in which people remain opaque to themselves, operating under the influence of forces and factors foreign to their self-images and yet, at the same time, absolutely constitutive of and integral to their very being. One might be tempted here to invoke the French psychoanalyst Jacques Lacan's[3] neologism "extimacy," a neologism referring to that which is simultaneously intimate and exterior, the core of a subject's structure, which the conscious self of this same subject nonetheless cannot directly identify with and make its own. Along these lines, economic class struggles (Marx), historical power relations (Nietzsche), and fraught past experiences (Freud) are all posited as central determinants of the human condition usually misrepresented and/or obfuscated by mechanisms that conspire to keep such unsettling truths from being openly acknowledged and addressed – these mechanisms being ideology according to Marx, morality according to Nietzsche, and repression according to Freud.

---

*3. For a discussion of Lacan, see the essay by Ed Pluth in *The History of Continental Philosophy: Volume 5*.

However, one might already be wondering: What sets Freud apart from Marx, Nietzsche, and other thinkers in the continental philosophical tradition with whom he shares some overlapping conceptual ground? What is distinctive about Freudian psychoanalysis with respect to post-Kantian European philosophy? There are many fashions in which one could go about answering such questions. In fact, considering both the sizable intellectual scope of Freud's own voluminous writings as well as the veritable mountain of literature by clinicians, philosophers, and many others dealing with Freud, a small library's worth of books could be written on the differences Freudian ideas make in the history of nineteenth- and twentieth-century continental philosophy.

What is more, Freud analyzes many matters of direct concern to philosophers of various stripes: temporality, embodiment, subjectivity, inter-subjectivity, affectivity, and countless other objects and phenomena. So, given that the present discussion is constrained by the length limitations of a single essay, difficult decisions must be made about what will be focused on here (as Spinoza remarks, "all determination is negation"). Despite these difficulties, one notion clearly thrusts itself forward as the leading candidate for the status of being Freud's crucial and unique contribution to the history of ideas, including the history of continental European philosophy: the unconscious (*das Unbewusste*). Psychoanalysis is born with the discovery of the unconscious in the late 1890s. It thereafter remains the defining object of inquiry for analysis as a particular discipline unto itself.

As Freud himself admits, he does not invent the unconscious *ex nihilo*, instead arriving at this notion through a combination of clinical experience with patients (including himself as the analysand of his in-depth self-analysis) and extensive reading across a range of material. He readily concedes that quite a few poets, artists, and philosophers before him discerned significant aspects and contours of these nuanced shades of mental life. Additionally, against a nineteenth-century intellectual background colored by the concepts of F. W. J. von Schelling, G. W. F. Hegel, Søren Kierkegaard, Marx, Schopenhauer, and Nietzsche, among others, it initially appears to be the case that much of what seems original in Freud involves, in actuality, modifications, inflections, and embellishments added to ideas that were already, as it were, "in the air" before he invents psychoanalysis at the turn of the century.

But this initial appearance is misleading. Although Freud's elaborations of psychoanalysis (as centered on the unconscious) over the decades of his mature career draw much inspiration from a whole series of other thinkers and disciplines, one must not lose sight of those characteristics and features of the specifically Freudian unconscious that make it an absolutely unprecedented idea distinct from its historical precursors. Lacan laments that Freud chose to designate what he discovered with a word bearing a negative prefix (i.e. "un-"). His "return to Freud" endeavors to undo the damage done to the picture of Freud by misunderstandings generated, at least in part, by the proliferation of false renditions of the unconscious flourishing in the vagueness and indeterminacy opened up by a concept-term superficially appealing to everything that is simply not conscious; a brief moment of consideration ought to lead one to conclude that the unconscious of psychoanalysis, as a set of components and operations at play in the human psyche, cannot be the mere equivalent of the indefinite number of things that could be said to be "not conscious." Following Lacan's lead, only a correct positive conception of the unconscious (as more than just the negation of consciousness) will suffice in order to situate Freud properly *vis-à-vis* both his predecessors and successors in the history of continental philosophy. Lacan (sometimes referred to as "the French Freud") is arguably the most important interpreter of the philosophical import of Freudian psychoanalysis for continental Europe, and the approach to Freud adopted here is unashamedly guided in certain ways by his teachings.

What follows is organized into two parts. In the first part, the peculiar features of the unconscious as the object of Freudian psychoanalysis will be outlined, with an eye to highlighting those of its traits that identify it as a unique contribution to the history of ideas. This task of outlining will be structured by the six sorts of questions one can ask about a thing (i.e. Who? What? Where? When? Why? and How? – of course, each of these questions will require further specification to become precise enough to guide a fruitful discussion of Freud). Then, in the second part, this thus-established delineation of the unconscious will be used to situate Freudian psychoanalysis in its relations to some of the major European philosophical orientations of the past two centuries. This latter half of the essay will strive to bring into view the convergences and divergences between Freud and those surrounding him in nineteenth- and twentieth-century continental philosophy.

II. THE UNCONSCIOUS – THE OBJECT OF FREUDIAN PSYCHOANALYSIS

Who? – the subject of the unconscious

Although Freud does not explicitly employ the terms "subject" and "subjectivity" as found throughout the bodies of literature constituting continental philosophy – more than anyone else, Lacan is responsible for putting such philosophical language into circulation within Freudian discourse – what these terms refer to is constantly at stake throughout the entire span of his psychoanalytic theorizations. However, even granting this, one might nevertheless wonder whether Freud's descriptions of the unconscious are the appropriate places to go looking for a Freudian account of subjectivity; surely his musings and speculations about the conscious dimensions of the ego, for instance, are more likely to furnish a depiction of the subject relevant to the concerns of philosophical orientations situated in a tradition rooted in Kantian and post-Kantian German idealism (these being conceptual frameworks evidently centered on consciousness and self-consciousness). Is the unconscious not something nonsubjective? Would images of it along the lines of either an utterly asubjective roiling mass of impulses and urges and/or a static storehouse of inert, frozen tableaus of episodic memories not be more fitting?

The unconscious posited by Freud is reducible to neither a seething sea of irreducible instinctual energies nor an accumulated jumble of snapshots of the childhood past. Rather, the unconscious of Freudian psychoanalysis is a thing that thinks (albeit in modes intimately connected to libidinal and mnemic factors). What is most revolutionary about Freud's "Copernican Revolution" – Freud himself compares his mental decentering of the psyche to the shift from geo-centrism to helio-centrism – is the implication that one can think without thinking that one thinks, that one can know without knowing that one knows. Much of Western philosophy assumes that the mental and the conscious are synonymous and coextensive (this assumed equivalence has been empirically falsified by a wealth of psychological and neuroscientific research apart from the critiques to which psychoanalysis has submitted it). Consequently, many philosophers have presupposed (and some still persist in presupposing) that thinking and knowing exemplify and are inextricably bound up with the reflexive structures of a consciousness transparent to itself (i.e. to think is to think that one thinks, to know is to know that one knows). What Freud uncovers in his clinical work with patients and his examinations of sociocultural materials are the traces of sophisticated and complex processes of mentation (i.e. highly elaborate and clever mental maneuverings often involving intricate constellations of words and symbols) foreign to and disowned by the very authors of the evidence exhibiting these traces.

From the perspective opened up by Freud's analytic ears, a far-from-mindless "it," akin to an alien other of equal (yet utterly different-in-kind) intelligence to the familiar self-conscious "I," appears to dwell within psyches whose forms of consciousness tend to ignore or deny the muffled presence of this it. Mentioning Lacan's twin twists on René Descartes's famous "*Cogito, ergo sum*" is perhaps helpful here: "I think where I am not" – that is, the unconscious involves a thinking that the "I" of conscious selfhood does not believe or suspect is happening – and "I am not where I think" – that is, the true kernel of one's subjectivity resides not in the ego of one's self-awareness, but, instead, in this thinking that circumscribed conscious awareness does not think is thinking. The Freudian unconscious is, first and foremost, an ensemble of nonreflexive mental dynamics, a thinking that one (*qua* conscious ego) does not reflectively think while (it is) thinking.

What? – the substance of the unconscious

Although the unconscious is a style of thinking, a set of distinctive modes of mentation, it is not this exclusively. Of course, for anyone even minimally familiar with Freud, the unconscious also can be conceived of as both a particular place in the mind (i.e. a specific sector of the psyche topographically distinct from consciousness and the preconscious) and certain sorts of ideational materials (such as painful memories, inadmissible intentions, threatening desires, and the like). The knowing involved with this aspect of mental life is closely related to such materials as a kind of knowledge that one knows without knowing that one knows, relegated to mental regions resistant to self-conscious reflective assessment.

Hence, insofar as the unconscious is not pure form without content, a philosopher, especially one situated in the continental tradition, is likely to ask: What is the ontological status of the unconscious? Of what sort of "stuff" does it consist? What types of being(s) are involved with it? Freud himself does not address such queries directly, in part owing to his aversion to philosophy as he views it. His craving for scientific legitimacy in the eyes of the natural scientific positivism of his time, coupled with his bad impressions of highly speculative varieties of philosophizing inspired by the German idealists, lead him to be generally quite dismissive and disparaging of philosophy as a discipline, despite the obvious wealth of philosophical consequences entailed by his psychoanalytic theories. Nonetheless, whole books could be written in response to the preceding questions.

In terms of the ontological–material essence of the Freudian unconscious, several key points must be made. To begin with, the young Freud embarks on his path as a medical student researching matters neurological; as evinced by the posthumously published *Project for a Scientific Psychology* (1895), this training (under the direct influence of Brücke and the indirect influence of Gustav Fechner and Hermann von Helmholtz) remains a pervasive influence shaping his metapsychological reflections across the entire span of his intellectual itinerary. However, he soon comes to realize the limitations of the neurology of his day. Freud awaits an eventual biological articulation of psychoanalytic metapsychology, but starts laying the theoretical foundations of analysis without it. Whether the insights he thereby arrives at can and should be put back into relation with the natural sciences has been and continues to be the focus of much lively debate both within and outside of philosophical circles.

Contra a plethora of popular misrepresentations, Freud is not the vulgar biological materialist that he too frequently is portrayed as being, namely, a scientistic reductionist in the mold of eighteenth-century French monistic materialism. The psyche, including the unconscious, is admittedly not without its relations to the body. But, in addition to defying a complete and exhaustive reduction to corporeal being alone, the body with which the psychical apparatus maintains a *rapport* is not just mechanistic matter moved solely by efficient causes (i.e. the matter at stake in crude science-inspired materialisms). The (sexualized) body-image, as the ideational representations (*Vorstellungen*) of the body, is a crucial mediating matrix conjoining, as Freud puts it, soma and psyche. In this vein, through his concept of drive (*Trieb*) – this concept is another of Freud's major contributions to the history of ideas, one as unprecedented with respect to the philosophical tradition as the unconscious – Freud depicts human being as taking shape at the complex, tangled intersection of body and mind, nature and nurture.

Furthermore, as is particularly apparent in the early founding texts of psychoanalysis (such as, most notably, *The Interpretation of Dreams*, *The Psychopathology of Everyday Life*, and *Jokes and Their Relation to the Unconscious*), much of the "stuff" of the unconscious consists of elaborate webs of images, words, symbols, and concepts (i.e. *Vorstellungen*, themselves accumulating over the course of the individual's ontogenetic life history, chained together in incredibly sophisticated networks by the thinking activity of unconscious mental processes). Succinctly stated, the Freudian unconscious is not the familiar bastardized version of his later notion of the id (*das Es*). In other words, it is far from being simply a bubbling cauldron of primitive animalistic instincts held in check by nothing more than external social prohibitions and their psychical internalizations. Nor, by contrast with the Jungian unconscious and its archetypes, is the Freudian unconscious determined from the beginning by any innate meaningful contents wired into the foundations of the psyche.

Where? – the place of the unconscious

In addition to the form and content of the unconscious, there is the matter of the place of the unconscious. In continental European psychoanalytic circles, the 1923 publication of *The Ego and the Id* marks a transition from the "first topography" (i.e. the fundamental map of the mind as divided into conscious, preconscious, and unconscious domains) to the "second topography" (i.e. the id, ego, and super-ego trinity). Anglo-American psychoanalysts refer to this pivotal shift in Freud's metapsychology as the replacement of the "topographic model" with the "structural model." Additionally, one should note that, for the later Freud, the terms "conscious," "preconscious," and "unconscious" are not straightforwardly supplanted by (or correspond in any direct one-to-one manner with) the terms "id" (*das Es*), "ego" (*das Ich*), and "super-ego" (*das Über-Ich*). Instead, "conscious," "preconscious," and "unconscious" change from being nouns in the first topography (i.e. names for places in the psyche) to being adjectives in the second topography, adjectives modifying the nouns "id," "ego," and "super-ego" (e.g. in Freud's later work, there are unconscious portions of the ego and super-ego, hidden dimensions of selfhood and conscience of which one normally is unaware). Moreover, the latter terminological triad, as with other of Freud's German terms (such as *Trieb* or *Schicksal*), poses serious questions of translation on which hinge fundamental psychoanalytic issues with clinical and practical as well as theoretical and philosophical implications. For instance, whether every occurrence of "*das Es*" or "*das Ich*" should be translated with the technical terms "id" and "ego" respectively, rather than the words "It" and "I," makes a genuine difference to one's understanding of Freud's writings about analysis from 1923 onwards. Lacan's disputes with American ego psychology come out quite clearly through the differences between how he exegetically translates Freud's German versus the fashions in which his English-speaking adversaries read *The Ego and the Id* (like the German, the French terms for the three psychical entities of the second topography ["*ça*," "*moi*," and "*surmoi*"] preserve the same ambiguity between the technical and the nontechnical).

These difficulties aside, attention ought to be paid to the obvious here: Freud speaks of a psychical "topography," namely, a (metaphorically) spatial depiction of the mental apparatus. The first association one might have in response to this, especially those who buy the image of him as a naturalizing biological reductionist, is the idea of the project of anatomical localization. However, Freud, painfully aware of the limitations of even the most cutting-edge of what was then-contemporary neurology, warns against efforts to pin down the "places" of the psyche in relation to the anatomy of the central nervous system (with a hindsight informed by today's neurosciences, this decision against the project of localization was the right move insofar as the vast majority of complex mental dynamics, including ones operative in the Freudian unconscious, are nonlocalized *qua* widely distributed across bodily systems and environs).

Another association people often make as regards visual metaphors for the unconscious as a mental space is to the motifs of so-called "depth psychology," to imaginings of the unconscious as the concealed corners and recesses of the mind, as a psychical container for unpleasant things shrouded from view by the veil of repression. This conception of it as a deep, overshadowed repository is incredibly problematic (Lacan's recourse to mathematical topology is driven, in part, by the struggle to purge metapsychological theorizing of any reliance on a misleading picture-thinking tethered to the spontaneous, intuitive Euclidian geometrical register of macro-level sensory-perceptual experience). Unconscious phenomena frequently are on display out in the open (as instances of "the psychopathology of everyday life"), transpiring on the very surface of quotidian reality in publicly visible words and deeds – and yet, of course, usually somehow going unnoticed nonetheless. Furthermore, insofar as, on the Freudian account, consciousness itself is shaped by the unconscious, the latter is woven into the fabric of the former (rather than consciousness standing over and above the depths of the unconscious). Finally, certain dimensions of the unconscious even could be said to be distributed across individual psyches, situated in the intersubjective and trans-subjective structures arising between human beings via exchanges occurring within a diverse array of sociosymbolic milieus.

When? – the temporality of the unconscious

Freudian psychoanalysis, along with such roughly contemporaneous continental philosophical movements as both transcendental and existential phenomenology, takes significant strides in the direction of reconsidering the nature of being human in light of reflections on time. The temporal dynamics organizing psychical life are absolutely essential components of Freud's analytic theories. And yet, not only does Freud himself fail to realize the full extent of the contributions his work makes to a new philosophical conceptualization of temporality – this is related to his insistence on the "timelessness" of the unconscious – but popular consciousness comes to consider the discipline he founds as, so to speak, a science of the past. That is to say, owing to a combination of some of Freud's own remarks with impressions circulating among the general public, the unconscious phenomena of the psyche are at risk of being envisioned as either impervious to the passage of time and/or restricted to the effects of a limited number of repressed episodic memories from childhood. These misleading notions regarding the relevance (or, more accurately, irrelevance) of time to Freudian psychoanalysis obscure from view its many far-reaching ramifications for theories of temporality in philosophy.

Admittedly, the past is indeed very important in Freud's account of mental life, as evinced through such things as infantile sexuality, the return of the repressed, repetition compulsion, transference, and so on. But, beginning with his earliest proto-psychoanalytic texts of the 1890s, Freud indicates that the past at stake in the psychical facets with which he is concerned is a past dialectically intertwined with a present continually unfurling itself off into the uncharted terrain of the future, a future filled with an indefinite multitude of unpredictable contingencies. Such phenomena as deferred action (*Studies on Hysteria*), mnemic re-transcription ("Letter 52" to Fliess), screen memories ("Screen Memories"), day-dreams ("Creative Writers and Day-Dreaming"), and, most notably, the interaction between "infantile wishes" and "day-residues" in the formation of the "manifest texts" of dreams via the "dream-work" (*The Interpretation of Dreams*) all reveal that what the unconscious retains of the past in the form of encoded ideational representations is subjected to repeated retroactive alterations in connection with the ongoing lived history of ontogenesis. As a result of this dialectical oscillation between past and present, the unconscious past exerts its influence over the present only insofar as the present provides associative catalysts for the reactivation of this past, a past then modified by these same reactivations. Consequently, in psychoanalysis, a pure, undiluted repetition of or regression to a past "as it was" is impossible for several metapsychological reasons. This is a far cry from the image of the unconscious as a repository of fixed memories, a closed album of unchanging snapshots of early life events.

Additionally, the formations of the unconscious tend to orbit around enigmas pertaining to the temporal character of the human condition. More precisely, the entanglement of sexuality with the topics of birth and death is revealed through both the symptoms of certain neurotics and the fundamental fantasies situated at the core of each and every psyche. Many of the mysterious questions of existence that these fantasies attempt to answer bear on matters of mortality (and an unconscious that is allegedly ignorant of chronological time and logical negation struggles to comprehend such matters).

Lastly, although Freudian psychoanalysis could be identified as deploying developmental models of the mind, its developmentalism is not that of developmental psychology as it is commonly understood. To be more specific, when Freud insists on the timelessness of the unconscious, what he means is that prior phases of development (i.e. past periods of psychical experience and structure) are not eliminated and replaced by subsequent phases of development. Instead, the effects of the passage of time on the psyche involve the cumulative sedimentation of interacting layers (interactions in which layers of the long ago can and do continue to bend and warp current processes), rather than successive demolitions of the old by the new.

Why? – the reasoning of the unconscious

One of the more common misconceptions of the Freudian unconscious depicts it as a homunculus-like mind-within-the-mind, a sort of second mind as a lustful and violent *Doppelganger* of the conscious mind familiar to the first-person self. Freud takes great care to argue against such notions. By contrast with, for instance, the depth psychology of Pierre Janet (1859–1947; one of Freud's contemporaries who posits a "subconscious" *qua* a split-off double of consciousness), the unconscious of Freudian psychoanalysis does not think in the manners and modes of the thinking with which consciousness is acquainted. Unconscious mentation works quite differently than conscious mentation – so differently, in fact, that traces of the former, often writ large out in the open, easily and usually go unrecognized by the latter. The strange, unfamiliar thinking of the unconscious is not bound by the same logical and chronological laws and patterns as conscious cognition. In outlining elements of his metapsychology, Freud highlights the peculiarity of the unconscious in noting that it has no cognizance of either negation (including the law of noncontradiction foundational to the bivalent logic relied on by forms of conscious rationality) or time (in terms of the linear ordering of phenomena through the skeletal schema of past, present, and future). The Freudian distinction between "primary processes" (associated with the unconscious) and "secondary processes" (associated with consciousness) emphasizes precisely this: the rules and procedures of unconscious mentation are different in kind from those of conscious thinking. Hence, primary-process-style cognition is not to be conceived of along the lines of secondary-process-style cognition. In other words, the unconscious cannot be thought of as a duplicate of consciousness, a second consciousness operating apart from, yet in ways similar to, the first consciousness of the experiencing "I."

Some of the philosophically crucial upshots of Freud's insistence on the thinking (of the) unconscious as radically other in relation to conscious thought have to do with the statuses of reason and meaning in human existence. The unconscious is not "irrational" in the sense of being an inner primitive animality of crude instinctual whims and caprices, an opaque maelstrom of murky energies alien to more sophisticated, higher-order conceptual and linguistic reasoning. Nonetheless, the unconscious also is not "rational" relative to standards for rationality related to consciousness and self-consciousness. It does not pursue ends, weigh means, calculate outcomes, and ponder consequences as the conscious mind constantly does. The unconscious does not even recognize a firm, black-and-white line of demarcation between reality and fantasy, between fact and fiction. Freud, in connection with his later theories centered on the death drive, the super-ego, and masochism, goes so far as to hypothesize that the psyche even sometimes deviates from the rudimentary rationality embodied in the self-interested aiming at well-being, sabotaging its own pleasurable pursuits and inflicting pain and suffering on itself.

Likewise, although the formations of the unconscious are far from meaningless, they cannot be interpreted according to criteria of meaning derived from the recognizably meaningful phenomena of conscious life as experienced by the self of the ego. For example, the primary-process mentation characteristic of the unconscious, a style of thinking reflected in the dreams and free associations focused on by analysts, pays no heed to whether its manipulations of words, ideas, and images "mean something" according to the standards for meaning upheld by grammar, syntax, logic, and chronology. Unconscious cognition chains together ideational representations according to looser, more liberal principles of association, forging links between fragments of mental content that consciousness would never think to link. Consequently, psychoanalysis *à la* Freud is not (exclusively) a hermeneutic endeavor in search of deep meaning insofar as it necessarily involves paying attention to how facets of consciousness are configured and constrained by (sometimes quite elaborate and intricate) forms of nonsense and meaninglessness (nonsensical and meaningless from the perspective of mundane conscious contemplation).

How? – the manifestations of the unconscious

What evidence is there revealing the operations of the unconscious supposedly at play within the psyche? Asked differently, how does this un-thought thinking related but irreducible to libidinal economies manifest itself in analytically interpretable manners? Some of the first pieces of evidence prompting Freud to propose the revolutionary thesis that not all of what is mental is conscious come from his attempts to address hysteria therapeutically. This particular variety of neurosis involves psychosomatic conversion symptoms and/or affective reactions of a seemingly exaggerated and inappropriate degree of intensity in response to their apparent experiential stimuli. As regards the medically mysterious bodily ailments of hysterics, Freud's 1890s writings on hysterical patients and phenomena postulate, below the threshold of explicit conscious thematization and awareness, a psychical (rather than strictly physical) body cobbled together out of images, words, and concepts. This more-than-physiological body, a body of *Vorstellungen*, is identified as being responsible for the distribution of conversion symptoms across the body (i.e. symptoms that convert painful psychical conflicts into a decipherable "language" of physical pain). And, as regards the apparently irrational emotional outbursts of hysterics, Freud surmises that there invariably is, as it were, method to the madness. If there is a glaring discrepancy between a circumstance and someone's affective response to it, then, hidden behind (but associatively linked to) the circumstance, there must be another circumstance (a repressed idea or memory) as the unconscious determinant in relation to which the response is indeed justified and understandable. That which at first glance appears to be simply irrational turns out to be complexly structured by an idiosyncratic (quasi-)rationality, namely, the peculiar logics of mental processes typically unrecognizable to conscious cognition.

In the years that follow (especially 1900–1905), Freud proceeds to divulge a plethora of examples buttressing his axiomatic insistence that the mental and the conscious are anything but equivalent to or synonymous with each other. This deluge of evidence allegedly speaking in favor of the hypothesis of there being unconscious dimensions and dynamics in the mind comes in the forms of dreams, lapses of memory, slips of the tongue, and bungled actions, among other phenomena constituting the psychopathology of everyday life. Whereas the symptoms of hysteria are not experienced by all people, everyone is acquainted with these sorts of instances regularly occurring in the course of quotidian existence. Freud's interpretive gamble here is to wager that, contrary to widespread presumptions that nocturnal imaginings and accidental blunderings are obviously without any real significance, these seemingly unimportant occurrences are, in fact, of great import. Such occurrences, Freud contends, are encoded manifestations of another type of thinking able to be thoroughly decoded only through analytic interpretation. Given the pervasive ordering and organization of mentally mediated life, Freud considers it unreasonable simply to write off puzzling dreams and perplexing behaviors as merely meaningless, as marginal and disconnected in relation to the intricate linguistic–conceptual webs woven throughout the fabric of human being.

But perhaps the strongest evidence in favor of the Freudian case for the unconscious comes from people's amorous and sexual lives. Starting with his groundbreaking 1905 text *Three Essays on the Theory of Sexuality*, Freud brings to light a range of features of this prominent portion of human existence for which explanatory strategies based on the assumptions that the sexual is instinctually dictated by biological nature alone and/or that love is either self-evident or entirely inexplicable quickly prove to be inadequate and unsatisfactory. Individuals do not just fall in love with whoever comes along who happens to be a fitting partner for the animal–organic endeavor of reproduction. Nor do they confine their pleasures to heterosexual genital copulation; sometimes they do not take pleasure in this, but fancy other things instead. People often cannot articulate a cogent account for who they become enamored with or why they enjoy what they enjoy sexually. Through his conceptions of and reflections on infantile sexuality, homosexuality, drives, the Oedipus complex, transference, perversions, fetishism, gender identity, and sexual difference, Freud re-examines love and sexuality as blossoming at the tangled intersections of soma and psyche. Moreover, the powerful influences helping to configure these amorous and sexual phenomena usually remain opaque to ordinary conscious reflection. And yet, despite appearing to be illogically devoid of any rhyme or reason, love and sexuality, from the Freudian perspective, are not without their reasons, however rational or irrational, however visible or invisible.

III. FREUD AND … – THE RELATIONS OF PSYCHOANALYSIS TO EUROPEAN PHILOSOPHICAL ORIENTATIONS

German idealism

Freud directly and indirectly refers to Immanuel Kant on several occasions. Most of these references occur in the context of discussions dealing with the super-ego and moral masochism. Kant's metaphysics of morals, his ethics of pure practical reason, is clearly what Freud has in mind when he talks about the merciless harshness of super-egoistic morality as a "pure culture of the death drive." On Freud's anti-Kantian account, seemingly disinterested rational conscience often serves as the disguised conduit for the nonrational interests of the sadistic id, with the id's sadism inwardly discharged, via the super-ego, against the ego as its brutalized object. The ego's consciously baffling guilt is a price paid for the satisfaction of the vicious id. One could say that, from a Freudian perspective, ethical renunciations and sacrifices, contrary to superficial appearances, are not without pathological enjoyment (*qua* the sating of aggressive impulses).

Freud rarely mentions the German idealists. J. G. Fichte does not appear even once in the index of names occurring in the *Standard Edition*. The one citation of Hegel is a reference, in *The Interpretation of Dreams*, to someone else quoting Hegel. Schelling is explicitly invoked somewhat more frequently, most notably in the 1919 essay "The Uncanny." However, based on his acquaintance with certain nineteenth-century intellectual currents inspired by German idealism, Freud tends to dismiss this late-modern philosophical orientation as pseudo-scientific obscurantism, as unsubstantiated spiritualist silliness unworthy of serious consideration.

However, Freud's dismissive poor estimation of German idealist *Naturphilosophie* (philosophy of nature) is based more on its use and abuse by subsequent figures than on a careful assessment of the writings of Schelling and Hegel. Had he looked more closely at these two philosophers, Freud might have discerned in them precursors of and resources for his metapsychological model of the human psyche. Freudian psychoanalysis posits conflict, in various forms and on multiple levels, as a pervasive (even ubiquitous) power conditioning the ontogenetic emergence of full-fledged subjectivity and thereafter continuing to shape subjects. Freud's later speculations lead him to propose that psychical conflict, as grounded in the antagonisms and tensions reigning between *Eros* and the *Todestrieb* (death drive), goes right down to the bare bones and raw flesh of the biological body; human corporeality, rather than being harmoniously self-integrated and internally synthesized, is shot through with discord. In terms of this hypothesized fundamental strife between the forces of life and death, Freud credits the pre-Socratic thinker Empedocles with being an early predecessor in relation to his dual-drive theory of 1920 and after. But, in greater historical proximity to Freud, Schelling and Hegel conceive of material nature as saturated by proto-subjective negativity. The substance of German idealist *Naturphilosophie*, like the conflict-ridden somatic underpinnings of psychical life theorized by Freud, is at war with itself, permeated by the violence of clashing forces and the agitating disturbances of unsettling affects.

Moreover, thanks to Lacan putting Freud into dialogue with Hegel, one can perceive retroactively important precedents for Freud's specifically psychoanalytic conception of the unconscious in Hegel's philosophy (the 1930s rudiments of Lacan's own theoretical framework emerge at the intersection of Freudian psychoanalysis and Kojèvian Hegelianism). Some of these precedents include the dialectical self-subverting structure of the figures of consciousness in the 1807 *Phenomenology of Spirit*, the insistence on the thoroughly all-encompassing conceptual and linguistic mediation of human being in the 1812 *Science of Logic*, and the invocations of an unconscious entangled with sociohistorical forms of existence in the 1821 *Philosophy of Right*, to name a few psychoanalytically resonant lines of thought in the Hegelian philosophical apparatus. Like Freud, Hegel insists that the hidden dimensions of human subjectivity are not to be conceived of simply as the dark depths of a brute, bestial nature. Hegel and Freud concur on a point of great significance: the unconscious side of the subject is traversed by and enmeshed with intersubjective and trans-subjective configurations of great complexity and sophistication, networks of elaborately organized words, images, and ideas.

Materialism

The brand of materialism with which Freud obviously entertains a relationship is that of such nineteenth-century materialists as Fechner and Helmholtz, namely, a scientism inspired by physics and chemistry. In particular, Freud's metapsychological theories, from his 1895 *Project for a Scientific Psychology* through some of his final writings of the 1930s, display evidence of the influence on his thinking of so-called "psycho-physics." Psycho-physics is a nineteenth-century version of a quite well-known type of (speciously) scientific materialism, a materialism that believes it is both possible and desirable to reduce mental life and everything with which such life is bound up to corporeal substance (i.e. matter as physical particles mechanically interacting with each other according to the laws of efficient causality). Simply put, the psycho-physicists known to Freud strove to construct a psychology in which the psychical is investigated and described in the same fashion in which the natural sciences of the time handled material objects.

The influence of naturalistic, science-inspired materialism on Freud is glaringly manifest through several features of his corpus. First of all, Freud's earliest metapsychological formulations borrow images and ideas from the neurology in which Freud had been trained, speaking of the psyche (at least metaphorically if not literally) as a system of interconnected neurons through which circulate the excitations and stimuli of quotas of energy (both endogenous and exogenous). These neurology-derived metaphors persist, disguised and undisguised, throughout the entire subsequent span of Freud's intellectual itinerary. Additionally, Freud repeatedly appeals to the natural sciences; in particular, he forecasts future biological confirmations of his controversial hypotheses regarding human sexuality. More generally, the mechanistic language with which Freud depicts the dynamics of the psyche sometimes strongly resembles the discourse of psycho-physics, making mental processes sound like the workings of an asubjective, inhuman mechanical contraption.

But there are several very good reasons for rejecting the notion that Freud himself remains a committed psycho-physicist. And some of these reasons disclose resonances between psychoanalysis and the materialism(s) developed by and after Marx and Friedrich Engels. Although Freud makes no overt proclamations about historical and/or dialectical materialism (apropos Marxism, he briefly comments on the Russian Revolution of 1917 in *Civilization and Its Discontents*), his theoretical framework, like that of Marx and Engels, would not allow for unreservedly embracing any sort of mechanistic materialism. Stated much too succinctly, the relation between body and mind in Freudian psychoanalysis is a dialectical one. More precisely, soma participates in giving rise to psyche; but, thereafter, the psyche thus generated can and does exert reciprocal transformative powers over its libidinal–material sources in the body. Hence, by contrast with the mechanistic materialism of, for instance, psycho-physics, the treatment of mental life in analysis does not reduce it to an epiphenomenal status *vis-à-vis* the physical body.

Finally, as regards Marx's historical materialism, Freud's later work leads him implicitly to break with certain Enlightenment principles and biases presupposed by Marx (and, like Marx, Freud too is deeply marked by the beliefs and ideals of the Enlightenment). The traditional Marxist vision of history involves assuming that, at least in the long run, people are inclined to think and act in accordance with their own best interests (as exemplified by Marx's prediction that, eventually, the oppressed proletarian masses will awaken from their ideological slumber and revolutionarily smash their capitalist shackles so as to create a radically egalitarian socioeconomic arrangement in which true justice reigns). This is to attribute a minimal underlying rationality to human beings, one postulating that if somebody fully and genuinely knows what is "better" for himself or herself, then he or she will desire this good and behave so as to obtain it (an old article of faith going back to Socrates). Through such concepts as the death drive and "disavowal" (*Verleugnung*), the later Freud indicates not only that human beings can and do become libidinally invested in self-defeating and self-destructive projects, but they also are able openly to acknowledge things (say, that given values and institutions are based on bankrupt ideological foundations) while, regardless, continuing to live in ways unaltered by these acknowledgments. Knowing the truth is not automatically and inevitably liberating. Marxist critiques of ideology, as motivated by revolutionary political pursuits, are faced with some additional daunting difficulties by certain of Freud's insights into the contradictions and inconsistencies of desiring subjectivity and its defense mechanisms.

Existentialism

Although the label "existentialism" originates in the first half of the twentieth century as a term of journalistic convenience used with reference to Jean-Paul Sartre in particular, it has come to designate a movement beginning with the later Schelling (of the 1809 *Freiheitschrift* and after) and running through Kierkegaard, Fyodor Dostoevsky, Nietzsche, Franz Kafka, Martin Heidegger, Sartre, Albert Camus, and Samuel Beckett, among others. The existentialists' focus on the affective lives of human beings, especially their emphases on the relative frailty of reason *vis-à-vis* the emotions and the disturbing details of the gloomier side of negative affects, seems to be strikingly similar to what is involved with some of the concerns central to Freud's analytic perspective. And, if Nietzsche is deemed to be an existentialist, then, as a chorus of authors engaged in an academic sub-industry unto itself never tire of claiming, Freud is profoundly indebted to existentialism. Admittedly, Nietzsche is almost certainly one of the figures Freud has in mind when, in a moment of modesty, he portrays psychoanalysis as a theoretical systematization and practical instrumentalization of the insights and discoveries of various key predecessors. However, this momentary modesty aside, it would be utterly unjustifiable to maintain that Freudian analysis is simply a clinical recapitulation of Nietzschean philosophy. Apart from there being much in Freud's *oeuvre* that is not to be found in any developed or explicit form in Nietzsche's writings, there are many important differences between these two thinkers even at the level of overlapping concepts (such as the unconscious, drives, and so on). Moreover, whether any of the versions of the libidinal economy hypothesized by Freud are seamlessly compatible with the infamous "will to power" posited by Nietzsche is quite doubtful.

Countless comparisons and contrasts could be elaborated here as regards looking at Freud alongside the existentialist tradition. One could spell out a Freudian problematization of the possibility of reasonless action represented by the character Meursault in Camus's novel *The Stranger*. One could weave together Heidegger's treatment of temporality in his analytic of Dasein with the delineation of the temporal structures of the psyche sketched by Freud. Numerous other things could be said as well. Incidentally, along these lines, it is worth noting that Freud showed little interest in the bridge-building efforts of "existential psychoanalysts" such as Ludwig Binswanger and Medard

Boss.[4] Reciprocally, Heidegger was blithely dismissive of psychoanalysis and Sartre was highly critical of it. Both Heidegger and Sartre viewed Freud's vision of the human condition as too mechanistic and determinist to capture what is most essential in being human.

Despite their disagreements, Heidegger and Sartre share a picture of Freud as pursuing a fundamentally reductive project, as seeking to collapse the being of human beings into the law-governed workings of ultimately bio-material forces. This vulgar, commonplace portrayal of Freudian psychoanalysis is terribly mistaken. On the one hand, it is indeed true that Freud's notions of intrapsychical defense mechanisms and the overdetermination of states of consciousness undermine certain standard, quotidian senses of oneself as being an autonomous self, a free agent. But, on the other hand, psychoanalysis is anything but a straightforward discourse of determinism, a set of narratives about how people are nothing more than inherently ignorant puppets dancing on the end of strings held by an invisible master called "the unconscious." For Freud, not only are individuals usually unaware of the degree to which their seemingly self-determined words and deeds actually are determined by influences operating below the level of conscious cognizance; they are also, at the same time, heavily invested in avoiding any direct realizations of the frightening extent to which their modes of life and styles of being are not imposed and held in place by the authority of an extra-mental external reality such as fate, God, society, and/or childhood. In other words, behind the veil of repression lurk not only the heteronomous determining matrices and machinations of the unconscious, but also an often obfuscated "abyss of freedom," that is, an unsettling autonomy as the groundless ground beneath all constructed and constraining fashions of living. This freedom is normally just as unconscious as the hidden powers of psychical overdetermination.

Phenomenology

Freud shares with his contemporary Edmund Husserl, the founder of phenomenology, a debt to the teachings of Brentano. More precisely, Freud and Husserl appropriate, each in his own way, Brentano's "intentionality thesis" according to which the mental is distinct from the physical insofar as the former involves

4. Binswanger (1881–1966) and Boss (1903–90) were both mental health practitioners who sought to integrate clinical and theoretical psychoanalysis with phenomenology and existentialism, in particular the existential phenomenology of Heidegger. In philosophical circles, Binswanger today is perhaps best known for his essay "Dream and Existence," thanks to Foucault's translation of it (a translation accompanied by an introduction longer than the essay itself). Boss, advocate of "Daseinanalysis," is responsible for prompting Heidegger to give his *Zollikon Seminars* addressing philosophy and psychological matters.

an intentional directedness. Additionally, this directedness requires psychical "presentations" forming the (mental) objects with which the acts and operations of the mind concern themselves. Apart from influencing certain of Freud's metapsychological models having to do with *Vorstellungen* and their roles apropos reality (as psychical reality, the reality principle, etc.), Brentano's notion of intentionality informs the so-called "fundamental rule" of clinical analytic practice, namely, free association on the part of the analysand. When a patient in analysis says that he or she has "nothing" to say or "nothing" on his or her mind, this is never taken as literally true by the analyst. Due to the abiding, inherent "aboutness" of mental life (i.e. its intentional structure), there always and necessarily are things occurring to the analysand lying on the couch. Hence, his or her protests that he or she cannot think of anything to talk about should be interpreted, in nearly all instances, as resistance to associating freely.

However, despite having Brentano in common as a source of early inspiration, Freudian psychoanalysis and Husserlian phenomenology part company when it comes to the topic of the unconscious. Bluntly put, transcendental phenomenology *à la* Husserl contains no equivalent to the specifically analytic unconscious. When Husserl and his followers address aspects of mental subjectivity apart from the domain of conscious awareness, what they usually refer to are features of the mind that Freud would qualify as either preconscious (i.e. features that can become conscious on deliberate, focused reflection) or nonconscious (i.e. features that simply cannot be rendered within the parameters of possible representation holding for first-person conscious mentation). Unlike what is preconscious or nonconscious, what is unconscious is kept outside of the circumscribed sphere of (self-)consciousness thanks to the workings of defense mechanisms (i.e. repression and other intrapsychical defenses). The contents of the unconscious, although in most cases capable of being brought to light through an analytic process (by contrast with the nonconscious), cannot easily be called to mind at will (by contrast with the preconscious). Husserlian phenomenology lacks a proper unconscious insofar as it does not posit anything resembling the defense mechanisms so central to the Freudian understanding of mental life.

Whereas transcendental phenomenology shows little interest in psychoanalysis *qua* theory of the unconscious, existential phenomenology proves to be a much more promising philosophical partner for analysis. Although Heidegger turns a blind eye to Freud on the basis of ill-informed opinions of the latter's ideas, Binswanger and Boss, as well as many others, are not without their good reasons for sensing some potential points of theoretical co-augmentation between a metapsychological model of the psyche and an existential analytic of Dasein. One of the tragedies of the missed encounter between Freud and Heidegger is that the two twentieth-century figures carrying out the most radical reconsiderations of the human condition in light of temporality did not end up collaborating.

With respect to psychoanalysis, Maurice Merleau-Ponty is the most sympathetic and engaged of the great thinkers of the phenomenological orientation. Not only does he explicitly take up Freud's concepts and the ontogenetic schemas contained in analytic metapsychology – he also draws on Kleinian object-relations theory[5] and certain ideas formulated by his friend Lacan. In particular, the Merleau-Pontian account of embodiment, involving a distinction between the exogenously mediated "lived body" and the corporeality at stake in the natural sciences, is quite relevant to Freudian analysis. But, at the same time, the images and themes of harmony, integration, and fusion permeating Merleau-Ponty's philosophical discourse are at odds with the psychoanalytic stress on both pervasive antagonism and conflict as well as the psychical subject's insurmountable out-of-joint-ness with its surrounding environs.

Critical theory

Although Freud himself does not engage with Marx, several twentieth-century figures and movements in the Marxist tradition see in Freudian psychoanalysis a set of useful theoretical tools for political analysis and critique (and this despite Freud's bourgeois sensibilities as well as the suspicions that analysis is a form of "class therapy" excluding those not sufficiently blessed with spare time and disposable income). The most notable and well-known instance of this is the selective appropriation of Freud's ideas by members of the Frankfurt School of critical theory. Theodor Adorno's famous 1950 study *The Authoritarian Personality* attempts to sketch a psychoanalytically informed portrait of a purported type of individual character structure allegedly susceptible to fascist-style authoritarianism. As regards Adorno, it also should be mentioned here that his criticisms of scientism in the social sciences, with this scientism's insistence on quantitative and statistical methods of study, dovetails with the position of Freudian and post-Freudian psychoanalysis *vis-à-vis* those psychologies

5. Melanie Klein (1882–1960) is the founder of object-relations theory, a post-Freudian psychoanalytic approach that, as its name suggests, emphasizes the centrality of fantasy-mediated relationships with objects and others as the driving motor mechanisms of psychical development. Relations, rather than endogenous libidinal forces and factors, are identified as the formative fundaments of the psyche, fundaments allegedly established starting in very early infancy. Along with ego psychology (an outgrowth of Anna Freud's analytic doctrines, with the 1940s split between Anna Freud and Klein having had a decisive impact on the subsequent history of psychoanalysis, especially in the English-speaking world) and Lacanianism and its permutations, object-relations theory is one of the three major orientations shaping psychoanalysis over the course of the past several decades.

basing themselves on the numerical parsing of data from large test-subject sample pools. Freud does not shy away from offering evidence for his metapsychological claims about the organization and operation of the psyche: quite the contrary. But, nonetheless, analyses are always-unique experiences taking shape between singular subjects in intimate circumstances, circumstances whose private and unrepeatable qualities make them ill suited for a methodology based on replicable experiments open to public scrutiny. For practical as well as philosophical reasons, psychoanalysis cannot survive reduction to a "scientific psychology" according to the standards of the sort of scientism argued against by Adorno.

However, the key manifesto of Frankfurt School Freudo-Marxism in its most robust incarnation is Herbert Marcuse's 1955 book *Eros and Civilization*. In this text and elsewhere, Marcuse, through his particular manner of combining Freud with Marx, contends that psychoanalysis both falls prey to aspects of the ideology of capitalism's "repressive society" and, simultaneously, also harbors the conceptual resources for seeing through this same ideology. In Marcuse's eyes, Freud erroneously treats as ahistorical constants of human psychology facets of psychical life shaped by the temporary historical features of capitalism as a particular socioeconomic system. More specifically, Marcuse maintains that the material conditions peculiar to Freud's era – these conditions ostensibly require renunciations and sacrifices (i.e. "repressions" as per Marcuse's rather loose construal of Freudian vocabulary) on the part of individuals as cogs in a collective machine involving "alienated labor" and artificial scarcity – mislead Freud into positing extreme libidinal inhibition as an inherent, contextually invariant symptom afflicting every (discontent) individual ensconced within "civilization" (defined as any group order in which the price of membership is submission to restrictive rules). Along Marxist lines, Marcuse imagines a new ensemble of historico-material conditions yet to come in which the pointless toiling of commodity-propelled capitalism and the curbs on satisfaction it demands are eliminated; and, with this revolutionary change, neurosis-inducing repression as conceived of by Freud supposedly is eliminated too. While criticizing Freud in this fashion, Marcuse avowedly continues to rely on Freudian psychoanalysis, especially its theories of the libidinal economy, to explain the psychological and subjective workings of capitalism as well as to articulate his vision of a future society beyond repression. But Marcuse's political deployment of Freud's ideas arguably is based on some far-from-insignificant misunderstandings of these ideas. In a nutshell, Marcuse tends to equivocate illegitimately between instinctual needs and psychical drives as well as between intrapsychical repression and external social suppression. A better metapsychological appreciation of drive dynamics in relation to their enveloping milieus problematizes Marcuse's picture, calling into question whether the revolutionary liberation he anticipates can or would ever occur as envisioned by him.[6]

Blending psychoanalysis with Marxism is not the sole prerogative of the Frankfurt School. Starting in the 1960s, Lacan attracts an audience outside clinical analytic circles, an audience containing leftists of various stripes (including Maoist students of Louis Althusser, himself committed to a careful Marxist consideration of psychoanalysis, such as Jacques-Alain Miller and Alain Badiou[7]). Claude Lefort, Cornelius Castoriadis, and Slavoj Žižek, to name several of the most prominent representatives of continental political thought as inflected by psychoanalysis, draw on analytic concepts in their reflections on democracy and capitalism.

Feminism

The feminist reception of Freud, even when limited to those varieties of feminism forming part of the continental philosophical tradition, cannot be summarized easily or adequately given its sophistication and complexity. Needless to say, Freudian psychoanalysis has sparked a range of reactions from feminist thinkers, spanning a spectrum running from outright rejection to enthusiastic appropriation. What follows are a few highly selective remarks about a topic (i.e. Freud and feminism) around which has formed a sizable mass of diverse texts and debates.

Before mentioning some of the most noteworthy continental feminists concerned with Freudian psychoanalysis, a couple of claims ought briefly to be made against a certain feminist tendency to dismiss Freud as a misogynistic turn-of-the-century Viennese male whose views reflect those of his sexist culture and time. To begin with, Freud's female analysands are themselves products of a sexist culture and time. As such, their psyches are marked by the effects of a phallocratic system; through analysis, Freud reveals just how deeply ingrained are the imprints of patriarchy. But there is a world of difference between description and prescription, with Freud describing the sexualities and libidinal subjectivities of his patients without thereby aiming to endorse in a normative mode what he describes. Furthermore, despite moments when Freud admittedly does seem to fall back into aspects of the misogyny of his era, his sustained examination of sexual difference and gender identities, itself a deviation from his predecessors'

*6. For a detailed discussion of Marcuse, see the essay by John Abromeit in *The History of Continental Philosophy: Volume 5*.

*7. Miller and Badiou are discussed in detail in the essay by Patrice Maniglier in *The History of Continental Philosophy: Volume 7*, while Badiou is the focus of an essay by Bruno Bosteels in *The History of Continental Philosophy: Volume 8*.

and contemporaries' general tight-lipped silence apropos such matters, arguably opens up a whole horizon of new possibilities for considering the multifarious relationships between sexuality and subjectivity.

Along related lines, Freud launches his clinical analytic career by being one of the first people to start genuinely listening to suffering women. He treats female hysterics not as irrational creatures of emotion buffeted about by a crazy vortex of feelings and sensations (perhaps discombobulated by a "wandering womb"), but as proper human beings with rich mental lives that, even when riddled with psycho-neurotic symptoms, exhibit the rhyme and reason of the psychical logics uncovered by analysis. Additionally, Freud is not the simple-minded biological determinist that many, including many feminist critics, make him out to be on the basis of flawed partial interpretations of his writings. For him, human physiology, with "the anatomical distinction between the sexes," indeed crucially contributes to shaping the contours and characteristics of people's subjectivities. But these bio-material factors do not predestine someone in the direction of a single subjective *telos*; nor do they enjoy a final determining authority over who and what (sexed) individuals are or become.

French feminism and those feminist thinkers drawing from this particular strain of feminism are the most favorably disposed toward Freud and his legacy (especially his legacy in France as influenced by Lacan). While being critical of Freudian psychoanalysis in her classic 1949 book *The Second Sex*, Simone de Beauvoir's discussions of femininity therein are prefigured by Freud's groundbreaking de-essentialization of gender identity and his revelatory analytic dismantling of the sociopsychical constructions contributing to configurations of a denaturalized sexual difference. In Beauvoir's wake (and continuing up through the present), others tackle the issues of sex and gender in fashions that openly employ psychoanalytic concepts. Judith Butler, Hélène Cixous, Catherine Clément, Luce Irigaray, and Julia Kristeva, to list just a handful of theorists of diverse outlooks, maintain a nuanced, multifaceted dialogue with Freud, simultaneously pointing to limitations plaguing his conceptions of femininity while also deploying his ideas in projects striving to reconceptualize the status of sexual difference (these two endeavors sometimes come together as an immanent critique, namely, a critique of Freud's account of sexual subjectivity relying on Freud's own notions). Admittedly, even for those feminists drawing on Freud, there is much in his corpus (such as versions of the Oedipus complex and the notorious conjecture about penis envy in women) that must be reworked or discarded in light of feminist critical insights. Some of the most far-reaching explorations of the places of embodiment and inter-subjectivity in Freudian psychoanalysis are due to feminist interventions in the analytic field.

Structuralism

Of course, when one considers the link between psychoanalysis and structuralism, the primary association that immediately comes to mind is Lacan's return to Freud. During the first six years of his annual seminar (1953–59) and in contemporaneous writings, Lacan endeavors to re-read Freud through the lens of Saussurian structuralism (his version of Ferdinand de Saussure is heavily reliant on that of the structural linguist Roman Jakobson[8]). Paying close attention to both the role of language in Freud's theories and the linguistic–conceptual details of Freud's texts, Lacan asserts that Freud unknowingly already was a proto-structuralist of a Saussurian sort. Much of his evidence for this assertion comes from the prevalence of elaborate word-plays in the numerous examples of dreams, jokes, and parapraxes analyzed by Freud, especially in his early writings. Lacan insists that interpreting Freud's works in this fashion is crucial for avoiding the deviations from the essential tenets of Freudian psychoanalysis of which Lacan thinks Anglo-American psychoanalytic orientations are guilty. Lacan's quasi-structuralist return to Freud is a sustained effort to combat the image of Freudian psychoanalysis marketed by the American ego psychology of the 1950s in particular.

Claude Lévi-Strauss,[9] a structural anthropologist who epitomizes what is referred to as classical French structuralism, also significantly informs how Lacan understands Saussure and his successors in connection with psychoanalysis. What is more, Lévi-Strauss, taken on his own apart from Lacan's references to him, champions a conception of "structure" audibly resonating with the Freudian notion of the unconscious in manners echoing the resonances between Hegel and Freud. To be more precise, in his 1949 *Elementary Structures of Kinship* and similar studies, Lévi-Strauss claims to uncover the workings of formally expressible laws and patterns organizing and underpinning identity, status, and familial–social relations in given human groups. For the most part, the members of these groups are not directly or explicitly aware of these laws and patterns, although their thoughts and actions testify to the rule of these orders of nonconscious structures. Like the Freudian unconscious, Lévi-Straussian structures, rather than being sets of nonconscious instinctual tendencies, are networks of sophisticated codes and algorithms palpably molding individuals' existences without, for all that, these networks being self-reflexively grasped as such by those caught in their grip.

*8. For a discussion of Saussure and Jakobson, see the essay by Thomas F. Broden in *The History of Continental Philosophy: Volume 5*.

*9. For a detailed discussion of Lévi-Strauss, see the essay by Brian C. J. Singer in *The History of Continental Philosophy: Volume 5*.

According to the conventions of certain philosophical journalists and intellectual historians, Michel Foucault (at least in his youth) and Roland Barthes both also qualify, along with Lévi-Strauss and Lacan, as structuralists. In some of his first and some of his final works (in such texts as 1961's *History of Madness* [early] and 1976's initial volume of *The History of Sexuality* [late]), Foucault situates Freud historically, using this historical framing to call into question Freud's seemingly revolutionary, unprecedented status. From these critical Foucaultian perspectives, Freud appears to be surprisingly complicit with longstanding prior psychiatric traditions as well as part of a growing Western cultural tendency toward valorizing sexuality as the supposed secret truth of who and what one is. However, in between the early and late phases of his *oeuvre*, Foucault, near the end of *The Order of Things* (1966), approvingly speaks of psychoanalysis as participating in "the erasure of the figure of man," that is, the dawn of a new antihumanist thought (although Foucault does not mention him by name here, he undoubtedly is appealing to Lacan's structuralist version of analysis).

Carrying out a project called for by Saussure himself, Barthes develops semiotics as a "science of signs" beyond linguistics proper (i.e. a theory of sign-systems encompassing not only the signs of natural languages, but the signifying elements functioning in cuisine, fashion, art, etc.). Kristeva, perhaps Barthes' most prominent student, weaves together semiotics and Freudian–Lacanian psychoanalysis. The semiotic sensitivity to the multiple dimensions of signifying materials and practices – neither semiotics nor psychoanalysis limits signs and signifiers to meaningful instances of communicative language – meshes well with analytic approaches to the symbolically shaped texture of psychical subjectivity and its contexts.

Poststructuralism

Lacan's seventh seminar of 1959–60 (*The Ethics of Psychoanalysis*) justifiably could be identified as the first poststructuralist (albeit *avant la lettre*) treatment of Freudian psychoanalysis. Therein, Lacan enacts what is often described as a sort of turn in his thinking, a shift of emphasis in his foundational "register theory" from the Imaginary and the Symbolic to the Real. Whereas previously he focuses on the effects of images and signifiers in the structuring of the speaking subject, at the end of the 1950s he turns his attention to things (for instance, *das Ding*, *jouissance*, *der Nebenmensch*, and so on – in short, Things of the Real) that impact the Imaginary–Symbolic structures of reality without themselves being captured by or reducible to such structures. The signifier-supported scaffoldings of desiring subjectivity in its relations with intersubjective and trans-subjective constellations are no longer, in and after the seventh seminar, the sole foci of analytic metapsychology. Succinctly stated, for the later Lacan, structure is (in his own parlance) "not all."

However, the inaccurate picture of Lacan as a classical Lévi-Straussian structuralist, a picture based on his teachings from the years prior to the seventh seminar, informs a poststructuralist rebellion against the Lacanian return to Freud. This rebellion is intertwined with the events of May 1968 in Paris. In the climate of France in the late 1960s, Gilles Deleuze and Félix Guattari mount their anti-Oedipal critique of psychoanalysis, a critique portraying Freud and Lacan as insidious normalizers of desire, as representatives of an effort to codify an anarchic, nomadic, impersonal, and machine-like libidinal economy within the constraining coordinates of narratives centered on the nuclear family and its familiar anthropomorphic actors.[10] Deleuze and Guattari manage powerfully to channel and express the sociopolitical concerns of many of their contemporaries. But, under the influence of these turbulent times, this anti-Oedipal duo indulge in the tactics both of representing the Oedipus complex as the be all and end all of Freudian psychoanalysis (itself a debatable, dubitable representation) as well as of depicting Lacan as fundamentally a structuralist advocate of the utterly Oedipal Freud (this too is questionable and problematic).

In fashions more sympathetic to psychoanalysis, other poststructuralist discontents of Lacanianism play Freud off against Lacan. Arguably animated by a vaguely Bergsonian conceptual and theoretical aesthetic, André Green, Jean Laplanche, Paul Ricoeur, and others (such as Kristeva) appeal to Freudian energetics (supposedly encompassing the concepts of libido, drive, affect, and similar notions) *contra* the purported dominance of bloodless formal structures in the Lacanian model of psychical subjectivity. This poststructuralist strain of psychoanalytic theory is primarily responsible for the now-familiar allegations that Lacan-the-analyst indefensibly neglects body and emotion (themselves said to be sidelined by him in tandem with his ostensibly lopsided privileging of signifiers as conceived of via such disciplines as linguistics and mathematics). As with Deleuze and Guattari, these sorts of readings of Freud and Lacan are contentious and contestable.

Lastly, there are multiple connections between, on the one hand, psychoanalysis *à la* Freud, and, on the other hand, Jacques Derrida and the "deconstructionism" associated with his name. Derrida repeatedly addresses Freud and Lacan.[11] Moreover, his novel methods and techniques of philosophical exegesis are avowedly indebted to psychoanalytic practices of listening and reading.

10. See Gilles Deleuze and Félix Guattari, *Anti-Oedipus: Capitalism and Schizophrenia*, Robert Hurley *et al.* (trans.) (New York: Viking Press, 1977).
11. See, for example, Jacques Derrida, *The Post Card: From Socrates to Freud and Beyond*, Alan Bass (trans.) (Chicago, IL: University of Chicago Press, 1987).

Nonetheless, Derrida shares many of his fellow poststructuralists' concerns and reservations apropos Freudian and Lacanian analysis. Additionally, from a certain angle one can perceive deconstruction and psychoanalysis as mirror-image inversions of each other: whereas the former tends to discern a chaotic, nonsystematic heterogeneity behind a textual façade of ordered, systematic homogeneity, the latter tends to discern the opposite, namely, an ordered homogeneity behind a textual façade of chaotic heterogeneity (for example, the apparently fragmented and disjointed free associations of analysands are, in actuality, governed by an integrated, coherent order of unconscious formations). The texts interpreted by deconstructionists and analysts often differ, and, appropriately, so too do their interpretive procedures.

Declarations of Freud's death have become a journalistic cliché in an age dominated by the alliance between insurance companies and the pharmaceutical–industrial complex. However, although no longer enjoying the anomalous, strange success of its mid-twentieth-century years as the preferred psychological treatment of celebrities and the privileged theoretical framework governing psychiatry departments, psychoanalysis is far from perishing and disappearing. Part of what has been crucial to keeping Freud and his followers alive is continental philosophy's lively interest in psychoanalytic ideas (not to mention the creative applications of these ideas carried out by various sectors of the humanities and social sciences influenced by European philosophical currents). Today, philosophers and theorists rooted in the philosophies of continental Europe continue to appropriate, modify, and refine concepts from the Freudian tradition, using psychoanalysis to interrogate a range of contemporary cultural, political, religious, and scientific issues. Considering his continuing relevance to how people understand themselves and their world, Freud is anything but dead.

MAJOR WORKS

All references to the English translations refer to *The Standard Edition of the Complete Psychological Works of Sigmund Freud* (24 vols), edited and translated by James Strachey, in collaboration with Anna Freud, assisted by Alix Strachey and Alan Tyson (London: The Institute of Psycho-Analysis, 1953–74); hereafter abbreviated *SE*, followed by the volume number and, if a given text is one of two or more in a single volume, the inclusive page numbers. The dates in parentheses mark the dates of publication of the original German texts; those in brackets, when they occur, mark the dates of composition if these differ from the dates of publication.

Entwurf einer Psychologie ([1895] 1950). Published in English as *Project for a Scientific Psychology*. *SE* 1: 281–397.

Studien über Hysterie (with Josef Breuer) (1893–95). Published in English as *Studies on Hysteria*. *SE* 2.

Die Traumdeutung (1900). Published in English as *The Interpretation of Dreams*. *SE* 4–5.

Zur Psychopathologie des Alltagsleben (1901). Published in English as *The Psychopathology of Everyday Life*. *SE* 6.

Drei Abhandlungen zur Sexualtheorie (1905). Published in English as *Three Essays on the Theory of Sexuality*. *SE* 7: 123–245.

Der Witz und Seine Beziehung zum Unbewussten (1905). Published in English as *Jokes and Their Relation to the Unconscious*. *SE* 8.

Über Psychoanalyse ([1909] 1910). Published in English as *Five Lectures on Psycho-Analysis*. *SE* 11: 1–56.

Totem und Tabu ([1912–13] 1913). Published in English as *Totem and Taboo*. *SE* 13: vii–162.

Vorlesungen zur Einführung in die Psychoanalyse ([1915–17] 1916–17). Published in English as *Introductory Lectures on Psycho-Analysis*. *SE* 15–16.

Jenseits des Lustprinzips (1920). Published in English as *Beyond the Pleasure Principle*. *SE* 18: 1–64.

Massenpsychologie und Ich-Analyse (1921). Published in English as *Group Psychology and the Analysis of the Ego*. *SE* 18: 65–143.

Das Ich und das Es (1923). Published in English as *The Ego and the Id*. *SE* 19: 1–66.

Hemmung, Symptom und Angst (1926). Published in English as *Inhibitions, Symptoms and Anxiety*. *SE* 20: 75–175.

Die Zukunft einer Illusion (1927). Published in English as *The Future of an Illusion*. *SE* 21: 1–56.

Das Unbehagen in der Kultur ([1929] 1930). Published in English as *Civilization and Its Discontents*. *SE* 21: 57–145.

Neue Folge der Vorlesungen zur Einführung in die Psychoanalyse ([1932] 1933). Published in English as *New Introductory Lectures on Psycho-Analysis*. *SE* 22: 1–182.

Der Mann Moses und die Monotheistische Religion: Drei Abhandlungen ([1934–38] 1939). Published in English as *Moses and Monotheism: Three Essays*. *SE* 23: 1–137.

Abriss der Psychoanalyse ([1938] 1940). Published in English as *An Outline of Psycho-Analysis*. *SE* 23: 139–207.

Apart from the books listed above, many of Freud's most important texts are article-length essays as well as novella-length case studies. The most important of these would include (but not be limited to): the Fliess correspondence, the five famous case studies (Dora, Little Hans, the Rat Man, Schreber, and the Wolf Man), the writings on psychoanalytic technique, the papers on metapsychology, the later pieces on sexuality and gender identity, as well as numerous analyses of social, cultural, and political phenomena. The reader interested in these texts should turn to *The Standard Edition*.

13

RESPONSES TO EVOLUTION: SPENCER'S EVOLUTIONISM, BERGSONISM, AND CONTEMPORARY BIOLOGY

Keith Ansell-Pearson, Paul-Antoine Miquel, and Michael Vaughan

Darwin's *On the Origin of Species* was published towards the end of 1859 and although its influence on the intellectual life of the second half of the nineteenth century was immense and dramatic, it alone did not generate the rise of interest in questions about evolution. As one commentator has noted, most nineteenth-century evolutionists were Lamarckians or Spencerians rather than Darwinians: Jean-Baptiste Lamarck (1744–1829) had published his theory of progressive evolution in *Philosophie zoologique* in 1809 and Herbert Spencer (1820–1903) had developed an evolutionary theory of mind and behavior in his *Principles of Psychology* of 1855.[1] It is often assumed that Spencer and Darwin adhere to the same theory of evolution, but this is not the case; and it is Spencer who, at least for philosophers, was the major intellectual figure of the period. Some of philosophy's most original minds, such as Charles Sanders Peirce (1839–1914) and Henri Bergson (1859–1941), took note of the Darwinian revolution and the rise of philosophical evolutionism and sought to respond to them.[2] Bergson captures the mood well when he writes in his great text of 1907, *Creative Evolution*, that "the language of transformism forces itself now upon all philosophy, as the dogmatic affirmation of transformism forces itself upon science."[3] Let us note at the outset that Darwin's aim in the *Origin of Species* was not to promote the concept of evolution – the word appears only at the very end of the

1. Louis Menand, *The Metaphysical Club* (London: HarperCollins, 2001), 121.
2. For insight into Peirce and evolution, see Carl R. Hausman, *Charles S. Peirce's Evolutionary Philosophy* (Cambridge: Cambridge University Press, 1993).
3. Henri Bergson, *Creative Evolution*, Arthur Mitchell (trans.) (Basingstoke: Palgrave Macmillan, 2007), 17. Hereafter cited as CE followed by the page number.

book[4] – but rather to do away with the notion of supernatural intelligence, that is, the view that the universe is the result of an idea or plan. As one commentator has noted,[5] what is radical about Darwin's book is not its evolutionism but its materialism: species evolve according to processes that are entirely natural, chance-generated, and blind. Indeed, Darwin's choice of the word "selection" may be unfortunate since it suggests an intention at work in nature, while the process of evolution is a blind one: "The selection of favorable characteristics is therefore neither designed nor progressive. No intelligence, divine or otherwise, determines in advance the relative value of individual variations."[6] There is, then, no ideal type or essence of a species toward which adaptive changes are leading. In his *The Variation of Plants and Animals under Domestication* (1868), Darwin makes it clear that the process by which living things evolve can be explained without making use of any theory of design.

In this essay, we focus attention on Bergson's *Creative Evolution*, since this is without doubt the most important text on evolution by a continental philosopher. It contains an important critique of Spencer's evolutionism; it is intellectually ambitious and rich in showing how philosophy and science can reach a new rapport concerning questions of life; and it has inspired major developments in both postwar philosophy (notably the work of Gilles Deleuze) and recent biology (notably in applications of complexity theory and nonlinear thermodynamics to the study of living systems).

I. HERBERT SPENCER AND EVOLUTIONISM

Spencer's ideas on evolution are primarily contained in his *First Principles* (1862) and his two-volume work, *The Principles of Biology* (1864, 1867). In the first work, he sets himself two main tasks: first, to come up with an adequate definition of the aims and scope of philosophy; and, second, to provide an adequate conception of evolution. Spencer accepts that philosophy has limits of knowledge and affirms the idea that philosophy is unable to formulate "Being" in

4. The idea of evolution is presented at the end of the *Origin of Species* in a way that permits one to speak of a kind of Darwinian sublime: "Thus, from the war of nature, from famine and death, the most exalted object which we are capable of conceiving, namely, the production of the higher animals, directly follows. There is grandeur in this view of life, with its several powers, having been originally breathed into a few forms or into one; and that, whilst this planet has gone cycling on according to the fixed law of gravity, from so simple a beginning endless forms most beautiful and most wonderful have been, and are being, evolved" (*The Origin of Species* [Harmondsworth: Penguin, 1985], 459–60).
5. Menand, *The Metaphysical Club*, 121.
6. *Ibid.*, 122.

distinction from "Appearance." In short, philosophy is not an ontology.[7] But what is its character once these limits have been acknowledged? Spencer considers the rivalry between German and English philosophy in which "the English criticism" repudiates everything regarded as absolute knowledge. What they share, however, he notes, is a commitment to philosophy as the discipline that is concerned with systematized knowledge. What is needed is a useful contrast between philosophy and science. Spencer proposes that science "means merely the family of Sciences" and consists of "truths more or less separated"; by contrast philosophy stands for truths that have been integrated (FP 37). He writes:

> How, then, is Philosophy constituted? … So long as these truths are known only apart and regarded as independent, even the most general of them cannot without laxity of speech be called philosophical. But when, having been severally reduced to a mechanical axiom, a principle of molecular physics, and a law of social action, they are contemplated together as corollaries of some ultimate truth, then we rise to the kind of knowledge which constitutes Philosophy proper. (*Ibid.*)

Philosophy's job is to "comprehend and consolidate the widest generalizations of Science" (*ibid.*). If science is partially unified knowledge, philosophy is completely unified knowledge. Knowledge begins with crude and isolated observations; it then seeks to establish propositions of a broad scope that are separate from particular cases; and finally, it culminates in the articulation of universal propositions. It is important to note that Spencer is placing the stress not simply on knowledge as a process but rather on philosophy being able to express definite pieces and truths of knowledge; that is, his concern is not with the validity of the act of knowing but with the actual product of knowledge, such as an ultimate proposition that "includes and consolidates all the results of experience" (FP 42). For example, philosophy shows that we always think in terms of "relations" and their elements, such as likenesses and differences. Our thought enjoys a status of "relativity" and is thus forever debarred from "knowing or conceiving Absolute Being" (FP 47).

In the case of "evolution" the concern is with specifying its most general laws, for example, showing that "in its primary aspect" it denotes a change "from a less coherent to a more coherent form consequent on the dissipation of motion and integration of matter." Spencer takes this to be a *universal process*, that is, one through which "sensible existences," both individually and as a whole, pass

7. Herbert Spencer, *First Principles* (London: Watts & Co., 1937), para. 36. Hereafter cited as FP followed by the paragraph number.

during the "ascending halves of their histories" (FP 115). He contends that this holds for both the earliest changes in the visible universe and the changes that can be traced in societies and the products of social life, including science itself. Spencer is thus identifying a law of development that can be applied to all things that undergo evolution, be it a solar system, a planet, an organism, or a nation: "From the lowest living forms upwards, the degree of development is marked by the degree in which the several parts constitute a co-operative assemblage – are integrated into a group of organs that live for and by one another" (*ibid.*). Spencer is seeking again the most general and comprehensive principles by which the phenomenon of "Life" (a word he comes to be suspicious of[8]) can be understood, for example, "integration" and "differentiation." His central and most well-known claim is that in evolution there is a change from the homogeneous to the heterogeneous. We see this, he contends, in the case of the human animal, in the progress of every tribe and nation as well as every civilization (FP 122). The initial definition of "evolution" can now be finessed, then, as a change from an indefinite, incoherent homogeneity to a definite, coherent heterogeneity (FP 127, 138).

Spencer's *The Principles of Biology* takes the form of a theoretical inquiry into the meaning of life and not a contribution to the growth of any particular biological science.[9] His specific aim was to combat the "continental" tradition of inquiry and deny that living things possessed meaning on account of their being directed by an internal force or power. He was keen to avoid any probing into what may lie beneath surface shapes and instead seeks to restrict knowledge, in true empiricist fashion, to what is causally visible; in short, knowledge is "superficial" and, as such, uncovers rational and functional laws.[10] Spencer places himself in opposition to two continental currents of thought: on the one hand, the philosophical idealism associated with the likes of Lorenz Oken (1779–1851) and Goethe; and, on the other hand, a materialistic current stemming from Comtean positivism. Any appeal to transcendentalism (such as a vital principle of life) was to be avoided, along with innate principles and teleological perfection. At the same time, a crude positivism that held life to be meaningless was also to be avoided. There is "meaning" in life but this will be discovered only in the detailed interpretation of the functions and structures of life, such as plants and animals, and in the examination of their relations with an environment.[11] Life is not a separate force and the science of biology will demonstrate that living things are all subject to the same laws as the rest

8. See Mark Francis, *Herbert Spencer and the Invention of Modern Life* (Stocksfield: Acumen, 2007), 206, 226.
9. *Ibid.*, 211.
10. *Ibid.*
11. *Ibid.*, 212.

of the physical universe: "Nothing would be hidden; for Spencer the meaning of life was plainly visible in the forms and structures of the material world."[12] Where Spencer is radical is in his denial that classifications of living forms correspond to anything natural in the world; systems of classification are an artificial means for organizing our knowledge. The further we carry the analysis of things, he holds, the more obvious it becomes that divisions and classifications are essentially human inventions and scientific artifices by which we limit and arrange the matter under investigation and as a way of facilitating human inquiry.

The issue that intrigues Spencer in *The Principles of Biology* is not the natural selection of species but species' self-persistence and perpetuation; in short, their continuation over time. This means, therefore, focusing on the "static" aspect of life. He explains the exhibition of species' stability by recourse to a vital impulse, which he calls the protoplasm, but this impulse is not progressive, that is, it is an agent not of change but of stasis. For him what causes change is not the inner life force but some harsh novelty caused in the environment that serves to jerk a species out of equilibrium. Evolution, then, exhibits no drive towards perfection. On this issue he takes his inspiration from Darwin: evolution does not work toward specific goals. Moreover, "Spencer's biological evolution had become a matter of responses to physical forces that shaped or formed organic entities in the same way they did inorganic ones."[13] Curiously though, he holds to the view that the evolutionary destiny of human beings is separate from the rest of nature. His hope is that in time evolution will move beyond its "red in tooth and claw" character and result in the general abolition of "evil," or life beyond the cruelty, competition, pain, and fear that characterize nature.[14]

II. BERGSON'S *CREATIVE EVOLUTION*

Bergson began his intellectual life as a follower of Spencer but soon broke with him on core philosophical issues. In *Creative Evolution*, while acknowledging the powerful attraction Spencerian evolutionism has exerted on contemporary thought, he goes so far as to contend that this evolutionism deals in fact neither with becoming nor with evolution (CE 232). We shall return to his criticism of Spencer later in the next section. First, it will be helpful to provide insight into some of the main arguments of Bergson's great text, the text that turned him into a philosophical sensation in his own time and which various biologists of

12. *Ibid.*
13. *Ibid.*, 218.
14. *Ibid.*, 221, 225.

our own time, such as Steven Rose, Brian Goodwin, and Mae-Wan Ho, refer to as containing rich resources for understanding the evolution life as an open, dynamical system.

Bergson may well be the most important philosopher of life in the twentieth century, the one most seriously committed to it for philosophical ends. *Creative Evolution* was an audacious work when it was first published in 1907, and it remains so today. Here we encounter a continental philosopher taking seriously the insights of modern evolutionary theory and biology, attempting to assess their implication for matters of concern to philosophy, and seeking to demonstrate how philosophy can illuminate and clarify our thinking of life in its evolutionary aspects. Bergson is not afraid to speculate. However, for him "speculation" should be neither abstract nor idle, but grounded in facts that are empirically intelligible and testable. In *Creative Evolution,* Bergson attempts to show that the problem of knowledge, the problem of accounting for the faculties of intellect (*intelligence*) and intuition, is one with the metaphysical problem of gaining access to the real: the two form a circle, the center of which is "the empirical study of evolution." The double form of consciousness (intuition and intellect) is shown to reveal "the double form of the real" itself (dynamic and static). For Bergson, intellect reveals only the static aspect of reality, but through intuition we may gain access to the dynamic reality that intellect misses. The attempt to demonstrate this constitutes what we might call the Bergsonian Revolution. It is an effort to enter "into life's own domain," conceived as "reciprocal interpenetration, indefinitely continued creation" (CE 115). Life is to be approached as a "current of creative energy … precipitated into matter" that endeavors "to wrest from it [matter] what it can" (CE 209).

The significance of the science of the nineteenth century for Bergson is that it places at the center of its inquiry the "study of living beings." He concedes that even here science may still be governed by mechanics, but what we are dealing with is a mechanics of transformation, which is a mechanics that cannot be developed by relying on geometrical and spatialized schemas of thought. Change, transformation, and evolution are bound up with living and open systems, and the features of novelty that characterize such systems will always elude a mathematical treatment. A major critical point that Bergson makes in *Creative Evolution* concerns the way in which an exclusively physico-chemical study of organisms cannot grasp the real growth and change that are essential to life, because it treats its object of study – be it a single cell or a whole organism – mathematically, that is to say, as a constant, isolable, and self-identical unit. For Bergson, the physical sciences become merely symbolic when they treat life, which displays dynamic properties, within this static framework. Further, if science claims that it is justified in doing so because life *is* essentially mathematical, it ceases to be descriptive and becomes hypothetical. Through his studies of cytology, embryology, and paleontology, Bergson is well aware that the evidence suggests the contrary, that life is *not* essentially mathematical. In Bergson's terms, treating life within a static mathematical framework is dogmatic, and betrays a metaphysics that haunts science.

In an unorganized body or material object, Bergson accepts that change may be only a displacement of the ultimate parts of which an object is made, parts that themselves do not change, meaning there is no real growth, no history, nothing to prevent the object returning to its previous state (CE 5). What biology reveals, for Bergson, is that living organisms do not change through a mere rearrangement of parts, but that each part itself changes by splitting in an unpredictable way. Hence "the distinctive feature of the organized body is that it grows and changes without ceasing" (CE 9) because this growth or change "does not proceed by the association and addition of elements but by dissociation and division" (CE 58). This means that unlike unorganized matter, change in living systems cannot be charted and predicted as a rearrangement of parts because the parts themselves do not remain unchanged throughout the process. Indeed, they do not even remain self-identical, as it is their nature to multiply: "because there are several individuals now, it does not follow that there was not a single individual just before … it was *one* in the first instance and afterwards *many*" (CE 9). For Bergson, this is not a hypothesis: it is observable fact, evident in cell division, in the development of the embryo, and in the evolutionary process of speciation. In each case we see that what was once one is now literally two (or four, or eight, etc.). Thus, the very language of ultimate parts with a constant numerical value, which is the basis of a mathematical treatment, cannot express this process in which the parts that we identify continually multiply, and what is more, multiply in an unpredictable way.[15]

In contesting a purely mathematical treatment of life Bergson does not, as has been widely supposed, espouse a naive vitalism. Vitalism entails an appeal to some mysterious vital stuff that is then held to be the transcendent motor or agent of evolution, while Bergson explicitly eschews any appeal to a vital force or principle. He notes that when the mind considers the infinity of infinitesimal elements and causes that come together in the genesis of a living being, in which the absence or deviation of any one of them would ruin everything, its first impulse is to take "this army of little workers as watched over by a skilled foreman, the 'vital principle,' which is forever repairing faults, correcting effects of neglect or absentmindedness, putting things back in place" (CE 145). For

15. We should note that mathematics has found new applications since Bergson's time, and that within complexity theory in particular it is now used to model the behavior of systems that are held to be in principle dynamic and unpredictable, while in fact giving rise to patterns of regularity – a view that is very close to Bergson's own, but which the mathematics of his day did not entertain.

Bergson, however, there is no such foreman; nor are there any workers that need such supervision. Furthermore, "the position of vitalism is rendered very difficult by the fact that, in nature, there is neither purely internal finality nor absolutely distinct individuality" (CE 27).

Bergson claims that time has not been taken seriously in previous science. He contends that both common sense and science deal with isolated systems, which are systems that realize themselves in the course of time. Time is reduced to a process of realization on account of the fact that mechanical explanation treats both the past and the future as calculable functions of the present. As a result, time is deprived of efficacy and, in effect, reduced to nothing, having just as much reality for a living being as an hourglass. This is true of both mechanism and finalism for Bergson. Indeed, he contends that finalism is merely an inverted mechanism, substituting the attraction of the future for the compulsion of the past and conceiving the order of nature on the model of a realization of a plan. Bergson claims that both mechanism and finalism are, ultimately, attempts to conceive evolution along the lines of the workings of the human mind (for good reasons did Emmanuel Levinas locate in Bergson's text a source for Heidegger's question concerning technology).[16] He thus claims, somewhat radically, that mechanism's reproach against finalism – that it is anthropomorphic – can also be applied to mechanism itself. Both conceive of nature working like a human being in bringing parts together and proceeding via association and the addition of elements. Bergson suggests that a glance at the development of an embryo will readily show that life works in a very different manner, namely, via dissociation and division (self-differentiation).

Bergson's conception of life draws heavily on his notion of a virtual multiplicity made up of heterogeneous elements, in which the relations between them are ones of fusion and interpenetration. Considered in terms of its contact with matter, life can be likened to an impetus or an impulsion that in itself "is an immensity of potentiality [*virtualité*], a mutual encroachment of thousands and thousands of tendencies," which are such only when spatialized (CE 165–6). It is matter that carries out in actuality the division of this virtual multiplicity, and individuation is to be treated as in part the work of matter and in part the result of the inclination of life. In the opening part of *Creative Evolution*, Bergson states that there is no universal biological law that applies "precisely and automatically to every living being." Rather, "there are only *directions* in which life throws out species in general" (CE 10–11). This seemingly innocuous statement provides the key to understanding Bergson's attempt to stage an encounter between the

16. See Levinas's interview with Richard Kearney, "Dialogue with Emmanuel Levinas," in *Dialogues with Contemporary Continental Thinkers: The Phenomenological Heritage*, Richard Kearney (ed.) (Manchester: Manchester University Press, 1984), 13.

discoveries of modern biology and an enlarged perception of the "whole" of life and evolution, one that endeavors to go beyond the uncritical assumptions of "evolutionist philosophy" (the reference is to Spencer).

What challenge to thought did Bergson think the new biology presented? First, and most obviously, there is the rejection of Aristotle's thinking. In his discussion of the development of animal life in chapter two of *Creative Evolution*, he says that the cardinal error that has vitiated almost all philosophies of nature from Aristotle onward lies in seeing in vegetative, instinctive, and rational life successive degrees in the development of one and the same tendency. In fact, they are "*divergent directions of an activity that has split up as it grew*" (CE 88). This is in accord with one crucial aspect of his conception of "life," namely that it proceeds not by the association and addition of elements but by dissociation and division. Bergson argues that one of the clearest results of modern biology is to have shown that evolution has taken place along divergent lines (CE 113). This means that it is no longer possible to uphold the biology of Aristotle in which the series of living beings is regarded as unilinear.

The second challenge to thought raised by the new biology was located in the modern doctrine of "transformism," a doctrine that Bergson says he accepts "as a sufficiently exact and precise expression of the facts actually known" (CE 15). On the one hand, it shows us that the highest forms of life – highest in terms of complexity – emerge from a very elementary form of life, thus "the most complex has been able to issue from the most simple by way of evolution." On the other hand, it shows that life can no longer be treated as an abstraction. Life can now be described in terms of the continuity of genetic energy that cuts across the bodies "it has organized one after another, passing from generation to generation, [and that] has become divided among species and distributed amongst individuals without losing anything of its force, rather intensifying in proportion to its advance" (CE 17).

Bergson insists that we need to display a readiness to be taken by surprise in the study of nature and life and learn to appreciate that there might be a difference between human logic and the logic of nature. We cannot approach nature with any *a priori* conceptions of parts and wholes or any *a priori* conception of what constitutes life, including how we delimit the boundaries of an organism and hence define it. We must resist the temptation to place or hold nature within our own ideas or shrink reality to the measure of them. We should not allow our need for a unity of knowledge to impose itself on the multiplicity of nature. Life challenges the essential categories of thought: unity, multiplicity, mechanical causality, intelligent finality all fall short. A consideration of life in its evolutionary aspects makes it virtually impossible to say where individuality begins and ends, whether the living being is one or many, whether it is the cells that associate themselves into an organism or the organism that dissociates itself into cells. Unity and multiplicity, or the one and the many, are categories of inert matter; the vital impetus can be conceived as neither pure unity nor pure multiplicity.

The need for a new thinking of life arises for Bergson, in particular, out of the deficiency of the intellect and its inability to think duration.

> The more duration marks the living being with its imprint, the more the organism differs from a mere mechanism, over which duration glides without penetrating. And the demonstration has most force when it applies to the evolution of life as a whole … inasmuch as this evolution constitutes, through the unity and continuity of the animated matter which supports it, a single indivisible history.
> (CE 24)

Time is written and engrafted – it is inscription: "*Wherever anything lives, there is, open somewhere, a register in which time is being inscribed*" (CE 11). Bergson insists that this is no metaphor; rather, it is of the essence of mechanism to consider as metaphorical every effort to ascribe positive attributes to time. For mechanism, change is reducible to an arrangement or rearrangement of parts, while the irreversibility of time is depicted as an appearance relative to our ignorance. But if there is no direction of time for physics, this cannot be the case for biology. On every level we care to examine it, be it embryology, morphology, or the process of evolution itself, time is the indicator of life and of individuated living systems. This inscription and recording of time is, in fact, the time and place of the vital:

> [W]hat is properly vital in growing old is the insensible, infinitely graduated, continuance of the change of form … The evolution of the living being, like that of the embryo, implies a continual recording of duration, a persistence of the past in the present, and so an appearance, at least, of organic memory. (CE 13)

III. BERGSON ON SPENCER'S EVOLUTIONISM

Bergson opposes his conception of evolution to the Spencerian one, arguing that Spencer's method consists in reconstructing evolution with fragments of the evolved (CE 232). In short, Bergson's argument is that Spencer is unable to think genuine evolution since he lacks a principle of genesis and instead supposes that we can posit at the beginning what can only be the result of an actual evolution:

> Already, in the field of physics itself, the scientists who are pushing the study of their science furthest incline to believe that we cannot reason about the parts as we reason about the whole; that the same principles are not applicable to the origin and to the end of a progress; that neither creation nor annihilation, for instance, is inadmissible when we are concerned with the constituent corpuscles of the atom. Thereby, they tend to place themselves in the concrete duration, in which alone there is true generation and not only a composition of parts. (CE 235)

For Bergson, the illusion is generated when we define the evolution of life as a passage from the homogeneous to the heterogeneous. In effect, he is criticizing a specific variety of finalism, what Stephen Jay Gould and Richard C. Lewontin baptized "the Panglossian paradigm" or "adaptationist program":

> We call it the adaptationist programme, or the Panglossian paradigm [which] is rooted in a notion popularized by A. R. Wallace and A. Weismann, (but not, as we shall see, by Darwin) toward the end of the nineteenth century ... This programme regards natural selection as so powerful and the constraints upon it so few that direct production of adaptation through its operation becomes the primary cause of nearly all organic form, function, and behavior."[17]

However, Bergson is not being completely fair to Spencer since the principle of the passage from the homogeneous to the heterogeneous does not, in fact, specify the evolution of life but is to be applied to the physical universe. It is not the simplistic idea Bergson takes it to be, since before the invention of statistical mechanics it was not possible to understand life, or the formation of the solar system in our galaxy, except as a simple growth of entropy or of homogeneity in a closed system. Life needs an open structure to evolve, and this means for Spencer that evolution cannot be a closed system. For example, living organisms, which are made of "crystalloids" and "colloids," integrate nitrogenous compounds to which, through the absorption of heat, they add more motion. In short, they are not simple monatomic closed gas systems but are open systems. This means that "living aggregates" are not simply to be thought as "associated facts."[18] By

17. Stephen Jay Gould and Richard C. Lewontin, "The Spandrels of San Marco and the Panglossian Paradigm: A Critique of the Adaptationist Programme," *Proceedings of The Royal Society of London, Series B* 205(1161) (1979), 584–5.
18. Herbert Spencer, *The Principles of Biology: Volume One* (London: Williams & Norgate, 1864), para. 104.

this process a variety of heterogeneous elements and of heterogeneous functions in the same organism come to be diversely proportioned in diverse places and rendered more complex by evolution.

The details of Spencer's account of the evolution of life cannot be traced here. Bergson takes issue with it for a specific reason: the concepts that Spencer utilizes to account for evolution in the direction of the heterogeneous, such as integration, equilibrium, and maximization, and which come from the integral calculus, suggest that the process of evolution can be explained and *predicted* by natural laws (which are not laws of fate). Darwin, it needs to be noted, does not conceive of evolution in these terms. Although he admits the existence of natural laws, and endeavors to come up with a theoretical explanation concerning the origin of new species, he does not connect this explanation with a possible prediction of evolution. Darwin does not accept the idea of an intelligent design, such as an omniscient Creator who could have foreseen every consequence resulting from the laws he imposes.[19] He thus takes issue with the idea that evolution could have been intentionally ordered. Had this been the case, natural selection would not be the law or mechanism by which the Creator achieves his design because natural selection would not have been foreseen at the beginning.[20] Of course, Darwin did not hold this position from the start of his intellectual inquiries but came to it gradually as a result of intense and searching reflection. His mature stance is that the good of each being depends on the way by which this good is selected. Moreover, different ways of selection give different meanings to the concept of goodness, so that good and bad, fitting and ill-fitting, are *emergent properties*. This means that the substrate is not neutral. Rather, it can change in different circumstances.

What, then, as Daniel Dennett puts it, is Darwin's most dangerous idea? Is it that natural selection acts only through and for the good of each being, or for the good of a species, but without any intention? If so, we can then conclude, as does Dennett, that natural selection acts as a mindless and mechanical meta-engine that modifies biological engines, which in turn generate the growth in complexity and adaptability.[21] Dennett advances his idea of the accumulation

19. Charles Darwin, *The Variation of Animals and Plants under Domestication* (London: J. Murray, 1868), vol. 2, 427.
20. *Ibid.*, 428.
21. Dennett writes: "Here, then, is Darwin's dangerous idea: the algorithmic level *is* the level that best accounts for the speed of the antelope, the wing of the eagle, the shape of the orchid, the diversity of species, and all the other occasions for wonder in the world of nature. … No matter how impressive the products of an algorithm, the underlying process always consists of nothing but a set of individually mindless steps succeeding each other without the help of any intelligent supervision; they are 'automatic' by definition: the workings of an automaton" (*Darwin's Dangerous Idea: Evolution and the Meanings of Life* [London: Allen Lane, 1995], 59). According to Dennett, the key lesson to be learned from Darwin's revolution is this: Paley

of design based on a mindless algorithm in contraposition to the conception of a creative order that produces novelty from nothing that he attributes to Gould. In Dennett's view, natural selection is a crane and not a skyhook, and this means that natural selection is just a functional property that is not directly connected with its material structure. Like different clocks that can all keep good time, natural selection can be realized by different natural substrates. This is the argument of "substrate neutrality."

However, one of Bergson's main arguments is that time is acting in biology and so we need to pay attention to what natural selection is doing in each specific set of circumstances: evolution is never ready-made but always making itself. The Darwinian tree of evolution is full of singularities; it does not lead to a state in which all possible events are equiprobable. New "possibles" for life are invented. To conceive this, we need only think about genes that are not eternally conserved but can be modified; or let us think about how the world of RNA has been changed in the world of DNA. Bergson's insight into "creative evolution," then, is that constraints in biology do not have the same meaning they have in classical physics because they are *flexible*.

The reduction of real complexity to mathematical computation is one that Bergson locates in both nineteenth-century physics and biology. He quotes the following passage from Emil Du Bois-Reymond's *Über die Grenzen des Naturerkennens* of 1892:

> We can imagine the knowledge of nature arrived at a point where the universal process of the world might be represented by a single mathematical formula, by one immense system of differential equations, from which could be deduced, for each moment, the position, direction, and velocity of every atom of the world. (CE 25)

Life cannot be understood simply in terms of a mechanical realization of preexisting goals or problems. Rather, the problems of life are general ones, evolving within a virtual field that is responded to in terms of specific solutions.[22] Bergson's main argument, then, is that to adequately conceive of life we

---

was right in holding Design to be not only a wonderful thing but also to involve intelligence. Darwin's contribution was to show that this intelligence could be broken up into "bits so tiny and stupid that they didn't count as intelligence at all, and then distributed through space and time in a gigantic, connected network of algorithmic process" (*ibid.*, 133).

22. An example to illustrate this would be cases of convergent evolution, such as the eye, representing solutions to general problems that are common to different phylogenetic lineages, in this case that of light and the tendency "to see," or vision, and which involve a heterogeneity in the mechanisms actually involved.

need to appeal to a duration in which novelty is constantly springing forth and in which evolution is genuinely creative.

IV. ON THE SIGNIFICANCE OF EVOLUTION

At the end of chapter three of *Creative Evolution*, Bergson turns his attention to a consideration of the question of the "significance" (*signification*) of evolution, and the way in which this is revealed in "man." This should not be taken to reintroduce teleology or anthropomorphism into evolution, for Bergson states that it is in a "quite special sense that man is the 'term' and 'end' of evolution." How, then, is this "special sense" to be understood? He is not, of course, claiming that the phenomenon of human consciousness mysteriously lies at the very beginning of the evolution of life as some kind of concealed destiny. His point is that the key characteristics of consciousness – indetermination, hesitation, delay, the quantity of choice with respect to a field of action, and so on – are also tendencies or potentialities of life itself (life as a current of "creative" energy). It is in this specific sense that Bergson argues that consciousness – and what he calls "supra-consciousness" (*supraconscience*) – lie at the very origin of life. This expanded notion of consciousness means before all else an "exigency of creation" that can become manifest to itself only where creation is possible: "It lies dormant when life is condemned to automatism; it wakens as soon as the possibility of a choice is restored" (CE 261). Bergson is not suggesting that the evolution of life miraculously transcends the domain of contingency and accident in order for consciousness to realize itself. Evolution remains contingent in every aspect, and Bergson is not reintroducing teleology when he locates man as the "end" of evolution. Rather, he maintains that with the human being the "life" of consciousness reaches, at least potentially, its highest state of emancipation from the restrictions imposed on it by matter. He accepts that "there has not, properly speaking, been any project or plan" (CE 265), and that the evolution of life "takes directions without aiming at ends" (CE 102). Indeed, it is a crucial aspect of his conception of a creative evolution, be it a question of a work of nature or a work of art, that forms are created without an end in view, and Bergson works out his account of the significance of man in the context of a treatment of the part played by contingency in evolution, which he takes to be enormous and extends as far as life assuming a carbonic form and being developed and concentrated in organisms.

In his book *Wonderful Life*, Gould suggests that the fossils of the Burgess Shale challenge the traditional frameworks of progress and predictability for interpreting evolutionary history, revealing instead that the nature of that history is essentially contingent. The reason these fossils demand a new explanatory framework is because they show that the diversity of life during the "Cambrian explosion" – the earliest known proliferation of multicellular organisms – was much greater than it is today.[23] Today, there are thought to be twenty to thirty different phyla (basic anatomical designs) within the animal kingdom. What the Burgess fossils reveal is that at the very origin of the animal kingdom there were at least fifteen to twenty additional phyla. On the basis of this evidence, Gould rejects what he calls "the ladder of progress" and "the cone of increasing diversity" as models of evolutionary change[24] and develops a new explanatory framework in which diversification (of species) follows only from a prior decimation (of phyla). He states that it was a lottery as to which phyla survived[25] and does not shy away from the implications this has for our understanding of ourselves as human beings and our place in evolution:

> Invariant laws of nature impact on the general forms and functions of organisms; they set the channels in which organic life must evolve. … But the physical channels do not specify arthropods, annelids, mollusks and vertebrates, but, at most, bilaterally symmetrical organisms based on repeated parts. The boundaries of the channels retreat even further into the distance when we ask the essential questions about our own origin: Why did mammals evolve among vertebrates? Why did primates take to the trees? Why did the tiny twig that produced *Homo sapiens* arise and survive in Africa? When we set our focus upon the level of detail that regulates most common questions about the history of life, contingency dominates and the predictability of general form recedes to an irrelevant background.[26]

Gould's account of the decimation of phyla, among which humanity's distant ancestors must have survived, coupled with the contingency of our subsequent

23. More specifically, the number of phyla, or basic anatomical designs, was much greater during the Cambrian explosion, while today there are thought to be a greater number of species based on fewer phyla. See Stephen Jay Gould, *Wonderful Life: The Burgess Shale and the Nature of History* (London: Century Hutchinson, 1989), 98–100.
24. Bergson himself explicitly rejected the ladder of progress and the cone of diversity as images of evolutionary development in *Creative Evolution*: "the impression derived [from the study of organisms] is not always that of an increasing complexity … Nor does it suggest the idea of steps up a ladder" (CE 110).
25. As Gould says, "We do not know for sure that the Burgess decimation was a lottery, but we have *no evidence* that the winners enjoyed adaptive superiority," nor is there evidence that the survivors could have been predicted on the basis of any prior characteristic: "twentieth-century paleontology portrays the Burgess losers as adequately specialized and eminently capable" (*Wonderful Life*, 239, emphasis added).
26. *Ibid.*, 289–90.

evolution, leads him to take seriously the contingency of the human mind itself: "wind back the tape of life to the early days of the Burgess Shale; let it play again from an identical starting point, and the chance becomes vanishingly small that anything like human intelligence would grace the replay."[27] What would grace the replay then? What would take our place? Gould does not develop a positive account of the alternatives except to infer rightly from the extinct members among the Burgess fossils that they would be forms of life radically different from the vertebrates, mollusks, arthropods, and so on that are familiar to us today.

How is it, then, that if Bergson acknowledges the tremendous role played by contingency and accidents in evolution, which make it entirely conceivable that we could have evolved in ways that would make us physically and morally different from what, in fact, we are, he can also claim that man is the highest achievement of life, and as such reveals its nature most clearly? The brilliance of Bergson's account of the significance of the human is that from a comprehensive analysis of the variety of contingent evolutionary forms, he is able to discern certain functions that he sees as universal, and the expression of which is what marks out man as the most significant of its products. Hence, the empirical details of evolution constitute the factual basis not only for an understanding of the actual form of the human, but also for any speculation regarding its evolutionary significance.

Whereas it is the examination (in paleontology and comparative anatomy) of material forms that revealed contingency, it is the examination of organisms in terms of their function, and specifically their relation to energy, that allows Bergson to attribute significance to the human in particular. As Bergson says, "life as a whole, whether we envisage it at the start or at the end of its evolution, is a double labor of slow accumulation and sudden discharge" of energy. It is along these lines that Bergson distinguishes plant and animal life, which "develop two tendencies which at first were fused in one" (CE 76). The accumulation and release of energy "at first completed each other so well that they coalesced," but in the history of evolution we see that "the animal evolved … toward a freer and freer expenditure of discontinuous energy" while "the plant perfected rather its system of accumulation" (*ibid.*). Their tendency to emphasize different aspects of energy flow leads to the development of different modes of feeding, of movement, and ultimately of consciousness in the plant and the animal. However, his characterization of the evolution of animal life in terms of an increasing ability to use energy leads Bergson into a direct confrontation with the second law of thermodynamics, which states that all energy tends to degrade into heat, which is distributed throughout matter in a uniform manner. Bergson considers this to be "the most metaphysical of the laws of physics" because it attempts to

27. *Ibid.*, 14.

describe the very direction of existence (CE 156). While it may apply within a closed material system – which Bergson describes as "a thing unmaking itself" (CE 157) – it does not apply to life, in which we find an effort to remount the incline that matter descends and that in its creative passage through matter is "*a reality which is making itself in a reality which is unmaking itself*" (CE 159).[28]

Is Bergson here, for once, in direct contradiction to empirical evidence? His is an extreme claim, and demands some kind of support. This can be provided, however, by Mae-Wan Ho, one of the few biologists to adopt Bergson's work as a valid resource within science. In *The Rainbow and the Worm*, Ho develops an account of living systems in terms of nonequilibrium thermodynamics. Like Bergson, she claims that living organisms are "irreconcilable with the statistical nature of the laws of thermodynamics," hence those laws cannot be applied to life without some reformulation, which Ho develops under the name "a thermodynamics of organized complexity."[29] The difference for Ho is this: whereas in material systems, energy tends toward undifferentiated distribution or "equilibrium" as stated by the second law of thermodynamics, living systems are highly differentiated as a consequence of the way "energy flow organizes and structures the system in such a way as to reinforce the energy flow."[30] For this to work, an organism's ability to store energy is key. Hence, in Ho's definition, an organism is a coherent structure maintained far from thermodynamic equilibrium by the ability to store energy, and then release it in a way that magnifies its effect well beyond any potential it would have had in a purely material context. Bergson's description of animal life as a counter-entropic movement can be refined, through Ho's work, into an account of life as a local magnification of potential energy resulting through the differentiation of storage and release.

The excess of energy that the animal has at its disposal is, then, the condition for the development of human freedom as much as the brain itself. That is to say, human consciousness is not to be explained with reference only to its material conditions, but also to the contingent conditions of its evolutionary history. Gould too has noted this: "We shall then finally understand that the answer to such questions as 'Why can humans reason?' lies as much (and as deeply) in the quirky pathways of contingent history as in the physiology of neurons."[31]

Hence Bergson is not being materialistic, or providing an emergent account of the mind when he argues, for example, that the difference between animal consciousness and human consciousness lies in the number and range of motor

28. For Bergson's discussion of Boltzmann's interpretation of the second law of thermodynamics, see CE 157.
29. Mae-Wan Ho, *The Rainbow and the Worm: The Physics of Organisms* (London: World Scientific, 1998), xi.
30. *Ibid.*
31. Gould, *Wonderful Life*, 281.

mechanisms that have been set up in the human brain, which serve to give an almost unlimited field of choice in their release. Thus, from the fact that the brains of human and ape are alike, "we cannot conclude that consciousnesses are comparable or commensurable" (CE 263), because from the limited to the unlimited there is all the distance between the closed and the open (in fact, what we have here is a difference of kind and not merely degree). Unlike the case of the animal, the powers of invention within the human are not simply variations on the theme of routine. Rather, we have a machine that has the potential to triumph over mechanism and closure. The human is not a captive of the mechanisms its brain has set up. It is as a complex, open machine, therefore, that the human can be said to be the "interesting" animal. Bergson then duly notes the importance of the role played by language, social life, and technics in the creation of this "exceptional life" of the human animal (elsewhere Bergson calls man "the sporting animal" and conceives the brain as an organ of sport).[32] The complication of the brain, for Bergson, is an effect of evolutionary freedom as much as a condition of human freedom. The development of the brain itself is contingent on the excess of energy that allows the development of free action along the animal line of evolution. The brain is not an originary material base that allows consciousness to emerge. Rather, it is material so organized by evolutionary "consciousness"[33] as to allow it to re-emerge in the human:

> Things have happened just as though an immense current of consciousness, interpenetrated with potentialities of every kind, had traversed matter to draw it towards organization and make it, notwithstanding that it is necessity itself, an instrument of freedom. But consciousness has had a narrow escape from being itself ensnared. Matter, enfolding it, bends it to its own automatism, lulls it to sleep in its own unconsciousness. … So, from the highest rung of the ladder of life, freedom is riveted in a chain which at most it succeeds in stretching. With man alone a sudden bound is made; the chain is broken.[34]

The human form, then, is not prefigured in the evolutionary movement and cannot be said to be the outcome of the whole of evolution since this has been accomplished on several divergent lines, and the human species is simply at the

32. Henri Bergson, "Psychophysical Parallelism and Positive Metaphysics," in *Continental Philosophy of Science*, Gary Gutting (ed.) (Malden, MA: Blackwell Publishing, 2005), 68.
33. Again, this is not to anthropomorphize evolution: consciousness here means freedom, contingency, creation, and so on.
34. Henri Bergson, *Mind-Energy*, Keith Ansell-Pearson and Michael Kolkman (eds), H. Wildon Carr (trans.) (Basingstoke: Palgrave Macmillan, 2007), 19.

end of one of them: "[man] does not draw along with him all that life carries in itself" (CE 266). Nevertheless, for Bergson man is more significant than the species that occupy the other lines of vegetable and animal evolution because he is the being in whom the vital movement of life reaches its highest expression, and hence the being in whose freedom the creative nature of evolution is made most evident. This point is worth stressing so that Bergson is not misheard when he advances these kinds of insights. There is nothing anthropomorphic in Bergson's claim that man reveals the significance of evolution, primarily because it is not the specific form of man but his function as a free and creative being that constitutes his significance. It is as if "*a vague and formless being*" (*un être indécis et flou*) – call it, Bergson says, man *or* superman – had sought to realize itself but could succeed in this effort only by abandoning parts of itself in the process (such losses are represented by the animal and vegetable worlds and what is positive in them).

In subsequent essays and texts, Bergson does think outside the restrictions he himself had placed on speculation in *Creative Evolution*, speaking of the appearance of the human – "or of some being of the same essence" – as the "*raison d'être* of life on our planet."[35] However, we should not suppose that the metaphysician in Bergson has simply got the better of him and now overrides the stress he had previously placed on the empirical study of evolution. He still maintains that "experience is the only source of knowledge,"[36] and he seeks to develop his insights on the basis of a synthesis of an intellectual cognition of facts and the accumulation of probabilities. With the word "experience" Bergson means something rich and varied, but the objects of experience we refer to must be ones that can become objects of scientific inquiry and research. Bergson's thinking of life and of creative evolution culminates in a conception of "creative emotion" and the claim that philosophical certainty, which admits of degrees, requires the extension of intuition – supported by science – by "mystical intuition." He ends his final book, *The Two Sources of Morality and Religion* (1932), by describing the universe as a machine for the production of gods and declaring that the task now facing human beings is whether they wish to go on living or not. In order to address the tremendous social, political, and international problems of the planet, we need to refine the "spirit of invention" that to date has been cultivated largely on the basis of mechanism. It is not more and more reserves of potential physico-chemical energy that need releasing but those of a moral energy: "the body, now larger, calls for a bigger soul" and "mechanism should mean mysticism."[37]

35. Bergson, *The Creative Mind*, 59; see also Henri Bergson, *The Two Sources of Morality and Religion*, R. Ashley Audra and Cloudesley Brereton (trans.), with the assistance of W. Horsfall Carter (Notre Dame, IN: University of Notre Dame Press, 1977), 255–6.

36. Bergson, *The Two Sources of Morality and Religion*, 248.

37. *Ibid.*, 310.

It is perhaps this kind of reflection on the meaning of evolution that has generated some of the more far-out speculations we encounter in work on evolution in the twentieth century, such as the writings of Pierre Teilhard de Chardin (1881–1955), as well as in positions advanced in our own time that propose that we are currently witnessing on earth a takeover of mindless Darwinian evolution by controlled and self-directed evolution.[38] De Chardin, a priest and paleontologist, claimed to have been inspired in part by Bergson's *Creative Evolution* as well as by Nietzsche's conception of the superhuman. What concerns him most is not that there is evolution, a fact he considers indisputable, but whether evolution is directed or not. In *The Phenomenon of Man*, he holds that evolution does have a precise orientation as well as a privileged axis, and he thinks that he can show this while "leaving aside all anthropocentrism and anthropomorphism."[39] In his attempt to establish his case, he resurrects almost all the notions that Darwin's revolution had cast into intellectual oblivion: "The impetus of the world, glimpsed in the great drive of consciousness, can only have its ultimate source in some *inner* principle, which alone could explain its irreversible advance towards higher psychisms."[40] In short, for de Chardin the meaning of evolution comes from it having a definite direction and this is a psychic one centered on man or, rather, consciousness and the fact that the story of life on earth is to be understood as the spreading of "spirit" around it. The future of evolution for de Chardin consists in the attainment of what he calls "super-life," which is a "superior form of existence" beyond mere survival and an opening "onto limitless psychic spaces" in the universe.[41] He explicitly uses the word "superhuman" to depict this future and speaks of it in terms of a "spiritual renovation of the earth."[42] In an attempt to add intellectual substance to his ill-defined concerns, de Chardin comes up with an armory of strange new terms,

38. In a statement that takes one's breath away on account of its reckless personification of evolution, Kevin Kelly writes: "My larger point is that the advantages of Lamarckian evolution are so great that nature *has* found ways to make it happen," and adds, "Evolution daily scrutinizes the world not just to find fitter organisms but to find ways to increase its own ability. … Evolution searches the surface of the planet to find ways to speed itself up … not because it is anthropomorphic, but because the speeding up of adaptation is the runaway circuit it rides on. … What evolution eventually found in the human brain was the complexity needed to peer ahead in anticipation and direct evolution's course" (*Out of Control: The New Biology of Machines* [London: Fourth Estate, 1995], 361). He goes on: "What evolution really wants – that is, where it is headed – is to uncover (or create) a mechanism that will most quickly uncover (or create) possible forms, things, ideas, processes in the universe" (*ibid.*, 363).
39. Pierre Teilhard de Chardin, *The Phenomenon of Man*, Bernard Wall (trans.) (London: Collins, 1959), 157.
40. *Ibid.*, 165.
41. *Ibid.*, 256–7.
42. *Ibid.*, 269.

such as the noosphere and the Omega Point,[43] and together they are meant to support his claim that evolution can be interpreted as the story of the ascent of consciousness and spirit that culminates in an era of "hyper-personalization"[44] – or, one might say, Hegel meets biology and evolution: "There can be no doubt about it," he claims after stating that modern totalitarianism is the distorted truth of something magnificent, "the great human machine is designed to work and *must* work – by producing a super-abundance of mind."[45]

De Chardin's appreciation lacks the subtlety of Bergson's speculations about the significance of evolution and the possible "meaning" within it of the appearance of the human. Moreover, he fundamentally distorts the sense of Nietzsche's "superhuman" figure. For Nietzsche, of course, the emphasis is to be placed on the *body*, not on consciousness or spirit,[46] and he was keen to separate his idea from association with evolutionary thought, insisting that the question to be posed was not what should now replace or succeed humanity in the order of being, but rather what kind or type of human should now be willed and bred as having greater value and being more certain of a future.[47]

V. DELEUZE AND BERGSONISM

The influence of Bergson on Deleuze cannot be overestimated. Indeed, Alain Badiou calls Bergson Deleuze's "real master, far more than Spinoza, or perhaps even Nietzsche."[48] He further insightfully notes that it was Deleuze's immense

43. By "noosphere," de Chardin means a new era in evolution centered on the emergence of the "thinking layer" or the "soul" of the Earth and achieved through hominization: "outside and above the biosphere there is the noosphere" (*ibid.*, 202). The "Omega Point" names the centered point around which the noosphere revolves, namely, consciousness as "hyper-personalization": "Because it contains and engenders consciousness, space-time is necessarily *of a convergent nature*. Accordingly its enormous layers, followed in the right direction, must somewhere ahead become involuted to a point which we might call *Omega*, which fuses and consumes them integrally in itself" (*ibid.*, 285). In short, de Chardin is claiming that the more the "sphere" of the world expands and grows in consciousness, the richer and deeper it becomes and is concentrated at a point that allows us to speak of "the volume of being."
44. *Ibid.*, 284–5.
45. *Ibid.*, 82.
46. In a note of 1883–84, Nietzsche writes: "we are in the phase of the modesty of consciousness … Put briefly: perhaps the entire evolution of the spirit is a question of the body … The organic is rising to yet higher levels. Our lust for knowledge of nature is a means through which the body desires to perfect itself … In the long run, it is not a question of man at all: he is to be overcome" (Nietzsche, *The Will to Power*, §676).
47. Nietzsche, *The Antichrist*, §2.
48. Alain Badiou, *Deleuze: The Clamor of Being*, Louise Burchill (trans.) (Minneapolis, MN: University of Minnesota Press, 2000), 39.

merit to have "modernized the Bergsonian filiation." He did this by extricating Bergson from what he had laid himself open to:

> a recuperation of the injunctions of the Open [an important category in Bergson's *The Two Sources of Morality and Religion*] by Christian spiritualism and an adjustment of his cosmic vision to a certain global teleology of which Father Teilhard de Chardin was for a time the herald.[49]

According to Badiou, then, Deleuze's appropriation of Bergson is of great significance since it "secularizes" him and in so doing connects his concepts "to the creations at the forefront of our time."[50]

Deleuze identifies a number of philosophical innovations in Bergson's project and he accords a special importance to the accomplishment of *Creative Evolution*, locating in it the seeds of a new thinking of difference and the prospect of thinking beyond the human condition (beyond, that is, our spatialized habits of representation). There are a number of places in his writings where Bergson explicitly approaches philosophy as the discipline that "raises us above the human condition" (*la philosophie nous aura élevés au-dessus de la condition humaine*) and makes the effort to "surpass" (*dépasser*) the human condition.[51] In *Creative Evolution*, Bergson conceives philosophy as "an effort to dissolve again into the Whole." Moreover: "Intelligence reabsorbed into its principle, may thus live back again in its genesis" (CE 123). Such a method of thinking has to work against the most inveterate habits of the mind and consists in an interchange of insights that correct and add to each other. For Bergson, as Deleuze notes, such an enterprise ends by expanding the humanity within us and so allows humanity to surpass itself by reinserting itself in the Whole.[52] This is accomplished through philosophy, for it is philosophy that provides us with the means (methods) for reversing the normal directions of the mind (instrumental, utilitarian), so upsetting its habits. Deleuze stresses that for Bergson this makes philosophy's task a modest one. If we suppose that philosophy is an affair of perception, then it cannot simply be a matter of correcting perception but only of extending it. There is nothing at fault with the human condition, and its fundamental errors and habits do not require correction. Rather, the task is to extend the human present, which is the aspect of time in which the human necessarily dwells, a necessity to be explained through the dictates of evolution

49. *Ibid.*, 99.
50. *Ibid.*
51. Bergson, *The Creative Mind*, 50, 193.
52. CE 124; Gilles Deleuze, "Lecture Course on Chapter Three of Bergson's *Creative Evolution*," Bryn Loban (trans.), *SubStance* 36(3) (2007), 79–80.

such as adaptation: "The human condition is the maximum of duration concentrated in the present, but there is no co-exclusivity to being, that is to say that there is not only the present."[53]

For Deleuze, Bergson's philosophy contains a new thinking of difference: "The notion of difference must throw a certain light on Bergson's philosophy, but inversely Bergsonism must bring the greatest contribution to a philosophy of difference."[54] It is a quasi-phenomenological venture since the aim, Deleuze declares, is to "return" to things themselves. The promise, if this is got right, is nothing less than one of difference delivering Being to us. A careful consideration of the differences of nature will lead us to the nature of difference. Hitherto, thinking has confused two kinds of difference and covered one with the other: differences of degree over differences of kind or nature. The task of philosophy is to grasp the thing itself in its positivity, and this requires a notion of internal difference. Deleuze fully appreciates that a certain strand of modern philosophy finds such a notion of difference to be absurd. In the Hegelian schema of difference, a thing differs from itself only because it differs in the first place from all that it is not. Difference is, therefore, said to be constituted at the point of contradiction and negation. The novel modernity of Bergsonism lies, for Deleuze, in its critique of metaphysics and of a science that has forgotten the durational character of life and imposed on it an abstract mechanics. It rests on a schema that homogenizes difference by selecting only differences of degree through a spatialized representation of the real. General ideas simply present for our reflection completely different givens that get collected in utilitarian groupings. The task for Deleuze is one of breaking out of a merely "external state of reflection," so that philosophy no longer has a merely negative and generic relation with things in which it remains entirely in the element of generality.

For Deleuze the ultimate aim is to reconnect human thought and existence to, as he puts it, the "universal consciousness" of the Whole (*le Tout*). If Nietzsche's philosophy rests on an inversion of Platonism and a parody of metaphysics, the Bergsonian has found a different path, one that is able to articulate a philosophy of becoming that enables us to reverse the normal directions of thinking and its spatial habits. As Deleuze points out, for Bergson metaphysics begins not with Plato but with Zeno.[55] In his work on Bergson, Deleuze's singular contribution is his ability to see with tremendous clarity the significance of Bergson's project

53. Deleuze, "Lecture Course on Chapter Three," 79.

54. Gilles Deleuze, "Bergson's Concept of Difference," Melissa McMahon (trans.), in *The New Bergson*, John Mullarkey (ed.) (Manchester: Manchester University Press, 1999), 42.

55. "Metaphysics dates from the day when Zeno of Elea pointed out the inherent contradictions of movement and change, as our intellect represents them" (Bergson, *The Creative Mind*, 17); and, "Metaphysics … was born of the arguments of Zeno of Elea on the subject of change and movement. It was Zeno who, by drawing attention to the absurdity of what he called

for philosophy. In his 1960 lecture course on *Creative Evolution*, Deleuze indicates precisely where Bergson's importance lies, namely in the effort to radicalize the post-Kantian project commenced by Solomon Maimon and J. G. Fichte: the need to pass from a transcendental philosophy to a genetic one.[56] Exposing the "myth of the given" has, of course, been a preoccupation of much of twentieth-century philosophy and with respect to both analytical and continental sources of thought. Deleuze focuses attention in large measure on the nature of Bergson's singular contribution to this project. Neither the intellect nor matter can be taken as given (today the polarity is cashed out as one of "mind" and "world'); rather, there is a need for a double genesis. It is this conception of genesis that constitutes such an essential aspect of the Bergsonian revolution. If successful, it means that we will be able to enter into the Whole, or what Deleuze calls the universal consciousness of life. Deleuze stresses that the Whole enjoys neither interiority nor totality; individuated forms of life have a tendency toward closure but this is never accomplished on account of life. As Bergson puts in *Creative Evolution*, "finality is external or it is nothing at all" (CE 27). That the Whole is not given should fill us with delight since it is only our habitual confusion of time with space, and the assimilation of time into space, that makes us think the Whole is given, if only in the eyes of God.[57]

Informing Deleuze's Bergsonism is a philosophical critique of the order of need, action, and society that predetermines us to retain a relationship with things only to the extent that they satisfy our interest, and of the order of general ideas that prevent us from acquiring a superior human nature. This "ethical" impulse of Bergsonism has been taken up, as we shall now see, within contemporary biology.[58]

VI. "CREATIVE EVOLUTION" TODAY: BERGSON AND CONTEMPORARY BIOLOGY

A major innovation of Bergson's work on biology is the shift away from a focus on parts and toward the view that it is the whole that is important. This is not

movement and change, led the philosophers – Plato first and foremost – to seek the true and coherent reality in what does not change" (*ibid.*, 141).

56. Deleuze, "Lecture Course on Chapter Three," 77–8.
57. Gilles Deleuze, *Bergsonism*, Hugh Tomlinson and Barbara Habberjam (trans.) (New York: Zone Books, 1988), 104.
58. Deleuze continues his interest in Bergson and in evolution, including Darwinism and other models of life such as the ethological one provided by Jakob von Uexküll and his *Umwelt* research, in his subsequent texts such as *Difference and Repetition* (1968) and, with Félix Guattari, *A Thousand Plateaus* (1980).

to say that the analytic study of the parts of organisms, or of organisms as parts of evolution, is unimportant to Bergson, but that such research must itself take its direction from the whole context within which the parts find their sense. In *Creative Evolution* this move is evident in Bergson's definition of life as a whole that splits up into parts through dissociation rather than a whole that is constructed through the association of parts. This has several consequences: first of all, it rules out mechanism as a complete account of life because the focus on ultimate parts means it cannot think life except as constructed from matter; and second, it rules out vitalism as an account of life because the focus on an immaterial life-force means it cannot think its relation to matter except as a mysterious kind of animation. We might say, then, that while mechanism lacks an adequate philosophy of life as a whole, vitalism lacks an adequate physics of particular living organisms.

In *Creative Evolution*, Bergson presents a third way of approaching the problem that avoids the dogmatic stand-off between mechanism and vitalism by providing an account of life in expanded material terms: as dissociation, as the freeing up of energy, as an unpredictable and ultimately *creative* evolution. Bergson eschews dogmatic theorizing and retains of mechanism and vitalism only what is based on experience: from mechanism, this is the analytic study of organisms (the forms of which now are understood as contingent rather than determined), and from vitalism, the idea of life (which is now understood as immanent rather than transcendent to the forms of organisms). In *Creative Evolution*, Bergson was working with an expanded understanding of matter that was not widely recognized at the time, and this, as well as his choice of the term *élan vital*, led to him being broadly categorized as a vitalist. Today, however, there are no longer the same mechanistic limitations on our understanding of matter, and Bergson's dynamic account finds corroboration in many areas of contemporary biology (although we can still, of course, find the same dogmatic mechanism that Bergson opposed). What we can also find is that in place of vitalism (which is now largely consigned to history) are a number of models for thinking life as an open, dynamic system and for thinking through the implications of this for scientific practice itself.

How, then, do we locate *Creative Evolution* in the context of biology today? We do not want to limit our treatment of *Creative Evolution* to its reinstatement in a revisionist history of biology that, in the light of recent alternatives, would seek to expand the story of twentieth-century biology beyond that of the development of a mechanistic science leading from neo-Darwinism to modern genetics, but nor can we claim that *Creative Evolution* was a canonical text for the development of those alternatives. More than anything, it is the failure of the human genome project to "explain" life in mechanical terms (its greatest discovery was that there are not enough genes to do this, hence raising new questions rather than answering old ones) that necessitated a change of approach from determinism to a consideration of nonlinear causality, feedback mechanisms, and context-dependent behavior.[59] What *Creative Evolution* can offer is a model for thinking through these kinds of problems in biology, and, what is more, a model that relates these problems in biological research practices both to a more general epistemology (an engagement with which runs through all Bergson's work, and *Creative Evolution* in particular) and to their broader social and historical context (something that Bergson develops in *The Two Sources of Morality and Religion*, particularly in its fourth and final chapter).

Biologist Steven Rose has stated the need for resources exactly like this in the preface to *Lifelines*, where he describes how his attempt to establish a perspective on biology that transcends genetic reductionism made it necessary to "draw upon those powerful alternative traditions in biology which have refused to be swept along by the ultra-Darwinist tide into accepting that living processes can be reduced to mere assemblages of molecules driven by the selfish urges of the genes to make copies of themselves."[60] For Rose, Bergson (along with Georges Cuvier, Étienne Geoffroy Saint-Hilaire, and Hans Dreisch) is part of "an alternative, almost underground nonreductionist tradition in biology [whose] voices were and still are drowned out by an almost universal reductionist consensus which insists that, whatever the theoretical critique, reductionism works."[61] And we should note here that Dreisch, Bergson, and others are no longer described as vitalists but as "nonreductionists," signifying an important shift in the intellectual landscape: we no longer have vitalism as a metaphysical hypothesis opposed to "scientific" mechanism, but nonreductionism as a valid position within science that is opposed to what is now recognized as the metaphysical hypothesis of reductionism.[62]

59. "The lesson that has emerged with blinding clarity from the whole genome project is the error of regarding an organism as a kind of supermolecular machine whose parts are written in the genetic code" (Brian Goodwin, *Nature's Due: Healing Our Fragmented Culture* [Edinburgh: Floris Books, 2007], 89). "No amount of information on genes and protein interactions will ever add up to the complex, entangled whole that is the organism" (Mae-Wan Ho, "Human Genome: The Biggest Sell-Out in Human History," International Society for Science in Society report (2000). www.i-sis.org.uk/humangenome.php [accessed January 2010]).
60. Steven Rose, *Lifelines: Life Beyond the Gene* (Oxford: Oxford University Press, 1997), xii.
61. *Ibid.*, 78–9.
62. Indeed, in *Creative Evolution* Bergson had described the mechanistic treatment of life according to mathematical principles as "a certain new scholasticism that has grown up during the latter half of the nineteenth century around the physics of Galileo" (CE 236; cf. 13). Brian Goodwin also suggests that the modern science for which Galileo, Bacon, and Descartes laid the groundwork has now reached its limit as our primary way of knowing and relating to the world (*Nature's Due*, 11).

The reductionistic or mechanistic focus on parts that Bergson criticized in neo-Darwinism is today most clearly evident in genetics, and is subjected to a similar criticism by a number of biologists. For example, Brian Goodwin writes:

> Organisms have been replaced by genes and their products as the basic elements of biological reality. … There is no lack of highly persuasive books whose objective is to demonstrate why organisms are not what they seem to be – integrated entities with lives and natures of their own – but complex molecular machines controlled by the genes carried within them. … It is the absence of any theory of organisms as distinctive entities in their own right, with a characteristic type of dynamic order and organization, that has resulted in their disappearance from the basic conceptual structure of modern biology.[63]

For Goodwin, evolution is not the realization of a genetic program, but a dynamic process of emergent order (morphogenesis) "in which genes play a significant but limited role."[64] It is an approach that, like Bergson's, reintegrates the quantifiable facts of scientific analysis in a broader appreciation of the qualitative process that is their true context. As Goodwin expresses it:

> in an extended view of the living process, the focus shifts from inheritance and natural selection to creative emergence as the central quality of the evolutionary process. … Inheritance and natural selection continue to play significant roles in this expanded biology, but they become parts of a more comprehensive dynamical theory of life which is focused on the dynamics of emergent processes.[65]

---

63. Brian Goodwin, *How the Leopard Changed its Spots: The Evolution of Complexity* (London: Phoenix, 1994), ix–x. It is worth noting here that while Goodwin's statement might call to mind Richard Dawkins's *Selfish Gene,* Dawkins cannot straightforwardly be assimilated to a reductionist position. True, organisms are vehicles for the survival of atomistic genes in Dawkins's work, but only in the sense that it is the genes, and not the whole organism, that are the true subject of natural selection. In other respects, the organism is an "integrated and coherent" unit in which "genes may interact and even blend" in their effects on the organism. Dawkins's point as regards selection is that "they do not blend when it comes to being passed on to future generations" (*The Extended Phenotype* [Oxford: Oxford University Press, 1982], 114). While the reduction of inheritance to the passing on of genes is itself highly questionable, Dawkins does not reduce properties of organisms to the action of their genes, remaining sensitive to the environmental and social factors that affect gene expression.
64. Goodwin, *How the Leopard Changed its Spots*, xiii.
65. *Ibid.*

Denis Noble is another biologist whose work foregrounds the necessity of placing genes in their wider context. Whereas Goodwin uses a language of emergence derived from complexity theory, Noble develops what he calls "systems biology" as an alternative to the view that the instructions for the development of an organism lie in its genes: "there is no such program and there is no privileged level of causality in biological systems."[66] Noble denies any metaphors that would attribute causal agency exclusively to genes, as if they "control," "determine," "code for," or "contain" organic events in advance of their realization:

> From the systems biology viewpoint the genome is not understandable as "the book of life" until it is "read" through its "translation" into physiological function. My contention is that this functionality does not reside at the level of genes. It can't because, strictly speaking, the genes are "blind" to what they do, as indeed are proteins and higher structures such as cells, tissues and organs.[67]
>
> There is a complex interaction between genes and their environment – both the cellular environment and the wider environment of the organisms in which they exist. The organisms in turn have a relationship with their environment, and this also will have an impact on gene expression.[68]
>
> Moreover, this environment crucially determines which genes are expressed and to what degree. The passage of information is not simply one way, from genes to function. There is two-way interaction.[69]

However, despite the theoretical sophistication of the nonreductionist thinking of life, the shift toward this perspective within biology remains a mere stirring when compared to the landslide that its interpretive success might lead us to expect.[70] To understand why this is the case, let us highlight another impor-

66. Denis Noble, *The Music of Life: Biology Beyond the Genome* (Oxford: Oxford University Press, 2006), xii
67. *Ibid.*, 34.
68. *Ibid.*, 33. Here and in the next extract, Noble is specifically referring to the cellular environment, although, in his view, what he says is also true of wider environments.
69. *Ibid.*, 35.
70. Both Goodwin and Noble, for example, have demonstrated the value of emergence and nonlinear causality as strategies for understanding the heart organ. See Goodwin, *Nature's Due*, ch. 2, in which he also discusses cancer as an emergent property of cells, and Noble, *The Music of Life*, ch. 5.

tant point in the passage we cited from Rose: *whatever the theoretical critique, reductionism works.*

Who cares if the behavior of a gene is context dependent if we can isolate that context and show that within it the gene behaves in a predictable way? Or if we can isolate the aspects of a gene that are independent of a particular context and on this basis predict how it will behave when transplanted to a different one? Who cares about context dependence *in principle* when we can ignore it *in fact*? Well, philosophers such as Bergson do, and biologists such as Rose, Goodwin, Ho, and Noble do. But why do they? And what practical alternatives do they offer to the genetic technologies we are alluding to?[71] In order to answer this, let us turn Rose's statement that "reductionism works" into a question, or rather a series of questions: *how does reductionism work, what does it work on, and with what results?*

In their critical assessment of mechanistic practices in science, writers such as Rose, Goodwin, Noble, and Ho raise many of the same points as Bergson, emphasizing the utilitarian bent of the intellect toward fabrication, the historical contingency of scientific methods and principles, and the way mechanistic approaches actualize only a small part of a potentially far richer relationship to nature. However, they also emphasize two key issues that have developed only since Bergson's time: that research projects today are largely dictated by the requirements of technological and corporate interests, and that scientific practices constitute a significant intervention into natural processes – so much so that they are considered to make a significant contribution to the current environmental crisis. Now, in the terms of the mechanistic hypothesis, the intellectual reduction of nature to its fundamental parts is a process of discovery; but from a critical perspective, such an activity is not one of discovery but of intervention. If nature is a holistic process, then the isolation and manipulation of certain natural processes constitute a fundamental alteration of nature itself.

In *Creative Evolution*, Bergson's account of life as an integral whole was accompanied by an extensive critique of the intellect as that which resolves life into parts, describing it as an instrument of useful action rather than of disinterested speculation. Its main characteristic is the fabrication of instruments from matter, and when it turns to consider life it cannot help but do so from its utilitarian perspective: "it makes us consider every actual form of things, even the form of natural things, as artificial and provisional; it makes our thought efface from the object perceived, even though organized and living, the lines that outwardly mark its inward structure" (CE 101). This ability to regard living form

71. The word alternative is not entirely appropriate here; the issue is not about abandoning mechanistic science, but delimiting for it an appropriate field of application and complementing its method with others that may be more appropriate to different areas.

as provisional – to literally see in life only raw material for our use – gives us "an unlimited power of decomposing according to any law and of recomposing into any system" (*ibid.*). In *Creative Evolution*, this remains an epistemological point, and Bergson is primarily concerned with accounting for the "bewilderment" of an intellect designed to organize matter "when it turns to the living and is confronted with organization" itself, but the problem today is a different one: the "recompositions" that the intellect organizes are at odds with the "inward structure" or "organization" of organisms or ecosystems, and actually disrupts those systems (CE 104).[72]

Goodwin has demonstrated very clearly that the presuppositions of genetic reductionism "make it legitimate to shunt genes around from any one species to any other species."[73] If the gene is ultimately the only biological reality, then "species don't have natures" and "we can manipulate them in any way."[74] Life itself loses all significance in such a view, and nature becomes "a set of parts, commodities that can be shifted around."[75] As Goodwin notes, the rhetoric that goes along with biotechnology is totally at variance with the reality: genes are not stable bits of information, they are defined by context, and if you change the context you change the activity of the gene, leading to unexpected modifications and transgenic transference between species.[76] For Goodwin, contemporary genetic technologies mark the highest point of a "science of quantities" that was formally introduced by Galileo and has, during its relatively short history, enabled an exceptional rate of technological development. He suggests that the advancement of scientific knowledge, which now suggests that life is not made up of parts, and the worsening environmental crisis, which results from treating life as if it is made up of parts, both indicate the necessity of a fundamental shift toward what he calls "a science of qualities" that would take into account the properties of living systems as a whole.[77] In his most recent work he has argued

72. In *The Two Sources of Morality and Religion*, Bergson suggests that "the spirit of invention has not always operated in the best interests of humanity" and that we should "allot to the machine its proper place, I mean the place where it can best serve humanity," although his beef is largely with the social implications of technology, which fosters an artificial need for luxury and widens the gap between capital and labor, rather than with the environmental implications that would be revealed only years later. See Bergson, *The Two Sources of Morality and Religion*, 305–7.
73. Brian Goodwin, with David King, "An Interview with Professor Brian Goodwin," *GenEthics News* 11 (March–April 1996), 7.
74. *Ibid.*
75. *Ibid.*
76. *Ibid.*
77. See Brian Goodwin, "From Control to Participation via a Science of Qualities" (1999), at http://www.schumachercollege.org.uk/learning-resources/from-control-to-participation-via-a-science-of-qualities (accessed January 2010).

that living systems have qualities such as health that are in no sense "secondary" to those usually observed by science. They are properties that pertain to the whole system and cannot be explained in terms of the properties or interaction of its parts.[78]

In the *Origin of Species* Darwin introduced his new concept of natural selection by using an analogy between variation under domestication and variation under nature. The work of contemporary biologists, no less than that of Bergson, suggests that it is time to move beyond this analogy. The effects of the contemporary techno-scientific "domestication" of nature are so much more powerful than the selective breeding that Darwin considered that they defy comparison (after Bergson, we could say that this is a difference of degree that is so great it amounts to a difference in kind). Rather than suggesting an analogy with nature, the evidence today indicates that "domestication" suggests the opposite: the technological manipulation and control of nature is the most short-sighted and destructive line of action we could have taken, disrupting nature and inhibiting creative evolution. Alongside her laboratory practice, Ho has also developed an extensive critique of mechanism, characterizing it as an adolescent phase in the development of the life sciences and claiming that the application of methods and principles drawn from the mathematical and physical sciences is inadequate to an understanding of life: in order to reach maturity, biology must adopt a more holistic perspective, using an intuitive as well as intellectual approach. She emphasizes a view of life as symbiotic, with humans as participants in a creative – we could say, a *healthy* – evolution. Such participation cannot be grounded in an intellectual – that is to say, an *instrumental* – disposition toward nature: a disposition that makes us alienated from nature and from ourselves.[79]

Life is holistic, and the manipulation of parts has effects on the whole that cannot, in principle, be predicted. Reductionists may well object that, given a complete knowledge of the parts, prediction is possible, but what Bergson originally revealed was that analytic knowledge alone is by definition inadequate, because it reveals not what life is, but only what we can do to it. In this context, a concept such as "conservation" can find a new application, no longer as simply the preservation of life as it is, but rather as the preservation of the dynamism of life so that it can continue to evolve creatively. As the Bergson scholar and environmentalist Pete Gunter has pointed out, Bergson's focus on the whole of

78. See Goodwin, *Nature's Due*, ch. 3. Another example of reductionism at work on a larger scale is the industrial farming practice of monoculture: "This monoculture mentality arises directly out of a reductionist science of quantities that looks at species in terms of specific traits that can be maximized to give high yields of particular products" (Goodwin, *How the Leopard Changed its Spots*, 211). The Bergson scholar and environmentalist Pete Gunter also investigates the effects of monocultural farming in North Texas in his book *The Big Thicket*.

79. This is a central theme of Goodwin's *Nature's Due*.

evolution "locates man squarely *in* nature and stresses man's kinship to all living creatures."[80] Bergson's model of evolution as the differentiation of a common impetus clearly emphasizes the importance of studying the evolution of ecosystems as well as individual species. The concept of divergent tendencies within a single evolutionary process means that all evolution, in principle, is symbiotic, and places ecology at the very heart of biology.

A biology of organisms that is not complemented by an ecology of the whole context within which they evolve is incapable of supporting an adequate concept of creative participation in life, leaving the scientist unable to comprehend life, able only to make use of it. Farming practices based on genetic technologies such as the annual use of neutered and patented seeds, or based on industrial technologies such as clearcutting and monoculture, effectively abolish the dynamic conditions of a creative evolution. Indeed, when Goodwin describes the way in which "mechanism works," he uses an analogy with drug addiction: "farmers become enslaved to 'scientific' methods of production that are intrinsically unsustainable, and new technological 'fixes' are needed to sort out new problems."[81] We cannot solve the problems that techno-science has created through further interventions. Indeed, this line of thinking has more in common with indigenous knowledge than it does with European epistemology, but it is important to note (as against readings that would suggest Bergson is an "irrationalist" and "anti-science") that this is not essentially at odds with science – only with the intellectual and industrial appropriation of science. What is required is – in Bergson's terms as well as those of contemporary biologists – intuition of the self and sympathy with life; only in this way can "humanity … set about simplifying its existence with as much frenzy as it devoted to complicating it."[82]

Creative Evolution is only now receiving the attention it deserves. More than any other work in the philosophy of life, this text is predominantly understood in light of what came after it. This is not to say merely that we interpret it in retrospect, but that the philosophical community has had a century to acclimatize itself to the scientific worldview that Bergson recognized at its inception. It stands as a lesson in how philosophy can accompany rather than follow science, and how both disciplines gain from this partnership. Dynamic theories of biology and evolution can operate only through the recognition of the temporal character of living systems, ecological theories can operate only through the recognition of sympathy between organisms, and both these approaches were developed by Bergson at a time when biological science on the

80. P. A. Y. Gunter, "Bergson and the War against Nature," in *The New Bergson*, John Mullarkey (ed.) (Manchester: Manchester University Press, 1999), 168.
81. Goodwin, *How the Leopard Changed its Spots*, 210.
82. Bergson, *The Two Sources of Morality and Religion*, 307.

whole operated by treating organisms as raw material. Our thinking of life today is moving away from control and toward participation, away from exploitation and toward sustainability, and only now is scientific thought embarking on the path that Bergson pointed out a century ago, a path that he had seen indicated in the evolutionary biology of the late nineteenth and early twentieth centuries. Bergson's visionary ideas are not of course the only resource for this project,[83] but they surely merit being placed at the center of any serious philosophical response to questions of life and evolution.

83. Mention should be made of Uexküll's *Umwelt* research, which sought to show the extent to which the "environment" is structured and mediated by the specific *Umwelt* of the organism and which has been taken up by continental philosophers such as Heidegger (*The Fundamental Concepts of Metaphysics*), Merleau-Ponty (*In Praise of Philosophy and Other Essays*), and Deleuze & Guattari (*A Thousand Plateaus*).

CHRONOLOGY

	PHILOSOPHICAL EVENTS	CULTURAL EVENTS	POLITICAL EVENTS
1620	Bacon, *Novum organum*		
1633		Condemnation of Galileo	
1634		Establishment of the Academie Française	
1637	Descartes, *Discourse on Method*		
1641	Descartes, *Meditations on First Philosophy*		
1642		Rembrandt, *Nightwatch*	English Civil War begins
1651	Hobbes, *Leviathan*		
1662	*Logique du Port-Royal*		
1665		Newton discovers calculus	
1667		John Milton, *Paradise Lost*	
1670	Pascal, *Les Pensées* (posthumous) Spinoza, *Tractatus theologico-politicus*		
1675		Leibniz discovers calculus	
1677	Spinoza, *Ethics*		
1687		Newton, *Philosophiae naturalis principia mathematica*	
1689	Locke, *A Letter Concerning Toleration* (–1690) Locke, *An Essay Concerning Human Understanding* and *Two Treatises of Civil Government*		

	PHILOSOPHICAL EVENTS	CULTURAL EVENTS	POLITICAL EVENTS
1695		Bayle, *Dictionnaire historique et critique, vol. I*	
1714	Leibniz, *Monadologie*		
1739	Hume, *A Treatise of Human Nature*		
1742		Handel, *Messiah*	
1748	Hume, *An Enquiry Concerning Human Understanding*		
1751	Diderot and D'Alembert, *Encyclopédie, vols 1 & 2*		
1755	Rousseau, *Discours sur l'origine et les fondements de l'inégalité parmi les hommes*		
1759		Voltaire, *Candide*	
1762	Rousseau, *Du contrat social* and *Émile ou de l'éducation*		
1774		Goethe, *Sorrows of Young Werther*	
1776	Death of Hume	Adam Smith, *Wealth of Nations*	American Declaration of Independence
1781	Kant, *Kritik der reinen Vernunft*		
1783	Kant, *Prolegomena zu einer jeden künftigen Metaphysik*		
1784	Kant, "Beantwortung der Frage: Was ist Aufklärung?"		
1785	Kant, *Grundlegung zur Metaphysik der Sitten*		
1787			US Constitution
1788	Birth of Arthur Schopenhauer Kant, *Kritik der praktischen Vernunft*	Gibbon, *The Decline and Fall of the Roman Empire*	
1789	Death of d'Holbach	Adoption of *La Déclaration des droits de l'Homme et du citoyen*	French Revolution and the establishment of the First Republic
1790	Kant, *Kritik der Urteilskraft*	Edmund Burke, *Reflections on the Revolution in France*	
1791		Mozart, *The Magic Flute* Tom Paine, *The Rights of Man*	
1792	Mary Wollstonecraft, *Vindication of the Rights of Woman*		
1794		Creation of the École Normale Supérieure	Death of Robespierre

	PHILOSOPHICAL EVENTS	CULTURAL EVENTS	POLITICAL EVENTS
1795	Schiller, *Briefe über die ästhetische Erziehung des Menschen*		
1797	Schelling, *Ideen zu einer Philosophie der Natur als Einleitung in das Studium dieser Wissenschaft*	Hölderlin, *Hyperion, vol. 1*	
1798	Birth of Auguste Comte	Thomas Malthus, *Essay on the Principle of Population*	
1800	Fichte, *Die Bestimmung des Menschen* Schelling, *System des transcendentalen Idealismus*	Beethoven's First Symphony	
1804	Death of Kant		Napoleon Bonaparte proclaims the First Empire
1805		Publication of Diderot, *Le Neveu de Rameau*	
1806	Birth of John Stuart Mill	Goethe, *Faust, Part One* Reinstatement of the Sorbonne by Napoleon as a secular university	Napoleon brings the Holy Roman Empire to an end
1807	Hegel, *Die Phänomenologie des Geistes*		
1812	(–1816) Hegel, *Wissenschaft der Logik*		
1815		Jane Austen, *Emma*	Battle of Waterloo; final defeat of Napoleon
1817	Hegel, *Encyclopedia*	Ricardo, *Principles of Political Economy*	
1818	Birth of Karl Marx	Mary Shelley, *Frankenstein, or, The Modern Prometheus*	
1819	Schleiermacher, *Hermeneutik* Schopenhauer, *Die Welt als Wille und Vorstellung*	Byron, *Don Juan*	
1821	Hegel, *Grundlinien der Philosophie des Rechts*		Death of Napoleon
1823		Beethoven's Ninth Symphony	
1830	(–1842) Comte, *Cours de philosophie positive* in six volumes	Stendhal, *The Red and the Black*	
1831	Death of Hegel	Victor Hugo, *Notre Dame de Paris*	
1832	Death of Bentham	Clausewitz, *Vom Kriege*	
1833	Birth of Wilhelm Dilthey	Pushkin, *Eugene Onegin*	Abolition of slavery in the British Empire

	PHILOSOPHICAL EVENTS	CULTURAL EVENTS	POLITICAL EVENTS
1835		The first volume of Alexis de Tocqueville's *Democracy in America* is published in French	
1837		Louis Daguerre invents the daguerreotype, the first successful photographic process	
1841	Feuerbach, *Das Wesen des Christentums* Kierkegaard, *On the Concept of Irony with Constant Reference to Socrates*	R. W. Emerson, *Essays: First Series*	
1842	Birth of Hermann Cohen	Death of Stendhal (Marie-Henri Beyle)	
1843	Kierkegaard, *Either/Or* and *Fear and Trembling* Mill, *A System of Logic*		
1844	Marx writes *Economic-Philosophic Manuscripts*	Alexandre Dumas, *The Count of Monte Cristo*	
1846	Kierkegaard, *Concluding Unscientific Postscript*		
1847	Boole, *The Mathematical Analysis of Logic*	Helmholtz, *On the Conservation of Force*	
1848	Birth of Wilhelm Windelband	Publication of the *Communist Manifesto*	Beginning of the French Second Republic
1851		Herman Melville, *Moby Dick* Herbert Spencer, *Social Statics* Great Exhibition staged in the Crystal Palace, London	
1852			Napoleon III declares the Second Empire
1853			(–1856) Crimean War
1854	Birth of Paul Natorp	H. D. Thoreau, *Walden*	
1855	Helmholtz, *Über das Sehen des Menschen*	Walt Whitman, *Leaves of Grass*	
1856	Birth of Sigmund Freud		
1857	Birth of Ferdinand de Saussure Death of Comte	Charles Baudelaire, *The Flowers of Evil* Gustav Flaubert, *Madame Bovary*	
1858	Birth of Émile Durkheim		
1859	Birth of Henri Bergson, John Dewey, and Edmund Husserl Mill, *On Liberty*	Charles Darwin, *Origin of Species*	(–1866) Italian Unification, except Venice (1866) and Rome (1870)
1861		Johann Jakob Bachofen, *Das Mutterrecht*	Tsar Alexander II abolishes serfdom in Russia

	PHILOSOPHICAL EVENTS	CULTURAL EVENTS	POLITICAL EVENTS
1862		Victor Hugo, *Les Misérables*	
1863	Birth of Heinrich Rickert Mill, *Utilitarianism*	Édouard Manet, *Olympia*	Abraham Lincoln issues the *Emancipation Proclamation*
1865		(–1869) Leo Tolstoy, *War and Peace* Premiere of Richard Wagner's *Tristan und Isolde*	Surrender of General Robert E. Lee signals conclusion of American Civil War
1866	Lange, *Die Geschichte des Materialismus*	Fyodor Dostoevsky, *Crime and Punishment*	The Peace of Prague ends the Austro-Prussian War
1867	Marx, *Das Kapital, vol. I*		
1868	Birth of Émile Chartier ("Alain")	Creation of the École Pratique des Hautes Études (EPHE) Birth of W. E. B. Du Bois	
1869	Birth of Léon Brunschvicg Mill, *The Subjection of Women*	(–1870) Jules Verne, *Twenty Thousand Leagues Under the Sea* (–1876) Wagner, *Der Ring des Nibelungen*	Completion of the Suez Canal
1870			(–1871) Franco-Prussian War Establishment of the Third Republic
1871	Cohen, *Kants Theorie der Erfahrung* Lachelier, *Du fondement de l'induction*	Darwin, *The Descent of Man* Eliot, *Middlemarch*	Unification of Germany: Prussian King William I becomes Emperor (*Kaiser*) of Germany and Otto von Bismarck becomes Chancellor Paris Commune
1872	Birth of Marcel Mauss Nietzsche, *Die Geburt der Tragödie*		
1873	Death of Mill	(–1877) Tolstoy, *Anna Karenina*	End of German Occupation following France's defeat in the Franco-Prussian War
1874	Birth of Ernst Cassirer and Max Scheler Émile Boutroux, *La Contingence des lois de la nature* Brentano, *Psychologie vom empirischen Standpunkt*	First Impressionist Exhibition staged by the Société anonyme des peintres, sculpteurs et graveurs (Cézanne, Degas, Guillaumin, Monet, Berthe Morisot, Pissarro, Renoir, Sisley)	
1875	Birth of Emil Lask Death of Lange	Premiere of Georges Bizet's *Carmen*	
1876		Death of George Sand (Amantine Aurore Lucile Dupin)	
1877	Cohen, *Kants Begründung der Ethik*	Henry Morton Stanley completes his navigation of the Congo River	

	PHILOSOPHICAL EVENTS	CULTURAL EVENTS	POLITICAL EVENTS
1878			King Leopold II of Belgium engages explorer Henry Morton Stanley to establish a colony in the Congo
1879	Frege, *Begriffsschrift*	Henrik Ibsen, *A Doll's House* Georg Cantor (1845–1918) becomes Professor of Mathematics at Halle Thomas Edison exhibits his first incandescent light bulb	
1882		Premiere of Wagner's *Parsifal* in Bayreuth	
1883	Birth of Karl Jaspers and José Ortega y Gasset Death of Marx Dilthey, *Einleitung in die Geisteswissenschaften* (–1885) Nietzsche, *Also Sprach Zarathustra*	Cantor, "Foundations of a General Theory of Aggregates"	
1884	Birth of Gaston Bachelard Frege, *Die Grundlagen der Arithmetik* Windelband, *Präludien*	Mark Twain, *Adventures of Huckleberry Finn*	
1886	Nietzsche, *Jenseits von Gut und Böse*		
1887	Nietzsche, *Zur Genealogie der Moral*		
1888	Birth of Jean Wahl		
1889	Birth of Martin Heidegger, Gabriel Marcel, and Ludwig Wittgenstein Bergson, *Essai sur les données immédiates de la conscience*		
1890	William James, *Principles of Psychology*		
1891	Birth of Rudolf Carnap, Fritz Kaufmann, and Edith Stein		
1892	Frege, "Über Sinn und Bedeutung" Rickert, *Der Gegenstand der Erkenntnis*		
1893	Birth of Roman Ingarden Xavier Léon and Élie Halévy cofound the *Revue de métaphysique et de morale*		
1894	Natorp, *Religion innerhalb der Grenzen der Humanität*		

	PHILOSOPHICAL EVENTS	CULTURAL EVENTS	POLITICAL EVENTS
1894			Captain Alfred Dreyfus (1859–1935), a Jewish-French army officer, is arrested and charged with spying for Germany
1895	Birth of Max Horkheimer and Felix Kaufmann	The Lumière brothers hold the first public screening of projected motion pictures Wilhelm Conrad Röntgen discovers X-rays	
1896	Bergson, *Matière et mémoire: Essai sur la relation du corps à l'esprit*	Athens hosts the first Olympic Games of the modern era	
1897	Birth of Georges Bataille Durkheim, *Le Suicide*		
1898	Birth of Herbert Marcuse	Zola, article "J'accuse" in defense of Dreyfus	
1899	Rickert, *Kulturwissenschaft und Naturwissenschaft*		Start of the Second Boer War
1900	Birth of Hans-Georg Gadamer Death of Nietzsche and Félix Ravaisson (–1901) Husserl, *Logische Untersuchungen*	Freud, *Interpretation of Dreams* Planck formulates quantum theory	
1901	Birth of Jacques Lacan		
1902	H. Cohen, *Logik der reinen Erkenntnis*		
1903	Birth of Theodor W. Adorno and Jean Cavaillès Natorp, *Platons Ideenlehre*	Death of Herbert Spencer Du Bois, *The Souls of Black Folk*	
1904	H. Cohen, *Ethik des reinen Willens* (–1905) Weber, *Die protestantische Ethik und der Geist des Kapitalismus*		
1905	Birth of Raymond Aron and Jean-Paul Sartre	Einstein formulates the special theory of relativity	Law of separation of church and state in France
1906	Birth of Hannah Arendt and Emmanuel Levinas	Birth of Léopold Sédar Senghor	The Dreyfus Affair ends when the French Court of Appeals exonerates Dreyfus of all charges
1907	Birth of Jean Hyppolite Death of Octave Hamelin Bergson, *L'Evolution créatrice*	Pablo Picasso completes *Les Demoiselles d'Avignon*	
1908	Birth of Simone de Beauvoir, Claude Lévi-Strauss, Maurice Merleau-Ponty, and W. V. Quine		

	PHILOSOPHICAL EVENTS	CULTURAL EVENTS	POLITICAL EVENTS
1910	Cassirer, *Substanzbegriff und Funktionsbegriff*		
1911	Death of Dilthey Lask, *Die Logik der Philosophie und die Kategorienlehre* Victor Delbos, first French journal article on Husserl: "Husserl: Sa critique du psychologisme et sa conception d'une Logique pure" in *Revue de métaphysique et de morale*	The Blaue Reiter (Blue Rider) group of avant-garde artists is founded in Munich	
1912	H. Cohen, *Ästhetik des reinen Gefühls* Natorp, *Allgemeine Psychologie*		
1913	Birth of Albert Camus and Paul Ricoeur Husserl, *Ideen I* Jaspers, *Allgemeine Psychopathologie* Scheler, *Der Formalismus in der Ethik und die materiale Wertethik* Unamuno, *Del sentimiento tragic de la vida*	Freud, *Totem and Taboo* Marcel Proust (1871–1922), *Swann's Way*, the first volume of *Remembrance of Things Past* First performance of Stravinsky's *Rite of Spring*	
1914	Death of Charles Sanders Peirce Ortega y Gasset, *Meditaciónes del Quijote*		Germany invades France
1915	Birth of Roland Barthes Death of Lask and Windelband	Franz Kafka, *Metamorphosis*	
1916	Saussure, *Cours de linguistique générale*	James Joyce, *A Portrait of the Artist as a Young Man*	
1917	Death of Durkheim	Lenin, *State and Revolution*	Russian Revolution
1918	Birth of Louis Althusser Death of Georg Cantor, H. Cohen, Lachelier, and Georg Simmel		First World War ends Proclamation of the Weimar Republic
1919		German architect Walter Gropius (1883–1969) founds the Bauhaus School	
1920	Death of Weber	Freud, *Beyond the Pleasure Principle*	Ratification of the 19th Amendment to the US Constitution extends suffrage to women
1921	Rosenzweig, *Der Stern der Erlösung*		

	PHILOSOPHICAL EVENTS	CULTURAL EVENTS	POLITICAL EVENTS
1922	Birth of Karl-Otto Apel Wittgenstein, *Tractatus Logico-Philosophicus* Bataille begins his twenty-year career at the Bibliothèque Nationale	T. S. Eliot, *The Waste Land* Herman Hesse, *Siddhartha* James Joyce, *Ulysses*	
1923	Scheler, *Wesen und Formen der Sympathie* Institut für Sozialforschung (Frankfurt School) is founded (and 1925, 1929) Cassirer, *Philosophie der Symbolischen Formen* (3 vols)	Freud, *The Ego and the Id* Kahil Gibran, *The Prophet*	
1924	Birth of Jean-François Lyotard Death of Natorp Brunschvicg, *Le Progrès de la Conscience dans la Philosophie Occidentale* Sartre, Raymond Aron, Paul Nizan, Georges Canguilhem, and Daniel Lagache enter the École Normale Supérieure	André Breton, *Le Manifeste du surréalisme* Thomas Mann, *The Magic Mountain*	Death of Vladimir Lenin
1925	Birth of Zygmunt Bauman, Gilles Deleuze, and Frantz Fanon Death of Frege Mauss, *Essai sur le don*	Franz Kafka, *The Trial* First Surrealist Exhibition at the Galerie Pierre, Paris	
1926	Birth of Michel Foucault Jean Hering publishes the first French text to address Husserl's phenomenology: *Phénoménologie et philosophie religieuse*	The film *Metropolis* by German director Fritz Lang (1890–1976) premieres in Berlin The Bauhaus school building, designed by Walter Gropius (1883–1969), is completed in Dessau, Germany	
1927	Heidegger, *Sein und Zeit* Marcel, *Journal métaphysique*	Virginia Woolf, *To the Lighthouse*	
1928	Birth of Noam Chomsky Bachelard, *Essai sur la connaissance approchée* Husserl, *Zur Phänomenologie des inneren Zeitbewußtseins* The first work of German phenomenology appears in French translation: Scheler's *Nature et formes de la sympathie: Contribution à l'étude des lois de la vie émotionnelle*	The first television station begins broadcasting in Schenectady, New York Bertolt Brecht (1898–1956) writes *The Threepenny Opera* with composer Kurt Weill (1900–1950)	

	PHILOSOPHICAL EVENTS	CULTURAL EVENTS	POLITICAL EVENTS
1929	Birth of Jürgen Habermas Heidegger, *Kant und das Problem der Metaphysik* and *Was ist Metaphysik?* Husserl, *Formale und transzendentale Logik* Wahl, *Le malheur de la conscience dans la philosophie de Hegel* Husserl lectures at the Sorbonne	Ernest Hemingway, *A Farewell to Arms* Erich Maria Remarque, *All Quiet on the Western Front*	
1930	Birth of Pierre Bourdieu, Jacques Derrida, Félix Guattari, Luce Irigaray, and Michel Serres Levinas, *La Théorie de l'intuition dans la phénoménologie de Husserl* Rickert, *Die Logik des Prädikats und das Problem der Ontologie*	Freud, *Civilization and its Discontents*	
1931	Heidegger's first works appear in French translation: "Was ist Metaphysik?" in *Bifur*, and "Vom Wesen des Grundes" in *Recherches philosophiques* Levinas and Gabrielle Peiffer publish a French translation of Husserl's *Cartesian Meditations* Husserl's *Ideas* is translated into English	Pearl Buck, *The Good Earth* Gödel publishes his two incompleteness theorems	
1932	Birth of Stuart Hall Bergson, *Les Deux sources de la morale et de la religion*	Aldous Huxley, *Brave New World* BBC starts a regular public television broadcasting service in the UK	
1933	Death of Émile Meyerson Cassirer, Cohn, Hönigswald, and Marck are dismissed from their university positions owing to the new Nazi civil service law, which declares Jews as non-Germans (–1934) Heidegger becomes Rector at Freiburg University (–1939) Alexandre Kojève lectures on Hegel at the École Pratique des Hautes Études University in Exile founded as a graduate division of the New School for Social Research	André Malraux, *Man's Fate* Gertrude Stein, *The Autobiography of Alice B. Toklas*	Hitler becomes Chancellor of Germany

	PHILOSOPHICAL EVENTS	CULTURAL EVENTS	POLITICAL EVENTS
1935		Penguin publishes its first paperback	
1936	Death of Rickert Husserl, *Krisis der europäischen Wissenschaften und die transzendentale Phänomenologie* Sartre, "La Transcendance de l'égo" in *Recherches philosophiques*	Benjamin, "The Work of Art in the Age of Mechanical Reproduction" First issue of *Life Magazine*	
1937	Birth of Alain Badiou and Hélène Cixous	Picasso, *Guernica*	
1938	Death of Husserl	Sartre, *La Nausée*	
1939	Establishment of Husserl Archives in Louvain, Belgium Founding of *Philosophy and Phenomenological Research* (–1941) Hyppolite publishes his translation into French of Hegel's *Phenomenology of Spirit*	Joyce, *Finnegans Wake* John Steinbeck, *The Grapes of Wrath*	Nazi Germany invades Poland (September 1) and France and Britain declare war on Germany (September 3)
1941	Death of Bergson Marcuse, *Reason and Revolution*	Death of Joyce Arthur Koestler, *Darkness at Noon*	Japan attacks Pearl Harbor, and the US enters the Second World War Germany invades the Soviet Union
1942	Birth of Étienne Balibar Death of Edith Stein Camus, *L'Étranger* and *Le Mythe de Sisyphe: Essai sur l'absurde* Merleau-Ponty, *La Structure du comportement* Lévi-Strauss meets Roman Jakobson at the École Libre des Hautes Études in New York		
1943	Death of Simone Weil Farber, *The Foundations of Phenomenology* Sartre, *L'Être et le néant*	Herman Hesse, *The Glass Bead Game* Ayn Rand, *The Fountainhead*	
1944	Cassirer, *An Essay of Man*	Jorge Luis Borges, *Ficciones* Jean Genet, *Our Lady of the Flowers*	Bretton Woods Conference and establishment of the International Monetary Fund (IMF) Paris is liberated by Allied forces (August 25)
1945	Death of Cassirer	George Orwell, *Animal Farm*	End of the Second World War in Germany (May)

	PHILOSOPHICAL EVENTS	CULTURAL EVENTS	POLITICAL EVENTS
1945	Merleau-Ponty, *Phénoménologie de la perception*	Sartre, Beauvoir, and Merleau-Ponty begin as founding editors of *Les Temps modernes*	Atom bombs are dropped on Hiroshima and Nagasaki; end of war in Japan (September) Establishment of the United Nations
1946	Hyppolite, *Genèse et structure de la "Phénoménologie de l'esprit" de Hegel* Sartre, *L'Existentialisme est un humanisme*	Eugene O'Neill, *The Iceman Cometh* Bataille founds the journal *Critique*	Beginning of the French Indochina War Establishment of the Fourth Republic
1947	Adorno and Horkheimer, *Dialektik der Aufklärung* Beauvoir, *Pour une morale de l'ambiguïté* Heidegger, "Brief über den Humanismus" Jaspers, *Von der Wahrheit*	Camus, *The Plague* Anne Frank, *The Diary of Anne Frank* (posthumous) Thomas Mann, *Doctor Faustus*	(–1951) Marshall Plan
1948	(–1951) Gramsci, *Prison Notebooks* Althusser appointed *agrégé-répétiteur* ("caïman") at the École Normale Supérieure, a position he holds until 1980	Debut of *The Ed Sullivan Show*	The United Nations adopts the Universal Declaration of Human Rights
1949	Beauvoir, *Le Deuxième sexe* Lévi-Strauss, *Les Structures élémentaires de la parenté* Heidegger's *Existence and Being* is translated	Arthur Miller, *Death of a Salesman* George Orwell, *1984* Cornelius Castoriadis and Claude Lefort found the revolutionary group and journal *Socialisme ou Barbarie*	Foundation of NATO
1950	Death of Mauss Ricoeur publishes his translation into French of Husserl's *Ideas I*		Beginning of the Korean War
1951	Death of Alain and Wittgenstein Arendt, *The Origins of Totalitarianism* Quine, "Two Dogmas of Empiricism"	J. D. Salinger, *The Catcher in the Rye* Marguerite Yourcenar, *Memoirs of Hadrian*	
1952	Death of Dewey and Santayana Merleau-Ponty is elected to the Chair in Philosophy at the Collège de France	Samuel Beckett, *Waiting for Godot* Ralph Ellison, *Invisible Man*	
1953	Wittgenstein, *Philosophical Investigations* (posthumous) Lacan begins his public seminars	Lacan, together with Daniel Lagache and Françoise Dolto, founds the Société française de psychanalyse	Death of Joseph Stalin Ceasefire agreement (July 27) ends the Korean War

	PHILOSOPHICAL EVENTS	CULTURAL EVENTS	POLITICAL EVENTS
1953		Crick and Watson construct the first model of DNA	
1954	Jaspers and Bultmann, *Die Frage der Entmythologisierung* Lyotard, *La Phénoménologie* Scheler, *The Nature of Sympathy*, appears in English translation		Following the fall of Dien Bien Phu (May 7), France pledges to withdraw from Indochina (July 20) Beginning of the Algerian revolt against French rule
1955	Marcuse, *Eros and Civilization* Cerisy Colloquium *Qu'est-ce que la philosophie? Autour de Martin Heidegger*, organized by Jean Beaufret	Vladimir Nabokov, *Lolita*	
1956	Sartre's *Being and Nothingness* appears in English translation		Hungarian Revolution and Soviet invasion The French colonies of Morocco and Tunisia gain independence
1957	Chomsky, *Syntactic Structures* Founding of *Philosophy Today*	Jack Kerouac, *On the Road* Camus receives the Nobel Prize for Literature	Rome Treaty signed by France, Germany, Belgium, Italy, the Netherlands, and Luxembourg establishes the European Economic Community The Soviet Union launches *Sputnik 1*, the first man-made object to orbit the Earth
1958	Lévi-Strauss, *Anthropologie structurale*	William S. Burroughs, *Naked Lunch* (–1960) The first feature films by directors associated with the French "New Wave" cinema, including, in 1959, *Les Quatre Cent Coups* (*The 400 Blows*) by François Truffaut (1932–84) and, in 1960, *A bout de souffle* (*Breathless*) by Jean-Luc Godard (1930–) The Sorbonne's "Faculté des Lettres" is officially renamed the "Faculté des Lettres et Sciences Humaines"	Charles de Gaulle is elected president after a new constitution establishes the Fifth Republic
1959	Lévi-Strauss is elected to the Chair in Social Anthropology at the Collège de France	Günter Grass, *The Tin Drum*	
1960	Death of Camus Gadamer, *Wahrheit und Methode* Sartre, *Critique de la raison dialectique*	First issue of the journal *Tel Quel* is published The birth control pill is made available to married women	

	PHILOSOPHICAL EVENTS	CULTURAL EVENTS	POLITICAL EVENTS
1960	Spiegelberg, *The Phenomenological Movement*		
1961	Death of Merleau-Ponty Derrida, Introduction to *Edmund Husserl: L'Origine de la géométrie* Fanon, *Les Damnés de la terre*, with a preface by Sartre Foucault, *Histoire de la folie à l'âge classique* Heidegger, *Nietzsche* Levinas, *Totalité et infini: Essai sur l'extériorite*		Erection of the Berlin Wall Bay of Pigs failed invasion of Cuba
1962	Death of Bachelard Deleuze, *Nietzsche et la philosophie* Thomas Kuhn, *The Structure of Scientific Revolutions* Lévi-Strauss, *La Pensée sauvage* Heidegger, *Being and Time* appears in English translation Merleau-Ponty, *Phenomenology of Perception* appears in English translation First meeting of SPEP at Northwestern University	Rachel Carson, *Silent Spring* Ken Kesey, *One Flew Over the Cuckoo's Nest*	France grants independence to Algeria Cuban Missile Crisis
1963	Arendt, *Eichmann in Jerusalem*	Betty Friedan, *The Feminine Mystique* The first artificial heart is implanted	Imprisonment of Nelson Mandela Assassination of John F. Kennedy
1964	Barthes, *Eléments de sémiologie* Marcuse, *One-Dimensional Man* Merleau-Ponty, *Le Visible et l'invisible* (posthumous)	Lacan founds L'École Freudienne de Paris The Beatles appear on *The Ed Sullivan Show*	Gulf of Tonkin Incident US Civil Rights Act outlaws discrimination on the basis of race, color, religion, sex, or national origin
1965	Death of Buber Althusser, *Pour Marx* and, with Balibar, *Lire "Le Capital"* Foucault, *Madness and Civilization* appears in English translation Ricoeur, *De l'interprétation: Essai sur Freud*	Truman Capote, *In Cold Blood* Alex Haley, *The Autobiography of Malcolm X*	Assassination of Malcolm X
1966	Adorno, *Negative Dialektik* Deleuze, *Le Bergsonisme* Lacan, *Écrits*	Jacques-Alain Miller founds *Cahiers pour l'analyse*	(–1976) Chinese Cultural Revolution

	PHILOSOPHICAL EVENTS	CULTURAL EVENTS	POLITICAL EVENTS
1966	Foucault, *Les Mots et les choses: Une archéologie des sciences humaines*	Johns Hopkins Symposium "The Languages of Criticism and the Sciences of Man" introduces French theory to the US academic community *Star Trek* premieres on US television	Foundation of the Black Panther Party for Self-Defense by Huey P. Newton and Bobby Seale
1967	Derrida, *De la grammatologie, La Voix et le phénomène,* and *L'Écriture et la différence*	Gabriel Garcia Marquez, *One Hundred Years of Solitude*	Confirmation of Thurgood Marshall, first African American Justice, to the US Supreme Court
1968	Deleuze, *Différence et répétition, Spinoza et le problème de l'expression* Habermas, *Erkenntnis und Interesse*	Carlos Castaneda, *The Teachings of Don Juan: A Yaqui Way of Knowledge* Stanley Kubrick, *2001: A Space Odyssey* The Beatles release the White Album	Events of May '68, including closure of the University of Nanterre (May 2), police invasion of the Sorbonne (May 3), student demonstrations and strikes, and workers' occupation of factories and general strike Prague Spring Assassination of Martin Luther King Tet Offensive
1969	Death of Adorno and Jaspers Deleuze, *Logique du sens* Foucault, *L'Archéologie du savoir*	Woodstock Music and Art Fair Neil Armstrong is the first person to set foot on the moon	Stonewall riots launch the Gay Liberation Movement
1970	Death of Carnap Adorno, *Ästhetische Theorie* Foucault, *The Order of Things* appears in English translation Husserl, *The Crisis of European Philosophy* appears in English translation Foucault elected to the Chair of the History of Systems of Thought at the Collège de France Ricoeur begins teaching at the University of Chicago Founding of the *Journal of the British Society for Phenomenology*	Millett, *Sexual Politics* Founding of *Diacritics* First Earth Day	Shootings at Kent State University Salvador Allende becomes the first Marxist head of state to be freely elected in a Western nation
1971	Lyotard, *Discours, figure* Founding of *Research in Phenomenology*	Reorganization of the University of Paris	End of the gold standard for US dollar
1972	Death of John Wild		Watergate break-in

	PHILOSOPHICAL EVENTS	CULTURAL EVENTS	POLITICAL EVENTS
1972	Bourdieu, *Esquisse d'une théorie de la pratique* Deleuze and Guattari, *Capitalisme et schizophrénie. 1. L'Anti-Oedipe* Derrida, *La Dissémination*, *Marges de la philosophie*, and *Positions* *Radical Philosophy* begins publication Colloquium on Nietzsche at Cerisy		President Richard Nixon visits China, beginning the normalization of relations between the US and PRC
1973	Death of Horkheimer Derrida, *Speech and Phenomena* appears in English translation Lacan publishes the first volume of his *Séminaire*	Thomas Pynchon, *Gravity's Rainbow* (–1978) Aleksandr Solzhenitsyn, *The Gulag Archipelago* Roe *v.* Wade legalizes abortion	Chilean military coup ousts and kills President Salvador Allende
1974	Derrida, *Glas* Irigaray, *Speculum: De l'autre femme* Kristeva, *La Révolution du langage poétique* Levinas, *Autrement qu'être ou au-delà de l'essence*	Founding of *Critical Inquiry* Creation of the first doctoral program in women's studies in Europe, the Centre de Recherches en Études Féminines, at the University of Paris VIII–Vincennes, directed by Hélène Cixous	Resignation of Nixon
1975	Death of Arendt Foucault, *Surveiller et punir: Naissance de la prison* Irigaray, *Ce sexe qui n'en est pas un* Foundation of GREPH, the Groupe de Recherches sur l'Enseignement Philosophique	*Signs* begins publication The Sixth Section of the EPHE is renamed the École des Hautes Études in Sciences Sociales	Andrei Sakharov wins Nobel Peace Prize Fall of Saigon, ending the Vietnam War Death of Franco First US–USSR joint space mission
1976	Death of Bultmann and Heidegger Foucault, *Histoire de la sexualité. 1. La Volonté de savoir* Derrida, *Of Grammatology* appears in English translation Barthes is elected to the Chair of Literary Semiology at the Collège de France	Foundation of the International Association for Philosophy and Literature	Death of Mao Zedong Uprising in Soweto
1977	Death of Ernst Bloch	240 Czech intellectuals sign Charter 77	Egyptian president Anwar al-Sadat becomes the first Arab head of state to visit Israel

	PHILOSOPHICAL EVENTS	CULTURAL EVENTS	POLITICAL EVENTS
1977	Deleuze and Guattari, *Anti-Oedipus* appears in English translation Lacan, *Ecrits: A Selection* appears in English translation	Centre Georges Pompidou, designed by architects Renzo Piano (1937–) and Richard Rogers (1933–), opens in Paris	
1978	Death of Kurt Gödel Arendt, *Life of the Mind* Derrida, *La Vérité en peinture*	Edward Said, *Orientalism* Birmingham School: Centre for Contemporary Culture releases *Policing the Crisis* Louise Brown becomes the first test-tube baby	Camp David Accords
1979	Death of Marcuse Bourdieu, *La Distinction: Critique sociale du jugement* Lyotard, *La Condition postmoderne: Rapport sur le savoir* Prigogine and Stengers, *La Nouvelle alliance* Rorty, *Philosophy and the Mirror of Nature*	Francis Ford Coppola, *Apocalypse Now* The first cognitive sciences department is established at MIT	Iranian Revolution Iran Hostage Crisis begins Margaret Thatcher becomes prime minister of the UK (the first woman to be a European head of state) Nicaraguan Revolution
1980	Death of Barthes and Sartre Davidson, *Essays on Actions and Events* Deleuze and Guattari, *Capitalisme et schizophrénie. 2. Mille plateaux* Derrida, *La Carte postale* Kristeva, *Pouvoirs de l'horreur: Essai sur l'abjection* Foucault, *The History of Sexuality, Vol. One* appears in English translation	Lacan officially dissolves the École Freudienne de Paris Murder of John Lennon Cable News Network (CNN) becomes the first television station to provide twenty-four-hour news coverage	Election of Ronald Reagan as US president Solidarity movement begins in Poland Death of Yugoslav president Josip Broz Tito
1981	Death of Lacan Habermas, *Theorie des kommunikativen Handelns* Bourdieu is elected to the Chair in Sociology at the Collège de France	First cases of AIDS are discovered among gay men in the US Debut of MTV	Release of American hostages in Iran François Mitterrand is elected as the first socialist president of France's Fifth Republic Confirmation of Sandra Day O'Connor, first woman Justice, to the US Supreme Court
1982	Foundation of the Collège International de Philosophie by François Châtelet, Jacques Derrida, Jean-Pierre Faye, and Dominique Lecourt	Debut of the Weather Channel	Falklands War
1983	Death of Aron Lyotard, *Le Différend*	Alice Walker, *The Color Purple* Founding of *Hypatia*	

	PHILOSOPHICAL EVENTS	CULTURAL EVENTS	POLITICAL EVENTS
1983	Sloterdijk, *Kritik der zynischen Vernunft*		
1984	Death of Foucault Davidson, *Inquiries into Truth and Interpretation* Irigaray, *Éthique de la différence sexuelle* Lloyd, *The Man of Reason*	Marguerite Duras, *The Lover* Milan Kundera, *The Unbearable Lightness of Being*	Assassination of Indira Gandhi Year-long strike of the National Union of Mineworkers in the UK
1985	First complete translation into French of Heidegger's *Sein und Zeit* Habermas, *Der philosophische Diskurs der Moderne* Irigaray's *Speculum of the Other Woman* and *This Sex Which Is Not One* appear in English translation	Don Delillo, *White Noise* Gabriel Garcia Marquez, *Love in the Time of Cholera*	Mikhail Gorbachev is named General Secretary of the Communist Party of the Soviet Union
1986	Death of Beauvoir Deleuze, *Foucault* Establishment of the Archives Husserl de Paris at the École Normale Supérieure	Art Spiegelman, *Maus I: A Survivor's Tale*	Chernobyl nuclear accident in USSR Election of Corazon Aquino ends Marcos regime in Philippines
1987	Derrida begins his appointment as Visiting Professor of French and Comparative Literature at the University of California, Irvine	Toni Morrison, *Beloved* Discovery of Paul de Man's wartime journalism damages the popularity of deconstruction in America	In June, Gorbachev inaugurates the perestroika (restructuring) that led to the end of the USSR The First Intifada begins in the Gaza Strip and West Bank
1988	Badiou, *L'Être et l'événement*	Salman Rushdie, *The Satanic Verses*	Benazir Bhutto becomes the first woman to head an Islamic nation Pan Am Flight 103, en route from London to New York, is destroyed by a bomb over Lockerbie, Scotland
1989	Death of Sellars Guattari, *Les Trois Écologies* Heidegger, *Beiträge zur Philosophie (Vom Ereignis)* Žižek, *The Sublime Object of Ideology*	*Exxon Valdez* oil spill in Alaska Tim Berners-Lee submits a proposal for an information management system, later called the World Wide Web	Fall of the Berlin Wall Students protest in Tiananmen Square, Beijing
1990	Death of Althusser Butler, *Gender Trouble*	The World Health Organization removes homosexuality from its list of diseases Beginning of the Human Genome Project, headed by James D. Watson	Nelson Mandela is released from prison Lech Walesa is elected president of Poland Reunification of Germany

	PHILOSOPHICAL EVENTS	CULTURAL EVENTS	POLITICAL EVENTS
1990			Break-up of the former Yugoslavia and beginning of the Yugoslav Wars Sandinistas are voted out of power after ten years of war against the US-backed Contras
1991	Deleuze and Guattari, *Qu'est-ce que la philosophie?*	Fredric Jameson, *Postmodernism, or, The Cultural Logic of Late Capitalism* The World Wide Web becomes the first publicly available service on the internet	First Gulf War begins Election of Jean-Bertrand Aristide as president of Haiti
1992	Death of Guattari Guattari, *Chaosmose*		Guattari runs unsuccessfully as a regional Green Party candidate in France Maastricht Treaty is signed, creating the European Union Dissolution of the Soviet Union
1993	Gilroy, *Black Atlantic*		Dissolution of Czechoslovakia; Vaclav Havel is named the first president of the Czech Republic Pablo Escobar, Colombian drug lord, is killed
1994	Death of Karl Popper Brandom, *Making it Explicit* Foucault, *Dits et écrits* Grosz, *Volatile Bodies* McDowell, *Mind and World*	Death of Ralph Ellison and Eugène Ionesco Bhabha, *The Location of Culture* The Channel Tunnel opens, connecting England and France	Genocide in Rwanda End of apartheid in South Africa; Nelson Mandela is sworn in as president North American Free Trade Agreement (NAFTA), signed in 1992, goes into effect
1995	Death of Deleuze and Levinas		End of Bosnian War World Trade Organization (WTO) comes into being, replacing GATT
1996		Cloning of Dolly the sheep (died 2003)	Death of Mitterrand
1998	Death of Lyotard Dussel, *Ética de la liberación en la edad ded la globalización y la exclusión*		Socialist–Green Coalition under Helmut Schmidt in Germany
1999	Spivak, *A Critique of Postcolonial Reason* Badiou leaves Vincennes to become Professor and Head of the Philosophy Department at the École Normale Supérieure	Death of Iris Murdoch	Introduction of the Euro Antiglobalization forces disrupt the WTO meeting in Seattle

	PHILOSOPHICAL EVENTS	CULTURAL EVENTS	POLITICAL EVENTS
2000	Death of Quine Negri and Hardt, *Empire*		The Second Intifada
2001	Balibar, *Nous, citoyens d'Europe? Les frontières, l'état, le peuple*		Terrorist attack destroys the World Trade Center
2002	Death of Bourdieu and Gadamer		Luiz Inacio Lula da Silva is elected president of Brazil
2003	Death of Blanchot and Davidson	Completion of the Human Genome Project	Start of the Second Gulf War Start of conflict in Darfur
2004	Death of Derrida and Leopoldo Zea Malabou, *Que faire de notre cerveau?*	Asian tsunami	Madrid train bombings
2005	Death of Ricoeur	Hurricane Katrina	Bombings of the London public transport system
2006	Badiou, *Logiques des mondes. L'Être et l'événement, 2.*		Evo Morales is elected president of Bolivia Bombings of the Mumbai train system
2007	Death of Jean Baudrillard and Rorty		
2008	Publication of first of Derrida's Seminars: *La Bête et le souverain*	Death of Robbe-Grillet, Aimé Césaire, Aleksandr Solzhenitsyn	Election of Barack Obama, the first African American president of the US International banking collapse
2009	Death of Lévi-Strauss, Leszek Kolakowski, Marjorie Grene	Death of Frank McCourt and John Updike	
2010	Death of Pierre Hadot and Claude Lefort	Death of Tony Judt and J. D. Salinger	Arab Spring uprisings begin in Tunisia
2011	Death of Michael Dummett and Elizabeth Young-Bruehl SPEP celebrates 50th anniversary		Death of Václav Havel US special forces kill Osama Bin Laden Occupy movement
2012		Death of Eric Hobsbawm and Adrienne Rich	

BIBLIOGRAPHY

Major works of individual philosophers are collected at the end of the relevant essay in the text.

Adair-Toteff, Christopher. "Neo-Kantianism: The German Idealism Movement." In *The Cambridge History of Philosophy 1870–1945*, edited by Thomas Baldwin, 27–43. Cambridge: Cambridge University Press, 2003.

Adorno, Theodor W., with Else Frenkel-Brunswik, David J. Levison, and R. Nevitt Sanford. *The Authoritarian Personality*. Edited by Max Horkheimer and Samuel H. Flowerman. New York: Harper & Brothers, 1950.

Allen, N. J. *Categories and Classification: Maussian Reflections on the Social*. Oxford: Berghahn, 2000.

Ansell-Pearson, Keith. *Viroid Life: Perspectives on Nietzsche and the Transhuman Condition*. London: Routledge, 1997.

Antliff, Mark. *Inventing Bergson: Cultural Politics and the Parisian Avant-Garde*. Princeton, NJ: Princeton University Press, 1993.

Arendt, Hannah. *Eichmann in Jerusalem: A Report on the Banality of Evil*. New York: Viking Press, 1963. Rev. and enl. ed. 1965.

Arendt, Hannah. *The Human Condition*. Chicago, IL: University of Chicago Press, 1958.

Arendt, Hannah. *The Life of the Mind*. New York: Harcourt Brace Jovanovich, 1978.

Arendt, Hannah. *The Origins of Totalitarianism*. New York: Harcourt Brace Jovanovich, 1951. 3rd ed. with new prefaces, 1973.

Babich, Babette. "Heideggers 'Beiträge' zwischen politische Kritik und die Frage nach der Technik." Translated by Harald Seubert. In *Eugenik und die Zukunft*, edited by Stefan Sorgner, H. James Birx, and Nikolaus Knoepffler, 43–69. Freiburg: Karl Alber, 2006.

Babich, Babette, ed. *Hermeneutic Philosophy of Science, Van Gogh's Eyes, and God: Essays in Honor of Patrick A. Heelan, SJ*. Dordrecht: Kluwer, 2002.

Babich, Babette. "Mach, Duhem, Bachelard." In *Twentieth-Century Continental Philosophy*, edited by Richard Kearney, 175–221. London: Routledge, 1996.

Babich, Babette. *Nietzsche's Philosophy of Science: Reflecting Science on the Ground of Art and Life*. Albany, NY: SUNY Press, 1994.

Babich, Babette. "'The Problem of Science' in Nietzsche and Heidegger." *Revista Portuguesa de Filosofia* 63 (2007): 205–37.

Bachelard, Gaston. *Essai sur la connaissance approchée*. Paris: Vrin, [1927] 1981.

Badiou, Alain. *Being and Event*. Translated by Oliver Feltham. London: Continuum, 2005.

Badiou, Alain. *The Century*. Translated by Alberto Toscano. Cambridge: Polity, 2007.

Badiou, Alain. *Deleuze: The Clamor of Being*. Translated by Louise Burchill. Minneapolis, MN: University of Minnesota Press, 2000.

Bambach, Charles. *Heidegger, Dilthey, and the Crisis of Historicism*. Ithaca, NY: Cornell University Press, 1995.

Barth, Kai-Henrik. "The Politics of Seismology." *Social Studies of Science* 33(5) (2003): 743–81.

Basso, Louis. "Induction technique et science expérimentale." *Revue philosophique de la France et de l'etranger* 99 (1925): 41–76.

Baudrillard, Jean. *Symbolic Exchange and Death*. Translated by Iain Hamilton Grant. London: Sage, 1993.

Bearn, Gordon. "Nietzsche, Feyerabend, and the Voices of Relativism." *Metaphilosophy* 17(2–3) (1986): 93–204.

Beauvoir, Simone. *The Second Sex*. Translated by Howard Madison Parshley. New York: Alfred A. Knopf, 1952. Originally published as *Le Deuxième sexe*. Paris: Gallimard, 1949.

Bell, David. "A Brentanian Philosophy of Arithmetic." *Brentano Studien: Internationales Jahrbuch der Franz Brentano Forschung* 2 (1989): 139–44.

Bellamy, Richard. *Liberalism and Modern Society: A Historical Argument*. University Park, PA: Pennsylvania State University Press, 1992.

Benrubi, Isaac. *Contemporary Thought of France*. Translated by Ernest B. Dicker. London: Williams & Norgate, 1926. Published in French as *Les Sources et les courants de la philosophie contemporaine en France*. Paris: Félix Alcan, 1933.

Bensaud-Vincent, Bernadette. "Chemistry in the French Tradition of Philosophy of Science: Duhem, Meyerson, Metzger and Bachelard." *Studies in History and Philosophy of Science Part A* 36(4) (December 2005): 627–49.

Bergson, Henri. "Life and Consciousness." In *Mind Energy*, edited by Keith Ansell-Pearson and Michael Kolkman, translated by H. Wildon Carr, 1–28. Basingstoke: Palgrave Macmillan, 2007.

Bergson, Henri. "On the Pragmatism of William James: Truth and Reality." Translated by Melissa McMahon. In *Key Writings*, edited by Keith Ansell-Pearson and John Mullarkey, 267–84. New York: Continuum, 2002. Originally published as "Sur le pragmatisme de William James," in his *La Pensée et le mouvant*, 267–80. Paris: Presses Universitaires de France, 1969.

Bergson, Henri. "Psychophysical Parallelism and Positive Metaphysics." In *Continental Philosophy of Science*, edited by Gary Gutting, 59–69. Malden, MA: Blackwell Publishing, 2005.

Berlin, Isaiah. *The Crooked Timber of Humanity*. Edited by Henry Hardy. London: John Murray, 1990.

Bernet, Rudolf, Iso Kern, and Eduard Marbach. *An Introduction to Husserlian Phenomenology*. Evanston, IL: Northwestern University Press, 1993.

Berthelot, Jean-Michel. *1895: Durkheim: L'Avènement de la sociologie scientifique*. Toulouse: Presses Universitaires du Mirail, 1995.

Berthelot, René. *Un Romantisme utilitaire: Etude sur le mouvement pragmatiste. 1, Le pragmatisme chez Nietzsche et chez Poincaré*. Paris: Félix Alcan, 1911.

Besnard, Phillippe, ed. *The Sociological Domain: The Durkheimians and the Founding of French Sociology*. Cambridge: Cambridge University Press, 1983.

Biberian, Jean-Paul. "Condensed Matter Nuclear Science (Cold Fusion): An Update." *International Journal of Nuclear Energy Science and Technology* 3(1) (2007): 31–42.

Bolzano, Bernard. *Theory of Science*. Dordrecht: Reidel, 1973. Originally published as *Wissenschaftslehre: Versuch einer ausführlichen und grösstentheils neuen Darstellung der Logik mit steter Rücksicht auf deren bisherige Bearbeiter*. 4 vols. Sulzbach: J. E. v. Seidel, 1837.

Bolzano, Bernard. "A Translation of Bolzano's Paper on the Intermediate Value Theorem." Translated by S. B. Russ. *Historia Mathematica* 7 (1980): 156–85. Originally published as *Rein analytischer Beweis des Lehrsatzes, dass zwischen je zwei Werthen, die ein entgegengesetztes Resultat gewähren, wenigstens eine reelle Wurzel der Gleichung liege*. Prague: Gottlieb Haze, 1817.

Borlandi, M. "Informations sur la rédaction du Suicide et sur l'état du conflit entre Durkheim et Tarde de 1895 à 1897." *Durkheim Studies* 6 (Fall 1994): 4–13.

Bouglé, Célestin. "Spiritualisme et Kantisme en France: Jules Lachelier." *La Revue de Paris* (May 1, 1934): 198–215.

Boutroux, Émile. *William James*. Translated by Archibald Henderson and Barbara Henderson. New York: Longman's, Green, 1912.

Bouwsma, O. K. *Wittgenstein: Conversations 1949–1951*. Edited by J. L. Craft and Ronald E. Hustwit. Indianapolis, IN: Hackett, 1986.

Bowler, Peter J. "The Whig Interpretation of Geology." *Biology and Philosophy* 3 (1988): 99–103.

Brochard, Victor. *De l'erreur*. Paris: Berger-Levrault, 1879.

Brenner, Anastasios, and Jean Gayon, eds. *French Studies in the Philosophy of Science*. Frankfurt: Springer, 2009.

Brooks, John I. *The Eclectic Legacy: Academic Philosophy and the Human Sciences in Nineteenth-Century France*. Newark, DE: University of Delaware Press, 1998.

Brunschvicg, Léon. "L'Idée critique et le système Kantien." *Revue de métaphysique et de morale* 31(2) (1924): 133–203.

Brunschvicg, Léon. *Préface* to *Œuvres de J. Lachelier*, i–xlv. Paris: Félix Alcan, 1933.

Brunschwig, Jacques. "Goldschmidt and Guéroult: Some Facts, Some Enigmas." *Archiv für Geschichte der Philosophie* 88 (2006): 82–106.

Brush, Stephen. "Mach and Atomism." *Synthese* 18 (1968): 192–215.

Brush, Stephen. *The Temperature of History: Phases of Science and Culture in the Nineteenth Century*. New York: Bart Franklin, 1978.

Bruzina, Ronald. *Edmund Husserl and Eugen Fink: Beginnings and Ends in Phenomenology, 1928–1938*. New Haven, CT: Yale University Press, 2004.

Buckley, Philip. "Husserl's Göttingen Years and the Genesis of a Theory of Community." In *Reinterpreting the Political*, edited by Lenore Langsdorf, Stephen H. Watson, and Karen Anne Smith, 39–50. Albany, NY: SUNY Press, 1998.

Burwick, Frederick, and Paul Douglass, eds. *The Crisis in Modernism: Bergsonism and the Vitalist Controversy*. Cambridge: Cambridge University Press, 1992.

Butterfield, Herbert. *The Whig Interpretation of History*. New York: Norton, 1931.

Caeymaex, Florence. *Sartre, Merleau-Ponty, Bergson: Les Phénoménologies existentialistes et leur héritage bergsonien*. Hildesheim: Olms, 2005.

Caillé, Alain. *Don, intérêt et désintéressement: Bourdieu, Mauss, Platon et quelques autres*. Paris: La Découverte, 1994.

Camilleri, Kristian. *Heisenberg and the Interpretation of Quantum Mechanics: The Physicist as Philosopher*. Cambridge: Cambridge University Press, 2009.

Camus, Albert. *The Stranger*. Translated by Stuart Gilbert. New York: Knopf, 1946. Originally published as *L'Étranger*. Paris: Gallimard, 1942.

Čapek, Milič. *Bergson and Modern Physics*. The Hague: Martinus Nijhoff, 1971.

Čapek, Milič. "Bergson's Theory of the Mind–Brain Relation." In Papanicolaou and Gunter, *Bergson and Modern Thought*, 129–48.

Čapek, Milič. *The Philosophical Impact of Contemporary Physics*. New York: Van Nostrand-Reinhold, 1961.

Capeillères, Fabien. "Généalogie d'un Néokantisme français: À propos d'Émile Boutroux." *Revue de Métaphysique et de Morale, Néokantismes* 3 (1997): 405–42.

Capeillères, Fabien. "To Reach for Metaphysics: Émile Boutroux's Philosophy of Science." In Luft and Makkreel, *Neo-Kantianism in Contemporary Philosophy*, 192–249.

Carnap, Rudolf. "The Elimination of Metaphysics through Logical Analysis of Language." In *Logical Positivism*, edited by A. J. Ayer, 60–81. New York: Free Press, 1959. Originally published as "Überwindung der Metaphysik durch logische Analyse der Sprache." *Erkenntnis* 2 (1932): 219–41.

Carnap, Rudolf. "Intellectual Autobiography." In *The Philosophy of Rudolf Carnap*, edited by Paul A. Schilpp, 3–84. La Salle, IL: Open Court, 1963.

Carnap, Rudolf. *The Logical Structure of the World*. Translated by Rolf A. George (from the 2nd ed.). Berkeley, CA: University of California Press, 1967. Originally published as *Der logische Aufbau der Welt*. Berlin: Weltkreis, 1928. 2nd ed. Hamburg: Felix Meiner, 1961.

Carnap, Rudolf. *The Logical Syntax of Language*. Translated by Amethe Smeaton. London: Kegan Paul, 1937. Originally published as *Logische Syntax der Sprache*. Vienna: Springer, 1934.

Carnap, Rudolf. *Der Raum: Ein Beitrag zur Wissenschaftslehre*. Berlin: Reuther & Reichard, 1922.

Carnap, Rudolf. "Replies and Systematic Expositions." In *The Philosophy of Ernst Cassirer*, edited by Paul A. Schilpp, 859–1013. La Salle, IL: Open Court, 1963.

Carnap, Rudolf. "Von der Erkenntnistheorie zur Wissenschaftslogik." In *Actes du Congrès international de philosophie scientifique*, vol. 1, 36–41. Paris: Hermann, 1936.

Carnap, Rudolf, Hans Hahn, and Otto Neurath. "The Scientific Conception of the World: The Vienna Circle." In *Otto Neurath: Philosophical Papers: 1913–1946*, edited by R. Cohen and M. Neurath. Dordrecht: Reidel, 1983. Originally published as *Wissenschaftliche Weltauffassung: Der Wiener Kreis*. Vienna: Wolf, 1929.

Carus, André. *Carnap and Twentieth-Century Thought: Explication as Enlightenment*. Cambridge: Cambridge University Press, 2007.

Casey, Edward S. "Habitual Body and Memory in Merleau-Ponty." *Man and World* 17 (1984): 279–97.

Casey, Edward S. *Remembering: A Phenomenological Study*. Bloomington, IN: Indiana University Press, 1987.

Cassirer, Ernst. *Determinism and Indeterminism in Modern Physics: Historical and Systematic Studies of the Problem of Causality*. Translated by O. Theodor Benfey. New Haven, CT: Yale University Press, [1936] 1956.

Cassirer, Ernst. *The Individual and the Cosmos in Renaissance Philosophy*. Translated by Mario Domandi. New York: Dover, 2000.

Cassirer, Ernst. "Kant und die Gegenwärtige Kritik der Naturwissenschaften in Frankreich." *Kant Studien* 35(2/3) (1929): 273–88.

Cassirer, Ernst. "Das Problem des Unendlichen und Renouviers 'Gesetz der Zahl.'" In *Philosophische Abhandlungen: Hermann Cohen zum 70: Geburtstag Dargebracht*, 85–98. Berlin: Bruno Cassirer, 1912.

Cassirer, Ernst. "Review of Ch. Renouvier, *Essais de Critique Générale*." *Die Geisteswissenschaften* 1 (1914): 634–5.

Cassirer, Ernst, and Martin Heidegger. "Davos Disputation Between Ernst Cassirer and Martin Heidegger." In Martin Heidegger, *Kant and the Problem of Metaphysics*, translated by Richard Taft, 193–205. Bloomington, IN: Indiana University Press, 1997.

Cavaillès, Jean. "On Logic and the Theory of Science." In Kockelmans and Kisiel, *Phenomenology and the Natural Sciences*, 353–409.

Clark, Ronald W. *The Life of Bertrand Russell*. London: Jonathan Cape, 1957.

Clark, Simon. *The Foundations of Structuralism: A Critique of Lévi-Strauss and the Structuralist Movement*. Brighton: Harvester Press, 1981.

Clarke, Terry N. *Prophets and Patrons: The French University and the Emergence of the Social Sciences*. Cambridge, MA: Harvard University Press, 1973.

Cleland, Carol E. "Methodological and Epistemic Differences between Historical Science and Experimental Science." *Philosophy of Science* 69 (September 2002): 474–96.

Cloud, John. "Imaging the World in a Barrel: CORONA and the Clandestine Convergence of the Earth Sciences." *Social Studies of Science* 31(2) (2001): 231–51.

Cobb-Stevens, Richard. *James and Husserl: The Foundations of Meaning*. The Hague: Martinus Nijhoff, 1974.

Cockburn, David. *Other Human Beings*. London: Macmillan, 1990.

Coffa, J. Alberto. *The Semantic Tradition from Kant to Carnap: To the Vienna Station*. Cambridge: Cambridge University Press, 1991.

Cohen, H. *Logik der reinen Erkenntnis*. 3rd ed. Berlin: Bruno Cassirer, 1922.

Conrad, Peter. *Modern Times, Modern Places: Life and Art in the Twentieth Century*. London: Thames & Hudson, 1998.

Critchley, Simon, and William R. Schroeder, eds. *A Companion to Continental Philosophy*. Oxford: Blackwell, 1998.

Crowell, Steven Galt. *Husserl, Heidegger, and the Space of Meaning: Paths Towards Transcendental Phenomenology*. Evanston, IL: Northwestern University Press, 2001.

Crowell, Steven Galt. "Husserlian Phenomenology." In *A Companion to Phenomenology and Existentialism*, edited by Hubert L. Dreyfus and Mark A. Wrathall, 9–30. Malden, MA: Blackwell, 2006.

Darwin, Charles. *The Origin of Species*. Harmondsworth: Penguin, 1985.

Darwin, Charles. *The Variation of Animals and Plants under Domestication*. 2 vols. London: J. Murray, 1868.

Dawkins, Richard. *The Extended Phenotype*. Oxford: Oxford University Press, 1982.

Dawson, Jr., J. W. "What Hath Gödel Wrought?" *Synthese* 114 (1998): 3–12.

Delacampagne, Christian. *A History of Philosophy in the Twentieth Century*. Translated by M. B. DeBevoise. Baltimore, MD: Johns Hopkins University Press, 1999.

Deleuze, Gilles. *Bergsonism*. Translated by Hugh Tomlinson and Barbara Habberjam. New York: Zone Books, 1988.

Deleuze, Gilles. "Bergson's Concept of Difference." Translated by Melissa McMahon. In *The New Bergson*, edited by John Mullarkey, 42–66. Manchester: Manchester University Press, 1999.

Deleuze, Gilles. *Difference and Repetition*. Translated by Paul Patton. London: Continuum, 1994.

Deleuze, Gilles. "Lecture Course on Chapter Three of Bergson's *Creative Evolution*." Translated by Bryn Loban. *SubStance* 36(3) (2007): 72–91.

Deleuze, Gilles. *Negotiations 1972–1990*. Translated by Martin Joughin. New York: Columbia University Press, 1995.

Deleuze, Gilles, and Félix Guattari. *Anti-Oedipus: Capitalism and Schizophrenia*. Translated by Robert Hurley, Mark Seem, and Helen R. Lane. New York: Viking Press, 1977.

Deleuze, Gilles, and Félix Guattari. *A Thousand Plateaus*. Translated by Brian Massumi. London: Continuum, 1988.

Deleuze, Gilles, and Félix Guattari. *What is Philosophy?* Translated by Graham Burchell. London, Verso, 1994.

Dennett, Daniel C. *Darwin's Dangerous Idea: Evolution and the Meanings of Life*. London: Allen Lane, 1995.

Dennis, Michael Aaron. "Earthly Matters: On the Cold War and the Earth Sciences." *Social Studies of Science* 33(5) (2003): 809–19.

Derrida, Jacques. *Given Time. I: Counterfeit Money.* Translated by Peggy Kamuf. Chicago, IL: University of Chicago Press, 1994.

Derrida, Jacques. *The Post Card: From Socrates to Freud and Beyond.* Translated by Alan Bass. Chicago, IL: University of Chicago Press, 1987. Originally published as *La Carte postale: De Socrate à Freud et au-delà*. Paris: Flammarion, 1980.

Derrida, Jacques. *Speech and Phenomena, and Other Essays on Husserl's Theory of Signs.* Translated by David B. Allison. Evanston, IL: Northwestern University Press, 1973. Originally published as *La Voix et le phénomène: Introduction au problème du signe dans la phénoménologie de Husserl*, Paris: Presses Universitaires de France, 1967.

Derrida, Jacques. "Violence and Metaphysics." In *Writing and Difference*, 79–153. New York: Routledge, 1997.

Descombes, Vincent. *Modern French Philosophy.* Translated by L. Scott-Fox and J. M. Harding. Cambridge: Cambridge University Press, 1980. Originally published as *Le Même et l'autre: Quarante-cinq ans de philosophie française (1933–1978)*. Paris: Éditions de Minuit, 1979.

Di Gregorio, Mario. *From Here to Eternity: Ernst Haeckel and Scientific Faith.* Göttingen: Vandenhoeck & Ruprecht, 2005.

Dillon, Wilton. *Gifts and Nations.* The Hague: Mouton, 1968.

Dilthey, Wilhelm. *The Formation of the Historical World in the Human Sciences.* Edited and translated by Rudolf A. Makkreel and Frithjof Rodi. Princeton, NJ: Princeton University Press, [1910] 2002.

Douglas, Mary. "Foreword." In Marcel Mauss, *The Gift: The Form and Reason for Exchange in Archaic Societies*, ix–xxiii. London: Routledge, 2002.

Driesch, Hans. *Analytische Theorie der organischen Entwicklung.* Leipzig: Engelmann, 1894.

Dreyfus, Hubert, ed. *Husserl, Intentionality and Cognitive Science.* Cambridge, MA: MIT Press, 1982.

Duhem, Pierre. *Études sur Leonard de Vinci: Ceux qu'il a lus et ceux qui l'ont lu.* Paris: A. Hermann, 1906.

Duhem, Pierre. *German Science: Some Reflections on German Science and German Virtues.* Translated by J. Lyon. La Salle, IN: Open Court, 1991. Originally published as *La Science allemande*. Paris: A. Hermann, 1915.

Dummett, Michael. *Frege, Philosophy of Mathematics.* Cambridge, MA: Harvard University Press, 1991.

Dummett, Michael. *The Origins of Analytic Philosophy.* Cambridge, MA: Harvard University Press, 1993.

Durkheim, Émile. *Contributions to L'Année sociologique.* Edited by Yash Nandan. New York: Free Press, 1980.

Durkheim, Émile. "The Dualism of Human Nature." In *Essays on Sociology and Philosophy*, edited by Kurt Wolff, 325–40. New York: Harper, 1960.

Durkheim, Émile. *Durkheim on Institutional Analysis.* Edited and translated by Mark Traugott. Chicago, IL: University of Chicago Press, 1978.

Durkheim, Émile. *Durkheim's Philosophy Lectures: Notes from the Lycée de Sens Course, 1883–1884.* Translated by Neil Gross and Robert Alun Jones. Cambridge: Cambridge University Press, 2004.

Durkheim, Émile. "L'Enseignement philosophique et l'agrégation de philosophie." In *Textes*, vol. 3, edited by Victor Karady, 403–34. Paris: Éditions de Minuit, [1895] 1975.

Durkheim, Émile. *The Evolution of Educational Thought in France.* Translated by Peter Collins. London: Routledge & Kegan Paul, [1938] 1977.

Durkheim, Émile. *"Germany Above All": German Mentality and War.* Paris: Armand Colin, 1915.

Durkheim, Émile. "Individualism and the Intellectuals." *Political Studies* 17(1) (1969): 19–30.

Durkheim, Émile. *Lettres à Marcel Mauss.* Paris: Presses Universitaires de France, 1998.

Durkheim, Émile. *Moral Education.* Translated by Everett K. Wilson and Herman Schnurer. London: Collier, [1925] 1973.

Durkheim, Émile. *On Morality and Society: Selected Writings*. Edited by Robert N. Bellah. Chicago, IL: University of Chicago Press, 1973.

Durkheim, Émile. *Pragmatism and Sociology*. Translated by J. C. Whitehouse. Cambridge: Cambridge University Press, 1983.

Durkheim, Émile. *Professional Ethics and Civic Morals*. Translated by Cornelia Brookfield. London: Routledge, [1950] 1992.

Durkheim, Émile. *Socialism and Saint-Simon*. Translated by Charlotte Sattler. New York: Collier, [1928] 1962.

Durkheim, Émile. *Sociology and Philosophy*. Translated by D. F. Pocock. Glencoe, IL: Free Press, 1953.

Durkheim, Émile, and Marcel Mauss. *Primitive Classification*. Translated by Rodney Needham. Chicago, IL: University of Chicago Press, [1903] 1963.

Dusek, Val. "Brecht and Lukács as Teachers of Feyerabend and Lakatos: The Feyerabend–Lakatos Debate as Scientific Recapitulation of the Brecht–Lukács Debate." *History of the Human Sciences* 11(2) (1998): 25–44.

Edel, Geert. *Von der Vernunftkritik zur Erkenntnislogik*. Freiburg and Munich: Alber, 1988.

Eger, Martin. "Hermeneutics as an Approach to Science, Parts 1 and II." *Science and Education* 2 (1993): 1–29, 303–28.

Ehrlich, Leonard H. *Karl Jaspers: Philosophy as Faith*. Amherst, MA: University of Massachusetts Press, 1975.

Einstein, Albert. "Zur Elektrodynamik bewegter Körper." *Annalen der Physik* 17 (1905): 891–921.

Érdi, Péter. *Complexity Explained*. Frankfurt: Springer, 2007.

Espagne, Michel. *En deçà du Rhin: L'Allemagne des philosophes français au XIXe siècle*. Paris: Éditions du Cerf, 2004.

Evellin, François. *Infini et quantité*. Paris: Germer Baillière, 1880.

Farber, Marvin. *The Foundation of Phenomenology: Edmund Husserl and the Quest for a Rigorous Science of Philosophy*. Albany, NY: SUNY Press, 1943.

Fédi, Laurent. *Le Problème de la connaissance dans la philosophie de Ch. Renouvier*. Paris: L'Harmattan, 1999.

Ferrari, Massimo. *I Dati dell'esperienza: Il neokantismo di Felice Tocco nella filosofia Italiana tra ottocento e novecento*. Florence: L. S. Olschki, 1990.

Ferrari, Massimo. *Introduzione a il neocriticismo*. Rome: Laterza, 1997.

Feyerabend, Paul. *Farewell to Reason*. London: Verso, 1989.

Feyerabend, Paul. *Science in a Free Society*. London: Verso, 1978.

Fleck, Ludwik. *The Genesis and Development of a Scientific Fact*. Translated by Frederick Bradley and Thaddeus J. Trenn. Chicago, IL: University of Chicago Press, 1980. Originally published as *Die Entstehung und Entwicklung einer wissenschaftlichen Tatsache: Einführung in die Lehre vom Denkstil und Denkkollektiv*. Frankfurt: Suhrkamp, [1935] 1979.

Flynn, Thomas. "Sartre." In Critchley and Schroeder, *A Companion to Continental Philosophy*, 256–68.

Fogelin, Robert. *Wittgenstein*. 2nd ed. London: Routledge, 1987.

Føllesdal, Dagfinn. "Husserl and Frege: A Contribution to Elucidating the Origins of Phenomenological Philosophy." In *Mind, Meaning and Mathematics: Essays on the Philosophical Views of Husserl and Frege*, edited by Leila Haaparanta, 3–47. Dordrecht: Kluwer, 1994. Originally published as *Husserl und Frege: Ein Beitrag zur Beleuchtung der Entstehung der phänomenologischen Philosophie*. Oslo: Aschehoug, 1958.

Føllesdal, Dagfinn. "Response (to Mohanty)." In Dreyfus, *Husserl, Intentionality and Cognitive Science*, 52–6.

Forman, Paul. "*Kausalität, Anschaulichkeit,* and *Individualität*, or How Cultural Values Prescribed the Character and the Lessons Ascribed to Quantum Mechanics." In *Society and Knowledge:*

Contemporary Perspectives in the Sociology of Knowledge, edited by Nico Stehr and Volker Meja, 333–47. New Brunswick, NJ: Transaction Books, 1984.

Forman, Paul. "The Primacy of Science in Modernity, of Technology in Postmodernity, and of Ideology in the History of Technology." *History and Technology* 23(1) (2007): 1–152.

Foucault, Michel. *History of Madness*. Translated by Jonathan Murphy and Jean Khalfa. London: Routledge, 2006. Originally published as *Folie et déraison: Histoire de la folie à l'âge classique*. Paris: Plon, 1961.

Foucault, Michel. *The History of Sexuality, Vol. One: An Introduction*. Translated by Robert Hurley. New York: Vintage, 1980. Originally published as *Histoire de la sexualité, 1: La Volonté de savoir*. Paris: Gallimard, 1976.

Foucault, Michel. *The Order of Things: An Archeology of the Human Sciences*. New York: Vintage, 1970. Originally published as *Les Mots et les choses: Une archéologie des sciences humaines*. Paris: Gallimard, 1966.

Fournier, Marcel. "Durkheim's Life and Context: Something New about Durkheim?" In *The Cambridge Companion to Durkheim*, edited by Jeffrey C. Alexander and Phillip Smith, 41–69. Cambridge: Cambridge University Press, 2005.

Fournier, Marcel. *Marcel Mauss*. Paris: Fayard, 1994.

Francis, Mark. *Herbert Spencer and the Invention of Modern Life*. Stocksfield: Acumen, 2007.

Frege, Gottlob. *The Basic Laws of Arithmetic: An Exposition of the System*. Berkeley, CA: University of California Press, 1967. Originally published as the first part of vol. 1 of *Grundgesetze der Arithmetik, begriffsschriftlich abgeleitet*. 2 vols. Jena: Pohle, 1893–1903.

Frege, Gottlob. "*Begriffsschrift*, a Formula Language, Modeled upon that of Arithmetic, for Pure Thought." In *From Frege to Gödel: A Source Book in Mathematical Logic, 1879–1931*, edited by Jean van Heijenoort, 1–82. Cambridge, MA: Harvard University Press, 1967. Originally published as *Begriffsschrift, eine der arithmetischen nachgebildete Formelsprache des reinen Denkens*. Halle: 1879.

Frege, Gottlob. *The Foundations of Arithmetic: A Logico-mathematical Enquiry Into the Concept of Number*. Oxford: Blackwell, 1950. Originally published as *Die Grundlagen der Arithmetik: Eine logisch-mathematische Untersuchung über den Begriff der Zahl*. Breslau: Koebner, 1884.

Frege, Gottlob. "Function and Concept." In *The Frege Reader*, edited by Michael Beaney, 130–48. Oxford: Blackwell, 1997. Originally published as *Funktion und Begriff*. Jena: Hermann Pohle, 1891.

Frege, Gottlob. "On Concept and Object." In McGuiness, *Frege*, 182–94. Originally published as "Über Begriff und Gegenstand," *Vierteljahrsschrift für wissenschaftliche Philosophie* 18 (1892): 192–205.

Frege, Gottlob. "On Sinn and Bedeutung." In *The Frege Reader*, edited by Michael Beaney, 151–71. Oxford: Blackwell, 1997. Originally published as "Über Sinn und Bedeutung." *Zeitschrift für Philosophie und philosophische Kritik* 100 (1892): 25–50.

Frege, Gottlob. "Review of E. Husserl, *Philosophy of Arithmetic*." In McGuiness, *Frege*, 195–209. Originally published as "Besprechung der E. Husserl, Philosophie der Arithmetik, I." *Zeitschrift für Philosophie und philosophische Kritik* 103 (1894): 313–32.

Frege, Gottlob. "Thought." In McGuiness, *Frege*, 351–72. Originally published as "Der Gedanke: Eine logische Untersuchung." *Beiträge zur Philosophie der deutschen Idealismus* 1 (1918): 58–77.

Freudenthal, Gad. "Maimonides' Guide of the Perplexed and the Transmission of the Mathematical Tract 'On the Asymptotic Lines' in the Arabic, Latin, Hebrew Medieval Tradition." *Vivarium* 26 (1988): 113–40.

Friedman, Michael. "The *Aufbau* and the Criticism of Metaphysics." In Friedman and Creath, *The Cambridge Companion to Carnap*, 129–52.

Friedman, Michael. "Ernst Cassirer." *Stanford Encyclopedia of Philosophy*, 2004 (http://plato.stanford.edu/entries/cassirer).

Friedman, Michael. "Introduction: Carnap's Revolution in Philosophy." In Friedman and Creath, *The Cambridge Companion to Carnap*, 1–18.

Friedman, Michael. *A Parting of the Ways: Carnap, Cassirer, and Heidegger*. Chicago, IL: Open Court, 2000.

Friedman, Michael, and Richard Creath, eds. *The Cambridge Companion to Carnap*. Cambridge: Cambridge University Press, 2007.

Frodeman, Robert. *Geo-Logic: Breaking Ground between Philosophy and the Earth Sciences*. Albany, NY: SUNY Press, 2003.

Gabriel, Gottfried. "Introduction: Carnap brought Home." In *Carnap Brought Home: The View from Jena*, edited by S. Awodey and C. Klein, 3–23. Chicago, IL: Open Court, 2004.

Gadamer, Hans-Georg. "Paul Natorp." In Paul Natorp, *Philosophische Systematik*, xi–xvii. Hamburg: Felix Meiner, 2000.

Gadamer, Hans-Georg. *Wahrheit und Methode*. Tübingen: J. C. B. Mohr, 1960.

Gaita, Raimond. *The Philosopher's Dog: Friendship with Animals*. New York: Routledge, 2003.

Game, Ann. *Undoing the Social: Towards a Deconstructive Sociology*. Toronto: University of Toronto Press, 1991.

Gane, Mike. "The Deconstruction of Social Action: The 'Reversal' of Durkheimian Methodology." In *Durkheim's Suicide: A Century of Research and Debate*, edited by W. S. F. Pickering and Geoffrey Walford, 22–35. London: Routledge, 2000.

Gane, Mike. "Durkheim contre Comte." In *La Méthode Durkheimienne d'un siècle à l'autre*, edited by Charles-Henri Cuin, 31–8. Paris: Presses Universitaires de France, 1997.

Gane, Mike. *On Durkheim's Rules of Sociological Method*. London: Routledge, 1988.

Gane, Mike, ed. *The Radical Sociology of Durkheim and Mauss*. London: Routledge, 1992.

Gane, Mike. "Woman as Outsider." In Gane, *The Radical Sociology of Durkheim and Mauss*, 85–132.

Gehlen, Arnold. "Rückblick auf die Philosophie Max Schelers." In *Max Scheler im Gegenwartsgeschehen der Philosophie*, edited by Paul Good, 179–88. Bern: Francke, 1975.

Geiger, Moritz. *The Significance of Art: A Phenomenological Approach to Aesthetics*, edited and translated by Klaus Berger. Washington, DC: University Press of America, 1986.

Geiger, Moritz. *Zugange zur Ästhetik*. Leipzig: Der Neue Geist, 1928.

Giedion, Siegfried. *Mechanization Takes Command: A Contribution to Anonymous History*. Oxford: Oxford University Press, 1948.

Giedymin, Jerzy. "Polish Philosophy in the Interwar Period and Ludwik Fleck's Theory of Thought Styles and Thought Collectives." In *Cognition and Fact: Materials on Ludwik Fleck*, edited by Robert Cohen and Ludwig Schnelle, 179–215. Boston, MA: Reidel, 1986.

Giere, Ronald. *Explaining Science*. Chicago, IL: University of Chicago Press, 1988.

Gill, Jerry H. "Saying and Showing: Radical Themes in Wittgenstein's *On Certainty*." *Religious Studies* 10(3) (September 1974): 279–90.

Gillies, Mary Ann. *Henri Bergson and British Modernism*. Montreal: McGill-Queen's University Press, 1996.

Ginev, Dmitri. *The Context of Constitution: Beyond the Edge of Epistemological Justification*. Dordrecht: Springer, 2006.

Ginev, Dmitri. *A Passage to the Idea for a Hermeneutic Philosophy of Science*. Amsterdam: Rodopi, 1997.

Gladigow, Burkhardt. "Pantheismus und Naturmystik." In *Die Trennung von Natur und Geist*, edited by Rüdiger Bubner, 119–44. Munich: Fink, 1990.

Glendinning, Simon. *On Being With Others: Heidegger, Wittgenstein, Derrida*. London: Routledge, 1998.

Glock, Carl Theodore. *Wilhelm Diltheys Grundlegung einer wissenschaftlichen Lebensphilosophie*. Berlin: Junker & Dünnhaupt, 1939.

Gödel, Kurt. *On Formally Undecidable Propositions of Principia Mathematica and Related Systems.* Translated by Bernard Meltzer. New York: Basic Books, 1962.

Gödel, Kurt. "Über formal unentscheidbare Sätze der Principia Mathematica und verwandter Systeme I." *Monatshefte für Mathematik* 149(1) [1931] (September 2006): 1–29.

Goodwin, Brian. "From Control to Participation via a Science of Qualities." (1999). Available at www.schumachercollege.org.uk/learning-resources/from-control-to-participation-via-a-science-of-qualities (accessed January 2010).

Goodwin, Brian. *How the Leopard Changed its Spots: The Evolution of Complexity.* London: Phoenix, 1994.

Goodwin, Brian. *Nature's Due: Healing Our Fragmented Culture.* Edinburgh: Floris Books, 2007.

Goodwin, Brian, with David King. "An Interview with Professor Brian Goodwin." *GenEthics News* 11 (March–April 1996): 6–8.

Gordon, Peter E. "Neo-Kantianism and the Politics of Enlightenment." *The Philosophical Forum* 39(2) (2008): 223–38.

Gould, Stephen Jay. *Wonderful Life: The Burgess Shale and the Nature of History.* London: Century Hutchinson, 1989.

Gould, Stephen Jay, and Richard C. Lewontin. "The Spandrels of San Marco and the Panglossian Paradigm: A Critique of the Adaptationist Programme." *Proceedings of The Royal Society of London, Series B* 205(1161) (1979): 581–98.

Gourd, Jean-Jacques. *Le Phénomène.* Paris: Félix Alcan, 1888.

Gower, Barry. "Cassirer, Schlick, and 'Structural' Realism: The Philosophy of the Exact Sciences in the Background to Early Logical Empiricism." *British Journal for the History of Philosophy* 8(1) (2000): 71–106.

Granger, Gilles-Gaston. *Concept, structure et loi en science économique: Essai d'épistémologie comparative.* Paris: Presses Universitaires de France, 1955.

Granger, Gilles-Gaston. *Pensée formelle et sciences de l'homme.* Paris: Éditions Montaigne, 1960.

Grant, Edward. *The Foundations of Modern Science in the Middle Ages: Their Religious, Institutional and Intellectual Contexts.* Cambridge: Cambridge University Press, 1996.

Gregory, Frederick. *Nature Lost? Natural Science and the German Theological Traditions of the Nineteenth Century.* Cambridge, MA: Harvard University, 1992.

Greisch, Jean. "Ethics and Lifeworlds." In *Questioning Ethics: Contemporary Debates in Philosophy*, edited by Richard Kearney and Mark Dooley, 44–61. New York: Routledge, 1999.

Grogin, R. C. *The Bergsonian Controversy in France, 1900–1914.* Calgary: University of Calgary Press, 1988.

Gross, Neil. "Introduction." In *Durkheim's Philosophy Lectures: Notes from the Lycée de Sens Course, 1883–1884*, 1–30. Cambridge: Cambridge University Press, 2004.

Gross, Neil. "A Note on the Sociological Eye and the Discovery of a New Durkheim Text." *Journal of the History of the Behavioral Sciences* 32(2) (1996): 408–23.

Guerlac, Suzanne. *Thinking in Time: An Introduction to Henri Bergson.* Ithaca, NY: Cornell University Press, 2006.

Guéroult, Martial. *Descartes selon l'ordre des raisons.* 2 vols. Paris: Aubier, 1953.

Guéroult, Martial. *Dianoématique.* Paris: Aubier-Montaigne, 1979.

Guéroult, Martial. *L'Évolution et la structure de la doctrine de la science chez Fichte.* 2 vols. Paris: Les Belles Lettres, 1930.

Gunn, John Alexander. *Modern French Philosophy: A Study of the Development since Comte.* Foreword by Henri Bergson. London: T. F. Unwin, 1922.

Gunter, P. A. Y. "Bergson and the War against Nature." In *The New Bergson*, edited by John Mullarkey, 168–82. Manchester: Manchester University Press, 1999.

Gunter, P. A. Y. *The Big Thicket: An Ecological Reevaluation*. Denton, TX: University of North Texas Press, 1993.

Gunter, P. A. Y. "The Dialectic of Intuition and Intellect: Fruitfulness as a Criterion." In Papanicolaou and Gunter, *Bergson and Modern Thought*, 3–18.

Gurwitsch, Aron. *The Field of Consciousness*. Pittsburgh, PA: Duquesne University Press, 1964. Originally published as *Théorie du champ de la conscience*, translated by Michel Butor. Paris: Desclée de Brouwer, 1957.

Gurwitsch, Aron. *Studies in Phenomenology and Psychology*. Evanston, IL: Northwestern University Press, 1966.

Gutting, Gary. *French Philosophy in the Twentieth Century*. Cambridge: Cambridge University Press, 2001.

Haeckel, Ernst. *Systematische Phylogenie: Entwurf eines natürlichen Systems der Organismen auf Grund ihrer Stammesgeschichte*. Berlin: Georg Reimer, 1894–96.

Hamelin, Octave. *Essai sur les éléments principaux de la représentation*. Paris: Félix Alcan, 1907.

Hamelin, Octave. *Fichte*. Strasbourg: Presses Universitaires de Strasbourg, 1988.

Hamelin, Octave. *Les Philosophes présocratiques*. Strasbourg: Association des publications de l'université de Strasbourg, 1978.

Hamelin, Octave. *Le Système d'Aristote*. Paris: Félix Alcan, 1920.

Hamelin, Octave. *Le Système de Descartes*. Paris: Félix Alcan, 1911.

Hamelin, Octave. *Le Système de Renouvier*. Paris: J. Vrin, 1927.

Hanson, Norwood Russell. *Patterns of Discovery: An Inquiry into the Conceptual Foundations of Science*. Cambridge: Cambridge University Press, 1958.

Hausman, Carl R. *Charles S. Peirce's Evolutionary Philosophy*. Cambridge: Cambridge University Press, 1993.

Heelan, Patrick A. "Husserl, Hilbert and the Critique of Galilean Science." In *Edmund Husserl and the Phenomenological Tradition*, edited by Robert Sokolowski, 157–73. Washington, DC: The Catholic University of America Press, 1988.

Heelan, Patrick A. "Preface." In Gaston Bachelard, *The New Scientific Spirit*, iii–viii. Boston, MA: Beacon Press, 1984.

Heelan, Patrick A. *Quantum Mechanics and Objectivity: The Physical Philosophy of Werner Heisenberg*. The Hague: Martinus Nijhoff, 1965.

Heelan, Patrick A. *Space-Perception and the Philosophy of Science*. Berkeley, CA: University of California Press, 1983.

Heidegger, Martin. "The Age of World Picture." Translated by William Lovitt. In *The Question Concerning Technology*, 115–54. New York: Harper & Row, 1977.

Heidegger, Martin. *Basic Writings*. Edited by David F. Krell. New York: Harper & Row, 1977.

Heidegger, Martin. *Introduction to Metaphysics*. New York: Doubleday, 1961. Originally published as *Einführung in die Metaphysik*. Tübingen: Niemeyer, 1953. Published in collected works, *Gesamtausgabe*, vol. 40. Frankfurt: Klostermann, 1983.

Heidegger, Martin. *Martin Heidegger: Supplements: From the Earliest Essays to "Being and Time" and Beyond*. Edited by John van Buren. Albany, NY: SUNY Press, 2002.

Heidegger, Martin. *The Metaphysical Foundations of Logic*. Translated by Michael Heim. Bloomington, IN: Indiana University Press, 1984. Published in collected works as *Metaphysische Anfangsgründe der Logik im Ausgang von Leibniz*. *Gesamtsausgabe*, vol. 26. Frankfurt: Klostermann, 1978.

Heidegger, Martin. "My Way to Phenomenology." In *On Time and Being*, translated by Joan Stambaugh, 74–82. New York: Harper & Row, 1972. Originally published as *Zur Sache des Denkens*. Tübingen: Max Niemeyer, 1969.

Heidegger, Martin. "Overcoming Metaphysics." In *The End of Philosophy*, edited and translated by Joan Stambaugh, 84–110. New York: Harper & Row, 1973. Reprinted in *The Heidegger*

Controversy: A Critical Reader, edited by Richard Wolin, 67–90. New York: Columbia University Press, 1991. Originally published as "Überwindung der Metaphysik," in his *Vorträge und Aufsätze*, 71–99. Pfullingen: Neske, 1954.

Heidegger, Martin. "Phenomenological Interpretations in Connection with Aristotle: An Indication of the Hermeneutical Situation." Translated by John van Buren. In *Supplements*, 111–45. Originally published as "Phänomenologische Interpretationen zu Aristoteles (Anzeige der hermeneutischen Situation)," edited by Hans-Ulrich Lessing. *Dilthey-Jahrbuch* 6 (1989): 229–74.

Heidegger, Martin. "Postscript" to "What is Metaphysics?" In *Existence and Being*, 349–61. Chicago, IL: Henry Regnery, 1949. Originally published as "Nachwort" to *Was ist Metaphysik?* 4th ed. Frankfurt: Klostermann, 1943.

Heidegger, Martin. "Recent Research in Logic." In *Becoming Heidegger: On the Trail of his Early Occasional Writings, 1910–1927*, edited by Theodore Kisiel and Thomas Sheehan, 30–50. Evanston, IL: Northwestern University Press, 2007.

Heidegger, Martin. *Towards the Definition of Philosophy*. Translated by Ted Sadler. London: Continuum, 2000.

Heidegger, Martin. *What is Called Thinking?* Translated by F. D. Wieck and J. G. Gray. New York: Harper & Row, 1968.

Heidegger, Martin. "Wilhelm Dilthey's Research and the Struggle for a Historical Worldview." Translated by Charles Bambach. In *Supplements*, 147–76.

Heilbron, Johan. "Les Métamorphoses du durkheimisme, 1920–1940." *Revue française de sociologie* 26 (1985): 203–37.

Heller, Erich. *The Importance of Nietzsche: Ten Essays*. Chicago, IL: University of Chicago Press, 1988.

Henckmann, Wolfgang. *Max Scheler*. Munich: C. H. Beck, 1988.

Hentschel, Klaus. "Der Vergleich als Brücke zwischen Wissenschaftsgeschichte und Wissenschaftstheorie." *Journal for General Philosophy of Science* 34 (2003): 251–75.

Herbert, Christopher. *Victorian Relativity: Radical Thought and Scientific Discovery*. Chicago, IL: University of Chicago Press, 2001.

Hering, Jean. *Phénoménologie et philosophie religieuse*. Paris: Félix Alcan, 1925.

Hilbert, David. "Mathematical Problems." *Bulletin of the American Mathematical Society* 8 (1902): 437–79.

Hill, Clair Ortiz. "Did Georg Cantor Influence Edmund Husserl?" *Synthese* 113 (1997): 145–70.

Hill, Clair Ortiz. "Frege's Attack on Husserl and Cantor." *The Monist* 77(3) (July 1994): 345–57.

Hill, Clair Ortiz. *Word and Object in Husserl, Frege, and Russell*. Athens, OH: Ohio University Press, 1991.

Ho, Mae-Wan. "Human Genome: The Biggest Sell-Out in Human History." Institute of Science in Society report (2000). www.i-sis.org.uk/humangenome.php (accessed January 2010).

Ho, Mae-Wan. *The Rainbow and the Worm: The Physics of Organisms*. London: World Scientific, 1998.

Höffding, Harald. *Modern Philosophers and Lectures on Bergson*. Translated by Alfred C. Mason. London: Macmillan, 1915.

Holzhey, Helmut. "Cohen and the Marburg School in Context." In *Hermann Cohen's Critical Idealism*, edited by Reinier Munk, 3–37. Dordrecht: Springer, 2004.

Holzhey, Helmut. *Cohen und Natorp*. 2 vols. Basel and Stuttgart: Schwabe, 1986.

Holzhey, Helmut. "Neukantianismus." In *Historisches Wörterbuch der Philosophie*, vol. 6, 747–54. Darmstadt: Wissenschaftlichen Buchgesellschaft, 1984.

Holzhey, Helmut. "Der Neukantianismus." In *Geschichte der Philosophie*, vol. 12, edited by H. Holzhey and W. Röd, 13–129. Munich: Beck, 2004.

Howard, Don. "Einstein and Duhem." *Synthese* 83(3) (June 1990): 363–84.

Husserl, Edmund. "Adolf Reinach." Translated by Lucinda Vandervort Brettler. *Philosophy and*

Phenomenological Research 35(4) (June 1975): 571–4. Originally published as "Adolf Reinach," *Kantstudien* 23 (1919): 147–9.

Husserl, Edmund. *Aufsätze und Rezensionen (1890–1910)*. Published in collected works, *Husserliana*, vol. 22, edited by Bernard Rang. Dordrecht: Kluwer, 1997.

Husserl, Edmund. *Briefwechsel*. Published in collected works, *Husserliana*, Edmund Husserl Dokumente 3/1–10, edited by Karl Schuhmann. Dordrecht: Kluwer, 1994.

Husserl, Edmund. *Erster Philosophie, I*. Published in collected works, *Husserliana*, vol. 7, edited by Rudolf Boehm. The Hague: Martinus Nijhoff, 1956.

Husserl, Edmund. *The Idea of Phenomenology*. Translated by William P. Alston and George Nakhnikian. Dordrecht: Kluwer, 1964. Published in collected works as *Die Idee der Phänomenologie*, *Husserliana*, vol. 2, edited by Walter Biemel. Dordrecht: Kluwer, 1964.

Husserl, Edmund. *Introduction to the Logical Investigations: A Draft of a Preface to the Logical Investigations 1913*. Translated by P. J. Bossert and C. H. Peters. The Hague: Martinus Nijhoff, 1975. Originally published as "*Entwurf einer 'Vorrede' zu den Logischen Untersuchungen*," edited by Eugen Fink. *Tijdschrift voor Philosophie* 1 (1939): 106–33, 319–39.

Husserl, Edmund. *Méditations cartésiennes: Introduction à la phénoménologie*. Translated by Gabrielle Peiffer and Emmanuel Levinas. Paris: Armand Colin, 1931.

Husserl, Edmund. "The Origin of Geometry." In *The Crisis of European Sciences and Transcendental Phenomenology*, 353–78. Originally published as "Der Ursprung der Geometrie als intentional-historisches Problem." *Revue internationale de philosophie* 1 (1939): 155–81.

Husserl, Edmund. *Philosophy of Arithmetic: Psychological and Logical Investigations*. Translated by Dallas Willard. Dordrecht: Kluwer, 2003. Originally published as *Philosophie der Arithmetik: Psychologische und Logische Untersuchungen*, vol. 1. Halle–Saale: C. E. M. Pfeffer, 1891.

Husserl, Edmund. "A Reply to a Critic of My Refutation of Logical Psychologism." In *Husserl: Shorter Works*, edited by Peter McCormick and Frederick Elliston, 152–8. Notre Dame, IN: University of Notre Dame Press, 1981. Originally published as "Rezension von Palágyi." *Zeitschrift für Psychologie und Physiologie der Sinnesorgane* 31 (1903): 287–94.

Ingarden, Roman. *The Cognition of the Literary Work of Art*. Translated by R. A. Crowley and K. R. Olson. Evanston, IL: Northwestern University Press, 1973. Originally published as *Vom Erkennen des literarischen Kunstwerks*. Tübingen: Max Niemeyer, 1968.

Ingarden, Roman. *The Literary Work of Art*. Translated by G. G. Grabowicz. Evanston, IL: Northwestern University Press, 1973. Originally published as *Das literarische Kunstwerk*.Tübingen: Max Niemeyer, 1965.

James, William. *Pragmatism and Four Essays from "The Meaning of Truth"*. New York: Meridian, 1974.

James, William. "The Present Dilemma in Philosophy" (1907). In *Pragmatism*, edited by Bruce Kuklick, 7–21. Indianapolis, IN: Hackett, 1981.

Jankélévitch, Vladimir. *Henri Bergson*. Paris: Presses Universitaires de France, 1959.

Jaspers, Karl. "Heidegger." Translated by Hans R. Rudnick. In *The Philosophy of Karl Jaspers*, rev. 2nd ed., edited by Paul. A. Schilpp, 75/1–75/16. La Salle, IL: Open Court, 1974.

Jaspers, Karl. *Notizen zu Martin Heidegger*. Edited by Hans Saner. Munich: Piper, 1978.

Jaspers, Karl. "Philosophical Autobiography." Translated by Paul A. Schilpp and Ludwig B. Lefebre. In *The Philosophy of Karl Jaspers*, edited by Paul A. Schilpp, 1–94. New York: Tudor Publishing Company, 1957.

Jaspers, Karl. *Philosophy is for Everyman: A Short Course in Philosophical Thinking*. Translated by R. F. C. Hull and Grete Wels. New York: Harcourt, Brace & World, 1967. Originally published in German as *Kleine Schule des philosophischen Denkens*. Munich: Piper, 1965.

Jaspers, Karl. *Psychologie der Weltanschauungen*. Berlin: Springer, 1919.

Jaspers, Karl. *Reason and Existenz*. Translated by William Earle. New York: Noonday Press, 1955.

Jaspers, Karl. *Way to Wisdom: An Introduction to Philosophy.* Translated by Ralph Manheim. New Haven, CT: Yale University Press, 1951. Originally published as *Einführung in die Philosophie.* Zurich: Artemis, 1950.

Jones, Susan Stedman. *Durkheim Reconsidered.* Cambridge: Polity, 2001.

Kaegi, Dominic, and Enno Rudolph, eds. *Cassirer–Heidegger: 70 Jahre Davoser Disputation.* Hamburg: Felix Meiner, 2000.

Kaelin, Eugene. *An Existentialist Aesthetic: The Theories of Sartre and Merleau-Ponty.* Madison, WI: University of Wisconsin Press, 1962.

Kallen, Horace. *William James and Henri Bergson: A Study in Contrasting Theories of Life.* Chicago, IL: University of Chicago Press, 1914.

Kaplan, Robert. *Forgotten Crisis: The Fin-de-Siècle Crisis of Democracy in France.* Oxford: Berg, 1995.

Karsenti, Bruno. *L'Homme total: Sociologie, anthropologie et philosophie chez Marcel Mauss.* Paris: Presses Universitaires de France, 1997.

Karsenti, Bruno. "The Maussian Shift: A Second Foundation for Sociology in France?" In *Marcel Mauss: A Centenary Tribute*, edited by Wendy James and N. J. Allen, 71–82. Oxford: Berghahn, 1998.

Kaufmann, Fritz. *Das Reich des Schönen: Bausteine zu einer Philosophie der Kunst.* Stuttgart: Kohlhammer, 1960.

Kearney, Richard, ed. *Dialogues with Contemporary Continental Thinkers.* Manchester: Manchester University Press, 1984.

Kearney, Richard. *Modern Movements in European Philosophy.* 2nd ed. Manchester: Manchester University Press, 1986.

Kelly, Kevin. *Out of Control: The New Biology of Machines.* London: Fourth Estate, 1995.

Kerzberg, Pierre. *Critique and Totality.* Albany, NY: SUNY Press, 1997.

Kerzberg, Pierre. *Kant et la nature.* Paris: Les Belles-Lettres, 1999.

Kierkegaard, Søren. *The Sickness unto Death.* Translated by Howard V. Hong and Edna H. Hong. Princeton, NJ: Princeton University Press, 2001.

Kisiel, Theodore. *The Genesis of Heidegger's "Being and Time"*. Berkeley, CA: University of California Press, 1993.

Kisiel, Theodore. *Heidegger's Way of Thought.* London: Continuum, 2002.

Kisiel, Theodore. "Science, Phenomenology and the Thinking of Being." In Kockelmans and Kisiel, *Phenomenology and the Natural Sciences*, 167–83.

Kisiel, Theodore, and Thomas Sheehan, eds. *Becoming Heidegger: On the Trail of his Early Occasional Writings, 1910–1927.* Evanston, IL: Northwestern University Press, 2007.

Kleeberg, Bernhard. "God–Nature Progressing: Natural Theology in German Monism." *Science in Context* 20(3) (2007): 537–69.

Kleinberg, Ethan. *Generation Existential: Heidegger's Philosophy in France, 1927–1961.* Ithaca, NY: Cornell University Press, 2005.

Kleinpeter, Hans. *Der Phänomenalismus: Eine naturwissenschaftliche Weltanschauung.* Leipzig: Johann Ambrosius Barth, 1913.

Kockelmans, Joseph J. "The Era of the World-as-Picture." In Kockelmans and Kisiel, *Phenomenology and the Natural Sciences*, 184–204.

Kockelmans, Joseph J. "Science and Discipline: Some Historical and Critical Reflections." In *Interdisciplinarity and Higher Education*, edited by Joseph J. Kockelmans, 11–48. University Park, PA: Pennsylvania State University Press, 1979.

Kockelmans, Joseph J., and Theodore J. Kisiel, eds. *Phenomenology and the Natural Sciences.* Evanston, IL: Northwestern University Press, 1970.

Köhnke, Klaus Christian. *Entstehung und Aufstieg des Neukantianismus: Die Deutsche Universitätsphilosophie zwischen Idealismus und Positivismus.* Frankfurt: Suhrkamp, 1986. Abridged English translation, *The Rise of Neo-Kantianism: German Academic Philosophy Between Idealism and Positivism*, translated by R. J. Hollingdale. Cambridge: Cambridge University Press, 1991.

Kremer-Marietti, Angèle. *Seven Epistemological Essays*. Paris: Buenos Books America, 2007.

Krijnen, Christian. *Nachmetaphysischer Sinn: Eine Problemgeschichtliche und Systematische Studie zu den Prinzipien der Wertphilosophie Heinrich Rickerts*. Würzburg: Königshausen & Neumann, 2001.

Krijnen, Christian. *Philosophie als System: Prinzipientheoretische Untersuchungen zum Systemgedanken bei Hegel, im Neukantianismus und in der Gegenwartsphilosophie*. Würzburg: Königshausen & Neumann, 2008.

Kuper, Adam. "Durkheim's Theory of Kinship." *British Journal of Sociology* 36(2) (1985): 224–37.

Lacan, Jacques. *The Ethics of Psychoanalysis, 1959–1960*. Translated by Dennis Porter. New York: Norton, 1992. Originally published as *Le Séminaire. 7: L'Éthique de la psychanalyse, 1959–1960*. Paris: Éditions du Seuil, 1986.

Lammana, Mary Ann. *Emile Durkheim on the Family*. London: Sage, 2002.

Lask, Emil. *Gesammelte Schriften*, volume 2. Tübingen: Mohr, 1923.

Lask, Emil. *Die Lehre vom Urteil*. Tübingen: Mohr, 1912.

Laudan, Rachel. *From Mineralogy to Geology: The Foundations of a Science, 1650–1830*. Chicago, IL: University of Chicago Press, 1987.

Lawlor, Leonard. *Derrida and Husserl: The Basic Problem of Phenomenology*. Bloomington, IN: Indiana University Press, 2002.

Lawlor, Leonard. "The Legacy of Husserl's '*Ursprung der Geometrie*': The Limits of Phenomenology in Merleau-Ponty and Derrida." In *Merleau-Ponty's Reading of Husserl*, edited by Ted Toadvine and Lester Embree, 201–23. Dordrecht: Kluwer, 2003.

Lawn, Chris. *Wittgenstein and Gadamer: Towards a Post-Analytic Philosophy of Language*. London: Continuum, 2005.

Leck, Ralph M. *Georg Simmel and Avant-Garde Sociology: The Birth of Modernity 1880–1920*. New York: Humanity Books, 2000.

LeGrand, Homer Eugene. *Drifting Continents and Shifting Theories*. Cambridge: Cambridge University Press, 1989.

Lejbowicz, Max. "Pierre Duhem et l'histoire des sciences arabes." *Revue des questions scientifiques* 175(1) (2004): 59–84.

Lembeck, Karl-Heinz. *Platon in Marburg: Platon-Rezeption und Philosophiegeschichtsphilosophie bei Cohen und Natorp*. Würzburg: Königshausen & Neumann, 1994.

Lévi-Strauss, Claude. *The Elementary Structures of Kinship*. Edited by Rodney Needham. Translated by James Harle Bell and John Richard von Sturmer. Boston, MA: Beacon Press, 1969. Originally published as *Les Structures élémentaires de la parenté*. Paris: Presses Universitaires de France, 1949.

Lévi-Strauss, Claude. *Introduction to the Work of Marcel Mauss*. Translated by Felicity Baker. London: Routledge, 1987.

Levinas, Emmanuel. *Basic Philosophical Writings*. Edited by Adriaan T. Peperzak, Simon Critchley, and Robert Bernasconi. Bloomington, IN: Indiana University Press, 1996.

Levinas, Emmanuel. *Collected Philosophical Papers*. Translated by Alphonso Lingis. The Hague: Martinus Nijhoff, 1987.

Levinas, Emmanuel. *Difficult Freedom: Essays on Judaism*. Translated by Seán Hand. Baltimore, MD: Johns Hopkins University Press, 1997. Originally published as *Difficile liberté: Essais sur le judaïsme*. Paris: A. Michel, 1976.

Levinas, Emmanuel. *Entre Nous: Thinking-of-the-Other*. Translated by Michael B. Smith and Barbara Harshav. New York: Columbia University Press, 1998. Originally published as *Entre nous: Essais sur le penser-à-l'autre*. Paris: B. Grasset, 1991.

Levinas, Emmanuel. *Ethics and Infinity: Conversations with Philippe Nemo*. Translated by Richard A. Cohen. Pittsburgh, PA: Duquesne University Press, 1985. Originally published as *Ethique et infini*. Paris: Librairie Arthème Fayard et Radio France, 1982.

Levinas, Emmanuel. "Ethics of the Infinite." In *Dialogues with Contemporary Continental Thinkers: The Phenomenological Heritage*, edited by Richard Kearney, 57–69. Manchester: Manchester University Press, 1984.

Levinas, Emmanuel. *Existence and Existents*. Translated by Alfonso Lingis. Pittsburgh, PA: Duquesne University Press, 2001. Originally published as *De l'existence à l'existent*. Paris: Vrin, 1947.

Levinas, Emmanuel. *The Levinas Reader*. Edited by Seán Hand. Oxford: Blackwell, 1996.

Levinas, Emmanuel. *Otherwise Than Being, Or Beyond Essence*. Translated by Alfonso Lingis. The Hague: Martinus Nijhoff, 1981. Originally published as *Autrement qu'être ou au delà de l'essence*. Paris: Vrin, 1974.

Levinas, Emmanuel. *Outside the Subject*. Translated by Michael B. Smith. London: Athlone, 1993. Originally published as *Hors sujet*. Fontfroide-le-Haut: Fata Morgana, 1987.

Levinas, Emmanuel. "The Paradox of Morality: An Interview with Emmanuel Levinas." Translated by Andrew Benjamin and Tamra Wright. In *The Provocation of Levinas: Rethinking the Other*, edited by Robert Bernasconi and David Wood, 168–80. New York: Routledge, 1988.

Levinas, Emmanuel. "Reflections on the Philosophy of Hitlerism." *Critical Inquiry* 17 (August 1990): 62–71. Originally published as "Quelques réflexions sur la philosophie de l'hitlérisme." *Esprit* 2 (1934): 199–208.

Levinas, Emmanuel. *The Theory of Intuition in Husserl's Phenomenology*. Translated by André Orianne. Evanston, IL: Northwestern University Press, 1973. Originally published as *La Théorie de l'intuition dans la phénoménologie de Husserl*. Paris: Félix Alcan, 1930.

Levinas, Emmanuel. *Time and the Other and Additional Essays*. Translated by Richard A. Cohen. Pittsburgh, PA: Duquesne University Press, 1987.

Levinas, Emmanuel. *Totality and Infinity*. Translated by Alfonso Lingis. Pittsburgh, PA: Duquesne University Press, 1969. Originally published as *Totalité et infini*. Paris: Vrin, 1961.

Levinas, Emmanuel, and Richard Kearney. "Dialogue with Emmanuel Levinas." In *Face to Face with Levinas*, edited by Richard A. Cohen, 13–33. Albany, NY: SUNY Press, 1986.

Liard, Louis. *La Science positive et la métaphysique*. Paris: Germer-Baillières, 1879.

Liegener, Christoph, and Giuseppe Del Re. "Chemistry versus Physics, the Reduction Myth, and the Unity of Science." *Zeitschrift für allgemeine Wissenschaftstheorie* 18 (1987): 165–74.

Lindsay, A. D. *The Philosophy of Bergson*. London: Dent, 1911.

Logue, William. *Charles Renouvier, Philosopher of Liberty*. Baton Rouge, LA: Louisiana State University Press, 1993.

Loiskandl, Helmut, Deena Weinstein, and Michael Weinstein. "Introduction." In Georg Simmel, *Schopenhauer and Nietzsche*, translated by Helmut Loiskandl, Deena Weinstein, and Michael Weinstein. Amherst, MA: University of Massachusetts Press, 1986.

Lotze, Rudolf Hermann. *Logic*. Oxford: Oxford University Press, 1884. Originally published as *Logik*. Leipzig: Hirzel, 1874.

Luft, Sebastian. "Reconstruction and Reduction: Natorp and Husserl on Method and the Question of Subjectivity." In Makkreel and Luft, *Neo-Kantianism in Contemporary Philosophy*, 59–91.

Lukes, Steven. *Emile Durkheim*. London: Allen Lane, 1973.

Lyon-Caen, Charles. "Notice sur la vie et les travaux de M. Louis Liard." *Séances et travaux de l'Académie des Sciences Morales et Politiques* 81 (1921): 25–60.

Lyotard, Jean-François. *The Differend: Phrases in Dispute*. Translated by Georges Van Den Abbeele. Minneapolis, MN: University of Minnesota Press, 2002.

Lyotard, Jean-François. *Just Gaming*. Translated by Wlad Godzich. Minneapolis, MN: University of Minnesota Press, 1985.

Lyotard, Jean-François. *The Postmodern Condition: A Report on Knowledge*. Translated by Geoff Bennington. Minneapolis, MN: University of Minnesota Press, 1984.

Lyotard, Jean-François. *The Postmodern Explained to Children: Correspondence 1982–1985*. Edited by Julian Pefanis and Morgan Thomas. Translated by Don Barry. London: Turnaround, 1992.

Lyotard, Jean-François. *Postmodern Fables*. Translated by Georges Van Den Abbeele. Minneapolis, MN: University of Minnesota Press, 1997.

Makkreel, Rudolf and Sebastian Luft, eds. *Neo-Kantianism in Contemporary Philosophy*. Bloomington, IN: Indiana University Press, 2010.

Malcolm, Norman. *Ludwig Wittgenstein: A Memoir*. Oxford: Clarendon, 2001.

Mannheim, Karl. *Essays on the Sociology of Knowledge*. Edited by Paul Kecskemeti. London: Routledge & Kegan Paul, 1952. Originally published as *Die Strukturanalyse der Erkenntnistheorie*. Berlin: Reuthes and Reinhard, 1922.

Marcuse, Herbert. *Eros and Civilization: A Philosophical Inquiry into Freud*. Boston, MA: Beacon, 1955.

Martínez, Alberto A. "Handling Evidence in History: The Case of Einstein's Wife." *School Science Review* 86(316) (March 2005): 49–56.

Matthews, Eric. *Twentieth-Century French Philosophy*. Oxford: Oxford University Press, 1996.

Mauchaussat, Gaston. *L'Idéalisme de Lachelier*. Paris: Presses Universitaires de France, 1961.

Mauss, Marcel. *Écrits politiques*. Paris: Fayard, 1997.

Mauss, Marcel. *The Nature of Sociology*. Translated by William Jeffrey. Oxford: Berghahn, 2005.

Mauss, Marcel. *On Prayer*. Translated by Susan Leslie and W. S. F. Pickering. Oxford: Berghahn and Durkheim, [1909] 2003.

Mauss, Marcel. "A Sociological Assessment of Bolshevism." In Gane, *The Radical Sociology of Durkheim and Mauss*, 165–215.

Mauss, Marcel. "Sociology: Its Divisions and Their Relative Weightings." In *The Nature of Sociology*, translated by William Jeffrey, 31–85. Oxford: Berghahn, 2005.

Mauss, Marcel. *Techniques, Technology and Civilization*. Edited by Nathan Schlanger. Oxford: Berghahn, 2006.

McGinn, Marie. *Routledge Philosophy Guidebook to Wittgenstein and the Philosophical Investigations*. London: Routledge, 1997.

McGuiness, Brian. *Frege: Collected Papers on Mathematics, Logic, and Philosophy*. Oxford: Blackwell, 1984.

Medawar, Peter. *The Art of the Soluble*. London: Methuen, 1967.

Menand, Louis. *The Metaphysical Club*. London: HarperCollins, 2001.

Merleau-Ponty, Maurice. *Merleau-Ponty à la Sorbonne*. Grenoble: Cynara, 1988.

Merleau-Ponty, Maurice. *Phenomenology of Perception*. Translated by Colin Smith. New York: Routledge & Kegan Paul, 1962. Originally published as *Phénoménologie de la perception*. Paris: Gallimard, 1945.

Merleau-Ponty, Maurice. *In Praise of Philosophy and Other Essays*. Translated by John Wild, James Edie, and John O'Neill. Evanston, IL: Northwestern University Press, 1988. Originally published as *Elogie de la philosophie et autres essais*. Paris: Gallimard, 1960.

Merleau-Ponty, Maurice. *Signs*. Translated by Richard C. McCleary. Evanston, IL: Northwestern University Press, 1964. Originally published as *Signes*. Paris: Gallimard, 1960.

Merleau-Ponty, Maurice. *The Visible and the Invisible*. Translated by Alfonso Lingis. Evanston, IL: Northwestern University Press, 1968. Originally published as *Le Visible et l'invisible: Suivi de notes de travail*. Paris: Gallimard, 1964.

Meštrović, Stjepan G. *Durkheim and Postmodern Culture*. New York: Aldine de Gruyter, 1992.

Milet, Jean. *Bergson et le calcul infinitésimal: Ou, la raison et le temps*. Paris: Presses Universitaires de France, 1974.

Mill, John Stuart. *An Examination of Sir William Hamilton's Philosophy*. Boston, MA: William V. Spencer, 1865.

Miller, Watts Willie. *Durkheim, Morals and Modernity*. London: UCL Press, 1996.

Mirowski, Philip. *The Effortless Economy of Science*. Durham, NC: Duke University Press, 2004.

Mohanty, J. N. *Husserl and Frege*. Bloomington, IN: Indiana University Press, 1982.

Mohanty, J. N. "Husserl and Frege: A New Look at Their Relationship." In Dreyfus, *Husserl, Intentionality and Cognitive Science*, 43–52.

Montebello, Pierre. "Matter and Light in Bergson's *Creative Evolution*." Translated by Roxanne Lapidus. *SubStance* 114, 36(3) (2007): 91–100.

Moore, G. E. "A Defense of Common Sense." In *Classics of Analytic Philosophy*, edited by Robert R. Ammerman, 47–67. Indianapolis, IN: Hackett, 1994.

Moore, G. E. "Proof of an External World." In *Classics of Analytic Philosophy*, edited by Robert R. Ammerman, 68–84. Indianapolis, IN: Hackett, 1994.

Moran, Dermot, and Sebastian Luft, eds. *The Neo-Kantian Reader*. London: Routledge, 2010.

Mormann, Thomas. *Rudolf Carnap*. Munich: C. H. Beck, 2000.

Mourélos, Georges. *Bergson et les niveaux de réalité*. Paris: Presses Universitaires de France, 1964.

Mulhall, Stephen. *Inheritance and Originality: Wittgenstein, Heidegger, Kierkegaard*. Oxford: Oxford University Press, 2001.

Mullarkey, John. *Bergson and Philosophy*. Edinburgh: Edinburgh University Press, 1999.

Mullarkey, John. "Life, Movement, and the Fabulation of the Event." *Theory, Culture, and Society* 24(6) (2007): 53–70.

Munk, Reinier, ed. *Hermann Cohen's Critical Idealism*. Dordrecht: Springer, 2004.

Nagel, Ernest, and James R. Newman, *Gödel's Proof*. New York: New York University Press, 1958.

Natorp, Paul. "Kant und die Marburger Schule." *Kant-Studien* 17 (1912): 193–221.

Natorp, Paul. *Die logischen Grundlagen der exakten Wissenschaften*. Leipzig: Tuebner, 1910.

Natorp, Paul. "On the Objective and Subjective Grounding of Cognition." Translated by L. Phillips and D. Kolb. *Journal of the British Society for Phenomenology* 12(3) (1981): 245–66. Originally published as "Ueber Objective und Subjective Begründung der Erkenntniss." *Philosophische Monatshefte* 23 (1887): 257–86.

Neumann, Günther. *Die phänomenologische Frage nach dem Ursprung der mathematisch-naturwissenschaftlichen Raumauffassung bei Husserl und Heidegger*. Berlin: Duncker & Humblot, 1999.

Nietzsche, Friedrich. *The Antichrist*. Translated by R. J. Hollingdale. Harmondsworth: Penguin, 1968.

Nietzsche, Friedrich. *Beyond Good and Evil*. Translated by R. J. Hollingdale. Harmondsworth: Penguin, 1987.

Nietzsche, Friedrich. *Daybreak: Thoughts on the Prejudices of Morality*. Translated by R. J. Hollingdale. Cambridge: Cambridge University Press, 1987.

Nietzsche, Friedrich. *Ecce Homo*. Translated by Duncan Large. Oxford: Oxford University Press, 2007.

Nietzsche, Friedrich. *The Gay Science*. Translated by Josefine Nauckhoff. Cambridge: Cambridge University Press, 2001.

Nietzsche, Friedrich. *Human, All Too Human*. Translated by Marion Faber and Stephan Lehmann. Harmondsworth: Penguin, 1994.

Nietzsche, Friedrich. *On the Genealogy of Morality*. Edited by Keith Ansell-Pearson. Translated by Carol Diethe. Cambridge: Cambridge University Press, 1992.

Nietzsche, Friedrich. *Sämtliche Werke: Kritische Studienausgabe*. 15 vols. Edited by Giorgio Colli and Mazzino Montinari. Berlin: de Gruyter, 1980.

Nietzsche, Friedrich. *The Wanderer and His Shadow*. In *Human, All Too Human*, translated by R. J. Hollingdale. Cambridge: Cambridge University Press, 1986.

Nietzsche, Friedrich. *The Will to Power*. Translated by R. J. Hollingdale and Walter Kaufmann. New York: Random House, 1967.

Nizan, Paul. *Les Chiens de garde*. Paris: Rieder, 1932.

Noble, Denis. *The Music of Life: Biology Beyond the Genome*. Oxford: Oxford University Press, 2006.

Nolen, Désiré. *La Critique de Kant et la métaphysique de Leibniz*. Paris: Germer-Baillière, 1876.

Nolen, Désiré. *Kant et la philosophie du XIX siècle*. Montpellier: Martel Aîné, 1877.

Nye, Mary Jo. "The Boutroux Circle and Poincaré's Conventionalism." *Journal of the History of Ideas* 1 (1979): 107–20.

Ollig, Hans-Ludwig. *Der Neukantianismus*. Stuttgart: Metzler, 1979.

Overgaard, Søren. *Wittgenstein and Other Minds: Subjectivity and Intersubjectivity in Wittgenstein, Levinas, and Husserl*. London: Routledge, 2007.

Paneth, Friedrich A. "The Epistemological Status of the Chemical Concept of Element." *Foundations of Chemistry* 5 (2003): 113–45.

Papanicolaou, A. C., and P. A. Y. Gunter, eds. *Bergson and Modern Thought: Towards a Unified Science*. London: Harwood, 1987.

Paradis, Bruno. "Indétermination et mouvements de birfurcation chez Bergson." *Philosophie* 32 (1991): 11–40.

Parodi, Dominique. *La Philosophie contemporaine en France*. Paris: Félix Alcan, 1919.

Parrochia, Daniel. *Formes et systématiques philosophiques*. Thesis. 1988. Available from the Atelier National de Reproduction des Thèses, University of Lille III.

Parrochia, Daniel. *La Raison systématique: Essai d'une morphologie des systèmes philosophiques*. Paris: Vrin, 1993.

Parsons, Talcott. *The Structure of Social Action*. New York: McGraw Hill, 1937.

Pascher, Manfred. *Einführung in den Neukantianismus*. Munich: UTB, 1997.

Paumen, Jean. *Raison et existence chez Karl Jaspers*. Brussels: Éditions du Parthenon, 1958.

Pears, David. *Wittgenstein*. London: Collins, 1971.

Peiffer, Jeanne. "France." In *Writing the History of Mathematics*, edited by Joseph W. Dauben and Christoph J. Scriba, 3–44. Basel: Birkhäuser, 2002.

Pfänder, Alexander. *Phenomenology of Willing and Motivation and Other Phaenomenologica*. Edited and translated by Herbert Spiegelberg. Evanston, IL: Northwestern University Press, 1967.

Pfänder, Alexander. *Die Seele des Menschen*. Halle: Max Niemeyer, 1933.

Philipse, Herman. "The Phenomenological Movement." In *The Cambridge History of Philosophy 1870–1945*, edited by Thomas Baldwin, 477–97. Cambridge: Cambridge University Press, 2003.

Pickering, Mary. *Auguste Comte: An Intellectual Biography*. Cambridge: Cambridge University Press, 1993.

Pilkey Orrin H., and Linda Pilkey Jarvis, *Useless Arithmetic: Why Environmental Scientists Can't Predict the Future*. New York: Columbia University Press, 2007.

Plant, Bob. *Wittgenstein and Levinas: Ethical and Religious Thought*. London: Routledge, 2005.

Politzer, Georges. *Écrits*. Edited by Jacques Debouzy. Paris: Éditions Sociales, 1969.

Polt, Richard. *Heidegger: An Introduction*. Ithaca, NY: Cornell University Press, 1999.

Pöggeler, Otto. "Heidegger's Political Self-Understanding." In *The Heidegger Controversy: A Critical Reader*, edited by Richard Wolin, 198–244. New York: Columbia University Press, 1991.

Poma, Andrea. *The Critical Philosophy of Hermann Cohen*. Albany, NY: SUNY Press, 1997.

Porter, Roy. "Charles Lyell and the Principles of the History of Geology." *British Journal for the History of Science* 9(32) (1976): 94–6.

Quirk, Tom. *Bergson and American Culture: The Worlds of Willa Cather and Wallace Stevens*. Chapel Hill, NC: University of North Carolina Press, 1990.

Raab, Thomas, and Robert Frodeman, "What is it Like to be a Geologist? A Phenomenology of Geology and its Epistemological Implications." *Philosophy and Geography* 5(1) (2002): 69–81.

Ragep, F. Jamil. "Duhem, The Arabs, and the History of Cosmology." *Synthese* 83 (1990): 210–14.

Ravaisson-Molien, Félix. *La Philosophie en France au XIXème siècle*. Paris: Imprimerie impériale, 1868.

Readings, Bill. "Pagans, Perverts or Primitives? Experimental Justice in the Empire of Capital." In *Judging Lyotard*, edited by Andrew Benjamin, 168–91. London: Routledge, 1992.

Reck, Erich. "Carnap and Modern Logic." In Friedman and Creath, *The Cambridge Companion to Carnap*, 176–99.

Renaut, Alain. *Les Révolutions de l'université*. Paris: Calmann-Lévy, 1995.

Renz, Ursula. *Die Rationalität der Kultur: Zur Kulturphilosophie und ihrer transzendentalen Begründung bei Cohen, Natorp und Cassirer*. Hamburg: Felix Meiner, 2002.

Reschke, Renate. *Denkumbrüche mit Nietzsche: Zur anspornenden Verachtung der Zeit*. Berlin: Akademie, 2000.

Richardson, Alan. *Carnap's Construction of the World: The "Aufbau" and the Emergence of Logical Empiricism*. Cambridge: Cambridge University Press, 1998.

Rickert, Heinrich. *Allgemeine Grundlegung der Philosophie*. Tübingen: J. C. B. Mohr, 1921.

Rickert, Heinrich. "Das Eine, die Einheit und die Eins." *Logos* 2 (1911): 26–78.

Rickert, Heinrich. *Der Gegenstand der Erkenntnis*. Tübingen: J. C. B. Mohr, 1882. 3rd ed. 1915.

Rickert, Heinrich. *Grundprobleme der Philosophie*. Tübingen: J. C. B. Mohr, 1934.

Rickert, Heinrich. "Zwei Wege der Erkenntnistheorie." *Kant-Studien* 14 (1909): 169–228.

Ricoeur, Paul. *Freedom and Nature: The Voluntary and the Involuntary*. Translated by Erazim Kohak. Evanston, IL: Northwestern University Press, 1966.

Rohrhuber, Julian. "Intuitions/Anschaungen." *Faits divers* 1 (2007): 1–3.

Rose, Steven. *Lifelines: Life Beyond the Gene*. Oxford: Oxford University Press, 1997.

Roubach, Michael. "Heidegger, Science, and the Mathematical Age." *Science in Context* 10(1) (1997): 199–206.

Ruderman, David B. *Jewish Thought and Scientific Discovery in Early Modern Europe*. New Haven, CT: Yale University Press, 1995.

Ruthenberg, Klaus. "Chemistry Without Atoms." In *Stuff: The Nature of Chemical Substances*, edited by Klaus Ruthenberg and Jaap van Brakel, 55–70. Würzburg: Königshausen & Neuman, 2008.

Ryckman, Thomas. "Carnap and Husserl." In Friedman and Creath, *The Cambridge Companion to Carnap*, 81–105.

Ryckman, Thomas. "Hermann Weyl and 'First Philosophy': Constituting Gauge Invariance." In *Constituting Objectivity: Transcendental Perspectives on Modern Physics*, edited by Michel Bitbol, Pierre Kerszberg, and Jean Petitot, 279–98. Dordrecht: Springer, 2009.

Ryckman, Thomas. *The Reign of Relativity: Philosophy in Physics 1915–1925*. Oxford: Oxford University Press, 2005.

Safranski, Rüdiger. *Martin Heidegger: Between Good and Evil*. Translated by Ewald Osers. Cambridge, MA: Harvard University Press, 1998. Originally published as *Ein Meister aus Deutschland: Heidegger und seine Zeit*. Munich: Hanser, 1994.

Salanskis, Jean-Michel. "Die Wissenschaft denkt nicht." *Tekhnema* 2 (1995): 60–85.

Sander, Angelika. *Max Scheler zur Einführung*. Hamburg: Junius, 2001.

Sartre, Jean-Paul. *Being and Nothingness*. Translated by Hazel E. Barnes. New York: Washington Square Press, 1956. Originally published as *L'Être et le néant*. Paris: Gallimard, 1943.

Sartre, Jean-Paul. *The Transcendence of the Ego: An Existentialist Theory of Consciousness*. Translated by Forrest Williams and Robert Kirkpatrick. New York: Farrar, Straus & Giroux, 1972. Originally published as "La Transcendance de l'ego: Esquisse d'une description phénomenologique." *Recherches Philosophiques* 6 (1936–37): 85–123.

Scerri, Eric. "Normative and Descriptive Philosophy of Science and the Role of Chemistry." In *Philosophy of Chemistry: Synthesis of a New Discipline*, edited by David Baird, Eric Scerri, and Lee McIntyre, 119–28. Dordrecht: Springer, 2006.

Scerri, Eric. *The Periodic Table: Its Story and its Significance*. Oxford: Oxford University Press, 2006.

Scerri, Eric. "Realism, Reduction and the 'Intermediate Position.'" In *Of Minds and Molecules*, edited by Nalini Bhushan and Stuart M. Rosenfeld, 51–72. Oxford: Oxford University Press, 2000.

Scharff, Robert C. *Comte after Positivism*. Cambridge: Cambridge University Press, 1995.

Scharfstein, Ben-Ami. "Bergson and Merleau-Ponty: A Preliminary Comparison." *Journal of Philosophy* 52 (1955): 380–86.

Scheler, Max. *Die deutsche Philosophie der Gegenwart: Gesammelte Werke Band 7*. Bern/Munich: Francke, 1973.

Scheler, Max. *On Feeling, Knowing, and Valuing: Selected Writings*. Edited with introduction by Harold Bershady. Chicago, IL: University of Chicago Press, 1992.

Scheler, Max. *Nature et formes de la sympathie: Contribution à l'étude des lois de la vie émotionnelle*. Translated by M. Lefebvre. Paris: Payot, 1928.

Scheler, Max. *Schriften aus dem Nachlaß I: Zur Ethik und Erkenntnislehre. Gesammelte Werke Band 10*. Bern: Francke, 1957.

Schilpp, Paul A. *Albert Einstein: Philosopher-Scientist*. New York: Tudor Press, [1949] 1957.

Schlanger, Nathan. "Technological Commitments: Marcel Mauss and the Study of Techniques in the French Social Sciences." In *Techniques, Technology and Civilization*, 1–29. Oxford: Berghahn, 2006.

Schrift, Alan D., ed. *The Logic of the Gift: Toward an Ethic of Generosity*. New York: Routledge, 1998.

Schrift, Alan D. *Twentieth-Century French Philosophy: Key Themes and Thinkers*. Malden, MA: Blackwell, 2006.

Schmaus, Warren. "Kant's Reception in France: Theories of the Categories in Academic Philosophy, Psychology and Social Sciences." *Perspective on Science* 11(1) (2003): 3–34.

Schmaus, Warren. "Renouvier and the Method of Hypothesis." *Studies in History and Philosophy of Science* 38 (2007): 132–48.

Schmaus, Warren. *Rethinking Durkheim and his Tradition*. Cambridge: Cambridge University Press, 2004.

Schnädelbach, Herbert. *Philosophy in Germany 1831–1933*. Translated by Eric Matthews. Cambridge: Cambridge University Press, 1984.

Schuhmann, Karl. *Husserl-Kronik*. The Hague: Martinus Nijhoff, 1977.

Schumann, Karl, and Barry Smith. "Adolf Reinach: An Intellectual Biography." In *Speech Act and Sachverhalt: Reinach and the Foundations of Realist Phenomenology*, edited by Kevin Mulligan, 3–27. The Hague: Martinus Nijhoff, 1987.

Schummer, Joachim. "The Philosophy of Chemistry." *Endeavor* 27(1) (2003): 37–41.

Schutz, Alfred. *Collected Papers I: The Problem of Social Reality*. Edited by Maurice Natanson. The Hague: Martinus Nijhoff, 1971.

Schutz, Alfred. *Collected Papers II: Studies in Social Theory*. Edited by Arvid Brodersen. The Hague: Martinus Nijhoff, 1964.

Schutz, Alfred. *Collected Papers III: Studies in Phenomenological Philosophy*. Edited by I. Schutz. The Hague: Martinus Nijhoff, 1966.

Schutz, Alfred. *The Phenomenology of the Social World*. Translated by George Walsh and

Frederick Lehnert. Evanston, IL: Northwestern University Press, 1967. Originally published as *Der sinnhafte Aufbau der sozialen Welt*. Vienna: Julius Springer, 1932.

Schutz, Alfred. *Reflections on the Problem of Relevance*. Edited by Richard M. Zaner. New Haven, CT: Yale University Press, 1970.

Schutz, Alfred. "Scheler's Theory of Intersubjectivity and the General Thesis of the Alter Ego." *Philosophy and Phenomenological Research* 2 (1942): 323–47.

Schutz, Alfred, with Thomas Luckmann. *The Structures of the Life-World*. Translated by Richard M. Zaner and H. Tristam Engelhardt, Jr. London: Heinemann, 1974.

Serres, Michel. *Hermès*. Paris: Éditions de Minuit, 1968.

Serres, Michel. *Le Système de Leibniz et ses modèles mathématiques*. 2 vols. Paris: Presses Universitaires de France, 1968.

Sieg, Ulrich. *Aufstieg und Niedergang des Marburger Neukantianismus: Die Geschichte einer philosophischen Schulgemeinschaft*. Würzburg: Königshausen & Neumann, 1994.

Sluga, Hans. *Gottlob Frege*. London: Routledge, 1980.

Sluga, Hans. *Heidegger's Crisis: Philosophy and Politics in Nazi Germany*. Cambridge, MA: Harvard University Press, 1993.

Smith, David Woodruff. "What is 'Logical' in Husserl's Logical Investigations? The Copenhagen Interpretation." In *One Hundred Years of Phenomenology: Husserl's Logical Investigations Revisited*, edited by Dan Zahavi and Frederik Stjernfelt, 51–65. Dordrecht: Kluwer, 2002.

Smith, David Woodruff, and Ronald McIntyre. *Husserl on Intentionality*. Dordrecht: Reidel, 1982.

Sokal, Alan, and Jean Bricmont. *Impostures intellectuelles*. Paris: Éditions Odile Jacob, 1997.

Spencer, Herbert. *First Principles*. London: Watts & Co., 1937.

Spencer, Herbert. *The Principles of Biology: Volume One*. London: Williams & Norgate, 1864.

Spiegelberg, Herbert. *The Context of the Phenomenological Movement*. The Hague: Martinus Nijhoff, 1981.

Spiegelberg, Herbert. *The Phenomenological Movement: A Historical Introduction*. 3rd rev. and enl. ed. The Hague: Martinus Nijhoff, 1982.

Stein, Edith. *Finite and Eternal Being: An Attempt at an Ascent to the Meaning of Being*. Translated by Kurt Reinhardt. Washington, DC: ICS Publications, 1999. Originally published as *Endliches und ewiges Sein: Versuch eines Aufsteigs zum Sinn des Seins*. 1950. Republished posthumously in *Edith Steins Werke*, II. Freiburg: Herder, 1987.

Stein, Edith. *On the Problem of Empathy*. Translated by Waltraut Stein. Washington, DC: ICS Publications, 1989. Originally published as *Zum Problem der Einfühlung*. Halle: Buchdrucheri des Waisenhauses, 1917.

Steinle, Friedrich. "Experiment, Concept Formation and the Limits of Justification: 'Discovering' the Two Electricities." In *Revisiting Discovery and Justification*, edited by Jutta Schickore and Friedrich Steinle, 183–95. Frankfurt: Springer, 2006.

Stone, Gregory, and Harvey Farberman. "On the Edge of Rapprochement: Was Durkheim Moving Towards the Perspective of Symbolic Interaction?" *Sociological Quarterly* 8 (1967): 149–64.

Strenski, Ivan. *Durkheim and the Jews of France*. Chicago, IL: University of Chicago Press, 1997.

Tarde, Gabriel. *On Communication and Social Influence*. Edited by Terry N. Clark. Chicago, IL: University of Chicago Press, 1969.

Tarot, Camille. *De Durkheim à Mauss: L'Invention du symbolique*. Paris: La Découverte, 1999.

Teilhard de Chardin, Pierre. *The Phenomenon of Man*. Translated by Bernard Wall. London: Collins, 1959.

Thorndike, Lynn. *History of Magic and Experimental Science*. New York: Columbia University Press, 1941.

Tieszen, Richard. *Phenomenology, Logic, and the Philosophy of Mathematics*. Cambridge: Cambridge University Press, 2005.

Tilghman, Benjamin R. *Wittgenstein, Ethics and Aesthetics: The View from Eternity*. Albany, NY: SUNY Press, 1991.

Tilliette, Xavier, SJ. *Karl Jaspers: Theorie de la verité, métaphysique des chiffres, foi philosophique*. Paris: Aubier, 1960.

Turner, A. Richard. *Inventing Leonardo*. New York: Knopf, 1992.

Turner, Stephen. "Durkheim among the Statisticians." *Journal of the History of the Behavioral Sciences* 32(4) (1996): 354–79.

Van Brakel, Jaap. "Chemistry as the Science of the Transformation of Substances." *Synthese* 111 (1997): 253–82.

Van Brakel, Jaap. "On the Neglect of the Philosophy of Chemistry." *Foundations of Chemistry* 1 (1999): 111–74.

Vidal-Rosset, Joseph. "De Martial Guéroult à Jules Vuillemin, analyse d'une Filiation." In *Le Paradigme de la filiation*, edited by Jean Gayon and Jean-Jacques Wunenberger, 213–26. Paris: L'Harmattan, 1995.

Vinnikov, Victor. "We Shall Know: Hilbert's Apology." *Mathematical Intelligencer* 21 (1999): 42–6.

Visvanathan, Shiv. "On the Annals of the Laboratory State." In *Science, Hegemony, and Violence: A Requiem for Modernity*, edited by Ashis Nandy, 257–88. Oxford: Oxford University Press, 1988.

Von Wolzogen, Christoph. *Die Autonome Relation: Zum Problem der Beziehung im Spätwerk Paul Natorps; Ein Beitrag zur Geschichte der Theorien der Relation*. Würzburg and Amsterdam: Rodopi, 1984.

Vuillemin, Jules. *L'Héritage Kantien et la révolution Copernicienne, Fichte, Cohen, Heidegger*. Paris: Presses Universitaires de France, 1954.

Vuillemin, Jules. *Nécessité ou contingence: L'Aporie de Diodore et les systèmes philosophiques*. Paris: Éditions de Minuit, 1984.

Vuillemin, Jules. *What are Philosophical Systems?* Cambridge: Cambridge University Press, 1986.

Wallace, William. "Duhem and Koyré on Domingo de Soto." *Synthese* 83(2) (1990): 239–60.

Wallwork, Ernest. "Religion and Social Structure in The Division of Labor." *American Anthropologist* 86(1) (1984): 43–64.

Wegener, Alfred. "Die Entstehung der Kontinente." *Geologische Rundschau* 3 (1912): 276–92.

Weizsäcker, Carl Friedrich von. "Nietzsche: Perceptions of Modernity." In *Nietzsche, Epistemology, and Philosophy of Science*, edited by Babette Babich and Robert S. Cohen, 221–40. Dordrecht: Springer, 1999.

Wetterstein, John R. "The Philosophy of Science and the History of Science: Separate Domains vs. Separate Aspects." *The Philosophical Forum* 14(1) (Fall 1982): 59–79.

Weyl, Hermann. *Raum-Zeit-Materie: Vorlesungen über allgemeinen Relativitätstheorie. Dritte Auflage*. Berlin: J. Springer, 1919.

Whitehead, Alfred North, and Bertrand Russell. *Principia Mathematica*. 3 vols. Cambridge: Cambridge University Press, 1910–13.

Wigner, Eugene. "The Unreasonable Effectiveness of Mathematics in the Natural Sciences." *Communications in Pure and Applied Mathematics* 13(1) (1960): 1–14.

Willard, Dallas. *Logic and the Objectivity of Knowledge: A Study in Husserl's Early Philosophy*. Athens, OH: Ohio University Press, 1984.

Willey, Thomas. *Back to Kant: The Revival of Kantianism in German Social and Historical Thought, 1860–1914*. Detroit, MI: Wayne State University Press, 1978.

Winch, Peter. "Nature and Convention." *Proceedings of the Aristotelian Society* 20 (1960): 231–52.

Winch, Peter. "Understanding a Primitive Society." *American Philosophical Quarterly* 1(4) (October 1964): 307–24.

Wittgenstein, Ludwig. *Culture and Value*. Edited by G. H. von Wright. Translated by Peter Winch. Oxford: Blackwell, 1994.

Wittgenstein, Ludwig. *Lectures and Conversations on Aesthetics, Psychology and Religious Belief.* Edited by Cyril Barrett. Oxford: Blackwell, 1994.

Wittgenstein, Ludwig. "On Heidegger on Being and Dread." Translated by Michael Murray. In *Heidegger and Modern Philosophy: Critical Essays*, edited by Michael Murray, 80–83. New Haven, CT: Yale University Press, 1978.

Wittgenstein, Ludwig. *Philosophical Occasions 1912–1951.* Edited by James Klagge and Alfred Nordmann. Indianapolis, IN: Hackett, 1993.

Wittgenstein, Ludwig. "Remarks on Frazer's *Golden Bough*." Translated by John Beversluis. In *Wittgenstein: Sources and Perspectives*, edited by C. G. Luckhardt, 61–81. Bristol: Thoemmes Press, 1996.

Wittgenstein, Ludwig. *Zettel.* Edited by G. E. M. Anscombe and G. H. von Wright. Translated by G. E. M. Anscombe. Oxford: Blackwell, 1990.

Windelband, Wilhelm. "Geschichte und Naturwissenschaft." In *Präludien; Aufsätze und Reden zur Philosophie und ihrer Geschichte*, vol. 2, 136–60. Tübingen: Mohr/Siebeck, 1924.

Worms, Frédéric. *Introduction à "Matière et mémoire" de Bergson.* Paris: Presses Universitaires de France, 1997.

Worsley, Peter. "Emile Durkheim's Theory of Knowledge." *The Sociological Review* 4 (1956): 47–62.

Wurtz, Adolphe. *Dictionnaire de chimie: Pure et appliquée.* Paris: Librairie Hachette, 1874.

Yourgrau, Palle. *A World Without Time: The Forgotten Legacy of Gödel and Einstein.* New York: Basic Books, 2005.

Zahar, Eli. *Poincaré's Philosophy: From Conventionalism to Phenomenology.* La Salle, IL: Open Court, 2001.

Zaner, Richard M. *The Problem of Embodiment: Some Contributions to a Phenomenology of the Body.* The Hague: Martinus Nijhoff, 1971.

Zittel, Karl Alfred von. *Geschichte der Geologie und Paläontologie bis Ende des 19. Jahrhundert.* Munich: Oldenbourg, 1899.

INDEX